MODERN AUSTRIA

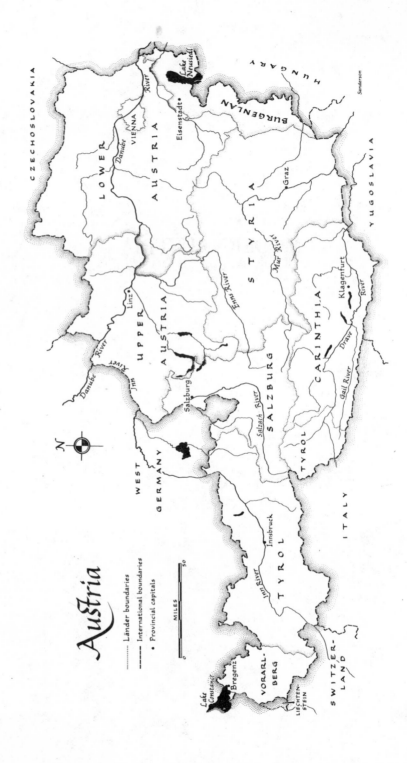

Austria

.... Länder boundaries
——— International boundaries
• Provincial capitals

MILES

0   50

N

CZECHOSLOVAKIA

HUNGARY

Lake
Neusiedl

Danube River

VIENNA

LOWER

AUSTRIA

Eisenstadt •

BURGENLAND

Graz

STYRIA

YUGOSLAVIA

Linz •

UPPER

AUSTRIA

Enns River

Mur River

Salzburg •

SALZBURG

CARINTHIA

Klagenfurt •

Drave River

Gail River

Salzach River

Danube River

Inn River

WEST

GERMANY

TYROL

ITALY

Innsbruck •

Inn River

TYROL

VORARL-
BERG

Bregenz •

Lake
Constance

LIECHTEN-
STEIN

SWITZER-
LAND

Sanderson

MODERN AUSTRIA

Editor: Kurt Steiner

Co-editors: Fritz Fellner

Hubert Feichtlbauer

Editorial Committee

Hubert Feichtlbauer   Gottfried Scholz

Fritz Fellner   Kurt Steiner

Eduard März

SPOSS
INC

The Society for the Promotion of Science and Scholarship Inc.
(a non-profit corporation)
835 Page Mill Road, Palo Alto, California 94304 USA

The Society for the Promotion of Science and
Scholarship Inc. Palo Alto, California, USA

International Standard Book Number: 0-930664-03-5
Library of Congress Catalog Card Number: 80-53944

PRINTED AND BOUND IN THE UNITED STATES OF AMERICA

093676

ABOUT THE PUBLISHER

The publisher is a nonprofit corporation: The Society for the Promotion of Science and Scholarship (SPOSS, INC.). As applies to other nonprofit corporations, any surplus arising from its operations must be used exclusively to further the Society's purposes as set forth in its Articles of Incorporation; that is, the Society seeks to promote through its publications selected works of educational value in science and the humanities.

The Trustees of the Society invite inquiries regarding the publication of books of appropriate quality and educational value.

OTHER PUBLICATIONS FROM SPOSS, INC.

Modern Switzerland

Editor: Professor J. Murray Luck. Coeditors: Dr. Lukas F. Burckhardt, Professor Hans Haug. Editorial Committee: Professors Josef von Ah, Hugo Aebi, Erich Gruner, Hans Haug, J. Murray Luck, and Dr. Lukas F. Burckhardt.

Modern Switzerland provides a comprehensive cross-sectional view of many aspects of Switzerland, of her people, and their institutions. Some twenty-seven Swiss scholars, gifted with expert knowledge in their special fields of interest, have cooperated in this unusual effort to describe Switzerland in the 1970's.

Hard cover, 531 pages, illustrations, index
(ISBN 0-930664-01-9, $22.00 USA, $23.00 elsewhere per copy).

"Each contributing author writes with authority and perception and frequently supplies minute details on such matters as the education system or leisure-time activities . . . Whether the reader seeks some general information about Switzerland or whether he seeks technical details, this book will be of great assistance and it is therefore highly recommended for every library, no matter whether public or college."

Choice, Oct. 1978

"Its aim is to describe present-day Switzerland to the English-speaking world, and in this it succeeds admirably."

Peninsula Living, June 3, 1978

". . . unequalled in English, and possibly any other language, as a survey of an exemplary country."

World Affairs Report 8, No. 4, 1978

"Modern Switzerland does an outstanding job of providing a comprehensive cross-sectional view of many aspects of Swiss life."

Bulletin Credit Suisse, Vol. 84, Summer 1978

Art and Society: The New Art Movement in Vienna, 1897–1914

By Prof. James Shedel, Dept. of History, Georgetown University, Washington DC

The book describes a period in Vienna of great contemporary interest. Otherwise known as the Wiener Secession, its beginnings in 1897 marked the entrance of Austria into the ranks of the European avant-garde. The Austrian term for the new art form referred to both an act of rebellion and the artistic movement it brought into being.

To be published Nov. 1981, about 250 pages, hard cover, illustrations, index.

(continued next page)

Population Pressures: Emigration and Government in Late Nineteenth-Century Britain

By Prof. Howard L. Malchow, Dept. of History, Tufts University, Medford, Mass.

This book is a study of the politics of emigration, and specifically of those organizations lobbying to persuade the government to assist emigration. The focus is on the National Emigration League in the period 1869–1871 and on the National Association for Promoting State-directed Emigration and Colonization from 1883 to 1891.

Hard cover, 323 pages, illustrations, index
(ISBN 0-930664-02-7, $18.00 USA, $19.00 elsewhere per copy).

". . . Malchow presents these efforts and the opposition to them, as well as the response of the various governments to their efforts, in a readable and suggestive narrative . . . This is a most useful book. The research is extensive, with the author bringing together in a relatively short compass the activities of men and organizations supporting emigration during the latter part of the Victorian period . . . it will be consulted by anyone working in the field of emigration or in the related fields of charity, the role of the state, the relation between labor and emigration, and intra-imperial relations . . . it is a useful case study of lobbying tactics and strategies, and the discussion of J. H. Boyd and Lord Brabazon (later Earl of Meath) is most illuminating."

Albion, Vol. 12, No. 1

"Malchow admirably succeeds in identifying the reasons advanced by those favoring state-assisted emigration . . . Both the author and his publishers have produced a fine book . . . the plates from the *Illustrated London News* do much to add life to the subject. Malchow should be complimented, not only for his thorough use of a wide variety of sources but also for his excellent grasp of peripheral issues."

The American Historical Review, Oct. 1980

"An addition to the growing literature on Victorian pressure groups. Malchow describes the attempts to pressure government into initiating state-aided emigration to relieve social distress in England and to help build colonies in the empire. His focus is on the large but unsuccessful National Association for Promoting State Colonization of the 1880's . . . We now know what happened to large-scale emigration schemes after Edward Gibbon Wakefield. Recommended for university libraries."

Choice, July/Aug. 1980

Tradition and Innovation in Contemporary Austria

Editor: Prof. Kurt Steiner, Dept. of Political Science, Stanford University, Stanford, Calif.

Based on a symposium on the occasion of the twenty-fifth anniversary of the Austrian State Treaty, 1955, held at Stanford University, this volume contains contributions by Austrian and American experts. The articles focus on the polarity of tradition and innovation in various aspects of contemporary Austrian life.

To be published fall 1982, about 250 pages, hard cover, index.

Orders may be placed through booksellers or directly from SPOSS, INC., 835 Page Mill Road, Palo Alto, CA 94304, USA
(California residents add applicable sales tax.)

Der Bundespräsident

What associations does the name of Austria evoke in the mind of
an American citizen? In the first instance perhaps the thought of Vienna
as the home of waltzes and operettas. The city of Salzburg is linked with
Mozart and its annual Festival. Especially in the United States the
teachings of Sigmund Freud have found many students and interpreters.
The manifold problems of the former multinational polity in the Danube
area and the reflection of them in its literature are to an increasing degree
becoming a discipline at numerous universities in the United States, and
valuable contributions have been made there towards the elucidation of
Austria's intellectual history. For Americans interested in politics a
series of important international meetings during recent years, above all
between President Jimmy Carter and the Chairman of the Presidium of
the Supreme Soviet, Leonid Breschnev, has rendered Austria familiar as
a focal point and land of encounter.

Perhaps in this way there has been aroused interest in contemporary
Austria and the life that its people lead. How has today's permanently
neutral republic at the centre of Europe emerged from the remainder,
shaken by political and economic crises, of the Austro-Hungarian Dual
Monarchy? What are the political and economic forces which shape it?
What is the nature of its social and economic structure? To give an answer
to these and a row of other questions is what the compilation "Modern
Austria", published by the Society for the Promotion of Science and
Scholarship Inc., Palo Alto, California, seeks to do. The editors, Professor Steiner, Professor Fellner, Dr. Feichtlbauer, and the names of
their collaborators ensure that American readers will obtain comprehensive
and carefully consolidated information.

I genuinely welcome the publication of this book. It performs a
valuable task for the dissemination of knowledge about Austria at the most
up-to-date level and at the same time it constitutes a meritorious contribution to better understanding between the citizens of the United States and
the Austrian people. My best wishes accompany "Modern Austria" on its
journey to as wide a circle of readers as possible.

[Federal President of Austria]

CONTENTS

List of Contributing Authors   xi

Foreword, *Kurt Steiner*   xix

INTRODUCTION: The Genesis of the Austrian Republic,
Fritz Fellner   1

PART I: GEOGRAPHY AND DEMOGRAPHY

1. Austria: Landscape and Regional Structure,
Helmut Wohlschlägl   23

2. Demography and Population Problems, *Helga Leitner*   75

3. Religions and Their Relations to State and Parties,
Erika Weinzierl   99

PART II: ECONOMY

4. Austria's Economic Development, 1945–1978, *Edward März
and Maria Szecsi*   123

5. The Economic Structure, *Felix Butschek*   141

6. Development and Problems of Austrian Industry,
Ferdinand Lacina   155

7. Monetary and Budget Policy, *Stephan Koren*   173

8. Social Partnership in Austria, *Maria Szecsi*   185

Appendix to Part II: A Note on Energy in Austria,
compiled by *Kurt Steiner*   203

PART III: GOVERNMENT AND POLITICS

9. Government Structure: The Principles of Government,
Peter Gerlich   209

10. Political Parties, *Anton Pelinka*   223

11. Elections and Parliament, *Heinz Fischer*   241

12. Public Administration: The Business of Government,
Raoul F. Kneucker   261

13. The Media, *Hubert Feichtlbauer*   279

PART IV: SOCIAL, EDUCATIONAL, AND LEGAL POLICY

14. Social Policy Since 1945: Democracy and the Welfare State,
   Rudolf Strasser   301

15. Education and Educational Policy, *Kurt Steiner*   321

16. Higher Education, *Kurt Steiner*   335

17. Legal Policy Since 1970, *Franz Pallin and Herbert Ent*   345

PART V: AUSTRIA AND THE WORLD

18. Foreign Policy, *Peter Jankowitsch*   361

19. Defense Policy from the Austrian Point of View,
   Emil Spannocchi   381

20. Austria and the World: Image and Impact, *Gottfried Heindl* 393

PART VI: CULTURE AND THE ARTS

21. Contemporary Literature in Austria,
   Wendelin Schmidt-Dengler   409

22. Music in Austria, *Gottfried Scholz*   431

23. Performing Arts and Festivals, *Ernst Haeusserman
   and Sigrid Wiesmann*   449

24. Contemporary Art, *George Eisler*   471

Epilogue: Intellectual Trends in Austria Since 1945, *Norbert Leser* 485

Index   509

LIST OF CONTRIBUTING AUTHORS

Univ. Doz. Dr. FELIX BUTSCHEK, born 1932, is a member of the managing staff of the Austrian Institute of Economic Research. His areas of interest are labor economics, regional economics, social policy and recent Austrian economic history. He is the author of *Die österreichische Wirtschaft zwischen 1938 und 1945* (Stuttgart, 1978), *Vollbeschäftigung in der Krise—die österreichische Erfahrung 1974 bis 1979* (Wien, forthcoming) and, with H. Seidel and A. Kausel, *Die regionale Dynamik der österreichischen Wirtschaft* (Wien, 1966). He edited *EWG und die Folgen* (Wien, 1966) and *Ökonomische Aspekte der Arbeitsmarktpolitik* (Wien, 1975), and has published a number of articles in professional journals.

GEORG EISLER, born in 1928, lives and works as an artist in Vienna. He spent the years from 1939 to 1946 in England, where he studied at various schools of art and where some of his work was first exhibited. He returned to Vienna in 1946. Since then his paintings, drawings, and graphics have been shown in various cities in Austria, Holland, Germany, Belgium, England, Italy, and the United States, and some of his work has been published in various portfolios as well as in a monograph (Vienna, 1970). Eisler also created stage and costume designs (Royal Opera House, Covent Garden, 1961; Schauspielhaus, Graz, 1973) and illustrated a number of books. An exhibition of his work, together with that of Hrdlicka, Martinz, Schönwald, and Schwaiger, held in Vienna in 1969, initiated an important programmatic trend in Austrian modern art. Georg Eisler was elected President of the Secession in Vienna in 1968 and held this position until 1971. He received the Austrian State Prize for Painting in 1965, the Prize of the City of Vienna in 1971, and the Cross of Honor for Science and Art in 1974. He was a Guest Lecturer at the University of New Mexico and the University of Southern California in 1976.

Ministerialrat Dr. HERBERT ENT, born 1923, is Chief of the section of the Ministry of Justice concerned with questions of family law. In this capacity he participated prominently in the family law reform as well as in the reforms of the laws regarding youth welfare and regarding psychologically handicapped persons. He dealt with these matters, together with Gerhard Hopf, in commentaries to various laws, published in 1975, 1976, and 1979. Recent articles (1978 and 1979) by Dr. Ent have appeared in *Österreichische Juristenzeitung* and in *Österreichische Notariatszeitung*. He was awarded the Great Silver Medal of Merit of the Republic of Austria.

Dr. HUBERT FEICHTLBAUER, born 1932, is presently Chief Editor of *Die Furche,* an independent weekly on cultural, social, and political affairs, addressing itself to intellectual readers. Formerly he was editor of the newspapers *Salzburger Nachrichten* and *Kurier,* and of the weekly *Wochenpresse.* During 1977 and 1978 he was correspondent on U.S. and UN affairs in Washington, D.C. and New York. He is a well-known lecturer, and serves frequently as moderator on TV programs.

Dr. FRITZ FELLNER, born 1922, is Professor for Modern and Contemporary History at the University of Salzburg (since 1964). Previously he was Lecturer at the University of Vienna, and Visiting Professor at the University of Texas (1960–61), Western Illinois University (1963), and Franklin and Marshall College (1964–65). In 1978 he held the newly established Visiting Professorship in Austrian Studies at Stanford University. Between 1954 and 1971 he also taught at the Institute of European Studies in Vienna. He held grants from the Theodor Körner Foundation (1954) and the Rockefeller Foundation (1957), and he received the Prize of the City of Vienna in 1960. He edited the political diaries of Josef Redlich (2 volumes, 1953–54) and is the author of a number of books, chapters, and articles on recent Austrian history, including diplomatic history. He serves on many commissions (e.g. Austrian UNESCO Commission, Commission on the History of the First Republic, Scientific Council of the Theodor Körner Foundation).

Dr. HEINZ FISCHER, born 1938, is a member of the National Council (first elected in 1971), Chairman of the Parliamentary Group of the Socialist Party (i.e. leader of the present majority in parliament) since 1975, and a Deputy Chairman of the Socialist Party since 1979. He also teaches political science at the University of Innsbruck (since 1978).

He studied law at the University of Vienna (1957–61). Before assuming his present positions he was Secretary of the Parliamentary Group of the Socialist Party.

Dr. Fischer is the editor of *Das politische System Österreichs* (2nd ed., 1977) and of *Rote Markierungen* (1980), and together with W. Czerny wrote the *Kommentar zur Geschäftsordnung zum Nationalrat* (1968). He has published many articles on parliament and on parties and elections. He was a founder of the Austrian Political Science Association.

Dr. PETER GERLICH, born 1939, is Professor of Political Science at the University of Vienna (since 1975). He studied law and political science at the Universities of Vienna, Munich and at Columbia University. He was engaged in post-doctoral studies at the Institute for Advanced Studies in Vienna, and from 1967 to 1973 chaired its division of political science. After a year as Professor at the University of Braunschweig (1973–74) he assumed his present position. From 1975 to 1979 he was Dean of the Faculty of Social Science. Among his books are *Abgeordnete in der Parteiendemokratie* (with Helmut Kramer, 1969) and *Parlamentarische Kontrolle im politischen System* (1973). He also published numerous articles and contributed chapters to various books on Austrian and comparative politics. From 1975 to 1977 he was Chairman of the Austrian Political Science Association.

Professor ERNST HAEUSSERMAN, born 1916, is Director of the Theater in der Josefstadt (since 1968). After emigration to the United States, he returned to Vienna, and was Director of the Theater in der Josefstadt, together with Franz Stoss, from 1953–59. From 1959–1968 he was Director of the Burgtheater, and then resumed his present position. He is also a member of the Board for the Salzburg Festival, responsible for the dramatic sector. Among his publications is *Die Burg: Rundhorizont eines Welttheaters* (1964).

Dr. GOTTFRIED HEINDL, born 1924, is Director for Cultural Affairs, Austrian Federal Theaters (since 1971). He received his Ph.D. from the University of Vienna (1951). From 1950–54 he was editor of *Neue Wiener Tageszeitung* and subsequently Press Secretary of the Austrian People's Party (1955–66). Prior to assuming his present position he was Director of the Austrian Institute in New York (1966–70).

Ambassador Dr. PETER JANKOWITSCH, born 1933, is Austria's Permanent Representative at the Organization for Economic Cooperation and Development (OECD) in Paris (since 1978). After receiving a doctorate in jurisprudence from the University of Vienna (1950) and a diploma from the Academie de Droit Internationale in the Hague (1959), he joined the International Law Division of the Federal Chancellory and, in 1962, the Embassy in London. In 1970 he became Chief of the Staff of the Chancellor (Kabinettschef). In 1972 he was appointed as the Permanent Representative of Austria at the United Nations, where he held important positions including the (elected) positions of Chairman of the Commission on Space, and (in 1973) President of the Security Council. He holds leading positions in various institutes and societies in the area of his activities. He contributed chapters on international relations to the Festschrift for H. Morgenthau (Washington, 1977) and for H. Firnberg (Vienna, 1965), and published many articles in various journals.

Dr. RAOUL F. KNEUKER, born 1938, is Secretary General of the Austrian Science Research Fund. He studied law at the University of Graz, political science at Brandeis University, and public administration at the Salzburg Seminar in American Studies, in Speyer and in Washington, D.C. He was Research Assistant at the Law Faculty of the University of Vienna (1964–

69). Prior to assuming his present position he was Secretary General of the Austrian Rector's Conference (1970–78). He serves presently as Chairman of the Austrian Political Science Association. He has contributed articles on public administration to *Österreichisches Jahrbuch für Politik 1977* and to other books, as well as to various periodicals.

Dr. STEPHAN KOREN, born 1919, is President of the Austrian National Bank (since 1978). He studied economics at the University of Vienna and was on the staff of the Austrian Institute of Economic Research from 1945 to 1965. He became Professor of Economics at the University of Innsbruck in 1965. In 1967 he was appointed Secretary of State for Economic Questions in the cabinet of Chancellor Klaus, and he became Minister of Finance in 1968, a position he held until 1970. In 1968 he also became Professor at the Economic University in Vienna. Elected to the National Council in 1970, he became Chairman of the Parliamentary Group of the Austrian People's Party in the same year. Reelected twice, he performed the function until he assumed his present position.

Professor Koren is the author of a number of books and articles, especially in the field of economic, industrial, and energy policy.

Diplomkaufmann FERDINAND LACINA, born 1942, is Chief of the Staff of the Chancellor (Kabinettschef, since 1980). He studied at the University of Economics in Vienna and worked since 1965 in the Economic Department of the Chamber of Labor in Vienna. In 1978 he became head of the Department for Financial Planning in the Österreichische Industrie-Aktiengesellschaft (ÖIAG), the holding company of the Austrian state-owned industry. His publications deal with Austria's economic structure and industrial policy, and with multinational enterprises.

Dr. HELGA LEITNER, born 1949, is Assistant Professor at the Institute for Geography of the University of Vienna (since 1979). She studied geography, regional science, and Anglistic at that university (Ph.D. 1978) and at the Technical University, Karlsruhe. She was Research Assistant at the International Institute for Applied Systems Analysis (IIASA) in Laxenburg (1975–76) and Visiting Assistant Professor of Geography at the University of Minnesota (1978). Her publications deal with international European labor migration and problems of integration and assimilation of migrant workers, with new approaches to high school geography teaching in Austria, and with multivariate statistical analysis (causal modeling, path analysis) in human geography.

Dr. NORBERT LESER, born 1933, is Professor for Social Philosophy at the University of Vienna (since 1980). Previously he was Honorary Professor of Political Science (since 1977), and Professor of Political Science at the University of Salzburg (since 1971). His primary research interest is in the history of political ideas (especially socialism and Marxism) and Austrian contemporary history (social philosophy). He has published six books and numerous articles. He is Vice-President of the International Hans Kelsen Institute, and received the Theodor Körner Prize (1961, 1963, and 1968), the Prize for the Promotion of Sciences of the City of Vienna (1962), and the Karl Renner Prize for Publicists (1967). He was awarded the Austrian Medal of Honor for Science and Art in 1978.

Professor Dr. EDUARD MÄRZ, born in 1908, is head of the Institute of Economic History at the University of Vienna. He studied at the University of Vienna and at Harvard University, and was Professor of Economics at Union College and Hofstra College (1948–53). Previously he was head of the Department of Economic Research in the Vienna Chamber of Labor (since 1956). Dr. März is the author of *Österreichische Industrie- und Bankpolitik in der Zeit Franz Josephs I, Österreichs Wirtschaft zwischen Ost und West, Einführung in die Marx'sche Theorie der wirtschaftlichen Entwicklung,* and of numerous other publications in the field of economic history and economic policy.

Professor Dr. FRANZ PALLIN, born 1909, is President of the Austrian Supreme Court (since 1972). After receiving his doctorate in jurisprudence from the University of Graz (1932) he became a judge in 1936, but was dismissed for political reasons after the Anschluss in 1938. He resumed his juridical activities in 1945 as public prosecutor, became *Generalanwalt* in 1951, *Erster Generalanwalt* in 1962, and *Generalprokuratur* (1966–71). Concurrently he was Chief of the Section on Criminal Affairs in the Ministry of Justice from 1960 to 1965. In 1971 he became Vice-President of the Supreme Court. Dr. Pallin, who was awarded the honorary title Professor and the Great Gold Medal of Merit by the City of Vienna, has published widely on the Penal Code.

Dr. ANTON PELINKA, born 1941, is Professor of Political Science at the University of Innsbruck (since 1975). He studied law at the University of Vienna, and political science at the Institute for Advanced Studies in Vienna. In 1966 and 1967 he served as editor of the weekly *Die Furche.* Before assuming his present position he was lecturer for political science at the University of Salzburg (1972), Associate Professor at the University of Essen (1973), and Professor at the Pedagogical College of Berlin (1974). He is the author (with M. Welan) of *Demokratie und Verfassung* (1971), *Stand oder Klasse?* (1972), *Dynamische Demokratie* (1974), *Gewerkschaften im Parteienstaat* (1980), and of other books and numerous articles on democratic theory and comparative and Austrian politics. He edited (with A. Kadan) *Die Grundsatzprogramme der österreichischen Parteien* (1979).

Dr. WENDELIN SCHMIDT-DENGLER, born 1942, is Associate Professor for Modern German Language and Literature at the University of Vienna. He studied classical philology and Germanic philology and literature (Germanistik) in Vienna and obtained his Ph.D. in 1965. Prior to assuming his present position, he was Lecturer at the same university (since 1974) and Visiting Professor in Klagenfurt (1975) and Salzburg (1978). He also teaches at the Stanford Study Center in Vienna. Professor Schmidt-Dengler is the author of *Genius: Zur Wirkungsgeschichte antiker Mythologeme in der Goethezeit* (1978) and of *Eine Avantgarde aus Graz* (1979) as well as of essays on Augustinus, Erasmus, the literature of Sturm und Drang and, especially, on the Austrian literature of the nineteenth and twentieth centuries. He is editing some of the writings left by Heimito von Doderer, of which three posthumous volumes have appeared, namely *Essays* (1970), *Tagebücher* (1976), and *Erzählungen* (1980), and is engaged in research on the Austrian literature between 1918 and 1938.

Dr. GOTTFRIED SCHOLZ, born 1936, is Professor of Music at the Hochschule für Musik und darstellende Kunst in Vienna, and since 1974 has been Director of the Institute for Music Analysis. He served as Vice-Rector of the Hochschule in 1974–76 and 1977–79. He was lecturer at Kabul, Afghanistan, where he organized the first music school, and Visiting Professor at Indiana University (summer 1969 and 1971–72) and at Stanford (1980). He also teaches at the Institute for European Studies (since 1965) and at the Stanford Study Center in Vienna (since 1974). Dr. Scholz was General Secretary of the European Regional Group of the International Music Council (1978–79) and presently is President of the Austrian Music Council. He was awarded the Great Medal of Merit of the Republic of Austria. Professor Scholz has published various books and articles on Haydn, Mahler, music of the twentieth century, music theory, musical forms and music pedagogy.

General EMIL SPANNOCCHI, born 1916, is Commandant of the Austrian Army. He comes from a family in which every generation has provided a general for the Austrian Army. General Spannocchi started his military career in the Austrian army, and continued it in the German army as officer of armored troops and in the General Staff. In the new Austrian army he rose to the position of Commandant of the Defense Academy after having been general of armored troops. He was also engaged in preparatory work for the establishment of the readiness troops. When, during the restructuring of the army's organization in 1973, the Army Command was instituted as the highest command for all army units, he was appointed to the position of Commandant of the Austrian Army. In this position he was instrumental in the ongoing reforms that he describes in his contribution to this volume.

Dr. KURT STEINER, born 1912, is Professor of Political Science (Emeritus) at Stanford University. After obtaining the degree of Doctor of Jurispru-dence from the University of Vienna and practicing law there, he emigrated to the United States in 1938. He became Director of the Berlitz Schools of Languages in Cleveland and Pittsburgh before joining the U.S. Army in 1943. In the army and subsequently in government service he was a prose-cuting attorney in the war crimes trial before the International Military Tribunal for the Far East, and a legislative attorney in the General Head-quarters of the Supreme Commander for the Allied Powers (1945–51). He received his Ph.D. in political science from Stanford University in 1955, and after a year at Princeton University, returned to Stanford as a faculty member in the field of comparative politics. He also was a Visiting Professor at the Free University of Berlin (1965) and at the University of Vienna (1977). He is the author of *Local Government in Japan* (1965) and *Politics in Austria* (1972), and co-editor and co-author of *Political Opposition and Local Politics in Japan* (1981). He also has contributed chapters to a num-ber of books and has published articles on Japanese government and law in various professional journals. He was awarded the Austrian Medal of Honor for Science and Art in 1981.

Dr. RUDOLF STRASSER, born 1923, is Professor for Private Law, Labor Law, and Social Welfare Law at the Johannes Kepler University in Linz. Between 1949 and 1967 he held various positions with the Chamber of Labor of Upper Austria, including Chief of the Legal Divisions. Having taught at the University of Vienna since 1958, he assumed his present position in 1965. He was Pro-Rector (1965–67) and Rector (1968–70) of his university, as well as Dean of the Faculty of Law (1975–77). He is President of the Ludwig Boltzmann Gesellschaft and Chairman of the Commission for Codification of Labor Law in the Ministry for Social Administration (both since 1968). Since 1978 he has also been editor of the journal *Das Recht der Arbeit.* He has published 29 books and 73 articles in his teaching fields as well as on broader aspects of social policy and the policies of higher educa-tion.

MARIA SZECSI, M.A., was a staff member of the Department of Economic Research in the Vienna Chamber of Labor and a member of the Economic and Social Advisory Board, and edited the quarterly journal *Wirtschaft und Gesellschaft.* She is the author of numerous studies, published by the Cham-ber of Labor, as well as a contributor to various journals in the field of economic policy.

Dr. ERIKA WEINZIERL, born 1925, is Professor of Modern History and Director of the Institute for Contemporary History at the University of Vienna (since 1979). After studies of history and art history at that university and at the Institute for Research in Austrian History, she joined the Haus-Hof und Staatsarchiv in Vienna. In 1964 she became Chairperson of the Institute for Contemporary Church History at the International Research Center, Salzburg. Prior to assuming her present position she was Professor of Austrian History with emphasis on contemporary history. She is the editor of the monthly journal *Zeitgeschichte* (since 1973) and Director of the Ludwig Boltzmann Institute for the History of Social Science (since 1977). Among other books, she has published *Die österreichischen Konkordate von 1855 und 1933* (1960), *Zu wenig Gerechte: Österreicher und Judenverfolgungen 1938–1945* (1969), and *Emanzipation? Österreichische Frauen im 20. Jahrhundert* (1975). She contributed a chapter on Austria to *The Catholic Church Today: Western Europe* (1969). Among works she has co-edited are *Kirche in Österreich* (with Ferdinand Klostermann et al., 2 volumes, 1966–67) and *Österreich: Die Zweite Republik* (with Kurt Skalnik, 2 volumes, 1972).

Dr. SIGRID WIESMANN, born 1941, teaches at the Hochschule für Musik und darstellende Kunst in Vienna (since 1974) and at the Forschungsinstitut für Musiktheater at the University of Bayreuth. She studied musicology, theater science, art history, and philosophy at the University of Vienna, as well as voice at the Academy of Music in Vienna and at the Juilliard School of Music in New York. Her fields of research and publication are contemporary musical and theatrical life, and especially the music theater.

Magister HELMUT WOHLSCHLÄGL, born 1949, is Assistant Professor at the Institute for Geography of the University of Vienna (since 1974). He studied geography and history at that university, as well as regional planning at the Technical University, Karlsruhe (1976–77). His publications deal with population research, demographic developments and internal migration, tourism, and the development of agriculture since the 19th century, as well as with new perspectives in geographical education and the application of multivariate statistical methods (causal modeling, path analysis, cluster analysis) in human geographic research.

FOREWORD

The subject of this book—"Modern Austria"—is relatively unknown to the world outside that country. As Gottfried Heindl notes in his contribution to this volume, the image of Austria abroad is largely determined by five "M's": Mountains, Music, Mozart, Maria Theresa, and Metternich. Except for the timeless mountains—a great asset for the tourist industry—all relate to a time long gone by.[1] It is as if, in this popular view, time had stood still in the center of Europe.

The scholarly literature of Austria in the English language also shows a bias toward the past. Much of it deals with the Austro-Hungarian monarchy, and thus with a time when present-day Austria did not exist as yet as a separate entity. For the time beyond the *fin de siècle* and the disintegration of the monarchy, the scholarly output drops sharply. There are few books dealing with the period between 1918 and the Anschluss of 1938, and even fewer dealing with the period since 1945, when an independent Austria arose from the devastation of World War II.

Aside from the overpowering influence of clichés—which are outdated, as the title of this book indicates and the contributions to it demonstrate —this popular and scholarly neglect of more recent developments is undoubtedly also due to the smallness of the country. However, the size of a country's area or population—or of its military power—may well be a poor yardstick for the interest it deserves. Pope John Paul I once referred to present-day Austria as an "island of the blessed." Such a characterization, even granting a hyperbolic element in it, would suggest that the country merits the attention of a world not so "blessed," especially if we consider that many Austrians delightedly agree with it.

Of course, everything is relative. We know that relative deprivation influences perception; it seems plausible that perception is also influenced by relative satisfaction, as expressed by the phrase "We never had it so good." The somewhat euphoric evaluation of their present situation by many Austrians of the older generation may well be explainable in terms of a contrast between the past and the present. Austrians who experienced the First Republic (1918–1938) remember it as a period of economic deprivation, of doubts in the future and self-doubts, of civil conflict and regime changes— a period that ended with the Anschluss and the cataclysm of war. From the beginning there were doubts about the economic viability of the country, and these doubts became a self-fulfilling prophecy, as Eduard März notes in his chapter. The monarchy had been an integrated economic unit, with

xix

a division of labor among its various parts, and a domestic market that permitted a flow of their products. The new republic—the remnant of the empire after all non-German nationalities left it to follow their own destinies —never overcame the severe economic dislocations resulting from the dismemberment of this economic unit. It suffered first from a runaway inflation, and then from the stagnation and rampant unemployment.

Domestic politics become highly polarized, and the conflicts between the political antagonists—significantly referred to by the military term *Lager* (camps)—were fought out increasingly in the streets by their paramilitary forces. In 1934, after a short but sharp civil war, parliamentary democracy was replaced by an authoritarian regime of the Right, which, however, failed to achieve the allegiance of major population groups. In international relations, Austria was more of an object than a subject. In the stormy interwar years, its foreign policy followed one or another "course," as dictated by the exigencies of the moment.[2] In 1938 its policy options seemed exhausted, and the way was open to the Anschluss. Austria not only disappeared as a state but was not even allowed to remain an administrative unit within the Third Reich. The First Republic had lasted a scant twenty years.

Paradoxically, the Nazi interlude was a prelude to the different Austria that was to emerge after the war. As Felix Butschek notes in this contribution, the Anschluss brought about the economic restructuring that the First Republic had failed to achieve. The traditional emphasis on consumer goods gave way to a greater emphasis on basic industries as Germany created a number of large-scale industrial enterprises. Since these enterprises were located away from the previous concentration in the eastern provinces (*Länder*), regional bifurcation into an industrial east and an agrarian west was lessened. Trade became oriented to the West. The experience of a short but explosive boom immediately after the Anschluss, and the acquaintance with the technological and organizational basis of an industrial economy that had been in high gear for a number of years conveyed a new know-how and new attitudes.[3] After the war, the question of Austria's economic viability was hardly ever raised even during the difficult period of postwar reconstruction. It was definitely laid to rest by the "economic miracle" of the 1950s. In terms of economic performance, Austria caught up with and in some aspects surpassed the rest of Europe. Inflation was contained, and it has been modest for some years; full employment not only is a commonly agreed upon policy goal, but has actually been achieved; the currency is stable and strong, and industrial strife is virtually unknown owing mainly to the arrangements known as "social partnership," described in the chapter by Maria Szecsi. Domestic politics is free of the rancor typical of the *Lager* mentality of the First Republic. In international relations Austria adopted a perpetual neutrality basically on the Swiss model in 1955, and the country maintains friendly, although not entirely equidistant, relations with the two power blocs. As the contribution by Peter Jankowitsch indicates, Austria plays an increasingly active role in international organizations. In short, if the First Republic was a failure, the developments since 1945 have many aspects of a success story.

As stated above, this contrast may explain the somewhat euphoric evaluation of the present situation by the older generation. But the positive attitude to the present situation is not limited to that generation.[4] Rather, it is shared by the great majority of the entire population. We can surmise that as far as the younger generation is concerned, the comparison is more with the rest of Europe than with the Austrian past. In such comparisons Austria need no longer feel inferior. The per capita product and per capita income are now up to the standards of Western Europe. The country no longer appears somewhat backward—"charmingly backward" according to the tourist cliché, but backward nevertheless—but it has fulfilled its "need to catch up" and has become "mature for Europe." (Such words as *Nachholbedarf* and *Europareife* were much in vogue in the 1960s.) Various chapters in this volume indicate this progress in such areas as technology, economy, law, the school system, and the bureaucracy.

Underlying this "modernization" is a change in attitudes, particularly in the area of political culture. As Fritz Fellner notes in the Introduction, after the breakup of the monarchy, Austrians found it difficult to accommodate themselves to the new reality of living in a small, relatively unimportant state. As mentioned above, they had never been a unit within the monarchy. The question was raised whether, having become the inhabitants of a separate state by the will of the victorious powers, they now also constituted a nation. Many answered it in the negative and saw Austrians as a part of the German nation.[5] Most of those who perceived differences between Austrians and Germans preferred a self-image that was backward-looking, conservative, and influenced by adherence to the preindustrial, nonsecular values of the past. An ambivalence regarding the Austrian national identity persisted throughout the First Republic.[6] In the Second Republic, however, an Austrian national consciousness has emerged. A number of opinion polls indicate clearly that the overwhelming majority now affirms the existence of an Austrian nation.[7]

As Peter Gerlich and Anton Pelinka note, the general framework of politics—the Constitution and the party system—is essentially identical with that of the First Republic. But attitudes toward politics have clearly changed. Austrians of the interwar period were ambivalent in regard to the form of government, namely parliamentary democracy. When the highest stake—the future of society—was fought about in the streets, the parliamentary discussions seemed somewhat futile. The polarization of the parties made fruitful cooperation also impossible within parliament. Because of its poor performance record—due, of course, also to other causes, including exogenous ones—parliamentary democracy was not accorded full legitimacy.

The experiences of the civil war of 1934, of the authoritarian regime, and of the Nazi period were not lost on the politicians of the two big parties, who emerged or reemerged in the Second Republic. Some of them had shared a common fate in Hitler's concentration camps. The resulting political tolerance, together with, paradoxically, a lingering distrust of each other which made it seem risky to entrust either party by itself with the reins of government, led the party elites to experiment with the model of a Grand Coalition form of parliamentary democracy.[8] The need for a united front against the occupying powers was, of course, an important motivation, but the Grand Coalition continued for eleven years beyond the end of the occupation in 1955. It is a sign of the general acceptance of parliamentary democracy in the Second Republic—shared, as Leser notes in the Epilogue, even by former Nazis readmitted to political life in 1949—that one of the criticisms of the Grand Coalition that led to its ultimate demise in 1966 was the doubt whether the model (including the lack of an effective opposition to the government) was a true parliamentary democracy. The decrease in the ideological polarization of the parties and their increasing pragmatism removed the risks of a return to the more common majoritarian model of democracy, and the transition to it proceeded smoothly. Since 1966 one of the big parties forms the government, while the other plays the role of opposition.

A further change in attitudes is indicated by an examination of the election campaigns of the last decade. Beginning at least in 1970, the parties vied for recognition by the voters as the pioneers of a "modern" Austria. In this appeal—which obviously tapped a latent popular mood—the Socialist Party (SPÖ) under Bruno Kreisky turned out to be more successful, especially among younger voters. "We received from the voters a mandate for the modernization of Austria," wrote the SPÖ ideologist Karl Czernetz in the party journal *Zukunft* in October 1971. However, this success of the SPÖ should not obscure the efforts of the People's party (ÖVP) to shed much of its conservative image and, indeed, of its actual conservatism and to become "a modern party of the progressive sector." These efforts are the more significant, since an appeal to modernity or progress would have been uncongenial to the tradition-minded clientele of the party's prewar predecessor, the Christian Socialist party.[9]

There are signs of another change in elite attitudes—and possibly popular attitudes as well—that deserve mention. As Norbert Leser, following the historian Adam Wandruszka, notes, the three dominant political tendencies (that in the form of the three *Lager* had carried over from the monarchy to the First Republic and then to the present) had developed out of the disintegration and, in fact, in opposition to the old liberalism which had experienced a short-lived ascendancy during the late 19th century.[10] It is thus somewhat surprising that, probably related to the preference for "modernity," the three present inheritors of these tendencies—the SPÖ, ÖVP, and FPÖ—have of late come to lay claim to representing liberalism. For the FPÖ (Freiheitliche Partei, usually translated as Liberal party) this claim is linked with the ongoing attempt to change the party from one of German nationalism (which was the attraction to its original clientele) to one that, having embraced parliamentary democracy, serves that form of government by opposing the collectivist tendencies of the two big parties.[11] As far as the big parties are concerned, liberalism has permeated the SPÖ in the form of cultural liberalism (as evidenced by some of the reforms of the Kreisky government), whereas the ÖVP tends more in the direction of economic liberalism.[12]

Summarizing these sketchy remarks, we may state that the preferred self-image is that of a national community that is democratic, modern, and liberal. It seems appropriate to state this at the outset of a book on modern Austria, because these desired attributes are at odds with customary clichés and with attitudes actually characteristic in Austria's more recent past.

In the foregoing we discussed prevailing attitudes in the area of political culture in a broad sense, i.e. attitudes in regard to national identity, the governmental system, and some basic attributes of the society. When we turn to culture in the sense of the various forms of artistic expression—the sense, by the way, in which the term is most frequently used in the German language—we find a widely shared general belief in the importance of the arts for society. The contributions by Wendelin Schmidt-Dengler, Gottfried Scholz, Ernst Haeusserman and Sigrid Wiesmann, and Gottfried Heindl indicate that this is reflected in cultural policy: Austria is well known as a "big spender in the arts." Beyond that, however, a certain heterogeneity is apparent. In the artistic establishment and in the evaluation of artistic achievement by the general public, conservatism is the prevailing tendency. Modernity is contained by tradition. Fifty years ago, the poet Anton Wildgans noted with approval that the idea that "every innovation might contain the gospel," the "barbaric pleasure in worthless glitter that loudly proclaims to be valuable and genuine," and the urge to be "with the times" are not as widespread in Austria as they are in some other societies.[13] This applies even today in the arts.

Yet, as a sort of counterpoint, we find also experimentation and avant-gardism in literature, music, the fine arts, and the performing arts, carried forward especially by the younger generation. Often this takes the form of endeavors to bring art closer to the life of the people and thus to a juxtaposition of "art for the elite" and "art for the people." Avant-gardism, too, is an Austrian tradition, although one that was stifled at times by conservatism or by the cultural policies of authoritarian regimes.[14]

The customary clichés make it appear as if the terms "Austria" and "modern" were somehow contradictory. The reality in present-day Austria is obviously more complex. The chapters of this book, written by prominent Austrians, will, among other things, indicate to what extent Austria is modern in the various aspects of life that they describe and analyze.

Habent sua fata libelli! If John McNeil, Chief Executive Officer of Annual Reviews, had not raised the question of a possible new edition of my book on *Politics in Austria* at a dinner conversation with our mutual friend Ruth Krow, this book might not have been written. Professor J. Murray Luck, Executive Officer of the Society for the Promotion of Science and Scholarship (SPOSS), subsequently asked whether, as an alternative, I would be willing to edit a book on *Modern Austria,* written by Austrian authors, as a sequel to the volume on *Modern Switzerland,* which he had edited. I agreed to this proposal. Before I had advanced very far in my planning, Professor Fritz Fellner of the University of Salzburg came to Stanford as the first Visiting Professor of Austrian Studies under a program initiated in 1977 through a grant of the Austrian government and people. I asked him to assist me as co-editor, and by agreement we coopted Dr. Hubert Feichtlbauer editor of the political and cultural weekly *Die Furche,* in the same capacity. Professor Luck's experience and wise counsel was of inestimable help to me throughout. I am also indebted to Professor Fellner and Dr. Feichtlbauer for carrying out their duties of communication with the authors, which were possibly more burdensome than any of us had anticipated.

Because of the multitude of disciplines represented by the various chapters of this book, we felt it desirable to have the advice of an economist and of an expert in the arts. We therefore invited Professor Eduard März and Professor Gottfried Scholz to join us on the Editorial Committee and to take charge of the chapters related to their fields. They graciously accepted. In our first meetings in Vienna in May 1979, we agreed on the structure of the volume, on the topics of the various chapters, and on a list of potential contributors. Another meeting of the Editorial Committee was held in May 1980 to assure reasonable compliance with the prepublication time schedule, and I am grateful for the cooperation of its members also in this phase. We are all grateful to the authors, who—in spite of their heavy public or academic duties—found time to contribute to this undertaking.[15]

Although some manuscripts were submitted in English, most had to be translated. Some authors made their own arrangements in this regard. The majority of the chapters were translated by Dr. Ulrike Lieder at Stanford University and by Fred Prager and Susan Perkins in Vienna. Elizabeth Spurr served as copy editor with efficiency and great common sense. The book's cover was designed by Witold Preyss. Dr. Peter Frank, curator of the Germanic collections of the Stanford Libraries, was unstinting in his help and advice. The Department of Political Science at Stanford University made secretarial services available to me, and Elizabeth Gretz typed, with cheerfulness and efficiency, the voluminous correspondence with co-editors and authors, retyped some manuscripts, and kept track of the progress of the project. The Society for the Promotion of Science and Scholarship proved to be an unusually supportive publisher. Sharon Hawkes, Richard Burke and other members of the staff of Annual Reviews Inc. were most helpful in keeping the production of the book reasonably close to its schedule. Of course, there were occasional delays and frustrations; at such times the moral support of John McNeil was particularly welcome. To all of them go my thanks.

It is my pleasant duty to acknowledge with sincere gratitude the support of the Austrian Ministry for Foreign Affairs, and particularly the friendly interest that the director of its Press and Information Section, Dr. Gregor Woschnagg, evinced for this undertaking from its beginning.

In the "destiny" of a book, publication is of course a beginning, not an end. It then has to make its way in the world. As we submit *Modern Austria* to its readers, we can only echo the hope expressed in the Preface by Austria's Federal President, Dr. Rudolf Kirchschläger, that the volume will contribute to the dissemination of knowledge about Austria at the most up-to-date level and thus to better understanding.

Kurt Steiner
Editor

Notes

1. The "music" referred to in the relevant survey responses was overwhelmingly that of Mozart, Johann Strauss, Haydn, Beethoven, and Schubert.
2. The nadir was reached prior to the Geneva Protocols of 1922, when the dissolution of the state and the distribution of its various parts among neighboring states was openly discussed. See, e.g., Kurt Waldheim, *The Austrian Example* (New York, 1971), pp. 29–30. Later Austria followed an "Italian course," leading to the Rome Protocols of 1934. For a while Mussolini played the role of a protector of Austrian independence against Hitler's designs. The *rapprochement* between Mussolini and Hitler led to the adoption of a "German course" in 1936, when the government declared that Austria's foreign policy would be determined by its being "a German state."
3. See also Felix Butschek, Österreichs Wirtschaft vom Zusammenbruch zum Staatsvertrag, in *Europäische Rundschau* (Wien, Frühjahr 1980), p. 71.
4. In surveys in 1959, 1964, and 1970, respondents were asked the question "When was Austria, in your opinion, best off?" In 1959, 8 percent opted for the First Republic; in 1964 and 1970 only 3 percent did so. The corresponding figures for the Second Republic were 74 percent, 83 percent, and 92 percent. See Peter J. Katzenstein, The Last Old Nation: Austrian National Consciousness Since 1945, in *Comparative Politics*, January 1977, pp. 147–71.
5. Friedrich Heer, in *Österreich—ein Leben Lang* (Wien, 1962), phrased the question as follows: "Who were these Austrians after 1918? Were they Germans in rump Austria, German Austrians, Austrian Germans, Germans in a 'second German state' or an Austrian nation?"
6. The ambivalence was particularly strong among the political elites. See Kurt Steiner, *Politics in Austria* (Boston, 1972), pp. 14–21.
7. Ibid., pp. 156–58. See also William T. Bluhm, *Building an Austrian Nation: The Political Integration of a Western State* (New Haven, 1973), and Peter J. Katzenstein, *op. cit.* For a reflection of this in the emergence of an identifiable modern Austrian literature, see the chapter by W. Schmidt-Dengler in this volume.
8. See Steiner, *op. cit.,* pp. 167–88, 409–26. The Grand Coalition is an example of the type of democratic system for which Arend Lijphart and other political scientists use the term "consociational democracy." See Lijphart's Typology of Democratic Systems in *Comparative Political Studies,* vol. 1 (1968–1969), pp. 3ff.
9. On the election campaigns of 1970 and 1971, see Steiner, *op. cit.,* pp. 271–76.
10. See Norbert Leser's Epilogue to this volume; also Steiner, *op. cit.,* pp. 39–44, 120–32.
11. See the chapters by Pelinka, Fischer, and Leser in this volume.
12. See Leser, Epilogue. The competing claims to being liberal were evidenced, for example, in the February 1980 issue of the journal *Berichte und Informationen,* in which ÖVP chairman Anton Mock called his party "a natural political home also for the liberal person," and Leopold Gratz, the Socialist mayor of Vienna, wrote about "the pseudo-liberalism of the ÖVP."
13. Quoted in the chapter by Gottfried Heindl in this volume.
14. One example is the "secession" of innovative artists from the artistic establishment in the *fin de siècle.*
15. Because the prospective authors of the chapters on energy and on the educational system were unable to meet required deadlines, I undertook to provide some information on these topics.

Modern Austria, pp. 1–20
Copyright © 1981 by SPOSS Inc. All rights reserved

INTRODUCTION: THE GENESIS OF THE AUSTRIAN REPUBLIC

Fritz Fellner

Professor of Modern and Contemporary History, University of Salzburg

1

When, during the Paris Peace Conference in the spring of 1919, a journalist asked French Premier Clemenceau which territories of the Habsburg monarchy the Austria under discussion consisted of, the old statesman is said to have answerd, *"L'Autriche, c'est ce qui reste"* (Austria, that is what is left over). Historians have meanwhile proved that Clemenceau never did make that statement—and yet they have accepted it as historically true, because it characterizes most fittingly not only the genesis of the Republic of Austria, but even more so the mentality of this small nation's citizens. People in the "hereditary lands," as the Danubian and alpine provinces of the Habsburg monarchy were called, and which were inhabited by Germans, had always considered themselves the center of the multi-national empire. They felt they were the core from which proceeded the formation of the great power in Central Europe and, even more, of the great Habsburg empire upon which, at one time, the sun did not set. Up until the collapse of the Habsburg rule at the end of World War I, these people felt responsible for the entire empire; they thought of solutions to the crises that had been shaking this empire for decades only in terms of reforms that would not have affected the extent of the empire's territorial holdings.

Of all the fourteen nationalities that lived under the rule of the Habsburg dynasty until 1918, the Germans were the only ones who had always thought in terms of the entire state and who had not called for "national liberation." With one exception, it had been German politicians and authors who had developed all the plans for reforming the multi-national state in

Translated by Ulrike E. Lieder, Stanford University

9306-6403/81/0415-0001$01.50

order to overcome the quarrels among the individual national groups.[1] The Czechs, Croats, Poles, and Romanians, even the Hungarians, had dreamed of liberation and had made plans for their independence. The German-Austrians had, at best, discussed a reform of the empire and were intellectually and politically unprepared when, during the military collapse of the last war months, the many nations left their common home and tried to take along what they considered their own. The German-Austrians remained behind—in their own eyes and emotions they were *ce qui reste*—and they found themselves confronted with the necessity of having to find a new goal, a new meaning for their lives and their history. Unprepared for this situation, and unable to imagine life as a small nation,[2] misunderstanding the interpretation of the cliché of self-determination, they believed they could secure their future only in a union of all Germans, in joining the German Reich—only to find themselves, one generation later, after the catastrophe of World War II, once again confronted with the problem of having to reorient themselves.

Again, the question of the "meaning of Austrian history" arose, and even more than at the time of the founding of the republic in 1918, the Austrians in 1945 sought refuge in the past; they began to repress the apparent hopelessness and meaninglessness of the present by resorting to the greatness of the past. The Austrians, more so than other nations, live in and by history, a history that has never really been their "own history" in the way in which they presently perceive it as their "own past." It was the misconception of the Germans of the Habsburg monarchy that they identified with the entire state and were unable to recognize and accept the independence and difference of the other nations and their political-social-constitutional organization. It is the misunderstanding of the Austrians of today that they usurp as "their" history everything that took place in Central Europe between antiquity and the end of World War I in 1918.

This problem is documented by a comparison of history textbooks and reference books of the various successor states: Hungarian, Yugoslav, Czech, Polish, and Italian history includes the fate of the Habsburg monarchy only inasmuch as it concerns their own nation and treats the rest as the history of a foreign nation. In present-day Austria, "Austrian" history is still considered to be the history of all countries that at one time or another were under the rule of the Habsburg dynasty—even in the case of only secondary or tertiary dynasties that were connected to the Empire only through family ties, but not politically and economically. Today's Austrians usurped the history of Central Europe, just as their ancestors, the Germans of the Habsburg monarchy, thought to speak on behalf of the entire Empire. This preoccupation with the concepts of the great empire, the incessant references to a past historical role, has, to this day, hampered Austria's finding its self-image, has made it difficult for Austrians to accept the national reality of a territorially small Republic of Austria. The modern-day Austria constantly measures itself against the "old" Austria, and it seems that a brief outline of this historical self-image and its critical confrontation with the real historical situation is more necessary for an understanding of this country's current problems than for most other small states in Europe.

2

The territory of present-day Austria is rich in historical traditions. An outline of Austria's history could—even should—begin in that early era of the Iron Age, about 800 B.C., that had been named the Hallstatt period after the great discovery site of remnants of the Celtic culture in Upper Austria. It could report on the research done on the Roman period, when the border of the Roman Empire followed the Danube, and to which all important Austrian cities can be traced back, either as settlements or as military camps. There have been those who wanted to derive a mission for the Austria of the present from this function of antiquity, this aspect of the cities and camps on the Danube as outposts of occidental culture. Others, with no less justification, thought to recognize for Austria the historical task of bridging cultures from the ethnic and ideological mixtures that characterize the history of the Austrian region during the transition from antiquity to the Middle Ages.

However, most experts agree that the beginning of Austrian historical identity dates back to the 10th century, when the Babenberg dynasty was given the margravate in the southeast of the country. The name *ostarrichi* first appears in a document from the year 996. Precisely with this agreement on the beginning of Austrian history begins the misunderstanding that is so characteristic of the Austrian conception of history. The Babenbergs' margravate was only a small area, situated approximately where the Monastery Melk on the Danube is located today; in the following decades it expanded in the direction of today's Upper and Lower Austria, and established a capital in Vienna in the middle of the 12th century. Vorarlberg, the Tyrol, Salzburg, Carinthia, Styria, Burgenland, and even large parts of Upper Austria had their own history, independent of the core of Austria, well into the Modern Age, and they never belonged to the Babenbergs' territory. For a brief period in the middle of the 13th century, after the Babenbergs had become extinct, there was the possibility of a union of the territories in the heart of Central Europe under the Bohemian king Ottokar Przemysl, when Ottokar added the estate of the Babenbergs to his Bohemian lands. But these ties were cut for two centuries when the Habsburgs moved into the Austrian patrimonial lands during the 1270s.

From the very beginning, the position of the Habsburgs in Central Europe was determined by the policy that was later pointedly expressed in the famous Latin saying, *Bella gerant alii, tu felix Austria nube* (Let the others wage war; you, fortunate Austria, marry!). The basic principle of feudal rule, marriage contract, and succession by inheritance formed the constituent elements of the conglomerate of counties, duchies, and kingdoms that the Habsburgs acquired one by one, beginning in the 13th century, building the empire that, at the time of its greatest expansion in the early 18th century, stretched from the coast of present-day Belgium to close to the Black Sea, and from Tuscany to far into Poland. We cannot rightfully include in the "Austrian" history those years at the beginning of the 16th century when, owing to Emperor Maximilian I's marriage policy, his grandson Charles V could call his own all Spanish possessions including the overseas colonies and could claim that the sun never set on his empire. But, to be sure, the Austrians are proud of the jewels and gems stemming from that union, which are being kept in the treasury in Vienna.

The early 16th century, or, more precisely, the years 1521–1522, when Emperor Charles V gave the Central European lands to his brother Ferdinand, thus separating the Austrian line of the Habsburgs from the Spanish line, and 1526, when the Austrian line of the Habsburgs inherited Bohemia and parts of Hungary, may be considered the decisive milestone of Austrian history. It was the time when the territories were united that were to remain united until 1918. In his excellent book on the essence and the problems of the history of Central Europe, united under the Habsburg rule, *The Habsburg Empire, A Study in Integration and Disintegration,* Robert A. Kann sets the year 1526 as the time when the domains, which the Habsburgs had acquired and expanded, became a state.[3]

Only thirty years later, Ferdinand I was elected Emperor of Germany, and, except for a single brief interruption, the imperial crown of the German Empire remained in the hands of the Austrian line of the Habsburg dynasty. The political weight and the historical tradition of the name Habsburg were so great that even after the death of the last male Habsburg, Charles VI, the succession of the Habsburg daughter Maria Theresa could be secured through the Pragmatic Sanction of 1713; her husband's name was simply appended to the dynasty name: Habsburg-Lorraine was the name of the house that then reigned over Central Europe for another two centuries. From a historical perspective, the Habsburg holdings represent themselves as the archetype of feudal power; the title of the Habsburg ruler with its enumeration of 33 "functions" and countries illustrates much more impressively than any analysis the feudal structure of the power of the "House of Austria".[4]

3

While the Habsburgs increased their holdings country by country through marriage and succession by inheritance—and, in repelling the Ottoman threat in Southeastern Europe, through war as well—a fundamental change of the economic and thus also of the social and political order was taking place in Europe. The transition from the feudal to the capitalist system, which had created a modern state in France during the 17th century, began to make itself felt in the Habsburg territories during the 18th century. The history of the "House of Austria" during the 18th century was shaped by the problems of changing the feudal order to a modern state. However, historians have only very recently begun to view the 18th century no longer exclusively from a dynastic perspective, but to investigate its socioeconomic conditions. It should be noted that the modernization of the Habsburg empire becomes apparent a short time after the kingdom of Lombardy and the Spanish Netherlands were incorporated into the Habsburg empire as a consequence of the Spanish succession; the character of these two countries with their advanced, industrial-capitalist structure differed vastly from the other, predominantly agrarian possessions of the Habsburgs. It is just as noteworthy that this process of change was first realized in the Bohemian-Moravian lands of the Habsburg empire, whose economic structure was closest to an industrial-capitalist system. Yet, disregarding Lombardy, the Spanish Netherlands, and Bohemia, the Habsburg possessions during the 18th century lacked the socioeconomic infrastructure from which the establishment of a territorially uniform state would have organically followed. The change of the feudal holdings of the House of Austria into a modern State of Austria was not the result of a change in the economic and social structure; rather, it was forced upon the lands from above; it was an attempt to modernize through administrative techniques by decree of the ruler. This historical peculiarity has remained a determining factor of the Austrian mentality until the present day. It is not the citizen's own economic and political interest that, in interaction with the other citizens' interests, molds public life, but the government functionary; the authorities tell the subject how to behave, tell him what is considered correct "above." The change of Central Europe from a feudal order to modern constitutional statehood took place not in the form of self-government by individuals but in the form of administration. The development of the modern structure of the state in the Habsburg countries is characterized not by the Anglo-Saxon formation of a local government, but by the establishment of a bureaucratic system. This bureaucracy, setting out to organize the economy and society without having real economic substance, found itself in its efforts confronted with the opposition of the traditionally feudal elements of the estates, which, up until the middle of the 19th century, represented the real, the agrarian, power in Central Europe. Joseph II wanted to push forward the reforms that were begun by the statesmen Kaunitz and Haugwitz in the 1770s and 1780s, but he failed to attain his goals. However, the system of "Josephinism," which he created, namely the dominance of the bureaucratic civil servant in public life, has survived all political upheavals and changes and has remained to this day the principle of state order in Austria.

Establishing a modern state administration requires a trained corps of functionaries who are the basis of this administration; it requires trained subjects who can read, understand, and implement the administration's orders. Therefore, it was only logical that Maria Theresa's and Joseph's reform policies concentrated in particular on the development of a general education system. The Habsburgs of the 18th century established in their territories a great and successful education system, ranging from the establishment of mandatory schooling for every child to the reorganization of the universities, a system whose essential elements remained valid well into the 20th century. But what was instrumental in forming a uniform consciousness of state, overcoming local and provincial traditions in the Western European countries, became a hindrance to the formation of a common patriotism in the countries of the Habsburg Crown, and finally became the element that would destroy the Habsburg empire: literacy made the population conscious of their language and thus of their nationality, and the introduction to higher education awakened among the students and the educated bourgeoisie the desire to assert ethnic and national characteristics. The opposition of the estates to the centralist state bureaucracy was joined in the 19th century by the demand of nationalist ideology for recognition of linguistic and cultural independence. The history of the Habsburg empire during the 19th century is the history of failure of state reform. Attempting to create a centrally organized uniform state, the government ultimately lost its battle on two fronts, against the tradition of the feudal estates on the one side and against the awakening of national liberation movements on the other. Beginning with the creation of an Austrian empire in 1804, which encompassed all kingdoms, duchies, counties, and lands, continuing with Metternich's attempt to overcome the claims of the individual nations by creating supranational federative structures, and reaching to the constitutional experiments of the revolutionary year 1848 and of the early 1860s, which culminated in a reform of the interior order of the Habsburg nations with the so-called *Ausgleich* (compromise) of 1867, the history of this conglomerate of nations has been shaped by the dilemma of trying to find a governmental order that, while respecting the states' rights stemming from feudal traditions, and while taking into consideration the national independence of the 14 nationalities that had coalesced under the Habsburg rule, would make possible a parliamentarization of the political life that was in accordance with the constitutional demands of the 19th century.

Since historiography concentrated on political, national, and cultural aspects in the representation of the history of the Habsburg multi-national empire, it has lost sight of the fact that the ultimate failure of the new order was due to the following factor: the nations of the Habsburg monarchy lacked the prerequisite economic structure that could have borne a spontaneous democratization from within the society. It is not a matter of chance that, when reflecting on Austrian history, what comes to mind primarily are the cultural achievements of the clerical and aristocratic dynasties, the great monuments of baroque culture, opera and music, theater, palaces, and painting, the documentation of mystical traditions. Rationalization, the technical modernization of Central Europe, took place from above, without the demographic bases being present. In Austria, secularization of thought during the Age of Enlightenment led from the religious complex of the Counter Reformation to the myth of nationalism. Only during two brief periods in the history of the Austro-Hungarian Empire, in the thirty years from 1850 to about 1880 and in the two decades around the turn of the 20th century, do we find the beginnings of a socioeconomic change to the capitalist system that had developed during the 19th century in Western Europe and even in the German empire and in the kingdom of Italy.

4

The first decades in the rule of Emperor Franz Joseph were shaped by the problems arising from the contrast between federalism and centralism. The so-called *Ausgleich* of 1867 sought to overcome this polarity by granting independence to the countries of the Hungarian crown. From that time on, the only things common to all parts of the monarchy were the dynasty and the empire's foreign policy. Each of the two parts of the Dual Monarchy, as it was known thenceforth, had its own parliament and its own government. The inhabitants of Vienna and of the hereditary lands, those parts of the Dual Monarchy of which present-day Austria is comprised, never did learn to accept the independence of the Hungarian half of the empire. After the loss of Lombardy and Venezia in the wars of 1859 and 1866, and after the expulsion from the German Confederation in 1866, the *Ausgleich* of 1867 signified the end of the dominating position the Germans believed to have achieved in the Habsburg monarchy. Still habituated to by the imperialistic-nationalist concepts of the state of the 19th century, they had presumed the medieval ideal of the supranational empire to contain a national concept of the state and had seen themselves on a political-cultural mission, given them by history. In a kind of manifest destiny, the Germans believed they had to fulfill some sort of civilizing duty toward the non-German nationalities in Eastern and Southeastern Europe. The dominating position of the Germans in the Habsburg empire found its institutional embodiment in the needs of a uniformly organized, modern administration of the state and was perceived as oppression by the non-German nationalities who had just discovered their national identity, especially so because of this identification of German dominance with the central administration and the requirement of German as the official language of the empire. Since the center of the national language of each of the nations united in the Habsburg monarchy was located outside the Habsburg territory, the pan-nationalist tendencies of the era of nationalism had to bring about the internal corrosion of the multi-nation empire.

Around the turn of the 20th century, the national disintegration of the Dual Monarchy had progressed to such an extent that the governments of the great European powers began discussing the restructuring of Central Europe in the event of the dissolution of the Habsburg empire, which was to be expected after the death of the aged Emperor Franz Joseph. But the empire seemed to find once again a new dynamism when a brief economic upswing during the first decade of the 20th century led to an attempt at expansive foreign policy in the Balkans, directed by the Foreign Minister, Count Aehrenthal. Because of the general impression of national anarchy, which could not even be coped with by the rise of democratic mass parties after the introduction of universal suffrage in 1907, historians had, for a long time, lost track of the fact that this flare-up of economic-capitalist and imperialist dynamics in foreign policy coincided with a new zenith in Austrian art and culture, with the work of Klimt, Mahler, and Schnitzler. Only in recent years have we once again become aware of this coincidence.[5]

The success of Aehrenthal's imperialism in the Balkans blinded the younger members of the Viennese leadership elite; they failed to see the limitations of the power of the Habsburg empire in both domestic and foreign policy and thought to be able to restore order at home through a ruthless show of force, to be able to ward off the irredentism threatening the empire from all sides through a belligerent act. The assassination of Heir Apparent Franz Ferdinand and his wife on June 28, 1914, in Sarajevo provoked punitive action against the kingdom of Serbia, which, in the course of a few weeks, escalated into world war. However, this did not generate a general patriotism in the entire empire; rather, the desire for national liberation intensified, and the internal disintegration of the Habsburg monarchy progressed parallel to its military defeat. Even before the military collapse, the Czechs and South Slavs had proclaimed their demand for independence. Emperor Franz Joseph's successor, Emperor Charles, attempted one last time to keep the dispersing nations together in a restructured empire when he ordered federalization of the empire in the October Manifesto of 1918. But the Manifesto ultimately turned out to be only the constitutional instrument for the legal dissolution of the Habsburg monarchy. Even before the armistice was signed, the Czechs, South Slavs, Poles, and Romanians had constituted themselves independent states, a development that took the representatives of the German-speaking nations of the Habsburg monarchy completely by surprise. Even the Social Democrats had, up to the very end, planned and developed concepts only for the Habsburg monarchy in its entirety. It is characteristic of the historical assessment of the events of 1918 that, half a century later, in 1968, the Hungarians, Czechs, South Slavs, Romanians, and Poles celebrated the 50th anniversary of the founding of their states, while the Austrians discussed the dissolution of the Habsburg monarchy.[6]

5

There were no German-Austrians in the fall of 1918 who, at home or in exile, would have fought for the establishment of a small Austrian republic. Karl Renner, head of the German-Austrian Social Democrats, who took over the direction of German-Austrian politics during those weeks, had always worked on programs for restructuring the entire multi-national empire since he became involved in politics around the turn of the century; he had never even considered the idea of an independent German-Austria. The German-Austrians of all political persuasions were so convinced that their historical mission was leadership of the Habsburg monarchy that there were no plans at all for the future of the empire's German-speaking countries in case of a dissolution of the Danubian monarchy. When it became obvious in October and November of 1918 that the non-German nations wanted to divorce themselves not only from their ties with the rule of the Habsburgs but also from their ties with the German-speaking hereditary lands, there was, in the area of present-day Austria, hardly a voice that spoke out for a solution that was confined to Austria itself.

Excluded from the union with the other former nations of the Habsburg crown, the Germans demanded the same "national solution" for themselves: the union of all Germans in a pan-German *Reich*.[7] The German dream of unity, which had failed during the revolution of 1848, was once again revived. The Proclamation of the Republic, which was published on November 12, 1918, following Emperor Charles' abdication, stated in Article 2: German-Austria is part of the German republic. This declaration of loyalty to a German identity and to the union with the German republic was common to all political persuasions. The small Austrian republic that was created at the time of the military and political collapse was only intended to be a temporary solution. It was the decision of the victorious Allies—who could not allow the German Reich they had just defeated to enlarge, with all the concomitant possibilities of a newly awakening Balkan imperialism—and not the will of the German-Austrian population that made the provisional solution of the fall of 1918 a finality. Article 88 of the Versailles Peace Treaty prohibited the incorporation of German-Austria into the German Reich; Article 80 of the state treaty of Saint-Germain stipulated the independence of the republic that had been constituted from the patrimonial lands of Lower and Upper Austria, Styria, Carinthia, the Tyrol, Vorarlberg, Salzburg, and the German-speaking part of western Hungary, which was now called Burgenland. The German-speaking provinces of Bohemia and Moravia, which had also been claimed for the small republic by its republican government, had to remain with Czechoslovakia, which was the successor of the kingdom of Bohemia and the margravate of Moravia. Some German-speaking border regions along the southeastern border of the republic were incorporated into the new Yugoslavian state, and South Tyrol was given to the kingdom of Italy for strategic reasons.

At a time of triumph for nationalist movements in Europe, this disregard for the national wishes of the Germans of the disintegrated Habsburg monarchy had to be especially offensive. The German-Austrians were never able to accept the new reorganization of Europe resulting from the Paris Peace Treaties; they had not wanted the state whose continued independent existence had been forced on them, and they reluctantly set about shaping it. It was the basic weakness of the First Republic, as the state of the time between the wars has become known since the reestablishment of Austria after World War II, that Austria had not evolved from an idea, had not been fought for, but had been forced upon the population. This basic situation, this attitude of aversion, explains and makes understandable the events that shaped the history of the years 1919–1938:[8] having grown up with concepts covering vast territories, the people could not get used to living in a small state. Ignaz Seipel, the leader of the Christian-Socialist party, and Otto Bauer, the leader of the Social Democratic party, ideological antagonists, agreed on this negation of the small Austrian state.

Not only was there nationalist aversion to existence as a small state, but valid economic reasons against it were believed to exist as well. The areas that were now united as the Austrian republic in their economic structure had never been oriented toward each other, but closely related to the other parts of the Habsburg monarchy. Vienna in particular, formerly the center of an empire of 50 million, was now, with its almost two million inhabitants, the disproportionately large capital of a republic of six million. The administrative machinery in Vienna, which the small republic had inherited from the monarchy, was much too large, and the country's industrial potential was much too small and had not been developed for the needs of the small state. Above all, the agricultural regions that had been left to the republic, could not, because of their alpine structure, provide the alimentation for the small state. Austria as a small state was not viable—not only was this conviction held by the Austrian republic's politicians, but it was shared by the statesmen of the great European powers. The small state could not exist on its own. Since it seemed to be in the interest of the balance of power in Central Europe to safeguard the independence of the Austrian republic, economic assistance was sought abroad. In the Geneva Protocols of October 1922, the League of Nations granted the Republic of Austria a loan for the stabilization of its currency, which had totally lost its value owing to inflation. The following stipulations were attached to the loan: Austria must not enter a union with the German Reich, and she had to obligate herself to make far-reaching budget cuts.

While the Geneva Protocols secured the international status of the republic, the financial aid turned out to be a factor of internal destabilization. Already during the last decades of the Habsburg monarchy, the conflict between three political camps had determined the political life in the provinces of the Republic of Austria:[9] the various German-nationalist-liberal groups of the bourgeoisie; the Christian Socialists, whose base at that time was still the shop owners in Vienna and the farmers in the country; and the Marxist-oriented Social Democrats, who represented labor. In the days of the founding of the republic, these three parties had formed an all-party government, headed by Karl Renner and had attempted to master the crises. In 1920, they jointly produced a parliamentary constitution. However, as Austria's international position stabilized, the political conflict among the parties erupted anew. This conflict was all the more dangerous as all three directions were distinctly ideological groupings with clear-cut social class structures. The domestic political scene in Austria, and even parliament, was dominated by animosity; it proved fatal to the democratic development that all three groupings made militant disputes the center of their activities. Clashes at rallies and political acts of violence dominated everyday life. The growing home defense forces—supported by the Italian Fascists—poisoned the climate even more. The democratic peace at home was finally broken when, in July 1927, more than 100 persons were killed during a shooting following a demonstration.

The world economic crisis hit the hardly restored Austrian economy especially hard, and the collapse of the Austrian *Creditanstalt** brought about a period of the most severe economic depression for the country. This

*Translator's Note: The *Creditanstalt* was the major bank in Austria.

came at a time when the growing national socialism had introduced a new, aggressive, ideological element in the political discussion. National social- ism, controlled by Germany, undermined the moderate German-nationalist camp, the so-called pan-Germans. The Christian Socialists, who had formed the government since 1920, were afraid of losing new elections and took refuge in an authoritarian course.[10] In 1933, Chancellor Dollfuss stripped parliament of its power and prohibited the political parties. In February 1934, during a three-day civil war, the Social Democratic party was smashed, and a new constitution with authoritarian-fascist traits was proclaimed.

The clerico-fascist regime, so called because of the Dollfuss government's close ties to the Catholic church, could only stay in power by means of harsh repression. Chancellor Dollfuss was assassinated during an attempted *Putsch* by the National Socialists. His successor, Schuschnigg, was unable to establish order and political stability in the country, which was endan- gered by both economic problems and external threats. The ideologically hostile concepts that permeated the ways of thinking snuffed any new beginnings of democratic cooperation, and the economic uncertainty opened Austria up to the National Socialist propaganda, which claimed to be the fulfillment of German-nationalist dreams. Not only the Germans and the Austrians but also the British and the Americans were convinced that it had been a historical mistake to prohibit the incorporation of Austria into the German Reich in 1919. The internal crises of the "state against its will" —as the First Republic is characterized in retrospect—convinced many who rejected national socialism because of its racist ideology that only an Anschluss would bring a solution to the problems and would safeguard the welfare of the population. The wish for economic stability, the opposition to the clerico-fascist regime and the pan-German tradition paved the way for the success of national socialism and were responsible for the surrender without a fight when Hitler, during yet another internal crisis, had German troops march into Austria and proclaimed the Anschluss of Austria the "coming home to the German Reich."[11]

At that time, in March of 1938, the majority of the Austrian population welcomed the Anschluss to the National Socialist German Reich, and it should not be overlooked that, besides the pan-German tradition, the Aus- trians' pronounced anti-Semitism, stemming from religious and economic causes, enabled them to collaborate with national socialism. To be sure, the results of the plebiscite of April 10, 1938, which claimed that more than 99 percent of the population were followers of Hitler, were falsified, but at that time resistance to national socialism was limited to very small circles; even the Catholic church and the Social Democrats were then opposed only to the ideology of national socialism, not to the union with the German Reich.

6

In the following months of the year 1938, Austria became completely absorbed by the German Reich. The Austrians awakened from the propaganda frenzy over the Anschluss to the sobering reality of a purposeful destruction of their traditional characteristics, and instead of being led to economic prosperity, they were led from the depression into a new world war. Yet, the disillusionment about the Anschluss did not result in the development of an Austrian independence movement during those years. After all, the great powers had recognized *de facto* or *de jure* the Anschluss of Austria to the German Reich in 1938, and the League of Nations had, without opposing, accepted the destruction of the national independence of one of its members. Even after the outbreak of World War II, the political objectives within and without Austria were solely the suppression of the German military might and of National Socialist ideology, but not the reinstitution of the small Austrian republic. For the second time within one generation, Austrians found themselves confronted with the problem of a complete reorientation: pan-Germanism, which had been envisaged as the new goal after the disintegration of the Habsburg monarchy, had turned out to be the wrong way, and there were no new alternatives for the time being. However, as the war progressed, there was an increasing willingness not only to resist national socialism but also to repeal the Anschluss of Austria to the German Reich, among both the population and those who had left Austria for reasons of politics or race. But only after the great powers, allied against Hitler Germany, had declared the Anschluss null and void in the Moscow Declaration of 1943 and had proclaimed the reinstitution of an independent Austria as their war objective did the idea of bringing the small state of Austria back to life begin to gain ground among the emigrants and among the Austrian population.[12] With all due respect to the heroism of those Austrians who fought against national socialism in the resistance movement or against the German Reich in the war, it would be wrong historically to attribute decisive significance to this resistance. The material as well as ideological prerequisites for an effective resistance movement were simply lacking; what was at stake during the last war years was much more the reality of physical survival than the idealities of Austria's future organization.

7

The Austria that emerged in April 1945 from the ruins of National Socialist rule was, just like the First Republic, not the fruit of an idea that swept the nation, but the result of a given political situation. But, in contrast to the time 27 years ago, the Austrians did not rebel against this reality but seized the chance offered to them. One would almost be tempted to say that the Austrians proved in 1945 and in the following decades that people can actually learn from history. The state against its will, which they had without serious concern allowed to be destroyed in 1938, became the state that everybody wanted—so much so that the Austrian national propaganda today, 35 years later, has made us forget how little the Austrians of 1945 had wanted to believe in the possibility of the reinstatement of the Republic of Austria.[13] The basic weakness that had doomed the First Republic to failure from the moment of its birth in 1918 did not exist in 1945: her inhabitants did not consider the reconstituted Austria a provisional solution until the time of her incorporation into a larger political unit (an idea, incidentally, that the British pursued for some time; by a vague concept of a Danubian federation they wanted to prevent economic weakness in Central Europe as well as a possible expansion of Soviet power politics), but a definitive solution for which they were willing to work with the utmost effort. They were loyal to this small state whose viability they did not want to doubt and for which they wanted to work.

The Austrians had learned from history in another respect as well: not only had the First Republic failed because of a lack of patriotism and because of economic problems; it had also been destroyed from the inside, by the discord among the parties and by the deeply antidemocratic attitudes of politicians and citizens. The camps that had fought each other without mercy during the years between the wars were now willing to cooperate. During the years of National Socialist oppression, they had learned to respect each other, and they wanted to jointly carry out the task that so unexpectedly confronted them for the second time in their history. The violent confrontation, which had determined the history of the First Republic, was replaced by cooperation after 1945, and the democratic coalition became the characteristic of the Second Republic.

Yet, the external conditions threatened the continued existence of Austrian independence and the country's economic viability much more in 1945 than had been the case in 1918. The country was exhausted from the ravages of war, the Allied air raids had caused severe damage in the cities and in industry, and communications were largely interrupted. Furthermore, in accordance with Allied plans, Austria had been occupied by the armies of the great powers. Hardly liberated, Austria was in danger of becoming the plaything of big power rivalries, the pawn in the poker game of the Cold War. That this twofold danger could be overcome, that Austria could become not only viable but prosperous as never before—albeit after considerable delays—was due to the willingness of the Allies, the USA in particular, to help Austria through economic aid programs, but it was also very much the result of the Austrian population's will to live.

Even before the war ended in Europe, a provisional government that had been formed by representatives of all political directions on the initiative of the old Social Democrat Karl Renner proclaimed on April 27, 1945 Austria's independence as a democratic republic. In September 1945, in a conference of the provinces, representatives from all former provinces acknowledged the authority of the Renner government for the territory of the entire nation. At about the same time, the Western Allies, after having first been distrustful of this government because it had begun its activities under Soviet auspices, accepted it as the spokesman for all of Austria. Democratic parliamentary elections were held in November 1945. They showed that the two large political groupings, which had already determined the policies pursued by parliament during the First Republic, had remained essentially the same: the Socialist Party of Austria (SPÖ, Sozialistische Partei Österreichs), the successor party of the Social Democrats, and the Austrian People's Party (ÖVP, Österreichische Volkspartei), the successor party of the Christian Socialists, turned out to be almost equally strong. The election regulations would have given the absolute majority in parliament to the rather conservative ÖVP.

However, the leading politicians of the two parties decided to cooperate in order to share the burden of responsibility for denazification, economic reconstruction, and policies. The government was formed according to the proportional strength of the two parties as the "grand coalition." Within a short time, this system of proportional representation developed into a system of shared responsibility which encompassed the entire public life in Austria. The parties had decided not to draft a new constitution, but rather to return to the constitutional system of the First Republic, the 1920 constitution in its amended form of 1929. For the time being, however, the effectiveness of this constitution was hampered by the presence of the occupying powers; only the so-called second control agreement, a statute agreed upon among the Allies, which regulated occupation policy, created in 1946 the prerequisites for a relatively unhampered democratic political life in Austria.

The years 1945 to 1952 were years of fighting for survival. The nationalization of heavy industry and of banking, jointly decided by all parties, the support by the United Nations Relief and Rehabilitation Administration, and, beginning in 1948, the support from the Marshall Plan created the prerequisites for the recovery of the Austrian economy.

In the spring of 1955, ten years after the fighting of World War II had ended, the victorious Allies were finally able to overcome the tensions of the

Cold War to the extent that they met for the signing of a State Treaty on and with Austria, a treaty that established the conditions for the withdrawal of the Allied occupation forces. Now Austria's independence and free sovereignty were also internationally recognized.[14] After the occupation forces had withdrawn, the Austrian parliament, in free resolve, declared Austria a permanently neutral state on October 26, 1955. In the following decades, Austria went freely and independently through a period of growing economic prosperity and growing national self-confidence. Yet the memories of the economic catastrophies of the world economic crisis and of the political dangers and subversion of the time between the wars, still on the minds of the Austrians, overshadowed the material well-being, although in addition to the material prosperity there was political stability at home, the likes of which the country had never known.

In 1949, the adherents of the former pan-German party, which had been banned from the first parliamentary elections immediately after the end of the war because of their affiliation with the National Socialists, were allowed to participate again in the elections. With the Association of Independents (VdU, Verband der Unabhängigen), they brought back into the sphere of forces in Austrian domestic politics the somewhat diminished so-called third camp with a declared German-nationalist political direction. However, this time this anti-Marxist group was denied the decisive role it had played in the 1920s; the bitter experience of the National Socialist war years had deprived the German-nationalist ideology of its attraction, and the economic stabilization of the 1950s also contributed to the development of an Austrian national consciousness.

It was not least due to the willingness of the two large parties, ÖVP and SPÖ, to continue their cooperation that Austria was able to participate in Europe's prosperity, undisturbed and in domestic peace. Even after having regained full sovereignty with the State Treaty of 1955, the generation of 1945, the generation of the founders of the Second Republic, in a peculiar mixture of trust, based on the experience of years of cooperation during the occupation, and of mistrust, based on the bitter experience of hatred and fighting during the years between the wars, always preferred the compromise of a coalition to the possible perils of a confrontation between a one-party government and the opposition. The belief in the indispensability of the two-party government by proportional representation as guarantor of domestic peace began to falter only when the generation of 1945, for reasons of old age, had to hand over the leadership of the two large parties to the next generation, who considered the disadvantages of the proportional coalition to be greater than its advantages.

When the ÖVP, benefiting from an internal crisis in the SPÖ, was able to gain the absolute majority in the National Council (Nationalrat) for the first time in the 1966 parliamentary elections, the leaders of the two parties were unable to agree on the conditions of a coalition pact, and the ÖVP formed the first one-party government of the Second Republic under the leadership of Chancellor Klaus. Quite a few experts on Austrian politics and history, not only on the side of the Socialists, felt uneasy about this decision. The Socialists had not forgotten the trauma of 1920, when they had voluntarily left the coalition government and had been forced to remain in opposition until the end of the republic, and the democratically inclined Conservatives were still afraid that the year 1935 might be repeated, when Dollfuss, as chancellor of a Christian-Socialist government, destroyed the parliamentary system and violated the constitution. But these fears turned out to be unjustified. The ÖVP under Chancellor Klaus did not have a very skillful hand in its policies, although it should be remembered that many of the reforms, which were later implemented under the Socialist government in the 1970s, had first been discussed at that time, as for instance the reform of the educational system. However, at no time were there any intentions of jeopardizing the constitution.

When, after the legislative period of the parliament elected in 1966 had expired, the government held new elections in the spring of 1970, it led the country unintentionally and unexpectedly to a historical turning point. Disappointed by the ÖVP's leading personalities and its programs, the Austrian voters turned to the reformed SPÖ, which had also undergone a replacement of top-ranking officials. In the spring of 1970, for the first time in the history of the Second Republic, the Socialist party of Austria was returned to parliament as the strongest party. Bruno Kreisky, chairman of the SPÖ, rejected a coalition with one of the two other parties represented in parliament, and, since he did not have a majority, he risked the uncertainty of forming a minority government. Early new elections, held one year later, made this risk pay off (and honored the carefully balanced policies of Kreisky's first cabinet) and gave the SPÖ an absolute majority for the first time. This majority was not only confirmed but even strengthened in the 1975 and 1979 elections.

The turn from the 1960s to the 1970s was characterized by political successes of the Socialist parties throughout Europe; thus, from a historical point of view, the SPÖ's electoral victory cannot be regarded as surprising. Yet, this SPÖ victory derives its unique historical significance from the specifically Austrian development. Since the Communist party of Austria (KPÖ) has always been only a negligible factor in Austrian politics and never a formative force in Austrian history, the SPÖ had become the only representative of labor. The victory of the SPÖ therefore signals the completion of Austria's transformation from a country of farmers to a country of workers and employees. The SPÖs victory must be seen as the documentation of a complete change of Austria's social structure—this is its primary historical significance.

Yet the historical significance of this electoral victory goes far beyond just this. Before 1966, the progressive elements in Austria had shown fear of a recurrence of the right-wing dictatorship, of a return to the system of the 1930s, while the conservative elements had retained their fear of a Marxist revolution-a trauma remaining from the so-called revolutionary years, from the time of the founding of the republic after the end of World War I— which they had again and again introduced into the political discussion as a polemic element. In the 1966 elections, the Austrians proved that they had overcome the first basic weakness of the First Republic, the tendency toward a right-wing, authoritarian government; the 1970–1971 elections demonstrated that the second basic weakness of the First Republic, the fear of the supposed danger of a Socialist-Marxist revolution, had also been overcome. Twenty years after its foundation, the First Republic, worn down by this contrast between right and left, had fallen victim to the National Socialist seizure of power. Twenty-five years after its foundation, the Second Republic demonstrated in the 1970–1971 elections that it had found democratic stability in the interplay of parliamentary majorities, a stability that guaranteed respect for the constitution as the basis of political life by any government, regardless of its political persuasion. Since 1970, it is a historical fact beyond debate for the citizens of the Second Republic that Austria is a nation, and democracy its unchallenged constitutional basis.

Yet, in addition to these aspects of social and national history, the elections of 1970–1971 also contain a personnel decision of fundamental historical significance. In the country where political and cultural anti-Semitism had almost become a basic element of political attitudes since the emancipation of the Jews in the middle of the 19th century; in the country where Adolf Hitler had been decisively formed, especially in his anti-Semitic philosophy; in this country not only had the SPÖ been elected in 1970, but, in voting for the SPÖ the majority of Austrians had elected Bruno Kreisky, an Austrian of Jewish descent, to be chancellor. A brief attempt by a small group of political radicals during the 1970 election campaign at propagandistic exploitation of Kreisky's Jewish origin had only met with indignation among the population, not only among the SPÖ voters. In my opinion, the true historical significance of the 1970 elections for Austria is contained in this decision of the majority of Austrians not to let the question of Jewish descent become the criterion of political considerations. Anti-Semitism, this destructive element of hatred in the domestic policy of the period between the wars, has lost its destructive power for the Austrians, although it may still haunt a few minds. With this personnel decision of 1970, Austrians have finally freed themselves of the burden of the ideological sins of the time between the wars. From this point of view, the year 1970 signals the historical turning point, the completion of the construction of the democracy of the Second Republic, the beginning of a new historical period.

Notes

1. Kann, *The Multinational Empire.* (See the Selected Bibliography for complete publishing information.)
2. Fellner, p. 26.
3. Kann, *The Habsburg Empire.*
4. "We . . . by God's grace, Emperor of Austria; King of Hungary, of Bohemia, of Dalmatia, Croatia, Slavonia, Galicia, Lodomeria, and Illyria; King of Jerusalem, etc.; Archduke of Austria; Grand Duke of Tuscany and Cracow; Duke of Lothringia, of Salzburg, Styria, Carinthia, Carniola, and Bukowina; Grand Duke of Transylvania, Margrave of Moravia; Duke of Upper and Lower Silesia, of Modena, Parma, Piacenza, and Guastolla, of Ausschwitz and Sator, of Teschen, Friaul, Ragusa, and Zara; Princely Count of Habsburg and Tyrol, of Kyburg, Görz, and Gradisca; Duke of Trent and Brixen; Margrave of Upper and Lower Lausitz and Istria; Count of Hohenembs, Feldkirch, Bregenz, Sonnenberg, etc.; Lord of Trieste, of Cattaro, and above the Windisch Mark; Great Voyvod of the Voyvodina, Serbia, etc., etc." Quoted after Jászi, p. 34.
5. Schorske, *Fin de Siècle Vienna,* and Gerschenkron, *An economic Spurt That Failed.*
6. Plaschka and Mack, *Die Auflösung des Habsburgerreiches.*
7. Stadler, *The Birth of the Austrian Republic, 1918–1921.*
8. Gulick, *Austria from Habsburg to Hitler.*
9. Adam Wandruszka, Österreichs politische Struktur. Die Entwicklung der Parteien und politischen Bewegungen. In Heinrich Benedikt, *Geschichte der Republik Österreich.*
10. Carstens, *Fascist Movements in Austria.*
11. Luža, *Austro-German Relations in the Anschluss Era.*
12. Maimann, *Politik im Wartesaal,* and Fritz Fellner, *Die aussenpolitische und völkerrechtliche Situation Österreichs, 1938. Österreichs Wiederherstellung als Kriegsziel der Alliierten. In Weinzierl and Skalnik.*
13. Stadler, *Austria.*
14. Stourzh, *Kleine Geschichte des Österreichischen Staatsvertrags.*

Selected Bibliography

Austrian History Yearbook. Vols. I–XIV (1965–1979) published annually by Rice University in Cooperation with the Conference Group for Central European History. From vol. XV on, published by The Center for Austrian Studies at the University of Minnesota.

Barker, Elisabeth. *Austria 1918–1972.* London, 1973.

Benedikt, Heinrich, ed. *Geschichte der Republik Österreich.* München, 1954.

Bluhm, William T. *Building an Austrian Nation. The Political Integration of a Western State.* New Haven, 1973.

Braunthal, Julius. *The Tragedy of Austria.* London, 1948.

Buttinger, Joseph. *In the Twilight of Socialism: A History of Revolutionary Socialists in Austria.* New York, 1953.

Carstens, Francis L. *Fascist Movements in Austria. From Schönerer to Hitler.* Berkeley, Calif., 1977.

Crankshaw, Edward. *The Fall of the House of Habsburg.* London, 1963.

———. *The Habsburgs.* Wien, 1971.

Diamant, Alfred. *Austrian Catholics and the First Republic.* Princeton, 1960.

Evans, R. J. W. *The Making of the Habsburg Monarchy, 1550–1700.* London, 1979.

Fellner, Fritz. The Dissolution of the Habsburg Monarchy and Its Significance for the New Order in Central Europe: A Reappraisal. In *Austrian History Yearbook,* vol. IV–V (1968–1969).

Gerschenkron, Alexander. *An Economic Spurt That Failed.* Four lectures in Austrian History. Princeton, 1977.

Gulick, Charles A. *Austria from Habsburg to Hitler.* 2 vols. Berkeley, Calif., 1948.
Jászi, Oscar. *The Dissolution of the Habsburg Monarchy.* Chicago, 1961.
Jelavich, Barbara. *The Habsburg Empire in European Affairs, 1814–1918.* Chicago, 1969.
Kahn, Robert A. *The Habsburg Empire.* London, 1957.
———. *A History of the Habsburg Empire.* Berkeley, Calif., 1974.
———. *The Multinational Empire. Nationalism and National Reform in the Habsburg Monarchy, 1848–1918.* 2 vols. New York, 1950.
———. *A Study in Austrian Intellectual History.* New York, 1960.
Luża, Radomir. *Austro-German Relations in the Anschluss Era.* Princeton, 1975.
Macartney, C. A. *The Habsburg Empire, 1790–1918.* London, 1968.
———. *Maria Theresa and the House of Austria.* London, 1969.
McGrath, William J. *Dionysian Art and Populist Politics in Austria.* New Haven, 1974.
Maimann, Helene. *Politik im Wartesaal. Österreichische Exilpolitik in Grossbritannien, 1938–1945.* Wien, 1975.
May, Arthur J. *Habsburg Monarchy, 1867–1914.* New York, 1961.
———. *The Passing of the Habsburg Monarchy, 1914–1918.* 2 vols. Philadelphia, 1966.
Pick, Robert. *Empress Maria Theresa.* London, 1968.
Plaschka, Richard G., and Karlheinz Mack, eds. *Die Auflösung des Habsburgerreiches. Zusammenbruch und Neuorientierung im Donauraum.* Wien, 1970.
Schorske, Carl. *Fin de Siècle Vienna. Politics and Culture.* New York, 1980.
Shell, Kurt. *The Transformation of Austrian Socialism.* New York, 1962.
Spielman, John. *Leopold I of Austria.* London, 1977.
Stadler, Karl R. *Austria.* London, 1971.
———. *The Birth of the Austrian Republic, 1918–1921.* Leyden, 1966.
Steiner, Kurt. *Politics in Austria.* Boston, 1972.
Stourzh, Gerald. *Kleine Geschichte des Österreichischen Staatsvertrages.* Wien, 1975. 2d rev. ed., 1980.
Taylor, A. J. P. *The Habsburg Monarchy, 1809–1918. A History of the Austrian Empire and Austria-Hungary.* London, 1948.
Wandruszka, Adam. *The House of Habsburg.* Transl. by Cathleen and Hans Epstein. New York, 1964.
Weinzierl, Erika, and Kurt Skalnik, eds. *Österreich. Die Zweite Republik.* Graz, 1972.
Zeman, Z. A. B. *The Breakup of the Habsburg Empire, 1914–1918. A Study in National and Social Revolution.* London, 1961.
Zöllner, Erich. *Geschichete Österreichs. Von den Anfängen bis zur Gegenwart.* Wien, 1961. 4th ed., 1979.

PART I

GEOGRAPHY AND DEMOGRAPHY

Modern Austria, pp. 23–73

1. AUSTRIA: LANDSCAPE AND REGIONAL STRUCTURE

Helmut Wohlschlägl

Assistant Professor, Institute of Geography, University of Vienna

1 AUSTRIA—A COUNTRY IN THE HEART OF EUROPE

The Republic of Austria, a landlocked state in south-central Europe, lies in the heart of the European continent. Today, however, political realities have made this a peripheral location between the two large power blocs and economic regions of East and West (Map 1). With an area of 83,853 km², inhabited by roughly 7.5 million people, it is one of Europe's smaller countries: about twice the physical size of Switzerland, or, to scale it by American standards, a little smaller than the State of Maine. With a population larger than that of Switzerland and a little smaller than that of Sweden, the two other neutral countries of Europe, it has, on the other hand, just a third of the area and an eighth of the population of the Federal Republic of Germany. Austria's population density of about 90 inhabitants per km² (1979) is comparatively low by European standards, and lower than that of all the neighboring countries with the exception of Yugoslavia. This figure reflects the Alpine character of the country (because of which it is often referred to as the "Alpine Republic") as well as its location outside the main industrial agglomerations and densely populated regions of the continent.

Placed at the borders of the settlement areas of the three large European ethnic groups, the Germanic, Romanic, and Slav peoples, and of the Magyars, Austria was, and is, an intermediary between their different cultures, a country of transit and of interchange at the intersection of the important European crossroads running north to south, and east to west. The relative position of Austria within Europe has, of course, undergone repeated and profound changes in the course of its history: alternating from border

23

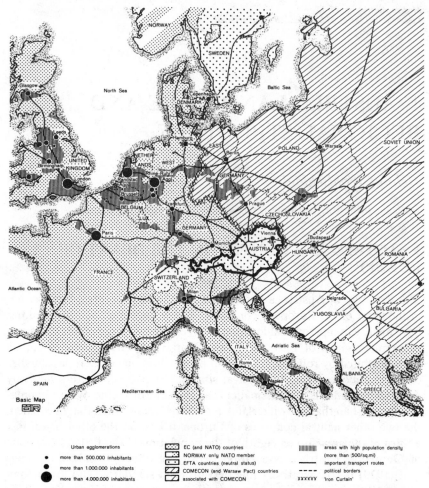

Urban agglomerations
- more than 500.000 inhabitants
- more than 1.000.000 inhabitants
- more than 4.000.000 inhabitants

EC (and NATO) countries
NORWAY only NATO member
EFTA countries (neutral status)
COMECON (and Warsaw Pact) countries
associated with COMECON

areas with high population density (more than 500/sq.mi)
important transport routes
political borders
'Iron Curtain'

Map 1. Austria's location in Europe.

outpost on the southeastern edge of the Occident in the Middle Ages to central position in that great power, the Habsburg Monarchy (and thus in the interplay of European power politics) and then once again to a peripheral location facing the "Iron Curtain" that divides the Europe of today.

Until 1918 today's Austria was a key component of the Habsburg empire with its 52 million inhabitants. After the dissolution of the empire Austria was left a truncated remnant, a small country that at its inception was meant to comprise the solid core of German-speaking peoples' territories of the erstwhile monarchy.[1] But the German-speaking border regions of Bohemia and Moravia went to Czechoslovakia, while the Alpine provinces of Tyrol, Carinthia, and Styria lost considerable portions of their territory to Italy and Yugoslavia. Thus the present state of Austria came into being, a country extending almost 600 km lengthwise from east to west, with a maximum width from north to south of only 280 km, its now excessively large capital city of Vienna oddly placed close to the eastern periphery.[2] The country's westernmost third only consists of a narrow corridor between 32 and 60 km wide that was left over after the southern Tyrol was ceded to Italy in 1918–1919. It connects Austria with Switzerland and separates the EEC (and NATO) member countries, the Federal Republic of Germany, and Italy, whereas the eastern portion of Austria, on the other hand, extends far into the bloc of COMECON countries, which together constitute almost half of the international frontiers, totaling 2640 km, that Austria shares with its seven neighboring countries (see Map 1).[3]

Austria's administrative division into nine federal provinces (Länder) of very uneven size (Table 1) is the result of historical developments dating back centuries in some cases, and of a gradual growing together of several ancient countries into one federal state.[4] There are distinct differences between the provinces, not merely in the customs and dialects of their populations, but to some extent also in economic structure and cultural landscape. That historically conditioned individuality is at the root of the federal structure of the Republic.

2 THE LANDSCAPE OF AUSTRIA

2.1 Overview

A characteristic feature of the Austrian landscape, and one that constitutes part of its particular charm, is the remarkable variety of topography, vegetation, and cultural landscape existing within a small area. Though its most important settlement cores and industrial centers lie in the vicinity, in the northern foreland, and near the eastern slopes of the Alpine massif, Austria is basically an Alpine country, since almost two thirds (62 percent) of the country's total area is occupied by the Alps, and thus its Alpine proportion is bigger even than that of Switzerland.

Little more than a quarter of Austria (28%) is flat or moderately hilly, well suitable for settlement and climatically favorable, curving along the Alpine region to the north and east in a band of variable width (Map 2). That portion is commonly subdivided into (a) the Northern Alpine Foreland including the Danube valley, (b) the lowlands and hilly regions of northeastern Austria including the Vienna Basin, and (c) the southeastern lowlands and rolling hills, also called the Southeastern Foreland (see Bobek 1957). The Austrian portion of the Bohemian Granite Massif constitutes the remaining tenth of the country's area; it is a barren upland of medium

Table 1 Federal provinces of Austria

	Area		Population, 1979		Changes in population, 1951–1979 (%)	Density of population, 1979 (pop/km²)	Structure of employment[a], 1971 (%)			Provincial capital (inhabitants, 1979, thousands)
	Km²	Percent	Thousands	Percent			AF	MIT	Serv.	
Vienna	415	0.5%	1,572	20.9%	-2.7%	3,788.0	0.8%	39.9%	59.3%	Vienna (1572)
Lower Austria	19,171	22.9	1,397	18.6	-0.2	72.9	21.7	43.7	34.6	(Vienna[b])
Burgenland	3,966	4.7	264	3.5	-4.5	66.6	26.9	45.3	27.8	Eisenstadt (11)
Styria	16,386	19.5	1,185	15.8	+6.8	72.3	20.4	42.1	37.5	Graz (250)
Carinthia	9,533	11.4	527	7.0	+11.0	55.3	13.6	41.1	45.3	Klagenfurt (85)
Upper Austria	11,979	14.3	1,242	16.6	+12.1	103.7	18.2	46.7	35.1	Linz (208)
Salzburg	7,154	8.5	432	5.8	+32.0	60.4	12.3	36.2	51.5	Salzburg-City (140)
Tyrol	12,647	15.1	583	7.8	+36.5	46.1	11.6	37.8	50.6	Innsbruck (120)
Vorarlberg	2,601	3.1	302	4.0	+55.7	116.1	6.1	58.6	35.3	Bregenz (26)
Austria	83,853	100.0%	7,504	100.0%	+8.2%	89.5	14.0%	42.7%	43.3%	Vienna (1572)

[a] Proportion of economically active persons by economic sectors Agriculture and Forestry (AF), Mining, Industry, and Manufacturing Trades (MIT), and Public and Private Services (Serv.), are in percent.

[b] Lower Austria has no capital of its own; Provincial Government and all central administrative institutions are domiciled in Vienna.

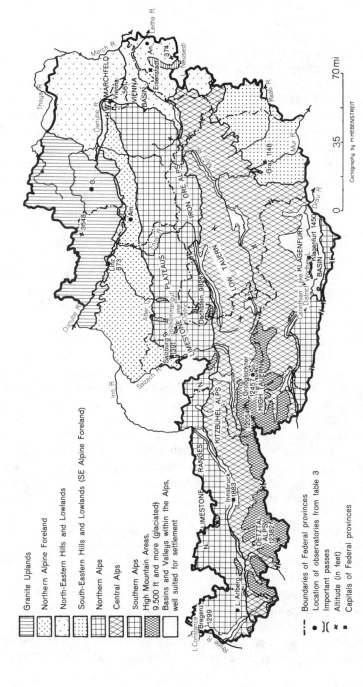

Granite Uplands

Northern Alpine Foreland

North-Eastern Hills and Lowlands

South-Eastern Hills and Lowlands (SE Alpine Foreland)

Northern Alps

Central Alps

Southern Alps

High Mountain Areas,
9,500 ft and more (glaciated)

Basins and Valleys within the Alps,
well suited for settlement

Boundaries of Federal provinces

Location of observatories from table 3

Important passes

Altitude (in feet)

Capitals of Federal provinces

Map 2. **Physiographic divisions of Austria.**

0   35   70mi

Cartography by H.HEBENSTREIT

L.Constance
Bregenz
1299
Rhine R.

L.Arlberg

OETZTAL
ALPS
(2382)

N.   LIMESTONE RANGES

Innsbruck
883

KITZBÜHEL ALPS

GroßGlockner
12457
HIGH TAUERN

Dachstein 9826

LIMESTONE
PLATEAUS

Salzburg Salzkammergut
1391   Lake
District

LOW TAUERN

IRON ORE ALPS

Carinthian Lake
District Wörther

KLAGENFURT
Klagenfurt 1450
BASIN

Mur R.

Drau R.

Raab R.

Graz 1148

Mur R.

After R.

Linz
873

Danube R.

Inn R.

Salzach R.

Enns R.

*3648

G.

Thaya R.

March R.

Danube R.

N.W.MARCHFELD
MARCHFELD

Vienna
561

VIENNA
BASIN

An.
374
Eisenstadt

Leitha R.

Neusiedl

height between the Bavarian and the Bohemian border and the Danube with several spurs across the river.

Corresponding to the physiographic structure, the spatial distribution of the population, too, is very uneven. Roughly two thirds of Austria's population live in the Danube valley and in the lowlands and hilly country north and east of the Alps; more than 25 percent are concentrated in Vienna and its environs. Within the Alps the population is concentrated in valleys, which are frequently rather narrow, and small basins, where high population densities are reached in some places. Above the valleys large areas are covered by forests, or offer pastures on high Alpine slopes, or are unproductive for agriculture and forestry at all. Isolated homesteads of mountain farmers formed the only kind of settlement above the lower slopes of the valleys until recent years when lodging, recreation and skiing facilities were provided in growing numbers in the course of the expanding tourist industry.

Altogether the so-called permanent settlement area, i.e. the area that is cultivated, built-up, or used for transportation but excluding mountain pastures, woodland, and barren land—amounts to barely 35,000 km^2, which is only about four tenths of Austria's total area. In Tyrol, the most mountainous and least densely populated province, that share amounts to only about 15 percent.[5]

The land use pattern (see Table 2) reflects this mountainous character of Austria. About 45 percent of the total area is used for agricultural purposes, but more than a quarter of this land consists of high-lying, extensively used pasturage. These Alpine pastures are of special significance for enlarging the limited space for agricultural economy, especially in the western Alpine regions (Tyrol, Vorarlberg, Salzburg).[6] Another four tenths of the Republic's area are covered by forests, and a tenth (i.e. an area even larger than the province of Salzburg) is unproductive wasteland. The rest consists of built-up areas, land covered by water (lakes, rivers, dams), etc. Within the intensively used agricultural areas (a bare third of the territory of Austria) tilled land preponderates over grassland, with considerable differences in spatial distribution.

In the Alpine regions with their livestock economy, plowed land after decades of steady decline has sunk to total insignificance with the exception of the Klagenfurt basin. In Tyrol and Vorarlberg, for instance, it comprises no more than 3 percent of the total area. But in the plains and hilly country of Austria's northeastern region it accounts for between 60 and 70 percent, whereas grassland is almost nonexistent. Only there and in the Southeastern Foreland do special crops, fruit-growing, and viticulture play an economically significant role. Yet despite its rather narrow natural basis, Austrian agriculture is very efficient—as will be discussed below (under 3.3).

Table 2 Types of land use in Austria from west to east, arranged by federal provinces (percent)

	Vorarlberg	Tyrol	Salzburg	Carinthia	Styria	Upper Austria	Lower Austria	Burgenland	Austria
Arable land	0.7	2.6	2.3	9.5	11,0	24.2	38.1	40.2	17.8
Vineyards	—	—	—	—	0.1	—	1.7	4.9	0.7
Orchards, market gardening, and other special cultivations	0.8	0.1	0.4	0.8	1.5	1.6	1.3	1.3	1.1
Meadows and pastures for intensive use	14.4	6.2	12.7	9.1	12.3	23.7	10.8	8.3	12.2
Meadows and pastures for seasonal use (excl. Alpine pastures)	9.5	3.8	5.8	5.6	4.6	2.1	2.6	3.6	3.9
Alpine pastures (Almen) (in the mountains in high altitude)	24.7	23.6	23.7	16.1	6.4	0.5	0.4	—	9.7
Woodland	29.3	33.4	34.2	46.6	52.1	36.2	36.6	28.2	39.3
Areas covered by water and moorland	2.3	1.2	1.5	1.8	0.7	2.1	1.1	7.3	1.6
Barren land, built-up areas, and roadways	18.3	29.1	19.4	10.5	11.3	9.6	7.4	6.2	13.7

With forests covering a 40 percent share of its area, Austria is one of the most heavily wooded countries of Western Europe. The timber production of its forest economy is surpassed only by the Scandinavian countries of Sweden and Finland. Large forest tracts are widespread, particularly in the eastern and north-eastern parts of the Alps, and in the Granite Uplands. Of all the provinces, Styria is richest in forests. Copper beech and fir and spruce mixed forests formed the natural forest cover at lower elevations in the Alps, and on the Granite Uplands, but systematic forestry replaced these mainly with spruce monoculture. As one proceeds upward, to higher elevations in the Alps, the species changes from the spruce to larch and stone pine, extending up to the timberline.

Climate, indigenous vegetation, and land use show significant differences between the eastern parts of Austria, influenced by a continental climate, and the west, which is subject to an oceanic influence, and also display a characteristic vertical zoning depending on varying altitude. The climate of the country is determined by three major climatic regions (Table 3).

The Northern Alpine Foreland and adjacent areas are characterized by the Central European intermediate climate. In these parts the prevailing west and northwest winds are the bearers of humid Atlantic air masses, which bring frequent and abundant precipitation at all seasons and comparatively mild temperatures. The higher-lying Granite Uplands, although subject to not dissimilar climatic conditions, have a more severe highland climate, colder winters and strong winds. The northern front of the Alps

Table 3 Average temperatures and rainfall of selected observation points in the different climatic regions of Austria

Climatic region	Observation point[a] (altitude)	Average temperature (Degrees Celsius)			Average annual precipitation (Millimeters)
		January	July	Annual	
Central European intermediate climate: Lowlands (from west to east)	Salzburg (430 m)	−1.9	18.1	8.3	1,359
	Amstetten (328 m)	−1.7	19.0	8.8	925
	Vienna (202 m)	−1.0	19.3	9.4	683
Uplands (granite)	Gutenbrunn (828 m)	−4.1	14.6	5.2	881
Alpine climate: Peaks	Sonnblick (3105 m)	−13.0	1.2	−6.2	2,580
Valleys at higher altitudes	Langen/Arlberg (1220 m)	−3.1	14.0	5.4	1,957
Basins	Tamsweg (1021 m)	−6.3	15.4	5.3	752
Pannonic climate	Andau (118 m)	−1.5	20.1	9.7	576

[a] See map 2 (abbreviations: Am, Amstetten; H.W., Vienna, Hohe Warthe; G. Gutenbrunn; So, Sonnblick; L, Langen/Arlberg; T, Tamsweg; An, Andau).

in particular, exposed to westerly winds, experiences orographic up-slope rainfalls and is rather wet. From there towards the Inner Alps and the East the intensity of precipitation decreases.

Within the Alpine region (Alpine climate) there are considerable differences in climate owing to the complex surface divisions and variations in altitude. Short, rather cool summers and long winters with copious snowfalls are a common feature. In many areas the snow cover stays for three or four months of the year even in the valleys. The notorious Föhn wind is a typical feature of the Alpine climate. It is a warm, dry "katabatic" (down-slope) wind that usually blows from the south, raising the temperature suddenly and melting the snow.

In contrast to the humid west, the east of Austria is under the influence of the continental-type Pannonian climate, which forms a transition to the climate of the east European steppes. It is characterized by little precipitation—though still sufficient for intensive cultivation of the land—and by hot summers causing severe desiccation of the soil. The winters are cold but there is little snow. Only in the south of Carinthia and on the southeastern rim of the Alps does a certain influence of the mild, sub-Mediterranean climate make itself felt.

The upper limits of vegetation, settlement and land use decrease significantly from the western to the eastern parts of the Austrian Alps and also from the central to the border areas of the massif, as do the average altitudes of the mountain ranges. Thus, the timberline is around 2,200 to 2,000 meters in the western reaches of the Central Alps, whereas it is 1,700 to 1,800 meters above sea level on the northern and eastern edges of the Alps. The upper limit of permanent settlement is as high as 1,900 m in a few extreme instances in the Tyrolean Central Alps, while it never exceeds 1,000 m in the eastern part of the Alps. There is a zone of dwarf pines and stunted shrubs above the timberline, changing at 2,000–2,400 meters to completely treeless Alpine tundra with patches of moss, which borders higher up on barren ground and a zone permanently covered by snow. In the western Central Alps the snowline runs at about 3,000 m, whereas in the east and in the northern part of the massif it is about 2,500 m.

2.2 The Austrian Alps

The Austrian Alps are very sharply structured in zones running in an east-west direction, the lengthwise division being accentuated by two longitudinal valley troughs separating the Central Alps from the Northern and Southern Alps respectively (Map 2). Apart from these, there are few broad valleys in the Alpine region, which generally is characterized by relatively small and narrow structures. Small basins and wider sections of valleys are connected together by valley steps, narrow valleys, passes or lines of tectonic depression. The remarkable scenic variety of the mountains may be mainly attributed to the contrasts of mineral composition of the rock formations, to differing surface features and water seepage, and to the variety of both vegetation and cultural landscape.

The narrow northern boundary zone of the Alps ("Flysch" zone) mainly consists of soft sandstone, marl, and argillaceous schist, and is characterized by rounded peaks and soft slopes covered by mixed (coniferous and deciduous) woods and meadows. Adjoining this zone to the south are the Lower Limestone Alps (Kalkvoralpen), a densely wooded mountain region consisting of permeable limestone and dolomite, never reaching heights above 2,000 m (6,600 ft). The light-colored rock walls, peaks, and ridges of these ranges are clearly differentiated from the rounded flysch hills. Further south, they turn into the mighty bulk of the Northern Limestone High Alps. The towering mountain chains in the west are most impressive; in the east they consist of large limestone massifs whose barren karstic plateaus show a great scarcity of water. Only their highest peaks (Dachstein, Hochkönig) are covered by glaciers. Reaching heights of up to 3,000 m, these mountains with their abruptly rising steep walls, narrow valleys and ravines, their scree slopes, and their stony valley bottoms covered with gravel are not favorable for agriculture, settlement or transportation, but they form a landscape that fascinates with memorable sights (Picture 1).

In stark contrast to the precipitous peaks of the Limestone Alps, the lower, undulating mountains of the 'greywacke' zone (slate and shale ranges) are well suited for mountain farming and mountain pasturage (Picture 2). They are also economically significant on account of their abundant mineral deposits (magnesite, copper, and iron ore). A special feature in this respect is the Erzberg ("iron-ore mountain"), a mountain in the eastern reaches of the Alps in Styria: it constitutes Austria's largest iron ore deposit and mining complex.[7]

The highest compact mountain ranges of Austria are situated in the Western Central Alps. Their bulky massifs and imposing ridges mainly consist of hard impermeable gneiss and crystalline shales. Their highest parts are covered by glaciers and they are intersected by deep U-shaped valleys that were fashioned through glacial erosion. The wooded zones on the steep sides of the valleys are narrow. Since there is very little land suitable for cultivation, some extreme forms of mountain farming have developed on steep rock terraces, on stretches where the steep slopes level out, and also in some side valleys. The predominant features, however, are mountain pastures and barren land. Austria's highest peak, the Grossglockner (3,797 m [12, 457 ft]) (Picture 3) is part of the range called Hohe Tauern. Plans are afoot to turn part of this area into a national park within

Picture 1.   View from the south of the Dachstein, one of the highest mountains in the Northern Limestone Alps. Photo: Austrian National Tourist Office.

the next few years. The existence of valley steps with numerous waterfalls and the abundance of water in the region have facilitated the construction of a number of large dams and hydroelectric power stations (the best known being at Kaprun). By the construction of mountain roads leading to the glacier regions (the most famous road known as Grossglockner-Hochalpenstrasse) and cableways, the opening-up of the mountain regions to mass tourism—which has already become the main source of income for the inhabitants of many valleys of western Austria—has reached a very advanced stage in the western Central Alps.

The eastern Central Alps are lower and more densely wooded and their division into individual ranges is more pronounced, since they are intersected by relatively wide basins. Because of their predominant forest cover, in literature often a distinction is made between the "pasture and rock mountains of western Austria" and the "wooded mountains of central

Picture 2.   Kitzbühel lies within the Slate and Shale ranges, which permit intensive mountain farming and Alpine pasturage in summer, and afford excellent possibilities for skiing in winter. The view is from the Hahnenkamm—famous for international skiing competitions—toward the northeast to the Kitzbühler Horn, the other well-known skiing area of Kitzbühel. Photo: Austrian National Tourist Office.

Austria." Here the rural population's livelihood mainly depends on forestry and stock farming. Tourism, as yet, is underdeveloped in wide areas of this region (see 3.6 below). The limited economic basis has led to a substantial drift away from some of the mountainous areas in the eastern Central Alps of Styria and Carinthia.

Besides forestry and farming, in the past and up to the present day the economic and social structure of central Austria has been largely shaped by and based on iron ore mining and smelting and iron shipping activities. The proximity of the Erzberg combined with the abundance of timber and of water-based energy sources gave rise to the development of a lively small-scale iron manufacturing industry very early in history. But these activities

Picture 3.   Heiligenblut in northwest Carinthia, with the Grossglockner and its glaciers in the
background. The village is the southern terminal of the panoramic Grossglockner-Hochalpenstrasse, which leads across the main ridge of the Alps. Since that road was opened, Heiligenblut
has become a significant place for tourism. Photo: Austrian National Tourist Office.

declined toward the end of the 19th century with the advent of large-scale
industrial production, which developed in more favorable locations along
the rim of the Alps. Only in Upper Styria, in the valleys of the Mur and
Mürz rivers did the old smelting and forging manufactures lead to the
development of a large industrial zone of heavy industry. However, this area
has recently been beset by structural problems (see 3.2 below).

The Southern Alps, of which Austria only has a share in Carinthia and
eastern Tyrol, resemble the Northern Alps in their mineral composition and
surface features, but they are less distinctly structured. The Southern Limestone Alps, including the impressive walls of the Lienzer Dolomiten and the
Karawanken ranges, are part of this area. But in contrast to the cool climate

of the Northern Alps, which is influenced by westerly winds, they have a somewhat milder climate and a richer vegetation.

The wide valleys and basins are the main areas of settlement in the Alps: the densely populated Inn valley is the principal settlement area of Tyrol, and Innsbruck is the only major Austrian city within the Alpine region. The plain bordering on the Rhine river contains the highly industrialized economic and settlement core of the province of Vorarlberg. The Mur-Mürz valley contains the most important industrial zone of Styria, aside from the area around the city of Graz. Finally, the Klagenfurt basin, the largest basin in the Eastern Alps, is the core and center of Carinthia. Here the climate and soil conditions favor agriculture, and the cultivation of potatoes and maize flourishes. The provincial capital of Klagenfurt and the traffic center of Villach are the traditional centers of this province, which has also become a favorite tourist area on account of the warm summer climate and the numerous lakes (Picture 4).

Scattered settlement, with isolated farmsteads or small hamlets, is the rule in the areas of Alpine mountain farming. In the valleys other characteristic types of rural settlement are unstructured villages and so-called church-hamlets, usually situated on sunny slopes, terraces, or alluvial cones, with houses clustered irregularly around a central church. In the tourist areas as well as in areas of industrial development extensive building activity has changed this traditional appearance considerably. In the whole Alpine region a specific Alpine ("Swiss cottage") style for newer buildings is gradually becoming prevalent over the different house and farm building types that have developed historically in various parts of the Alps (e.g. the picturesque old farmhouses still found in Tyrol, Vorarlberg, or Salzburg), thus unifying the regional variety of house types and layouts (Picture 5).

2.3 The Granite Uplands

Besides the Alps, there is a second mountainous area in Austria in the north near the Czechoslovakian border, apart from the main traffic routes. It is a rolling, low mountain range with bare and windswept plateaus, whose stony soil yields rather modest crops. The climate is rough, and only along its eastern edge are conditions more favorable for agriculture, which in the uplands mainly concentrates on the cultivation of rye, potatoes, and oats. The highest points of this area, at around 1,300 m, are covered by extensive spruce forests.

Since the middle of the 19th century, the pressure of population growth in these granite uplands with their traditional small-scale farming structure has been marked by a steady drift of young people to the metropolitan area of Vienna, and this trend persists to the present day. Tourism does not play a significant role in this area, the economic development of which is further

Picture 4. Millstättersee in Carinthia and (in the background) the valley of the Drau, an example of a densely populated valley within the Alps with internationally important transport lines. Millstatt is an important resort in the Carinthian lake region. Photo: Austrian National Tourist Office.

Picture 5.   Farm houses in Tyrol (Innervillgraten). Photo: Friedrich Muhr

hampered by its peripheral location near the Iron Curtain. The western reaches of this area, however, have profited since the termination of World War II by the dynamic growth of the provincial capital, of Upper Austria, Linz, situated near the southern rim of the uplands, on the banks of the Danube.

2.4 The Northern Foreland of the Alps

Between the Granite Uplands and the Alps there is a stretch of land of varying width known as the Northern Foreland of the Alps. It is undulating, terraced country of low knolls and hillocks intersected by pebbly rivers originating in the Alps and flowing toward the Danube. Abundant precipitation is brought by the humid westerly winds, especially to the western part of the foreland, and the climate is comparatively mild. This favors a productive mixed agriculture (cultivation of forage crops and clover, cattle breeding, and dairy farming). Toward the east the share of land under plow increases over meadows, and the fertile brown soil carries rich crops of cereals, maize, and sugar beets.

In the greater part of this area scattered farmsteads and hamlets with sometimes quite substantial homesteads, so-called "Vierkanthöfe" ("four-square"-farmsteads), interspersed with market-villages and small country-towns as central places, are the traditional form of settlement. Recently the Foreland has undergone rapid industrialization, accompanied by a considerable increase in population and rapid housing development along the main traffic route linking Vienna with Linz and Salzburg, especially in the core region of Upper Austria. This was stimulated by the establishment of several large industrial enterprises in this area (see section 3.1 below) as well as the area's favorable location between the capital of Austria and the Federal Republic of Germany.

2.5 The Lowlands and Hills of Northeastern Austria

The lowlands and hilly regions of the northeastern part of Austria, which differ considerably from all other Austrian landscapes with respect to climate and cultural landscape, are of great economic importance for the country as a whole. Climatically they belong to the Pannonian climatic region, i.e. they have little precipitation, hot summers, a protracted growing season, fertile black soils, and a natural vegetation of oak and hornbeam woods. Rudimentary forms of steppe flora are seen occasionally. This is Austria's most intensively cultivated agricultural region, the most important region for growing wheat, vegetables, and sugar beets. Wines of high quality, among them some that have won international renown, are produced in extensive vineyards situated in northern Burgenland, on the eastern rim of the Alps to the Vienna Basin, and also on the humps and hills of the "Weinviertel" covered with fertile loess (Picture 6).

This is the region of the only large plains in Austria—the Vienna Basin, the Marchfeld, and the lowlands east of Lake Neusiedl in the northern part of Burgenland. Lake Neusiedl, surrounded by reeds and only about 1.5 m in depth, is a typical lake of the steppes. The plain to the east of the lake is part of the Hungarian steppe, the "Puszta," with its typical steppe vegetation and salty ponds.

The characteristic types of settlement in this region are regularly laid out villages, the buildings either placed along the main street (roadside village) or grouped around an elliptic village green, a centrally located common

Picutre 6. Characteristic landscape of the northeastern hills and lowlands in the so-called Weinviertel, close to the Czechoslovak border. The picture shows the city of Retz with its historic center. Photo: Austrian National Tourist Office.

("Angerdorf"). These villages are surrounded by large field systems consisting of long but narrow strips of small fields. These so-called "Gewannfluren" form an obstacle to a rationalization of agricultural development.
Therefore large scale reallocation of the arable land (Flurbereinigung) has
been necessary to improve the system of field ownership. Despite some
changes in local architecture in recent years, the regularly laid out villages
with their low, longitudinal farmhouses are still in sharp contrast to the
unstructured villages, scattered settlements, and largely irregular arrangements of buildings and fields found in the Alps and in the northern foreland.

The western rim of the Vienna Basin, merging into the eastern edge of
the Vienna Woods—themselves the northernmost extension of the Alps—
is a very suitable location for the metropolitan area of Vienna. It is situated
on the banks of the Danube at the intersection of historically important
trade routes. To the south, in the Vienna Basin, thanks to the excellent
traffic situation, the availability of hydropower, and the proximity of the
large metropolitan market, a development had set in as early as the 19th
century that brought into being modern Austria's most important and
versatile industrial area. Today this is an almost totally built-up band-like
region extending along the eastern rim of the Alps from the city of Vienna
almost to the Semmering Pass, which connects Vienna with Styria, Carinthia, and the harbor, formerly Austrian, of Trieste.

By contrast, the Weinviertel, the Marchfeld, and the northern part of the
province of Burgenland are predominantly agricultural, hardly touched by
industrialization, with the exception of a few enterprises that process agricultural products. In the Weinviertel, situated northeast of Vienna, are
Austria's major crude oil and natural gas fields, currently supplying a
quarter of Austria's demand. The crude oil is processed by the large refinery
at Schwechat on the southern outskirts of Vienna.

2.6 The Southeastern Hills and Lowlands

The southeastern part of Austria, too, consists mainly of hilly country;
foothills of the Alps extending in undulating, long-drawn-out saddles and
knolls with gentle slopes, interspersed with broad, flat-bed valleys in a
predominantly southeasterly direction. Their comparatively mild climate is
subject to Pannonian and sub-Mediterranean (Illyric) influences, evidenced
by the region's sweet chestnut and mixed deciduous woods. This climate
favors agriculture and, in particular, fruit-growing and the cultivation of
maize. A modicum of industrial development and the predominantly small-
scale farming structure, in conjunction with their pheripheral location
within Austria, are responsible for the comparatively low degree of economic development of wide stretches of land. Here, on the southern and
eastern periphery as in most of the northern and easterly border regions—

living standards and economic potentialities are still lagging behind conditions in the more highly developed regions of Austria.

The basin of Graz, the provincial capital of Styria on the Mur River, is the center of settlement and development of this area, and a variety of industrial activities is found here. The brown coal workings of Köflach are the most important deposit of this mineral resource in Austria—apart from the deposit in the Hausruck Range, in the Upper Austrian Foreland of the Alps.

REGIONAL STRUCTURE AND PROBLEMS OF REGIONAL DEVELOPMENT

3.1 East-West Disparities in Regional Development

Today, Austria is a developed industrial nation. Industry and the manufacturing crafts contributed approximately 44 percent of the GNP in 1976. In 1977, 41 percent of all economically active persons were employed in manufacturing crafts and in industry, whereas only 11.8 percent were active in agriculture and forestry, and no less than 47.2 percent worked in the various branches of the tertiary sector. There are, however, considerable regional differences in the country's economic structure, and regional development since 1945 has by no means run evenly. Many problems associated with present-day regional structures and developments are due to the variegated political developments that took place in Central Europe in the course of this century.

The Habsburg Monarchy, a large economic entity with a functioning regional division of labor, was economically developing rapidly despite political tensions. Vienna with its 2.1 million inhabitants in 1910—as against a population of only 1.57 million in 1979—was able to utilize its favorable location in the center of the Danubian economic region. After World War I the truncated Austrian state was left with only 12 percent of its former territory and 13 percent of its population, but 30 percent of the former monarchy's industrial labor force were still living within the new national boundaries. This newly formed small country had to face grave problems of regional restructuring. The major part of Austria's industry had lost its basis of raw material sources and supplies of semifinished goods, and many branches of industry were disproportionately large, thus forcing a dependence on exports for survival. The old industrial regions of Lower Austria and Styria, cut off from their traditional markets, were overtaken by stagnation and crises. The outsize capital of Vienna was left with excess capacities in public and private administrative bodies, banking, and insurance.

In the period between the two world wars this was the situation that had been inherited from the Austro-Hungarian Empire: heavy industry was concentrated in the east of Austria, mainly in and around Vienna and in the Vienna basin; the old established iron-mining and processing industry of Upper Styria and near the outer reaches of the Alps—in Steyr, Waidhofen/Ybbs, St. Pölten, Ternitz, and Graz—represented the second industrial center; whereas the rest of Austria had no industrial areas of any significance, except for the highly industrialized Rhine valley of Vorarlberg, where a sizable textile industry had grown in the course of the 19th century.

Major shifts in Austria's regional economic structure were initiated only with the incorporation of the country into the German Reich in 1938 and its integration into the planning structure of a wartime economy. Hydropower and existing traffic routes were rapidly expanded. Major armaments industries were established in the "Alpine Fortress," boosting the economy of the western part of Austria, a region that had been barely touched by industrialization in the past. Linz in particular, the capital of the province of Upper Austria, was turned into a center of industry, where large-scale metallurgical and chemical enterprises were founded. These were further expanded after 1945. Today they are among the largest and most important state-owned industrial combines in Austria, e.g. the "VÖEST" (United Austrian Iron and Steel Works) in Linz, the chemical combine of Chemie-Linz AG, the aluminum works of Ranshofen, and the viscose staple fiber industry at Lenzing.

Ever since 1945 the dynamics of regional economic development in Austria—as well as regional population and settlement development[8]— have been characterized by a marked west-east differential, with a tendency gradually to reduce the considerable preponderance of the eastern part's economic potential, which is a legacy of the monarchy to this region, its former industrial core, carried over into the new republic. Since 1945, the western provinces of Vorarlberg, Tyrol, Salzburg, and Upper Austria have enjoyed better conditions for economic development than the eastern and southern parts, for a number of reasons: they had largely escaped damage during the war, whereas the eastern part had been subjected to military action and some areas had suffered large-scale destruction. In addition, the Russian occupation of Lower Austria and parts of Vienna up to 1955 had led to some flight of capital and to the relocation of some industrial enterprises to western Austria, and many enterprises in Lower Austria and in Vienna had been confiscated and partly dismantled. At the same time many enterprises in the western provinces expanded and new factories were erected and equipped with the help of Marshall Plan funds.

Other contributory factors are the open borders that the western provinces have with the West, and the proximity to industrial centers and populous regions of the Federal Republic of Germany and Switzerland, offering important siting and communication advantages and potential contacts. The eastern provinces, on the other hand, and the border regions in particular, are hampered by their closeness to the Iron Curtain, with all the difficulties encountered in traffic and trading with Eastern Europe. The western provinces, especially the Alpine rural areas, were further stimulated economically by the lively increase in international tourism. Its extensive development has since led to a certain leveling of the differences in per capita income between urban and rural areas that are still pronounced in eastern Austria, where they are a stimulating factor of the drift of population toward urban areas.

3.2 The Industrial Regions of Austria

Despite the fact that the western provinces have tended to gain economic importance, it must not be overlooked that the economic hub of Austria is still located in the east. The goods produced in the federal provinces of Vienna, Lower Austria, Burgenland, and Styria still make up about two-thirds of the Austrian GNP, even though the rate of growth of the GNP in this region has fallen below the Austrian average during the last two decades.[9] Nearly 40 percent of the production of manufactured and industrial goods is concentrated in Vienna and the Vienna basin.

Map 3 shows the most important industrial locations in Austria, listing different branches of industry, as well as the main industrial regions, mining centers, and the spatial pattern of agricultural economy.

Industry in Vienna shows a high degree of diversification, ranging over many branches, with particular emphasis on food and fine foods production, electrical engineering, chemicals, and the machine-building industry. Characteristic is the absence of truly large-scale industries in the capital, since the Habsburg emperors did not countenance the establishment of heavy industry within the boundaries of their residential city. Although industrial employment has been decreasing since the 1960s while the service sector has been gaining, the pattern of employment is nevertheless shifting toward more capital-intensive and research-oriented sectors, resulting in increases of productivity at rates in excess of the national average. The construction of a major motor engine factory, recently initiated by General Motors, will bring the largest industrial enterprise of Vienna into being.

The industrial structure of the Vienna Basin has also developed a great deal of diversity. The expansion of employment figures is due to the establishment of many new enterprises in branches of greater-than-average growth potential, related to the region's function as a complementary industrial region for Vienna. It profits from enterprise mobility and shifts of industrial location: some enterprises transfer their production units from the city to locations on its periphery. On the other hand the older factories, partly dating back to the pre-1918 period, are encumbered by structural weaknesses. This applies in particular to the metallurgical sector—includ-

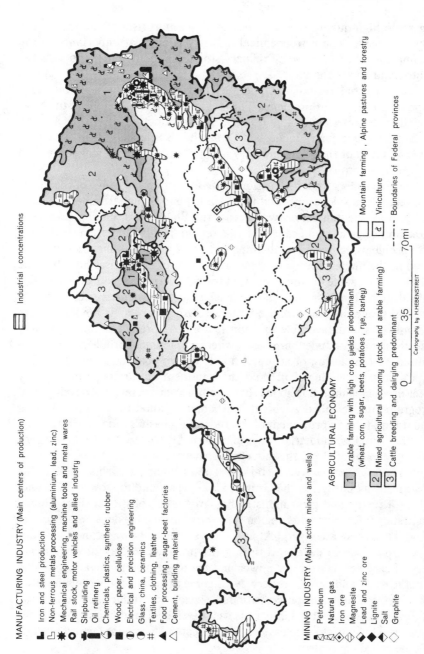

MANUFACTURING INDUSTRY (Main centers of production)

▙ Iron and steel production
⌐ Non-ferrous metals processing (aluminium, lead, zinc)
✳ Mechanical engineering, machine tools and metal wares
○ Rail stock, motor vehicles and allied industry
◖ Shipbuilding
◐ Oil refinery
◑ Chemicals, plastics, synthetic rubber
■ Wood, paper, cellulose
◨ Electrical and precision engineering
◧ Glass, china, ceramics
Textiles, clothing, leather
◀ Food processing, sugar-beet factories
△ Cement, building material

▥ Industrial concentrations

MINING INDUSTRY (Main active mines and wells)

Petroleum ▽
Natural gas ◁
Iron ore ◆
Magnesite ◇
Lead and zinc ore ◆
Lignite ◆
Salt ◀
Graphite ◇

AGRICULTURAL ECONOMY

▨ 1 Arable farming with high crop yields predominant
(wheat, corn, sugar, beets, potatoes, rye, barley)

▦ 2 Mixed agricultural economy (stock and arable farming)

▫ 3 Cattle breeding and dairying predominant

▦ Mountain farming, Alpine pastures and forestry

□ ♂ Viniculture

–·–·– Boundaries of Federal provinces

0   35   70mi

Cartography by H.HEBENSTREIT

Map 3. Austria. Agricultural economy, manufacturing, and mining industry.

ing some high-quality steel producers—and enterprises of the textile and paper industry. The petrochemical industry is of great importance in the Vienna basin, with a large oil refinery situated at Schwechat; and so is the rubber and tire industry.

The industrial region of Upper Styria is increasingly beset by grave regional development problems. That region is mainly a center of the locationally raw-material oriented iron and steel production (steel mills and the metal-working industry in Leoben-Donawitz, Kapfenberg, Mürzzuschlag, etc.), and also of the paper industry and mining (iron ore, magnesite, and —formerly—brown coal).

The area suffers from its location being far out on the fringe of the major markets of central Europe, and from inadequate Alpine transport connections up to now (an expressway across the Phyrn Pass, linking Linz with Graz and of great significance for this region, is now under construction). The problems caused by high transport costs and the difficulties encountered in the modernization and rationalization of enterprises have become all the more acute in times of world-wide overproduction of steel. The substitution of jobs through the establishment of new enterprises with production programs that promise better growth prospects is rendered more difficult by the unfavorable location factors. At present the most gravely affected area is the Judenburg basin, where employment problems have been caused by the closure of an unprofitable brown coal mine (featuring Europe's deepest hauling shaft) and the imminent closure of a high-quality steel-producing mill. It is hoped that a comprehensive regional development program (the so-called Aichfeld-Murboden regional program) will bring about long-term improvement of the Judenburg basin's economic structure.

Other, smaller, industrial zones of eastern Austria are located around the Styrian capital of Graz, the industrial structure of which is well balanced, with a certain emphasis on metal wares and vehicles; as well as close to the Czechoslovak border, in the Granite Uplands around the town of Gmünd, where a textile and glass industry has grown out of the local traditional domestic crafts. This latter region is facing considerable development problems. Then there are several Alpine valleys—in the Lower Limestone Alps —where industries developed during the previous century, taking advantage of easy access to water power and featuring mainly metal processing and the wood and paper industry. Next come the two rapidly growing cities of St. Pölten and Amstetten, situated astride the traffic axis connecting Vienna and Linz, whose industry is well diversified; and finally there is the industrial town of Weiz in eastern Styria, featuring a major factory producing electrical equipment.

Mention has already been made of the dynamic economic development of the industrial areas in the west of Austria—the core area of Upper Austria, the city of Salzburg and its surroundings, the lower Inn valley in

Tyrol, and the Rhine valley in Vorarlberg. Of these, the Upper Austrian industrial zone with its center, the city of Linz, is the most important. The establishment of large-scale industrial enterprises in the 1940s was a decisive stimulus for the development of this expanding industrial zone, which originally produced steel, metals, chemicals, paper, and cellulose, and has since widened its range considerably. This area has become the second largest industrial zone in Austria next to Vienna and the Vienna basin. Besides Linz, the towns of Wels and Steyr—the latter internationally significant for its metal goods, motor vehicles, and armaments producing combine —are also important industrial sites. The eventual completion of the Rhine-Main-Danube canal and the construction of a large new harbor to the east of Linz will further improve the development prospects of this region. But apart from this area, there are also numerous important industrial towns in Upper Austria within the rural expanse of the Alpine Foreland, e.g. Braunau on the banks of the Inn, with one of the largest aluminum works of Central Europe in Ranshofen; Ried-im-Innkreis, home of the world's second-largest ski factory; and Vöcklabruck.

The region of Salzburg, favored by its immediate proximity to the border with the Federal Republic of Germany, is growing into an important trading center, competing with Vienna by progressively taking over wholesale trading, and forwarding and shipping functions. This area, like the lower Inn valley, is profiting from the fact that a more-than-average number of big West German corporations are establishing branches in the western provinces of Austria. In the highly industrialized province of Vorarlberg in the far west of Austria, close economic links exist with eastern Switzerland. The textile and clothing industries are predominant and compete successfully in international markets. The city of Dornbirn is the most important textile center.

However, the open western borders are also a source of certain regional problems for the western provinces, since a sizable proportion of the labor force commutes across the border to work in the neighboring industrial centers of southern Bavaria and Switzerland. Furthermore, the central regions of Vorarlberg, Tyrol, and Salzburg are also exposed to a considerable influence and competition from the the regions beyond the borders— mainly the Bavarian metropolis of Munich and the eastern part of Switzerland with its financial and trading center of Zurich. The pull affects the labor market in a number of ways, as well as in terms of the use made of cultural services and shopping facilities of Munich or Zurich or other cities in the neighboring countries by the inhabitants of Western Austria.

3.3 Rural Austria and Structural Change in Agriculture

Since 1945, Austria's rural areas have been undergoing a significant process of change, which has not yet come to a close. The fundamental changes in the economic and social structure of the nation during the past three decades have resulted in agriculture and forestry no longer being the economic mainstay of the rural population. The process of "disagrarization" —of separation of the rural population from farming—is a feature common to all developed economies, which may also be observed in Austria.

The continual reduction of labor needs in agriculture, which may be expected to continue in the near future, has led only in part to a drift of population to industrial and urban areas. Instead, after World War II, there has been a marked increase in commuting—often over great distances—resulting in a gradual transformation of former farm villages into residential settlements of nonagricultural job holders. This transformation has been reinforced by the establishment of industrial enterprises in rural areas, assiduously promoted in regional planning to slow down the rural-urban migration process, and to prevent the trend towards increasing spatial concentration of economic potential and population in the densely populated urban industrial settlement areas. Besides, tourism has gained considerable importance as a major source of income for the rural population in the west and south of Austria.

The total number of persons employed in agriculture and forestry has dropped from 1.1 million in 1951 to 350,000 in 1977. In 1951, every third economically active person was employed in this sector, whereas in 1977 it was every tenth person. During the same period, about 70,000 (out of 433,000) land holdings went out of production. The peak of this trend occurred during the late 1950s and early 1960s, when the gap between agricultural and industrial incomes widened significantly during the economic boom, and rapid growth of the national economy resulted in a permanent shortage of labor, which exerted a strong pull on the rural working population.

Simultaneously agriculture underwent rapid mechanization and rationalization, sharply raising labor productivity and productivity per acre. In 1951, every person fully employed in agriculture and forestry produced food sufficient for approximately four persons. In 1977 this figure had risen to 23. Between 1950 and 1976, productivity per acre doubled for grain and trebled for maize. Average annual milk production per cow increased by 75 percent (see Krammer and Scheer 1978). This has resulted in Austria's being completely self-sufficient today with respect to nearly all major agricultural products (bread grain, milk and milk products, meat, sugar, maize), and in many instances there is even a surplus of domestic production.

Yet Austria's agricultural structure is still characterized by a predominance of small-scale farming: 80 percent of all agricultural holdings cultivate an area of less than 20 hectares (ha) (50 acres) and nearly 43 percent work fewer than 5 ha (12 acres). Just under 40 percent of all farms operate on a full-time basis today, agriculture being the only source of income (as against 64 percent in 1951). Part-time farming has become the predominant form of agricultural activity (55 percent of all farms) despite the tendency toward automation and rationalization in arable and stock farming, and toward "industrializing" crop and livestock production. In the near future the part-time farmer who is working in industry or in the service sector will continue to be a fixed element of Austria's agricultural structure, even though the share of this form of enterprise in agricultural production is decreasing continuously.

In the Vienna Basin, in the Marchfeld, and in the north of the province of Burgenland, as well as in the Northern Alpine Foreland, agriculture has become very efficient since World War II. The ecology of these regions is favorable, and they are close to the economically most highly developed parts of Austria. These circumstances, together with adequate farm size, make the transition from labor-intensive to capital-intensive farming feasible. Hence the transition from the traditional highly diversified production of farm products to increasing specialization of individual farms as well as of certain regions, governed by the laws of market economics, has been far-reaching. Of course, all these phenomena have long been characteristic of U.S. agriculture.

One consequence of this development has been the so-called "grain boom" (Greif 1979) in the dry areas of northeastern Austria, where now about 80 percent of all sugar beets and 70 percent of all bread grain are grown. Many farms specialize in wheat, sugar beets, and vegetables, and have completely abandoned animal husbandry, whereas areas where special crops—such as wine—are grown are extending. Outside the areas most suited to the cultivation of crops, much of the land has been reverted to grassland and meadows. Marginal land is often no longer used agriculturally at all. The consequence has been a decrease in the area used for agriculture in favor of woodlands in Austria since the 1950s.

In the western part of the northern Foreland of the Alps, the cultivation of fodder plants has extended, besides the cultivation of fertile meadows, and there is a high degree of specialization in dairy farming and the breeding of beef cattle, which makes for sharp competition with the Alpine regions.

The structural changes that took place in the agricultural core regions of Austria could not be equaled in the ecologically disadvantaged mountain regions and the areas near the "dead" eastern border with their predominantly small-scale farms. Consequently, Austria is faced today—in addition to the traditional disparity of incomes between urban and rural areas—with similar disparities between agricultural problem areas, with their mountain farmers and small-scale farmers in the border regions, and the agriculturally developed areas with their consolidated farm structure.

3.4 The Eastern Border Areas—A Rural Residuum

The border areas adjacent to Czechoslovakia, Hungary, and Yugoslavia pose special economic problems. Although extensive stretches offer the necessary climatic and soil conditions for intensive agriculture, a major part of this area suffers from the problems associated with small-scale farming, farmstead lands divided into a lot of scattered and small fields, lack of capital, and a high land/labor ratio, coupled with below-average incomes and a lack of nonagricultural employment opportunities. The Granite Uplands perhaps have the worst disadvantage, since the stony, rather barren soil and the rough climate aggravate existing problems.

Since there has been little industrialization in these areas and there is hardly any tourist trade, seasonal, weekly or daily commuting has increased considerably—a well-known example is that of the construction workers from Burgenland who work in Vienna. There have also been considerable population losses and an increase in the average age-structure, owing to selective out-migration of younger age groups to other areas. The cities and market towns have also come under the influence of the region's general economic stagnation. They have remained small, with an infrastructure that has been totally inadequate until recently, and there has been no new settlement worth mentioning. Problems were generally compounded by proximity to the eastern borders.

Great efforts have been made in recent years to improve the economic conditions of the border areas. A number of development plans were worked out—mostly by the provincial authorities of Lower Austria and Burgenland—encompassing impressive regional planning measures aimed at improving the central functions of the towns as centers of services and employment, in order to slow down the population drift and to improve the infrastructure. However, the creation of nonagricultural employment is encountering great difficulties, despite substantial government assistance. The industrial enterprises founded in the border areas are usually small labor-intensive factories employing a high percentage of female and unskilled labor, investing little capital and producing goods which are cheap to transport. For these reasons most of the newly established factories belong to the clothing and leather-processing sector. Certain enterprises located in the industrial zones, e.g. of the electrical industry, are also establishing branches in the border areas because of low labor costs and government subsidies.[10]

According to a prognosis of the labor market carried out by the Austrian Institute for Regional Planning, a shortfall of 80,000 jobs is expected in the eastern border areas in the first half of the 1980s. This is nearly 80 percent of the prospective employment deficit for all of Austria predicted for that period. Sweeping measures for regional development will continue to be needed in the near future. Otherwise, this deficit can only be met by commuting or migration to the economic core regions and cities, which will have negative consequences for the borderland's demographic and economic structure and land utilization (such as acreage ecologically suitable for cultivation lying fallow).

3.5 Mountain Farming in the Alps

The problem of mountain farming in the Alpine region deserves special attention. Austria is considered the country with the highest number of mountain farmers in Europe, since it has approximately 114,000 mountain farms (1970; about one-third of all its agricultural enterprises), which cover about half of all the area utilized for agriculture and forestry in Austria.

In the Middle Ages and at the beginning of modern times, the Alpine regions were cleared of forests in successive waves, so that the area usable for settlement and cultivation was extended to great altitudes reaching the utter limits of the ecologic possibilities. After that the upper limit of permanent rural settlement gradually declined and many mountain farms were abandoned. However, the contraction of settlements at high altitudes and of cultivated land reached its peak in the late 19th century, the time of the "industrial take-off" in Austria. This period is referred to as the so-called period of "crisis in mountain farming." The main reasons for that crisis were the "Grundentlastung" of 1848, which terminated the manorial system, the growing competition of the Alpine forelands in stock raising, and the competition of higher wage levels in industry. Additionally, especially in the wooded eastern parts of the Alps, the decline of charcoal burning and small-scale iron processing as well as the tendency of large landowners to consolidate their forests and hunting grounds caused a considerable rural exodus to the new industrial centers (see Lichtenberger 1965 and 1975).

The mountain farms of western Austria, which were mainly engaged in Alpine pastoral economy, were much better able to resist these tendencies. Perhaps this was partly due to the strong attachment to the land of the free farmers of the Tyrol, Vorarlberg, and Salzburg, which contrasted with the predominantly feudal structures which had existed in the east until 1848.

The decline of mountain farming in Austria was again accelerated by the dynamic development of the nation's economy in postwar times, in view of the lack of possibilities to rationalize the labor-intensive but not at all profitable holdings. However, the extent of this trend to close down Alpine farms must not be overrated, compared with the same process that was also taking place in the lowlands, and in the Granite Uplands. All this was part of the structural changes in agriculture. Between 1951 and 1960, for example, the number of farms in the provinces of Salzburg and Tyrol decreased by only 2 to 3 percent, as compared with an overall national average decrease of 6 to 7 percent. In particular, income from tourism, which the mountain farms receive either directly by letting rooms or indirectly through a great variety of part-time activities—from working as mountain guides and ski instructors to various kinds of employment in hotels and restaurants—has contributed considerably to their financial consolidation and to the improvement of their standard of living.

But part-time employment outside agriculture and mechanization more and more lead to a certain reduction of agricultural production and to its concentration on flat or modestly sloping stretches of mountain regions, and in consequence a significant shift occurred toward extensive land use on the steeper slopes and in higher areas, a problematical development from the point of view of landscape preservation. According to Greif (1979), an area of more than 300,000 ha of land in the mountains is no longer in agricultural use today, of which 160,000 ha represent mountain meadows, high up on steep slopes and difficult to reach ("Bergmähder"). The effort of using this land is much too strenuous, out of proportion to returns, because agricultural machinery and equipment cannot be used in this terrain and there is not enough labor to work these slopes by hand—nor would it pay to do so if the labor were available. Thus thousands of acres of land lying fallow are waiting to be afforested.

Similar development problems are encountered with respect to the mountain pastures ("Almen"), which used to be an important part of Alpine agriculture. In certain areas, large stretches of pasture are being progressively abandoned, thus endangering the ecological balance of the high Alpine areas and changing the cultural landscape. According to official statistics, one out of five mountain pastures was no longer used in 1974. However, it must be noted that the number of grazing cattle on Alpine pastures, again increased during the past decade—obviously in consequence of the great efforts made by federal authorities responsible for the improvement of mountain pastures, and also owing to general efforts and measures aimed at strengthening Alpine pastoral economy.

But in the Alpine regions it is not only land of marginal profitability that is no longer under cultivation. Owing to the change from full-time to part-time agriculture, or nonagricultural employment, even fertile and profitable fields in the valleys are no longer cultivated. According to Greif (1979), approximately 10 percent of the Alpine land lying fallow is some of the richest land available in the different regions.

All the developments outlined here lead to a certain deterioration of the attractive and varied scenery of Alpine cultural landscape. This in turn will affect tourism, which is the most important development branch of the Alpine economy in many valleys. It is therefore obvious that the problems of mountain farming are not merely agricultural ones, to be solved by agricultural policy measures, but also problems touching upon the economic developments of the regions, to be included in sweeping regional policy measures.

In this connection, a gradual revalorization of the function of the rural areas is increasingly gathering momentum in Austria (and incidentally also in Switzerland), inasmuch as agricultural production becomes confined to the most fertile land, whereas marginal land is gradually relegated to extensive use only. Besides agricultural production, the function of the countryside as the setting of recreational and leisure-time activities of the population of the metropolitan and industrial areas is gaining importance, and the role of the mountain farmer is increasingly becoming that of a guardian of cultivated land, providing the needed maintenance of ecological balance—for which services he is entitled to appropriate remuneration. Particularly in the Alpine region, which now may be considered Europe's "roof garden" and an international recreation area, the function of the countryside as an agriculturally productive area is definitely losing importance compared with its recreational function. The mountain farmers, therefore, receive subsidies and loans from diverse public bodies to safeguard their subsistence, since the maintenance of mountain farming is in the public interest to preserve the cultural landscape in the Alps.

3.6 Tourism in Austria

Attention has repeatedly been drawn to the role of tourism as a factor of regional development. Tourism has brought a rapid and continuous improvement of economic conditions to wide areas unsuited to intensive agriculture or to development of industry. Indeed, any survey of Austria would be incomplete that did not refer to this sector, which is of paramount importance for the national economy, since it generates a large share of primary income, in view of the high proportion of tourists from abroad.[11] Austria has become one of the leading countries of mass tourism, thanks to its lovely and varied scenery, its historical sites and places of cultural interest, its many recreational opportunities, and its wide range of tourist facilities. In 1978, approximately 12.3 million arrivals of foreign tourists were counted in Austria, placing it among considerably larger countries, such as Spain, France, Italy, and even the United States—the latter with a tourist influx from abroad of 17.5 million visitors in 1976.

While only about 21 million overnight stays were registered in Austria per annum in 1952–1953 (40% being overnight stays of foreign tourists)—

which corresponds to figures reached during the peak years between the two world wars—the volume of tourism has since increased more than fivefold. Two distinct periods of development may be distinguished: first, the dynamic period of growth and expansion of the late 1950s and of the 1960s, with an average annual growth rate of overnight stays of 8.3 percent (1952–1972), followed by a period of more moderate growth since 1972, characterized by stagnation of summer tourism at a high level, accompanied by a continuous rise in winter tourism.

In 1978, 108.4 million overnight stays of tourists were registered in hotels, inns, boarding houses, etc. as well as in private homes and on camping sites, the percentage of overnight stays of foreign tourists being 75%. These figures were even higher in 1979 and 1980, the latter being the peak year up to now. By far the largest share of all overnight stays by foreigners, i.e. 74 percent, came from the Federal Republic of Germany, followed by the Netherlands (11 percent).

Besides this specific concentration of tourists by nationality in Austria, two further typical features stand out (see Lichtenberger 1975): a slightly decreasing seasonal concentration of tourism, and a continued and marked regional concentration in the western provinces of Tyrol, Salzburg, and Carinthia.

Despite Austria's international renown as a country for winter sports, it must not be overlooked that tourism is still much concentrated in the summer season—except in a few areas—so that more than 40 percent of all annual overnight stays occur in only two months, in July and August (in Carinthia as much as 65 percent). Consequently, wide areas are faced with the problem of unused or sparely used capacities and consequent low returns from single-season tourism. The local authorities are therefore doing their utmost to expand the summer season into spring and autumn—or, wherever natural conditions permit, to provide facilities for winter sports in order to create a second tourist season in winter, since there are still considerable growth prospects in winter tourism, judging from international trends. Additionally, winter tourism usually tends to attract patrons spending more money per day than summer tourists. In the summer season Austria must increasingly compete for visitors with more distant countries due to the boom in long-distance tourism. Therefore a great number of skiing areas have been opened in recent years by the construction of cablecars, chair-lifts and tow-lifts, making the highest mountain regions accessible to the streams of visitors and skiers. Sometimes the ski-lifts and downhill runs together form a veritable system linking entire mountain ranges and valleys with each other. These ski circuits are, of course, augmented by the necessary infrastructure catering to the tourists' needs. In consequence, there has been an increase, since the beginning of the 1960s, in the percentage of overnight stays during the winter season, from 21 to 34 percent.

Between 1961 and 1978 the regional concentration of tourism has increased even further. Although at the beginning of this period around 56 percent of all overnight stays in Austria were registered in the three federal provinces mentioned above, this figure rose to 66 percent in 1978. During the same year 75 percent of all overnight stays of foreign tourists in Austria occurred in these provinces, 40 percent being in the single province of Tyrol. Here the proportion of overnight stays of visitors from abroad is about 93 percent, the complementary proportion of native tourists' overnight stays being only 7 percent. These figures clearly demonstrate the dominant position of Tyrol with respect to Austrian tourism, and its dominance in winter tourism is even more marked (more than half of all overnight stays of foreigners during the winter of 1977–1978). Considering that, on an average, Austria receives about 840 schillings (66 U.S. dollars) in foreign exchange per overnight foreign visitor, the contribution tourism makes to the economic prosperity of regions with intensive tourist traffic, where more than 100 overnight stays per inhabitant can be counted on an annual average, may easily be appreciated.

In comparison with the western parts of the country, the intensity of tourism is much lower in Austria's eastern provinces, although there are considerable possibilities of expansion in many places. During recent years, a dynamic growth of tourism has been witnessed in certain regions. One example is the area around Lake Neusiedl, with a topography totally different from the Alps. The eastern limit of the area of massive tourism, an area where all the large and internationally known holiday resorts—with the exception of Vienna and several spas—are located (see Map 4), extends from the lake district of Upper Austria ("Salzkammergut") and the Styrian part of the Enns valley in a south-southeasterly direction to the lake district of Carinthia. Whereas overnight stays of foreigners predominate to the west of this line, the area in the east is one of predominantly domestic tourism, where people mainly from Vienna take their leisure and spend their vacations. Relatively important tourist centers are situated in the Limestone Alps of Upper and Lower Austria, as well as in upper Styria and in the eastern part of this province. However, there are areas east of the above mentioned limit—even in the Alps—that have hitherto attracted no tourism at all. Certain traditional once famous tourist regions on the eastern edge of the Alps, for example the Semmering area, which used to be frequented by visitors from southeastern Europe,[12] have stagnated. It has to be mentioned that generally the old traditional lakeside resorts, spas, and other summer resorts, which are partly encumbered with types of accommodation, infrastructure and architectural features dating back to the last century and often unadaptable to modern conditions, have fallen behind the new centers of summer and winter tourism in the dynamics of tourist development.

Tourist traffic in Lower Austria, which used to enjoy the patronage of visitors from Vienna, is today handicapped by the fact that the Viennese are increasingly traveling to places farther afield, so that the traditional summer resorts are now being frequented only by older people. Furthermore, growing weekend and short-distance traveling brought about by increasing use of the automobile, and the noticeable trend of the metropolitan population to acquire second homes in the countryside have also had a negative effect on the tourist trade especially on the enterprises providing accommodation. A belt of second homes has expanded in recent years, particularly around Vienna. According to Lichtenberger (1980), approximately 50,000 houses or apartments have been acquired by Viennese in the province of Lower Austria since the beginning of the 1960s, comprising partly new housing construction, partly renovated farm buildings, readapted apartments, etc. In northern Burgenland and in Styria, too, many second homes have been bought or built.

The important centers of winter sports, which also enjoy an active summer season, have developed more dynamically than all other types of tourist areas. The Arlberg area (Tyrol-Vorarlberg), for example, and the region around Kitzbühel in Tyrol have acquired an international reputation, but they are also "classical" traditional resorts for foreign tourists in western Austria. Other areas are the Little Walser valley (Kleinwalsertal) in the province of Vorarlberg; the area around Innsbruck and Seefeld, internationally known from the Winter Olympics held there in 1964 and 1976; the Ötz valley and Ziller valley in Tyrol; the Gastein valley and the region around the Glockner massif, including Kaprun, Zell-on-See, and Saalbach in the province of Salzburg. In addition there are numerous recently fast-developing resorts at the eastern end of this western domain of intensive tourism in Austria catering to tourists from abroad in particular, but where domestic tourists also have a considerable share, especially during the winter season; places such as the area around the Radstätter Tauern Range; the Lungau area in the province of Salzburg; Schladming and the upper part of the Enns valley in the province of Styria; and Bad Kleinkirchheim in Carinthia (see Map 4).

Another kind of international resort, flourishing only during the summer season, has developed in the vicinity of lakes. In the famed lake district of Carinthia, a great number of important tourist centers, e.g. Velden, Pörtschach, and Millstatt, are situated near the five largest lakes of the province; best known of which is the Wörthersee. The Salzkammergut lake district is situated in the provinces of Salzburg, Upper Austria, and Styria, containing lakes such as Wolfgangsee, and Mondsee; but mention should also be made of Bodensee (Lake Constance) in Vorarlberg, which is also the site of the provincial capital of Bregenz.

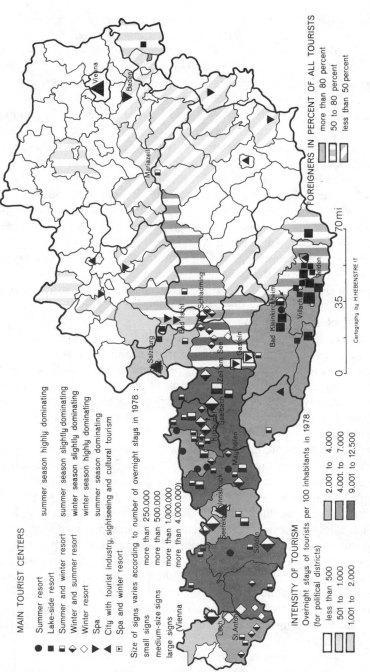

MAIN TOURIST CENTERS

- Summer resort
- Lake-side resort
- Summer and winter resort
- Winter and summer resort
- Winter resort
- Spa
- City with tourist industry, sightseeing and cultural tourism
- Spa and winter resort

summer season highly dominating
summer season slightly dominating
winter season slightly dominating
winter season highly dominating
summer season dominating

Size of signs varies according to number of overnight stays in 1978 :

small signs   more than 250.000
medium-size signs   more than 500.000
large signs   more than 1.000.000
(Vienna   more than 4.000.000)

INTENSITY OF TOURISM

Overnight stays of tourists per 100 inhabitants in 1978
(for political districts)

less than 500
501 to 1.000
1.001 to 2.000
2.001 to 4.000
4.001 to 7.000
9.001 to 12.500

FOREIGNERS IN PERCENT OF ALL TOURISTS

more than 80 percent
50 to 80 percent
less than 50 percent

Cartography by H.HEBENSTREIT

0   35   70mi

Map 4. Regional structure and intensity of tourism in Austria.

Internationally renowned spas and health resorts are among the largest tourist communities in Austria. Best known among them are probably Badgastein, also the center of a large winter sport area; Baden near Vienna; and Bad Ischl in the Salzkammergut area in Upper Austria. Besides these there are a great number of villages and towns offering facilities for recreation; and, finally, big-city tourism must not be left out of consideration.

Besides Innsbruck, the large town in the heart of the mountains, and the city of Salzburg with its internationally famed music festivals, its romantic architecture, and picturesque location on the fringe of the Alps (Picture 7), Vienna is, of course, the city attracting the largest stream of tourists. The federal capital of Austria is known throughout the world as the former residence of the Habsburg dynasty and is the largest tourist center of the country, with 4.3 million overnight stays in 1978. Its many interesting buildings and flourishing cultural life attract a wider spectrum of tourists from all over the world than all of the rest of Austria (Picture 8). In particular, American tourists traveling in Europe are attracted to this city. Although tourists from the United States account for only 1.6 percent of all overnight stays of foreigners visiting Austria, they are the second largest group among the visitors to Vienna, outnumbered only by those from the Federal Republic of Germany.

In Austria, the direct and indirect multiplier effects of income from tourist trade have a strong impact. There are two main reasons for this: The structure of the tourist trade, consisting predominantly of small and medium-scale enterprises; and the participation of a sizable section of the the population, mainly in the rural areas, in this field, e.g. through letting rooms to visitors. The positive impact of tourism is reflected in much building activity, too.

Large single or double family houses with a story added especially for renting rooms to tourists are now typical of the settlements in the western provinces. Often there is a separate building for use as a guest house, sometimes including breakfast facilities, adjoining the house used by the host family. Also a significant rise in the communities' income from local taxes and rates in most of the tourist regions has occurred. Of nearly 100,000 enterprises providing accommodation, about three-quarters are private homes letting rooms to tourists and providing breakfast, whereas only one quarter are professional establishments proper, such as hotels, inns, boarding-houses and the widespread hotels garni. The latter group, however, accounts for 55 percent of all available accommodations. Camping is of no great significance in Austria, with the exception of the lake district of Carinthia.

The boom experienced in the Austrian tourist trade could never have taken place without the initiative displayed by large sections of the popula-

Picture 7. Center of Salzburg, capital of the province of the same name and location of the internationally famous Salzburg Festival. The old city with its baroque churches, narrow streets, and interesting old houses lies at the foot of the largest, fully preserved medieval castle in Austria, Hohensalzburg. Photo: Austrian National Tourist Office.

Picture 8.   View of the inner city of Vienna, with St. Stephen's Cathedral and St. Peter's Church. Photo: Austrian National Tourist Office.

tion in renting private rooms, as well as in establishing enterprises for the accommodation of tourists. It has often been emphasized that the tourist trade in Austria has a strongly local nature. Outside the big cities, international hotel chains and hotels belonging to large enterprises are practically nonexistent. Owing to the small scale of the enterprises, investments and risks are well spread. The letting of rooms in private houses has almost become a "way of life" (Lichtenberger 1976); it constitutes an important supplementary source of income for many families—even though it is not always based on principles of economic rationality alone. The proportion of privately rented rooms is very high in those areas only now developing a significant tourist trade and at the fringes of the highly developed tourist regions, whereas it falls behind hotel business in the major tourist centers. In traditional tourist areas with hotels dating back to the beginning of the century and to the interwar years, and in the larger cities including Vienna, the number of privately rented rooms is minimal.

Without doubt the extension of the winter sports areas will be the major driving force in the development of Austrian tourism during the coming years, and considerable efforts will have to be made to maintain summer tourism at its present high level. It could already be observed during the economic recession of the early 1970s that there was no falling-off during the winter seasons but a drop did occur in some summer resorts. In many cases winter tourism upgrades high pasture areas in the mountains, which were formerly not intensively utilized; and even barren land is brought into use, becoming the setting of quite intensive economic activity (e.g. the region around the Arlberg, the Ötz valley, the Radstätter Tauern Range). However, the extension of winter sports to the highest mountain peaks— and there are already five large areas where skiing is possible on the glaciers in midsummer—constitutes a great risk for the ecological balance of the mountain areas. Consequently the problems are also increasing that relate to the resistance of Alpine ecosystems to damage, particularly through tourism, as well as to the determination of limits to the receptive capacity of tourist areas.

It will be imperative to strive harder than ever to keep the natural environment intact in the main tourist areas, since it constitutes the major capital asset of the tourist industry in Austria. One measure of paramount importance in this direction is to make sure of the continued accessibility of the lake shores that have not yet been built up. There is also a danger that the best parts of the recreation areas surrounding the cities, particularly of Vienna—but also famous tourist regions in the Alps—may be spoilt by indiscriminate building activities, as has already begun to happen. Tourism also requires the planned expansion of the infrastructure and increased efforts to preserve Austria's many monuments, cultural sites, and historical urban centers. It will be a task of regional policy to resolve the conflict that has arisen between the conservationists and those business interests intent on opening new areas for recreation, in order to bring about equitable development, guided both by the requirements of environmental preservation and the needs of the economy to guarantee economic welfare for the Alpine population. Only in this way will it be possible to avoid the negative concomitants of mass tourism, which could do irreparable damage to the Alpine ecosystem and natural milieu, and to the settlement pattern and cultural landscape.

3.7 The Interregional Traffic Network

As shown in Map 1, Austria is situated at the intersection of important European traffic routes, which lead across the Alps and along the Danube River. Whereas the west-east axis following the northern fringe of the Alps is a naturally favorable traffic route but one nowadays of diminished international importance because of the political situation in Europe, the north-south routes have to contend with the Alps—a major obstacle to intensive traffic. But these are the paths carrying heavy flows of transit traffic, since they link the economic and population centers of west- and of north-central Europe, on the one hand, with Italy and southeastern Europe, on the other. Besides considerable heavy goods traffic, there is a great stream of tourists traveling to the Mediterranean, and in addition Italian, Yugoslav, and Turkish workers follow these routes to jobs in the Federal Republic of Germany. In particular, the route from Salzburg to Graz, crossing the Alps, is known by the sobriquet the "guest workers' route."

The mountainous topography of Austria makes the construction and maintenance of a network of international highways very costly, and a high level of technological skill is required for providing high-capacity traffic routes across the Alps. The heavy traffic crossing the national borders has obliged Austria to build expressways and motorways that serve international rather than domestic traffic. This means that up to the present the Austrian economy has had to shoulder certain costs for other countries.

This is particularly true for the westernmost and most important of the three transalpine expressways, the Brenner Highway in Tyrol. Completed at the beginning of the 1970s, it traverses the Alps via the Brenner Pass, which is the route with the highest density of traffic in the whole Eastern Alps. It forms the shortest link between the two EEC countries, the Federal Republic of Germany and Italy. The other two transverse routes farther to the east, i.e. the Tauern expressway between Salzburg and Carinthia, completed in 1980, with a planned connecting expressway via the southern Alps into Yugoslavia, and the Phyrn expressway linking Upper Austria and Styria (see Map 5) are of high international but, conversely, also of significant regional economic importance. After the completion of the Tauern expressway the province of Carinthia, formerly frequently inaccessible from the north-west in the winter due to the high Alpine passes, is for the first time linked with western Austria by a connection that is open every day of the year and is now easily accessible from the populous centers of western Germany. After the completion of the Phyrn expressway, expected for the second half of the 1980s, Styria, which has no high capacity connection with the west, will be in a less peripheral position. Furthermore, Austria's two most important centers of the steel industry, in Upper Austria and upper Styria, will be linked by this route, which it is hoped will greatly improve regional stability in the latter. The transalpine routes constitute a remarkable technical achievement, with impressive bridges (the Europe Bridge of the Brenner Highway, shown in Picture 9, being the second highest bridge in Europe) and long tunnels piercing the mountain ridges.

Two other important traffic routes that are particularly important in serving the needs of inland traffic in Austria provide the links that connect Vienna with the west and south: the "West Expressway" connecting Vienna

Picture 9.   The Europe Bridge, south of Innsbruck on the Brenner Expressway leading across the Alps from the Federal Republic to Italy, is the second highest highway bridge in Europe. Photo: Austrian National Tourist Office.

and the Vienna Basin to Upper Austria, Salzburg, and the Federal Republic of Germany and the "South Expressway" not yet completed, which will link Vienna with Italy and the Mediterranean port of Trieste and connect the three southern and eastern provinces of Lower Austria, Carinthia, and Styria with each other. For the sake of the regional development of the southeastern border area, this expressway does not lead along the traditional traffic route through the Mur and Mürz valleys but runs closer to the eastern border areas and the city of Graz. This will help Austria's second largest city extract itself from its present dead-end position within the Austrian traffic network.

After the completion of the South Expressway and the Phyrn expressway all large urbanized areas in Austria will be interlinked by expressways with the exception of the Rhine valley in Vorarlberg. But that area has recently been provided with a secure, all-year-round connection with the rest of Austria through the Arlberg Tunnel, 14 km long, the second longest highway tunnel in Europe.

The great railway lines, which also cross the Alps mainly through long tunnels, had been partly built during the time of the Habsburg Monarchy. Unlike the expressways they follow the traditional traffic routes fairly closely. However, they are marred by bottlenecks, since certain stretches are negotiated by single-track lines and portions of the permanent road beds are not suitable for the high speeds required of modern rail traffic. Austria has provided pioneering feats in the history of Alpine railroad construction. In 1853, for example, the Semmering rail link between Vienna and the industrial zone of upper Styria was the first mountain railway to be constructed in Europe.

The Danube River, Austria's only navigable river, is of relatively little importance compared with other waterways such as the Rhine in West Germany. However, it is expected that the Rhine-Main-Danube Canal—to be completed in the mid-1980s—will change this state of affairs drastically. Land-locked Austria will then be situated astride a waterway traversing Europe. Although the scope and structure of future navigation can only be roughly estimated at present, it is certain that the opening of this canal will inaugurate many new possibilities for economic development along the Danube, especially for the core region of Upper Austria with its heavy industry and chemical industry. The city of Linz is already Austria's biggest inland port, followed by Vienna and Krems. A new, larger harbor, now in the planning stage, is to be built southeast of Linz, in the Danube valley. It will, however, be necessary to devise an integrated development plan encompassing the adaptation of the Danube as an internationally important navigation route and the generation of energy (major hydroelectric power stations), while simultaneously providing recreational facilities, combined with environmental protection measures since some parts of the valley are of great scenic beauty (see Picture 10).

3.8 Urban Growth and the Cities

Austria, like other industrialized countries, is highly urbanized. In 1971, approximately 64 percent of the total population lived in towns of more than 5,000 inhabitants, including surrounding communities.

Austria's urban system is dominated by Vienna, where around 21 percent of the country's population were living in 1977. The city next in size, Graz, has only 250,000 inhabitants, or one-sixth the population of Vienna. The four cities of more than 100,000 inhabitants—besides Graz, these are Linz, Salzburg, and Innsbruck—are also capitals of federal provinces; as is Klagenfurt, with 80,000 inhabitants. All of them developed during the previous centuries into residences of sovereigns, centers of administration and seats of institutions of the provinces, and thus have grown to become the principal cities of the Austrian central place hierarchy.

In 1976, there were just 17 towns in Austria of between 20,000 and 80,000 inhabitants; most already having been historically prominent as district capitals in their respective regions. The majority of the towns have, however, remained small, with fewer than 10,000 inhabitants. In the provinces of Salzburg and Tyrol, there are no medium-size cities between the provincial capitals and the small towns. The province of Burgenland has barely

Picture 10. The Danube in Lower Austria, where the river breaks through the Granite Uplands in the narrow valley known as Wachau, with the medieval castle ruin of Aggstein. Photo: Austrian National Tourist Office.

any cities at all. Its present capital, Eisenstadt, has only 11,000 inhabitants; the historical centers of the region remained with Hungary when the Burgenland was ceded to Austria.

Settlement in the forelands of the Alps has been continuous since Roman times—there were Roman settlements on the present sites of Vienna, Salzburg, and Linz—while in the Alps proper the Roman cities perished during the times of mass migration of eastern tribes in the middle of the first millenium A.D. Thereafter, many of the towns were founded by secular and ecclesiastical princes, prelates, and feudal lords, to serve as stopover and rest places along the trade routes, as trading centers or military strongholds. Other ones developed gradually from market towns and villages into bigger settlements that were later granted city charters. A number of Alpine towns flourished in former times because of mining activities in the vicinity. Many Austrian towns are spread at the foot of fortresses or castles. A number of the urban settlements were deliberately planned and laid out around rectangular town squares.

All the larger cities of Austria go back to medieval times, and medieval buildings still characterize many of the town centers. Some of them were transformed later on, their original medieval character being overlaid mainly in the baroque style, and later still in the style of the "founder era" of the late 19th century.

Vienna's specific position and historical development are inextricably linked with the rise and fall of the Habsburg monarchy. The urban core contains remnants of the medieval city, which remained unchanged in later periods, with St. Stephens Cathedral marking the city center, surrounded by the palaces of noble families and abbeys built in the baroque style. The core is encircled by the Ringstrasse, built after 1857, along which there are many splendid buildings, some belonging to the Imperial Court (dominated by the "Hofburg" Palace with its outer forecourt, the "Heldenplatz" or Heroes' Square), or to ecclesiastical authorities, and other famous buildings serving national and city administration and government (Parliament, City Hall); magnificent museum buildings; the well-known Opera House and the Burg Theater; the Vienna University; and many stately bourgeois palaces and apartment houses dating back to the founders period. The densely built up areas adjacent to the urban core were once suburbs outside the city walls ("Vorstädte") which grew in the 18th and 19th centuries, today forming the inner districts of the municipal area of Vienna characterized by an intermingling of economic activities with residential functions.

The time between 1840 and 1914 is known as the "Gründerzeit," or Founders' period. During this time, when railroads were built and Vienna was industrialized, the capital rose to the rank of a true world metropolis. From 440,000 inhabitants in 1840, its population increased to 2.1 million

Picture 11.   Aerial view of Vienna. Photo: Landesbildstelle Wien.

in 1914. That period witnessed the most profound changes in the city's layout and architectural appearance.

Expansion of the central business district took hold of large portions of the old medieval city quarters and proceeded along the old radial thoroughfares into the suburbs. Along the then urban periphery a circular, densely built-up belt of tenement buildings arose, with tiny apartments for the stream of immigrants converging on the city. These old tenement buildings with their tens of thousands of poorly fitted small flats, today additionally characterized by an overaged population structure, form a "strangulating ring" that poses great problems for city planners and for the housing market (see Bobek and Lichtenberger 1966, and Lichtenberger 1978). On the other hand, Vienna is still profiting today from certain achievements of that era, e.g. with respect to its cultural institutions, the boldly planned system of canalization, the transport network, and the streamlining of the Danube riverbed, carried out during the 1870s.

After the dissolution of the monarchy, the city went through a period of heavy population decrease and of economic stagnation—a decline that only came to a halt in 1955 with the signing of the State Treaty between Austria and the Allied Powers. The most important feat of architectural renewal in the time between the two world wars, which characterizes the face of the city in the residential areas up to now, was the Vienna municipal administration's social housing program for the construction of big blocks of flats for workers, designed to alleviate the pressing housing shortage. Its interesting forms of architecture today attract increasing international attention (e.g. the Karl Marx–Hof).

Since 1945, Vienna has experienced a lively renewal of building activity —between 1945 and 1965 more than 160,000 apartments were built, half of this number by the municipal administration of Vienna (social housing) and the built-up area of the municipality was extended by laying out extensive new residential districts on the urban periphery. At the same time, the inner districts of the city have lost inhabitants because of the poor condition of the buildings which very often do not provide adequate housing standards, and also through the conversion of apartments into offices in the now economically prospering city. Attempts are being made to slow this development by means of large-scale renovation and revitalizing projects in the old residential quarters. Strict building regulations, drawn up during the last century, have prevented the construction of excessively high buildings, so that the appearance of the city today can by no means be compared to that of the large U.S. cities with their skyscrapers. Much the same situation holds for most other cities in Central Europe. The social segregation of the urban population, too, is much less pronounced than in most metropolitan areas of the United States.

A number of major projects have been carried out or started in recent years. Besides the construction of many roads, three underground lines were completed (with additional ones still under construction); work is in progress on a second bed for the Danube, providing improved protection against flooding; Europe's largest hospital is under construction; and the quality of life and leisure of the population has been improved by the conversion of a portion of the city center into a pedestrian area. Important political and cultural projects have been carried out: construction of the Vienna International Center for the United Nations and organization of international congresses and symposia; outstanding artistic performances are taking place in opera, in theaters, and in the offerings of the Vienna Festival. All this has added to Vienna's image being still a world metropolis, a city of culture and an educational center, with its five universities and three university colleges for music and the arts, despite the city's peripheral position in close proximity to the Iron Curtain. Vienna's recent official designation as a third domicile of the United Nations, after New York and Geneva, is a special recognition of Vienna's efforts in these fields.

Of course, Vienna is also the center of the country's largest urbanized area. There are seven urbanized areas in Austria, so-called "core areas" (see Wurzer 1970), covering 14 percent of Austria's total area, but with approximately 60 percent of its population and three fourths of all persons employed in the manufacture of commodities. Map 5 shows, besides Austria's most important cities, the location of these seven core areas of population and economic activity. They are also the central areas of the seven principal regions that functionally divide the country (see Bobek & Fesl 1973) and whose borders roughly coincide with the borders of the federal provinces. The exception is the so-called East-Region with its growth-pole being the city of Vienna and its suburban zone, where Vienna, Lower Austria and Burgenland with the exception of its southern part together form a single functional region.

Next to the core area including Vienna and the Vienna Basin, the Upper Austrian core area around Linz, which recorded the fastest population growth in absolute terms of these seven areas, is the second largest in the country. Another is the Styrian core area, which is divided into two parts, one part grouped around the center of Graz, the other situated in the industrial zone of upper Styria, around the towns of Leoben and Kapfenberg. Furthermore, there is the Innsbruck-Kufstein core area in the lower Inn valley (Tyrol); other ones are the Salzburg core area and the Carinthian core area, and finally that around Bregenz, Dornbirn, and Feldkirch (Vorarlberg). With the exception of the last-mentioned and smallest core area, all those listed are monocentrically organized, the provincial capitals being the core cities and growth-poles. Only in the province of Burgenland has

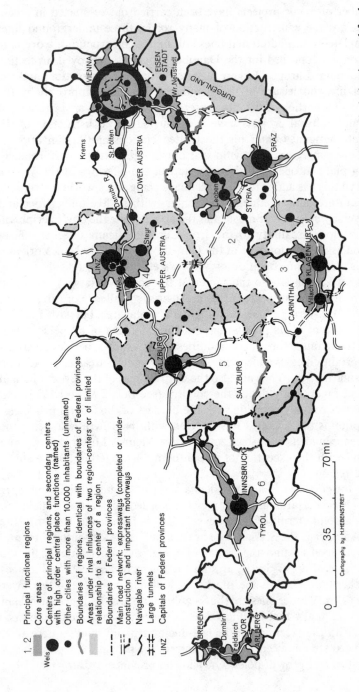

Map 5. Austria: core areas, major cities, regions, and interregional road network (core areas as defined by Wurzer 1970, principal regions as defined by Bobek and Fesl 1973).

no such concentration developed, since the predominance of Vienna has made the development of independent centers in the eastern region rather difficult.

The urbanized areas attract their population influx from the rural areas. However, as in other countries, the people moving in very often do not settle in the central cities but rather on the peripheries or in the adjacent outer communities. The process of suburbanization is compounded by the migration of some of the city-dwellers toward the periphery in search of residential space in the green belt. However, this trend has by no means reached the proportions observed in the metropolitan areas of the United States.

Outside the urban conglomerations, concerted and coordinated efforts are made to develop regional centers of employment and shopping facilities, augmented by public services—schools, hospitals, administrative offices, etc.—which are much needed in the eastern Alpine and eastern border regions of Austria. This design of selective promotion of viable subcenters, intended to function as stimulating agents of regional development, is an aspect of the basic aims of Austria's general policy for regional planning; it is hoped that the principle of decentralized concentration, applied in Austria's urban and economic development, will largely counteract the negative consequences of increasing settlement density and uninhibited sprawling urbanized areas, coupled with an increasing depopulation of the countryside, and yet meet modern demands for infrastructure and nonagrarian employment opportunities. Berentsen (1978) has pointed out that the principle of decentralized concentration has probably become the guiding principle for regional planning efforts in Austria, because of another fact, also: It is better suited to Austria's basic federalism and the independence of the federal provinces than any completely centralized planning model.

Notes

1. Concerning the birth of the Republic of Austria, see the contribution of F. Fellner in the present volume.
2. In 1920 there were 6.4 million inhabitants within Austria's borders, 1.9 million of them living in Vienna.
3. More than one-third of the national borders run along the Iron Curtain facing the COMECON and Warsaw Pact countries—Czechoslovakia (568 km) and Hungary (346 km); the border shared with Yugoslavia, which is associated with COMECON, is 311 km in length. The longest stretch of border is with the Federal Republic of Germany (784 km), with which country—as with Switzerland and the tiny principality of Liechtenstein (together 200 km of common borders)—Austria has close cultural ties. The 430 km of border shared with Italy runs mainly along Alpine ridges.
4. Following the extension of the German domain in the Middle Ages, which moved along the Danube valley toward the east, taking definite shape in 976 A.D. under the rule of the dukes of Babenberg with the establishment of the "Ostmark" or "eastern borderland"

(first mention of the name 'Österreich' in its medieval form, Ostarrichi in 996), the Danubian provinces of Upper and Lower Austria became the nucleus of political expansion. Next, Austria was extended southward, through the acquisition of Styria in 1192, and Carinthia in 1355, under the Habsburgs (since 1282), who endeavored to form a link-up with their ancestral possessions in Switzerland and southwestern Germany also in a westerly direction. Thus, in 1363 the country of mountain passes, the Tyrol, was incorporated into Austria, and Vorarlberg was acquired during the 15th century. Rather late—in 1805—the ecclesiastic principality of Salzburg was joined to Austria. The two most recently established provinces are Burgenland, which was the German-speaking part of western Hungary, incorporated into Austria after the dissolution of the Habsburg monarchy (1919–1921); and Vienna, the out-size capital, which was made a federal province by itself through separation from Lower Austria in 1922.

5. In consequence, the density of settlement is rather high for that 15 percent, i.e. 310 inhabitants per km² (1979), while the remaining 85 percent of the province is practically uninhabited, disregarding the temporary settlement during the seasons of Alpine stock farming and of tourism.

6. In the high parts of the Alps, in western Austria, Alpine mountain pastures (Almen) make up about 30 percent of the total area.

7. Nearly all of Austria's iron ore, i.e. 3.4 million tons (1977), which forms an important raw material basis for Austria's iron and steel industry, is mined on or around the Erzberg, largely by open-cast mining. Another, smaller iron ore deposit was worked at Hüttenberg in Carinthia until it was shut down recently.

8. See the contribution by H. Leitner in the present volume.

9. The share of the four provinces decreased from 65.9 percent in 1952 to 59.2 percent in 1977; that of the western provinces of Tyrol, Vorarlberg, and Salzburg rose from 13.2 to 17.9 percent; and the share of the province of Upper Austria with its heavy industry rose from 15.4 to 16.7 percent.

10. On the other hand, an above-average number of industrial enterprises is closing down in the border areas. According to a report of the Federal Chancellor's Office to the OECD on Austria's regional policy (1973), efforts in certain parts of the Granite Uplands to stabilize the population by the establishment of industrial enterprises ended in failure because a sufficient number of suitable and large enough enterprises could not be mustered.

11. In 1978, Austria received foreign exchange in the amount of 61.4 billion schillings from foreign visitors. After deduction of the foreign exchange spent by Austrian tourists abroad, a total of 31.3 billion schillings accrued to Austria, which was an important contribution toward covering the trade deficit.

12. During the 1936–1937 tourist season, 44 percent of all foreigners staying overnight in Austria came from southeastern Europe, and 47 percent from western Europe. In 1978, on the other hand, 1.2 percent came from southeastern or eastern Europe, and 95 percent came from western Europe.

Selected Bibliography

IN ENGLISH

Berentsen, W. H. 1978. Austrian Regional Development Policy: The Impact of Policy on the Achievement of Planning Goals. In *Economic Geography*, vol. 54, pp. 115–34. Worchester, Mass.

Bobek, H. 1974. The Formation of Regional Inequalities in Development: The Case of Austria. In *Proceedings of the Commission on Regional Aspects of Development of the International Geographical Union*. Vol. I, *Methodology and Case Studies*, ed. by R. S. Thoman. Pp. 779–94.

Federal Press Service. 1979. *Austria. Facts and Figures*. Vienna. 238 pp.

Hoffman, G. W. 1977. Central Europe. West Germany, Switzerland, Austria. In *A Geography of Europe. Problems and Prospects*, ed. by G. W. Hoffman. New York. 4th ed. Pp. 305–67.

Lichtenberger, E. 1975. *The Eastern Alps*. Problem Regions of Europe Series. London. 48 pp.

Rees, H. 1974. *Italy, Switzerland and Austria. A Geographical Study*. Part 3, Austria. Pp. 259–348. London.

Regional Planning in Austria. 1978. Published by the Austrian Conference for Regional Planning (ÖROK) on the occasion of the 4th European Conference of Ministers responsi-

ble for Regional Planning in Vienna. Österreichische Raumordnungskonferenz, Schriftenreihe Nr. 15a, Wien. 89 pp.
Salient Features of Regional Development Policy in Austria. 1974. Paris: Organization for Economic Cooperation and Development (OECD). 90 pp.

IN GERMAN

Atlas der Republik Örsterreich. Ed. Kommission für Raumforschung der Österreichischen Akademie der Wissenschaften, Director Hans Bobek. Wien: Freytag-Berndt und Artaria. 6 issues. 280 maps of high scientific level.
Bobek, H. 1957. Österreich—Schlüsselstellung in Europa—Lage und Raum. In *Spectrum Austriae.* Ed. O. Schulmeister. Wien. Pp. 21–49.
——— 1970. Ausgliederung der Strukturgebiete der österreichischen Wirtschaft. In *Strukturanalyse des Österreichischen Bundesgebietes.* Ed. by order of the Österreichsche Gesellschaft für Raumforschung und Raumplanung by R. Wurzer. Wien. Vol. 2, pp. 449–59
Bobek, H., and M. Fesl. 1973. Zentrale Orte und ihre Bereiche—Neuerhebung 1973. Sheet XII/6 of Atlas der Republik Österreich, see above.
Bobek, H., und E. Lichtenberger. 1966. *Wien: Bauliche Gestalt und Entwicklung seit der Mitte des 19. Jahrhunderts.* Wien. 382 pp.
Glatz, H. 1979. Regionale Disparitäten in Österreich. Konzepte und Mängel der Regionalpolitik. In *Österreichische Zeitschrift für Politikwissenschaft,* Vol. 8., Wien. Pp. 177–97.
Glauert, G. 1975. *Die Alpen, eine Einführung in die Landeskunde.* Geocolleg-Series. Kiel. 104 pp.
Greif, F. 1979. Gedanken zur Alm- und Bergbauernfrage. In *Österreich in Geschichte und Literatur,* Vol. 23, Wien. Pp. 96–108.
Krammer, J., und G. Scheer. 1978. *Das österreichische Agrarsystem.* Wien: Institut für Höhere Studien und Wissenschaftliche Forschung. 340 pp.
Krebs, N. (1928). Die Ostalpen und das heutige Österreich. Eine Länderkunde. 3. edition 1961, Darmstadt. 2 Vols.
Lichtenberger, E. 1965. Das Bergbauernproblem in den österreichischen Alpen. Perioden und Typen der Entsiedlung. In *Erdkunde,* Vol. 19, Bonn, Pp. 39–57.
———. 1978. *Stadtgeographischer Führer Wien.* In: Sammlung Geographischer Führer, Vol. 12. Berlin. 263 pp.
———. 1980. Die Stellung der Zweiwohnungen im städtischen System—Das Wiener Beispiel. In *Berichte zur Raumforschung und Raumplanung,* Vol. 24, Wien. Pp. 3–14
———. 1976. Der Massentourismus als dynamisches Phänomen. In: *Verhandlungen des Deutschen Geographentages,* Vol. 40. Wiesbaden
Luftbildatlas Österreich. 1969. Eine Landeskunde mit 80 farbigen Luftaufnahmen. Ed. L. Scheidl. Wien. 198 pp.
Regionalpolitik in Österreich. 1973. *Bericht des Bundeskanzleramts (Büro für Raumplanung) an die OECD,* Arbeitsgruppe Nr. 6 des Industriekomitees. In: *Österreichische Raumordnungskonferenz* (ÖROK), Schriftenreihe, Vol. 15, Wien. 96 pp.
Scheidl, L., und H. Lechleitner. 1978. *Österreich. Land, Volk, Wirtschaft in Stichworten.* Wien, 3. ed. 184 pp.
Seidel, H., F. Butschek, und A. Kausel. 1966. *Die regionale Dynamik der österreichischen Wirtschaft. In Studien und Analysen,* Band 1. Wien.
Strukturanalyse des österreichischen Bundesgebietes. 1970. Ed. by order of the Österreichischen Gesellschaft für Raumforschung und Raumplanung by R. Wurzer. 3 Vols. Wien, 834 Pp., and more than 200 maps.
Wichmann, H., ed. 1972. *Die Zukunft der Alpenregion.* München.
Wurzer, R. 1970. Struktur und Probleme der Verdichtungsgebiete. In *Strukturanalyse des österreichischen Bundesgebietes,* see above, Vol. 2, Pp. 505–33.

Modern Austria, pp. 75–97

2. DEMOGRAPHY AND POPULATION PROBLEMS

Helga Leitner

Institute of Geography, University of Vienna

1 INTRODUCTION

Austria's population development during this century is characterized by moderate growth with considerable regional variations. Between 1910 and 1971, the population grew by approximately 808,000 persons, from 6, 648,000 to 7,456,403. The development was not steady, of course: periods of growth are offset by periods of stagnation or decrease (see Table 1). With an annual average growth rate of 0.2 percent, Austria lies below the average for most Western and Central European countries.

There are three demographic components that are basic to an understanding of the development of the population figure and the demographic structure: fertility, mortality and migration movements. These are, of course, closely connected with economic, political, and social developments, some of which date back to the previous century. Part of Austria's demographic history is also part of the general demographic changes that had taken place over time in the industrialized nations, such as a decrease in the mortality rate, followed by a decline in the birth rate[1] and an increasing concentration of the population in urban areas. Independent of these changes, Austria's demographic development during the 20th century has been shaped by the following events: World Wars I and II, voluntary and forced population movements after the wars, and the increasing influx of foreign migrant workers.

2 DEMOGRAPHIC PERIODS AND REGIONAL POPULATION DEVELOPMENT

2.1 The Period 1910–1951

At the beginning of this century World War I caused a grave interruption in Austria's population growth, which had been continuous up until that

75

9306-6403/81/0415-0075$01.50

Table 1 Population growth in Austria since 1910, due to natural increases and migrations

Year	Population	Average annual growth rate (per thousand)	Change (in thousands)		
			Total	Natural increase[a]	Net migration[b]
1910	6,648,310	−1.4	−113.6	−128.6	15.0
1923	6,543,742	3.1	225.5	258.9	−33.4
1934	6,760,233	1,5	173.7	20.6	153.1
1951	6,933,905	2.0	139.9	268.9	−129.0
1961	7,073,807	5.2	· 382.6	340.8	41.8
1971	7,456,403	3.4	76.6	28.3	48.3
1974	7,533,046	−0.8	−24.6	−26.6	2.0
1978	7,508,950				

[a] Births minus deaths.
[b] Immigration minus emigration.

time. The loss of 190,000 men killed in action, increased mortality among the civilian population, and extremely low birth rates (in 1917, 13.8 per thousand compared with 25–30 per thousand between 1910 and 1913), owing to the absence of the men who were in military service, resulted in a decrease of Austria's population by more than 100,000 persons in the census interval between 1910 and 1923.[2] After the fall of the Austro-Hungarian Monarchy in 1918, extensive population transfers took place, but they essentially offset each other: The immigration of the German-speaking and Jewish population from the newly created national states was balanced by an almost equally high emigration. Further, the economic and political crisis in the Austria of the 1930s caused 72,000 Austrians to emigrate to non-European countries, in particular to the United States between 1921 and 1937.[3] The highest number of emigrants came from the province of Burgenland.

World War II had similarly disastrous consequences for the population of Austria; the country lost 271,000 persons in the course of this war. However, in contrast to World War I and with the exception of the year 1945, there was no birth loss. On the contrary, the number of births, which had reached an absolute low in 1937 (See Fig. 1), had already increased with the German annexation of Austria, primarily owing to the Nazi population policy, which attached special significance to families with a large number of children. The birth surplus of the war years continued into the postwar period, albeit at a lower level. After World War II, Austria was the destination as well as the transit country of large streams of refugees, which primarily consisted of German-speaking people uprooted by the ending of the war or expelled by the governments of the Eastern European countries in the course of their ethnic housecleaning policy.

per Thousands Inhabitants

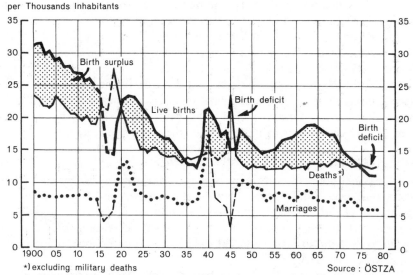

Figure 1 Development of fertility, mortality, and marriage rates since 1900.

2.2 The Period 1951–1961

Along with a stabilizing political and economic situation, the number of births rose relatively sharply in Austria, especially after 1955 (see Fig. 1). This trend, which occured in most other Western European countries, seemed to indicate the end of the historical trend of a declining birth rate. The high migration losses during this period are primarily due to the emigration of the refugees of World War II, who had been included in the resident population in 1951.

2.3 The Period 1961–1971–1978

During the census interval 1961–1971, Austria experienced a population increase unprecedented in the postwar period (see Table 1). There are two main reasons for this: the large excess of births over deaths and the influx of foreign workers, especially since the mid-1960s. However, midway through this period a break in the development of the birth rate occurred, known as the "pill drop-off." Since 1964, the birth rate and fertility rate have declined continuously up to the present. This decrease, which must be considered a serious problem for the demographic development in Austria, has become more pronounced since 1969; it caused a birth deficit in 1975 and reached a low point in 1978, with a birth rate of 11.4 per thousand. This puts Austria among the countries with the lowest birth rates in an international comparison; only the birth rates in the Federal Republic of Germany (9.3 per thousand in 1978) and in Luxemburg (10.9 per thousand) are lower.

The slightly increased mortality rate during this period is due to shifts in the age structure, not to a genuine increase in mortality.

In the early 1970s, the decline in the natural increase (excess of births over deaths) could still be compensated for by the immigration of foreign workers. However, the most recent period, 1974–1978, is, for the first time since World War II, characterized by a decrease in the population figure (see Table 1). This is due to a combination of an excess of deaths over births and a decrease in the immigration gains, caused by a stop to the immigration of foreign workers in the course of the economic recession.

2.4 Regional Population Development

The regional population development in Austria is characterized by two factors: a) growth differentials between the eastern, southern, and western provinces (*Länder*)—while the west and south experienced a population increase, the east has been lagging behind,[4] b) an increasing concentration of the population in urban areas at the cost of a population decline in the rural areas (see Table 3).

Whereas the growth differentials between the eastern and western provinces originally started in the interwar period, they were accelerated as a result of World War II and during the ten years of Soviet occupation of Austria's eastern provinces. In the period between 1934 and 1951, the provinces of Vienna, Lower Austria, and Burgenland lost 10.6 percent of their population. Vienna accounts for the greatest part of this loss; its population decreased by 320,000 inhabitants in this time period, mainly as a result of a high birth deficit. Apart from this, Vienna also lost population through the forced emigration of about 180,000 Viennese Jews, of which only a relatively small percentage resettled in Vienna after the war. In contrast, western Austria (Upper Austria, Salzburg, Tyrol, and Vorarlberg) and southern Austria (Styria and Carinthia) saw a rapid population growth, owing to a continuous excess of births over deaths as well as to both migration gains from the eastern provinces and immigration of resettlers and refugees, primarily Germans from Eastern Europe.

Between 1961 and 1971 the western provinces again experienced an above-average population growth. The primary reason for the more favorable population development in western Austria was not so much a migration gain as a higher level of fertility (birth rate, 1961: Vorarlberg, 25.3 per thousand; Vienna, 11.5 per thousand) and a more favorable age structure of the population (see *Fig. 2*). For the most recent period, 1971 to 1977, this trend continued: population losses of the three eastern provinces are contrasted with population gains in Upper Austria, Salzburg, Tyrol, and Vorarlberg, while the south and southeast, which hitherto had been growing although to a lesser extent than the west, now also experienced stagna-

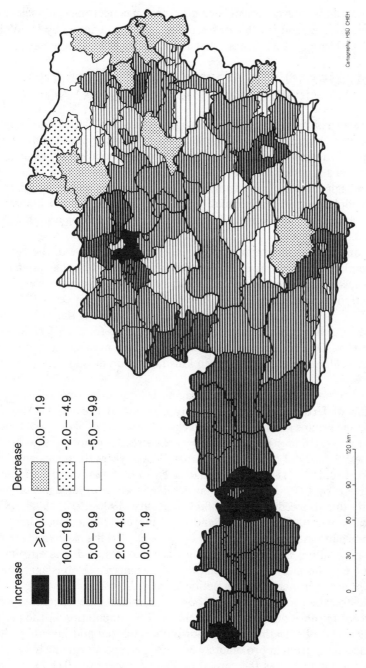

Figure 2   Rates of population growth, 1961–1971 (in percent).

tion in population development. For information concerning the social and economic background for this development, see the chapters by H. Wohlschlägl, E. März and M. Szecsi, and Felix Butschek in this book.

3 CHANGES IN THE POPULATION STRUCTURE AND THE PROBLEM OF DEMOGRAPHIC AGING

Since the turn of the century, Austria's age composition has changed gradually from the "pyramid shape" characteristic of growing populations to the "urn shape" indicative of a stationary or decreasing population (see *Fig. 3*). The age and sex composition of the Austrian population is now characterized by a high surplus of women in the older age groups and by a high ratio of old people in the total population; in fact, it is the second highest in Europe, with only the German Democratic Republic having a higher proportion of old people.

The long-term demographic process of aging, distinctive of the general demographic development in all Western industrialized nations, manifests itself in the age-sex composition of 1971, as do the incisive historical events discussed in section 2 (see Fig. 3). The birth deficits of the years 1945 and 1915–1919, as well as during the economic depression of the 1930s, have resulted in clearly visible indentations in the graph for the 1971 age-sex composition. One reason for the generally greater number of women 43 years and older is the loss of the men killed in action during the two world wars.

The phenomenon of demographic aging is primarily a consequence of reduction of fertility, which necessarily diminished the numbers in the younger age groups and increased the relative proportion of old people, and is only to a very minor degree caused by a decrease in mortality. Whereas the life expectancy of a newborn infant was 30.4 years for males and 33.1 years for females in 1865–1875, it had risen to 66.6 years and 73.7 years, respectively, by 1970–1972. The considerable increase in life expectancy is primarily due to a reduction in infant mortality (1906–1910, 197.4; 1978, 15.0 deaths per 1000 live births) and child mortality, and much less to a lower mortality rate among the other age groups. The life expectancy of the female population, higher in all age groups, has resulted in a surplus of women (sex ratio in 1971, 885 men per 1000 women), which is aggravated by the number of men killed in action during the wars.

In Austria the proportion of persons 60 years and older increased from 9.4 percent to more than one-fifth of the resident population in the period 1910–1971. Parallel to this, the proportion of children and juveniles (0-14 years) decreased from approximately 30 to 24 percent. Particularly affected by this development was the capital of Vienna, where in 1971 28 percent

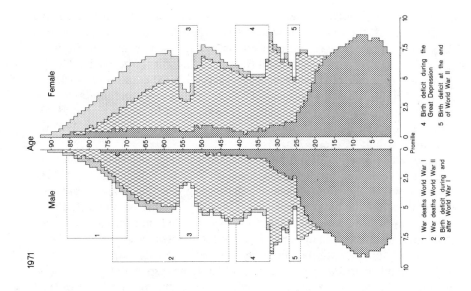

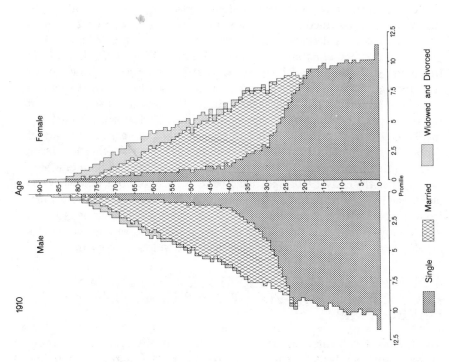

Figure 3 Age, sex, and family status composition, 1910–1971.

of the resident population were over 60 years, and only 16 percent under 15. In contrast, the western provinces have a much younger age structure. According to the most recent projections by the Österreichisches Statistisches Zentralamt (Austrian Central Bureau of Statistics), the aged-dependency ratio (number of persons 60 and older per 1000 persons of working age [15–60]) for the entire nation will not experience any more fundamental changes during the next two decades. It is expected to level off around 30 after having risen steadily from 15 to 37 between the end of World War iI and the first half of the 1970s.

The high proportion of old people in Austria gives rise to a number of social and economic problems, such as, for instance, the question of the extent to which the working-age population can bear the financial burden of providing for the older population. However, it must be noted that the problem of future provision for old age is dependent not only on the age structure but also on changes in the labor force participation rate[5] and on the capacity of the national economy.[6] At least equally important is the problem of adequate human care for the elderly, the responsibility for which has largely been left to the public, owing to the general separation of the generations, which is particularly prevalent in the large cities.

A brief survey yields the following changes of the marital-status composition of the Austrian population: a combination of an increased tendency to marry[7] and a lower median age at first marriage (1971: women 21.7, men 24.4) resulted in a decrease in the proportion of singles. Whereas 42.4 percent of the female population above the age of 15 were single in 1910, this figure had shrunk to 21.9 percent in 1971 (see Fig. 3). However, in recent years, the number of marriages has decreased to an extent that can no longer be interpreted as a cohort effect. The first-marriage rate (first marriages per 1000 singles) of women aged 16 to 39 decreased from 109.2 in 1971–1973 to 90.6 in 1975; that of men between the ages of 18 and 39 declined from 101.4 in 1961–1962 to 78.9 in 1975. On the other hand, the divorce rate (divorces per 1000 married persons), which had been climbing slowly since the early 1960s, reached a peak in 1975 for both women (11.9) and men (13.1).[8] Furthermore, the continuous increase of widowed women from approximately 8 percent in 1910 to about 15 percent in 1971 is noteworthy. Again, it is the capital of Vienna that is most affected by this development, having as its share 20 percent of widowed women.

4 THE PROBLEM OF FERTILITY DECLINE AND PROJECTIONS FOR FUTURE POPULATION DEVELOPMENT

The 135,000 live births recorded in 1963 represent the postwar maximum in the annual number of births in Austria. In spite of increased economic prospects, the number of births has been declining steadily since 1964, reaching a low point of 85,000 births in 1978. This development is caused by a genuine decline in the fertility rate (live births per 1000 women aged 15–45), not by a decrease in the birth rate as a consequence of changes in the demographic structure. The fertility rate decreased from 92 (1963) to 55 (1978). Interestingly, there is a leveling of the previously great differences in fertility between urban and rural areas in the course of this development. While in 1961 the general fertility rate of the communities with up to 5000 inhabitants was 105 percent higher than that of Vienna with its 1.6 million inhabitants, this difference had been reduced to 60 percent by 1971 (see Table 2).

There is still no definite answer to the conditions and causes of this recent decline in fertility, which also affects the neighboring Federal Republic of Germany and Switzerland, among others. The influencing factors are too complex to yield a simple answer. Recent studies on the problem show that a changed attitude on the optimal size of the family and the behavioral pattern of birth control play an important role. However, the approaches and hypotheses explaining the desire to limit family size are controversial in many ways. Often cited reasons for the decrease in births are the employment of women and a changed understanding of their role in society, as well as the "egotism" of the prevalent "ideology of privacy."[9] There was also a lengthy debate in Austria on whether the actual decline was caused by a high proportion of abortions, and if this was due to a liberalized abortion law. The debate was occasioned by the reform of the penal code regulations pertaining to the "termination of pregnancy."[10] However, clear, unambiguous arguments could not be found. The fact remains that it is not only in Austria that there is a certain perplexity with respect to the precise individual and societal conditions of pregnancy, birth, and abortion.

The drastic decline in fertility among the Austrian population and the high number of births among foreign workers brought dramatic questions in the mass media, such as "Are the Austrians dying out?" Apart from such

Table 2 Variations in the general fertility rate[a] by settlement size, 1951–1971

	1951	1961	1971
Communities up to 5,000 inhabitants (rural)	73.7	96.6	72.9
Communities with 5,001 to 250,000 inhabitants (urban)	48.6	65.7	55.3
Vienna (1.6 million inhabitants)	26.7	47.0	45.5
Austria	55.6	76.2	61.5

Source: P. Findl and H. Helczmanovszki, 1977, p. 48.
[a] General fertility rate is defined as live births per 1,000 women between the ages of 14 and 49.

superficial, pessimistic statements, what are the effects of the present fertility decline on the future population figure, population structure, and social reality? The projections on the development of the population figure and population structure until the year 2010, by the Austrian Central Bureau of Statistics, may serve as an indication. A total of three variants with different assumptions concerning the development of fertility were calculated, with the main variant representing the most plausible development.[11] According to its findings, the birth deficit that has been observed since 1975 will increase, especially after the year 2000, owing to the expected low numbers of births of the next five years. This will probably result in a decline in Austria's population figure by a quarter million, from 7,-508,000 in 1978 to 7,720,000 by 2010. Thus Austria would have the same population thirty years from now as it did in 1965.

The age structure will develop as follows: owing to the declining fertility, the number of children under 15 will decrease from 1,580,000 in 1979 to 1,320,000 by 1988. The subsequent increase is only temporary and would lead to a low of approximately 1,230,000 by 2010. For the near future we can expect a continued increase in the number of 15- to 60-year-olds, i.e. in the working-age population. The employment potential had already increased by approximately 350,000 persons between 1971 and 1979 and it will grow by another 147,000 by 1988. The subsequent decline will be slow initially and accelerate only shortly before the turn of the century. There will be no drastic changes in the proportion of old people in the Austrian population during the next two decades. The proportion of the elderly, measured as the number of persons 60 years and older, will remain relatively constant during this period and will increase to a figure of 22 percent by 2010 only after the turn of the millennium. Further, as the war generations with their great deficits of males are dying off, a normalization of the sex ratio of the population (by 2010, 940 men per 1,000 women) will occur during the period covered by this projection.

Projections of the future regional development of the population by the Österreichisches Institut für Raumplanung (Austrian Institute for Regional Planning) indicate that the decline in total population will primarily affect the rural areas unless there is a trend reversal in the migration movement (see Section 5).[12]

How are we to assess a zero population growth or a slight decline in the Austrian population, as well as the corresponding changes in the population structure?[13] There are, of course, the above-mentioned consequences of a declining population figure with regard to the financial burden of providing for the elderly. Further, there are significant effects on the educational system and on the labor market. Because the number of children is decreasing, the need for space in kindergartens and elementary and secondary schools will diminish, thus also lowering the demand for teachers. Yet, it should be noted that this consideration will be valid only if the quality of education is not increased by means of a more favorable student-teacher ratio. According to the projections of the Austrian Central Bureau of Statistics, the number of persons of working age in the total population will rise. As a result, there will be not only an increased demand for jobs but also a decreased chance for upward occupational mobility, because competition for the relatively fixed number of high-level positions will be greater in a stationary population with a higher proportion of 40- to 60-year-olds. Assuming that the decrease in total population will affect primarily the rural areas and economically weak regions, we can expect increased disparities between the growth regions and the disadvantaged areas and, as a result, a greater need for planning strategies that offer viable alternatives for further advancement in Austria's lagging regions.

5 INTERNATIONAL MIGRATION FLOWS AND THE PROCESS OF SPATIAL CONCENTRATION

In recent years, the regional distribution of the population in Austria has been considerably influenced by internal migration movements. The mobility of the Austrian population is low in comparison with other Western industrial countries. According to data provided by the Austrian Institute for Regional Planning (see Sauberer, 1976), only approximately 4.7 percent of the resident population changed their place of residence within the period of one year, whereas this figure amounted to 20.5 percent in the United States and 11.7 percent in England and Wales (1960). More than half of the interregional migrants moved less than 50 km, and less than 10 percent moved further than 200 km.

An analysis of the net migration rate of the period 1961–1971 and of the internal net migration rate between 1966 and 1971 in Austria's 98 political districts reveals the following trends:

1. As in all Western European countries, the economically attractive urban agglomerations generally registered migration gains. The highest relative gains were experienced by the agglomerations of the provincial capitals of Linz, Salzburg, Innsbruck, Graz, and Klagenfurt, followed by the metropolitan area of Vienna and the medium-sized cities and their surrounding communities (see Table 3).

2. Within the urban agglomerations, the suburban areas or surrounding communities registered the highest relative migration gains. These result from the interregional migration to the urban agglomerations, as well as the increased outmigration of the population from the inner cities to the suburban areas. The suburban areas offer not only better environmental condi-

tions but also a wide array of building sites, in particular for single-family houses and dwellings in apartment houses, often at better prices. However, this trend toward suburbanization in Austria has by no means reached an extent that would be comparable to that found in US cities. It is most pronounced in the region around Linz.[14]

3 The main outmigration areas (see Fig. 4) within Austria are, first, the peripheral areas in the north and east of the country, along the Czechoslovakian and Hungarian borders. These still predominantly agrarian border regions of Lower and Upper Austria and of central and southern Burgenland, whose residents have practically no additional source of income through tourism, experienced a migration deficit of 8 percent of the 1961 resident population. Equally serious was the exodus from the areas of the Low Tauern and the Gurktaler Alpen in the provinces of Carinthia, Styria, and parts of Salzburg. The outmigration trends in these alpine regions were enhanced by unfavorable agrarian incomes, relatively little tourism, and stagnation or decline in the typical industries, such as mining, lumber, and paper.

4. In contrast to the development in the alpine regions of southern and central Austria, the alpine areas of Western Austria recorded a more favorable, partially even positive net migration rate. It is especially the great expansion of tourism with its two seasons per year (winter and summer) that has provided new sources of income in these regions, thus halting outmigration.

Because of the selective effect of migrations—almost 60 percent of the internal migrants are between 15 and 35 years—the areas with continuous migration losses suffer a reduction in the economically active population and in the most fertile age groups. In contrast, this selective character of migration results in a more favorable population composition in areas with continuous migration gains. The inevitable consequence for the outmigration areas is an adverse effect on fertility rate, employment potential, and social life. This qualitative "demixing" in the regional population distribution is a serious and consequential process, and it is to be expected that it will even accelerate unless fundamentally new regional development strategies are implemented.

6 THE FOREIGN WORKER PROBLEM

Besides the internal migration movement, international migration, through the inmigration of foreign workers, is playing an increasingly significant role in Austria. Up until the early 1960s the growing Austrian economy could satisfy its demand for labor on the domestic market. However, beginning in the mid-1960s, a marked shortage of domestic labor, in particular in

Table 3 The Austrian population by urban and rural areas, 1961–1971

	Resident population, 1971		Average annual change 1961–1971 (per thousand)		
	Absolute (thousands)	Percent	Total change	Natural increase	Net migration
Agglomeration of Vienna	2024.5	27.2	0.8	−3.6	4.4
Central city	1614.8	21.7	−0.8	−4.6	3.9
Suburban communities	409.7	5.5	7.4	0.8	6.7
Other large urban agglomerations[a]	1247.2	16.7	11.5	5.7	5.9
Central cities	769.7	10.3	7.8	2.4	5.4
Suburban communities	477.4	6.4	17.9	11.1	6.7
Medium-sized urban agglomerations[b]	762.6	10.2	10.0	7.6	2.4
Central cities	377.6	5.1	7.1	4.9	2.2
Suburban communities	385.0	5.2	12.9	10.3	2.5
Rural areas outside the urban agglomerations	3422.1	45.9	4.5	8.6	−4.0
Communities with more than 5000 inhabitants	711.4	9.5	8.6	9.0	−0.4
Communities up to 5000 inhabitants, 1971	2710.7	36.4	3.5	8.4	−4.9
Rural areas in eastern Austria[c]	1081.2	14.5	0.2	4.7	−4.4
Rural areas in southern Austria[d]	1031.8	14.1	3.7	9.1	−5.4
Rural areas in western Austria[e]	1232.0	17.3	9.0	11.5	−2.5
Austria	7073.8	100.0	5.2	4.6	0.6

Source: *Regionalpolitik in Österreich*. Bericht des Bundeskanzleramtes (Büro für Raumplanung) an die OECD, Arbeitsgruppe No. 6. In *Österreichische Raumordnungskonferenz, Schriftenreihe*, No. 3 (Wien, 1973), p. 16.

Note: Delimitation of the urban agglomerations according to the concept of R. Gisser, 1971.

[a] Graz, Linz, Salzburg, Innsbruck, Klagenfurt.

[b] Wiener Neustadt, Sankt Pölten, Krems, Steyr, Wels, Bergenz, Dornbirn, Feldkirch, Villach, Leoben, Kapfenberg-Bruck an der Mur.

[c] Lower Austria and Burgenland.

[d] Styria and Carinthia.

[e] Upper Austria, Salzburg, Tyrol, and Vorarlberg.

unskilled and semiskilled jobs, became noticeable. This was compensated for by recruiting foreign labor from the economically less developed countries of Southeastern Europe.

The inmigration of the so-called *Gastarbeiter* (guest workers), mainly from Yugoslavia (approximately 90 percent) and Turkey (about 10 per-

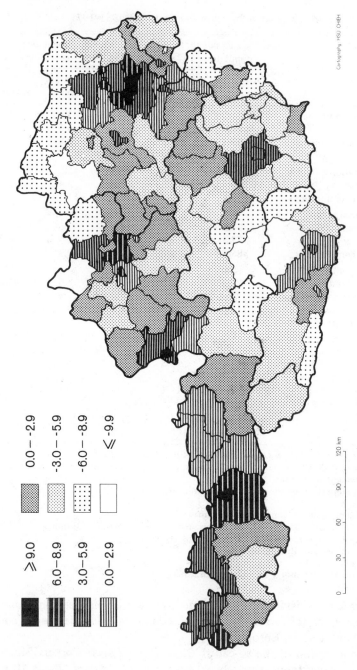

Figure 4   Net migration rates, 1961–1971 (in percent).

cent), reached a peak in 1973, when about 205,000 Yugoslavs and Turks were working in Austria, equaling 8.7 percent of the total number of employed persons. There are clear regional differences in their share of the domestic labor force. In 1973 the highest proportions were found in the industrial areas of Vorarlberg (23 percent of the total labor force), followed by Vienna (approximately 12 percent), Salzburg (12.2 percent), and Tyrol (9.1 percent). In the latter two provinces, a large percentage were employed as manual workers in the tourist industry. Vienna was the center of immigration of foreign workers, having about 40 percent of all guest workers employed in Austria in 1973. Since 1974, the number of foreign workers has decreased continuously, parallel to the development in other Western European countries and primarily owing to the economic crisis. As of 1978, the number of foreign workers employed in Austria was only 158,800.

An essential function of the employment of foreign workers is balancing the seasonally and economically fluctuating need for labor in the domestic market (see Fig. 5). The demand for less qualified labor mainly determines the structure of the foreign workers. For example, in 1972 the overwhelming majority of the guest workers in Vienna were unskilled or semiskilled manual workers (almost 90 percent); only about 9 percent were employed in skilled manual occupations and virtually none were either self-employed, office workers, or professionals.[15]

Until the late 1960s, inmigration of guest workers to Austria consisted of mostly married or single, predominantly male individuals. With a high rate of fluctuation, caused primarily by the so-called rotation policy, which aims at an administratively controlled limitation of the length of stay in the host country and which regards employment of *Gastarbeiter* as a temporary phenomenon, the foreign workers provided an elastic labor supply, which could be drawn on limitlessly as required but turned off when no longer needed in times of crisis. During the early 1970s, there was an increased incidence of families following the foreign workers to Austria, and of inmigration of married couples or of entire families, which resulted in a longer stay of the foreign workers. The opinion that the employment of foreign workers would be only a temporary phenomenon had to be revised.

These changes in the composition of inmigrants and in the length of stay brought about a number of problems, primarily in the large cities and in the industrial centers, their main destinations. Some of these problems will be outlined briefly here. One of the greatest problems for foreign workers, but also for the host country, is the problem of housing. Because of their low income and partly owing to their desire to save money, either to send to relatives or to invest at home, the guest workers, in general, have only limited economic resources to spend on housing. Therefore they look for cheap rentals when seeking accommodations, thus aggravating already ex-

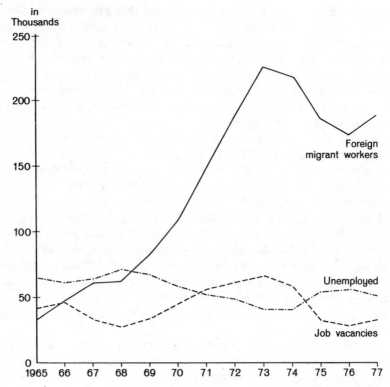

Figure 5 Numbers of foreign migrant workers, job vacancies, and unemployed persons, 1965–1977.

isting scarcities in the low-cost housing market. Besides, the housing market is one field where foreign workers are most likely to face formal and informal discrimination by the indigenous population. In the major towns, all this leads to a concentration of migrant workers in a) old and run-down housing within the densely built-up areas of the old city centers, which are badly in need of redevelopment, or b) in areas, mostly occupied by industrial and warehousing activities, that had not been zoned as residential by the city planners. It also happens frequently that owners of old run-down buildings, particularly in and around the central business district, take advantage of the guest workers' demands for low-rent housing. By overcrowding these buildings, they not only generate very high rents per square meter, but also speed the rate of physical deterioration. This practice increases short-run profits, and in the long run allows landlords a quicker replacement of these buildings by new office buildings and commercial developments. However, in general it must be said that the spatial segregation of foreign workers in Austrian cities does not reach dimensions comparable with those of ethnic minorities in American cities. There are positively no foreign workers' ghettos in Austrian cities.

The cultural differences and the language barrier between the indigenous population and the foreign workers, which make mutual adjustment difficult, have resulted in a number of social and human problems. In particular, the different culture of the *Gastarbeiter* from Southeastern Europe is often resented by the local population and is frequently the cause of discrimination. The low esteem in which the Austrian population holds the guest workers and the regulations of the Ausländerbeschäftigungsgesetz (Law Concerning the Employment of Foreign Workers) are two essential barriers to the integration and assimilation of foreign workers. But there have not been any massive actions against the employment and presence of foreign workers in Austria similar to those in Switzerland that culminated in a series of "Foreignization Initiatives." However, it must be said that the number of foreign workers employed in Switzerland is more than three times as high as in Austria.

Despite the problems outlined above, Austria did derive significant benefits from the employment of foreign workers. Space limitations permit only a somewhat sketchy discussion of these. From the demographic point of view there are advantages in the population development, especially in stagnating areas like Vienna. Because of their favorable age structure—about 97 percent were less than 50 years old in 1972—foreign workers play an important role in restoring the balance of the Austrian age composition, which is characterized by a high proportion of old, dependent people. Not only do they add to the population at work, helping to support the growing number of inactive persons, but with their high number of births[16] they also have a favorable influence on the birth rate in Austria.

Furthermore, it can be stated that social upward mobility for the local population was facilitated by the influx of foreign workers and by their acceptance of socially undesirable jobs. This also results in an increase in the average income of the local employees because they move up to higher and better-paid positions, leaving their former functions to the foreign workers. However, the influx of guest workers gains an interesting ambivalent significance in the context of this process. On the one hand, it promotes upward mobility of the indigenous lower classes; on the other hand, however, the immigration of foreign workers hampers the tendency toward equalization of the entire class structure by filling up the lower social classes.[17]

From the point of view of the national economy, the effects are similarly ambivalent. Without a doubt, the economy as a whole derives short- and medium-term benefits from the employment of foreign workers, as is shown by an economic cost-benefit analysis up to the year 1980, carried out by the Institut für Empirische Sozialforschung (Institute for Empirical Social Research).[18] On the other hand, there is, for example, the problem of old, relatively low-capacity enterprises remaining in business through the employment of foreign workers, thus lessening the pressure toward structural reforms and the introduction of modern technologies and economic techniques.

7 ETHNIC AND LINGUISTIC MINORITY GROUPS

Although present-day Austria is predominantly a German-speaking country (in 1971, 97.6 percent of the total population indicated that they use German as their primary language of communication), there are a number of ethnic and linguistic minorities. They live in the southern and eastern border regions of the country and amount to no more than 1.2 percent of the total population.

The numerically largest group are the Croats in Burgenland. By 400 years ago, they were settled here to offset the population losses during the Turkish wars, or they came as refugees. However, when the borders were redrawn after World War I, about one-third of the Croat minority remained in Hungary and Czechoslovakia. Today, the Croats in Burgenland and in the neighboring areas are an ethnic minority in linguistic enclaves, whose situation is further aggravated by being split up over three countries. The difficulties of the Burgenland Croats in maintaining their identity are also reflected in their declining numbers after World War II. While the Croats still represented about 12.5 percent of the total population of Burgenland in 1951, only 9 percent of the province's population (a total of 24,526 persons) indicated that Croatian was their language of communication during the most recent official census.[19] The causes of this decline which also affects the other minorities, will be discussed later.

The second largest native ethnic group are the Slovenes, living in the southern province of Carinthia. According to the 1971 census, in the mixed-language areas of southern Carinthia they amounted to 16,082 persons, or about 3.3 percent of Carinthia's population, with only about 3,930 persons indicating that they use Windisch as their language of communication.[20]

Like the Croats and Slovenes, the Hungarian-speaking minority in Burgenland has been characterized by a constant decline since the turn of the century. However, there was a slight increase of the Hungarian-speaking population living in Burgenland and in Vienna as a result of the Hungarian Crisis of 1956. Today, the larger part of this language group lives in Vienna (about 6,000 persons, presumably refugees from 1956–1957), and not in Burgenland, their traditional area of settlement (about 5,600 persons).

Finally, there is the Czech minority, especially in Vienna. Compared to the turn of the century, when Vienna was often called the "largest Czech city," but even in comparison to the time between the wars (1923, 81,353 Czechs and Slovaks), they are now a negligible minority of 8,110 (1971 census). This fact is explained by the repatriation of Czechs and Slovaks after World War I and during the 1930s and 1940s, but also by a gradual assimilation and integration into the German-speaking Viennese population in the course of the decades.

A series of internal and external economic changes as well as the development of the formal and informal relations between the minority and majority may be considered the causes of the decreasing number of the minority population in the southern and eastern border regions. For the Burgenland Croats and Hungarians and for the Carinthian Slovenes, maintaining their language had traditionally been closely linked to their occupation in agriculture.[21] Through the increasing automation of agriculture, many people lost their jobs and were forced to seek employment in other fields often outside their home community.[22] It was, further, the markedly lower income in agriculture that caused many to commute or to migrate to employment centers outside their linguistic area. In Carinthia, there is the additional influence of tourism, which requires the exclusive use of the German language.[23]

What does the Federal Government do to protect and maintain the ethnic minorities in Austria? From the standpoint of constitutional norms in particular, their legal situation is quite good, since the regulations of the 1976 Volksgruppengesetz (Law Concerning Ethnic Minorities) apply to them.[24] This law aims to safeguard the rights of all ethnic and linguistic minorities in Austria in order to assure their further existence. Among other things, the law requires bilingual topographic signs in mixed-language areas; and, through reform of the Official Languages Law, it provides for recognition of the ethnic minority's language as the official language in addition to and on an equal basis with German. Furthermore, through the institution of ethnic minority advisory boards, the minorities are legally authorized to participate in decisions about all cultural, social, and economic affairs that concern them, including measures of financial support.[25] In summary, it can be said that some of the provisions of the law concerning ethnic minorities have already been implemented, but, besides the support by the appropriate authorities at the federal and provincial level, it is especially an understanding on the part of the majority population, which is imperative for the continued existence of the ethnic and linguistic minorities in Austria.

8 SOME REMARKS ON POPULATION POLICY

In recent years, the fundamental significance of demographic development for all social and economic planning efforts, as well as for regional planning, has become increasingly apparent. This applies to the so-called natural demographic development, i.e. the development of births and deaths, as well as to internal and international migrations. The problems outlined in this article—the continually declining birth rate since the mid-1960s and the fact that fertility fell short of replacement levels, the process of aging in the Austrian population, the immigration of foreign workers from Mediterranean countries, and distinct regional disparities in population growth as well as their economic, social, and demographic consequences—all have played a major role in making demographic questions topical.

The close and complex interrelation between demographic processes, on the one hand, and economic and social developments, on the other, points to the necessity of coordinating population policy with other policies, as for instance social policy, in particular family policy and regional and economic policy. Population policy therefore does not serve to attain individual, isolated goals, but must essentially be an integrated part of any healthy, future-oriented governmental policy. For a long time, population policy in Austria was taboo, just as it was in Germany, a fact probably due to the onus attached to this political issue stemming from Nazi times. In many cases, the government followed and still follows a "strategy of adjustment" to the current demographic trends, which are, at any rate, not unaffected by the daily political decisions in the various spheres of social and economic life. This type of strategy seems to be problematic because of the long-term effects characteristic of demographic processes. Thus, for example, the consequence of the currently low fertility level will appear only much later, and cannot be reversed by short-term corrective measures. The necessity of a foresighted government policy that reacts at a sufficiently early stage to foreseeable changes in the number, structure, and spatial distribution of the Austrian population becomes obvious (at the present time, for instance, by making provisions for an adequate number of jobs and by pursuing a regional and structural policy to lessen regional disparities).

In conclusion, an overview of legal measures directed at influencing the above-mentioned demographic trends and diminishing the existing imbalances will be given. However, it is difficult to determine to what extent legal instruments can influence demographic processes, and the effectiveness of the various measures is quite frequently controversial. In general, it is impossible to say to what extent changes in behavior are due to a law or to the economic and social pressures that occasioned the law.

As for fertility, efforts are being made in Austria to assist parents in realizing their wishes with regard to the number and timing of birth of their children. This assistence consists of counseling (Familienberatungsförderungsgesetz [Law to Promote Family Counseling]) and financial support. For instance, the Familienlastenausgleichsgesetz of 1967 (Law Providing for Equalization of Family Burdens), aimed at easing the financial burdens associated with marriage and child rearing, provides, among others birth and family allowances, subsidies for travel costs or free trips to and from school for children, and free textbooks. Furthermore, the legislation provides tax benefits for the family, i.e. indirect tax cuts for sole providers, as well as deductions for children, and since 1972, a one-time marriage allowance. In addition to these, a series of protective and assistance measures[26] in connection with pregnancy and birth, school and occupational training, are worth mentioning; for instance, maternity insurance, the possibility of a one-year paid maternity leave, emergency relief for single mothers, subsidies for school and university education, and apprenticeships.

With respect to the variable "housing," important when starting a family and when determining its size, significant measures have been taken through the construction of publicly subsidized housing as well as through the introduction of rent subsidies.

Owing to the increased immigration of foreign workers from Yugoslavia and Turkey and its associated problems, the law Concerning the Employment of Foreign Workers was passed in 1975.[27] The regulations of this law assign the foreign workers more or less a buffer function for balancing economic and seasonal fluctuations on the domestic labor market. Foreigners who have lived at least ten years in Austria can, under certain circumstances, acquire Austrian citizenship.

In order to prevent further draining of peripheral and economically less developed regions and of ecologically unfavorable areas, the Federal Government, the provinces, local authorities, and various associations—such as employers' and employees' associations, chambers of agriculture, commerce, trade, and labor—have, for some time, taken a series of measures in regional economic policy, employment policy, and infrastructure policy. These measures are directed at decreasing the existing regional differences in performance and prosperity levels and at reducing the regional disparities in population development.[28]

Notes

1. Birth rate equals live births per year per 1000 inhabitants. Death rate equals deaths per year per 1000 inhabitants.
2. For details, see P. Findl and H. Helczmanovszki, 1977, pp. 26ff. (See the Selected Bibliography for complete publishing information.)
3. For details, see H. Helczmanovszki, 1973, pp. 140ff.

4. On the economic and political causes of the east-west difference in Austria's population dynamics, see the chapter by H. Wohlschlägl in this volume.

5. Changes in the labor force participation rate during recent years were primarily caused by lowering of the retirement age, lengthening of full-time education, and increase in the employment of women.

6. For details, see G. Feichtinger, 1977.

7. See P. Findl and H. Helczmanovszki, 1977, pp. 100ff.

8. For details, see H. Hausa, "Familie," in M. Fischer-Kowalski and J. Bucek, 1979, p. 87.

9. For details, see R. Münz, 1977, pp. 30–34.

10. Penal Code, Articles 96–98, in the version published in the *Federal Law Gazette* No. 60/1974. On this reform, see also the chapters by E. Weinzierl, and by F. Pallin and H. Ent in this volume.

11. For the main variant it was assumed that the decline in fertility will, to a lesser extent, continue for several years (1982, net reproduction rate of 0.73, i.e. 5 percent lower than in 1978). For the period 1983–1991, an increase in the net reproduction rate to 0.85 was assumed, to be constant until the year 2000. The projections of the mortality rate were based on an extrapolation of trends observed during recent decades. For the years 1978–80 a slight net migration loss was assumed (minus 2000 persons each year), and a balanced net migration for the following years. For a more detailed explanation of the assumptions on which the prognosis is based, see P. Findl, 1979, pp. 273–85.

12. See. M. Sauberer, "Raumordnung und zukünftige Tendenzen der regionalen Bevölkerungsentwicklung in Österreich," *Mitteilungen und Berichte des Salzburger Instituts für Raumforschung,* vol. 4 (Salzburg, 1978), pp. 30ff.

13. For details, see G. Feichtinger, 1977.

14. See H. Wohlschlägl, 1977, pp. 321–43.

15. Further details on the structure of the foreign workers and on questions of their segregation and integration are in H. Leitner, 1978.

16. Although the total foreign worker population in Vienna amounts to only a little more than 5 percent of the resident population, it accounts for more than 15 percent of all live births (1978).

17. See "Grenzen und Probleme der Beschäftigung von Gastarbeitern im Land Salzburg," *Schriftenreihe des Salzburger Instituts für Raumforschung,* vol. 2 (Salzburg 1974), pp. 60ff.

18. See E. Gehmacher, "Economic and Social Cost-Benefit Analysis of Foreign Workers' Occupations" (unpublished paper, Institut für Empirische Sozialforschung; Wien, 1973).

19. Persons who declared their own language in combination with German are included in the lingual minority.

20. Windisch is a Slovenian dialect.

21. See F. Pacher, 1977, pp. 36–56.

22. Development, especially of the secondary sector, in the mixed-language areas of southern Carinthia and in the settlement areas of the Croats in Burgenland, is greatly hampered by their location on Austria's borders.

23. See F. Pacher, *ibid.*

24. *Federal Law Gazette,* No. 396/1976.

25. However, there was no uniform regulation with regard to the languages to be used in school. According to the 1955 State Treaty, the Slovenian and Croat minorities in Austria are entitled to elementary schooling in Slovenian and in Croatian and to a proportional number of their own high schools.

26. On these measures and their significance, see also the chapter by R. Strasser in this volume.

27. *Federal Law Gazette,* No. 218/1975.

28. For details on these measures, see *"Regional Development Policy in Austria"* (report by the Federal Chancellor's Office to OECD, Working Group No. 6; Wien 1973).

Selected Bibliography

Bodzenta, E., ed. *Die österreichische Gesellschaft. Entwicklung-Struktur-Probleme.* Wien, 1972.

Feichtinger, G., ed. Stationäre und schrumpfende Bevölkerungen. Demographisches Null- und Negativwachstum in Österreich. *Lecture Notes in Economics and Mathematical Systems,* vol. 149. Wien, 1977.

Feichtinger, G., and H. Hansluwka. The Impact of Mortality on the Life Cycle of the Family in Austria. In *Zeitschrift für Bevölkerungswissenschaft,* vol. 3, pp. 51–79. Boppard, 1977.

Findl, P. Bevölkerungsprognose für Österreich, 1978–2010. In *Statistische Nachrichten,* vol. 34, pp. 273–85. Wien, 1979.

Findl, P., and H. Helczmanovszki. The Population of Austria. *Schriftenreihe des Instituts für Demographie der Österreichischen Akademie der Wissenschaften,* vol. 1. Wien, 1977. Also published in *CICRED Series. World Population Year 1974* by the Committee for International Coordination of National Research in Demography (CICRED), United Nations, Population Division. Paris, 1974.

Fischer-Kowalski, M., and J. Bucek, eds. *Ungleichheit in Österreich.* Wien, 1979.

Gaspari, Ch., and H. Millendorfer. *Prognosen für Österreich. Fakten und Formeln der Entwicklung.* Wien, 1973.

Gastarbeiter-Wirtschaftsfaktor und soziale Herausforderung. Ed. by Arbeitskreis für ökonomische und soziologische Studien. Wien, 1973.

Gisser, R. Bevölkerungsentwicklung 1951–1961–1971 der städtischen Agglomerationen Österreichs. In *Institut für Stadtforschung Information,* No. 10, pp. 70–78. Wien, 1971.

Hansluwka, H., K. Schubert, and K. Stiglbauer. Grundzüge der Veränderungen in der Verteilung der österreichischen Bevölkerung seit dem Jahre 1869. In *Internationaler Bevölkerungskongress Wien 1959,* ed. by the International Union for the Scientific Study of Population, pp. 586–97. Wien 1959.

Helczmanovszki, H. Die Entwicklung der Bevölkerung Österreichs in den letzten 100 Jahren nach den wichtigsten demographischen Komponenten. In H. Helczmanovszki, ed., *Beiträge zur Bevölkerungs- und Sozialgeschichte Österreichs,* pp. 113–65. Wien, 1973.

Kuhn, D. *Der Geburtenrückgang in Österreich.* Wien, 1975.

Leitner, H. Migrant Workers in Austria: Social, Demographic and Economic Impacts. In *Austrian History Yearbook,* forthcoming, 1980.

———. *Segregation, Integration und Assimilation jugoslawischer Gastarbeiter in Wien—eine empirische Analyse.* Ph.D. thesis, University of Vienna. Wien, 1978.

Münz, R. Die Erforschung des generativen Verhaltens in Österreich. In *Österreichische Zeitschrift für Soziologie,* vol. 5, pp. 30–34. Wien, 1977.

Pacher, F. Bemerkungen zur Situation der Kärntner Slovenen aus sozialwissenschaftlicher Sicht. In *Österreichische Zeitschrift für Soziologie,* vol. 5, pp. 36–56. Wien, 1977.

Rosenmayr, L. Selected Problems of the Family in Urban and Rural Austria. In *International Journal of Comparative Sociology,* vol. 1, pp. 89–102. Dharwar, India, 1960.

Sauberer, M. Migration Patterns in Austria—Conclusions from Recent Studies of the Austrian Institute for Regional Planning. *Österreichisches Institut für Raumplanung—Materialien,* No. 7. Wien, 1976.

———. Regional Demographic Analysis and Projections—Experiences of the Austrian Institute for Regional Planning. *Österreichisches Institut für Raumplanung—Materialien,* No. 5. Wien, 1975.

Schlag, W. A. Survey of Austrian Emigration to the United States. In O. Hietsch, ed., *Österreich und die angelsächsische Welt. Kulturbegegnungen und Vergleiche,* pp. 139–96. Wien, 1961.

Volksgruppen in Österreich. Jahrbuch "Integratio," No. 11, ed. by Europa-Club. Wien, 1979.

Volksgruppen. Die rechtliche Stellung der Volksgruppen in Österreich. Eine Dokumentation, ed. by the Federal Chancellor's Office (Bundeskanzleramt). Wien, 1977.

Wohlschlägl, H. Bevölkerungswachstum und Wanderungsvorgänge im Raum Linz. In *Österreich in Geschichte und Literatur,* vol. 21, pp. 321–43. Wien, 1977.

Unless a different source is stated, all data for graphs and figures were taken from the following publications of the Austrian Central Bureau of Statistics (Österreichisches Statistisches Zentralamt): *Statistisches Handbuch der Republik Österreich,* annually. *Demographisches Jahrbuch Österreichs,* annually. *Ergebnisse der Volkszählungen* (Population Census Data) for the years 1910, 1923, 1934, 1951, 1961, 1971

Modern Austria, pp. 99–120
Copyright © 1981 by SPOSS Inc. All rights reserved

3. RELIGIONS AND THEIR RELATIONS TO STATE AND PARTIES

Erika Weinzierl

Professor of Modern History, University of Vienna, and Director of the Institute for Contemporary History

1

According to the 1971 census, 6,540,294 Austrians were Roman Catholic, 444,307 Protestant [both Augsburger Bekenntnis (Augsburg Confession) and Helvetisches Bekenntnis (Reformed Confession)], 320,031 did not belong to any denomination, and 149,771 were members of other religious groups, which were not enumerated in detail.[1] A brief description of these latter religions will be found in the last part of this essay. However, the essay will focus on the relations of the Christian churches, and of the Catholic Church in particular, to the State, to the parties, and to politics. This focus may require a word of explanation.

In countries in which there is a historical tradition of a strict separation of Church and State, the relationship of these two institutions to each other is undoubtedly of much less relevance than is the case in Austria. In such countries, the regulation of the relationship between Church and State by concordats—treaties with the Holy See on ecclesiastical matters—and the question of the position of the churches vis-à-vis the parties have relatively little political significance. Historically, the situation has always been different in Austria and, as will be shown, it is different today. Second, there has been a fundamental change in policies relating to the Catholic Church, between the First Republic and the Second Republic. This fundamental change has contributed essentially to the pacification and stabilization of Austrian domestic politics. For these reasons it seemed appropriate to concentrate on these problems. Given the limitation of space, this meant

Translated by Ulrike E. Lieder, Stanford University

99

9306-6403/81/0415-0099$01.50

also that the relations of the churches to each other and the internal activities of the religions or churches and of church-related organizations could not be dealt with in any depth.

2

The statistics, mentioned above, indicate that almost 87 percent of the population are nominally members of the Catholic Church, which has thus maintained a strong position in social policy. Until 1938, this position was characterized by strong ties to political power, a consequence of a specifically Austrian development since the Counter Reformation.

Up until the fall of the Habsburg empire, the Habsburg rulers were the patrons of the Church, in spite of the *Kulturkampf* [struggle between Church and State] during the 1860s and 1870s. Afterward, the Christian Socialist party took over this function. That party's most important politician of the time between the wars, Ignaz Seipel, who held the office of Chancellor several times, was a priest himself. Between 1934 and 1938, the ties with the authoritarian Christian Socialist corporative state were, at least officially, especially close, a fact that further increased the long-existing tensions between the church and the Social Democratic party, which had been prohibited since the civil war of February 1934.[2]

During the National Socialist time, the Church, which had even been courted by the new regime before the so-called plebiscite, did not succeed in establishing a situation resembling a concordat, in spite of a declaration by the Austrian bishops in favor of the *Anschluss.* Realizing that they had been put off and deceived for months, the bishops took the initiative in September 1938 and broke off the negotiations over a *modus vivendi.* One of the resultant punitive actions was the Hitler Youth attack on the *archiepiscopal palais* in Vienna on 8 October 1938. From that point on, the Church —legally just as unprotected as in the so-called Warthegau, a part of the former Poland, since 1939—found itself in a situation of "persecution and resistance" for which numerous priests and laymen gave their lives. In fact, the clergy had one of the highest percentages of victims of the Austrian resistance.[3]

However, the prosecuted Church gained authority far beyond the circles of the so-called practicing Catholics, a fact from which the bishops drew clear-cut consequences by the fall of 1945. They decided to maintain the withdrawal of the clergy from active politics, which had taken place in December 1933 for totally different reasons, to avoid one-sided political ties in the future and announced this in a joint pastoral letter.[4] Although all Austrian bishops basically adhered to this policy, it did not gain its full effectiveness in cultural policy until 1956. This is due to several reasons.

Franz König became Archbishop of Vienna in 1956, and since he had always especially advocated this policy,[5] he is considered by many to be its initiator, a fact that has not always won him friends among the Catholics who have political ties to the Austrian People's Party (Österreichische Volkspartei, ÖVP). In any case, the present relationship between the Church and the large political parties of the Second Republic is the result of the painful process of reorientation to which all Austrians were subject between 1933 and 1945. It is also the result of manifold efforts that have not been free of setbacks, and it is not totally immune to partial relapses into the past, as is demonstrated by events of the 1970s, which will be discussed later, and by the present discussion on schools.

3

To be sure, the new, 1978 party program of the Socialist Party of Austria (Sozialistische Partei Österreichs, SPÖ) goes beyond the old one of 1958, which had also been very positive on the question of "Socialism and religion,"[6] when, after recognizing the freedom of religion, it states expressly:

> The Socialists are deeply sympathetic to the Christian message that prescribes charity as well as support for the weak and underprivileged. Today, millions of Christians are members of the Socialist movement because they are convinced that they can advocate their basic moral values in this movement. They are Socialists not in spite of their being Christians but because of it.[7]

By comparison, the statements of principle in the ÖVP's 1972 "Salzburg Program" on the ÖVP and Christianity generally do not appear to have a more decisively Christian orientation:

> The ÖVP regards Christianity as the constant challenge to shape our world according to the principles of justice, charity, brotherhood, and peace. It is open to Christians and to all who, for different motives, profess to a humanist philosophy. The ÖVP recognizes the independence of the churches and of the religions and supports their unhindered activities in the public domain. It does not commit itself to any denomination or ecclesiastical institution.

The actual differences are found in the individual subject matters of the programs and in political practice, such as, for instance, the economy and the schools, where the SPÖ, in contrast to the ÖVP, which merely demands a differentiated educational program, demands the "realization of a joint school for all 10- to 14-year-olds," thus the "comprehensive school." Different views also prevail with regard to the family, whose basic value to society is not contested by the Socialists. However, the ÖVP, while approving of family planning in the sense of responsible parenthood, declares further: "Our respect for life also includes the unborn life. Therefore, abortion as a means of birth control is to be rejected. Criminal prosecution of abortion must take into consideration situations of conflict.[8]

The present state of the discussion is outlined by the comparison of the statements on this issue in the two party programs. In this context, the programs of the Liberal Party of Austria (Freiheitliche Partei Österreichs, FPÖ) and of the Communist Party of Austria (Kommunistische Partei Österreichs, KPÖ) may safely be disregarded, although the FPÖ's 1968 Bad Ischl Program states that information at an early age on methods of contraception was not least necessary in order to "help to avoid the often chosen solution of termination of pregnancy."[9]

However, going back to the year of the founding of the Second Republic, we find the following picture, not insignificant for the 35 years that have passed since then: the first declaration similar to a program is the ÖVP's Programmatic Guidelines of June 1945. Their Item 7 contains the following declaration of intent with regard to cultural policy:

> Freedom of conscience, of religion, and free practice of the religions recognized by the State. Freedom and independence of the Church and of the religions in the State, conclusion of a state treaty, which takes into account the prevailing circumstances, with the Catholic Church, to which the majority of the citizens belong. Protection of the rest from work on Sundays and holidays, safeguarding of religious welfare (chaplaincy) in public institutions, e.g. hospitals, orphanages, asylums; also in the army. Autonomy and material independence of the Church and of the religions, and the right to levy dues on their members. A marriage law that provides for the option of civil marriage, but in such a way that Church weddings, which are to be reported immediately to the registry, will also enjoy civil validity.

The 1947 SPÖ Program for Action, based on the more or less explicit continued validity of the 1926 Austro-Marxist Linz Program, was that party's first programmatic declaration. It advocated religious freedom and spoke against moral constraint: "Religion is a person's private affair: rejection of any type of moral constraint, safeguarding of religious freedom and of the free practice of one's religion. No preferences to be given to one denomination, no support from public funds to be granted to any denomination or religious institution." With regard to schools, the program demanded that the upper division of elementary schools and the four grades of the lower division of intermediate schools be joined in a general intermediate school. The "unrestrained termination of pregnancy" was regarded as "the primary danger to a woman's health"; however, criminal prosecution of cases of termination of pregnancy was rejected.[10]

On the part of the so-called official Church there was, at that time, only the declaration of the fall of 1945, mentioned above. Priests and lay persons joined in clarifying the declaration's statements. In preparation for the first

Austrian Katholikentag* after the war, in 1952, the so-called Mariazell Manifesto evolved from a study conference: "Let us not return to the union of Throne and Altar . . . , Let us not return to having one party patronize the Church . . . !" However, the Church was all the more ready to "[cooperate] with the State on all matters of common interest, i.e. marriage, family, and education."[11]

4

Owing to the difficult situation of the Republic, which was occupied by the four Allied powers, the Church did not press for a "state treaty," a concordat, directly after 1945. This concordat had already been demanded in the first ÖVP program and was later included only once more, in the 1958 program.[12]

After 1945, the Church also won a considerable victory in court with the abrogation of Article 67 of the Personenstandsgesetz [Law Concerning a Person's Civil Status], which the Constitutional Court had declared unconstitutional. This article had provided for the criminal prosecution of those clergymen who performed a Church wedding without prior civil marriage. On 20 December 1955, one day after the Constitutional Court had handed down its verdict, the National Council passed a law to implement the stipulations of Article 26 of the State Treaty (obligating Austria to make reparations for the loss of properties or assets suffered by individuals or groups because of their race or religion after 13 March 1938), also with respect to the property of the Church.

Since 1956, a new attitude of the SPÖ toward the Church has begun to emerge as well. Several reasons were decisive for this new attitude: the take-over of a new leadership generation within the party, where cultural policy was now no longer solely determined by anticlerical Austro-Marxists; the efforts of a small but active committee on Church and Socialism (from 1959 to 1977 "Committee of Socialist Catholics"; since 1977 "Committee on Christianity and Socialism"); and not least the realization of the party leaders of that time that, with a population of almost 90% at least nominal Catholics, the party could only become a party with broad popular appeal if its relations to the Church were improved. From the side of the Church, it was above all the pastoral letter of the Austrian bishops of October 1956, drafted by the Bishop of Innsbruck, Paulus Rusch, that contributed to the improvement of relations. This pastoral letter unambiguously rejected only Manchester capitalism and communism as well as the

*Translator's Note: The Katholikentag is a decennial general assembly of the Catholics of a country.

Socialist-Marxist philosophy, but it explicitly recognized the efforts by the moderate Socialists to create a socially more just society. During the 1956 SPÖ party convention, the then Vice Chancellor of the ÖVP/SPÖ coalition government, Adolf Schärf, therefore expressed his "great satisfaction that, for the first time in Austria, a serious attempt is being made in a pastoral letter to do justice to democratic socialism."[13]

The improved relations between the Church and the SPÖ are also due to contacts between Church organs and individual Socialist party and union officials who had an open ear for the concerns of the Church. These officials were Franz Olah; Minister of Justice Otto Tschadek, a practicing Catholic himself; and the president of the Vienna municipal school board, Max Neugebauer. The subject of better relations between the Church and the SPÖ were also suggested in the speech that new Federal President Adolf Schärf gave at his inauguration in May 1957. Schärf declared his happiness about the fact that there was a new, different atmosphere in the country's cultural policy: "I will do everything possible to see to it that the relations between the State and the Catholic Church are regulated in this atmosphere, without reawakening past sentiments."[14] Six days later, the Council of Ministers, chaired by Chancellor Raab, decided to tackle the question of a concordat. In his governmental declaration of July 4, 1956, Chancellor Raab had already expressed his hope for an amicable regulation of the relation between Church and State. A committee of ministers was appointed to work on the concordat. On December 19, 1957, this committee approved the draft of a note to the Holy See, informing the addressee that the Austrian government had unanimously resolved to recognize the principal significance of the 1933 concordat. However, events that occurred since the signing of the concordat had created a situation where, in a number of points, the stipulations of the concordat were in contradiction to the Austrian legal system. In making this statement, the Austrian government assumed that the Holy See, too, considered it necessary to start as soon as possible "negotiations on a new concordat that should regulate all relevant questions, such as, in particular, questions of marriage and of schools."[15]

A detailed and reserved response to the Austrian note came on 30 January 1958. The communication from Rome first describes the repeated efforts by the Holy See to gain recognition of the concordat. The unanimous decision by the government to recognize the 1933 concordat was noted "with pleasure." However, immediately following, the Holy See expressed its regret that the government had not only avoided any binding declaration on the validity of the concordat, but also neglected the application of important stipulations as, e.g. in the question of schools, in the question of payments by the State to the Church, and, above all, in the question of marriage. Concluding, the Holy See declared that it could not be satisfied with the mere recognition of the validity of the concordat, but that it had to demand the recognition and exercise of the obligations entered into. However, it was willing to negotiate "those touch-ups, i.e. small changes that might be deemed necessary."

Although such a reaction by Pope Pius XII, who, in 1933, in his function as the secretary of state to Pope Pius XI, had signed the concordat, could almost have been expected, it so surprised and disappointed even the leading politicians of the People's party that the negotiations reached a deadlock. Negotiations were not taken up again until after the death of Pius XII in October 1958, under Pius's successor John XXIII. The Vienna nuncio, Dellepiane, and his then assistant at the Vienna nunciature, Bruno Heim (who is now an archbishop, working in London as a representative of the Vatican), informed John XXIII of the specifically Austrian problems.

Since the hope seemed to be justified that the goal could be attained by way of partial solutions, the Austrian government decided on March 17, 1959, quoting the pertinent stipulations of the 1933 concordat, to request that the Holy See elevate the Apostolic Administration of Burgenland to a diocese. The reaction of the Vatican was swift and friendly and contained the suggestion to regulate at the same time the relations between the Church and the State with respect to property. On April 21, 1959, the government decided to enter into such negotiations. Because of the Austrian elections of May 1959 and the subsequent negotiations for the formation of a coalition government, the negotiations between the Foreign Ministry and the Vienna nunciature did not progress expeditiously until November 1959.

By the turn of the year 1959–1960, the preliminary discussions were already concluded, and, following approval by the Holy See, the wording of the treaties was made final by the spring of 1960. On 23 June 1960, Nuncio Dellepiane, Foreign Minister Kreisky, and Minister of Education Drimmel signed the treaties between the Holy See and the Republic of Austria on the proprietary relations and on the elevation of the Apostolic Administration of Burgenland to the rank of diocese. On 12 July 1960, these treaties were submitted to the National Council for discussion. Only the liberal representative, Gredler, spoke against ratification, since his party considered them to be the explicit recognition of the "Dollfuss concordat." The speaker for the SPÖ, Neugebauer, discussed the relations between Church and State in Austria in detail and stated that the United States had separated Church and State, but "our tradition is different; we have the principle of cooperation." The ÖVP representative, Weiss, stressed especially the historical significance of this day, when two concordats—which, however, covered only partial areas—were, for the first time in Austria, given constitutional consent by a freely elected parliament. "It is therefore to be hoped there will be no doubts in the future as to the legality of the two treaties that are to be ratified today."[16] During the following vote, both treaties passed with the votes of the government parties.

As far as the contents of the two treaties are concerned,[17] the first one establishes the Eisenstadt Diocese. The proprietary relations were regulated as follows: in reparation for properties and rights expropriated during the Nazi era, the Church receives an annual 100 million schillings from the State. All but 10 percent of the religious funds, established by Emperor Joseph II from expropriated Church properties for the purpose of stipends for the clergy, and which the State had administered on behalf of the Church until 1938, is turned over to the State.

This solved all open questions of property—some of which had been open for more than 150 years—between the Church and the Catholic Church in Austria. The amicable settlement of these questions with the Catholic Church resulted in the legal regulation of the payments by the State to the other religions in the course of the same year. In October 1960, the Catholic Church was guaranteed an annual amount of 300,000 schillings, the Israelite religion was granted a one-time sum of 30 million schillings, payable in five installments and, beginning retroactively with the year 1958, an annual subsidy of 1.8 million schillings. On 13 December 1960, the question of compensating the Protestant Church of the Augsburg Confession and of the Reformed Confession for the requisition of Church-owned real estate and objects in Burgenland for educational purposes was settled. It received a one-time sum of 2.1 million schillings.[18]

Owing to the efforts of Minister of Education Heinrich Drimmel, the new Protestantengesetz [Law Concerning the Protestant Church], which had been demanded in the ÖVP's basic program of 1958, was already realized on 6 July 1961 in the Bundesgesetz über äussere Rechsverhältniss der evangelischen Kirche [Federal Law Concerning the External Legal Situation of the Protestant Church]. This law provides for the explicit and separate recognition of the Protestant Church of the Augsburg Confession, of the Protestant Church of the Reformed Confession, and of the Church of the Augsburg and Reformed Confessions, with the latter being recognized as an association of churches. The churches have full organizational autonomy and are entitled to levy church dues. The parishes at all levels are corporations under public law and are, as such, entitled to legal assistance by the authorities. The continued existence of the Department of Protestant Theology with at least six full professorships at the University of Vienna is guaranteed. Moreover, the Protestant Churches receive an annual subsidy of 3,250,000 schillings in four equal installments from the State as well as a sum equivalent to the salaries of 81 employees in a given salary classification (A IV/4).

The law of 6 July 1961 revoked the Protestant Patent of 8 April 1861 and the 1939 law on the legal position of the supreme consistory in Vienna.

After the law was passed, Bishop Gerhard May stated expressly that the equal rights of the Churches now had a basis in the law.[19]. The most pressing problems of the other major religions had thus been settled relatively quickly, which was undoubtedly also due to the impression left by the successful negotiations between the Second Republic and the Catholic Church. After the treaty regulating the property rights had been signed, negotiations on the clarification of school problems in conjunction with the concordat were begun with the Catholic Church.

5

By 9 July 1962, the treaty on the regulation of questions concerning the educational system between the Holy See and the Republic of Austria was signed.[20] In essence, this treaty took note of the situation created by the 1949 law on religious instruction in schools, without invalidating Article VI of the 1933 concordat. This article stated that Catholic schools might be given State subsidies, pending the improvement of the economic situation. Since there were no essential changes in Austria's unfavorable economic situation until 1938, these provisions were never implemented. According to the treaty of 9 July 1962, Article VI is fully valid, with the exception of a few explicitly stated changes concerning the recognition of the possibility of withdrawal from religious instruction. Schools will continue to offer religious instruction to the same extent as before.

An innovation is the guarantee of State subsidies of up to 60 percent of the personnel costs (100 percent since 1971) for Catholic schools. This disposed of the last obstacle for the long-planned educational reform for which Minister of Education Heinrich Drimmel had worked hard and with great willingness to negotiate with the coalition partner. On August 18, 1962, the amended constitutional law[21] on the educational system was passed by the National Council with the votes of the coalition parties. This closed a gap in the Austrian constitution that had been open since 1920. Pursuant to the eight Educational Acts, which were passed by the National Council, together with the treaty of 9 July 1962 on the basis of the amended constitutional law of 25 July 1962, denominational schools were, for the first time in Austrian History, given a legal guarantee of State subsidies. These Educational Acts must therefore be seen as a significant result of a new democratic cultural policy in Austria, even though they did not totally fulfill the expectations of some of the Catholic teachers, and although, compared to the time before 1938, they restricted the monopoly of denominational schools in Burgenland.

Pursuant to the treaties with the Holy See of 7 July 1964 and 7 October 1968,[22] the dioceses of Innsbruck and Feldkirch were established. During the tenure in office of the SPÖ minority government of Kreisky, the Catholic schools were granted subsidies of 100 percent of their personnel expenses in 1971. The valorization agreement of 1976 (an additional 29 million schillings annually) contains the dissolution of the religious funds which had already been agreed on in 1960. Of all the questions of the concordat that were open after 1945, the only one to remain open is the issue of marriage. Since the German marriage law, introduced in 1938, was not repealed, civil marriage is still obligatory. In the long run, there should be no serious obstacle to the solution sought by the Catholics, namely to make civil marriage an option. In general, it can be said that the stipulations of the concordat, which were relatively explosive politically, were implemented quite satisfactorily for the Church. This, however, would not have been possible without the Grand Coalition between the ÖVP and SPÖ, which spanned two decades.

6

Far less satisfactory, from the point of view of the Church, were the reforms of the criminal law and of parts of the marriage law. During the time of the ÖVP government of Klaus, Hermann Withalm, then secretary general of the ÖVP, had given political Catholicism an unmistakable rebuff.[23] Yet the ties of the Chancellor and of leading cabinet members of the Church were strong enough, following the wishes of the bishops, to modify the 1966 ministerial draft of the criminal law reform.[24] This draft had been essentially worked out by the Commission on the Reform of the Criminal Law, which had been laboring on this task since 1954, and it included freedom from criminal prosecution for abortion, homosexual relations between consenting adults, and adultery. According to reports by the daily press of that time, the 1968 government bill differed from the drafts only in two points, which were described as "hot problems," i.e. legal sanctions against abortion and against homosexual relations between consenting adults. It also contained some other changes, as, for instance, "a significant extension of the definitions of felonies as opposed to misdemeanors, and an extension and tightening of various provisions with regard to religious and sexual offenses." Public reaction to this development was not very positive, and the opposition (SPÖ and FPÖ) took a negative attitude. Therefore, only a relatively short general debate on the government bill took place in the legal committee of the National Council during the XIth legislative period.[25]

Under Kreisky's first SPÖ government the bill was redrafted following the lines of the original draft of the Commission on the Reform of the Criminal Law. In that commission, the regulation of the abortion issue had already been passed in 1957 with 14 votes in favor, 1 against, and 3 abstentions.[26] This regulation was almost identical to that contained in the government bill of November 1971. According to the bill, termination of pregnancy was permissible only on medical grounds, but social, ethical, and eugenic grounds were to be included as well. This still met with resistance among Catholic circles and caused the Aktion Leben (Right to Life Movement) to collect 823,000 signatures against this solution. However, at this point it could be expected that the People's party would not refuse its parliamentary consent to legalizing abortion on the expanded grounds mentioned above (Indikationslösung). When this solution seemed to be imminent, a group of young Socialist women, who had collected 30,000 signatures in favor of abolishing Article 144—which the Social Democrats had unsuccessfully demanded in the parliament of the period between the wars—succeeded during the SPÖ party convention in Villach in April 1972 in winning over the SPÖ's Womens' Movement for their demand of legalizing abortion up to three months after conception (*Fristenlösung*). The party convention accepted this demand, as did Minister of Justice Broda. The passionate protests by the Right to Life Movement were of no avail, and neither were the concerned admonitions of the Austrian Conference of Bishops or the threats of the opposition (ÖVP and FPÖ) to withhold their consent on the great reform of the criminal law. On 29 November 1973, the National Council passed the reform only with the votes of the absolute majority of the SPÖ. The objections of the Federal Council were overridden by the National Council on 23 January 1974, so that the reform became law.

The Austrian bishops, led by Cardinal König, considered legalized abortion to be a severe burden on the relationship between the Church in Austria and the party currently in power. However, at least as early as 1974, they ruled out the possibility that the Catholics might form a front against the SPÖ similar to the *Kulturkampf,* which would have meant a return of the atmosphere in cultural policy of the First Republic.[27] However, even before the National Council overrode the Federal Council's veto, one of the leading spokesmen of the Right to Life Movement, the president of the judicial senate of the Higher Court in Vienna, Friedrich Lehne, suggested two measures against legalized abortion during a conference of the Salzburg Catholic Academy. These two measures were implemented in 1974, namely an appeal in the Constitutional Court and a petition for a referendum. In their extraordinary conference on 26 January 1974 in Liñz, the Austrian bishops ratified a communiqué on legalized abortion which, they said, "violated the inalienable right to the protection of human life in Austria." They pointed out that the general synod of the Protestant Church had also spoken out in favor of the unborn's right to live, and they welcomed the plans of the Right to Life Movement to prepare a petition for a referendum.[28]

The action committee of the Right to Life Movement decided in June 1974 to initiate and carry out a petition for a referendum requesting a "federal law on the protection of human life." The Conference of Bishops of 2 July 1974 hailed this as an "independent initiative of Austrian Catholics."[29]

As had been announced, on 16 October 1974, the Right to Life Movement began to collect signatures: 10,000 signatures were needed initially (200,000 are necessary to bring the matter of a law before the National Council for its consideration). There were isolated incidences of relapses into the style of the *Kulturkampf* of the past[30] on both the Socialist and the Catholic sides. This happened in spite of the repeated and sincere assurances of the chairman of the referendum committee, Eduard Ploier, that the referendum was interdenominational and nonpartisan, and in spite of the decision by the Austrian Conference of Bishops not to publish a pastoral letter on the 1975 National Council elections,[31] since it did not wish to establish a connection between the referendum and the election campaign. Therefore, it must definitely be considered an honest effort to maintain domestic peace in Austria when the Right to Life Movement decided to begin its main referendum only after the elections to the National Council on 5 October 1975.

In these elections the SPÖ again won an absolute majority, as it had in 1971. This meant that yet another reform of the new criminal law, which had only been in force since 1 January 1975 in favor of the goals sought by the Right to Life Movement was improbable, and, in fact, it did not take place. This circumstance and the interruption in the campaign of the Right to Life Movement have certainly contributed to the fact that the movement did not reach its set goal, 1 million votes in the main referendum. It fell short with 896,000 votes. Yet, this result was the best of all Austrian referenda, and although it was not an official activity by the official Church, the reason for the referendum, legalized abortion, is even today still not accepted by many Austrian Catholics.

As is demonstrated by the pastoral letters alone, which the Austrian bishops have written since 1970, they have always, in joint or in individual declarations, unequivocally spoken out against the "limited reform of the criminal law" (no criminal prosecution of adult homosexuals and of persons who disrupt the marriage of others, and milder penalties for adultery) as well as against the 1978 reform of the divorce law (right to divorce after a six-year separation).[32] They have also again and again spoken out against legalizing abortion up to three months after conception.

Before the parliamentary committee in charge made its decision, the public was just as aware of the bishops' opinion as it was of that of the party in power. Even while he was still opposition leader, Chancellor Kreisky had consciously worked toward improvement of relations between the SPÖ and the Church. These efforts culminated in the conference "The Socialists and the Catholic Church" in St. Pölten in November 1967,[33] which attracted considerable attention, and in 1975 in the choice of the independent Foreign Minister Rudolf Kirchschläger, a practicing Catholic, as the SPÖ's candidate in the elections for the office of Federal President. By January 1977, Kreisky had assured representatives of the Right to Life Movement that he would recommend that a rigid position be not taken during the further debates of the referendum, but that he saw no chance that legalized abortion might be abolished.[34]

In April 1977, the new governor of Salzburg, Haslauer, and the then ÖVP *Klubobmann* (leader of the ÖVP's parliamentary faction), Professor Koren, accused the Church of a "double strategy" in the issue of legalized abortion. By this they meant that the Church expected the ÖVP to support the referendum, while indicating to the SPÖ that this issue would not constitute a *casus belli.* [35] These attacks in the spring of 1977 led Cardinal König to deny the validity of the views expressed by the ÖVP, and by Koren in particular, whose statements he considered to be a personal opinion. On the other hand, he declared on television that the ÖVP, which professed adherence to a "Christian image of man, a Christian world order," was, at the present time, fundamentally and in principle closer to the Church than "the Socialist party, which based its program on a general humanism." During their meeting in early May, the ÖVP party leadership then declared the issue officially closed.[36]

However, Kreisky's reaction to this development was harsh. In a newspaper interview, he stated that he considered Cardinal König's statements on television to be discrimination against the SPÖ.

> After all, our party, merely by virtue of its size, has more Catholics than the ÖVP. As far as I am concerned, these statements represent a setback in our relations with the Church—but I hope that this will not continue. . . . Our future relations will certainly depend on the question whether the Cardinal's statements were accidental or whether they signaled a new, different course of the Church.[37]

7

Three years after this controversy, we can safely say that they did not signal a new course. Of course, before and also after April 1977 there were other problems that resulted in differences of opinion between the SPÖ and the Church and that caused the latter concern. Among these were the attacks by Young Socialists from Vienna, Linz, Styria, and Carinthia on religious instruction in schools, but these were immediately rejected as groundless by the SPÖ leadership.[38] Other problems included the revival of the Associa-

tion of Free Thinkers[39] in late 1976 by the chairman of the Young Generation of the SPÖ, Albert Konecny, and the 1978 reform of the divorce law,
already mentioned. The discussion on the schools, which has already been
hinted at,.caused quite an uproar in the fall of 1979.[40] However, this issue
will probably not be as explosive, at least not in the immediate future, since
government and opposition decided jointly in February 1980 to extend the
current school experiments for another two years. In this question, the
bishops have repeatedly stressed the importance of the family in a child's
education and have also rejected an all-day school *mandatory* for all students, but they have not committed themselves to one principle. They all
followed the course that Cardinal Innitzer proclaimed in 1945 and that
Cardinal König, the only Austrian bishop ever to be considered *papabilis*
in two Papal elections, has maintained unswervingly, namely to keep the
Church as free as possible from all unilateral political ties. This is probably
primarily due to the fact that the majority of the Austrian bishops had
already consciously experienced the very different situation during the years
1934–1938 and 1938–1945 and that the episcopates are unusually long in
the Second Republic. This applies to Archbishop Rohracher of Salzburg
(1943–1977), just as it does to Bishop Rusch of Innsbruck (Suffragan and
Administrator since 1938), Bishop Köstner of Klagenfurt (since 1945), and
Cardinal König (since 1956). It has also contributed considerably to the
continuity of Austrian ecclesiastical policy, which has also been confirmed
by the Second Vatican Council. Ecclesiastical policy, especially with respect
to the relationship between Church and State and the political parties, has
also been supported by all significant Austrian theologians of the past
decades, such as Michael Pfliegler (1891–1972); Karl Rudolf (1886–1964);
the pastor of academics and artists, Otto Mauer (1907–1973); and the
Viennese pastoral theologian, Ferdinand Klostermann (b. 1907), who is the
best known internationally since Karl Rahner left Innsbruck. It can therefore be assumed that Cardinal König's clear statement before the 1976
Salzburg assembly of the delegates of the Catholic Men of Austria will also
determine the future "political" attitude of the Church in Austria:

The bishops are only as strong as the Catholic people and the faith that they live. In a
democracy, policy is made by the parties. Should the Catholics in this country found
their own political party? There would probably be no objections to more political parties
in Austria, among them a Catholic party. It is irrelevant how many seats such a party
could win, and it is not our place today to sit in judgment on the past when there was
such a party. Time has passed over that. In our view, the Church cannot be a party; it
cannot exist in a relationship of friendship with or animosity toward other parties. In
a country that is 90% Catholic, a Catholic party would not be an element of integration;
rather, it would be an element of disintegration. The Catholics in this country vote for

different parties. But they should not merely be voters; they should work there where they stand in their political opinions, in order to help determine the policy of these parties, of their party.

I know, dear friends, that many of you have found your political home in the People's party. You should stay there, work there, and cooperate. I would also like to take this opportunity to thank you for your involvement in politics. But I also believe that many things in Austria, especially in our most recent past, would have gone differently if the Catholics in the Socialist party had spoken up more. I do not presume to pass judgment on the position of the Catholics in the Socialist party. However, in the Church there are no differences between the social classes; there is no hierarchy according to a person's political beliefs. It is not the task of the Church to make political proselytes but to support Catholics, wherever they may stand politically, and to ask them to base their political actions, too, on their faith.

Of course, this also applies to those Catholics who are members or voters of the Liberal party. We must not create the impression that the Church is concentrating only on the two large parties; there are Catholics in other large parties as well; they, too, have the right to be treated equally as Catholics.

When, in 1945, after the tragic experiences of the past, the Austrian bishops followed a new course, dictated by the country's best interest, but also by the Church's mission to bring salvation, many Catholics misunderstood us and thought they, too, should abstain from politics. The political distance of the Church has resulted in an apolitical attitude in many Catholics. But such an attitude is totally erroneous. You cannot avoid politics, you cannot escape from politics.[41]

Of course, this appeal was directed primarily at the representatives of the "intensive segment" of the Austrian Catholics. However great the number of Catholics mentioned at the beginning of this essay may be, their participation in Church life is decreasing. Since 1974, more than 20,000 Austrians withdrew annually from their Church membership; only one-third of all baptized Catholics participate in Sunday Mass; the membership in Catholic organizations is declining. Hundreds of thousands of men and women are still members, particularly in suborganizations or movements of the Katholische Aktion*; there are still Catholic university communities and Catholic fraternal student organizations in all university towns, organizations that are still very active. However, these organizations, too, are presently not as attractive to the general student body as they were, for instance, at the time of the Second Vatican Council. The number of young people following a calling in the priesthood or in a religious order is also decreasing. The Linz pastoral theologian Wilhelm Zauner considers these phenom-

*Translator's Note: The Katholische Aktion is the official Catholic lay organization, with a structure that reaches from the federal and diocesan levels to the parish level. It has a number of subdivisions (e.g. Catholic Action for Men, which also includes the Catholic Workers' Movement).

ena to be a direct result of the decreasing social effectiveness of the Church.

Apart from all theological and pastoral consequences[42] arising from the present trend, it must be said that this trend corresponds to the development found wherever industrialization and urbanization are increasing. As the essays elsewhere in this book on those developments indicate, this happened extensively in the Second Republic. In 1951, 22 percent of the population were still making their living in agriculture; in 1978 this figure had shrunk to not quite 12 percent. Hundreds of thousands are emigrating from the rural areas to industry and to the service sector. Thus their ties to the Church and to the ÖVP loosened. All pertinent studies prove that, at least around 1970, there was a correlation between participation in religious services and a preference for the ÖVP. Two-thirds of the persons who withdrew from church membership live in cities with more than 100,000 inhabitants; one-third live in Vienna, where withdrawals from church membership amounted to 41% in 1965, a proportion that has increased further since 1967. The age group in which the majority of withdrawals from church membership occurs, the 30- to 50-year-olds, is also the one with the lowest attendance of church services. The wish for constancy and an unwavering faith are strongest among women, older people, inhabitants of communities with fewer than 2,000 inhabitants, and among persons with less formal education. Still, more than 70% of the population have a church wedding, 90% have their children baptized, and more than 90 percent are given a church funeral ceremony.[43]

So the traditional demonstrations of church membership on the occasion of the significant events of a lifetime—baptism, wedding, funeral—are still very pronounced. In addition, 86–91 percent of those questioned in Salzburg, Upper Austria, Carinthia, and the Tyrol indicated that they believe in the existence of God. The answers to all other questions concerning aspects of their faith were much less positive and varied more.

8

Yet Austria is still a Catholic country, at least nominally. All other religions, although they are recognized by the State, their relations to the State and to the political parties, receive much less attention from the public and from contemporary historical research. However, the Protestant Christians (whose legal position within the State has been discussed earlier) have, especially during the past ten years, succeeded in attracting more attention for their potential in social policy from the two large parties. This is, among other factors, also due to the discussions on legalized abortion, on which there was no unified official position in the Protestant churches. Although the leadership of the Protestant Church did support the Catholic position, as already mentioned, Superintendent Reingrabner of Burgenland and the well-known Protestant theologians Professor Dantine (Augsburg Confession) and Professor Lüthi (Reformed Confession) were in favor of legalizing abortion up to three months after conception.[44]

Moreover, in 1977, a Protestant Committee of the ÖVP was constituted. It sponsored its first conference in May 1978 on the topic Protestant Responsibility for Austria. In March 1978, the Committee on Christianity and Socialism of the SPÖ held an official inquiry in Vienna on the topic Protestants and the New SPÖ Program; and plans were made to establish a Protestant section within the committee. Before the inquiry was held, Superintendent Temmel of the Protestant Church in Upper Austria said in an interview that the Protestant Church could "definitely join [the SPÖ] for part of the way" in a number of practical social issues. This opinion is shared by Superintendent Reingrabner. However, Temmel ruled out a *political* Protestantism, as did the secretary general of the Protestant Committee of the ÖVP, Kauer.[45] There is an absolute agreement with the Catholic Church on this question of principle. As a result of the Second Vatican Council, there were also more opportunities for discussions in the area of theology, and more opportunities for joint activities, even though major difficulties have again arisen here and there for the ecumene, more so than during the great upswing of the 1960s.

9

Of the other religions that are not individually mentioned in the 1971 census, the Jewish religion is the oldest. Documentary evidence indicates that Jews lived in the territory of present-day Austria by the 9th century. The culture of Vienna at the turn of the 20th century, now often and justly extolled,[46] had been largely created by Jews. But when the Israelitische Kultusgemeinde (Community of the Israelite Faith) was resurrected in 1945, there were only 2,000 of the 190,000 Jews left in Vienna as a result of the "final solution" of the National Socialist regime.

At present, 8,000 Jews belong to the Kultusgemeinde in Vienna. Approximately 2,000 Jews do not register as such because of the municipal tax that would be involved.[47] In the remaining eight provinces, there are maximally 300 Jews,[48] so that the community in Vienna is the largest and the leading Jewish community in Austria, as it was before 1938.

The question of the party political orientation of the Jewish community is, relatively speaking, not problematical. The Viennese community is the only one in Europe in which "political" elections take place. Within it, the Bund werktätiger Juden (League of Working Jews), an auxiliary SPÖ organization, has a majority on the executive committee, which was an absolute majority (14 out of 24 seats) between 1952 and 1976. In the 1976 elections, the Bund lost three seats, while the Vereinigter Jüdischer Wahlblock (United Jewish Election Bloc) gained three seats, winning seven seats as compared to its previous four seats. The Wahlblock is a coalition of the List Simon Wiesenthal, which is close to the ÖVP, and the General Zionists and two other groups. The Zionists obtained two seats, and the strict Orthodox group retained their seat.[49] In spite of this, the leader of the Bund, Anton Pick, president of the Kultusgemeinde since 1970, retained his position on the basis of a coalition with a moderate Orthodox group, Khal Israel (Community of Fighters for God), which had obtained three seats.

In spite of the clearly differentiated political preferences of the various groups, there is unity when difficult situations arise. The 1975 Wiesenthal/ Peter/Kreisky affair may serve as an illustration. When Wiesenthal exposed the then chairman of the Liberal Party (FPÖ), Friedrich Peter, as a member of one of the infamous SS details during World War II, and when the Socialist Chancellor Kreisky defended Peter just as vehemently as he attacked Wiesenthal, the Kultusgemeinde backed Wiesenthal.[50]

However, differences seems to arise more frequently in the area of religion. The majority of the community, also including the Bund, is liberal. The Orthodox Jews, numbering between 500 and 600, the Misrachi (those from the east), and the even stricter Machsike Hadass feel that they do not receive adequate support from the Kultusgemeinde.[51] For instance, Machsike Hadass not only requires their own rabbi and their own butcher, but also maintains their own elementary school for only 44 students and a kindergarten for 45 children in the Viennese district of Leopoldstadt. The Vienna municipal school board pays the salaries of two of the nine teachers, and the Kultusgemeinde subsidized the Talmud Thora School, which is attached to the school, with 220,000 schillings in 1977. In spite of the annual subsidies of approximately 3 million schillings it receives from the Federal Government and the City of Vienna and from the municipal tax, the Kultusgemeinde was unable to fulfill the request for 800,000 schillings, made at that time. This inability was due to its other financial commitments: the maintenance of the temple on Seitenstettengasse in Vienna; a new Jewish community center, the House of Encounter; the maintenance of other synagogues and of schools for the rabbinate, and of several periodicals; and the maintenance of the old people's home with a geriatric hospital in the Viennese suburb of Döbling, and of Jewish cemeteries "which had once been intended for 200,000 Jews" (Anton Pick).[52]

However, Austria's youngest religious community, recognized by the State since 1978, does not have any financial problems at the present time. The Islamic faith according to Hafemitic Rites had already been granted recognition by the State in 1912, following the 1908 annexion of Bosnia and Herzegovina by the Habsburg monarchy. However, the Department for Religious Affairs in the Ministry of Education, which had been working on the application for recognition since 1968, felt that the 1912 law, which had never been repealed, was not in agreement with the present Austrian constitution.[53] In addition, there was the issue of the organization of the practicing Muslims, some of whom were Austrian citizens while others were foreigners living in Austria, predominantly foreign workers. It was due to their relatively large number that the question of recognition became relevant again. However, an exact figure can hardly be given because of fluctuations that are also caused by the current economic situation; figures given range from 80,000 to 35,000, the latter given for 1978 by the Ministry of Education.[54] Among the foreigners, the greatest contingent are the Turks, followed by Yugoslavs, primarily from Bosnia, whereas the smaller groups (Persians, Egyptians, Arabs, and East Indians) are predominantly students, but there are also 3,000 old Austrian Muslims. The first institution to be established was a Muslim Social Service, which set up centers for foreign workers with a Koran school and a prayer room in Vienna's 1st and 3rd Districts. It was Abd el Rahimsai, a naturalized Austrian citizen born in Afghanistan, who started the initiative for recognition in 1968. In the course of the same year, owing to the efforts of members of the Islamic embassies, a foundation for the construction of a mosque was started. The basic capital, $200,000, came from Saudi Arabia. Part of this money was used to purchase a site on Hubertusdamm in the Vienna suburb of Floridsdorf, where the cornerstone was laid in 1968.[55] In 1978, the Islamic Centre was completed. Saudi Arabia alone had paid 55 million schillings toward its construction, and other oil-producing nations had financed the interior. The Centre, located near the new United Nations city, provides cultural and social services and also has a mosque. However, the Muslim Social Service is still dependent on its own financial power and on donations. Its application for State recognition of the Islamic faith was granted in 1978.[56]

Other religious communities recognized by the State are the Greek Orthodox Church, the Old Catholic Church, the Methodists, the Mormons, and the Armenian Apostolic Church (since 1976). The Bund der Baptistengemeinden (League of Baptist Parishes) applied for State recognition as early as 1966, but this application could not yet be ruled on because of the League's own reservations with respect to the extent of State supervision. In 1976 the Department for Religious Affairs received applications by Buddhists and by the Church of Scientology,[57] the latter church belonging to the so-called youth religions, mentioned below. The Salvation Army considers itself a "free Protestant Church," and, in spite of its low membership in Austria (50–100), it maintains a home for women in Vienna and a social asylum, Europahaus, in Linz.[58] Just like the Quakers, who are also active in social matters, the Salvation Army is a society, a legal status, which, in the opinion of officials in the Department for Religious Affairs, could also be granted to other applicants.[59]

The Methodists, recognized by the State, consider themselves a Free Evangelical Church. They have small parishes in almost all Austrian provinces and their own bookstore in Vienna. Administratively, the Austrian Methodists belong to their church's Geneva diocese.[60] More detailed figures can be provided on the membership of other religious communities: the Mormons and Adventists have approximately 6,500 members; Jehovah's Witnesses have increased their membership from 2,200 in 1950 to 13,000 in 1977. They were also the ones to most consistently bear witness to their faith during the Nazi era, and they accepted incarceration in concentration camps and death for their faith.

The so-called youth religions, which often only serve to make their founders richer, cannot be compared to the religious communities enumerated above. However, these sects have in recent years attracted young Austrians or have tried to court them with dubious means. Among them are the sect of the Reverend Moon, the International Unification Church or God's Children; the Transcendental Meditation/Austrian Association for the Promotion of the Science of Creative Intelligence; and the Church of Scientology. According to estimates, these sects have a total of approximately 5,000 followers in Austria.[61]

Notes

1. *Statistisches Handbuch für die Republik Österreich* 29 Jg. N. F. 1978.
2. Alfred Diamant, *Austrian Catholics and the First Republic* (Princeton, 1960); Paul Michael Zulehner, *Kirche und Austromarxismus* (Wien, 1967); and Ernst Hanisch, *Die Ideologie des politischen Katholizismus in Österreich 1918–1938* (Wien, 1977).
3. Still the most complete source for all of Austria is Jakob Fried, *Nationalsozialismus und katholische Kirche in Österreich* (Wien, 1947); also Gerhard Wanner, *Kirche und Nationalsozialismus in Vorarlberg* (Dornbirn, 1972); *Zeugen des Widerstandes. Eine Dokumentation über die Opfer des Nationalsozialismus in Nord-, Ost- und Südtirol von 1938–1945,* bearbeitet von Dr. Johann Holzner, P. Anton Pinsker, S. J.
4. Richard Barta, Religion—Kirche—Staat, *Bestandsaufnahme Österreich* (Wien, 1965); *Kirche in Österreich, 1918–1965,* ed. by Ferdinand Klostermann, Hans Kriegl, Otto Mauer, and Erika Weinzierl (2 vols., Wien, 1966–1967); Hans Magenschab, *Die Zweite Republik zwischen Kirche und Parteien* (Wien, 1968); Erika Weinzierl, Die katholische Kirche, *Österreich—die Zweite Republik,* II, ed. by Erika Weinzierl and Kurt Skalnik (Graz, 1972).
5. Erika Weinzierl, Die gesellschaftspolitischen Grundlinien des Kardinals König, *Österreichisches Jahrbuch für Politik 1979* (München, 1980), p. 153.
6. *Österreichische Parteiprogramme, 1868–1966,* ed. by Klaus Berchtold (Wien, 1967), p. 289.
7. Albert Kadan and Anton Pelinka, *Die Grundsatzprogramme der österreichischen Parteien —Dokumentation und Analyse* (St. Pölten, 1979), pp. 144ff.
8. The quotations in the text are based *seriatim* on ibid., pp. 191, 197, 177, 167, 21.

9. Ibid., p. 227.
10. Berchtold, op. cit., pp. 377 and 268ff. The programmatic guidelines of the KPÖ from 1946 do not contain statements on religion and the church. The Liberal Party, (FPÖ) and its predecessor, the Association of Independents, (Verband der Unabhängigen, VdU) did not yet exist.
11. Quoted according to Barta, op. cit., pp. 270ff.
12. "We profess to freedom of conscience, freedom of religion, and free practice of the religions recognized by the State. A citizen who lives his life according to the teachings of the church must not be disadvantaged because of it. Therefore, a solution of the question of the concordat and a new law concerning the Protestants are to be sought as soon as possible" (ibid., p. 388).
13. Magenschab, op. cit., pp. 25ff.
14. *Wiener Zeitung,* 5/23/57. This statement is in some contrast to Schärf's position as Vice Chancellor in 1950, when he espoused the Theory of Annexation, according to which Austria ceased to exist as a state in 1938 and all international treaties entered previously lost their validity. See Adolf Schärf, Gilt das Konkordat?, *Die Zukunft,* 1950, pp. 34–37, 117–25.
15. The negotiations on the ministerial level were preceded by talks with dignitaries of the Church, initiated by Olah and participated in by the new SPÖ chairman, Bruno Pittermann. See Gerhard Silberbauer, *Österreichs Katholiken und die Arbeiterfrage* (Graz, 1966); Alfred Kostelecky, Die Situation Kirche-Staat seit dem Abschluss des Staatsvertrages 1955, *Religion, Wissenschaft, Kultur 9* (1958): 150.
16. Stenographische Protokolle des Österreichischen Nationalrates, IX Gp., 37 Sitzung, 7/12/60, p. 1497.
17. *Federal Law Gazette,* 195 and 196/1960.
18. Sten. Prot., op. cit., IX Gp., 41 Sitzung, 10/26/60, pp. 1629ff.
19. *Archiv der Gegenwart,* 7/9/61.
20. *Federal Law Gazette,* 273/1962.
21. *Federal Law Gazette,* 215/1962. (Translator's Note: A constitutional law is a law that is declared as such and the passage of which requires a two-thirds majority.)
22. *Federal Law Gazette,* 227/1964 and 101/1968.
23. *Wiener Kirchenzeitung,* 6/4/67. See also Hermann Withalm, *Aufzeichnungen* (Graz, 1973), pp. 156ff.
24. *Kathpress,* 4/6/67.
25. Eugen Serini, Die Entwicklung des Strafrechts, *Österreich—die Zweite Republik,* op. cit., II, p. 131.
26. Friedrich Nowakowski, Zur Neuregelung des Abtreibungsstrafrechtes in Österreich, in Johannes Gründel, *Abtreibung—pro und contra,* (Innsbruck, München, no year of publication indicated), pp. 44, 50.
27. See *Kathpress,* 1/2 and 1/23/74; *Kurier,* 1/14/74.
28. *Kathpress,* 1/21/74 and 1/28/74, supplement.
29. An interview with Cardinal König in October 1974 subsequently led to some tensions between him and followers of the Right to Life Movement. In the meantime, the Constitutional Court had rejected the motion of the provincial government of Salzburg to declare the relevant legal provisions (Article 97, paragraph 1) unconstitutional. See *Kathpress,* 10/7, 10/9, and 10/11/74, also 6/5/74 and 7/3/74.
30. See *Kathpress,* 10/14/74 and 11/11/74, and profil, 11/20 and 11/27/74.
31. *Kathpress,* 11/6/74.
32. *Federal Law Gazette,* 273/1971 and 303/1978. See statements by the Austrian bishops on the reform of the criminal law, dated 6/8 and 7/8/71, pastoral letters 1971 from Germany, Austria, and Switzerland, published by the Institut für kirchliche Zeitgeschichte Salzburg, 1974, pp. 202–4, and statements by the Austrian Conference of Bishops on the reform of the divorce law, dated 1/30/78, pastoral letters 1978, p. 249.
33. All papers read during this conference are published in *Die Furche,* 11/22/67.
34. *Kathpress,* 1/21/77.
35. *Salzburger Nachrichten,* Kurier, 4/30/77.
36. *Salzburger Nachrichten,* 5/6/77.
37. *Neue Kronen-Zeitung,* 5/9/77.
38. *Kathpress,* 10/1, 10/15, and 11/5/75; also Paul M. Zulehner, Kirche–SPÖ: Beispiel des Reiligionsunterrichts, *Zukunft,* March 1971, pp. 31ff.; *Kathpress,* 10/13/77, and *Wochenpresse,* 10/20/77.

120   WEINZIERL

39. *Kathpress,* 11/19/76. The Association of Free Thinkers (Freidenkerbund), consisting of persons who had disaffiliated from the Catholic Church, had played a not insignificant role in the First Republic.
40. See also Heiner Boberski, Ganztags zur Schule, *Die Furche,* 11/14/79.
41. Pastoral letters, 1976, Salzburg, 1977, pp. 321ff.
42. Wilhelm Zauner, Kirche in Österreich. Überlegung zu einem Entwurf, in Theodor Piffl-Perčevič, *Zuspruch und Widerspruch* (Graz, 1977), pp. 178ff.
43. *Die Religion im Leben der Oberösterreicher,* 2 parts; *Zur religiösen Situation in Innsbruck,* 1970, 2 parts; *Glaube und Kirche in Kärnten,* 2 parts, all published by the Institut für kirchliche Sozialforschung, 1970; and Paul M. Zulehner, *Verfällt die Kirchlichkeit in Östereich?* (Graz, no year of publication indicated), pp. 16ff (for Vienna).
44. *Arbeiter-Zeitung,* 4/2/78, and präsent, 6/1/78.
45. *Linzer Tagblatt,* 3/23/78; Robert Kauer, Passagiere statt Wegbegleiter, *präsent,* 6/1/78; and his Evangelische und Evangelische Kirchen in der Österreichiselen Politik, *Österr. Jahrbuch für Politik 1979* (München, 1980), p. 121. Helmut Gamsjäger, Evangelische Kirche und Sozialdemokratie, *Die Zukunft,* 1978.
46. For an important source, see Carl E. Schorske, *Fin-de-Siècle Vienna. Politics and Culture* (New York, 1980).
47. *Die Presse,* 11/9/76.
48. Courtesy Anton Pick, leader of the Bund werktätiger Juden.
49. *Die Presse,* 12/14/76, and *Wochenpresse,* 12/15/76.
50. *Die Presse,* 11/9/76.
51. *Die Presse,* 2/27/79, and *trend* 1979/5.
52. Ibid., and *Kurier,* 11/21/77.
53. *Die Presse,* 3/1/76, and *Arbeiter-Zeitung,* 8/5/78, supplement.
54. Ibid.
55. *Berichte und Informationen,* 1977/1.
56. *Die Presse,* 7/4/78, and *Arbeiter-Zeitung,* 8/5/78, supplement.
57. *Die Presse,* 3/1/76.
58. The Salvation Army Sees Itself in a Different Light, in *Arbeiter-Zeitung,* 7/23/78, letter to the editor from Major Paul Nef, Chairman of the Society, Salvation Army.
59. *Die Presse,* 3/1/76.
60. Gerald Kennedy, *Weltweite Methodistenkirche. Ihre Geschichte und ihr Auftrag* (Zürich, 1956), p. 256.
61. *Profil,* 3/7/78.

Selected Bibliography

The extensive notes to this essay refer to much of the pertinent literature and can therefore serve at the same time as a basic biliography for works in the German language. Tangentially relevant publications in English are as follows:

Diamant, A. *Austrian Catholics and the First Republic.* Princeton, 1960.

Pulzer, P. G. *The Rise of Political Antisemitism in Germany and Austria.* New York, 1954.

Rusinow, D. The Retreat from Josephinism. In K. Silvert, ed. *Churches and States.* New York, 1967.

Weinzierl, E. Austria. In M. A. Fitzsimmons, ed. *The Catholic Church Today: Western Europe.* Notre Dame, Indiana, 1969.

PART II

ECONOMY

Modern Austria, pp. 123–40

4. AUSTRIA'S ECONOMIC DEVELOPMENT, 1945–1978

Eduard März

Head of the Institute of Economic History, University of Vienna

Maria Szecsi

Former staffmember of the Department of Economic Research, Vienna Chamber of Labor

1   1945—A NEW BEGINNING

Students of recent Austrian history are invariably struck by the contrast between the development of the country after World War I and after World War II. Although the first Austrian Republic (1918–1938) remained economically the weakest of all the countries of Central Europe, forever on the brink of total disaster, present-day Austria can look back on thirty years of unprecedented prosperity and stability. To be sure, an important part of the explanation lies in the vastly superior climate of the international economy in the second of these two periods. However, looking back at the immediate postwar situation of Austria, one might have expected even in this more favorable external setting a rather slow and uneven recovery, which would put the economy at best on a path of sluggish growth, highly vulnerable to the impact of international recessions. Thus an equally important part of the explanation must be looked for in factors internal to the history of the Second Republic.

1.1   The Doctrine of Nonviability—a Self-Fulfilling Prophecy

Any attempt to identify these factors leads back to the question after the causes of the extremely poor performance of the Austrian economy in the between-the-wars period. At the end of World War I the sudden dissolution of the Austro-Hungarian Monarchy had left the German-speaking frag-

123

9306-6403/81/0415-0123$01.50

ment that constituted itself "Austria" (originally "German-Austria") in a state of complete exhaustion and disorganization, its economy cut off from its former supplies of food and raw materials and its former markets for industrial goods. Austrian industry, geared to a vast internal market and already depleted of machinery and materials by a war effort far beyond its strength, saw itself suddenly confronted by high tariff barriers which the successor states erected to build up their own economies and to gain economic as well as political independence from their former master-nation. The desperate situation of the whole country, especially of the starving population of its oversized capital city of Vienna, has so often been described in the literature on postwar Europe that there is no need to enter here into details.

Admittedly, the task of restructuring the economy to adapt it to its new conditions of survival was a formidable one; it would have taxed to the full all the energies of a people united in national purpose and political will. Unfortunately, the Austrian people at that time were neither. What had seemed the natural solution to Austria's economic problems, namely union with Germany, was vetoed by the Allies. The bourgeoisie, moreover, never became reconciled to the democratic Republic. Thus, Austria remained the "State that nobody wanted," without a defined national identity and lacking a basic consensus in support of its political system.

It was in this atmosphere that the doctrine of the economic "nonviability" of Austria took almost universal hold over the minds of the economic and political leaders of the country. The argument was largely based on the smallness of the internal market and the lack of natural resources. The not inconsiderable assets that the country still possessed in the form of industrial capacity and a highly skilled working population were overlooked or belittled, in any case underestimated. "Smallness" in itself is not, of course —and never was—an obstacle to economic advancement, as shown by the example of the prosperous small nations of Northern and Western Europe. But whatever the merits of the nonviability thesis may have been objectively, its psychological effects assuredly were such that it became a self-fulfilling prophecy. In fact, industrial production throughout the whole history of the First Republic barely surpassed the prewar level by a small margin in the prosperous years 1928–1929, only to fall far behind in the Great Depression of the 1930s. By comparison, Germany, equally hit by the war and its disastrous aftermath, by 1938 had reached a GNP level of about 50 percent above prewar.

1.2 The Heritage of German Rule

What were the new elements in 1945 that made for such a startling difference in the speed of recovery? Certainly the devastations of World War II were, if anything, much more severe than those of World War I. This time there were the heavy direct effects of war as well as occupation damages, since the Soviets seized what was left of machinery and equipment in their zone. Housing was in a terrible condition, about 177,000 units having been completely or partly destroyed. And again, Austria was torn away from the larger economic area into which it had been integrated. In these respects, then, its situation was rather worse than in 1918. But there were compensating advantages.

First of all, we note the complete reversal of the people's attitude toward the existence of Austria as an independent and democratic state. Seven years of domination by Hitler's Germany had cured the great majority of Austrians of their age-old hankering for union with the big brother. The "State that nobody wanted" became almost overnight a state that almost everybody wanted. On the political level the new sense of national identity found expression in the formation of a coalition government between the leading political forces of the country, the Socialists and the People's party, The coalition held for twenty years. This created an entirely novel psychological, political and social setting in which doubts about economic viability had no place. There developed, on the contrary, quite a lively "industrial spirit" hitherto foreign to tradition-bound Austrian entrepreneurs.

A second favorable factor, whose significance emerged only in the course of time, was the large industrial complex built up by Nazi Germany on Austrian territory for armaments requirements. Most important were the Hermann Goering Werke, a large iron and steel complex that was added to Austria's older one in Styria. Further new capacities had been created in the fields of heavy chemicals, aluminum, and machinery; a number of hydroelectric power plants had been built, and others had been left in various stages of completion or planning. To be sure, all of these new works had been destroyed in the war and denuded of their equipment; most had not even been finished by the Germans. Hence, it is not surprising that many voices were raised in favor of liquidating the entire complex, which seemed so overdimensioned for Austrian needs, calling for investments that it was thought would far exceed the possibilities of the impoverished country. In spite of these weighty arguments, it was immediately decided to rebuild these works and to restructure the Austrian economy around a greatly enlarged basis of heavy industry. Given the uncertain prospects of European recovery at the time, this decision took some courage. As it turned out, the new capacities were well adapted to the needs of Austria's expanding postwar economy. Especially in the period of reconstruction, but also thereafter as long as the almost unlimited demand of world markets for steel and steel products lasted, they served as "pacemakers" of export growth and industrial modernization. In following this ambitious course Austria benefited not so much by the fragmentary remainders of physical plant it had inherited as from a certain transfer of technology and know-how that had taken place during the German occupation. Thus it is perhaps no accident that its most successful innovation, the LD steel-making process (named after the steel centers at Linz and Donawitz), which has found world-wide application, originated in the newly built VOEST mills (Vereinigte Österreichische Eisen-und Stahlwerke), successor to the Herman Goering Werke.

2   THE PHASE OF RECONSTRUCTION

The reconstruction of the shattered economy after 1945 proceeded at a fast pace, not only compared with the past but also by any absolute standard. In 1946 the indexes of industrial and agricultural production stood at less than half of prewar (1937), and Austria was once more, according to American observers, the country with the lowest standard of nutrition in Europe. Only three years later the 1937 level was reached; five years after that the peak level of the interwar period (1929) was surpassed. Thus it can be said that by 1952 the reconstruction period was ended; a new phase of development was about to begin.

2.1   The Marshall Plan

Unquestionably the Marshall Plan was an essential factor in this "economic miracle." There is no need to enter here into the history and motivation of this remarkable enterprise, which became known by the initials ERP (European Recovery Program). Considering Austria's singular position as a country committed to the West but still in part occupied by Soviet troops, its aid requirements clearly had high political priority for the USA. Even before the Marshall Plan went into effect, recognition of Austria as a "liberated country" had made it eligible for UNRRA aid, which set in at the end of 1945 and consisted mostly of foodstuffs. From then on aid was given under various titles until in 1948 the ERP was set up. Altogether, under all programs, Austria received some 1.6 billion dollars of Allied aid (1.4 from the US). By far the most important economic effects resulted from the so-called direct aid part of the program, which was principally utilized to create a revolving fund for the purpose of supplying cheap credit to Austrian enterprises. A total of 678 million dollars was spent for this purpose. The system worked as follows: the goods that the US sent as free gifts were sold to the Austrian public at relatively moderate prices. The revenue from these sales was paid into a special account, the "counterpart account," from which credits flowed back into the economy, mostly for investment purposes, at subsidized interest rates varying between 3 and 5 percent according to the priority rating of the project. Although the US authorities retained final control over the utilization of the counterpart credits, basic policy goals were worked out in agreement with Austrian plans. When the Marshall Plan wound up in 1952, the remaining assets in the counterpart account were turned over to the Austrian government. The ERP fund remained an important, though with the progress in inflation a necessarily dwindling, source of investment finance throughout the 1950s. Another significant form of aid ("indirect aid," 284 million dollars) served to cover deficits in the balance of trade, first on a bilateral, later on a multilateral, basis in the framework of the European Payments Union (EZU).

In the first two years (1947–1948) the bulk of US aid was used to feed a hungry population and to provide coal and other essentials for survival. Starting in 1950 the major effort could be diverted to capital investment in industry, agriculture, and infrastructure. Of the 11 billion Austrian schilling counterpart credits pumped into the economy until 1953, roughly 3 billion went into coal mining and power plants, 4 billion were devoted to industrial investment, 1.6 billion to agriculture, and the rest to the reconstruction of the transportation and communications systems. Over the whole period this source of finance accounted for roughly 30 percent of total net and 20 percent of gross investment.

2.2   The Nationalization Acts

Another big problem Austria was confronted with in 1945 was the fate of the huge bulk of former German property, comprising not only the afore-mentioned new industries but also a number of older Austrian enterprises that had been transferred after 1938 to German owners. There were no legal claimants to this property, nor was private domestic capital available to acquire these assets and to get production going. Transfer to foreign owner-ship was impossible for political reasons, even if there had been serious bidders. The problem was further complicated by the fact that the Soviet Union laid claim to all German property under the title of war reparations. In its own occupation zone it had already seized the enterprises falling into this category and established its own administrative authority (USIA). In the Allied zones the claim was not recognized, but there was no certainty about the future settlement of the whole reparations complex. In view of all these open questions, the political parties quickly reached agreement on the only sensible solution—nationalization. Undoubtedly the impulses be-hind this extraordinary political act were mixed. In the Socialist party, though it was by no means of a revolutionary bent, ideological reasons strongly supported the practical considerations involved. And even in con-servative circles there was widespread skepticism about the chances of revival of the old capitalist order. But the decisive factor was certainly the pressure of the singular circumstances outlined above. The hope of foiling the Russian designs by this expedient of course played a major role.

The Nationalization Acts of 1946 and 1947 transferred huge industrial holdings to the Republic. They covered the extractive industries (coal, iron ore, oil, aluminum), with the sole but significant exception of American- and French-owned magnesite mines, practically the entire steel industry, and most of the large enterprises in the field of machinery, chemicals, and electrical equipment. At the same time the three largest banks of the country, which in turn held considerable industrial assets, were nationalized. Full public property was also established in the field of electric power generation. Since before the war all major public utilities (railroads, gas, communications, etc) had been run by the state or the municipalities, Austria emerged after the war as the country with the largest nonprivate economic sector in the Western world. This fact has decisively shaped its sociopolitical structure. However, in the course of time, heavy foreign investment occurred, which resulted in the creation of an industrial establishment of comparable size by multinational (especially German) concerns, primarily active in more modern, "brain-intensive" fields such as electronics, chemicals, and machinery.

The reconstruction period also saw the first—though short-lived—experiment in large-scale economic planning on the basis of an Investment Program covering the allocation of ERP funds as well as all other public investment. In this way the main structural decisions were implemented, along with nationalization. But in the degree to which private investment strengthened and the nationalized enterprises were able to finance themselves, largely by internal accumulation, the economics of the market prevailed over the concept of planning. Even so, the sheer volume of public ownership and investment made the presence of the State in the economy felt more ubiquitously than in countries with a purer form of capitalism. Altogether, one may characterize the resulting institutional framework as that of a "mixed economy" with rather strong elements of State intervention on both the macro- and the micro levels.

3   ECONOMIC ACHIEVEMENT, 1950–1978

3.1   Inflation and Stabilization

As could be expected, the most threatening danger to the economy in the immediate postwar period was inflation, with the specter of a runaway inflation like that of 1920–1922 ever present. The strict price and wage controls imposed immediately after the war necessarily broke down as huge price differentials developed between rationed and black-market goods, leading inevitably to upward pressure on wages. The beginnings of a wage-price spiral were clearly visible. By July 1947 even the official price index (including only legal prices) stood at 275 on the basis of 1945. This was the setting for another novel experiment made possible through the close cooperation of the highly centralized organizations of trade unions and employers—the Austrian Trade Union Federation (Österreichischer Gewerkschaftsbund) and the Federal Chamber of Trade and Industry (Bundeskammer der gewerblichen Wirtschaft). In 1947 the first of five wage-and-price pacts was concluded between the representatives of these bodies, with the concurrence of the government. The agreements covered prices of all essential goods and provided for across-the-board flat wage and pension increases, which aimed at controlling inflation while securing at least minimum wage standards. This was the first trial run of the procedures that later came to be known as "social partnership."

Although some initial success could be registered after each of these pacts, it was soon recognized that the rising pressure on costs could not be effectively dealt with by voluntary regulation alone. In 1951–1952 a harsher course was decided upon; stabilization was enforced by radical fiscal and monetary restrictions, with the unavoidable sequel of a severe recession. In 1953 the rapid recovery of the economy came to a halt, and the rate of employment rose to almost 9 percent, the highest figure in all of postwar history. However, though its impact was shocking, the stabilization crisis was to be overcome fairly rapidly. Though the price index had already passed the 800 mark, the threat of a breakdown of the monetary system had been removed, and the Austrian economy was launched upon a course of stable growth and high employment for the next two decades.

3.2   Top Place in the Growth Race

As shown in Tables 1 and 5, Austria was able to maintain a consistently high rate of growth. From 1950 to 1960 Gross National Product (GNP) increased on the average by 6 percent annually, in the following decade by 4.7 percent, and from 1970 to 1979 by 4.3 percent. Since population growth was slight, per capita figures were almost correspondingly great. In the same periods industrial production increased by 7.2, 5.6, and 4.4 percent, real wages have by and large kept pace with the growth of productivity so as to leave distributive shares—wages and profits—constant in the long run.

With this performance Austria occupies a top place in the international growth league, slightly ahead of Germany and well above the average of the OECD countries. Consequently, the economic distance between Austria and the historically richer countries has drastically diminished, although per capita income (7,710 dollars in 1978) today is still well below that of the very rich countries like Sweden and Switzerland. The improvement

Table 1   Average growth rates (in percent)

	1950–1959	1960–1969	1970–1979
Gross Domestic Product	6.0%	4.9%	4.3%
Industrial production	7.2[a]	5.6	4.4
Real wages (all employed persons)	4.7[b]	5.2	3.6
Exports	9.3[b]	9.0	7.6

Source: Official statistics.
[a] 1951–1959.
[b] 1954–1959.

since prewar times is impressive. Thus, for instance, per capita income of Germany—measured in dollars—was two and a half times as great as that of Austria before the occupation. Today the distance has shrunk to about 35–40 percent (FRG only). Since Germany in this same period has overtaken the USA by a small margin, about the same or even a slightly better relation obtains now between Austria and the USA, whose productive powers before the war generated an income 4.5 times as great. Since 1955, too, Austria has made steady if not quite as large gains, and can now boast of a rating, still by the same measuring rod, 10 percent above the OECD —Europe average instead of trailing behind, as in 1955, by 30 percent (see Table 3).

Admittedly the dollar standard in international income comparisons has lost some of its validity in recent years on account of the violent fluctuations in exchange rates, which do not necessarily reflect comparable shifts in real terms. Also, living standards depend not only on current income alone but also on the accumulated wealth of households in the past. Thus, for instance, housing conditions in Austria still bear the stamp of its former poverty. But even if all that is taken into account, a solid advance in Austria's position cannot be denied. Comparisons in terms of purchasing power are always difficult and debatable. But as far as they have been attempted, they show at least as good a picture, or even a better one, than the usual dollar scale.

Table 2   International comparison of growth rates (in percent)

	1955–1959	1960–1969	1970–1979
Austria	5.6%	4.9%	4.3%
Germany (FRG)	7.1	5.0	3.2
Sweden	3.2	4.4	2.1
Netherlands	3.6	5.4	3.5
United Kingdom	2.2	3.0	2.0
USA	3.3	4.1	2.8
OECD—world	3.9	5.1	3.5

Source: OECD.

Table 3 Per capita Gross National Product (in dollars)

	1955		1977		1978	
	Absolute	Index	Absolute	Index	Absolute	Index
Austria	$ 603	100.0	$6,378	100.0	$ 7,711	100.0
Germany (FRG)	821	136.2	8,407	131.8	10,345	134.2
Switzerland	1,298	215.3	9,576	150.1	13,350	173.1
Sweden	1,350	223.9	9,482	148.7	10,377	134.6
Netherlands	724	120.1	7,680	120.4	9,249	119.9
Belgium	1,025	170.0	8,058	126.3	9,796	127.0
United Kingdom	1,039	172.3	4,370	68.5	5,494	71.2
USA	2,417	400.8	8,664	135.8	9,586	124.3
OECD—world	1,190	197.3	6,482	101.6	7,684	99.6

Source: OECD.

3.3 Structural Change

Growth of this order of magnitude implies rapid structural change, between the agricultural, manufacturing, and service sectors on the one hand, and the various branches of industry and services on the other. Sectorial change, following the well-known laws of Fourastié and Colin Clark, resulted primarily in a large-scale net shift of the labor force from agriculture to services, whereas the manufacturing sector increased only moderately. Over the whole period the share of agriculture in the total labor force (including self-employed) decreased from its high starting point of 32 percent (1950) to 9.5 percent (1978), a figure only slightly above that of Switzerland (8.5 percent), which has similar natural conditions for agriculture. Not less than half of this shift occurred after 1970, a fact that points up vividly the special dynamism of the economy in this short period. Since the agricultural share generally counts as one of the most important indicators of economic development, it may be said that by that standard too full industrial maturity has been reached (see Table 4).

The increase in agricultural productivity was sufficient not only to offset the decline in labor input but to meet fully the rising internal demand and

Table 4 Share of main economic sectors in total employment, employees and self-employed (in percent)

	Agriculture and forestry	Manufacturing (incl. mining)	Services
1934	37.1%	32.1%	30.8%
1959	23.7	41.2	35.1
1977	9.9	40.8	49.3

Source: Institute of Economic Research (WIFO).

to produce, beyond that, sizable surpluses of milk and cereals. The differential between agricultural and industrial incomes remained higher, however, than in most fully developed countries. Whether the system of agricultural subsidies plus controlled prices—which is practiced in Austria, as in most other Western countries—has held back the incomes of this sector or merely failed to raise them sufficiently is a moot question. (At present farmers in high Alpine regions receive some support, not only on economic grounds but also for reasons of preserving the natural environment for tourism.)

Employment in the manufacturing sector rose in the same period by only a few percentage points, from 38 to 42 percent, fluctuating somewhat with the cyclical movement. Accordingly, the service sector expanded rapidly, from 30 to 48 percent. Owing mainly to flourishing tourism and the growth of public services of all kinds, this sector has been able so far to absorb the labor set free in slack times by industry. Its high elasticity of demand for labor has also been an important factor in maintaining employment in times of sudden inflows into the labor market owing to demographic reasons. Fears expressed by some economists in the mid-1960s, when industrial employment decreased for several years, that the shift to the service sector indicated a "premature aging" of the economy implying a permanent weakening of its industrial backbone, were not borne out by later developments.

3.4   High Investment, High Employment

In view of a practically stable population, high investment was required to sustain growth. Gross investment rose steadily throughout the 1950s to reach 26 percent of GNP in 1960. It then remained remarkably constant through the entire decade. In the 1970s there was a significant upward push, resulting in an average of 28.4 percent for the years 1970–1978. Among the Western countries, only Norway and Japan have higher investment rates. A further characteristic feature is the high share of public investment. Adding together direct public investment, investment in nationalized industries, and various indirect forms of investment subsidies, the public share has been estimated to amount to not less than 50 percent of total gross investment. This also explains the steadiness of the investment rate, which was hardly affected by cyclical swings; the impact of cycles, however, has been much more marked on industrial investment taken by itself (see Table 5).

The trend of employment follows that of investment rather closely. The unemployment rate, which had been over 6 percent in the first half of the 1950s, was down to 2.9 percent by 1960 and stayed below 3 percent throughout the decade; in the 1970s it was below 2 percent in all years up to 1980. At the same time the number of wage earners rose from around 2 million (1955) to 2.7 million. The point of full employment was reached

Table 5   Investment rates as percent of GNP

	1950–1959	1960–1969	1970–1979
Austria	20.5%	26.2%	28.4%
Germany (FRG)	22.3	24.0	22.5
Sweden	18.8	21.8	20.8
United Kingdom	13.5	19.4	19.7

Source: OECD.

in 1960–1961; from then on, labor shortages made themselves felt increasingly as a restraint on growth. In this situation trade union resistance to the inflow of foreign workers weakened, and ever larger contingents of foreigners, mostly Yugoslavs and Turks, were admitted. Their number reached its absolute and relative peak in 1973 with 227,000 (8.7 percent of the employed labor force). As everywhere else, foreign workers filled the least attractive jobs in heavy construction, unskilled factory work, and services for tourism (see Table 6).

We round off this brief account of the overall economic performance with a few words about cyclical movement. In general, with the one significant exception mentioned below, business cycles in Austria followed rather closely the European pattern, being of short duration and leading only to a deceleration of growth without marked employment effects. Although the recession of 1957–1958 following the boom of the mid-1950s was quickly overcome, leading to another high in 1960, the period between the two following recessions of 1962 and 1967 was one of sluggish growth accompanied by high inflation. The malaise in the first place affected industrial investment and exports, causing a great deal of pessimism concerning the future prospects of the economy. The fear of chronic stagflation was more widespread among experts and businessmen. But in retrospect, there was a temporary maladaptation of the industrial structure to the rapid changes in demand that were taking place in the course of the increasing integration of the European and world economies; this could be identified as the root cause of this trough in the growth curve. Its dark forebodings were soon refuted by the course of events. From 1968 to well into 1974, the country

Table 6   Labor market

	1955	1960	1973	1978
Employees (1,000)	2.074	2,282	2,608	2,758
Foreign workers (1,000)			227	177
Rate of unemployment	5.4%	3.4%	1.2%	2.1%

Source: Hauptverband der österreichischen Sozialversicherungsträger and Bundesministerium für soziale Verwaltung.

experienced the longest boom in its history, bypassing the general recession of 1971–1972, which, though not especially severe, was felt in most European countries. In these two years Austria registered growth rates of 5.6 and 6.0 percent, compared with 3.2 and 3.7 percent in Germany, its most important trade partner. To the surprise of all, it was possible for the first time to break the link between the Austrian economy and the international cyclical movement. Evidently this miracle could not be repeated in the oil-shock crisis of the mid-1970s. But before we go into the story of these critical years, we will deal briefly with the problem of European integration as it affected Austria.

4   AUSTRIA AND EUROPEAN INTEGRATION

Integration was easily the most widely discussed issue confronting the country in the 1950s and 1960s. This is hardly surprising in a small country with a foreign trade share amounting to roughly one-third of its social product. For an industry traditionally habituated to high protective tariff barriers, the transition to an open economy was certainly fraught with danger. But the risk had to be taken if Austria did not want to forgo participating in the rapid progress of the international division of labor. At an early stage the first steps toward liberalization had to be taken in compliance with general international treaties (GATT and OECD). But the real problem arose when two integration blocks, EFTA and the Common Market (EEC), were forming in Europe.

Since the countries of the Common Market accounted for the bulk of Austria's foreign trade (roughly 60 percent of imports and 50 percent of exports), a strong export interest was ranged on the side of those favoring association with this block. Producers for the domestic market were just as naturally on the other side of the fence. Moreover, there were important political aspects to the matter. On many sides fears of German domination over the Austrian economy amounting to a cold *Anschluss* were expressed. Such a development would, it was feared, jeopardize the delicate balance of Austria's position between East and West based on the State Treaty of 1955. In this dilemma a dilatory course was chosen. In 1959 Austria joined the EFTA, whose member countries at that time accounted for only 12–13 percent of its foreign trade. However, with the beginning of negotiations between Great Britain and the EEC, the EFTA soon found itself in a state of impending dissolution, and the trend toward an all-European integrated market became irresistible. Thus Austria too approached the EEC in the early 1960s seeking a special arrangement compatible with its neutral status. After a whole decade of difficult negotiations, agreement was finally reached in 1972, providing for a gradual lowering of tariff barriers to the point of zero in 1977. The treaty covered generally manufactured goods with the exception of a few "sensitive goods" for which the transition period was extended. (Later, provisions for some agricultural products were added, but Austria remained outside the EEC Agricultural Market.)

The final step in the integration process, opening Austrian markets to the competition of the strongest industrial powers in Europe, luckily fell into the period of the "long boom." The structural difficulties that had caused so much concern in the mid-1960s were quickly overcome, or at any rate overcompensated for, in the climate of a strong export-led expansion. To be sure, imports grew even faster, leading in the late 1970s to a large deficit in the foreign balance. But this development had—as we shall see presently —specific causes not directly connected with free trade.

Integration certainly speeded up the modernization of industrial and export structure, which had been taking place slowly in the 1960s. Thus the share of higher-order industrial goods—machinery, industrial equipment, and finished consumer goods—in Austrian exports rose from 18 percent (1955) to 42 percent (1978), accompanied by a corresponding decline of the share of raw materials and semifinished goods from 76 to 43 percent in the same period. There were also marked changes in the regional distribution of exports reflecting the two-step integration process. Whereas in the EFTA period the export share of this region more than doubled (from 13 to 29 percent), it fell again after 1973, but remained higher than before. The share of the Common Market countries moved in reverse order, first falling sharply (from 49 to 39 percent) and then recovering about half of the loss. It should be noted that exports to the Eastern countries, always considered of great importance, were maintained more or less throughout at the same level, of about 13–15 percent.

5   MAIN FEATURES OF ECONOMIC POLICY

The basic problem of postwar economic management was of course the same in Austria as anywhere else in the Western world, namely the trade-off between employment, inflation, and the balance of payments—the famous "magic triangle." Creeping inflation began soon after the stabilization crisis of 1953 and became a matter of principal concern in the 1960s, when the inflation rate rose higher, threatening to surpass that of Austria's major trade partners. To cope with this problem, fiscal and monetary restrictions were imposed from time to time, with the usual doubtful effects. Yet, though the emphasis varied between different periods and governments, on the whole the fear of inflation never dominated economic policy in Austria as much as it did, say, in Germany or the USA.

5.1   Priority for Full Employment

If it is true, as has been sometimes said, that German inflation fears can be traced back to the traumatic experience of the galloping inflation of the early 1920s, in Austrian psychology the trauma of the enormous unemployment of the 1930s seems to have played a larger part. However that may be, it is a fair generalization to say that Austrian economic policy has given priority consistently to full employment over price stability, whatever the fashionable doctrines of the moment may have been. The socialist government, in power since 1970, explicitly adheres to this principle as a keystone of its entire program. In keeping with this Keynesian bias of policy, there has also generally been a marked preference for fiscal over monetary instruments of countercyclical steering. Among Austrian economists too, especially among those acting as advisers to the government, Keynesianism has retained a stronger hold in the face of the monetarist counterattack than in most other countries.

The success of this policy hinged ultimately on the support it received from the institutions of "social partnership" that had been established on a permanent basis in the late 1950s. The formal procedures for wage and price control set up in this framework are described elsewhere in this volume. Here it must suffice to point out the importance of the social climate engendered by this unique form of consensual conflict settlement for keeping inflationary cost rises in bounds without resorting to the remedy of unemployment. Specific labor market policies, such as subsidies for retraining and relocating workers set free by the closing down of operations in nonprofitable enterprises or branches of production, have also been applied fairly extensively. But measures of this type, although useful in raising the mobility of labor, cannot affect the level of employment significantly.

5.2   Crisis Management since 1974

In concluding this brief survey, special treatment must be given to the difficult period that set in with the world-wide recession in the aftermath of the oil shock and the breakdown of the Bretton Woods system. The fact that Austria managed to maintain high employment as well as relative price stability in these years, which elsewhere were haunted by rising unemployment and/or inflation, has aroused a great deal of international attention. The initial shock hit Austria no less severely than other countries, though with a certain delay. In 1974 the inflation rate rose to 9.5 percent, still below the OECD average of 13.5 percent, but uncomfortably high. Belying all forecasts of continuing prosperity, the boom came to an abrupt end; 1975 brought a negative growth rate for the first time since 1953, causing an unexpected jump in the budget deficit. Yet, in spite of the simultaneous fiscal and inflation problems, the Socialist government decided on a course of further deficit spending. To cope with the threat of being drawn into the international inflationary trend, it was decided to maintain the exchange rate of the schilling tied to the German mark, regardless of mounting pressure from exporters calling for devaluation and without paying heed to the well-meaning advice of international authorities. This was a risky policy, which needed full trade-union backing on the wage front. The government could rely more surely on receiving this backing, since the old habits of social partnership were now reinforced by the political loyalty of the unions to the Socialist leadership—an experience radically different from that of the British Labour Government in the same period. Thus the rate of wage increases was brought down successively, along with the falling inflation rate; there were only slight—or no—real wage gains for a few years. As a result, Austria became the most stable country after Germany and Switzerland, with an inflation rate of only 3.6 percent in 1978, compared with the OECD average of 9.3 percent. At the same time employment was kept high, not only by fiscal demand management and public investment but also by selective supports of various kinds. For this purpose subsidies to enterprises in temporary difficulties were combined with the more generous use of facilities provided under the Labor Market Act (retraining of labor). In the Nationalized Industries redundant labor was kept on temporarily, especially to avoid dismissals in the steel industry during the international steel slump. Also some "export of unemployment" took place as the number of foreign workers was reduced, so as to diminish their share in the total labor force from over 8 to about 6 to 7 percent. But these were only supplementary remedies which would have been exhausted quickly if the overall strategy had not been, on the whole, highly successful —a fact the more remarkable in view of the specially strong influx of young people into the labor market in this period.

On the other side of the balance sheet the price of this strategy cannot be ignored. From 1972 to 1978 the budget deficit increased in nominal terms sevenfold to over 50 billion AS (Austrian schillings), in relative terms from a little over 7 to nearly 20 percent of total expenditure. The national debt rose, even so, to only about 200 billion AS, still a moderate amount compared to that of many other countries. But the psychological effects of the steep rise in the deficit, together with the growing load of servicing the debt, set limits to further fiscal expansion. To reduce the deficit—or, at any rate, to prevent its further increase—became imperative. Another phenomenon darkening the horizon in the mid-1970s was the unfavorable development of the balance of trade and "invisibles" (balance on current account) in spite of a steady rise in tourism and consistently high export gains. This was partly a direct consequence of prosperity, since Austrian consumers tend to spend a disproportionate part of rising incomes on imported goods, especially motor cars. In part, of course, the rising oil bill added to the trouble. In 1977 the deficit reached 49 billion AS. Though it fell considerably in the two following years (to 22 and 26 billion respectively) the existence of a long-run structural problem had to be faced. Thus another factor restraining expansive policies came into the picture.

Though up to the time of writing, these difficulties could be kept within manageable bounds by various expedients, the limits of the special "Austro-Keynesian" practice of crisis management have become apparent. A small country with such a high degree of dependence on its foreign trade cannot, of course, remain an island of stability in an unstable world.

5.3 Problems and Perspectives

The difficulties indicated above arise not only on a technical plane. The rapid changes the world has undergone in the last decade have everywhere raised questions outside the traditional concerns of economists and economic policy makers, whether Keynesian, monetarist, or other. It is neither possible nor necessary to list here in detail all these new issues that bedevil the governments of the Western world, more baffling every day. It suffices to point to the energy crisis, the growing awareness of environmental restraints, and the increasing political instability in wide parts of the world. All of these tend to reinforce the stagnation tendencies, that for a variety of economic reasons, seem to have made their appearance on the international scene since 1973–1974. Thus, according to almost unanimous expert opinion, the Western world must prepare for an extended period of slow growth. From these deeper-lying roots of the present social and economic problems Austria is not and cannot be exempt.

To begin with the question of energy, Austria is dependent at present for over two-thirds of its energy requirements and 85 percent of its oil requirements on import. This dependence will increase, since its own oil wells are nearing exhaustion. Coal and bituminous gas are imported in large quantities, mostly from Eastern Europe and the Soviet Union. Austria's biggest asset in the field of conventional energy is hydroelectric power, where there are still some reserves for new capacity—unless blocked by environmental activism. As for nuclear power, Austria is so far the only country to have outlawed its use by legislative action after a referendum (1978) that denied permission to operate the completed nuclear plant at Zwentendorf. Although strong efforts are made at present to initiate another referendum overturning that decision, the outcome of this initiative is doubtful. Energy planning and energy saving must therefore have high priority in future policy making.

Further problems of industrial structure will appear with the accelerating shift of simpler manufacturing processes from Western countries to those of the Third World—already well under way. In spite of the great progress made in the past in the modernization of industry, Austria still has too large a sector of traditional manufactures, too small a basis in modern electronics and other "brain-intensive" productions. Here the consequences of long-standing neglect of research and development—notwithstanding considerable efforts in this direction in the recent past—will make themselves increasingly felt, as much as the persisting risk aversion of Austrian entrepreneurs.

One of the most difficult hurdles in the transition to slower growth, which seems in any case unavoidable, will probably arise in the social and political sphere. This readjustment will necessarily raise issues of income distribution, which will put a severe strain on the hitherto smoothly functioning instruments of conflict regulation. As long as the demands of all groups could be satisfied more or less proportionately out of the increase in social product, distributive shares remained—again more or less—constant. Dissatisfaction with the existing income distribution never reached a high pitch. This condition may change when the rising expectations of the various social groups can no longer be met in the same measure, in view of social considerations and the needs for public services on a growing scale. Redistribution policies will have to take effect that are bound to sharpen the edge of social conflict. Whether the problem-solving capacity of the present institutional system of Austria, with its built-in mechanisms of flexibility, will be adequate to these new challenges only time will tell. Evaluation of its past performance perhaps allows some hope that the Austrian model will prove workable even under the highly unpropitious conditions prevailing on the international economic scene on the threshhold of the 1980s.

Selected Bibliography

BACKGROUND MATERIAL (BEFORE 1945)
Brusatti, Alois, ed. *Die Habsburgermonarchie, 1848–1918.* Vol. I, *Die wirtschaftliche Entwicklung.* Wien, 1973.
Butschek, Felix. *Die österreichische Wirtschaft, 1938–1945.* Wien, 1978.
Gross, Nachum *Industrialization in Austria in the Nineteenth Century.* Berkeley, Calif., 1947.
Hertz, Friedrich. *The Economic Problem of the Danubian States.* London, 1947.
————. *Die Produktionsgrundlagen der österreichischen Industrie.* Wien, 1917.
März, Eduard. *Österreichische Industrie- und Bankenpolitik im Zeitalter Franz Joseph I.* Wien, 1968.
Otruba, Gustav. *Die österreichische Wirtschaft im 20. Jahrhundert.* Wien, 1968.
Rothschild, Kurt. *Austria's Economic Development Between the Wars.* London, 1947.

CONTEMPORARY AUSTRIA (SINCE 1945)
Ausch, Karl. *Licht und Irrlicht des österreichischen Wirtschaftswunders.* Wien, 1965.
Beirat für Wirtschafts-und Sozialfragen. *Die Landwirtschaft in der Industriegesellschaft.* Wien, 1968.
————. *Untersuchung des Preis- und Kostenauftriebs.* Wien, 1968.
————. *Zehn Jahre ERP in Österreich.* Wien, 1958.
Haberler, Gottfried. *Austria's Economic Development: A Mirror Picture of the World Economy.* Washington, D.C., 1980.

Kausel, Anton, et al. *Österreichs Volkseinkommen, 1913–1963.* Wien, 1965.
Koren, Stefan. Die Industrialisierung Österreichs—vom Protektionismus zur Integration. In Wilhelm Weber, ed., *Österreichs Wirtschaftsstruktur gestern-heute-morgen.* Berlin, 1961.
März, Eduard. *Österreichs Wirtschaft zwischen Ost und West.* Wien, 1965.
Rothschild, Kurt. Wurzeln und Triebkräfte der österreichischen Wirtschaftsstruktur. In Wilhelm Weber, ed., *Österreichs Wirtschaftsstruktur gestern-heute-morgen.* Berlin, 1961.
Seidel, Hans. *Struktur und Entwicklung der österreichischen Industrie.* Wien, 1978.
Weber, Wilhelm, Stefan Koren, and Karl Socher. *Die Verstaatlichung in Österreich.* Berlin, 1964.

CURRENT PUBLICATIONS

Arbeit und Wirtschaft. Österreichischer Gewerkschaftsbund und Arbeiterkammertag.
Monatsberichte des Instituts für Wirtschaftsforschung and *Statistische Übersichten.* In cooperation with Statistisches Zentralamt.
Quartalshefte der Gironzentrale. Girozentrale der österreichischen Sparkassen.
Wirtschaftspolitische Blätter. Bundeskammer der gewerblichen Wirtschaft.
Wirtschaft und Gesellschaft. Wiener Kammer für Arbeiter und Angestellte. Quarterly, since 1974.
Wirtschafts- und Sozialstatistisches Handbuch. Kammer für Arbeiter und Angestellte für Wien. Annually.

Modern Austria, pp. 141–54
Copyright © 1981 by SPOSS Inc. All rights reserved

5. THE ECONOMIC STRUCTURE

Felix Butschek

Member of the managing staff of the Austrian Institute of Economic Research

1 THE HISTORICAL DETERMINANTS OF AUSTRIA'S ECONOMIC STRUCTURE

An understanding of the structure and of the structural problems of the Austrian economy is possible only by reference to its historical development. Anything even remotely approaching continuity was granted Austria as little in the economic field as in its political history. To begin with, industrialization proceeded in a much more complicated manner than it did in most other Western and Central European countries. The Industrial Revolution, spreading east, west, and south from England, gradually took hold in each region's socioeconomic development. In this process the Austrian monarchy occupied a special position: of its diverse areas some had attained a level similar to that of Western and Central European countries (e.g. that portion that now constitutes the Federal Republic of Austria, as well as Bohemia and Moravia), whereas others resembled comparatively backward eastern and southern regions of Europe (Galizia, Bukovina, Dalmatia, Hungary). Although growth spread rapidly in the industrial centers, the monarchy as a whole lagged behind Western and Central European countries.

Nor did the monarchy identify with the role of an industrial country; but rather it identified with that of a partly industrialized, partly agricultural country, with many characteristics of the latter finding expression in narrow-minded, guild-bound policies internally and protectionism in foreign trade. Such foreign-trade policies could, of course, only be pursued in a country the size of the monarchy, which was self-sufficient in agricultural products and to some extent also in raw materials and fuel supplies. Industrial production was concentrated on the needs of the domestic market,

Translated by Fred Prager, Vienna.

9306-6403/81/0415-0141$01.50

whereas foreign trade aimed at regions where competitive pressures from Western Europe were less prevalent or where they could be counteracted by political influence. This meant that a considerable portion of exports went to the Southeast.

The result was an industrial structure with basic industries produced at comparatively high cost, and with a preponderance of consumer-goods industry. It also led to a fairly sharp division of labor between the comparatively highly industrialized portion of the country that is today the Federal Republic of Austria, also containing the capital city of Vienna, and the rest of the monarchy. The former supplied industrial goods and services, exchanging them for the agricultural products and fuel supplies from the latter.

The dissolution of the monarchy was accompanied by a fundamental rupture in the basic elements of economic existence. This Austria—the "leftover"—had suddenly become a tiny country. For such a state, conditions apply that are totally different from those that obtain in large countries. What used to be an internal flow of goods had suddenly become a problem of foreign trade. Gone were the days when Austria was self-supporting in its food supplies, in raw materials and in fuels. In the past, Austria could reckon on largely secure markets, whereas now not only was it exposed to free competition but also it had to struggle against the attempts of the successor states to secure autarky through the erection of customs barriers. The situation was further aggravated by the fact that Austrian industries were ill adapted to international competition; and they remained faithfully oriented toward their markets in the South and Southeast—or at least they tried to.

A consequence of this situation was, of course, the emergence of a structurally adverse balance of payments. True, in the beginning Austria experienced an uninterrupted upswing lasting until 1929. It compensated, at least in part, for the losses suffered after World War I. Agriculture and hydraulic energy generation were especially emphasized in this period. But this expansion, partly induced by inflation, did not suffice to eliminate the balance-of-payments deficit.

The multitude of unsolved economic problems was one of the reasons for the fact that the world-wide recession hit Austria with particular force. At the height of the depression in 1933 the Gross National Product had fallen to 81 percent of the level of 1913, and unemployment had passed the mark of 557,000, that is, 26 percent of wage and salary earners. In subsequent years the aim to contain the balance-of-payments deficit remained the primary goal of economic policy. This was indeed achieved in 1937—by means of a determinedly thorough restrictive policy, albeit at the cost of deep and persistent stagnation: Gross National Product rose by a mere 12 percent in real terms between 1933 and 1937, and unemployment was still 21.7 percent in that year. Agriculture alone could be partly shielded from the effects of the world recession by means of a comprehensive system of market controls and foreign-trade regulations.

The German occupation caused yet another deep break in the pattern of the Austrian economy. Austria was speedily integrated into the German economy in 1938, which meant adaptation of its formerly relatively liberal foreign trade to a restrictive system.

In the years between the two world wars Austrian foreign trade had gone through a slow and painful process of reorientation, away from its former traditional trading regions, toward the West. With the German occupation this changed at one stroke. Germany had urgent need of the unused Austrian reserves in raw materials, productive capacities, and labor reserves, and now a drastic reorientation of trade routes was set in motion. On the other hand, German economic policy did not confine itself to commercial policy measures: efforts were made to stimulate Austrian domestic demand by means of expanded spending, and this led to a precipitate increase of economic growth in 1938 and 1939.

The most lasting interventions into the Austrian economic structure resulted directly from measures related to rearmament and war economy. A number of major industrial installations were set up on Austrian territory because the National Socialist government assumed that Austrian territory would be well out of the way of future potential theaters of war and also because there were considerable unused capacities on hand—especially human resources. With the onset of the wartime bombing raids in Germany, the transfer to Austria of major industrial installations took on growing proportions. Despite heavy ravages in the last phases of the war, these investments were destined to exert a decisive impact on the Austrian industrial structure after the end of hostilities.

When the Austrian government after the war decided to rebuild these ruined installations, a number of consequences followed for the Austrian economy. The productive structure shifted to raw materials to a considerable degree; large-scale enterprises came to the fore and the economic potential of the western provinces (*Länder*) was more fully utilized. The forced integration into the German economy had brought a more decisive orientation toward the West generally. Although foreign-trade contacts had been reestablished in the immediate postwar period with the traditional Eastern trading partners, the division of Europe into political and economic blocs resulted in an almost complete severance of these contacts.

In spite of this renewed rupture and in the face of new conditions that were much worse than in 1919, the Austrian economy made an unexpectedly rapid comeback after World War II. The extensive damage resulting from the war could be rapidly repaired, thanks to the generous economic assistance offered by the United States. By 1949 the Gross National Product had already surpassed the level of 1937, and with the currency reform and stabilization of 1953 the ground had been prepared for the startling economic revival of the 1950s. This has been termed the Austrian economic miracle because the expansion of that period surpassed that of most of the OECD countries. Rapid growth continued—with few interruptions—right up to the onset of the oil crisis in 1975, and even that crisis has been mastered astonishingly well. Since then Austria has managed to maintain full employment and keep inflation in check.

In this period Austria succeeded in reducing the huge income differential in relation to other industrial countries which had resulted from stagnation in the interwar years. This is clearly confirmed by a comparison with the United States. In 1950, the gross national per capita income in the USA—calculated on the basis of the official exchange rate—surpassed its Austrian counterpart by 424 percent, and in 1960 by 215 percent; in 1970, the US lead had diminished to 140 percent, and in 1978 it was a mere 24 percent. Even taking into account the fluctuations in the exchange rate and in the demographic structure, these figures give an indication of how rapidly the Austrian economy was catching up.

This favorable development in income leads us to conclude that basically the Austrian economy has achieved the type of structure appropriate to a country in its position; i.e. the transition from a region serving the industrial and administrative needs of a semiagrarian major power to a highly industrialized small country has been successfully accomplished.

2 THE CHARACTERISTICS OF AUSTRIA'S ECONOMIC STRUCTURE

The economic structure of Austria today is basically that of an industrialized small country. In 1978 it produced a Gross Domestic Product of 845,000 million Austrian schillings, the equivalent of 57,900 million US dollars, or $7,700 per capita. The per capita income level is still below that of comparable European countries (Sweden, Norway, Denmark, the Netherlands, Belgium, Switzerland). The catching-up process described in the foregoing did not yet suffice completely to compensate the consequences of two world wars and of long-standing stagnation. To this result[1] agriculture and forestry contributed 4.8 percent, manufacturing 43.9 percent, and services 51.3 percent.

A high degree of economic interlocking exists with the outside world, as must be expected with a small country. In 1978, 34.8 percent of Gross Domestic Product was exported (exports in the broad sense, i.e. including services). However, the intensification of Austrian foreign trade and the removal of customs barriers and quota system obstacles was a process drawn out over several decades. The strict administrative regulations of postwar foreign trade were gradually removed after the schilling devaluation of 1953, and from that moment on Austria was exposed to international competition. European integration initiated powerful thrusts toward liberalization. Prompted by its policy of perpetual neutrality, Austria joined the more loosely organized economic bloc, the European Free Trade Association (EFTA).[2] This decision brought some burdens for the Austrian economy. Although Austrian exporters succeeded to a considerable extent in adjusting to the new markets in geographically often unfavorable regions, their gains in market shares in the EFTA region could not fully compensate for market losses in EEC markets. This again led to balance-of-payments deficits—for the first time since the liberalization of the 1950s. The slowing-down of the economy in the mid-1960s, the so-called structural crisis, was also connected with the European economic integration. Conversely, it is assumed that the conclusion of the trade agreement with the EEC—signaling once again a rerouting of trade but this time toward familiar markets —acted as one strong impulse among others for the sustained expansionist thrust of the early 1970s.

As a result, 52.6 percent of Austrian exports went to the EEC countries in 1978, and 72.3 percent went to the countries comprising the industrialized West. The historical and geographic components—and, to a lesser extent, political influences—find expression in a 13.7 percent share of trade with the East, this being the highest share of any Western country, excepting only Finland. Overseas trade, however (USA, 3.0 percent; Japan, 0.6 percent), and trade with the developing countries, including OPEC, remained rather limited, at 10.4 percent (Table 1).

The structural deficit of the balance of trade is usually compensated for by the favorable balance of services. This surplus is based on Austria's highly developed tourist traffic, which in 1978 accounted for 8.5 percent of the gross added value in all economic sectors.

Agriculture, once a major economic sector, has lost much of its former importance. After World War II Austria, in common with other industrial countries, subjected almost the entire agricultural market to fairly strict marketing controls; these were intended to preserve agriculture and to adjust the income of the rural population to the national average.

Labor productivity rose faster in agriculture than in industry; however, since the income elasticity of demand for food products is very low, there is strong pressure for migration from villages to towns. Although agricultural policy in the first postwar period aimed at maintaining the agricultural labor force, tolerating migration only as far as it proved inevitable, a change

Table 1   Regional structure of Austrian exports and imports, 1978 (in percent)

	Share in total exports	Share in total imports
Western industrialized countries[a]	72.3%	81.0%
Western Europe[b]	67.6	75.5
European free-trade association[c]	65.4	74.5
EEC 73	52.6	65.4
FRG	29.1	43.3
Italy	8.8	8.9
UK	4.9	3.1
EFTA 73	12.8	9.0
Switzerland	7.8	6.1
Southeastern Europe[d]	5.6	1.7
Overseas industrialized countries[e]	5.0	6.1
USA	3.0	3.0
Japan	0.6	1.8
Eastern Europe	13.7	8.8
OPEC	4.9	3.9
Developing countries without OPEC	5.5	4.9

[a] OECD countries.
[b] European OECD countries.
[c] EEC 73 and EFTA 73.
[d] Yugoslavia, Greece, Turkey, Spain.
[e] Overseas OECD countries and the Republic of South Africa.

occurred at the beginning of the 1960s. Now it became policy to encourage migration away from agriculture, for reasons of income parity. However, an income policy relying on price and marketing controls must contend with specific difficulties in Austria, because the country's agriculture is heterogeneous: there are very considerable differences in productivity between the Alpine foothills and the higher Alpine regions.[3]

The timber trade, too, is of considerable importance within the primary sector. Though the features of the land make timber production more difficult and hence more costly in Austria than in other well-wooded countries, Austria's situation and transportation facilities in relation to its main markets are favorable and promise some security of export outlets. The bulk of Austrian timber exports goes to Italy and South Germany.

Industry is the principal source of growth of the Austrian economy. It happens often in small countries that growth impulses originate abroad and are transmitted to the other branches of the economy by export industries. Between the two world wars the industrial sector had been particularly hard hit, its production growing more slowly than the total Gross National Product; by contrast, the opposite happened after World War II. However, this rapid expansion of industrial production did not proceed at a steady pace but in spurts. Up to the 1960s industry dominated economic development. Whereas industry had contributed only 17.6 percent to the total net social product in 1946 (at 1954 prices), compared with 21.9 percent in 1937, the net value added by industry to the social product reached its highest share in 1962, with 32.4 percent.

A period of sluggish growth followed in the middle of the decade. In this phase changes in international demand coincided with the effects of European integration, precipitating difficulties for Austria in its most important export markets. Only toward the end of the 1960s did a renewed growth thrust set in, lasting until the onset of the oil crisis. Of course another slowdown, especially in industrial development, did set in again after 1975, as happened in all industrialized countries.

It must be remembered that the Austrian industrial structure had undergone considerable changes in consequence of the German occupation. After reconstruction the country had at its disposal a comparatively highly developed primary (raw materials) sector—compared, that is, with its prewar state—and this sector participated fully in the West European postwar boom. But the traditional manufacturing and consumer goods industries also profited from the rapidly increasing demand. True, the expansion of demand went hand in hand with structural changes in demand, and this in turn necessitated changes in the industrial structure. Growth rates in production over the long term differed widely between various branches of industry. Chemicals took the lead, followed by electrical engineering, the woodworking industry, and paper processing. Leather processing and mining, including magnesite production, stagnated, and foundries and vehicle production achieved only modest growth rates. These differences in the speed of expansion brought about shifts in the shares of the respective branches of industry within total industrial production. The pace of these structural changes appears to advance quite rapidly. At any rate, investigations have shown that the changes in Austrian industrial structure during the last big boom of 1968 were more rapid than in the Federal Republic of Germany. Yet significant differences remain, especially compared with the Federal Republic of Germany (FRG). Thus Austrian industry shows a marked preponderance in textiles, foodstuffs, paper, quarries and ceramics, metal smelting, wood processing, and the garment industry, while vehicles, machinery, iron and steel products, chemicals, and electrical engineering have a lesser weight.

If, following Clark and Fourastié, we accept the idea that certain income levels (Gross Domestic Product per capita) go hand in hand with a particular structure of production, then a "standard structure" can be computed for each country. The findings of a study along these lines lead to the conclusion that about half the structural differences, compared with the FRG, originate in the difference in income and half in different specialization.

But this hypothesis must also be taken with some caution, for even accepting the connections between income and structure of production, the question remains whether the "standard structure" of such small countries as Austria, highly dependent on export trade, is not more dependent on external factors. Besides, the question remains whether the division by branches is not too crude, simply overlaying essential differences in product distribution.

At any rate, labor productivity in Austrian industry ranks below that of the FRG. In 1960 the latter surpassed Austrian per capita net social product by about 30 percent. However, Austria has succeeded since in reducing that difference to 20 percent, thanks to faster productivity growth. It is worth noting that this productivity differential is due not to differences in capital endowment—which, at any rate, is quantitatively equal in the two countries—but to differences in the utilization of capital goods.

The two large economic sectors—goods production and services—developed at a very different pace. Industrial development was the keynote of economic expansion during the first half of the 1950s. Employment in the tertiary sector grew much more slowly: its share in employment and its contribution to the domestic product—its value added—showed a relative decrease. Only after the first big wave of demand for material goods had been satisfied did the service sector begin to grow, as a number of services started to "return to normal." Thus tourist traffic began to expand during the second half of the 1950s, and at the same time banking and the insurance business regained importance in a measure appropriate to the general income level. Last but not least, personal services gained in importance.

Although the pace of employment increase in the tertiary sector diminished during the 1960s—surely in part a consequence of the onset of manpower shortages—the share of employment in services rose substantially, since, conversely, industry had stagnated since the middle of the decade. The question arose in Austria at that time whether a "premature aging" of the Austrian economy was in the offing, in view of the early and rapid decrease in the share of industry. Though the "longest-lasting boom of the postwar period" at the end of the 1960s was accompanied by renewed rapid expansion of production and employment in industry, employment in the service sector nevertheless showed a constant and more rapid increase. And when industry reverted to a state of stagnation after 1975, the tertiary sector continued its expansion uninterruptedly, though at a lower rate of growth.

The expansion was evident in the great majority of the service branches. Educational and health services took the lead, followed by legal and business services, tourism, and banking. But the chief elements of growth were the two large fields of retail trade and public services. In these sectors employment expanded at a pace that reduced the increase in productivity in the tertiary sector to a level well below its long-term average, thereby contributing substantially to the preservation of full employment in Austria.

3 THE STRUCTURAL PROBLEMS OF THE AUSTRIAN ECONOMY

Basically, a national economy is faced with structural problems when the supply structure no longer keeps pace with the demand in domestic and foreign markets. As a rule, defective adjustment is both signalized and penalized by the emergence of balance-of-payments difficulties. Such adjustment crises appear periodically in the Austrian economy, but they tend to differ both in cause and in the means employed to overcome them.

The whole history of the economy of the First Republic was characterized by just such an adjustment crisis. Actually, the adaptation of the supply structure of this remnant of the old monarchy to the structural needs of a small country was never successfully accomplished. True, the country succeeded in achieving an approximate equilibrium in its balance of payments in the last year before the German occupation—but at the price of deep and persistent stagnation. The government of those days tried to achieve that end by restricting domestic demand and by a hard-currency policy. The apparently successful adjustment brought unemployment to a quarter of the working population and stagnating consumption, while at the same time economic activity in the rest of the world showed a gradual return to normal in the late 1930s. Even a modest expansion of domestic demand would probably have led to a deficit in the balance on current account within a short time.

Initially the destruction caused by the war and the largely obsolete installations and equipment in plants and factories prevented the integration of the Austrian economy into the international markets at the end of World War II. But after reconstruction, after elimination of war damages and following liberalization of Austrian foreign trade initiated in 1953, it became apparent that the Austrian industrial structure—at prevailing exchange rates—had become adjusted to domestic and foreign demand. The stage was set for the phase of the "Austrian economic miracle," during which no serious balance-of-payments problems ever had to be faced.

The next adjustment crisis made its appearance about the middle of the 1960s, in the course of European integration. The international monetary system in force at that time (Bretton Woods) scarcely made it possible for

Austria to resort to devaluation to counteract the balance-of-payments deficits—but, at any rate, government policy showed no particular interest in doing so. Nor did the government show any inclination to achieve equilibrium in the balance of payments through a curb on domestic demand. Such global economic policies as were applied at that time emanated from employers' and employees' organizations acting in concert—the so-called social partnership (*Sozialpartnerschaft*)—that attempted to improve the competitiveness of Austrian industry by controlling costs by means of income policies. The government had already turned its attention to structural policies, trying to alter the industrial structure without interfering in exchange rates and unit costs.

It appears that all these measures bore fruit, for a spectacular boom set in toward the end of the 1960s, in the course of which the growth of industrial production surpassed that of many other industrialized countries. Only after the crisis of 1975 did balance-of-payments difficulties reappear. However, it is doubtful that these problems resulted solely from an insufficiently adapted production structure. The government's economic policy, geared primarily to the maintenance of full employment, may also have contributed to the problem by changing the framework of economic activities so as to impair the competitiveness of the Austrian industry.

As a first step, the attempt was made to counteract the setback of 1975 through an expansive fiscal policy, but efforts were made simultaneously to oppose the inflationary trend through a systematic hard-currency policy. Both goals were achieved; but since wage policy could only be adjusted to the new situation after 1975, the export industry came under heavy cost and profit pressure. Conversely, the deep depression prevalent abroad, combined with the rising exchange rate of the Austrian schilling, created favorable conditions for the import trade.

All these circumstances lead to the following conclusions: The First Republic was beset, so to speak, by "absolute" structural problems; the structural defects were of such scale and magnitude that adjustments were virtually unattainable. In the Second Republic, on the other hand, the situation was quite different, and only "relative" structural crises were to be met. Basically, industry was extraordinarily dynamic. It proved, in the end, to be the true agent of the "miracle": it grew faster than did its counterpart in most other industrialized countries. Structural crises made their appearance mostly following external impacts, or on occasions when economic policies had for some particular reason temporarily impaired the competitive position of Austrian industry. But from this it follows that Austrian industry is basically capable of sufficiently rapid change. Its structure has undergone quicker adjustments since the middle of the 1960s than has the industry of the FRG. Such conditions as were prevalent in the mid-1960s, and again after 1975, merely required uncommonly quick structural adjustments.

This is also how the recent discussions on structural policies in Austria must be viewed, i.e. as an ambitious attempt to create an industrial and economic structure capable of meeting the most vigorous challenges; and in this respect the FRG and Switzerland must, to a certain extent, be considered models.

Of course, this realization should not obscure the undoubtedly existing problems in the Austrian economic structure. Weak enterprises are often kept going by means of subsidies from public funds, and too few such enterprises in both the private and the nationalized sector were shut down, particularly during the last big boom. It is equally certain that political considerations delayed needed adjustments in some fields immediately under public ownership. Keeping totally superfluous and loss-producing branch railway lines operative is only one glaring example.

One grave charge is that Austrian industry conducts too little research under its auspices; and this is somewhat due to its structure. The comparatively high share of traditional consumer-goods industries has a retarding effect on the research expenditure average. It would seem, on the other hand, that particularly in these fields enterprises can survive against competition from the developing countries only if they specialize in outstanding quality or design. At any rate, the field of research needs to be analyzed in depth, even though Austrian industry has largely succeeded in remaining competitive despite its backwardness in this area.

The thesis of a "premature aging" of the Austrian economy, i.e. the overproportional growth of its tertiary sector, must be viewed from a similar angle. To begin with, there are few criteria to assess this phenomenon with. Econometric surveys have shown that the services ratio in Austria, despite vigorous growth in recent years, is by no means higher than is concordant with the general economic level of the country.

But, in principle, what applies to industry applies to the service sector too. If it accords with the demand structure, then it accords with the structure of a small industrialized country. An overproportional services sector would in the end also be expressed in balance-of-payments problems. It would mean by implication that too few goods are produced to cover domestic demand and to compensate for imported goods through the country's own exports.

Of course, such considerations do not nullify the question whether this expansion was sensible—but this is something other than "premature aging." Such problems arise from the fact that a portion of these services—that is, the public services—are only in part offered on the market. They are mainly public goods, paid for out of taxes. The OECD surveys have pointed out that governments apparently lose control over the rapid rise of costs for educational and health services; and in the long run the question will no doubt arise whether public services should be allowed to continue expanding at the same rate as in the past. But in the short term these problems will have to be handled with great caution in Austria because they have contributed in no small measure to the maintenance of full employment, and since, at least until the middle of the 1980s, a considerable increase in the potential labor force must be reckoned with.

In agriculture, despite enormous changes during the past thirty years, a level appropriate to our "standard" small country has not been reached. No doubt the disparity in incomes is a general problem that farmers of Western industrial countries have to contend with; and the size of the labor force in farming is decreasing everywhere. But Austria still seems to lag in this respect (see Table 2). The proportion of the labor force in any sector in Western industrial small countries appears to be equal to the sector's share in Gross Domestic Product; yet Austrian agriculture requires twice the labor to produce its share in domestic product.

Table 2 Share of the labor force in agriculture and share of agriculture in Gross Domestic Product (in percent)

	Year	Share of economically active person	Year	Share in GDP
Austria	1976	10.6%	1976	5.3%
	1977	9.9	1977	4.8
	1978	9.5	1978	4.8
FRG	1977	7.8	1977	2.9
France	1977	9.7	1976	5.2
Italy	1977	15.9	1977	8.7
Netherlands	1977	6.3	1977	4.7
Belgium	1977	3.3	1977	2.7
Luxemburg	1977	5.9	1976	5.0
UK	1977	2.7	1977	2.8
Ireland	1977	23.1	1976	17.5
Denmark	1977	9.1	1976	6.9
EEC (9)	1977	8.2	1977	4.5
USA	1977	3.7	1976	2.9
Sweden	1977	6.1	1976	5.0
Switzerland	1977	8.5		

Source: OECD, Labor force statistics, 1966–1977, and National Accounts, 1976; EEC, *Agrarstatistisches Jahrbuch, 1974–1977*, and *Gesamtrechnungen der Landwirtschaft*.

Even taking into consideration the possible effects of tourism, the low productivity of Austrian agriculture is surprising. True, it must be accepted that the conditions of agricultural production are geographically unfavorable in Austria. But apart from this, the problem needs to be further investigated, since the share in Gross Domestic Product is calculated on the basis of current prices, and these are dependent on the type and extent of market regulation. But it may be that the conserving policy after the world economic crisis has preserved the work force of Austrian agriculture at a higher level than would be appropriate to a small Western country. At any rate, the same relation prevails in the FRG. Be that as it may, further migration from the country is at present rather limited in view of the state of the labor market now and probably until the middle of the 1980s.

With this enumeration of the structural problems, it is not intended to give the impression that Austria is suffering from economic malaise. Problems of this kind are encountered in every country—and many countries might consider themselves fortunate if all they had to face were problems like those confronting Austria. At all events, the period since World War II is an important historic epoch: after the turbulent upheavals of the past, Austria has now consolidated its economic structure, in keeping with the needs of a highly developed Western industrialized small country. It has found its identity.

Notes

1. Without considering indirect taxes, import duties, and bank service charges.
2. See also März & Szecsi in this volume.
3. See also Wohlschlägl in this volume.

Selected Bibliography

Bayer, K. Charakteristika der österreichischen Industriestruktur. *Monatsberichte des Österreichischen Institutes für Wirtschaftsforschung,* No. 8, 1978.
Bayer, K., J. Skolka, and J. Stankovsky. Structural Adjustments of Austrian Industry to Changing Patterns of International Division of Labour (hektographiert). Wien, 1979.
Butschek, F. *Die Österreichische Wirtschaft 1938 bis 1945.* Wien, 1978.
————. Umschichtungen in der Struktur der Erwerbstätigen. *Monatsberichte des Institutes für Wirtschaftsforschung,* No. 2, 1970.
————. Dienstleistungssektor und Vollbeschäftigung. *Monatsberichte des Österreichischen Institutes für Wirtschaftsforschung,* No. 10, 1978.
Fink, Krisztina M. *Die österreichisch-ungarische Monarchie als Wirtschaftsgemeinschaft.* München, 1968.
Gross, N. Austrian Industrial Statistics, 1880–85 and 1911–13. *Zeitschrift für die gesamten Staatswissenschaften,* February 1968.
————. Industrialization in Austria in the Nineteenth Century. Dissertation. Berkeley, Calif., 1966.
————. Die Stellung der Habsburgermonarchie in der Weltwirtschaft. In A. Wandruszka and P. Urbanitsch, eds., *Die Habsburgermonarchie, 1848–1918,* Bd. I. Wien, 1973.

154   BUTSCHEK

Hertz, F., *The Economic Problem of the Danubian States.* London, 1947.
———. *Die Produktionsgrundlagen der österreichischen Industrie vor und nach dem Kriege.* Wien, 1917.
Kausel, A., N. Nemeth, and H. Seidel. *Österreichs Volkseinkommen 1913 bis 1963.* Wien, 1965.
Koren, Stefan. Die Industrialisierung Österreichs—vom Protektionismus zur Integration. In W. Weber, ed., *Österreichs Wirtschaftsstruktur gestern-heute-morgen.* Berlin, 1961.
———. Sozialisierungsideologie und Verstaatlichungsrealität in Österreich. In W. Weber, ed., *Die Verstaatlichung in Österreich.* Berlin, 1964.
———. Struktur und Nutzung der Energiequellen Österreichs. In W. Weber, ed., *Österreichs Wirtschaftsstruktur gestern-heute-morgen.* Berlin, 1961.
März, E. *Österreichische Industrie- und Bankpolitik in der Zeit Franz Josephs I.*—Am Beispiel der k.k. privilegierten Österreichischen Creditanstalt für Handel und Gewerbe. Wien, 1968.
Meihsl, P. Die Landwirtschaft im Wandel der politischen und ökonomischen Faktoren. In W. Weber, ed., *Österreichs Wirtschaftsstruktur gestern—heute—morgen.* Berlin, 1961.
Puwein, W. Arbeitskräfte in der Land- und Forstwirtschaft. *Monatsberichte des Österreichischen Institutes für Wirtschaftsforschung,* No. 8, 1975.
Rothschild, K. W. Wurzeln und Triebkräfte der Entwicklung der österreichischen Wirtschaftsstruktur. In W. Weber, ed., *Österreichs Wirtschaftsstruktur gestern-heute-morgen.* Berlin, 1961.
Rudolph, R. L. Quantitative Aspekte der Industrialisierung in Cisleithanien 1848–1914. In A. Wandruszka and P. Urbanitsch, eds., *Die Habsburgermonarchie, 1848–1918,* Bd. I. Wien, 1973.
Schneider, M. Die Bezugs- und Absatzstruktur der Land- und Forstwirtschaft und der Agrarkomplex in Österreich. *Monatsberichte des Österreichischen Institutes für Wirtschaftsforschung,* No. 8, 1973.
———. Die Land- und Forstwirtschaft, 1980–1985. *Monatsberichte des Österreichischen Institutes für Wirtschaftsforschung,* No. 5, 1975.
Schausberger, N. *Der Griff nach Österreich.* Wien, 1978.
———. *Rüstung in Österreich.* Wien, 1970.
Schwödiauer, E. Der tertiäre Sektor in Österreich. *Monatsberichte des Österreichischen Institutes für Wirtschaftsforschung,* No. 2, 1971.
Seidel, H. *Struktur und Entwicklung der österreichischen Industrie.* Wien, 1978.
Tichy, G. Zahlungsbilanz- und beschäftigungsrelevante Strukturprobleme von Industrie und Gewerbe sowie Ansatzpunkte zu ihrer Überwindung (hektographiert). Wien, 1979.

Modern Austria, pp. 155–71

6. DEVELOPMENT AND PROBLEMS OF AUSTRIAN INDUSTRY

Ferdinand Lacina

Chief of the Staff of the Chancellor (Kabinettschef)

INDUSTRIAL DEVELOPMENT POST-1918

One of the main causes for doubt in the viability of "residual" Austria—the rump of Austria-Hungary that was left over after World War I—was the feebleness of its industry. Among the weak points was the disequilibrium in productive structure: an absence of important branches and the preponderance of certain others. A further weakness was the concentration of the country's industrial potential within certain selected regions: in Vienna and adjoining zones in the east; in Upper Styria; and in the province at the western tip of the Republic, in Vorarlberg.

The dismemberment of the Austro-Hungarian Monarchy had dealt the industrial structure of the whole region a heavy blow. The reorganization of enterprises on the basis of the new national states meant a tearing asunder of interconnected productions; the existing system of work specialization and division of labor was destroyed. Austrian industry lost a considerable portion of its network of branches and the bulk of its domestic markets.

These handicaps virtually prevented the country from benefiting from the short-lived postwar boom from 1925 to 1928. Potential investors, the major banking houses in particular, fought shy of the risk of making long-term investments in the industrial field because of the unstable political conditions of the 1920s with their constantly recurring social conflicts. The institutional investors would only consider short-term credits. Considerable portions of the means of production came under the effective control of foreign investors. This happened as early as 1919 in the case of Austria's largest enterprise, the iron and steel producer Alpine Montan. Many Austrian affiliates of foreign companies were reduced to an auxiliary role, later

Translated by Fred Prager, Vienna

9306-6403/81/0415-0155$01.50

to remain partially idle or finally to be shut down in the course of the subsequent world economic crisis. This was one of the causes for the severity and long duration of the crisis that hit Austria.

Other explanations may be found in the field of economic policy. The hard-currency policy imposed on Austria in 1922 in connection with the reconstruction of Austrian finances by an international loan[1] hampered the efforts to compensate the loss of protected domestic markets by the capture of new markets abroad. The branches geared to domestic demand were hit by restrictive budget policies and the general deflationary course pursued by the Republic's conservative governments. On top of all this, the collapse of the banking system hampered industrial recovery—both indirectly and directly—since a large number of the major industrial enterprises were under the direct control of the banks. The era of the First Republic was thus characterized by stagnation in the industrial sector. New industrial impulses became operative following Austria's annexation by Nazi Germany through the country's integration into the German war economy. New industries—steel, chemicals, aluminum—came into being under the aegis of large German corporations, in the course of the latters' expansionist drive to the east. Considerable capacities for the manufacture of armaments and munitions were switched to Austria, where they would be less easily accessible to Allied bombing attacks than in the industrial centers of Germany.

RECONSTRUCTION AND NATIONALIZATION AFTER 1945

Conditions for reconstruction of Austrian industry were more difficult in 1945 than they had been after World War I. Following the German occupation, most of the larger enterprises had been combined with German corporations. At the end of the war such plants were put under the control of the military authorities in the Soviet zone. Oil production and processing came under the Soviet Mineral Oil Administration; the other industrial installations were administered by the so-called USIA (Uprawlenije Sowjetskowo lmushtshestwa Awstrii, Administration of Soviet Properties in Austria). Until the end of the occupation in 1955, a considerable portion of the capacities in the traditional industrial regions of Vienna and Lower Austria remained outside the sphere of influence of the Austrian government.

The decision to nationalize certain industrial undertakings by unanimous vote in the Austrian parliament in 1946 was an attempt to reorganize enterprises that had been abandoned by their former owners, and to bring a considerable part of the basic industries and important major enterprises in the manufacturing sector, staffed by more than 56,000 employees, under Austrian control. Within ten years the labor force in these enterprises was to increase to nearly 100,000. With the simultaneous nationalization of the big banks, which held a great deal of industrial stock, a further significant number of enterprises was brought under indirect state control.

Only some of the nationalization measures could be put into effect at once, while others were vetoed by the Soviets and had to be postponed. The partition of Austria into Western and Soviet zones of occupation was to have important consequences for the country's regional development. American aid under the Marshall Plan bore fruit mainly in regions that had formerly been barely touched by industrialization, whereas the traditional industrial centers remained at a disadvantage, suffering by the dismantling of technical installations and handicapped by lack of investments until 1955.

Two factors operated in support of the bold decision to reconstruct the capacities that had been created during the German occupation and to integrate them into the Austrian industrial structure. They were the generous injections of investment capital from Marshall Plan aid funds and the postwar boom that spread to Austria, later to be reinforced by the Korea boom, which offered special export chances for the basic industries.

The nationalization measures were meant to form part of a system of comprehensive economic planning in terms of politico-economic concepts of the immediate postwar era. In actual fact, economic planning fell far short of all such ambitious imaginings. Sectoral planning did actually extend to the fields of coal and steel, for these alone did actually become totally subject to state control.

Postwar inflation was brought under control, thanks to agreements on wages and prices entered into between the "social partners," i.e. management and labor unions. The substantial devaluation of the schilling improved the export chances of industry, which had become the motor of the country's economic development. The nationalized state enterprises were the chief agents and promotors of this expansion, but numerous medium-size, privately owned enterprises, including some founded only after 1945, were equally instrumental in this economic upswing.

Of this expansion an impressive balance sheet can be drawn up: by 1951 industrial production had already surpassed the level of 1937 by two-thirds. The paper and textile industries had by then narrowly attained the value of prewar production, but the metal foundries produced three times the prewar output in 1951, whereas the chemical industry, mining, and the building materials industry had more than doubled prewar production.

THE STATE TREATY—EUROPEAN INTEGRATION

With the conclusion of the State Treaty of 1955, the nationalization measures became fully effective; enterprises employing a labor force of more than 25,000 employees were newly integrated into the nationalized sector, and—an event of the first magnitude—the crude oil and natural gas fields of Lower Austria, the oil refinery of Schwechat, and the network of filling stations in the eastern part of Austria were absorbed into state ownership. The nationalized Austrian Mineral Oil Administration Corporation (Österreichische Mineralöl Verwaltung, ÖMV) developed the site at Schwechat just outside Vienna into a large-scale refinery, while the small and obsolescent refineries, which had reverted to the possession of the international oil corporations, closed down. This, and the speedy development of a pipeline network, gave the nationalized petroleum industry a strong position. Even today it owns the only refinery in the country; it is the most important producer of oil and gas, and it controls more than a quarter of the country's network of filling stations.

The Austrian foreign trade structure after World War II was deeply affected by the political changes in Eastern Europe. Whereas approximately 28 percent of exports had gone to Eastern Europe before the war, such exports amounted to a mere 10 percent in 1955 (imports from Eastern Europe in 1937 were 32 percent, and in 1955 were 9 percent). Trade with the West, conversely, had grown significantly. In 1937, around 44 percent of exports had gone to the five most important Western European countries (Germany, Italy, France, the United Kingdom, and Switzerland); in 1955 this figure had risen to 55 percent. The Federal Republic of Germany alone bought a quarter of Austrian exports, and more than 35 percent of imports came from that country (in 1937, only 16 percent of imports came from undivided Germany).

The founding of the EEC in 1957 and the failure to create an all-European free-trade zone endangered the market position of Austrian industry in its most important markets, since Austrian entry into the EEC was not considered possible in view of the Austrian declaration of neutrality. Under these circumstances the establishment of the "small free-trade zone," the EFTA (European Free Trade Association), comprising seven European countries—the United Kingdom, Sweden, Denmark, Norway, Switzerland, Portugal, and Austria—brought temporary relief. It presented Austria with an opportunity to compensate for the loss of market shares in the EEC through considerable gains in a few markets that had up until now been less intensively cultivated, such as the United Kingdom and Scandinavia. But the trade balance with the EEC countries deteriorated dramatically after 1957. The deficit in trade of goods with the six founding members of the Common Market rose from around 2.5 billion schillings in 1957 to approximately 13 billion schillings in 1965. As a consequence of the increasing effects of being discriminated against in important markets, Austrian industries suffered an adaptive period of weakness in the 1960s.

The decrease of the extraordinarily vigorous industrial growth, from almost 7 percent, on the average, from 1956 to 1960, to 5 percent in the period 1961–1965, can be ascribed to this development. The rapid expansion of industry after the conclusion of the State Treaty was bolstered by massive fiscal encouragement of investment activities; a revaluation of capital assets as shown in balance sheets brought a general relief of tax burdens; and regulations permitting fast depreciation of investments, introduced in 1955, brought a strong incentive to invest. According to these regulations one-fifth of the costs of buildings and 40 percent of the costs of machinery could be written off in the year of acquisition. (Higher scales—25 percent and 60 percent, respectively—were allowed in regions at a disadvantage through Soviet occupation.) That system, amounting in fact to the granting of a rollover tax credit in case of constant investment, remains in force to this day, with some changes. But the most far-reaching effects were felt when the measures were first introduced—when these interest-free "tax credits" considerably strengthened the self-financing ability of the enterprises. In view of the ownership structure of Austrian industry, where broadly spread ownership of equity is unknown, that measure was of strategic significance in financing the industrial expansion.

THE INFLOW OF FOREIGN CAPITAL

After the conclusion of the state treaty a substantial change occurred in the attitude of foreign investors toward Austria. The political risk of a threatening partition of the country after the German pattern had now been removed. Austria offered the further advantage of possessing a well-trained and—by Western European standards—comparatively cheap labor force. The quickly expanding domestic market and Austria's traditional position as a trading partner of Eastern European countries may be identified as further motivating factors for the potential investor. And the division of Western markets caused many enterprises in Common Market countries— West German firms in particular—to found affiliated firms in Austria to promote their commercial activities within the EFTA region.

A preliminary survey made in 1961 disclosed that about 17 percent of the joint stock companies' nominal capital was owned abroad. The foreign investors' main engagement was in the electrical industry, in chemicals, paper-making, and machine-building industries. The most important investing countries were the USA, with more than a quarter of investments, followed by Great Britain (15 percent), Switzerland (14 percent), the Benelux countries (13 percent), and the FRG (9.5 percent).

Until the end of the 1960s foreign shares in nominal capital increased to 22.5 percent. In 1969, more than a sixth of the labor force in industry worked for enterprises predominantly controlled from abroad, and if minority participations are included, almost a quarter of those engaged in industry can be counted in this group. At that time the number of employees in enterprises under foreign control had already surpassed those in nationalized industries. It is noteworthy that German investments had increased sevenfold, making the FRG the most important foreign investor in Austria, with more than a quarter of the investments. The FRG had thus pushed the USA into second place, with Switzerland following in third place.

The Austrian policy toward penetration by foreign capital may be characterized as extremely liberal. During the 1970s, there were numerous takeovers, and quite a number of new enterprises were established by foreign interests. The net annual inflow of foreign direct investments increased until 1974 to a high mark of 3200 million schillings. The latest available data show approximately 30 percent of the industrial labor force to be engaged in enterprises under foreign influence. Other areas of foreign interest are the commercial sector, especially retail trade, and insurance companies.

Besides nationalized enterprises and affiliates of the nationalized banks, the branches and subsidiaries of the multinational corporations are counted among the largest Austrian industrial enterprises. Among the most important of these latter are affiliates of the Western European corporations of Siemens, Philips, Unilever, AEG, Brown-Boveri, MAN, Arbed, Nestlé, and Hoechst. From among leading American corporations, quite a number, e.g. General Motors, Exxon, Ford, and IBM, have been represented only by marketing organizations up until now. ITT, Mobil, and CPC have established manufacturing companies in Austria, and General Motors has recently begun construction work on a motor engine and gear unit factory in Vienna.

It may be said that Austria is among the European countries with an above-average foreign capital share in the industrial sector. But the engagement of American corporations remains modest, compared with the Western European average.

LEVELING OFF OF INDUSTRIAL GROWTH—THE QUESTION OF STRUCTURE

The leveling off of industrial growth, the decline of the industrial labor force, and stagnation of industrial investment in the 1960s—signs of a medium term adjustment process in Austrian industry and of the intensification of international competitive pressures—triggered an intensive debate on the problem of structure. Economic policy focused increasingly on industry. Export promotion was intensified in this period, through guarantees, favorable credits, etc, and new instruments were instituted toward the end of the 1960s for promotion of research and development, as well as for promoting risk capital investments through state guarantees.

Considering the quickly advancing international concentration of capital, the comparatively small size and limited potency of the Austrian enterprises was identified as one of the competitive disadvantages of Austrian industry. The government undertook to counteract this deficiency by a comprehensive reorganization of its industrial participation. A holding company was founded for the Nationalized Industries, charged with the task of combining and concentrating enterprises in identical or related fields. During the first half of the 1970s the two large crude steel producers, VÖEST and Alpine-Montan, were incorporated to form the VÖEST-ALPINE AG., and the high-grade-steel producers, amalgamated into the VEW (Vereinigte Edelstahlwerke), were affiliated to the former combine. There were similar reorganizations in the fields of nonferrous metal enterprises, and nationalized enterprises in the field of petroleum and chemicals started to cooperate.

THE SECOND WAVE OF INDUSTRIALIZATION, 1969–1974

Thanks to the vigorous European boom at the beginning of the 1970s, the period of weakness in Austrian industry was overcome. The following slackening of demand in foreign markets due to recessive tendencies in Western Europe in 1972–1973 could be held off by a strong self-sustaining expansion of the Austrian economy, making those five years a period of uninterrupted, powerful growth. Industrial production underwent increases on a scale last experienced during the 1950s. With a share of 28.3 percent in real Gross National Product, industry achieved its highpoint; nominal investment in industry doubled in the period 1969–1974.

STRUCTURAL CHANGE IN INDUSTRY

If we examine industrial growth by branches, we find that Austrian industry developed in close conformity with the international pattern of change (see Table 1). Chemical industry took the lead, with an annual increase, in real terms, of an average 9 percent over the preceding ten years, followed by electrical engineering. However, two important growth industries are totally unrepresented, automobile and aircraft production. Austria also lags badly in the field of advanced electronics.

The Austrian government has been engaged in negotiations with numerous automobile manufacturers abroad, attempting to persuade them to initiate production in Austria. These efforts may be entering a successful stage. We have already mentioned General Motors' undertaking to build an engine factory in Vienna. Steyr-Daimler-Puch, a corporation that had been engaged in the independent manufacture of automobiles before World War II and that produced minicars in Austria in cooperation with Fiat as late as the 1960s, has entered into two joint ventures recently; in Graz, the firm is making cross-country jeep-type cars, and in Steyr a motor engine plant is being constructed, in cooperation with the German BMW (Bayrische Motoren-Werke), where engines will be built that are based on an Austrian development of a fuel-saving diesel engine. The French firm of Renault has built a small feeder plant in Styria in cooperation with the national holding corporation of ÖIAG[2] and the Creditanstalt, the largest nationalized bank. In addition, quite a number of German automobile producers have installed numerous feeder plants in Austria. The decisive impulse for these government initiatives in the industrial field were considerations of balance-of-trade policy. In the peak year 1977 Austria imported automobiles at a cost of almost 20 billion schillings, equivalent to almost one-third of the total balance-of-trade deficit.

A uniquely Austrian phenomenon may be seen in the strong growth of the woodworking industry, which has taken third place, behind chemicals and electrical engineering, among the expanding branches, followed by

Table 1 Industrial production by branches, 1956–1978

		Percent share in total production	
	1956 = 100	1956	1978
Mining	94.5	6.1%	1.9%
Petroleum	184.6	8.3	4.8
Iron and steel	233.0	5.6	6.9
Nonferrous metals	266.4	1.5	1.3
Stone and clay	289.7	5.6	5.1
Glass	196.0	1.7	1.3
Chemicals	641.5	7.7	16.4
Pulp and paper	260.1	4.0	3.5
Paper products	436.7	1.0	1.5
Wood products	541.1	2.6	4.3
Food and tobacco	225.4	16.9	13.2
Leather products	203.6	2.2	1.5
Textiles	205.0	8.4	5.5
Apparel	239.1	2.8	2.4
Foundries	131.6	1.4	0.6
Machinery (nonelectrical)	305.2	8.3	9.6
Vehicles	148.9	4.9	2.8
Metal products	301.2	5.4	5.5
Electrical engineering	628.0	5.5	11.8
Total	287.2	100.0%	100.0%

paper processing. The fact that wood or timber, as raw material, is abundantly available in Austria can only partly explain this boom. Austria's reputation as one of the leading nations in winter sports—and an early switch by a number of small-craft ski manufacturers to production on an industrial scale—has enabled Austria to rise to the rank of the world's foremost ski producer.

Mechanical engineering, too, expanded at above-average rates. In this context it should be kept in mind that the extremely expansive and export-intensive branch of planning and building plants abroad must be included here. It was possible in some fields to market Austrian know-how not simply by products. One of the first major projects in the 1950s was the creation and development of the Indian steel industry by the Austrian-nationalized VÖEST. The technological developments of the LD-process (basic-oxygen process) and of the continuous-casting process, both initiated by the nationalized Austrian iron-and-steel industry, have given VÖEST-ALPINE a strong position in international steel mill construction. Other focal points of installation construction by this group are chemical plants, refineries, cement factories, and mining gear. Besides the nationalized industries, some medium-size firms were able, because of their technological know-how, to advance into leadership positions in their industries; e.g. the firm of Plasser and Theurer, international leader in the field of rail-making machinery, and Gesellschaft für Fertigungstechnik und Maschinenbau (Company for Finishing Technique and Machine Building), a leading maker of forging machinery. The structure of exports improved accordingly (see Table 2).

First among stagnating branches is mining, where real production lagged during the past twenty years. However, it must be noted that Austria does not possess any rich mineral deposits. The last anthracite coal mine had to be abandoned at the beginning of the 1960s, and brown coal only is being mined at present. The only copper mine closed down during the 1970s; one of the smaller state enterprises carries on lead and zinc mining, and one American and one French corporation are engaged in magnesite extraction.

Relatively high importance in overall industrial production must be accorded two branches that show below-average growth: textiles and the

Table 2 Structure of exports (in percent)

	1956	1965	1979
Raw materials	27.8	16.3	9.9
Semi-finished goods	25.8	23.5	23.6
Finished goods	43.6	55.0	62.6
Machinery and equipment	13.3	20.4	28.2

foodstuff and beverages industry. True, textiles were able to increase their export rate to over 50 percent, but at the same time this branch is exposed to vigorous foreign competition domestically, being priced out of its home market by imported goods. Wage-intensive manufactures, favored until the 1960s by the then still comparatively low wage level in Austria, such as garments and leather processing, are also hard pressed by increasing competition, especially from the low-wage countries of the Third World.

International comparisons show that structural change is progressing somewhat more slowly in Austria than in other industrial countries of Western Europe although this does not appear to have any detrimental effects on the pace of industrial development. This may be due, on the one hand, to the fact that Austria is less affected, because of its industrial structure, by incisive sectoral crises such as the extensive contraction of coal mining. On the other hand, an explanation may be sought in Austrian industrial policy, which endeavored to secure as smoooth as possible an adjustment of endangered branches. It is the aim of this policy to avoid shock effects in the labor market, in close cooperation with trade unions and management of the firms and industries concerned. With the assistance of massive subsidies from public funds, new productions were initiated and funded in potentially depressed areas, and existing enterprises were reorganized. In recent years, "structural aid" was instituted by the government for a number of particularly exposed and endangered branches, by providing investment funds for the support of paper, textile, and high-grade steel industries.

Considering its status as a small industrialized country, Austria possesses a remarkably balanced structure, both from a regional point of view and in respect of the mix of branches. The regional distribution of industrial capacities, in the beginning rather unbalanced, has undergone change, partly owing to external factors—first through considerations of the war economy, followed by the industrial installations founded by the German occupiers, and subsequently by the increasing development of the Western zones of Austria in the postwar period.

The course of industrial development in Austria was not marred by the rise of centers of "industrial single-crop economics," or the growth of a dominant single branch, such as befell large regions as well the overall economy of some other small countries, e.g. steel and coal in the Walloon portion of the Benelux countries or the watchmaking industry in the Swiss Jura region. A recent study[3] on the subject states that, with respect to a number of important productive factors, "the Austrian economic region had for a long time occupied a median position (e.g. in wage level, availability of qualified and adaptable labor, raw materials, industrial tradition, distance from markets), offering a relatively broad spectrum of choices of production possibilities." This may explain the conspicuous imperviousness to trade cycles displayed by Austrian industry—in contrast, for instance, to its German counterpart—and its lesser dependence on structural changes in its markets.

Without doubt a degree of deficiency must be noted in Austrian industry in certain technology-intensive branches. The absence of substantial government contracts in the armaments and astronautics fields and a comparative weakness in industrial research have led to a lag in some important fields of production. Industrial electronics—both in component manufacture and in terms of application in products and processes—may be mentioned as an example. This backwardness can only be lessened with the aid of transfer of know-how from abroad. For this very reason the creation of a favorable climate for investment in these fields is an important element of the industrial policy of the country. First successes may be noted in this respect, too. The German Siemens corporation, for instance, has recently begun construction of a plant for the manufacture of highly integrated component parts, combining the plant with a research center, a minority equity being held by the ÖIAG.

It may be noted on the positive side of the balance sheet that Austrian industry is in possession of comparatively new productive capacities, compared, say, with German industry. Although we have not gone into this aspect here, no doubt the stability of social and economic conditions has also contributed to giving Austrian industry a considerable competitive advantage.

The process of internationalization has found Austria rather on the receiving end, so far, by way of multinational corporations setting up branches and affiliates in the country. Austrian enterprises have done little investing abroad in the past; but direct investments of Austrian enterprises in foreign countries have been strongly on the increase in recent years. The results of a survey published in 1978 show the value of such investments to have reached approximately 5.6 billion schillings, which is about a fifth of the volume of foreign investments in Austria.

No multinational corporation has its headquarters in this country; the largest Austrian enterprise, the state-owned VÖEST-ALPINE, occupies 187th rank in the *Fortune* magazine list of 500 giant corporations. Average enterprise size in Austria is well below the average of the FRG, the UK or the USA. This may well be due to the comparative smallness of domestic markets and the density of economic activity, but it may also be a reflection of differences in branch structures.

THE ROLE OF THE NATIONALIZED INDUSTRIES

The large share of publicly owned enterprises is one of the specific peculiarities of the Austrian economic structure. In the goods-producing sector (manufacturing), the share of public ownership amounts to a fifth of employed persons and a quarter of value added.

These enterprises are linked to the ÖIAG—the state-owned industrial holding corporation—or to one of the state-owned banks (Creditanstalt, Länderbank) that hold equity in these enterprises. The ÖIAG, with 115,000 persons employed, reached an overall turnover of 9 billion US dollars in 1979, a third of this turnover being produced for export. The affiliated enterprises of the large banks employ a labor force of 60,000.

The following branches are completely or predominantly controlled by affiliates of ÖIAG: iron and steel production, petroleum processing, petrochemicals, and coal mining. The largest enterprises in the fields of crude oil production, the chemical industry, aluminum production and processing, and railway carriage building are affiliates of ÖIAG. ÖIAG, also occupies a strong position in electric engineering, through its affiliate Elin and by virtue of a minority equity holding in the Siemens company.

Whereas the ÖIAG group has its main center of gravity in basic industry, affiliates of the state-owned banks hold leading positions in many branches of the processing industries, e.g. in vehicle building, paper making and processing, cement and brick making, tire production, and chemical fiber production. The state monopoly in tobacco products must also be mentioned.

Private business circles and conservative political groups used to consider the nationalized industries an alien body in the Austrian economy. But with the passing of time, relations have become normalized to a large degree. This process of accommodation has been helped by the undeniable successes of the enterprises in question. While maintaining generally sound balances, the nationalized industry lies above the average with respect to investment, export intensity, and expenditure for research and development.

No doubt the nationalized enterprises are bound to take the purposes of the government's economic policy into account in their decisions to a greater extent than is the case with private enterprises. Thus, for instance, during the recession of 1974–1978 they reduced their labor force by only 3.3 percent compared with a decrease of 7.6 percent in industry as a whole. To be sure, redundant workers had to be kept on the payroll to some extent to achieve this result. Although this policy was instrumental as a support of the government's efforts to maintain full employment, it is a method that can only be used temporarily and within narrow limits. For all concerned —government, management, and the trade unions—are agreed that the nationalized sector must not become an industrial "sickbed"—in constrast to the development that can be observed at present in Italy and Great Britain.

TAXES AND PUBLIC SUBSIDIES

Austria is supposed to be a country with high taxes, judged by Western European standards. But the high rates of the schedule are considerably reduced, in fact, by a large variety of allowances for deductions and other tax privileges. Moreover, an extensive and complex system of public grants and subsidies exists. Some aspects of this system have been touched upon; we shall now try to describe its present range more fully.

Joint stock companies are subject to corporation taxes and tax on operating profits up to a combined maximum rate of 61 percent. The recipients are liable for income tax on distributed profits, but the effect of this double taxation is mitigated by a corresponding reduction of the corporation tax. Unincorporated firms and sole proprietorships are subject to income tax and operating profits tax up to a maximum (marginal) rate of 67 percent. Liberal allowances for accelerated depreciation of capital investment, especially machinery, have been mentioned. In addition, there are tax exemptions for a certain portion of investment and for retained profits in the form of an investment reserve. Altogether, by utilizing fully all these possibilities, total tax may be reduced to about a fourth of the nominal rate.

On top of investment promotion through the tax system, there exists an extensive system of direct state aid. It includes various forms of credit subsidies and credit guarantees for investments and exports, as well as direct state participation in investment projects.

The "classical" instrument of direct investment subsidies since the time of the Marshall Plann is the ERP Fund,[4] its resources having been substantially increased from Austrian sources. About half of the low interest credits are used for industrial projects. In 1978 a further form of interest subsidies was instituted, financed out of budget appropriations, of an order of magnitude that has in fact achieved a division of the money market into a long-term investment credit market and a commercial credit sector. This extensive program must be seen as a vital part of the policy instruments used to promote industrialization and to secure stability.

Besides those mentioned, there are other programs to take care of small and medium-size enterprises, and economic branches that are endangered by structural problems. The Österreichische Investitionskredit AG (Austrian Investment Credit Corporation) was organized on the basis of private enterprise, with the task of financing major investments; and the Österreichische Kommunalkredit-AG. (Austrian Communal Credit Co.) was organized to serve regional policy concerns.

A special fund was instituted for the promotion of applied research on the enterprise level; the fund participates with subsidies and low interest credits in financing precisely circumscribed research projects, providing a maximum share of 50 percent of the necessary finance. The state-owned Finance Guarantee Company assists projects in the industrial field by backing investment credits with guarantees; up to a certain amount it may also offer credit guarantees to finance the expansion of a firm's liquid assets, needed to sustain production after capital investment. It may also provide guarantees for the acquisition of shares in concentration processes considered desirable in the national economic interest. Finance to the limit of 10 billion schillings is available to guarantee the liabilities of the nationalized enterprises entered into for the purposes of investment.

New industrial ventures are supported within the framework of these programs, but for major industrial projects additional financial means are provided. Thus local and federal authorities often place cheap—or free— land at the disposal of investors; they subsidize the training of personnel and in certain cases give outright investment grants. The largest subsidy ever awarded to a single investor has gone to General Motors for the project mentioned above.

Export promotion is the task of a special institute, the Österreichische Kontrollbank, whose shares are owned by a consortium of banks and finance institutes. Backed again by state guarantees, it provides advance finance and guarantees mainly for longer term-export business. It would go beyond the scope of this study to describe in detail the programs for industrial promotion that exist on the local and regional level. Some of these are beginning to fill the gap that has always existed in the Austrian capital market, that is, the provision of risk capital. One institution of this type is the Vienna Innovation Corporation recently created with the assistance of the powerful Municipal Savings Bank (Zentralsparkasse) and the City of Vienna. It provides financing for the production and marketing of "ripe" innovations against a share in the revenue from the new product. Similar ventures are being undertaken by some private financial institutions to promote innovative developments by small and medium enterprises on the basis of the acquisition of shares.

It is undoubtedly an Austrian peculiarity that most of the programs and activities, described in this chapter, are based on close labor-management cooperation both on the enterprise level and in the general framework of "social partnership" described at length elsewhere in this volume. (See "Social Partnership in Austria".) This applies to the administration of all special funds as well as to structural measures affecting whole branches or regions. It also applies to the administration of a special instrument of labor market policy (*Arbeitsmarktförderung*), which enables the government to provide financial assistance from the Unemployment Compensation Fund to enterprises in acute difficulties.[5] This instrument aims at the prevention of sudden waves of dismissals, with their ill effects on regional labor markets, and at mitigating cyclical and seasonal employment difficulties; it makes possible timely reactions to threatening mass dismissals through a "DEWLINE," or early warning system.

Of course, it is difficult to judge the effects of this multifarious aid package, aimed at a variety of targets. The many instruments may well confuse the outsider. But in their application within a small industrialized country like Austria, it is usually possible to effect coordination and agreement between enterprise management, aid and promotional institution, political representation, and labor interests on an informal basis. This will be readily understood if one is aware of the climate in economic and social policy prevalent in Austria, which favors consensus of the groupings in society, not only in questions of national economic significance but also in specific problems and decisions of industrial policy.

INDUSTRY AFTER THE WORLD ECONOMIC RECESSION, 1974–1975

After the period of extraordinarily rapid industrial growth in the first half of the 1970s, Austria was hit, with some delay, by the international recession. The real level of industrial production receded by more than 6 percent in 1975. Only in 1977 did industrial production pass the 1974 level. Iron and steel production was most severely hit; in this sector the level attained before the recession could only be reached and passed in 1979.

Annual average growth of industrial production was only 1.5 percent in the period 1975–1978, and employment in industry decreased by 7.6 percent from the 1974 level. The stabilizing role of the nationalized industry was one factor ensuring that the recent recession touched Austria only to a limited degree. Other causes may be found in the well-timed and massive intervention of anticyclical fiscal policy, and in the active labor market and assistance policies, which helped avoid mass dismissals. It is clear that the consistent policy of job protection, which anticipated and helped circumvent a rise of even regionally limited unemployment, proved successful.

THE CURRENT DEBATE ON INDUSTRIAL POLICY

Although Austrian industry came off comparatively well during the recent crisis, a number of difficulties sparked a lively debate concerning reorientation of industrial policy. There was general agreement that Austria still has too high a share of basic industries and traditional finishing productions requiring little know-how. An analysis of the Austrian export structure also disclosed, in spite of great improvement, a comparative predominance in exports of goods that require a relatively low degree of skills to manufacture. The record foreign trade deficit of 1977, reaching more than 73 billion schillings, places the question of short-term strategies for raising the export quota, and medium-term strategies of import substitution, squarely in the focus of the debate. In the fields of research and development, there is persistent and serious backwardness in comparison with the leading industrialized countries. And the representatives of industrialists' interests, in particular, emphasized the increasing indebtedness of most enterprises, aggravated by the poor profits in the period 1975–1978.

In 1978, the Economic and Social Advisory Board[6] formulated an expert opinion advising the reorientation of industry to products embodying a high net value-added content and requiring a highly developed technology. This debate on structural policy focused on quality—in contrast to previous years, when the quantitative aspects had been given much prominence, as, for example, during the discussion about raising the level of investment, conducted in the 1960s.

Following this trend, the enterprises of basic industry decided—largely in the nationalized sector—to consolidate and rationalize the output of basic products while aiming principally at a vigorous increase in the final products. In the discussion of instruments for promoting the aims of industrial policy, the trade unions in particular demanded an approach directed at the quality rather than the amount of industrial investment, to be achieved by a shift from fiscal, or general, tax relief measures to selective direct subsidies. The Austrian hard currency policy was also scrutinized under the aspect of industrial policy. The points of view voiced in this connection differ strikingly from those in other countries. Whereas the trade unions favor close ties of the Austrian schilling with hard currencies in the interests of stability, employers point out that such a policy creates considerable difficulties in foreign trade.

Austrian industry again underwent considerable expansion in 1979, especially in consequence of the substantial growth of exports (up 17 percent) and the growth rate in industry amounting to approximately 6 percent. This growth also induced a break in the negative employment trend that had persisted since 1973; the number of employed persons in industry has again risen slightly since the middle of 1979. But the forecasts indicate that structural changes both in supplier markets (raw materials, energy) and in trading markets will proceed at an increased pace. The flexibility of the means and instruments of Austria's industrial policy will be severely strained, although up until now they have succeeded to a remarkable degree in safeguarding economic growth and the relative stability of employment.

Notes

1. This "reconstruction" was decided upon by a League of Nations conference in Geneva in 1922, to save Austria from bankruptcy. But the terms of the loan were severe and gave foreign creditors a great deal of influence over Austria's economic policy.

2. The *Österreichische Industrie Aktiengesellschaft* (ÖIAG) is actually, in the form of a holding corporation, the top-level administrative and planning agency for the entire sector of nationalized industries. Sole owner of its stock is the Federal Republic.
3. Hans Seidel, *Struktur and Entwicklung der Österreichischen Industrie* (Wien, 1978), p. 29.
4. This fund originated in the European Recovery Program under the Marshall Plan. Its workings are described in detail in Chapter 4.
5. Since there is little unemployment, this fund, which is part of the social security system, has means at its disposal over and above those needed for unemployment allowances.
6. For a description of this institution, see Chapter 8 in this volume.

Selected Bibliography

Brusatti, A. Wirtschaft, in Erika Weinzierl and Kurt Skalnik, eds., *Das Neue Österreich*. Graz, 1975.
Langer, E. *Die Verstaatlichungen in Österreich*. Wien, 1966.
Nemschak, F. *Österreich's Wirtschaft in den sechziger und siebziger Jahren: Rückschau und Ausblick*. Wien, 1970.
Nussbaumer, A. *Wirtschaftswachstum und Investitionsfinanzierung in Österreich*. Wien, 1968.
Seidl, H. *Struktur und Entwicklung der Österreichischen Industrie.* Wien, 1978.
Tautscher, A. (ed.). *Handbuch der Österreichischen Wirtschaftspolitik*. Wien, 1961.
Weber, W. (ed.). *Die Verstaatlichung in Österreich*. Berlin, 1964.
Weber, W. State-Controlled Enterprise in Austria, in *International Review of Administrative Sciences*. Brussels, 1962.

Modern Austria, pp. 173–83

7. MONETARY AND BUDGET POLICY

Stephan Koren

President of the Austrian National Bank

RECONSTRUCTION IN AUSTRIA

After World War I, the Republic of Austria emerged from the disintegrating Habsburg monarchy. During the first two decades of its existence it could barely master its economic and political problems. Depression, mass unemployment, and severe political controversies impaired the consolidation of the new state, prevented the coming into existence of a new consciousness of national identity, and encouraged doubts in the country's viability. The annexation by Hitler's Germany brought the era of the First Republic to an end.

The close of World War II made Austria a free country again. The external starting conditions were even more unfavorable than in 1918. Immense devastation caused by the war, the total collapse of the economy, a shortage of food and raw materials, as well as the division of the country into four occupational zones presented problems that were almost beyond solution. Nevertheless, the political conditions were more favorable. Occupation and the war had formed a new consciousness for their national identity in the Austrians, had strengthened the belief in the future and in the viability of the country, and had enhanced the readiness on the part of the political forces to join efforts in reconstructing Austria. Ideological antagonisms and group interests receded into the background. The will to overcome chaos and restore a functioning state structure dominated.

The monetary and budget policy covering the 35 years since 1945—during which Austria emerged from collapse and chaos into a modern industrial country—can be divided into periods that differ distinctly from one another. First came the years immediately following the war up to approximately 1947, during which the most essential elements of a new

9306-6403/81/0415-0173$01.50

state order had to be set up in all fields. Then were the following five years, during which the reconstruction of institutions destroyed by the war, of the infrastructure, of the manufacturing potential, and of housing was accorded priority. That was the period when the United States' European Recovery Program (ERP) contributed invaluably to the reconstruction of Austria. In 1952, when the postwar inflation had been successfully stopped and the currency stabilized, Austria's period of growth and modernization set in. Additional impulses were given when the occupational troops were withdrawn and Austria regained full freedom through its State Treaty of 1955. Finally, the time since the collapse of the Bretton Woods system and the world-wide impact of the oil crisis can be considered a new period, which has created problems that keep the international economic policy in suspense.

RESTORING ORDER OUT OF CHAOS

During the time immediately following the war, an economic policy in today's sense of the term was out of the question. First of all, emergency action had to be taken. There was no food available, traffic had completely broken down, tens of thousands of dwellings had been destroyed, and the production of goods had come to a standstill. The volume of money and goods was in gross disequilibrium and a large black market developed. The money supply was out of hand. The country had no currency of its own. The Reichsmark* and the currency issued by the occupying powers were the payments media.

Not before the end of 1945 could the Austrian schilling be reintroduced as national currency and the money supply thus brought under the jurisdiction of the Austrian National Bank, which had been reestablished in the meantime. Simultaneously with the reintroduction of the schilling currency, the excessive money supply was drastically reduced.

Inflation and the black market, however, could not be curbed by these measures. The supply of goods remained utterly insufficient—owing to the fact that raw materials, energy, and food were lacking. These could not be imported on account of the shortage of foreign payments media. On the other hand, without raw materials, exports could not be set going. The government had no alternative but to maintain strict controls of prices, imports, and exports, in order to at least safeguard the survival of the population (food was strictly rationed).

The setting-up of a new administration was a tedious process. The country was divided into four occupational zones and the military administra-

*The German currency unit up to 1948.

tion held the supreme authority. The first budget for the entire territory of the new Republic could not be passed by parliament before mid-1946. It could hardly contribute to bringing about stabilization. The need for government spending was almost unlimited; in addition, the costs of occupation had to be met. On the other hand, tax revenue was small. A credit and capital market could not develop because the propensity to save was practically nonexistent during that inflationary period. The actual extent of currency erosion during the first two postwar years cannot even be roughly calculated, since the officially authorized prices for all necessities were kept extremely low while prices on the black market, where a considerable part of the overall exchange of goods took place, were many times higher (in case of essential foodstuffs occasionally up to a hundred-fold). Only part of the public expenditure, including occupational costs, could thus be covered by tax revenue. The rest was, in practice, financed by increasing the money supply.

Foreign trade was small because the domestic output of goods set in very slowly and was immediately absorbed by the domestic market. (In 1946 and 1947, industrial output in Austria reached only 44 percent and 57 percent, respectively, of the last prewar year's level.) If goods were exported, this was mostly done by barter, that is, the goods were exchanged for other goods. The payment transactions with foreign exchange rates were officially fixed. Fixing was not guided by the market but by the official domestic price level. Accordingly, a black market for foreign payment media existed. The implementation of the necessary controlling measures was vested in the Austrian National Bank under the foreign exchange law.

All in all, efforts to restore order out of the existing chaos were soon successful, so that a functioning administrative structure was available by the end of 1947. Thus, the financial and monetary policy could eventually leave the period of improvising behind.

RECONSTRUCTION AND INFLATION

The start of a fairly orderly period of reconstructing the Austrian economy was made by stringent measures in the field of monetary policy. The currency protection law dating from the end of 1947 provided for the issue of new schilling bank notes that were exchanged against circulating schilling notes (including those of the Allied military administration) at a rate of 1 to 3. By this measure, inflation could be effectively curbed, although only temporarily. Since 1948, the United States' economic aid granted under the Marshall Plan contributed decisively to Austria's reconstruction. From 1948 to 1951, Austria received, free of charge, aid deliveries of raw materials, food, and capital goods, as well as direct financial aid within the framework of the European Payments Union (EPU) averaging 220 million dollars per annum. With this aid rapid expansion of production could be achieved. By 1949 industrial output was 23 percent, and in 1951 66 percent, above the level of the last prewar year. The schilling counterpart funds of the United States' aid deliveries were at the disposal of the Austrian government for financing important investments and were predominantly used for reconstructing the electrical supply industry as well as for rebuilding and modernizing nationalized basic industries. The private sector, on the other hand, was almost exclusively dependent on self-financing for its investments, because the ability to save remained at a low level and the basis for an evolving capital market was, therefore, still missing. By way of compensation, investments were greatly promoted via tax concessions.

Yet, the expansion of output and employment was accompanied by marked price increases, because the income policy was ahead of actual developments and constantly maintained a situation of excessive demand. During the four years from 1948 to 1951, the level of prices increased by no less than 140 percent.

Such domestic inflation blocked consolidation of the balance on current account that was in deficit, since this inflation promoted imports and hampered exports at stable rates of exchange. Therefore, the first stabilization attempt was made in November 1949. However, owing to the fact that the measures were insufficient, it was attended by no significant success. *Inter alia,* the Austrian schilling was considerably devalued (de facto by approximately 30 percent); yet, at the same time, a multiple exchange rate system was introduced, stipulating three different rates of exchange. For the purposes of foreign trade, goods and services were invoiced at differing rates of exchange, according to their priority. It is evident that the controls necessary for these measures were not exactly promoting exports.

All in all, the period up to 1951 brought enormous progress in repairing the war damage, in setting up industries again, and in modernizing and expanding output; on the other hand, it could not do away with growing budget deficits, a higher rate of inflation, and disequilibrium in foreign trade.

STABILIZATION AND ECONOMIC GROWTH

During the years 1950 and 1951, it became more and more clear that a decisive step toward stabilization of the Austrian currency was necessary. The population grew increasingly impatient with inflation, and economic cooperation with the major trading partners, which had quite stable currencies, became more difficult, owing to the fact that Austria continued to adhere to quantitative import restrictions at a time when its trading partners had already liberalized their foreign trade to a great extent. The decisive impetus that triggered a modification of the Austrian economic and monetary policy was, however, the drastic cut in the United States' foreign aid. With an unchanged policy, this cut would have led to disastrous balance-of-payments problems.

Therefore, the Austrian government decided on a thorough alteration of its course and carried out a tough austerity program. By means of expenditure cuts and tax increases the federal budget was consolidated. Through increases in interest rates and credit restrictions, the expansion of money supply was slowed down. Finally, the central bank abolished the system of multiple exchange rates and changed over once again to a uniform par value corresponding to the highest of the three exchange rates that had been applied so far (one U.S. dollar equal to 26 schillings). This implied, de facto, a devaluation of the schilling.

The success of the stabilization policy was startling. It was possible to stop inflation within a short period of time, and in 1952 the level of prices even dropped slightly. Simultaneously the growth of industrial output almost came to a standstill and the number of persons employed dropped by 3 percent, but by 1953 an amazingly strong upswing set in. Export growth surpassed all expectations, and within the shortest possible period of time Austria's position in the European Payments Union changed from a structural debtor country to a creditor country.

In the wake of currency stabilization and the favorable development of the balance of trade and the balance of payments, other far-reaching decisions in the field of economic policy were facilitated. The traditional protectionist practices could be dismantled at a relatively fast rate. Austria became a full member of the EPU and liberalized its foreign trade and service transactions. It was also able to enter gradually into all commitments in other international organizations and remove temporarily conceded exemption provisions.

ECONOMIC POLICY IN THE GROWTH PHASE

The efforts to harmonize international economic developments brought about numerous international agreements (OECD, GATT, EEC, EFTA). The common goal of these agreements was, first of all, the dismantling of foreign exchange controls and tariffs as well as the liberalization of world trade in order to obtain more economic growth. At that time, this was considered by many countries an essential precondition to catching up with the backlog of demand that had resulted from the simple fact that, after the end of the war, the gross national product of many Western countries was well below the level of the prewar period.

If one uses the growth rates of real GNP as an indicator of the increase in prosperity, the enormous forces triggered by this international economic policy become evident. During the period from 1955 to 1974, real gross national product of the European members of OECD increased by 132 percent (the Federal Republic of Germany 146 percent, France 167 percent, Italy 163 percent, Sweden 106 percent, Switzerland 110 percent, and Austria 156 percent). Japan even recorded growth on the order of 432 percent. On the basis of a strict international framework for conditions, this economic policy system aimed at coping with adjustment processes, above all by measures in the field of domestic economy—and, within the system, the budget policy soon assumed the role of a steering instrument.

The expansive forces making themselves felt in Austria after stabilization of the currency were primarily supported by financial policy measures in the following years. The vigorous economic growth increased tax receipts at an above-average rate. Yet, the government did not use this additional revenue for further public expenditure but implemented two successive income tax cuts. In addition, it introduced tax concessions for saving by means of securities and insurance. These incentives, and the confidence in the country's own currency inspired by stabilization, brought about rapid stimulation of the propensity to save, which eventually facilitated restoration of the capital market. Other impulses in the field of economic policy were also triggered by fiscal policy measures. In order to promote investments, entrepreneurs were granted the ability to write off new buildings and machinery prematurely, thus saving taxes. Similarly, the export of goods was promoted.

On the other hand, budget policy was scarcely used as an instrument to stimulate economic activity during the first years after stabilization. After the years of inflation, which were accompanied by constant problems over the budget, there was a strong desire to keep the budget balanced. As a consequence, during the phase of vigorous upswing to 1954, the federal budget was kept in equilibrium.

Yet, this course pursued by budget policy could not be continued in the following period; from 1955 to 1957, there were moderate deficits in the overall budget. In the recession year of 1958, however, the deficit ran to 5.5 billion schillings, and the national debt increased from 11 billion to 15.6 billion schillings.

The subsequent period, from 1958 to 1961, was significant from the angle of budget policy: it was characterized by transition to an active budget policy, prompted by economic policy considerations. The average budget deficit of that period was 2.3 billion schillings; the hard fact was again brought home that it is no problem to incur budget deficits (in 1958) during a recession, but very difficult to reduce them in the subsequent upward phase of the business cycle.

FURTHER UPSWING DURING THE 1960s

The international—and with it the Austrian—economic situation of the 1960s was characterized by growth rates of GNP that were above average, accompanied by slight fluctuations in growth. It was characteristic of the situation that this boom covered up erroneous structural developments, and this phenomenon finally made itself felt in accelerating upward price tendencies. Even if, from today's angle, we wistfully recall statements like the one saying that with a price increase of 5 percent the "high-water mark" was hit, stability had already become a fundamental problem by that time. There was agreement that stability was important; on the question of how this goal was to be reached in the actual practice of economic policy, interests clashed then as they do today.

Another problem of the 1960s boom was the shifting of priority to production of consumer goods. As a rather natural consequence, capital expenditure of the Austrian budget stagnated, and when no agreement on the budget estimate for 1966 could be reached, the Grand Coalition between the People's party and the socialists broke apart (a coalition that looked back on twenty years of cooperation, even if this cooperation did not always function smoothly). New elections were held, with the result that one party —the People's party—gained an absolute majority. For drawing up the fiscal policy, this was of little consequence because joint solutions continued to be sought and found within the framework of the social partnership: thus, in Austria, the absolute majority of one party was not linked—in contrast to many other countries—to playing a lone hand in the field of fiscal policy.

In 1967, recession gained more momentum world-wide than had been expected. Economic growth did not reach the forecasted 4 percent, but only 2.4 percent. The immediate consequence was a doubling of the budget deficit because the government compensated for the low tax receipts by additional borrowing. From 1966 to 1967, the net budget deficit went up from a 0.4 percent share in GNP to 1.9 percent. At the same time, inflationary pressure increased. The consumer price index, which had gone up by only 2.2 percent in 1966, hit the 4.0 percent mark in 1967.

This development during 1967 induced the government at the start of 1968 to implement a new economic policy program, which placed emphasis on two areas. On the one hand, it adopted measures designed to curb the budget deficit by means of tax increases and expenditure cuts. In this way, a restrictive effect on private consumption and on inflation was to be exerted. On the other hand, it provided for measures designed to have an impact in the longer run that were, above all, aimed at recovery of the investment and modernization dynamics of the Austrian economy. In particular, the instruments of investment financing were improved, research promotion was extended, enterprise mergers became tax-exempt, guarantee facilities for the formation of enterprises were established, and an investment program running over several years and designed to improve the infrastructure was adopted.

The recession of 1967 was followed by an exceptionally long boom period. The gross national product again increased by 4.4 percent in 1968, while the rate of inflation dropped to 2.8 percent. During the subsequent two years, growth expanded to reach 5.9 percent and 7.8 percent, respectively, and then remained at a level above 5 percent up to 1974. Since 1970, however, inflation was steadily increasing and reached 9.7 percent in 1974 —its highest rate since stabilization in 1952.

In letting the budget policy of the 1960s pass in review, one notes that, at first, the predominant opinion was that revenue and expenditure should be more or less in equilibrium. Since the close of the 1950s, the primary consideration had been the conception that budget deficits, incurred during a setback in economic activity, should and could be covered by net receipts stemming from the boom period. Such a policy should keep the national debt constant in absolute value—implying that in a growing economy the debt ratio would decrease in relative value. During the course of the 1960s, this conception was gradually growth-linked: in this context, the Advisory Board for Economic and Social Questions observed that the medium-term growth of the national debt should not exceed that of the gross national product. Toward the end of the 1960s and the beginning of the 1970s, the budget deficits could be kept more or less stable, the adjusted net deficit was reduced, and the transactions effective domestically even produced surpluses. During that time, the growth of the domestic economy was well above the average growth of other countries; thus, the income differential between Austria and the majority of highly developed industrial countries decreased.

The change of government in 1970 did not make much difference in this respect; after four years of one-party rule with the Austrian People's party in power, the Socialist party of Austria first formed a minority government and then gained the absolute majority for the first time in the fall of 1971. In spite of the obviously effective socialist electoral campaign slogan, that 3 percent inflation was too much, this change of government had little to do with economic questions.

In short, the politicians concerned with economic policy set out with the consideration that the trend of vigorous international growth would continue. That also was the time when the general conviction of the "manage-ability" of economic and monetary policy prevailed. Terms such as coarse control and fine control of the economy were discussed and certain techniques were associated with them—and believed in. The changes that had already been signaled with the collapse of the Bretton Woods system and that made their impact felt with the outbreak of the energy crisis in the wake of the oil boycott should teach us better.

THE PERIOD SINCE THE OIL CRISIS

The oil crisis in the fall of 1973 had a comparatively slight impact on Austria's domestic economic activity during the following year—in spite of the abrupt rise in oil prices and the severe disturbances of the international balance-of-payments equilibrium. Economic growth, forecast at 5 percent, finally ran to at least 4.1 percent. Inflation, however, accelerated from a level of 7.6 percent in 1973 to 9.5 percent in 1974. Relatively unnoticed, a considerable deterioration in the budget was already under way in 1974. The net deficit (deficit minus debt redemption) increased by over 60 percent and almost reached 2 percent of GNP.

Not before 1975 did recession set in fully, one year later than in many other countries; the national product shrank by 2 percent. As a consequence of this development, tax revenue fell considerably short of expectations. Since the government did not want to aggravate the crisis by cutting state expenditures, it covered the lacking tax receipts by additional borrowing. Thus, the net deficit of the budget went up again considerably in 1975, that is, by approximately 150 percent, or 4.5 percent of GNP. Since then, budget policy has repeatedly attempted to reduce the deficit. A number of tax increases during recent years as well as cuts in expenditure have alleviated the problem to some extent, but have not been able to provide adequate leeway for an active budget policy during the next phase of a more serious recession.

The problems of the federal budget and a policy on wage rates greatly outstripping economic growth during 1975 and 1976 soon shifted the key problems into the field of foreign trade and payments. In 1976 and 1977, the balance on current account rapidly showed a deficit at rates of 2.2 and 3.6 percent of GNP. The politicians in charge of economic policy took account of this development with a so-called "package of measures" designed to ease pressure on the budget with the help of tax increases and, above all, to curb imports of "non-essential goods," particularly those that brought about deterioration in the balance of payments. Even allowing for special factors—such as advance purchases in anticipation of the measures in question that were announced somewhat prematurely—the results were impressive. The deficit of the adjusted (actual) balance on current account dropped to approximately 6 billion schillings in 1978, i.e. approximately 0.7 percent of the national product; the following year, 1.9 percent of GNP was hit again by a current account deficit of 18 billion schillings, a fact certainly not to be considered a disaster.

PROBLEMS OF THE PRESENT TIME

Practically every historical investigation ending with the present time is inclined to describe the questions and problems of the immediate past more thoroughly and in greater detail. For readers in years to come, this may be of interest; for this presentation, I intend to discuss only the economic policy that was the focus of attention for practically all measures of the most recent past.

Austrian economic policy has adopted the view—at first with varying degrees of enthusiasm and later to an increasing extent almost unanimously —that full employment and the lowest possible price increases must be put ahead of other goals. The fact that full employment depends on a reasonable development of prices has been obvious. And the fact that the Austrian economy is closely interlocked with economies abroad is equally well known. Or, in other words, as a consequence of Austria's import surplus, the country's level of prices depends to a great degree on prices for imported goods.

The result of these considerations has been the so-called hard currency policy. In a nutshell, this implies nothing but the intention of keeping the schilling as unchanged as possible against the stable currencies of other countries with which Austria has significant economic relations. Naturally, during the past years this applied, above all, to the link between the German mark and the schilling. Over a longer period of time, the Austrian central bank was successful in keeping the exchange rate of the German mark stable in Austria, partly since the position of the schilling against the European monetary system was thus determined.

In the setting we live in, it has become exceedingly difficult to predict even the immediate prospects ahead. The periods of unambiguously definable economic development (business cycles)—that is to say, the go and stop distances—have become considerably longer, compared to the past. On the other hand, developments have become less visible at a glance: in former times, those who did the forecasting viewed events from the top of a tower, as it were, from which they could watch what was going on in the country. Today, they find themselves, at best, on a rostrum of very moderate height, which considerably hampers a sweeping view. Let us hope that they will not, sooner or later, be stationed in a trench with no horizon at all.

Selected Bibliography

Rothschild, K. W. 1977. Zyklisches Verhalten und Niveau der österreichischen Arbeitslosig-keit. In *Zeitschrift für Nationalökonomie*, vol. 37, 1–2:183–96.
Koren, Stephan. 1971. Die Industrialisierung Österreichs—vom Protektionismus zur Integra-tion. In *Österreichs Wirtschaftsstruktur—gestern—heute—morgen*. Berlin.
Sturc, Ernest. 1968. Stabilization Policies: Experience of Some European Countries in the 1950s. IMF Staff Papers, vol XV, no. 2: 198–204.
Haberler, Gottfried. 1979. Austria's Economic development: A Mirror Picture of the World Economy. In *Festschrift für Stephan Koren*. Berlin.
Nemschak, F. 1955. *Ten Years of Austrian Economic Development, 1945–55*. Wien.
Weber, W., and K. Socher. 1960. Inflation und Inflationsbekämpfung in Österreich seit 1945. In G. Bombach, Hrsg., *Stabile Preise in wachsender Wirtschaft. Das Inflationsproblem*. Tübingen.
Seidel, H. 1958. *Struktur und Entwicklung der österr. Industrie*. Wien.
Bayer, K., J. Skolka, and J. Stankovsky. 1979. Structural Adjustments of Austrian Industry to Champing Patterns of the International Division of Labour (hektographiert). Wien.
Oettl, Clement. 1971. *Funktionelle Gliederung der österr. Budgetausgabe, 1960–70*. Wien.

Modern Austria, pp. 185–201

8. SOCIAL PARTNERSHIP IN AUSTRIA

Maria Szecsi

Former member of the Economic and Social Advisory Board

The system of social partnership (*Sozialpartnerschaft*), recently sometimes referred to as "economic partnership" (*Wirtschaftspartnerschaft*), has grown in Austria bit by bit out of machinery originally established to deal with inflation by direct negotiations between trade unions and employers on wages and prices. For the first time the idea was applied in the conclusion of the five wage-and-price pacts mentioned in Chapter 4. Since that time it has developed wide ramifications for the effective participation of the representative organizations of the main social groups (or classes, if one prefers this term) in the shaping of economic and social policy. In certain sensitive fields of policy the consensual settlement of controversial issues by the "social partners" has come to be regarded as binding upon subsequent parliamentary and/or governmental action. Thus social partnership, to stick to the older and more familiar term, has assumed a crucial function in the general decision-making process, going far beyond the consultative procedures that most governments have established in some way. It is not surprising that the "Austrian model" has drawn a great deal of international attention.

That such permanent and institutionalized cooperation of the leading political and social forces could only come about in the general climate of social peace, which has characterized the history of the Second Republic, needs no further elaboration. A lasting arrangement of this kind necessarily requires a basic consensus concerning the socioeconomic structure, delineating the boundaries within which conflict must be contained. Though it has never been spelled out formally, there is no doubt that such a tacit agreement exists in this case. Principally it may be said to imply the maintenance

185

9306-6403/81/0415-0185$01.50

of the existing economic order, combining private property and the market system with strong elements of state interventionism and public property —in other words, the recognition of a "mixed economy." For the Socialists this means abandonment of further socialization plans; for the People's party it means respect for the status quo with regard to the main enterprises of the nationalized sector. In a more general way it may be said to include the stability of distributive shares between wages and profits in the longer term. This would preclude special efforts on either side to change these shares markedly and permanently.

Another, equally important precondition for the development of social partnership was the existence of highly centralized and stable organizations of economic interest groups (*Verbände*) capable both of internal conflict regulation and of strong outside representation. Since this institutional infrastructure is of a very special kind, its character and historical background must be described at some length.

CHAMBERS AND VOLUNTARY ASSOCIATIONS

For employers, employees, and agriculturists there exists a parallel structure of chambers and free associations with close interconnections. The chambers are self-governing corporate bodies in public law. Membership is compulsory for all persons engaged in the relevant economic activity; membership fees thus amount to a quasi-tax, providing the chambers with an independent, and today rather ample, financial basis; and the governing bodies of the chambers are correspondingly elected in quasi-public elections, voting rights being attached to membership. The construction goes back to 1849, when the Chamber of Trade was established in the aftermath of the Revolution of 1848. After World War I the Chamber of Labor came into being upon demand of the Social Democrats. To make the system complete, the peasants also received their chamber system at that time. All three chambers, which were abolished during the period of German rule, were reorganized after 1945. Apart from the right to review proposed laws on economic and social matters before they are submitted to parliament, they have been assigned a wide range of public functions, which will be discussed later. And beyond that they maintain numerous legal, advisory, social and educational services for their members. In keeping with the Federal Constitution of Austria, the chamber organization is also federally based, with separate chambers in each of the nine provinces (*Länder*). The employers' chambers are further subdivided along professional lines, forming an intricate edifice of sections and subsections, the details of which do not concern us here. Central activities are carried on for the employers by the Federal Chamber of Trade and Industry, for the employees by the

All-Austrian Assembly of Chambers of Labor, and for the peasants by the Presidents' Conference of Chambers of Agriculture. For the sake of clarity and brevity we shall hereafter refer simply to the Chambers of Trade, of Labor, and of Agriculture without respecting these awkward designations, always meaning the central organs. (A glossary giving the German terms is appended.)

To carry on their widely diverse activities, the chambers maintain a large and well-qualified staff, including special departments for economic and statistical research.

The chamber organization of Austria is often regarded as a variant of "corporatism," which formed the main ingredient of Italian fascism. As a matter of fact, concepts involving in one way or another the corporate organization of economic groups are much older than fascism; they have always played some part in the ideology of the Austrian Catholic movements. And it may well be that some elements of this tradition have gone into the genesis of present-day institutions. But the system as a whole is constructed on a principle opposite that of fascist "corporatism." The latter aimed at the *common* organization of employers and workers in each profession—an idea quite incompatible with free trade unions. The Austrian chambers were, on the contrary, based from the beginning on the separate representation of the social classes. Thus the Chamber of Labor, created by and in the spirit of the Social Democratic party, has always defined its role as a service to the trade unions, the arsenal of their "brain power."

Still it is interesting to note that the same law by which it was founded included certain provisions with a view to the cooperation of all chambers on matters of common interest. Even before that, in the later stages of World War I, trade union delegates had been given equal representation with the Chambers of Trade on various committees called into being by the government to aid in the management of the badly floundering war economy. Attempts to continue this type of cooperation in the immediate postwar period were soon broken off by the Federation of Industry. Thus, the antecedents of what later became "social partnership" can be traced back to these early beginnings. But in the following period of acute social conflict there was no chance of further development in this direction.

Among the voluntary associations actively participating in social partnership, first consideration must be given to the Austrian Federation of Trade Unions (Österreichischer Gewerkschaftsbund, ÖGB), one of the most powerful and highly centralized union organizations in the Western world. Traditionally organized on industrial lines, it has never experienced the fragmentation that goes with the crafts principle. National divisions haunting it in the days of the Empire were eliminated in 1918; political disunity

was ended in 1945 with the founding of a single, unified trade union organization. Thus today there are 15 industrial unions in all making up the
ÖGB, which boasts a membership varying between 55 and 60 percent of the
employed labor force. Though the individual unions are theoretically
largely autonomous, the central functionaries wield sufficient authority to
enforce general policy decisions within their ranks. On the employers' side
are the powerful Federation of Industrialists and the Federation of Business, which is affiliated with the People's party (ÖVP) and has dominant
influence in the Federal Chamber of Trade. Partners in the conclusion of
collective agreements (which always cover whole branches of industry) are
on labor's side the unions and on the employers' side the various industrial
sections of the Chamber of Trade. This reflects the fact that in the labor
domain the unions are the real center of power, the Chamber of Labor only
acting in their support. The situation is different on the other side, where
power is located in the chamber organization itself.

This whole structure ties in closely with the political two-party system.
Since the Socialists traditionally command the labor vote, they are assured
stable majorities in the organs of both the Chamber of Labor and the ÖGB.
Candidates in the elections for these organs run on party lists and are later
organized in separate caucuses (*Fraktionen*). Similarly, the dominance of
the People's party among small businessmen and peasants gives it the same
position in the two other chambers. A large organization of peasants
(Bauernbund) forms its backbone in the countryside. Moreover, on both
sides leadership positions in the parties, the associations, and the chambers
are closely interlocked, top positions usually being held by the same persons, thus forming a close network of personal and political loyalties.

It is easy to see how a constant process of bargaining and consensus-
finding, both internally and between the parties, is facilitated by such a
set-up, which provides permanent lines of communication between all decision-making factors. Quite rightly, an observant English commentator has
pointed to the vital importance of this system of overlapping memberships
in the leading bodies for the functioning of social partnership.[1] On the other
hand, it is equally easy to see how tidily the system reinforces the tendency
to bureaucratization, which—as we know at least since Robert Michels—
is the besetting evil of all large organizations.

THE JOINT COMMISSION FOR PRICES
AND WAGES

The idea of creating a formal instrument of social partnership goes back as
we have mentioned, to the price-wage pacts of the postwar period, which
were effectuated through a tripartite "Economic Commission." This com-

mission remained in abeyance afterward; attempts to revive it in the mid-1950s foundered on constitutional obstacles. But the underlying ideas were strongly advocated by forceful personalities in both camps. Foremost among them were Johann Böhm, the first president of the ÖGB, who, from the beginning, was convinced that in the new situation the trade unions must assume co-responsibility for the economy as a whole, not only for wages and working conditions; and, on the other side, Julius Raab, for some time Federal Chancellor, who was closely connected throughout his career with the chamber of Trade. In 1957, finally, the Joint Commission for Prices and Wages was established by consent of all participants, called into life by a simple resolution of the Council of Mininsters, without legislative action. It is composed of four representatives of government (the Federal Chancellor, Ministers of Interior, Trade and Industry, and Social Affairs) and two representatives each from the three chambers plus two from the ÖGB—an asymmetrical arrangement reflecting the real power structure: since there are two chambers affiliated politically with the People's party, the ÖGB had to be included to ensure equal representation for labor. The presence of so many ministers in the commission by no means signifies a preponderant role of government in its working. The responsibility for its decisions and their enforcement through voluntary discipline rests, on the contrary, mainly with the nongovernment bodies. In fact, at the top level, the commission acts through meetings of the four presidents of the organizations concerned. In these meetings the agenda for the commission is prepared, controversial issues are discussed, and disagreements among the lower ranks of the hierarchies are arbitrated. All questions left open in any of the subcommissions are referred to this "High Court" of social partnership. For some time the Joint Commission also met regularly with economic experts to discuss the state of the economy on the basis of the forecasts of the Institute of Economic Research, which enjoys a quasi-official status. These sessions have been less frequent lately.

Originally the commission's main task was seen in the field of price and wage policy. At first there was only a subcommission on prices (Price Commission), but after long wrangling a subcommission on wages (Wage Commission) was added. Finally, account was taken of the desire of the trade unions to extend the commission's agenda to the wider field of general economic policy and to put its work on a more scientific basis. With this purpose in view its third subcommission, the Economic and Social Advisory Board, was called into being (1963).

As shall be seen presently, the procedures on wages and prices are not exactly symmetrical. To begin with prices, the basic principle calls for all firms and enterprises whose prices are not subject to direct controls by governmental authorities to submit intended price increases to the Price

Commission. Official price control today applies to few, but important, goods such as milk, bread, gasoline, and electricity. Other exceptions are prices of public utilities such as railway and streetcar fares. Claimants may be individual firms, but more often the procedure covers whole branches of production whose costs—such as raw materials and wages—are assumed to be rising more or less to the same extent. The amount of the admissible increase is then fixed by the commission in terms of a flat percentage rate for all firms involved. The bargaining process centers around the evaluation of cost calculations submitted by the firms, and the result is usually a compromise quite a bit below their original demands, but probably not too far from what they really intended to achieve.

Unlike the Price Commission, the Wage Commission does not determine the *amount* of wage increases to be granted, but can only influence the *timing* of the next wage round. Formally its function is thus restricted to delaying as far as possible the beginning of negotiations for new branch-wide collective agreements. Its indirect influence on the wage level is exerted only through the informal consensus underlying the whole arrangement, assuring the necessary cooperation on the part of the ÖGB leadership. In this way the system works without official wage guide lines, which have always been rejected by the unions jealously guarding at least the appearance of full autonomy in wage bargaining.

There has been a great deal of controversy about the effectiveness of this system in influencing the actual movement of prices and wages. Owing to the well-known (and insoluble) problem of isolating the effect of a single factor in the economic process dependent upon so many interacting causes, this question cannot be answered conclusively. The statistical record of prices and wages in itself provides no clear evidence, since there is no way of knowing what would have happened in case of alternative stabilization policies. Certainly the activities of the Joint Commission left loopholes on all sides, and the upward pressures of the market on wages and prices could not be held in anything like a close grip. On the price side, its efficacy was limited for several reasons. It could deal in practice only with a small number of "key prices," leaving many important items of consumption, such as textiles, clothing, shoes, and many services, out of consideration. Imported goods were also excluded. New goods and real or purported quality changes presented an intractable problem. Quite frequently, the calculations submitted by firms were insufficient for a reliable appraisal of their cost situation. And in none too rare cases the decisions of the commission were ignored or circumvented by the firms. To prevent such breaches of discipline, the unions pressed strongly for a system of sanctions against violators. They obtained, in fact, a legal provision enabling the Minister of Interior to issue an order making the ceiling price set by the commission official, but only on application of all four chambers. For obvious reasons, the provision remained a dead letter; it was not applied in a single case. The most serious criticism, however, concerned the practice of the commision in dealing with whole branches of production. Quite rightly, it was charged that in this way the commission not only sanctioned but actually encouraged price collusion (cartel pricing) between firms.

With regard to wages, it has been pointed out before that the influence of the Joint Commission could be, even technically, only an indirect one. Moreover, the actual movement of wages always deviates extensively from the rates set in collective agreements. The demand for labor often drives wages well above these rates (the difference is called "wage drift"), especially in times of overemployment. The union's policy must take this into account; it cannot allow the gap to become too large. Actually, in Austria the unions have tried to counteract the cyclical swings by driving hard bargains in times of recession while forgoing exploiting to the full the chances of large increases in a boom period. This "anticyclical" wage policy has been applied with some success, but the timing has not always been too accurate. However, the idea behind it was a sound one, as most observers agree, namely, to support consumers' demand when investment demand is slack and, conversely, to dampen the cost rise when the economy is strong.

There have been many hitches in the functioning of the commission, accompanied by mutual recriminations and complaints of lack of cooperation. But, beyond these polemics, which should be regarded as part of the rules of the game, a sober appraisal of the record has led experts of both parties to a common conclusion: While the effect of the commission's activities on the average level of prices remains in doubt, it has nevertheless made an important contribution by "steering the time distribution of wage and price rises so as to prevent cumulative processes that would result in sudden shocks to the economy."[2] This aspect of its work has been of greatest importance in the mid-1960s, when the inflation problem assumed top priority for economic policy. Since then, the weight of responsibility for maintaining price stability has shifted, to some extent, away from individual price control. With the opening of Austrian markets to foreign competition, macroeconomic policies, especially with respect to the exchange rate, have assumed primary importance for regulating the interval price level. Although wage restraints have remained an essential prop of this policy, direct links between the ÖGB and the governing party would have been sufficiently strong to achieve this purpose even without the mediation of the Wage Commission. These trends, however, may be easily reversed with future changes in the political constellation or the economic situation.

THE ECONOMIC AND SOCIAL ADVISORY BOARD

The idea of this board was most actively propagated by the Economic Research Department of the Chamber of Labor, which took a leading part in the preparatory talks. It was set up with the task of studying the problems assigned to it by the Joint Commission within the context of the requirements of the economy as a whole and to formulate policy recommendations on the basis of its findings. Membership is composed on the same principle as the Joint Commission, consisting partly of functionaries but mostly of expert staff members nominated by the organizations. However, experts from the universities and other research institutes as well as the ministries are always invited to participate in the preparation of studies. Essentially the board is conceived as a kind of economic "brain trust" within the instrumentality of social partnership, with the double function of assembling expert advice and helping to resolve interest conflicts. This constitutes the main difference to similar institutions in other countries where the formulation of expert opinion and conflict settlement are strictly separated. The distinctive feature of the Austrian arrangement lies in the fact that it enables labor representatives to participate directly in shaping policy at a level from which they are generally excluded, since advisory bodies are usually drawn from academic establishments none too friendly to labor points of view.

The drawbacks of such a construction are also evident. Although theoretically members of the board are appointed *ad personam,* purportedly free to act on their personal views, the reality of the power structure behind the arrangement makes this a mere fiction. Actually, the work of the board is prepared—on both sides—in closed caucus meetings, where decisions are practically binding. Thus, in part at least, the findings of the board reflect predetermined conclusions rather than the independent judgment of its members. But since it may be rightly doubted that anything like absolute objectivity is possible in economic science, the political bias involved in this procedure is perhaps not greater than in other advisory bodies. It is only distributed more equally. And for that reason, its final results, being already based on compromise, are in closer touch with the political realities. Even so, the board's recommendations have never had the same weight as decisions taken in the Joint Commission. Although not without influence in guiding the general lines of policy, they have not always been followed by immediate action.

Still, the importance of the board's activities should not be underestimated. Especially in the critical years of the 1960s it has made an essential contribution in defining and clarifying the basic problems of the Austrian economy. Its thorough analyses of the inflationary process have elucidated the variety of interdependent factors acting on the price level, showing the wide range of measures needed to combat the phenomenon. Its studies of industrial policy have brought into focus the structural weaknesses of the economy, calling to attention the bearing of this problem on the prospects of economic growth. Other important issues dealt with were labor market policies, including questions of labor mobility, part-time work, and foreign workers. A study on the effects of shortening the work week led to an immediate settlement, detailing even the stages of the reduction from 45 to 40 hours in five years (1970–1974). Regular reviews of the budget and budgetary forecasts prepared by the board seek to provide a basis for long-term financial planning. Even if not always successful in particulars, all of this work, in sum, has certainly helped to bring about better coordination of economic policy, which all too often had relied on unconnected ad hoc measures. Above all, the board has, through plenary meetings and numerous work teams, provided a close network of communications between experts and functionaries, ideally suited for informal exchanges of views and equally informal understandings.

THE "SOCIAL PARTNERS" IN GOVERNMENTAL AGENCIES

In addition to the institutions described, there are innumerable government and semigovernment agencies and advisory bodies in which the chambers, and in important cases also the ÖGB, not only are represented by law but actually exercise public functions. It is impossible to list all these organs, but some of the more important ones should be mentioned to give an idea how deeply this type of participation and co-determination is anchored in the functioning of the political process. For instance, the "social partners" sit on the governing boards of the National Bank (of which the ÖGB and the three chambers own a sizeable part of the stock) and the Postal Savings Bank; they are engaged in the administration of the ERP Fund[3] and the Fund for the Promotion of Research, both of which dispose of various forms of public subsidies. A special domain of social partnership is the Agricultural Marketing Order, involving vast regulatory powers in prices, subsidies, and imports and exports of key agricultural products (milk, cereals, livestock, and meat). Here certain powers have been vested directly in commissions composed exclusively of the three chambers and the ÖGB, not only in making decisions (by four-fifths majority) but also in administering the execution of the system.

Other examples are the Cartel Commission, attached to the Cartel Court, which acts as expert adviser in matters relating to the execution of the Cartel Law and generally deals with restraints of competition. Nominees of the Chamber of Labor and the Federal Chamber of Trade also act as lay judges in cartel cases. In addition, the social partners have a place in all supervisory, advisory, and consultative bodies concerned with the running of public or semipublic institutions ranging from the Central Office of Statistics, the Institute of Economic Research, and the Food Codex Commission, to the Broadcasting Company (ORF). They are, in short, everywhere and at all levels tied into the vast network of everyday administrative and other public activities.

No wonder that Austria has often been called a "chamber state." From the juridical point of view, there are more peculiarities to the picture. As we have shown, the ÖGB is included in all the important bodies on an equal footing with the chambers. But, unlike the latter, it has no legal existence or standing in any way different from several thousand registered societies on the order of, say, a sports club or a society of stamp collectors. Moreover, although the chambers and ÖGB individually have functions assigned to them by law, the specific institution of "social partnership"—that is, the Joint Commission with its subcommissions—exists completely *extra legem*. It is not surprising that constitutional questions have frequently been raised in this connection.

SOCIAL PARTNERSHIP TODAY— RECENT EXPERIENCES

In some points of this account there has been vacillation between the present and past tense. There is a reason for this apparent lack of grammatical rigor. As originally conceived, the institutional edifice of social partnership fitted in ideally with the two-party coalition in government, which for twenty years was believed to be the only possible system for Austria. Any other solution—that is, either government by the majority party alone or a "little coalition" of either of the big parties with the small so-called Liberal Party—was believed to endanger the stability of the country and even to jeopardize its democratic foundations. When the coalition actually broke apart in 1966, giving way to a People's party government for four years, it quickly became clear that no such dire consequences were in the offing. Regarding social partnership, there was immediate consent to continue its activities on all levels. The new government, rather insecure in its unaccustomed position of sole power, was in fact anxious to avoid any break in the links of cooperation, since it feared that the unions might adopt a more aggressive course, seeing their party in the role of parliamentary opposition. In reality, the trade union establishment had no such intention; it had always regarded social partnership as a long-term proposition. Also it needed these links to maintain its influence on policy in the new situation.

There is another, more technical, point, which in fact compels any single party government to seek consensus on important economic legislation. The Austrian Constitution is in many ways an excellent piece of work, by the famous jurist Hans Kelsen. Unfortunately Kelsen had no idea of economic policy in the modern sense and failed to establish a clear competence of the Federal Government for the management of the economy. For this reason, the need arose to pass many important laws, such as the entire Agricultural Marketing Order and all laws relating to price control by providing them with a so-called "constitutional clause." This means they can only be abrogated, changed, or extended by a two-thirds majority, in Austrian practice obtainable only by previous agreement of the social partners. To the extent that this constitutional blockage applies, some form of consensus-finding on the level of the interest groups must therefore remain part of the political process.

Nevertheless, the advent of the Socialist government of Bruno Kreisky, followed by three successive electoral victories catapulting his party into power for the tenth year at this writing (with two more years to go), brought with it such a profound change in political scenery that it could not leave the style of decision making unaffected. Though the main institutions of social partnership, as described in this account, have been left intact, subtle changes have certainly taken place. On the whole, they have tended to diminish somewhat the place occupied by the system as a whole in the actual making of policy as well as in the eyes of the public. Some signals of this change have been mentioned: the grand policy meetings of the Joint Commission, always surrounded by much publicity, have become irregular, and the work of the Price Commission has diminished somewhat in importance.

On the whole, the iron rule of social partnership—that all laws affecting its domain must be passed by previous consent of the social partners—has been obeyed so far; it has been broken only in one case, albeit a not very significant one, concerning the improvement of provisions for workers' severance pay. But even in that case unanimity was restored by a subsequent agreement between the social partners on some relief measures for small business. (In parliament the People's party had voted for the original bill.)

But the most visible outward signal of a changing mood was the decline in the authority of the Advisory Board. Increasingly hampered by disagreements, arising not so much among the experts as at the top level of functionaries, its activities slowed down and almost stopped in the early 1970s after continued quarrels over its findings on the budget. Although this crisis was finally resolved, the board has never recovered its former importance. To avoid further breakdowns, sensitive issues were avoided in assignments, and it has been occupied with more or less innocuous general subjects—

such as the utilization of "social indicators" in measuring welfare or environmental problems—and with more technical matters of forecasting and improvement of statistics. Quite recently, though, there have been signs of a revival, inasmuch as the board has been asked to deal with the highly important, and highly sensitive, issue of energy.

It is too early to assess the significance of these developments for future prospects of social partnership. The reasons for its present malfunctioning are not difficult to see. The seeming permanence of Socialist rule has put the representatives of the Chamber of Trade in the uncomfortable position of sitting in the organs of social partnership with opponents who have direct links to the government while they have none. Understandably enough, they must fear that these organs are being turned into an instrument of government policy. Complaints of ÖGB dominance have been a constant theme in their public utterances, with the charge that Austria had become a "trade union state" rather than a chamber state. In reality, the government readily opened other channels of communication with the business world, bypassing the organs of social partnership. The Federation of Industrialists, in particular, often stymied in the Chamber of Trade by small business interests, found easy access to Finance Minister Hannes Androsch, who was bent on a course of industrial growth through investment incentives.

Neither did the old structures fit in too well on the Socialist side. The ÖGB, indeed, has stressed over and over again its willingness to continue on the road of social partnership. But, not unnaturally, its leaders have felt the increasing strain of having their hands bound by the consent rule in matters where they could use their majority. Over the matter of the extension of co-determination at the plant level (*Mitbestimmungsgesetz*), it almost came to a breaking point.

For different reasons, the interest of the government in the Advisory Board flagged as it gained experience and self-confidence. In this context, certain conflicts of view between the government and some of the Chamber of Labor experts on the board may have played a role, just as on the other side Chamber of Trade experts often had to be called to order by their superiors. Moreover, since the establishment of the board, there had been a marked increase in economic studies and research facilities, making available other sources of expert opinion. Thus, in this respect too, bypasses have been found and used, and the institutes of social partnership have lost their former near-monopoly position.

Quite apart from these political aspects in the narrower sense, the weakening of the links holding the system together may have deeper causes in the loss of the certainties that have guided economic policy through the

1950s and 1960s on a course of widely accepted goals—growth, employment, stability, and social welfare. Today, the concept of growth, the kingpin of this quartet, is clouded with doubts and confusion; traditional social welfare systems seem to have reached their limits; and further developments in this area are bound to raise sharply controversial issues. The new problems of ecology and energy cut through the old class lines, leading to strange alliances between social groups hitherto firmly attached to only one of the great political camps. At the same time, growing intellectual unrest is manifested in various movements, drawing from diverse sources, but generally directed against bureaucratic rule and technocratic management in the public domain, leading to the call for more democratization, decentralization, and participation of the citizens in the decision-making process.

Another factor that disturbs the tidy balance of the present system is the steady change in the sociological structure of the population. In proportion as the number of self-employed who form the traditional voting potential of the People's party dwindles with the progress of industrialization, the conservative camp is losing its former homogeneity. The People's party can only retain its voting strength by reorienting its policies to attract a larger number of wage earners. In consequence, the working class suborganization within its own ranks, the Austrian Federation of Workers and Employees (Österreichischer Arbeiter und Angestelltenbund, ÖAAB), which formerly played a minor role, is visibly gaining influence in the party; at present even the top leadership position is held by one of its members. Although remaining a definitie minority in the ÖGB, its spokesmen find themselves in agreement more often with the Socialist majority on social and economic issues than with the members of their own party in the Chamber of Trade. Thus the symmetrical construction of social partnership, originally based on the identity of interests between People's party and business, on the one side, and the Socialist party and labor, on the other, is gradually being undermined.

All this makes consensus-finding more difficult than it was in times of easy sailing under the winds of prosperity, guided by unquestioned standards of social progress along clear-cut lines. Moreover, ecological restraints and slower growth are bound to put questions of income redistribution on the agenda, which so far could be evaded by maintaining a distributive status quo fairly satisfactory to all contending groups. This too will sharpen conflicts between as well as within interest groups.

Against these strains and stresses, account must be taken of the relative flexibility and resilience that this deeply rooted system of cooperation has shown up to this point. It has already weathered some crisis situations; it may also prove able to adapt to the present problems. Although its formal procedures may have to be revamped or may even become obsolete, a total break with its essential principle of compromise and consensus does not seem to be considered by the leadership on either side. Even most of its critics, with the exception of those on the extreme right or left, would rather see wider participation in the system than see it abolished.

SOCIAL PARTNERSHIP IN THE EYES OF ITS CRITICS

Critical voices, of course, have always been heard. Criticism from the right has been less insistent and less ideological than from the left. It has centered mostly on constitutional aspects, inasmuch as the whole system of decision making by the "social partners" is, to say the least, extraconstitutional, if not—as some critics think—in some respects unconstitutional. Social partnership as seen by these critics is a particularly striking example of the contradiction between the norms of the Constitution and its real functioning. The gap between norm and reality, it is charged, "endangers the foundations of the constitutional order and finally tends to undermine the whole legal system (*Rechtsstaat*)."[4] But there is no unanimity on the subject even among jurists. Most of them would seek ways to legalize the existing institutions of social partnership while at the same time restraining their further encroachment upon the constitutional organs.

Apart from the juridical aspect, the democratic legitimacy of the system has also been questioned for other reasons. One of these is the preferential position it gives to three organized interest groups, excluding all others from direct access to the decision-making process. Originally this argument came more from the conservative side, especially from the associations of the free professions (doctors, lawyers, etc), which have strong lobbies anyway; lately it has also been taken up by a group of critical Socialists in connection with their general program of participatory democracy in all fields of social life. This idea has been strongly incorporated in the new program adopted by the Socialist party in 1978, but it is in no way clear how hitherto unrepresented groups—such as the old, housewives, the handicapped—should be included in a system designed to deal with basic class conflicts.

Much more pertinent seems the charge—at present raised by both right- and left-wing critics—that through the close network of social partnership actual power had been concentrated in the hands of a tiny group of functionaries at the top of the trade union and chamber bureaucracies, who were securely settled in their positions by practically noncontested elections. In this connection it will be remembered what has been said before about the dominant majorities in each of the organizations in question. Considering, in addition to the permanence of majorities, the interlocking of leadership positions in both camps, it stands to reason that this whole structure is not conducive to internal democracy. In fact, it can hardly be denied that the widening of the scope of co-determination at the top level has been generally accompanied by a decline of rank-and-file activity in all organizations. This is especially notable in the trade unions, where internal democracy forms an essential part of the value system. A prominent Socialist of the younger generation has put this point succinctly. The lack of an active feedback from below, he wrote, "carries with it the danger of alienation of the instutitions (of social partnership) from their original purpose of existence and thus also alienation between the representatives and those whom they represent."[5] This widely shared view generally does not imply total rejection of the system, but seeks to remedy its democratic insufficiency by revitalizing internal channels of communication.

And last, there has always been a current of fundamental opposition to the idea of social partnership on the grounds of Socialist principle. Though Communist influence in the Austrian labor movement is and has always been negligible, left-wing Socialists could not so easily cut loose from the strongly Marxist tradition of Austrian social democracy to approve of a concept of social peace diametrically opposed to class struggle. In the past decade, Marxist influences have received new impetus through various groupings loosely described as the "new left." The arguments in these circles, mostly composed of intellectuals and members of the student generation of the 1960s, lean heavily on the Marxist interpretation of class society, which denies any common interest between wage earners and capitalists. In the more extreme version, this view not only leads to outright rejection of "partnership" as such, but also asserts that even the everyday material and social interests of the workers have been sacrificed by the ÖGB to the interests of profit and capital. More moderate adherents of Marxism will readily admit that the workers have not fared badly by social partnership, as indeed is shown clearly by the record, but still find themselves unable to accept such a purely pragmatic approach, devoid of any Socialist ideology, even devoid of any perspective of social change.

Readers familiar with the generally negative attitude of American and English trade unions toward co-determination proposals may note that there has been no mention here of an analogous trend in Austria. As a matter of fact, opposition to co-determination as such, based on the rejection of any co-responsibility either at the plant level or higher, has never played a significant part in the debates about social partnership. As has been shown, all criticism, whether radical democratic or Marxist or both, leads to demands for more and more genuine participation rather than for a call to end it. Trade union spokesmen have often pointed out that the Austrian trade unions are simply "too powerful to evade responsibility," since the country cannot be governed without them. There is doubtless some truth to this, somehow felt by all but a small minority bent upon a straight revolutionary course. And it is only in recognition of this fact that the current trends of criticism have a chance of bearing fruit by showing the way to constructive alternatives.

Glossary

Österreichischer Gewerkschaftsbund (ÖGB), Austrian Federation of Trade Unions
  Caucuses (*Fraktionen*):
    Sozialistische Gewerkschafter (Socialists)
    Christliche Gewerkschafter (Christian unionists), loosely affiliated with the People's party
    Gewerkschaftliche Einheit (unity list), Communist-dominated

Industriellenvereinigung, Federation of Industrialists
Kammer für Arbeiter und Angestellte, Chambers of Labor
  Central organ: Österreichischer Arbeiterkammertag, All-Austrian Assembly of Chambers of Labor (the Vienna Chamber acts as head office)

Kammer der gewerblichen Wirtschaft (Handelskammern), Chambers of Trade
  Central organ: Bundeskammer, Federal Chamber of Trade and Industry

Landwirtschaftskammern, Chambers of Agriculture
  Central organ: Präsidentenkonferenz der Landwirtschaftskammern, Presidents' Conference of Chambers of Agriculture

Österreichische Volkspartei (ÖVP), People's party
  Suborganizations:
    Wirtschaftsbund, Federation of Business
    Bauernbund, Federation of Peasants
    Österreichischer Arbeiter, und Angestelltenbund (ÖAAB), Austrian Federation of Workers and Employees

Paritätische Kommission für Preis- und Lohnfragen, Joint Commission for Prices and Wages
  Subcommissions:
    Preisunterausschuss, Price Commission
    Lohnunterausschuss, Wage Commission

Beirat für Wirtschafts- und Sozialfragen and Economic and Social Advisory Board

Notes

1. Derek Robinson, "Prices and Incomes Policy: the Austrian Experience" (OECD, Paris, 1972), p. 64.
2. "Sozialpartnerschaft in Österreich," unpublished Study of the Economic and Social Advisory Board (Wien, 1976).
3. See chapters by März & Szecsi and Lacina, in this volume.
4. See note 2.
5. Egon Matzner, "Funktionen der Sozialpartnerschaft," in Heinz Fischer, ed., *Das politische System Österreichs* (Wien, 1974).

Selected Bibliography

Barbash, Jack. *Trade Unions and National Economic Policy,* esp. Chapter 3, "Austria: The Negotiation of Economic Policy." Baltimore, 1972.

Beirat für Wirtschafts- und Sozialfragen. "Sozialpartnerschaft in Österreich." Wien, 1978.

Edelman, Murray. *National Economic Planning by Collective Bargaining.* Urbana, Ill., 1954.

Klenner, Fritz. "Die Sozialpartner." In Jacques Hannak ed., *Bestandaufnahme Österreich.* Wien, 1964.

Klose, Alfred. Der Weg zur Sozialpartnerschaft. Wien, 1970.

Klose, Alfred, and Johann Farnleitner. "Die Rolle der Verbände in der Politik." In *Österreichisches Jahrbuch für Politik.* Wien, 1978.

Lackenbacher, Ernst. "Austria." In Adolf Sturmthal, ed., *White Collar Trade Unions.* Urbana, Ill., 1966.

Lachs, Thomas. "Wirtschaftspartnerschaft." In *Wirtschaft und Politik. Festschrift für Fritz Klenner.* Wien, 1976.

Matzner, Egon. "Sozialpartnerschaft." In Heinz Fischer, ed., *Das politische System Österreichs.* Wien, 1974.

Proksch, Anton. "The Austrian Joint Wage and Price Council." In *International Labour Review* (Geneva), March 1961.

Reithofer, Hans. "Der Beirat für Wirtschafts- und Sozialfragen." In *Festschrift für Eduard März.* Wien, 1973.

Suppanz, Hannes and Derek Robinson. Prices and Incomes Policy: The Austrian Experience (OECD, Paris, 1972).

Ucakar, Karl. "Die Entwicklung der Interessenorganisationen." In Heinz Fischer, ed., *Das politische System Österreichs.* Wien, 1974.

Schöpfer, Gerald. ed. *Phänomen Sozialpartnerschaft: Festschrift für Hermann Ibler.* Wien, 1980.

APPENDIX TO PART II:
A Note on Energy in Austria

Compiled by Kurt Steiner *

I.

Power supplies in Austria are provided by coal, natural gas, and hydroelectric plants. In 1976, the domestic production of coal (including lignite and coke) provided for approximately 29 percent of the domestic consumption; the rest had to be imported, mostly from Poland, the Soviet Union, Czechoslovakia, and the Federal Republic of Germany. Oil and natural gas are drilled primarily in Lower Austria between Vienna and Austria's northeastern border, and in upper Austria in the region between the Enns and Inn rivers. Oil and oil products accounted for less than 17 percent of the domestic consumption in 1976, natural gas for about 45 percent. The rest is supplied by imports. In the past, the major suppliers of crude oil were Iraq, Iran, the Soviet Union, and various African and Middle Eastern countries. Natural gas is imported mainly from the COMECON countries and, more particularly, from the Soviet Union. Since 1968 Austria has had a gas-pipe agreement with the Soviet Union, providing for the delivery of natural gas in return for the delivery of Austrian pipes.

Whereas Austria depends greatly on foreign countries in regard to the above-mentioned sources, the situation is different in regard to hydropower, which supplies most of Austria's electricity. As a mountainous country with a network of rivers, Austria is a major producer of hydroelectric power. More than 1,000 power stations of various sizes are in operation at present,

*I acknowledge that I benefited in compiling this note from a draft chapter by Diplom Ingenieur Dr. Wilhelm Frank, formerly chief of the section on energy and mining of the Austrian Ministry of Trade and Industry, to whom I am also indebted for the selected bibliography.

and others are being constructed or planned. Most of the power stations are located in the mountains; among the most important of these are the multistage installation at Kaprun in the province of Salzburg (with an output of 647,000 kilowatt hours per year), the Zemmwerke in Tyrol (with a similar output), and the Illwerke in Vorarlberg with installations at Vermunt (494,000 kWh) and Rodund (446,000kWh). Along the Danube an eleven-stage series of power stations is being constructed. Of the five stations, completed by 1976, the one at Aschach has the highest output, namely 1,602 million kWh per year. The economically exploitable hydroelectric power potential is estimated at close to 50,000 million kWh.

The existence of this hydroelectric power potential permits Austria to export electricity to neighboring countries via numerous international power lines. This export normally amounts to about 5,000 to 6,000 million kWh. On the other hand, because hydroelectric power is subject to seasonal variations, Austria also imports about 3,000 million kwh of electric power, mainly during the winter months. The accompanying table shows in simplified form Austria's electric power supply balance.

With the growth of the economy, the demand for electrical power is steadily rising, at a rate of at least 5 percent. At the same time there is an obvious necessity to limit the import of oil and oil products for energy production and to reduce the dependence on foreign sources. The available coal, mineral oil, and natural gas sources are, of course, nonrenewable and can be used for electric power production only to a very limited degree. Under these circumstances, it was decided to build a nuclear power plant at Zwentendorf, north of Vienna. Construction began in 1971, and operation was scheduled to start in 1978. However, before operation started, a referendum was held in November 1978, and the opponents of the plant's activation, concerned about its safety, won by a narrow margin. In consequence, parliament enacted a law prohibiting the utilization of nuclear power, and the political parties agreed that a future change of that law should be enacted only by a two-thirds majority. At this writing, another

Table 1 Austria's electric power supply balance, in million kWh

Hydroelectric power stations	18,800
Thermal power stations	11,500
Total power production	30,300
Imports	3,200
Total power supply	33,500
Exports	5,300
Austrian consumption	28,200

Source: *Österreich: Tatsachen und Zahlen*, 1977, p. 76.

referendum is being planned with the aim of overturning the earlier decision. In the meantime the production of hydroelectric and coal-based power is being stepped up.

II

The organizational structure in the field of energy, and particularly in the field of electric power production and distribution, based largely on the nationalization law of 1947, is complex. Characteristic is the prevalence of public corporations. In the field of electricity, these corporations are owned by the Federal Government, the provinces or larger municipalities.

Electricity production is mainly the responsibility of provincially owned companies, one in each of the provinces. The provincial capitals of Graz, Innsbruck, Klagenfurt, Linz, and Salzburg, however, have their own electrical companies. The construction and management of larger power plants is in the hands of special companies (*Sondergesellschaften*), in which the Federal Government must have a share of at least 50 percent. Together these special companies account for about half of the electricity production.

As for distribution, the high power-line network and major transformer stations are in in the hands of a central holding company, the Österreichische Elektrizitätswirtschaft A. G., commonly known as Verbundgesellschaft. This holding company is fully owned by the Federal Government. In addition to its responsibility for a uniform network, it regulates the export and import with foreign countries and represents the share of the Federal Government in the special companies.

Of course, this complex structure involves problems of coordination. An agreement regarding this coordination of their activities was first entered into by the Verbundgesellschaft and the provincial companies in 1967. Since then various plans for the extension of electricity production were established jointly. It was in this context of planning that a joint corporation for the production of nuclear energy (Gemeinschaftskernkraftwerk Tullnerfeld G.m.b.H.) was founded in 1970.

The public sector is also predominant in regard to other energy sources. A particular role is assigned to the state-owned Österreichische Mineralölverwaltungs A.G. (ÖMV), an integrated oil company. It is responsible for the largest part of the exploration and drilling activities in Austria, and it produces about 80 percent of the domestic mineral oil and about 60 percent of the domestic natural gas, mainly in the eastern and central fields. (The Western fields are exploited by the Österreichische Rohöl A.G., a subsidiary of Mobiloil and Shell.) The ÖMV has a majority share of the ownership of the mineral oil pipelines for domestic supply, and it owns the pipelines for the transit of mineral oil through Austria and for the import of natural gas into Austria. It also owns and operates Austria's only oil refinery, located at Schwechat, south of Vienna.

This refinery handles not only the crude oil produced in Austria—including that of the Österrichische Rohöl A.G.—but also the oil pumped along a pipeline from the Adriatic port of Trieste. It produces all grades of petroleum products, and it provides most of the raw material for the petrochemical industry, in which the ÖMV also plays an important role.

The coal-mining enterprises are also owned, wholly or in part, by the Federal Government. In sum, the private sector in the area of energy is quite insignificant, except for the trade in fuels, in which the branches of some multinational corporations also participate.

Selected Bibliography

Bundeskanzleramt. *Regierungsbericht Energie.* Wien, 1977.
Bundesministerium für Handel, Gewerbe, und Industrie. *Energiebericht 1979.* Wien, 1979.
Bundesministerium für Wissenschaft und Forschung. *Forschungskonzept für die Erschliessung und Nutzung geothermischer Energie.* Wien, 1976.
Frank, W. Strukturbilanzen der Energiewirtschaft. In *Unternehmungsforschung,* vol. 2. Würzburg, 1958.
Knauer, K., and A. Götz. Das Wasserkraftpotential Österreichs, Stand 1978. In *Österreichische Zeitschrift für Elektrizitätswirtschaft,* vol. 32. Wien, 1979.
Musil, K. *Energiebilanz für das Jahr 1978.* Wien, 1979.
———. Revision der Energieprognose bis 1990. In *Monatsberichte des Österreichischen Instituts für Wirtschaftsforschung.* Wien, 1978.
Schmidt, A., and H. Bauer. *Möglichkeiten zur Gewinnung von Energie aus biogenen Rohstoffen.* Wien, 1978.
General sources, including data, are:
Bundespressedienst, *Österreich: Tatsachen und Zahlen* (in English: *Austria: Facts and Figures*). Wien, about biannually.
Organization for Economic Cooperation and Development (OECD). *Country Surveys: Austria.* Paris, 1971.
Österreichisches Statistisches Zentralamt. *Statistisches Handbuch für die Republik Österreich.* Wien, annually.

PART III

GOVERNMENT AND POLITICS

Modern Austria, pp. 209–21
Copyright © 1981 by SPOSS Inc. All rights reserved

9. GOVERNMENT STRUCTURE:
The Principles of Government

Peter Gerlich

Professor of Political Science, University of Vienna

1 CONSTITUTION AND POLITICS

The political experiences of Austria before and after World War II provide a striking contrast: The so-called First Republic, created in 1918, could not maintain its democratic institutions and collapsed in the face of fascism. The Second Republic, recreated on an identical constitutional base in 1945, has overcome great difficulties and proved a thriving and viable democratic regime. This contrast, and especially the successful development after 1945, has intrigued quite a few outside observers. Austrians themselves were first somewhat startled to find their version of democracy proclaimed a model for societies confronted with great political difficulties, especially developing countries.[1] But since the general identification with their own state has in recent years been steadily increasing, they are now apt to consider this thesis a compliment.

As indicated, the institutional arrangements during both periods have been more or less identical. The Federal Constitution of 1920 provided the basic framework for the new Republic and created the institutions within which the process of democratic politics was to be carried out. It was suspended when the "authoritarian regime" took over in 1934, but put into force again in 1945. The fact that political failure as well as political success occurred within the same institutional framework proves that constitutional principles alone cannot explain the workings of politics in Austria—even though constitutional lawyers, a group influential in the country, generally feel this to be the case. Constitutional principles are one thing to look at to understand Austrian politics; trends of political practice—political principles if you will—constitute another factor at least as important. Partly

209

9306-6403/81/0415-0209$01.50

these principles contradict each other, partly they coexist side by side. Later on, examples will be given.

First, however, it might be of interest to reflect briefly on the reasons for this basic ambivalence. On the one hand, there is a strong sense of tradition dominating public affairs in Austria. When the Constitution of 1920 was drafted, leaders tended to look back rather than forward. Since they were influenced by the experiences of the 19th century and their struggles with the authoritarian tendencies of the monarchy, the new Constitution incorporated and expressed the principles of political liberalism, which had never quite succeeded during the monarchy. But liberalism had been connected with a certain stage of social, economic, and especially political development. In the meantime, new social groups had developed political identities and strong political organizations, as well as new and much increased demands on the state. The constitution builders of 1920 did not really want to face these new developments, perhaps because it appeared easier to reach a consensus on the basis of liberal principles.[2] There was a similar development in 1945; again political expediency prevented the discussion and adoption of a "modern" constitution.

Since then, society, the economy, and politics have further changed.[3] Some old and some new discrepancies have appeared between the model of politics the Constitution presupposes and political reality. One of the advantages of a liberal constitution is, of course, that it provides broad channels for the conduct of politics and asks only for certain formal procedures to be observed. In this sense its provisions have for the most part been carefully respected, especially since 1945. Nevertheless, the content and scope of modern politics often vastly exceed what early liberals may have had in mind.[4]

What are the partly contradictory principles of modern Austrian constitutional and political life? Jurists feel that the Constitution incorporates the principles of democracy, separation of powers, federalism, local autonomy, and liberalism.[5] It provides for the institutions of representative, parliamentary democracy, introduces the classical branches of government (including the concept of the rule of law), creates a federal state, introduces local self-government, and envisages a state limited in its activities by certain basic rights the citizens have reserved for themselves. From a social science point of view, these traditional principles may be supplemented by certain trends of Austrian politics: bureaucracy, consociationalism, corporatism, centralism, and interventionism. Representative institutions are confronted with the power of administrative organizations formally subordinated to them; separation of powers appears partly to be overlaid by a tendency of consociational cooperation of big parties, and especially corporatist interest groups; federalism and local autonomy are related to the strength of central authorities (especially within parties and interest groups); and, finally, the scope of government is still expanding—the liberal state of the earlier period has been succeeded, especially in Austria, by the interventionist modern welfare state.

Although the first two decades of the Second Republic were devoted to economic reconstruction, and later on economic development, the Grand Coalition government (1945–1966) was not much concerned with institutional reform. Since then, however, certain trends toward making Austria more "modern," observable also in other spheres of life, have spread to constitutional and political arrangements. The ambivalence of the institutional situation has been mirrored in these attempts. They have, on the one hand, proceeded along lines of liberal principles ("liberal" is a word highly respected in present-day political debates), expanding and perfecting traditional institutions. On the other hand, they have tried to come to grips with the new political phenomena as well as to extend the scope of state economic and social activities.[6]

We will now describe six basic dimensions of modern Austrian politics, starting with constitutional principles and describing the main institutional arrangements they imply; we will confront these with trends of political reality, show the attempts made to modernize and reform politics, and finally mention some areas of political conflict.

2   PRINCIPLES AND TRENDS

2.1   Democracy from Above

In its first article the Federal Constitution proudly proclaims: "Austria is a democratic republic. Its law originates from the people." There is agreement among constitutional lawyers that thus the principle of democracy is introduced into Austrian constitutional law, although it is sometimes felt that this programmatic clause is in itself rather meaningless.[7] To understand what is meant by it, one must study the concrete provisions regulating the way political decisions are arrived at. Closer inspection reveals that the Austrian Constitution provides mainly for institutions of representative democracy.[8] On the national, provincial, and local levels, major decisions are taken by representative assemblies, in the first two cases mainly in the form of statutes or laws.

The main legislative body on the federal level is the National Council (Nationalrat), composed of 183 deputies regularly elected for four-year terms (shorter sessions are possible) by the people on the basis of a proportional system of representation. The Federal Council (Bundesrat), established to represent provincial interests on the national legislative level, has little influence, even in law. The Federal Government (Bundesregierung), headed by the Federal Chancellor (Bundeskanzler) as a kind of Prime Minister, is fully responsible to the National Council, although not elected by it; it is appointed through the Federal President (Bundespräsident), the formal head of state. He in turn is elected by popular vote for a six-year term. Aside from his participation in the creation of a government, his functions are mostly ceremonial.[9]

On the provincial level, the legislative function is exercised by the Provincial Diets (Landtage), also elected by the people through a system of proportional representation. They, in turn, elect the provincial executive, called Provincial Government (Landesregierung), which is headed by the Governor (Landeshauptmann).

On the national level, the Constitution mentions the possibility of direct democratic participation in legislation in the form of popular initiative or referendum. But it does not encourage these forms of plebiscite democracy. A popular initiative, if supported by a relatively large number of citizens, has only to be formally voted on by the National Council. It is also completely left to this body whether to submit a draft law to popular referendum or not. A referendum cannot be initiated by the people. Not without justification has it been stated that the Federal Constitution resists popular participation in government decision making. To some extent this attitude reflects the strong traditions of Austrian politics. From the period of enlightened absolutism, a tendency to provide "government for the people, but not by the people" has dominated the practical ideology of political as well as bureaucratic functionaries.[10]

To a certain extent this tradition has been continued within the large political mass organizations, the parties and interest groups that dominate today's political reality. Even if the leadership within these organizations is selected by some form of internal voting, there are frequent complaints about the lack of effective internal democracy within parties, and especially among interest groups.[11] Although all this has been changing in recent years, not least as a consequence of attempts to modernize Austrian politics, a strong sense of hierarchy still permeates many spheres of public life. Popular political culture is correspondingly characterized by a tendency to be subject-oriented rather than participation-oriented.[12] In a sense these tendencies have been strengthened by the efficient use that party leadership makes of the modern means of influencing the public. Day-to-day politics is increasingly conducted with the help of opinion polls, marketing techniques, and shrewd use of the electronic mass media.

On the other hand, there have been attempts to improve some democratic elements of Austrian politics. Toward the end of the Grand Coalition government, growing dissatisfaction with discrepancies between constitutional principles and political reality became especially apparent. "Reform of democracy" became a slogan, and numerous reform plans were drafted, some of which have since been put into practice.[13]

Political parties have gained official status—neglected by the Constitution—by a statute according them explicit legal recognition and providing for state subsidies. Party academies have also been established to improve the political skills of party members and functionaries.

Direct democracy has been taken more serious, on the local as well as the national level. There have been several cases of popular initiatives and finally, in November 1978, the first referendum, in which the population, by a thin margin, decided not to put into action the first atomic power plant. In addition, a new institution has been created, after the model of the Skandinavian Ombudsman, which purports to handle complaints of the population concerning public institutions (*Volksanwaltschaft*).

Further attempts have been made to extend the principles of democracy into different spheres of life: penal law has been liberalized, family law made less authoritarian, the legal position of women strengthened, co-determination in industry improved, and aspects of participation in decision making introduced into school and university systems.[14] It is ironic that this general trend has stopped short of the area of politics itself: Unlike its models in other Western countries, the new party statute lacks provision for a democratic organization of Austrian parties.

2.2   Unseparated Powers

The Austrian Constitution follows the liberal theory of limiting misuse of power by distributing it and providing control mechanisms. It introduces the three traditional branches of government, albeit in a technically complicated form, establishing legislative, administrative, and judiciary institutions. A basic notion of the Austrian Constitution is that of the *Rechtsstaat,* which may be translated as "rule of law." All institutions are bound to adhere to the provisions of constitutional law, and a special Constitutional Court (Verfassungsgerichtshof) is established to control even the legislature. The administrative branch (including the government) and the judiciary branch are moreover bound to adhere to the statutory law. All executive action has its basis in parliamentary statute. Another special court, the Administrative Court (Verwaltungsgerichtshof), has been established to control the legality of administrative actions. The judiciary, or court system proper, is completely separated from the administration and is organized into a hierarchy of appellate courts, with the Supreme Court (Oberster Gerichtshof) at the top.[15]

Although the courts have been fairly independent in practice as well as in theory, the relationship between the legislative and executive branches has been much changed by the existence of disciplined parties. No longer does the parliament as a whole confront a government and administration. Rather, the majority party (or parties) that hold government office constitute a tight link between government and parliamentary majority. The control function has been taken over by the minority party (or parties) acting as opposition.[16]

Party influence, especially in Austria, does exceed the areas of parliament and government, however. Especially under the Grand Coalition all areas of public life were divided into spheres of influence under the so-called *Proporz* system. Much of this tradition lingers on. This is especially true of those numerous areas of public activity in which the state acts as a quasi-private business concern. Here the principle of legal determination is difficult to practice. But these areas are of great importance, since they include the nationalized industries, public contracts, business subsidies, and other public economic activities.

At the highest level of administration the role and influence of top civil servants should not be underestimated. Secure in their position—there are no political civil servants as in other countries—with the immense experience of lifetime duty within the same branch of government, they are often the equals of ministers with less experience and many duties. To this must be added the long tradition of bureaucratic influence of Austrian history. Here, too, the constitutional hierarchy subordinating civil servants to the authority of politically appointed officials may even be reversed.[17]

Actually, one main problem invalidating the principle of separation of powers in political reality is that individual functionaries hold important positions in different branches of government as well as in powerful parties and interest groups. There have been attempts to reduce the number of positions any politician may hold, but striking specimens of multifunctionaries may still be observed. Other attempts at reform in this area have included improvement in the position of the opposition in parliament and improvement of access to the courts, especially the Constitutional Court, which can now be approached not only by citizens who feel their constitutional rights have been infringed but also by opposition parties who failed to prevent a statute they considered unconstitutional from being passed in parliament.

2.3   Symbolic Federalism

As already mentioned, the Constitution provides not only for horizontal separation of powers but also for vertical division of powers establishing nine provinces (*Bundesländer*) as, in principle, autonomous elements below the level of national or federal government. This small country has a complicated constitutional structure that might seem necessary only in a large country with strong regional differences. The reasons are, of course, historical and political. The Austrian provinces had their separate histories within the Habsburg monarchy, which represented power bases that the different parties wanted to maintain when the Constitution was drawn up in 1920.[18]

There are discrepancies between principle and detail even in the Constitution itself. The distribution of spheres of influence is complicated and elaborate. Legislation and administration are in theory granted to one level or the other, or exercised jointly. Even if technically the Constitution provides that all matters not delegated to the federation shall be left to the provinces, in effect very few matters have been left to them. Almost all important political matters have in fact been delegated to the Federal Government. Not only are there no provincial courts of law, but matters of education, police, and fiscal and social affairs are mostly legislated in the National Council. Provincial autonomy extends to such matters as regional planning, aspects of agricultural affairs, hospitals, and electricity. However, in many spheres of administration the provincial administrative authorities have the task of executing federal laws under the supervision of federal authorities. Here a certain leeway in interpretation may exist, particularly if the factually strong position of civil servants vis à vis political representatives is taken into account.

As *Table 1* shows, the relative lack of functions assigned to the provinces is mirrored by the distribution of public finance. The provinces together spend only part of what the Federal Government spends. However, a marked trend can be observed increasing the relative share of the provinces. This is mostly due to the intensified economic activity of the provinces, for example in the areas of public housing and road construction.

This tendency corresponds to general developments. Federalism in Austria may still be mostly a symbolic, emotional matter. Inhabitants of the different provinces identify with their regional entity, its traditions, and, last, its politicians. But in recent years federalism has also increasingly become a matter of political concern. The provinces have jointly drafted a program of demands which the Federal Government has already accepted

Table 1   Proportions of total public expenditures, in percent

	1960	1974
Federal government	65.8%	54.9%
Provinces	20.7	30.4
Local government	13.5	14.7

Source: E. Matzner, ed., *Öffentliche Aufgaben und Finanzausgleich* (Wien, 1978).

in part. A general trend toward increased regional autonomy, which may be observed all over Europe, has found an already existing pattern in Austria, but it may lead, as recent developments suggest, to further intensification of the debate on provincial demands.[19]

2.4 Strained Local Government

Local autonomy, in the sense of local citizens determining their own affairs, was one of the minimal demands of 19th-century liberalism, especially in Austria.[20] The Constitution accordingly provides for municipalities or communes (*Gemeinden*) as basic territorial units within the provinces.[21] They are organized as autonomous entities and given certain tasks to carry out as suborgans of provincial and federal authorities. Municipalities can also become economically active, own property, and run enterprises. In the conduct of its affairs the municipality has an organization analogous to that of the provincial government; citizens elect a council, which in turn elects a committee and the mayor. It is probably characteristic of the trend in Austrian constitutional law to aim at regulations of highly abstract generality; namely, that all municipalities be treated more or less equally. The same regulations apply to the cities (there are 7 with a population of more than 50,000, and roughly 20 with more than 20,000), as well as to the smaller and rural communities (of which there are about 2,300 altogether).[22]

As can be deduced from *Table 2,* most of the small communities vote Conservative, and only the larger cities have Socialist majorities. Even more than on the provincial level, this signifies a certain tension vis à vis the higher levels of politics, made more relevant by the fact that the autonomous area is limited, especially in financial matters. Municipalities depend increasingly on contributions from provincial and federal authorities in order to carry out the ever increasing task of providing the necessary infrastructure for their citizens.[23]

This tight financial situation is a current political problem, especially in the larger, urban municipalities. Associated with it is the tendency (not so obvious on the federal or provincial level) toward citizen unrest. Mayors of parties long in power lost their office when they underestimated pop-

Table 2 Distribution of deputies among parties, 1977, in percent

	SPÖ	ÖVP	FPÖ	Other
Federal parliament	50.8%	43.7%	5.5%	
All provinces	47.3	48.2	5.2	
All municipalities	35.4	56.5	4.2	3.9%

Source: *Österreichisches Jahrbuch für Politik, 1978,* esp. p. 370.

ular dissatisfaction with projects threatening housing areas, which was sometimes expressed in the form of "citizens' initiatives." Conversely, local politicians have tried to learn from these experiences, and there is now an increased tendency to involve local citizens in decision-making processes.[24]

2.5   Consociationalism and Corporatism

When public law experts try to deal with political reality, which even to the legal mind no longer comfortably fits the general principles and institutions of the Constitution, they tend to describe recent political development as a trend toward the "party and interest group state" (*Parteien und Verbändestaat*). Indeed, powerful political organizations not even mentioned in the Constitution exercise a degree of apparently "official" power that is quite impressive.

How the parliamentary system of government has been transformed by the activities of disciplined mass parties has already been mentioned. Party influence became particularly strong during the period between 1945 and 1966, when Austria was ruled by the Grand Coalition of the Conservative and Socialist parties. In contrast to the First Republic, torn apart by political strife and even civil war, the two big "camps" were now cooperating, even if, especially in the beginning, rather reluctantly and with mutual distrust. Thus a system of consociational politics developed in which decision making by majority vote was replaced by mutual adjustments, distribution of spheres of influence, and mutual control.[25] This model was abandoned on the government level in 1966, and the traditional interplay between majority government and minority opposition was reintroduced, thus again activating, at least to a certain extent, the liberal principles of parliamentary government.

Consociational procedures were, however, maintained in the area of interest group cooperation—the so-called *Sozialpartnerschaft.*[26] During the Second Republic the big economic interest groups have achieved a position of great power. Characteristically, the Chambers of Commerce, Labor, and Agriculture (Handelskammer, Arbeiterkammer, and Landwirtschaftskammer) have a kind of semiofficial status in that every citizen economically active in the respective sphere is by law considered a member. To this has been added the Federation of Trade Unions (Österreichischer Gewerkschaftsbund), which, though a voluntary organization, has organized almost two-thirds of all workers and holds a virtual monopoly of trade union representation. These four large organizations realize the principle of corporatism,[27] the idea that political organization should follow economic position, and they effectively practice consociational politics within the framework of the so-called Joint Commission (Paritätische Kommission), which amounts to a second government for economic affairs. All wage and many price policies must, in fact, be approved by this body, which does not have any constitutional or even legal basis.

Sozialpartnerschaft has been instrumental in achieving the peaceful and, on the whole, prosperous development of the Austrian economy since 1945. However, criticism has been voiced about the immense concentration of power, which tends to further reduce the influence of constitutional institutions, and especially regarding the limited democratic legitimacy of the institutions of social partnership. Its leaders and representatives are in some ways elected within their organizations. But since they face no serious opponents there, they are practically unremovable, whereas parliamentary deputies or ministers are always open to this fate.[28]

2.6   Liberal to Welfare State

Liberalism not only proposed certain institutional arrangements but also had definite ideas about the content of politics, about the tasks to be performed by the state. The state was to concern itself only with providing necessary preconditions for the successful development of social and economic affairs by guaranteeing internal as well as external security, abolishing traditional regulations hampering the freedom of markets, and providing some aspects of social and technical infrastructure like education and transportation. In a negative way these ideas have been recognized by the Austrian Constitution, which refrains from defining any goals of state activities and limits itself to prescribing formal ways in which these activities are to be carried out. More explicitly, the list of citizens' rights incorporated in the bill of rights promulgated in 1867 and adapted in 1920, since no agreement could be reached on a more up-to-date list, stresses limits of state activity, especially if the right to freely exercise property rights is kept in mind.

These limited aims are not necessarily accepted any more. The state, no longer limited to the role of a sort of "night watchman" according to the ideas of liberalism, has been greatly expanding its areas of influence and spheres of activity. The modern "active state" (*Leistungsstaat*), the state of interventionism, has established an elaborate system of social policies on the one hand and is continuously intervening in the economy on the other. Austria now has an extended system of welfare legislation, which includes social insurance covering health, accidents, retirement, and unemployment; today this includes almost every citizen.[29] In addition, there are other welfare services e.g. for families.[30] In the economic sphere the state subsidizes industry and agriculture, maintains a large nationalized sector, and hands out contracts to a variety of private businesses.[31] All these activities, social and economic, have been continuously expanded in recent years in pursuance of what might be called the second aspect of modernity in Austrian politics. Figures showing taxes as a percentage of Gross National Product illustrate the fiscal effects of this trend through the years: 13 percent in 1913, 29 percent in 1955, 38 percent in 1969, and 42 percent (estimated) in 1978.[32]

The Constitution appears to be neutral: while not encouraging increased state activity, it certainly does not prohibit it. It must be noted, however, that the method of politics prescribed by constitutional procedure—legislation by statute and execution by administrative bodies—although quite appropriate for traditional regulative areas of politics like penal or civil law, is not at all adequate for distributive policies.[33] Here other forms of conducting decision making should be practiced, such as planning or introducing business methods like electronic data processing into the administration. Attempts to reform the bureaucracy in this respect have been numerous but not always successful. Special mention should be made of the establishment of a Federal Civil Service Academy (Verwaltungsakademie), which trains senior civil servants in modern management techniques.

3 CONCLUSION AND OUTLOOK

The political institutions of present-day Austria combine traditional and modern aspects. The Constitution, "a descendant from the world of yesterday,"[34] has been more or less successfully adapted to the necessities of a changed political environment. New procedures and institutions have been created that partly coexist with and partly change traditional arrangements. No radical reform has been seriously attempted—although the idea of drafting a completely new constitution has sometimes been discussed—but the pace of accommodation by reform of details has been increasing, especially during the last decade. Modernization implies partly improvement of liberal institutions, partly extension of democratic participation, and partly continuous expansion of social and economic policies.

The question of what factors explain the successful experience of the Second Republic, compared with the failure of the First remains difficult to answer, however. Both periods operated under the same constitution and maintained the same institutional setup. Of course the political culture changed drastically after 1945. Political as well as social consociationalism, made possible by Grand Coalition cooperation and the rise of a corporatist system of representative interests, contributed a great deal to the peaceful climate in which economic success became possible. But, conversely, might not economic success, made possible at least partly by a different and more secure international position, have led to cooperation and consociational-ism?[35]

The future may show whether the institutions of *Sozialpartnerschaft* will be able to maintain their cooperation in the face of a more difficult international and national economic situation.[36] But even if this somewhat precarious cooperation should break down, the traditional institutions of parliamentary democracy after thirty years of successful operation may be able to accommodate an increased amount of conflict. Some observers have noted that what has been gained in political stability in Austria since 1945 has been lost in intellectual and imaginative vitality. Reversals of this trend may become feasible.

Notes

1. See Bluhm, p. 257: "If Austrians could do so, why can't others?" See the Selected Bibliography for complete publishing information.
2. Pelinka and Welan, p. 13.
3. See Steiner, pp. 47ff, who describes geographic, demographic, and economic changes and their political consequences.
4. Gerlich, pp. 28ff.
5. See e.g. Walter, p. 101.
6. See e.g. the political aims of the present majority party summarized by Fischer, p. 14.
7. Klecatsky, p. 512.
8. The institutional framework of Austrian politics is well described by Steiner, pp. 98–118.
9. Since 1945 there have been five Federal Presidents: Karl Renner (1945–1951), Theodor Körner (1951–1957), Adolf Schärf (1957–1965), Franz Jonas (1965–1974), and Rudolf Kirchschläger (1974 to present; re-elected in May 1980).
   For a list of Federal Chancellors, see Chapter 11, note 5. For the results of the elections to the National Council, See Table 2 of Chapter 11.
10. Welan, pp. 1198ff.
11. See e.g. Pelinka and Welan, pp. 303 and 322.
12. See the recent comparative study on popular attitutes toward political action, with Austria one of the countries studied, in Barnes et. al., esp. p. 169.
13. A good summary of reform plans is provided by Hillbrand.
14. See Ermacora, esp. pp. 69ff.
15. See Steiner, pp. 397ff.
16. Gerlich, pp. 164ff.
17. Steiner, pp. 375ff.
18. Steiner, pp. 98ff.
19. For recent trends in Austrian federalism, see Motz.
20. See Ucakar and Welan.
21. Steiner, pp. 106–9.
22. See Bauer, pp. 16ff.
23. This limitation of local political capabilities is well brought out by one of the few case studies of an Austrian community; see Powell, p. 139.
24. A comparative study of citizen participation in urban planning describes and criticizes first attempts in this respect in Vienna. See Ulram, pp. 30–70.
25. For a definition of consociational democracy, see Steiner, p. 409.
26. See Matzner 1977; also Chapter 8 of this volume.
27. See Lehmbruch, pp. 158ff.
28. Matzner 1977.
29. See Talos; also Chapter 14 of this volume.
30. See Krebs and Schwarz.
31. A survey of contemporary industrial policy is provided by Raidl; see also Chapter 6 of this volume.

32. Data from Andreae, p. 172.
33. See a critique of the traditional technique of legislation by Öhlinger and Matzka, pp. 449f.
34. Welan, p. 1198.
35. See Bluhm, pp. 242ff.
36. Compare the projections by A. Klose and A. Pelinka in Marin, pp. 220ff.

Selected Bibliography

Andreae, C. A., ed. *Handbuch der österreichischen Finanzwirtschaft.* Innsbruck, 1970.
Barnes, S. H., M. Kaase, et al. *Political Action: Mass Participation in Five Western Democracies.* London, 1979.
Bauer, H., et al. *Aufgaben der Gemeinden.* Wien, 1977.
Bluhm, W. T. *Building an Austrian Nation.* New Haven, 1973.
Ermacora, F. Politische Aspekte der Verfassungsentwicklung in Österreich seit 1970. In *Österreichisches Jahrbuch für Politik.* Wien, 1978.
Fischer, H., ed. *Rote Markierungen '80.* Wien, 1980.
Gerlich, P. *Parlamentarische Kontrolle im politischen System.* Wien, 1973.
Hillbrand, H. Die bisherigen Vorschläge zur Demokratiereform in Österreich. In *Demokratie im Umbruch.* Innsbruck, 1969.
Klecatsky, H. R. Geht das Recht vom Volk aus? *Juristische Blätter,* 1976, pp. 512–15.
Krebs, E., and M. Schwarz. Austria. In S. B. Kamerman and A. J. Kohn, eds. *Family Policy, Government and Families in Fourteen Countries.* New York, 1978.
Lehmbruch, G. Liberal Corporatism and Party Government. In P. C. Schmitter and G. Lehmbruch, eds., *Trends Towards Corporatist Intermediation.* London, 1979.
Marin, B. *Wachstumskrisen in Österreich?* Wien, 1979.
Matzner, E. Sozialpartnerschaft. In H. Fischer, ed., *Das politische System Österreichs,* 2d ed. Wien, 1977.
Matzner, E., ed. *Öffentliche Aufgaben und Finanzausgleich.* Wien, 1978.
Mommsen and Reindl. Austria. In P. Merkl, ed., *Western European Party Systems.* New York, 1980.
Motz, M. Zur Lage des Föderalismus in Österreich. *Österreichisches Jahrbuch für Politik,* vol. 1. Wien, 1978.
Öhlinger, T., and M. Matzka. Demokratie und Verwaltung als verfassungsrechtliches Problem. *Österreichische Zeitschrift Für Politikwissenschaft,* Wien, 1975.
Pelinka, A., and M. Welan. *Demokratie und Verfassung in Österreich.* Wien, 1971.
Powell, G. B. *Social Fragmentation and Political Hostility, An Austrian Case Study.* Stanford, Calif., 1970.
Raidl, C. Aufgaben einer modernen Industriepolitik. *Österreichisches Jahrbuch für Politik,* vol. 2. Wien, 1978.
Steiner, K. *Politics in Austria.* Boston, 1972.
Talos, E. Zur Politik der sozialen Sicherung in der Zweiten Republik. *Beiträge zur historischen Sozialkunde,* 1978/2, Wien.
Ucakar, K., and M. Welan. *Kommunale Selbstverwaltung und konstitutioneller Rechtsstaat. In Forschungen und Beiträge zur Wiener Stadtgeschichte,* vol. 1. Wien, 1978.
Ulram, P. *Zwischen Bürokratie und Bürger.* Wien, 1978.
Walter, R. *Österreichisches Bundesverfassungsrecht.* Wien, 1972.
Welan, M. Demokratie und Demokratisierung. In M. Fischer et al, eds., *Dimensionen des Rechts.* Berlin, 1974.

Modern Austria, pp. 223–39
Copyright © 1981 by SPOSS Inc. All rights reserved

10. POLITICAL PARTIES

Anton Pelinka

Professor of Political Science at the University of Innsbruck

1 CHARACTERISTICS OF THE PARTY SYSTEM

The Austrian party system has two primary characteristics: continuity and concentration, which represent the essential difference between the Austrian system and most other European multiparty systems. Continuity means that the historical roots of the present Austrian parties go back to the 19th century, that the development of the party system can be traced back, without interruption, for about a century. Certain positions in today's party platforms, certain social interdependencies, certain historical identifications of today, can only be understood when this continuity is taken into consideration.[1] This continuity is also manifested in the party personnel. It is most pronounced in the Socialist party of Austria (Sozialistische Partei Österreichs, SPÖ), somewhat less so in the Austrian People's party (Österreichische Volkspartei, ÖVP), and least pronounced, yet still existent, in the Liberal party of Austria (Freiheitliche Partei Österreichs, FPÖ). In all three parties, a red thread of personnel continuity can be traced into the 19th century; there is also continuity of consciousness, of identification with the past.

Concentration means that the number of relevant parties is relatively small in Austria, that the voters concentrate to an unusual degree on very few parties. This concentration in the quantity of approval corresponds, in principle, to concentration in the quality of power. The number of parties that are actually able to influence the political process in the federation, the provinces, and the communities is conspicuously small.

In an international comparison, the Austrian party system can be categorized as a two-and-a-half-party system (or "limping party system"). Two

Translated by Ulrike E. Lieder, Stanford University

223

9306-6403/81/0415-0223$01.50

parties dominate, one is clearly smaller, and there are no fourth parties to speak of. This concentration on two large parties and one smaller one, along with actual exclusion of fourth parties, has remained essentially stable for decades and can be traced back to the early history of the Austrian party system.[2]

Concentration of the party system in Austria becomes all the more conspicuous in an international comparison because similar concentrations in Western multiparty systems are only observed in cases where an electoral law that promotes majorities (primarily the relative majority system in Great Britain and the USA, and in other political systems influenced by the Anglo-American system), favors the concentration of votes and seats on two parties. In Austria, this concentration on only a few parties occurred not because of a relative majority election system but in spite of a system of proportional representation.

2 DEVELOPMENTAL TRENDS IN THE PARTY SYSTEM

The development of Austrian parties is characterized by the concept of "camps." During the latter phase of the monarchy, during the First Republic and also the Second Republic, political parties have always been more than parties in a narrower sense. Besides the functions of political parties, i. e. besides the central function of participating in elections, parties in Austria have always been important as ideological communities. The parties and their auxiliary organizations in various interest areas formed camps that originally confronted each other with complete hostility.[3]

These camps are closely connected to continuity in the party system. The Socialist camp, which would be represented by the Socialist party in the Second Republic, was the speaker of the great majority of the Austrian labor movement, and it had close ties with the mainstream of the labor union movement. The Christian-Social-Conservative camp, which would be represented by the Austrian People's party in the Second Republic, was molded by political Catholicism, and to this day it is characterized by ties to Catholic associations and that segment of the population who are active Catholics. The German-Nationalist camp, today represented by the Liberal party, represented the bourgeois element, which was originally oriented especially toward a political union with Germany, and which emphasized its German background.

The problems of the dying monarchy can still be recognized in these three camps. The labor movement fighting for equality, political Catholicism representing the union of throne and altar, and German nationalism reflecting the conflicting nationalities—these phenomena are children of the monarchy, and they were passed on from the monarchy to the republic, even to the Second Republic. However, the conspicuous continuity of the camps is not to be understood as inflexibility. On the contrary, there is a concentration in favor of the two large camps at the expense of the third, smaller camp. Over a long period of time, the Socialist and the Christian-Social-Conservative camps have gained followers, whereas the German-Nationalist camp lost some of its support base. See Table 1.

This concentration in continuity has, so far, survived every emergence of a fourth party. For a short time, between 1945 and 1959, the Communist party of Austria (KPÖ) played the role of a fourth, at times even a third, relevant party. Yet, in spite of the role it played in the Resistance Movement, in spite of (or possibly because of) its close ties to Moscow, the KPÖ could not establish itself as a stable and essential factor in the Austrian party system. Owing to the delineation of the camps that had already been determined during the monarchy, it could not create a place for itself.

However, these developmental trends must not simply be extrapolated for the future. There are certain indications that the concentration of parties has reached its peak, or even passed it. For the first time in decades the combined votes of the two large parties decreased in 1979 National Council elections. New party groupings can be observed at the communal level, groupings that do not fit into the traditional tripartition of the party system —the phenomenon of fourth parties already exists at the lower levels.[4] It appears possible that, in the future, the party system will destabilize, or at least deconcentrate, beginning at the communal level. This development may be traced back to the system of proportional representation, perfected since 1971, which favors the emergence of small parties, combined with a progressing secularization of the entire party system. Decrease of the camp mentality, which will be discussed in detail later, is another intangible factor in the further development of the party system.

3   INTERNAL STRUCTURE OF THE PARTIES

3.1   Number of Voters and Members

The ratio of voters to party members is an unusual one, especially in the two large parties, compared internationally with other parties. The degree of organization expressed in the ratio of members to voters is highly developed in Austria. The SPÖ organization is above average, even compared with other extremely tightly organized member parties of the Socialist International. The ÖVP is the most tightly organized party in the European Union of Christian Democrats.

226   PELINKA

Table 1 Development of party concentration

National Council elections	Share of votes of the two large parties	Share of votes of all other parties
1920	77.8%	22.2%
1930	76.8	23.2
1949	82.7	17.3
1959	89.0	11.0
1970	93.1	6.9
1975	93.4	6.6
1979	92.9	7.1

Source: Compilation according to official election results.
Note: Large parties: Social Democrats and Christian Socialists until 1930, SPÖ (Socialist party) and ÖVP (People's party) since 1949.

The degree of organization in the parties is also determined by the structure of the organization, by the party's concept of what constitutes a member. SPÖ, FPÖ, and KPÖ adhere, without restrictions, to the principle of direct membership, which can only be acquired through a direct, individual act of joining the party. In the ÖVP, indirect membership has been prevalent, at least until 1980. See Table 2. Indirect membership arises out of membership in a subparty: the ÖVP consists of six suborganizations whose members are also members of the parent party. In comparison with membership in suborganizations, the number of direct members in the People's party is conspicuously small.[5]

This membership, which would indicate a degree of organization of more than 50 percent and thus represent an international record, includes many dual or multiple memberships, and precise figures are not available. It is possible—and not uncommon—for an ÖVP member to be a member in two or more suborganizations. It is impossible to record this in the membership statistics. Therefore, it is more realistic to base a determination of the membership on that of the three associations that dominate the recruiting structure of the entire People's party, and to neglect the membership of the other three suborganizations. In spite of this, the People's party shows an extreme degree of organization, which is supplemented by a considerable degree of organization in the SPÖ.[6] See Table 3.

Of course, the individual parties are not equally strong in all Austrian provinces. In the 1979 National Council Elections, the SPÖ had clearly above-average results in Vienna, Carinthia, and Burgenland. The results in Upper Austria and Styria corresponded roughly to the statewide average, whereas they were below average in Lower Austria, Salzburg, the Tyrol, and Vorarlberg. The regional distribution of ÖVP votes was the opposite of the SPÖ distribution. This regional concentration has essentially re-

Table 2   Members in the ÖVP and its suborganizations as of 1976

Organization	Number
Österreichischer Arbeiter- und Angestelltenbund, ÖAAB	
(Austrian Federation of Workers and Employees)	252,583
Österreichischer Bauernbund, ÖBB	
(Austrian Federation of Farmers)	405,734
Österreichischer Wirtschaftsbund, ÖWB	
(Austrian Federation of Business)	157,791
Österreichische Frauenbewegung, ÖFB	
(Austrian Women's Movement)	71,912
Junge Volkspartei, JVP	
(Young People's Party)	91,983
Österreichischer Seniorenbund, ÖSB	
(Austrian Federation of Senior Citizens)	201,400
Direct members	122
Total	1,181,525

Source: Compiled according to *19. ordentlicher Bundesparteitag, Bericht zur Parteiarbeit, 1974–1977* Wien, n.d.).
Note: Only at the 1977 Party Convention did the members of the Austrian Federation of Senior Citizens (until 1974 called "Österreichischer Pensionisten- und Rentnerbund" [Austrian Federation of Old Age Pensioners]) acquire full membership in the party, when their association was admitted as a suborganization with equal rights. Direct members are those members who have taken advantage of the theoretical possibility of joining the ÖVP directly and not indirectly (by way of a suborganization).

mained constant during the Second Republic, and, except for Lower Austria, we may speak of differences between east and west: the regional concentration of the ÖVP is in the west, that of the SPÖ in the east.[7]

3.2   Social Structure of Membership and Voters

The Austrian parties are supported by different social groups. As usual, the SPÖ represents the majority of labor, and the ÖVP represents the majority of farmers, independent small business men, and industrialists. However, in the process of the "second industrialization," these traditional social core groups are continuously decreasing. The large social group of white-collar workers (civil servants and employees), which benefits from this trend, distributes its votes relatively equally to both large parties. On this, the social level, the FPÖ voter structure is relatively similar to that of the ÖVP. See Table 4.

This social structure of the Austrian parties, in conjunction with the general social trend toward white-collar workers, means that the parties are becoming increasingly dependent upon the same large social group. Win-

Table 3 Degree of organization in the parties represented in the National Council (19)

	Voters (1979)	Membership	Degree of organization
SPÖ	2,412,778	706,039	29.3%
ÖVP	1,981,286	816,108	41.2%
FPÖ	286,644	34,000	11.9%

Source: Membership figures for the SPÖ are according to its Yearbook for 1979, report to the 25th party convention on the years 1978 and 1979 (Wien, no year of publication indicated). The ÖVP figures reflect only the membership of the three associations (ÖAAB, ÖBB, and ÖWB), according to *19. ordentlicher Bundesparteitag, Bericht zur Parteiarbeit, 1974–1977* (Wien, n.d.). Figures for the FPÖ are based on internal party estimates, since no official publications are available.

ning an election is becoming less dependent on the traditional core group; it is increasingly being determined by the behavior of the group of employees and civil servants, a group that is the most difficult to categorize.

.Another significant difference between the parties can be seen in the voter structure. The behavior of the Austrian voters is still clearly determined by their religious denomination, in spite of the factual secularization of the parties' policies. See Table 5. This corresponds to the traditional conflict between political Catholicism on the one side and anticlerical trends on the other. The great majority of active churchgoers (who, in view of the denominational structure of the total population, are Catholic) vote for the ÖVP; only minorities of these active Catholics regularly vote for the SPÖ or the FPÖ.

Table 4 Social structure of the voters, portion of party followers among the gainfully employed

	SPÖ			ÖVP			FPÖ		
	1971	1976	1978	1971	1976	1978	1971	1976	1978
Independent businessmen	4.1%	3.3%	3.2%	15.9%	11.9%	12.3%	18.7%	14.5%	14.4%
Employees in executive positions, sr. civil servants	3.4	4.1	4.4	4.7	6.2	7.4	8.3	10.4	10.6
Other employees and civil servants	35.7	37.9	41.2	29.3	28.2	35.3	33.3	31.8	44.1
Labor	53.1	52.0	48.1	15.9	21.0	21.2	29.0	28.7	21.1
Farmers	3.4	2.6	3.1	34.2	32.8	23.8	11.4	14.6	9.4
	99.7%	99.9%	100%	100%	100.1%	100%	100.7%	100%	99.6%

Source: Ernst Gehmacher, Franz Birk, and Herbert Berger, "Nationalratswahl-Analyse," in *Die Zukunft*, June 1979.
Note: Some columns do not add up to 100% due to rounding.

Table 5   Denominational structure of the voters, in percent

Sympathizers with	SPÖ	ÖVP	FPÖ	Others/ undecided
Go to church services:				
Several times a month	16%	57%	16%	27%
Once a month	7	10	5	10
A few times a year	32	21	31	23
(Almost) never	44	12	48	36
No answer				4
	99%	100%	100%	100%
Members go to church regularly	6%	63%		

Source: Compiled according to statistics from IFES or Fessl, in Joachim Raschke, ed., *Die politischen Parteien in Westeuropa. Geschichte-Programm-Praxis. Ein Handbuch* (Reinbek, 1978), p. 417.
Note: The first column does not add up to 100% due to rounding.

There is no real correspondence between the dynamics of the voter structure of the parties and that at the membership level. This is especially pronounced in the case of the ÖVP, which, owing to its structure, clearly reflects the social composition of the membership. The share of the traditional core groups—farmers, independent businessman—among the membership (of the Farmers' Association and the Economic Association) is clearly above the share of these groups among the voters of this party. It is not possible to make similar statements on the social composition of the membership of other Austrian parties because, owing to their party structure, there are no statistics on the occupational and professional categories of SPÖ and FPÖ members.

In conjunction with the general secularization, which has made popular and catch-all parties out of the former ideological and class parties, these structural changes at the voter level must be regarded as an additional drawing force toward the political center. Independent of their still existing, class-specific support among voters and members, the parties are forced to become parties representing the political center, attracting especially the white-collar workers, if they want to win the elections.

3.3   Party Finances

Several factors influence the finances of the Austrian parties: (*a*) the relatively high degree of organization results in relatively high revenues from membership dues; (*b*) the relatively high degree of interconnections between the parties and the State makes it possible that party functionaries, who owe their position to the party, be "taxed" by the party to a large extent; and (*c*) this degree of interconnection between the parties and the

State also results in various different items of direct or indirect State financing for the parties. The financing mandated by the 1975 Party Law represents only a part of these budget items.[8] See Table 6.

These three sources of revenue provide the two large parties already with an annual income of more than 300 million Schillings at the present time. In addition, there are revenues from donations. These are either collective donations—from economic associations, for instance—or individual donations made directly to the party by an individual. It is most difficult to estimate the magnitude of this source of revenue. However, a clear preponderance of collective donations over private ones is indicated by the organization of the Austrian economy in associations, by the Austrian laws which do not allow tax deductions for donations to political parties, as well as by individual reports.[9]

Excluding the revenues from donations, Table 6, below, shows the magnitude of the income of the two large parties during a non-election year.

A certain difference between the two large parties results from the magnitude of the donations. It is certain that the ÖVP receives more money from this budget item than does the SPÖ, a major reason being that labor unions in Austria must not directly finance the parties. The relatively small amounts that the Austrian Federation of Trade Unions (*Österreichischer Gewerkschaftsbund,* ÖGB) pays to its *Fraktionen* (caucuses or factions, structured according to party politics) are by no means comparable to the donations that the parties, i.e. primarily the ÖVP and the FPÖ, receive from the employers' associations.[10]

The FPÖ receives relatively less money from membership dues, because of its clearly lower degree of organization. Therefore, State financing is all the more important for this party. State financing of the parties, owing to the structure of the Party Law, favors smaller parties inasmuch as all parties represented in parliament are entitled to fixed base sums without consider-

Table 6   Revenues of the large Austrian parties

Revenue	Amount (million schillings)
Membership dues	131
Party taxes	42.5
State subsidies	170

Source: The compilation follows data given in Anton Kofler, *Parteienfinanzierung und deren Auswirkungen auf innerparteiliche Strukturen, dargestellt am Beispiel der ÖVP* (Diplomarbeit, University of Innsbruck, 1979), p. 152. The data for the ÖVP, based on an empirical study, were also used for the SPÖ. This is based on the assumption that revenues of the large parties are largely analogous (except for donations).

ation of the party's size. This makes the FPÖ that party of the three parties represented in parliament that benefits most from the State's financing of the parties.[11]

3.4 Democracy Within the Parties

The internal party process of formulating objectives is based on the principle of a representative democracy, oriented toward the party members. In all parties, the party convention plays the—formally—decisive role. The party convention is indirectly selected by the party members, and it serves as the party's parliament. However, in political practice, the significance of the party conventions has been reduced greatly. Informal patterns of formulating objectives have replaced the formality of the party's statutes; orientation has shifted away from the members toward the undecided voter. The party leadership—formally dependent on the party conventions—orients its behavior strongly toward the undecided voters, who are rarely organized as members within the parties, but who are the deciding factor in elections. This preponderance of informal patterns over the formally existing representative democracy is reflected especially clearly in the proceedings of the party conventions. Only in exceptional cases do the conventions have the function of deciding between several internal party alternatives that may concern objectives or personnel questions. As a rule, party conventions are instruments of acclamation which approve in retrospect the decisions already made by the party leadership.

The reality of the internal party decision-making process is also reflected in internal party political careers. Generally speaking, the pattern of seniority is predominant in Austrian parties: a person embarks on a career within the party and, in accordance with length of service and quality of performance, gradually works his way up. This pattern of seniority is essentially employed in the SPÖ, albeit with one important restriction: the "Faction of Socialist Trade Unionists" within the ÖGB is entitled to certain positions that are filled from this group, again following seniority rules. In the ÖVP, the pattern of seniority is used primarily within the associations themselves—it does not apply so much in the party itself as it does among the suborganizations that fill in this manner the positions to which they are "entitled."[13]

In addition to the pattern of seniority, there is also the pattern of technocracy. Technocracy means that the party leadership fills certain top positions while bypassing the traditional claims of groups within the party or of long-time functionaries. This makes extremely swift political careers possible in all three of the parties represented in parliament, even though the principle of seniority can still be observed. This second career pattern enables the party leadership to appoint candidates who would be particularly effective with the undecided voters, even against the latent resistance of the mid-level functionaries. Thus experts in any given field, who have not (or not yet) gone through the time-consuming career according to the seniority system, can achieve a top-level position.[14]

The seniority system and the technocracy system result in a party elite make-up increasingly different from the composition of the party base. The social composition of the parliamentarians in particular is more and more growing apart from its base. This is an indication that parliamentary and party efficiency have a clear priority over parliamentary and party representation. The "iron-clad law of oligarchy" is just as effective in the Austrian parties as it is in other parties in the Western democracies.[15]

4   EXTERNAL RELATIONS OF THE PARTIES

4.1   Roles in Government and Opposition

Because the two large parties are also in power at various levels, there has always been a close interconnection between the parties and the State in Austria. At the federal level, they governed together for a total of 21 years, from 1945 to 1947 still in coalition with the KPÖ, then as the "Grand Coalition" until 1966. Yet even the dissolution of this coalition did not result in a situation similar to the First Republic; neither of the two large parties felt it was the "opposition party on principle," having been denied the power to govern. Even after 1966, SPÖ and ÖVP remained the "natural parties in power." This is due to the following reasons:

1. The one-party government of the ÖVP (1966–1970) brought about a change of roles that prevented a possible rigid assignment of roles as party in power and opposition party similar to the First Republic.
2. The federalist structure of the Republic of Austria implied that the large party that was the opposition party at the federal level (the SPÖ from 1966–1970, the ÖVP since 1970) could still govern at the level of the provinces (*Länder*). Owing to the majority situation in the nine provinces, it is highly likely that, in the foreseeable future, each large party can expect absolute majorities and thus dominance in the governments of some of the provinces. The SPÖ can expect this above all in Vienna and Carinthia, the ÖVP primarily in the Tyrol and Vorarlberg.
3. Social partnership, the mechanism of compromise of the large economic associations, makes it possible for the large party in opposition to influence decisions via the indirect route of its ties with various associations. The SPÖ thus participates in government by way of the Socialist majority faction in the ÖGB and in the *Österreichischer Arbeiterkammertag* (Assembly of Austrian Chambers of Labor), whereas the ÖVP achieves

the same objective through its majority faction in the *Bundeskammer der gewerblichen Wirtschaft* (Federal Chamber of Trade) and in the *Präsidentenkonferenz der Landwirtschaftskammern* (Presidents' Conference of Chambers of Agriculture).[16]

This makes the exclusion from government of the opposition party quite bearable, since the party does participate in government at other levels and thus also participates in the distribution of positions, finances, etc. See Table 7. It is primarily the FPÖ that is excluded from the frequent crossings of the demarcation line between government and opposition. However, the FPÖ is attempting, by various means, to break out of its role as the permanent opposition party and to become a "natural party in power," primarily through alliances with a large party. The FPÖ came closest to this goal on the federal level through its parliamentary support of the Socialist minority government in 1970–1971, on the provincial level through its coalition with the ÖVP in Upper Austria (this gave the ÖVP the position of *Landeshauptmann* [head of the provincial government, governor]), and at the communal level through coalitions with one of the two large parties in various provincial capitals.

4.2 Interparty Relations

During the time of the Grand Coalition, the relations between the two large parties were institutionalized, its manifestations being the Coalition Committee and the Council of Ministers.[17] This tie between the two large parties

Table 7   Confrontations of government and opposition at the federal level

	Parties in power	Seats in National Council	Opposition parties	Seats in National Council
1945–47	ÖVP, SPÖ, KPÖ	100.0%		
1947–49	ÖVP, SPÖ	97.6	KPÖ	2.4%
1949–53	ÖVP, SPÖ	87.3	VDU, KPÖ	12.7
1953–56	ÖVP, SPÖ	89.1	VDU, KPÖ	10.9
1956–59	ÖVP, SPÖ	94.6	FPÖ, KPÖ	5.4
1959–62	ÖVP, SPÖ	95.2	FPÖ	4.8
1962–66	ÖVP, SPÖ	95.2	FPÖ	4.8
1966–70	ÖVP	51.5	SPÖ, FPÖ	48.5
1970–71	SPÖ	49.1	ÖVP, FPÖ	50.9
1971–75	SPÖ	50.8	ÖVP, FPÖ	49.2
1975–79	SPÖ	50.8	ÖVP, FPÖ	49.2
1979–	SPÖ	51.9	ÖVP, FPÖ	48.1

Source: Compilation according to official election results.
Note: The VDU (Verband der Unabhängigen [Association of Independents]) was the organization that preceded the FPÖ.

ceased to exist with the end of the coalition. Yet there have been other firm ties between SPÖ and ÖVP since 1966:

1. The Presidents' Conference of the National Council, whose members are the three presidents of the National Council and the chairman of the parliamentary groups (*Klubs*, caucuses) of the three parties, and the chief officers of the associations, thus the most important representatives of the SPÖ, the ÖVP, and the FPÖ. The Presidents' Conference carries out the functions of parliamentary switchboard and of parliamentary crisis management team.[18]
2. The governments of the provinces. Seven of the nine provincial constitutions expressly prescribe a government according to proportional representation, thus making cooperation between the SPÖ and the ÖVP a constitutional mandate. The two exceptions are Vienna and Vorarlberg.
3. The organs of social partnership, in particular the Joint Commission on Prices and Wages, which decides on wage and price matters. Members of the Joint Commission are the most important representatives of the economic associations, who generally are also representatives of one of the large parties. The Joint Commission provides them with a forum for regular meetings, during which important decisions are made.

Besides these three firmly institutionalized forms of regular cooperation, there are, of course, the normal forms of parliamentary cooperation in the various committees of the National Council and the Federal Council. Various constitutional laws (i.e. laws that are designated as such and that can be passed only by a two-thirds majority) require the two large parties to cooperate on certain matters. This is the case on all matters concerning education, which have been given constitutional status by the 1962 Education Acts, or on all matters concerning the agricultural marketing regulations, whose constitutional laws also require cooperation between the SPÖ and ÖVP.

Moreover, there are many formal and informal contacts between the parties, which are, however, generally bipolar and irregular. These contacts are bipolar in that one of the three parties represented in parliament consults with one other party, while the third party is excluded. They are irregular in that there is generally no regularly set time for such cooperation, and no permanent group.

The era of the coalition was characterized by the priority given to the relations between the two large parties over all other relations between one of the two large parties and a third or fourth party. This priority shifted to some extent when the coalition ended. In particular, since the first SPÖ government (1970–1971), when the FPÖ parliamentary group supported the Socialist minority government in decisive questions, a triangle of essentially equal relations between the SPÖ, ÖVP, and FPÖ has evolved. This basic triangle is supported by the fact that there are quite different forms of cooperation between the three parties at the lower level, in the provinces and the communities.

However, relations with fourth parties, especially with the KPÖ, are not as open. Since it left the Federal Government in 1947, the Communist party has not been able to break out of its self-imposed isolation, not even in 1966, when it supported the SPÖ in the election campaign. It therefore did not and does not now play a role in the area of interparty cooperation on all levels of Austrian politics.

4.3   Interconnections with Associations

The Austrian parties have many and varied ties with the economic associations. The four great economic associations that constitute the autonomous social partnership of the Joint Commission are generally dominated by groups that follow party lines. See Table 8. In the case of the three organizations, the Chambers of Trade, Chambers of Agriculture, and Chambers of Labor, this division into groups is a consequence of direct elections. Candidates for office in these chambers come from the parties, and the elections for the representative bodies of the chambers are similar to the elections for the organs of representation of the State. This results in the parties dominating the associations under the auspices of public law.

However, the association under the auspices of private law, the Austrian Federation of Trade Unions (ÖGB), is also influenced by party groups. The majority situation in these groups is determined by the elections at the level of the companies and factories. The results of the elections for the works councils and for the representative organs of personnel are the key to the distribution of positions among the party factions.

The strong position of the parties in the economic associations is also indicated by the conspicuously high percentage of association officials in the parliaments. It is a regular occurrence that more than 50 percent of all National Council members are not only representatives of the parties who were elected to parliament on the party slate but also officials in the economic associations. This means that more than half of the people's representatives nominated by the parties are also full- or part-time officials in employers' or employees' associations.[19]

The close ties between parties and associations widen and strengthen the parties' control, enabling them to exert influence in the economy and in the industrial relations between employers and employees. These close ties also serve to stabilize the entire political system by synchronizing and balancing the system of parliamentarianism, which is dominated by the parties, and the system of social partnership, which is dominated by the associations.

4.4   International Ties

The Austrian parties are embedded in the European party system. However, since Austria is not a member of the European Community, they are not integrated into the party federations that exist in the framework of the European Community. The international ties that the Austrian parties maintain make it possible to draw conclusions with respect to their programmatic and ideological positions.

The SPÖ is a member of the Socialist International, in which it is one of the strongest parties. One of the vice presidents of the Socialist International is an SPÖ member. Therefore, the SPÖ must clearly be classified as a party of democratic socialism, or of social democracy.

The ÖVP participates in the federations of the Christian Democratic parties; it is a member of both the World Union and the European Union of Christian Democrats. At the same time, the ÖVP is also a member of the European Democratic Union, which comprises some of the Christian Democratic parties and some of the conservative parties in Europe. The ÖVP is thus internationally recognized as a Christian Democratic and a conservative party.[20]

The FPÖ has been a member of the Liberal World Union only since 1979. Until then, it maintained ties with the Liberal World Union through the

Table 8   Shares of party groups in the economic associations as of late in 1979, in percent

	SPÖ	ÖVP	FPÖ	KPÖ	Others	Total
Chambers of Trade	9%	86%			4%	99%
Chamber of Agriculture	10	85	2%		4	101
Chambers of Labor	64	31	3	1%		99
ÖGB	77	20		3	1	101

Source: Compilation according to the results of the most recent chamber elections in each case (as of the end of 1979); and according to the grouping of the delegates of the 9th federal congress of the ÖGB (Austrian Federation of Trade Unions), 1979.
Note: For elections to Chambers of Commerce and of Agriculture, share of the seats in the Provincial Chambers; for elections to Chambers of Labor, share of all votes cast on the federal level; for the ÖGB, share of delegates to the 9th Federal Congress, 1979. In elections to the Chambers of Trade, the FPÖ runs on the same ticket as the Federation of Business of the ÖVP, which means that the share of the Federation of Business and of the lists ("Others") also includes FPÖ representatives. In the case of the ÖGB, all representatives of the Faction of Christian Trade Unionists, which is close to the ÖVP, have been included in the figure for the ÖVP.
Lines do not always add up to 100% due to rounding.

individual memberships of some of its officials. The fact that the FPÖ joined the Liberal World Union relatively late is indicative of the tension between the party's German-Nationalist roots and its liberal claims.

The KPÖ is not a member of any international federation of parties. However, it is considered a sister party by the CPSU, and it can be categorized as a party oriented toward the Soviet model and, since 1969, as clearly not oriented toward "Euro-Communism".[21]

5 IDEOLOGY AND PLATFORMS

The basic platforms of the Austrian parties are indicative of their changes from class and ideological parties to people's parties. Instead of unambiguous and clearly defined programmatic statements, still typical of the First Republic, the platforms are now pluralistic to the point of ambiguity, and their trends are obscure.[22]

The SPÖ has changed from the Austro-Marxist class party, which formulated its objectives accordingly in the 1926 "Linz Program," to a Social Democratic People's party at left center. The conspicuous modification of statements in the basic platform on the question of private property is typical of this trend. Whereas the old Social Democrats centered their statements on socialization of ownership of the means of production, the SPÖ emphasizes the significance of the issue of private property in its 1978 platform but does not propose concrete measures of socialization.

It is typical of the changes within the ÖVP that the party forgoes any denominational claims in the narrow sense of the word and that it has given up the old clerical positions of the Christian-Socialist party. Although the ÖVP does stress its adherence to certain basic Christian values in its 1972 basic platform ("Salzburg Program"), it emphasizes at the same time that it is open to everyone, even non-Christians. The ÖVP's present platform no longer emphasizes traditional clerical demands, such as the ecclesiastical marriage law applying to Catholics or a demand for parochial schools as norm.

In the case of the FPÖ, this programmatic change may be seen in the modification of its German-Nationalist ideas. During the First Republic, the Grossdeutsche Volkspartei (Greater German People's Party) emphasized the ideology of Anschluss in conjunction with national and racial elements. In contrast, the present-day FPÖ has overcome the idea of the Anschluss just as much as all the other parties. The 1973 "Freiheitliche Manifest zur Gesellschaftspolitik" (Liberal Manifesto on Social Policy) contains German-Nationalist remnants in just one sentence, which—almost covertly—declares the party's loyalty to the German national and cultural community.

This programmatic change in all the parties represented in parliament is an important indicator for the understanding of the parties' changed role. Today, the parties are largely secularized, in spite of a still existing, albeit decreasing, camp mentality. They have become "catch-all parties" or, at the least, people's parties with a broadly based appeal. This is indicated by the modifications in their basic platforms as well as by the changes in the structure of their membership and voters. This secularization is an ambivalent process. It facilitates finding a democratic consensus, thus promoting a stability that distinguishes the Second Republic from the First Republic. Yet it also promotes a fuzziness of the party system, making it more difficult for the voter, the democratic sovereign, to select among several, clearly distinguishable alternatives. The Americanization of the Austrian party system, which has been realized at least partially, facilitates the coherence and cooperation among the parties, but it obscures the transparency of the political process.

Notes

1. Adam Wandruszka, "Österreichs politische Struktur," in Heinrich Benedikt, ed., *Geschichte der Republik Österreich* (Wien, 1954). Kurt Steiner, *Politics in Austria* (Boston, 1972), espec. pp. 119–54. William T. Bluhm, *Building an Austrian Nation, The Political Integration of a Western State* (New Haven, 1973).
2. Jean Blondel, *An Introduction to Comparative Government* (London, 1969), espec. pp. 153ff. Joachim Raschke, ed., *Die politischen Parteien in Westeuropa. Geschichte-Programm-Praxis. Ein Handbuch* (Reinbek, 1978).
3. Wandruszka, op. cit.; Steiner, op. cit., espec. pp. 257–85. G. Bingham Powell, Jr., *Social Fragmentation and Political Hostility. An Austrian Case Study* (Stanford, 1970). Rudolf Steininger, *Polarisierung und Integration.* Eine vergleichende Untersuchung der strukturellen Versäulung der Gesellschaft in den Niederlanden und in Österreich (Meisenheim, 1975).
4. Erhard Angermann, Fritz Plasser, "Wahlen und Wähler in Österreich, 1976–1978," in Andreas Khol and Alfred Stirnemann, eds., *Österreichisches Jahrbuch für Politik, 1978* (Wien, 1979).
5. After the party's defeat in the 1979 elections, there have been discussions within the ÖVP on changing the principle of indirect to direct membership. A formal decision in favor of such a change was made at a party conference in early 1980, but the effect of this decision will not be clear before the next party conference in 1981 or 1982.
6. Cf. Data in Raschke's work, op. cit., regarding the other (West) European party systems.
7. Herbert Maurer, "Die Nationalratswahl vom 6. Mai 1979 in regionaler Sicht," in *Zeitschrift für Politik, Österreichische Monatshefte,* July/August 1979.
8. Anton Pelinka, "Parteienfinanzierung im Parteienstaat," in Andreas Khol and Alfred Stirnemann, eds., *Österreichisches Jahrbuch für Politik, 1977* (Wien, 1978).
9. Anton Kofler, *Parteienfinanzierung und deren Auswirkungen auf innerparteiliche Strukturen, dargestellt am Beispiel der ÖVP* (Diplomarbeit, University of Innsbruck, 1979).
10. Kofler, op. cit., pp. 127–40.
11. Pelinka, "Parteienfinanzierung," op. cit.
12. Cf. Bodo Zeuner, *Innerparteiliche Demokratie* (Berlin (West)), 1970.
13. Karl-Heinz Nassmacher, *Das österreichische Regierungssystem. Grosse Koalition oder alternierende Regierung?* (Köln, 1968), pp. 61–71.
14. Anton Pelinka, "Elitenbildung in den österreichische Grossparteien," in *Wort und Wahrheit* (1970).
15. Rodney Stiefbold, "Elites and Elections in a Fragmented Political System," in Rudolf Wildenmann, ed., *Sozialwissenschaftliches Jahrbuch für Politik,* vol. 4 (München, 1975). Anton Pelinka, "Volksvertretung als funktionale Elite. Der österreichische Nationalrat

auf dem Weg zum Arbeitsparlament," in Khol and Stirnemann, *Jahrbuch, 1978,* op. cit.
16. Alfred Klose, *Ein Weg zur Sozialpartnerschaft. Das österreichische Modell* (Wien, 1970). Thomas Lachs, *Wirtschaftspartnerschaft in Österreich* (Wien, 1976).
17. Frederick C. Engelmann, "Austria. The Pooling of Opposition," in Robert A. Dahl, ed., *Political Oppositions in Western Democracies* (New Haven, 1966). Wolfgang Rudzio, "Entscheidungszentrum Koalitionsausschuss. Zur Realverfassung Österreichs unter der grossen Koalition," in *Politische Vierteljahresschrift, 1971.* Gerhard Lehmbruch, *Proporzdemokratie. Politisches System und politische Kultur in der Schweiz und in Österreich* (Tübingen, 1967).
18. Helmut Widder, "Die Präsidialkonferenz des Nationalrates," in *Österreichische Zeitschrift für Politikwissenschaft* 1(1972). Heinz Fischer, "Die parlamentarischen Fraktionen," in Heinz Fischer, ed., *Das politische System Österreichs* (Wien, 1974). Peter Gerlich, "Funktionen des Parlaments," in Fischer, op. cit.
19. Pelinka, "Volksvertretung," op. cit.
20. Hans Janitschek, "Zur Entwicklung und Tätigkeit der Sozialistischen Internationale." Alfred Stirnemann, "Die Internationalen der politischen Mitte, der Europawahlkampf und seine Auswirkungen," both articles in Khol and Stirnemann, *Jahrbuch, 1978,* op. cit.
21. Leopold Spira, *Ein gescheiterter Versuch. Der Austro-Eurokommunismus* (Wien, 1979). Heinz Gärtner, *Zwischen Moskau und Österreich. Analyse einer sowjetabhängigen KP* (Wien, 1979).
22. Klaus Berchtold, *Österreichische Parteiprogramme, 1868–1966* (Wien, 1967). Albert Kadan and Anton Pelinka, *Die Grundsatzprogramme der österreichischen Parteien. Dokumentation und Analyse* (St. Pölten, 1979).

Selected Bibliography

Much of the relevant literature is referred to in the footnotes to this essay. The following list contains books and articles in English.

Bluhm, William T. *Building an Austrian Nation: The Political Integration of a Western State.* New Haven, 1973.
Diamant, Alfred. *Austrian Catholics and the First Republic: Democracy, Capitalism, and the Social Order, 1918–1934.* Princeton, 1960.
Engelmann, Frederick C. Austria: The Pooling of Opposition. In Robert A. Dahl, ed., *Political Oppositions in Western Democracies.* New Haven, 1966.
Powell, G. Bingham, *Social Fragmentation and Political Hostility: An Austrian Case Study.* Stanford, Calif., 1970.
Pulzer, Peter. Austria. In Stanley Henig, ed., *European Political Parties: A Handbook.* New York, 1969.
Shell, Kurt L. *The Transformation of Austrian Socialism.* New York, 1962.
Simon, Walter B. The Political Parties of Austria. Ph.D. dissertation, Columbia University, 1957.
Steiner, Kurt. *Politics in Austria.* Boston, 1972.
Stiefbold, Rodney. Segmented Pluralism and Consociational Democracy in Austria. In Martin O. Heisler, ed., *Politics in Europe: Structures and Processes in Some Postindustrial Democracies.* New York, 1973.

Other relevant books by Anton Pelinka include:

Demokratie und Verfassung in Österreich (together with M. Welan), Wien, 1971.
Gewerkschaften im Parteienstaat. Ein Vergleich zwischen dem Österreichischen und dem Deutschen Gewerkschaftsbund, Berlin, 1980.
Sozialdemokratie in Europa. Macht ohne Grundsätze oder Grundsätze ohne Macht? Wien, 1980.

Modern Austria, pp. 241–59

11. ELECTIONS AND PARLIAMENT

Heinz Fischer

Chairman of the Parliamentary Group of the Socialist Party

On October 1, 1980, Austria celebrated the 60th birthday of its Constitution. This Constitution had been ratified unanimously on October 1, 1920, two years after the collapse of the empire and the founding of the Republic, and after difficult but ultimately successful negotiations between Social Democrats and Christian Socialists. This anniversary gave rise to an intensified discussion of Austria's political and constitutional system, of the role of parliament and the election system. We shall refer to that discussion later in this essay.

1   THE HISTORICAL BACKGROUND

A brief outline of the historical background will help in reaching a better understanding of the present structures of parliamentarianism and the election system. The 1920 Constitution is based on the concept of parliamentary democracy, which strongly emphasized the parliamentary component. In spite of the principle of the separation of legislative and executive branches of government, the government was clearly dependent on parliament; and the Federal President—in an expression of rejection of the monarchical system—is given essentially only a representative function.

The legislation for the federal state is in the hands of a two-chamber legislative branch. The National Council, elected directly by the people, carries more political weight than does the Federal Council, which consists of representatives of the provincial parliaments and which essentially has only a suspensive veto at its disposal. This veto loses its effectiveness when the National Council overrides it (*Beharrungsbeschluss*).

Translated by Ulrike E. Lieder, Stanford University

241

9306-6403/81/0415-0241$01.50

With respect to the election system, Article 26 of the Austrian Constitution, which has remained in force essentially unchanged until today, stipulates the following:

> The National Council is elected directly by the people according to the system of proportional representation. It is elected in free elections by secret ballot, based on the equal and personal right to vote of those men and women who are 20 years old on January 1 of the election year. Within the national borders, the federal territory is divided into constituencies. The number of representatives is determined by the number of qualified voters of a constituency (election units), proportionate to the number of inhabitants of the constituency, i.e. the number of persons whose legal domicile was located in the constituency according to the most recent census. It is not admissible to organize the electorate in different election units.

In spite of the election system of proportional representation, a splintering distribution of the votes over a multitude of parties, thus creating a "Weimar situation,"* did not occur during the First Republic (1918–1938). This is primarily due to the fact that the country's political landscape was characterized even then (as it still is today) by the existence of two great political camps (the bourgeois Christian Social camp on the one hand and the Social Democratic camp on the other) and of one small third party, an inheritance from the German-nationalist movement and from parts of the liberal tradition. Left-wing (Communist) and right-wing splinter groups did not play a role until the National Socialists gained strength (see Table 1).

Table 1 Results of the elections to the National Council from 1920 until the end of the First Republic, by percentage of votes received and by seats

Party	1919 Seats	1919 Percent	1920 Seats	1920 Percent	1923 Seats	1923 Percent	1927 Seats	1927 Percent	1930 Seats	1930 Percent
Christian Social party	69	35.9%	85	41.8%	82	45.0%	85	49.0%	66	35.7%
Social Democratic party	72	40.8	69	36.0	68	39.6	71	42.0	72	41.1
German-Nationalist party (incl. Landbund[a] and Heimatblock[b]	27	20.8	28	17.2	15	12.8	9	6.0	27	17.8
Other	2	2.5	1	5.0		2.6		3.0		5.4
Total seats in the National Council	170	100%	183	100%	165	100%	165	100%	165	100%

[a] The Landbund was the rural component of the German-Nationalist movement.
[b] A wing of the right-wing militia, the Heimwehr, competed in the 1930 election under the label Heimatblock.

*Translator's Note: Reference is being made to the Weimar Republic (1919–1933) in Germany which was characterized by a multitude of small parties and splinter groups in parliament, making the formation of a stable and viable government all but impossible.

The position of the Federal President was greatly upgraded by the 1929 amendment to the Constitution. According to this amendment, the Federal President was to be elected no longer by the Federal Assembly—i.e. a joint session of the two houses of parliament—but directly by the people. Among other things, he was to be given the authority to dissolve the National Council under certain circumstances and to appoint or dismiss the Federal Government. There were no other significant changes in the constitutional positions of government and parliament in the period from 1920 to 1933.

However, even without incisive changes in the Constitution, the political development had remarkable effects on the functions of government and parliament—and, to be sure, not in the desired direction. In the elections to the National Council of October 17, 1920, the Social Democrats lost their position as the strongest party in parliament, a position they had gained in the 1919 elections to the provisional National Council. The bourgeois parties formed a coalition, and the Social Democrats became the opposition party. It must be kept in mind that from that time on, the position of the government strengthened continuously and developed into the true center of power, supported by the executive branch (army and police), while the political significance of the legislative branch diminished more and more.

One of the causes of this development may have been the fact that, even before the actual triumph of National Socialism in Austria—just as in Germany—there was a strong antiparliamentarian trend. This trend was further supported by a general disappointment in the parliamentary system's inability to solve the critical economic and social problems of the 1920s and early 1930s.

In addition, the political, ideological, and social differences between Social Democrats and Christian Socialists were so great during the First Republic that the parliamentary factions were able to develop a consensus only within the most restricted framework. An important element of fruitful legislative efforts was thus lacking. If the principle of majority, inherent and legitimate in a parliamentary democracy, is stretched to its limits, the basis of legitimation of this system is decisively weakened. Finally, it must also be emphasized that the parliament frequently was not the representative but only the sounding board of the actual political controversy. To a large extent, this controversy was carried on outside of parliament, not least in the clashes of militant paramilitary units of the two great camps, the Social Democrats' Republican Defense Corps and the right-wing militia's Heimwehr.

Seen from a global point of view, the parliamentary system in Austria did not gain a firm and definite foothold in the consciousness of the Austrian population, which was split into hostile camps, in the time between the wars —or rather, between 1920 (when the Constitution came into force) and 1933 (when parliament was dissolved).[1]

When, in March 1933, a conflict over the application of the rules of procedure caused the three presidents of the National Council to resign, the government was able to take advantage of this incident and dissolve parliament without meeting with determined resistance. The parliamentary system in Austria thus came to a rather inglorious end during the same year as it did in Germany—although under different circumstances—and gave way first to the authoritarian corporate state and then to Fascism.

2   THE ERA OF THE COALITION

Against this background, the picture of Austrian parliamentarism during the Second Republic, after 1945, is clearly different. For many years—and possibly up to today—its development was determined by the experiences of the First Republic.

The formation of a Grand Coalition by the Socialists and the Austrian People's Party (Österreichische Volkspartei, ÖVP, the successor party of the Christian Socialist), so vital to political stability in Austria—and probably also to gaining independence—responded to the need of including the two great political camps in the responsibility for government, and of thus avoiding the fatal confrontations of the period between the wars. However, it should also be noted that such a government, supported by nine-tenths of the voters and of the members of parliament, further strengthened the predominance of the government over parliament at least for the duration of the Coalition, and that this constellation had its effect even after the era of the Coalition had ended.

The political parties that presently exist in Austria, shown in *Table* 2, are as follows:

1. the Socialist party of Austria (Sozialistische Partei Österreichs or SPÖ), which continues the tradition of the Social Democratic party, founded in 1889;
2. the ÖVP, which is clearly the successor of the Christian Socialist party, but which was to make a fresh start in 1945;
3. the Communist Party of Austria (Kommunistische Partei Österreichs or KPÖ), which could count on a potential of approximately 4 to 5 percent of the valid votes during the first years of the Second Republic. However, after the State Treaty was signed and especially after the Soviet invasion of the CSSR in August 1968, its share of votes dropped to 1 percent. It has not been represented in the Austrian National Council since 1959; and
4. the Liberal Party of Austria (Freiheitliche Partei Österreichs or FPÖ), which evolved from the Association of Independents (Verband der

Unabhängigen, VdU), founded in 1949. It stems from the tradition of the German-Nationalist movement and has so far not been able to make a definite decision on whether to continue in this tradition or to develop following the pattern of the West German Free Democratic party (Freie Demokratische Partei Deutschlands, FDP). It is therefore oscillating between these two positions.

Based on the election results shown in Table 2 and the concomitant development in domestic policy, the following phases in Austrian parliamentarism since 1945 can be distinguished: (*a*) 1945 to 1955, the era of the "Grand Coalition" until the signing of the State Treaty; (*b*) 1955 to 1966, the era of the late Grand Coalition and of its crises; (*c*) 1966 to 1970, the era of the ÖVP government; and (*d*) 1970 to the present, the era of the SPÖ government.

3   THE PRIME OF THE GRAND COALITION

During the first phase, and the prime, of the Grand Coalition, the Austrian system of government was molded by the political and institutional pooling of all forces in order to attain the goal of securing the country's existence. The country, which was resurrected after the years of the Anschluss to Germany, had been devastated by the war and was now occupied by four Allied powers. The major goals were reconstruction, withdrawal of the occupying forces, and sovereignty. Socialists and ÖVP, worked together in government (led by an ÖVP Chancellor) and in parliament to attain these goals. It would be wrong to idealize this prime time of the Grand Coalition too much and to deny that there were considerable political differences

Table 2 Election results since 1945

	SPÖ		ÖVP		VdU/FPÖ		KPÖ	
	Percent	Seats	Percent	Seats	Percent	Seats	Percent	Seats
1945	44.6%	76	49.8%	85			5.42%	4
1949	37.71	67	44.03	77	11.67%	16	5.08	5
1953	42.11	73	41.26	74	10.95	14	5.28	4
1956	43.04	74	45.9	82	6.52	6	4.42	3
1959	44.79	78	44.19	79	7.70	8	3.27	0
1962	44.00	76	45.43	81	7.05	8	3.28	0
1966	42.56	74	48.35	85	5.35	6	—	—
1970	48.23	81	44.82	79	5.49	5	—	—
1971	50.04	93	43.11	80	5.45	10	—	—
1975	50.42	93	42.95	80	5.41	10	—	—
1979	51.03	95	41.90	77	6.06	11	—	—

regarding issues of domestic policy between the parties even during this period. These differences were reflected in heated election campaigns. First, reservations about the Coalition pacts were also expressed. The coalition pacts—binding agreements on the division and exercise of governmental power—resulted in the phenomenon that agreements made by the Coalition partners at the government level were rubber-stamped at the parliamentary level and at all other political levels.

However, the public was not very aware of the fact that parliament's latitude for action was greatly restricted, because many important political decisions did not even touch upon the area of the legislature because the government so clearly had the legitimation and the agreement of approximately 90 percent of the population and of 90 percent of the members of parliament, and because the advantages of the coalition system over the situation of the First Republic were so obvious.

4   THE LATTER PART OF THE ERA OF THE GRAND COALITION AND ITS CRISES

After the State Treaty had been signed and, in particular, after the 1959 elections (in which the Socialists won a small majority of the popular vote —as they had in 1953—but owing to the election arithmetic the ÖVP received one seat more in the National Council than did the SPÖ), the disagreements on domestic policy became more pronounced, the general political climate deteriorated, and the Coalition began to lose the respect it had enjoyed. There was no more external pressure on the Republic, nor was there the pressure of the occupying forces. The existential goals of the immediate postwar period had been reached, and the memories of the concentration camps of Fascism and of resolutions made jointly, which Socialists and Christian Socialists shared, began to fade. All these factors contributed to a certain strain on the Coalition, which obscured its advantages and made its disadvantages appear more glaring.

Parliament was bound by the decisions made by the government and by a "Coalition Committee," consisting of leading personalities from the two Coalition parties; it was thus reduced to the role of "State's notary," having no other task than that of ratifying decisions that had been made before they even reached parliament. Since there was no effective parliamentary opposition, the phenomenon of an "opposition by jurisdictional sphere" (Bereichsopposition) developed within the Coalition. The Socialists acted as opposition regarding matters that were under the jurisdiction of ÖVP ministers, and vice versa; or, in terms then in common usage, the "Socialist half of the country and of the government" was, as it were, in opposition to the ÖVP half, and vice versa.[2] Moreover, the Coalition's ability to reach compromises and to achieve results decreased continually, while the mountain of unsolved problems grew alarmingly.

The Socialists, being the weaker partner, especially after the 1962 elections, were still clinging to the Coalition, while the ÖVP began to develop ideas about areas to be exempted from the coalition arrangement and about facilitating majority decisions in some cases. This signaled the beginning of the end of the Coalition, not only because it increased the mistrust between the two large parties, but also because, just as in a bad marriage, both partners began to show interest in the third party, the FPÖ, which, until then, had not been considered fit to be a partner in a coalition or in a government. These overtures toward the FPÖ gave rise to additional conflicts among the Coalition partners.

5 THE ERA OF THE ÖVP GOVERNMENT

In the elections to the National Council of March 6, 1966, the ÖVP won 85 seats, the SPÖ 74, and the FPÖ 6, thus giving the ÖVP an absolute majority. The negotiations about the formation of a coalition, held after the elections, had no chance of succeeding, since the ÖVP was not willing to have the political latitude it had gained in the elections restricted by a coalition pact. So the ÖVP alone formed the government, and it had a strong parliamentary opposition of SPÖ and FPÖ, which had a combined total of 80 seats.

With this development, the role and the significance of parliament changed abruptly. In its legislative activities, the National Council was no longer reduced to the role of "State's notary," who would turn the Coalition Committee's decisions into laws. Now, government bills were considered the proposals of a one-party government and they were thoroughly debated in parliament. Of course, there was a great temptation for the majority party to keep these debates from going too far and to resolve the issues it considered important, by a majority vote. Yet, by comparison to the era of the Coalition, four circumstances are especially noteworthy and characteristic of the XIth legislative period (1966–1970):

1. During the XIth legislative period, a total of 175 plenary sessions took place, which lasted 1487 hours altogether. This was approximately three times longer than the average length of sessions during the previous legislative periods.
2. The number of government bills that the National Council passed with no changes at all or only minor ones decreased considerably. Although it was typical of the Coalition parliament to pass most government bills almost without any changes, the proportion of government bills that

parliament changed or redrafted now rose to about 50 percent. About one-eighth of all laws passed were changed extensively, and deviated strongly from the concepts contained in the original government bill.

3. In spite of this—or possibly because of it, since the opposition's intentions were also being considered—there was still a relatively high percentage of unanimous decisions in the National Council. During the time of the ÖVP government, a total of 517 laws were passed. Of these, 372 (70 percent) were passed unanimously, 62 (12 percent) were passed by the ÖVP alone, 43 (8.3 percent) were passed by the votes of ÖVP and SPÖ, and 40 (7.7 percent) were passed by the votes of ÖVP and FPÖ.

4. The role of the National Council changed even more in the area of parliamentary control. The SPÖ, having left the government, devoted itself intensively to this task, the effects of which can be found not only in certain accents in domestic policy and in the reporting by the media but also in statistics. Compared to the last legislative period of the Coalition (1962–1966), the application of various control measures proliferated during the time of the ÖVP government (1966–1970). (See also Table 4.)

The intensified parliamentary work, and especially the parliamentary confrontation between government and opposition, also increased the significance of parliament as a political forum. Media, especially TV, reporting increased, and the public became more aware and attentive and more conscious of parliamentary activities than it had been during the era of the Coalition.

Although parliament's significance increased after the end of the Coalition, it must not be assumed that it had thus fully regained the central role in the political process assigned to it by the Constitution. Such an assumption could not hold true for several reasons. First between 1966 and 1970, the government dominated parliament in the process of the development of political objectives (as is, incidentally, also the case since 1970). Being the "executive committee" of the party in power and of its parliamentary faction, and being in charge of the State administration, the Federal Government—led by the Federal Chancellor, who normally enjoys the political prestige of being the winner in the elections—plays a central role in the political process. Second not only should the development of political objectives be seen in the field of tension between parliament and government; extra-parliamentary and extra-constitutional power factors must also be taken into consideration. Especially significant are the representations of interests that cooperate within the scope of the so-called social partnership and that wield considerable power in the area of economic and social policy. Finally, although the significance of parliamentary control increased abruptly, it soon found its limitations, inasmuch as the minority could gain access to a great number of control measures only with the consent of the majority. This, of course, essentially diminished the practical significance of those measures. Some of these circumstances have turned out to be characteristics of the Austrian political system as such, independent of which party forms the government. Others were at least partially modified during the 1970s.

6 THE ERA OF THE SPÖ GOVERNMENT

The National Council elections of March 1, 1970, brought a marked change in the Austrian political landscape. Having won 81 seats, compared with the ÖVP's 78 seats and the FPÖ's 6, the Socialist party was, for the first time since 1920, the strongest party in the Austrian parliament even though it did not have an absolute majority. In spite of the latter circumstance, the SPÖ formed a minority government. In the elections of October 1971 (there had been a reform of the election law in the meantime), the SPÖ won the absolute majority with 93 seats (ÖVP 80, FPÖ 10), a majority that was confirmed in the 1975 and 1979 National Council elections. Therefore, the legislative periods since 1970 may be considered as a unit, all the more so as there was also continuity in personnel with the chancellorship of Bruno Kreisky.

Areas of the parliamentary system emphasized during the 1970s include the reform of the election law in 1970, the reform of the rules of parliamentary procedure in 1975, and a number of other amendments to existing laws and to the Constitution.

7 1970 REFORM OF THE ELECTION LAW

Since the early days of the Second Republic, Socialist politicians had repeatedly emphasized that the Austrian Constitution mandated the principle of proportional representation, but that this principle was not implemented consistently. Twice, in 1953 and in 1959, the SPÖ had won the majority of votes, and yet the ÖVP had received one seat more than the SPÖ (see Table 2).

In the National Council elections of March 1, 1970, as well, the SPÖ needed 27,432 votes for one seat in the National Council, whereas the ÖVP required only 25,962 votes. Between 1959 and 1970, the situation was even worse for the liberal party, which needed anywhere from 39,237 to 42,237 votes for one seat, i.e. on the average, almost 50 percent more votes than the ÖVP. These distortions were primarily determined by two factors: (*a*) The number of seats was distributed over the 25 constituencies, not according to the number of voters but according to the number of inhabitants; this gave an advantage to areas with many children (primarily rural and thus ÖVP dominated areas). (*b*) The seats were distributed in the course of two allocation processes (*Ermittlungsverfahren*), with the majority of seats being distributed during the first allocation process. Only the seats that had not been allocated in the first round came into the second allocation process, where the so-called remaining seats (*Restmandate*) were distributed according to the number of the remaining votes.[3] The smaller parties won only a small number of their seats directly, but received the majority of their seats in the second round. On the average, considerably more votes were necessary to receive a seat during the second round than in the first round, so that the election law that was in force until 1970 discriminated against small parties if the true principle of proportional representation is used as a measure.

The SPÖ felt discriminated against by the factor under (*a*), whereas the FPÖ felt at a disadvantage from the factor under (*b*). These parallel interests of the SPÖ and the FPÖ led to an SPÖ/FPÖ agreement on a reform of the election law in 1970. Of course, this reform came at the expense of the ÖVP, which had benefited from the old system and would therefore vote against it. This restricted the reform of the election law rather severely, since SPÖ and FPÖ did not have at their disposal the two-thirds majority that would have been necessary for an amendment to the Constitution. Therefore, the reform remained within the scope of the provisions of the existing Article 26 of the Constitution.

The reform of the election law was enacted on November 27, 1970. It reduced the number of constituencies in Austria from 25 to 9—the constituencies are now identical to the nine provinces—in order to adjust demographic differences between urban and rural areas as much as possible within each constituency. It also changed the methods of seat allocation so that seats distributed in the first and second rounds now require essentially the same number of popular votes. In fact, since the 1970 reform of the election law, the election system has become much more just, and it reflects more truly the principle of proportional representation, as indicated by Table 3.

However, it cannot be denied that the new, larger constituencies also have effects that are not as positive. There are now 39 seats for the constituency of Vienna, 35 for the constituency of Lower Austria, and 6 even for the smallest Austrian constituency of Vorarlberg. As a result, the ties between a representative and his constituents in an area that is supposed to be "his district" are not always as close as they would have been had there been only one representative for each constituency. For this reason, the discussion on the election law in Austria never ceased completely during the 1970s and has, in fact, again become more intensive at the turn of the decade.

Table 3   Number of votes necessary for one seat

National Council elections	SPÖ	ÖVP	FPÖ
1959	25,050	24,406	42,014
1962	25,798	24,994	39,237
1966	26,067	25,778	40,428
1970	27,432	25,962	42,237
Reform of the election law			
1971	24,518	24,559	24,847
1975	25,013	24,766	24,944
1979	25,402	25,737	26,067

8   REFORM OF THE RULES OF PARLIAMENTARY PROCEDURE

The second major change affecting the parliamentary system was the reform of the rules of parliamentary procedure in 1975. As was already mentioned, the SPÖ as the opposition party between 1966 and 1970 had complained that some of the control measures provided by the Constitution could only be utilized with the consent of the majority party. As a result, the tools of parliamentary control were not as effective as they should have been according to the concepts incorporated into the 1920 Constitution. After 1970, the ÖVP as the opposition party had similar experiences, and the SPÖ, although now the party in power, neither wished nor was able to dissociate itself from its own proposals and motions from the time when it was the opposition party. Thus, the prerequisites for a consensus of all parliamentary factions on this issue were present. After extensive negotiations, the National Council's new rules of procedure were unanimously approved on July 4, 1975. The new rules especially expanded the rights of control and the minority's rights, and also contained the following new regulations:

1. One-third of the members of parliament can appeal to the Constitutional Court any time, even without a concrete case or controversy, to have the constitutionality of a law checked.
2. Under certain circumstances, one-third of the members of parliament can ask the Board of Audits (Rechnungshof), the parliamentary organ of economic control of the Federal Government, to carry out a special investigation of economic conduct.
3. If a member bill, initiated by 8 of the total of 183 representatives, is not dealt with by the majority of the National Council, the proposers of that initiative can, after a period of six months, demand that their proposal be included in the agenda of a committee.

4. Twenty members of parliament can demand that a cabinet member's written response to a question raised in parliament be debated on the floor during the current or the following session of the National Council.
5. Newly instituted were parliamentary hearings as decided by the Main Committee (*Hauptausschuss*)[4]—an institution that has since been used numerous times.

Some of the developmental trends in Austrian parliamentarism during two decades, which are described above, can also be measured to a certain extent, as is shown by Table 4.

In summary, it can be said that, since the end of the Coalition and the beginning of single-party governments, parliamentary activity has clearly intensified. In the course of the 1970s, a stabilization and partially even a slight recession in parliamentary activity could be observed, which might be the first—not at all negative—results of the constantly growing criticism of the increasing "flood of laws," i.e. the production of too many laws.

9   OTHER REFORMS

Besides the reforms of the rules of parliamentary procedure and of the election law, a few other reforms of the 1970s that affect the parliamentary system should also be mentioned.

9.1   Public Advertisement of Open Positions

Until 1974, important positions within the Austrian system were publicly advertised only in isolated cases. A federal law, dated November 28, 1974, now mandates that all executive positions in the entire administration be advertised. According to the law, a commission must be established for each individual case of a position being advertised. This commission screens the incoming applications and then recommends an applicant to the person entitled to appoint someone to fill the vacant post (usually the Minister). Although the Minister is not obligated by this recommendation, he will need valid reasons for deviating from it. These provisions make for more openness in the appointments to leading functions, and they also facilitate parlimentary control.

9.2   Law Concerning the Political Parties (Parteiengesetz)

Although the political parties play a major role in the parliamentary and political system in Austria, their legal position was not clearly defined until 1975. A constitutional law* of 2 July 1975 states that "the existence and the diversity of the political parties [is] an essential component of the

*Translator's Note: A constitutional law is a law which is declared as such by the National Council. Its passage requires a two-thirds majority, as do all subsequent amendments.

Table 4   Trends in Austrian parliamentarianism

	1962–1966	1966–1970	1971–1975	1975–1979
Number of National Council sessions	95	175	151	123
Number of laws passed	376	517	573	410
Number of state treaties ratified	63	112	186	139
Number of reports debated	83	169	155	123
Number of written inquiries	384	1570	2432	2480
Number of oral inquiries	1182	2831	2274	702[a]
Urgent inquiries	3	34	23	23
Fact-finding committees	0	2	3	2
Number of committee sessions	444	170	420	351
Number of subcommittee sessions	205	111	427	382

[a] The new rules of procedure for 1975 gave the right to ask additional questions not only to the representative who made an oral inquiry, but also to a total of three other representatives. That, of course, reduced the number of inquiries dealt with during question time.

democratic order of the Republic of Austria" and regulates the legal position of the parties. The law also established regulations on party financing as well as a system of voluntary spending limits for election campaigns, limits that the parties observed during both the 1975 and 1979 elections.

9.3   Council on Foreign Policy

In order to intensify cooperation between government and parliament in the area of foreign policy, and in order to improve the information of the opposition on matters of foreign policy, thus creating the prerequisites for the broadest possible base of Austrian foreign policy, a federal law of 23 June 1976 establishes a Council on Foreign Affairs. This Council is chaired by the Chancellor; its members are the Vice Chancellor, the Foreign Minister, a representative of the Federal President, and representatives of the parliamentary factions. The law states that the Council on Foreign Affairs "is to be heard on all matters of foreign policy that are of fundamental importance in the opinion of the Chancellor, the Foreign Minister, or one of its members from the political parties." The Council on Foreign Affairs has proved itself in political practice and has undoubtedly increased its significance. However, the reservation, expressed when the Council was established, namely that its functions might be carried out at least partially at the expense of the Committee on Foreign Policy of the National Council, turned out to be not entirely unfounded.

9.4   The People's Advocates (Volksanwaltschaft)

For a time, the Scandinavian model of the Ombudsman as an additional institution of legal protection was being discussed in Austria. This discussion took place primarily on the journalistic and scientific levels, but also on the political level. A federal law of 24 February 1977 created a Volksanwaltschaft (People's Advocates' Office) as an additional constitutional institution. Anyone may complain to the People's Advocates because of alleged improprieties against the Federal Administration, including the Federal Government's activities as subject of private rights, as long as the complainant is affected by these improprieties and as long as he has no other legal recourse. What makes the Austrian People's Advocates' Office so special is the fact that it consists of three People's Advocates, who are selected by the National Council and who have equal rights. They work according to the principle of collective responsibility and competence, establish direct contacts with all authorities, are entitled to inspect files, and report regularly to the National Council. In order to gain experience, the People's Advocates' Office was initially established on an experimental bases for a period up to 1982. However, it has proved itself so that there can be no doubt that it will definitely be incorporated into the Constitution.

10   STRUCTURE AND METHODS OF THE NATIONAL COUNCIL

During recent years and decades, not only has there been further development of the legal bases and institutional conditions of the parliamentary system, but there has also been a change in the sociological structures. Although in the years after World War II the social barriers between the individual parties were also clearly reflected in the parliamentary factions, these barriers have since become more obscure.

After 1945, the ÖVP was primarily the party of the farmers and the bourgeoisie and partially the party of the civil servants, whereas the SPÖ represented labor and certain social strata of employees and civil servants, in particular the employees of the (nationalized) railroads. In the early 1980s, the ÖVP is attempting to strengthen its base of employed persons, while the SPÖ is undoubtedly advancing to the higher income levels. This development is also reflected in the composition of the National Council. During the past 25 years, the number of representatives trained in a manual trade declined from 33 percent (1950) to 10.4 percent, the percentage of farmers and independent small businessmen decreased slightly, while the proportion of white-collar employees increased from 17 to 31.7 percent, and that of civil servants from 9.7 to 21.9 percent. The rising number of white-collar workers in the National Council reflects especially the advancement of officials of interest associations (functionaries and officials of the labor unions, the Chambers, and the social insurance institutions) into the National Council (see Table 5).

Table 5 The composition of the Austrian National Council by occupation, 1956–1980

Occupational training	1956		1968		1976		1980	
	Absolute	Percent	Absolute	Percent	Absolute	Percent	Absolute	Percent
Blue-collar workers	55	33.33%	29	17.58%	26	14.21%	19	10.38%
White-collar workers	28	16.97	39	23.64	65	35.52	58	31.69
Farmers	23	13.94	23	13.94	17	9.29	21	11.47
Independent businessmen	23	13.94	26	15.76	19	10.38	22	12.02
Teaching professions	12	7.27	13	7.88	19	10.38	20	10.93
Civil servants (excl. teachers)	16	9.70	27	16.36	36	19.67	40	21.86
Other (e.g. household)	8	4.85	8	4.85	1	0.55	3	1.64
Total	165	100%	165	100%	183	100%	183	100%

The proportion of women in the Austrian National Council was 6.6 percent in 1955 and is presently 9.83 percent (11 out of 183). Although it is rising, it still reflects the fact that women are underrepresented at the political top levels.

In spite of these structural changes, one characteristic of European parliamentarism, which makes the latter essentially different from parliamentarism in the USA, has remained especially pronounced in Austria: the parliamentary factions act and vote as units. It almost never happens that the two great parliamentary factions of ÖVP and SPÖ do not cast a uniform vote, and such an occurrence is also extremely rare in the third faction, the FPÖ. In a somewhat simplified expression this is called *Klubzwang* (obligation to vote according to party). This obligation is primarily due to the fact that the representatives run not on their own individual political platform, but rather as the candidates of a political party. They are thus obligated to adhere to the party platform, and their chances of reelection depend largely on their being put on the ticket again by their party. Beyond that, the institution of *Klubzwang* is also undoubtedly connected to the process of formulating political objectives, which in Austria is characterized not so much by "individual lobbying" as by "collective lobbying" (by representations of interests), to which the parliamentary factions react as a unit.

The legislative path begins, as a rule, with a bill proposed by one of the federal ministries. At least when important matters are at issue, this bill is the product of consultations by bodies of leading specialists of the party in power. Cabinet members, representatives of the party and of its parliamentary faction, and, in the case of an SPÖ government, representatives of the Socialist faction of the Federation of Austrian Trade Unions (Österreichischer Gewerkschaftsbund, ÖGB) participate in these consultations. The bill is first subjected to a so-called *Begutachtungsverfahren* (solicitation of expert opinions), in the course of which some 30 to 70 institutions, among them all federal ministries, all provincial governments, all major representations of interests, as well as other institutions such as churches, youth organizations, and the conference of university presidents, are asked to give their views on the bill. In the case of important laws, public discussion of their contents begins, at the latest, at the same time.

Taking into consideration the views expressed and the positions taken in this procedure, and, if necessary, after renewed discussion by party organs, the government bill is then worked out. It must be passed unanimously by the Council of Ministers, and it is then sent to the National Council. Because of this process, every government bill has already been the subject of so much coordination that the parliamentary faction of the party in power can generally identify with the principles and objectives of such a government bill.

When the government bill is discussed in committee, it is primarily the opposition that is attempting to modify the bill according to its ideas, since it had not participated at all, or had participated only by way of representations of interests close to it, in the preparation of the government bill. However, the opposition, too, will endeavor to work out a unified—be it positive, negative, or differentiated—position on every government bill in order to achieve maximum effectiveness by maximum unity. The greater the interest of the majority party to have a matter passed unanimously, the greater will be the latitude for concessions to the opposition. It is a fact that a large portion of the most important laws passed in Austria in recent years were ratified unanimously.

Since Austria has a two-chamber system, laws passed by the National Council still require debate in the Federal Council before they can be promulgated. The Federal Council is a parliamentary body whose members are not elected directly but delegated by the provincial parliaments. However, according to the provisions of the Constitution, the Federal Council is not equal to the National Council. It has only a suspensive veto which can be overridden by the National Council (Beharrungsbeschluss).

During the past ten years, the Federal Council discussed a total of 1118 laws passed by the National Council, 22 of which it decided to veto. However, these vetoes came about only because there were times when the SPÖ majority in the National Council was offset by a slight ÖVP majority in the Federal Council. The latter would veto all those laws that had been passed by the National Council against the ÖVP vote. It can thus be said that the major portion of parliamentary work at the federal level clearly rests with the National Council.

Of course, each of the nine Austrian provinces has a parliament (*Landtag*) that is elected according to the principle of proportional representation.

These parliaments fulfill the tasks of doing the legislative work for the province and of controlling the provincial administration. At present, the ÖVP has a majority in six of the nine provincial parliaments, while the SPÖ has a majority in three, among them Vienna.

11 OUTLOOK

In assessing the political and, in particular, the parliamentary system of the Republic of Austria, the following factors deserve emphasis:

1. The great political and economic stability that distinguishes the Austria of today and that is such a remarkable contrast to the situation of the First Republic. In the persons of Leopold Figl, Julius Raab, Alphons Gorbach, Josef Klaus, and Bruno Kreisky, Austria has had only five chiefs of government in the 35 years between 1945 and 1980.[5]
2. Closely connected to the political stability and no less significant is the great social stability, especially since 1970. According to strike statistics of the Federation of Trade Unions, the total length of strikes in 1979 was only 7.9 seconds per employed person. The low number of strikes in order to attain social, economic, or political goals must not be considered an expression of the weakness of the labor union movement. On the contrary, it is the result of the fact that the unions, as a rule, do not need to resort to the instrument of strike in order to have proposals accepted that they feel can be borne by the economy as a whole.
3. In National Council elections, 93 percent of all votes are cast for the two large parties.
4. As a rule, the voter turn-out in National Council elections amounts to more than 90 percent.

There are, of course, also critical voices that point to the following circumstances, without denying the factors mentioned above: (*a*) The great influence of the political parties is also felt in areas where political parties really have no business. (*b*) The close political ties between the party in power, the government, and the parliamentary faction of the party in power have the effect of undermining the system of separation of powers of the legislative and executive branches because of the political alliance between the majority faction in parliament and the Federal Government. (*c*) The high voter turn-out and the concentration of votes cast for the two large parties, SPÖ and ÖVP, should not obscure the possibility that a significant number of voters of these parties might consider the party of their choice only the "lesser of two evils."

These factors also provide the starting point for discussion of the parliamentary system, a discussion that was particularly intensive in the year of the 60th birthday of the Constitution and that emphasized, among other things, the following points: efforts to reform, improve, and make more personal the election law by strengthening the links between candidates and their constituents; efforts to enlarge the powers of the provinces and of the communities by reallocating the tasks of the territorial authorities; efforts to expand the rights of control of the current minority at the federal level as well as at the level of the provincial parliaments; efforts to further reform the Austrian Constitution in order to better take into account the social and economic developments of the past 60 years; and efforts to strengthen the elements of direct democracy as a supplementary and corrective factor of representative democracy.

It will not be possible to realize some of the above-mentioned objectives in the near future—at least not in their entirety. But just as there were considerable developments in the political and parliamentary system of the Republic of Austria during the 1970s, so will there doubtless be a continuation of the "policy of small steps" in the 1980s. This seems to be a guarantee that the parliamentary system of the Republic of Austria will also be characterized during the 1980s by its proved mixture of stability and flexibility.

Notes

1. From a purely numerical point of view, there have been 671 National Council sessions between October 1920 and March 1933; that amounts to about 54 plenary sessions per year. With a few exceptions, there were hardly any epoch-making innovations or even merely remarkable codifications among the laws passed during this period. The political objectives were formulated outside of parliament, either in the government or on the streets.

2. The term "half of the country" (*Reichshälfte*), used facetiously, was a reference to the two parts of the Austro-Hungarian Monarchy in 1867. Governmental positions were distributed after each election among the Coalition partners according to the system known as *Proporz*. See Frederick C. Engelmann, "Haggling for the Equilibrium: The Renegotiation of the Austrian Coalition, 1959," *American Political Science Review*, 1962, pp. 651–62; and his "Austria: The Pooling of Oppositions", in Robert A. Dahl, ed. *Political Oppositions in Western Democracies* (New Haven, 1966).

3. In the first process, the sum of the votes cast for one party in a constituency is divided by the sum plus one of the number of seats allocated to this constituency. In the second process the so-called d'Hondt system is used.

4. The Main Committee is a parliamentary organ, established according to the Constitution. It is elected by the National Council under a system of proportional representation.

5. The tenure of these five chancellors is as follows: Leopold Figl—December 1945 to April 1953; Julius Raab—April 1953 to April 1961; Alphons Gorbach—April 1961 to April 1964; Josef Klaus—April 1966 to April 1970; Bruno Kreisky—April 1970 to the present. The Figl Cabinet was preceded by the Provisional Concentration Cabinet of Karl Renner, and was itself a concentration cabinet (including the KPÖ) until 1947. From then until April 1966, all cabinets were Grand Coalition cabinets. Josef Klaus formed the first single-party (ÖVP) cabinet in 1966, which was followed by single-party (SPÖ) cabinets under Bruno Kreisky.

Selected Bibliography

Adamovich, Ludwig. Aktuelle Tendenzen der Funktionsteilungen in der Gesetzgebung zwischen Parlament und Regierung. In *Österreichische Landesreferate zum VIII. Internationalen Kongress für Rechtsvergleichung in Pescara 1970.* Wien, 1970.

———. *Handbuch des österreichischen Verfassungsrechts,* vol. 6. Wien, 1971.

Bodzenta, Erich, et al. *Jungwähler in Österreich.* Linz, 1971.

Broda, Christian. *Die Stunde der Parlamentsreform ist gekommen.* Wien, 1970.

Engelmann, Frederick C., Austria: The Pooling of Oppositions. In Robert A. Dahl, ed., *Political Oppositions in Western Democracies.* New Haven, 1966.

———. Haggling for the Equilibrium: The Renegotiation of the Austrian Coalition 1959. *American Political Science Review,* 1962, pp. 651–62.

Fischer, Heinz, ed. *Das politische System Österreichs,* 2d ed. Wien, 1977.

Fischer, H., and W. Czerny. *Kommentar zur Geschäftsordnung des Nationalrates.* Wien, 1968.

Fornleitner, L., P. Gerlich, et al. *Die Transformation des österreichischen Parlamentarismus, Analysen des Struktur und Funktionswandels des Nationalrats,* 3 Teilbände. Wien, 1974.

Gehmacher, Ernst. Faktoren des Wählerverhaltens. In Heinz Fischer, ed. *Das politische System Österreichs,* 2d ed. Wien, 1977.

———. Die Meinung des Österreichers über sein Parlament. In *Die Republik.* Wien, 1973.

Gerlich, Peter. *Parlamentarische Kontrolle im politischen System.* Wien, 1973.

Gerlich, Peter, and Helmut Kramer. *Abgeordnete in der Parteiendemokratie, Eine empirische Untersuchung des Wiener Landtages und des Gemeinderates.* Wien, 1969.

Gerlich, Peter, et al. *Dynamische Demokratie, Macht und Kontrolle im politischen Prozess Österreichs.* Wien, 1973.

Goldinger, Walter. *Geschichte der Republik Österreich.* Wien, 1962.

Kadan, Albert, and Anton Pelinka. *Die Grundsatzprogramme der österreichischen Parteien Dokumentation und Analyse.* St. Pölten, 1979.

Kitzinger, U. W. The Austrian Election of 1959. In *Political Studies,* 1961, pp. 199–40.

———. The Austrian Electoral System. In *Parliamentary Affairs,* 1959, pp. 392–404.

Kohn, Walter S. G. The Austrian Parliamentary Election of 1971. In *Parliamentary Affairs,* 1971, pp. 163–77.

Koja, Friedrich. Entwicklungstendenzen des österreichischen Föderalismus. In *Schriftenreihe NÖ Juristische Gesellschaft,* H.2. St. Pölten, 1975.

Magenschab, Hans, and Heinrich Neisser. *Parlament und Opposition.* Wien, 1972.

Merkl, Adolph. *Die Verfassung der Republik Deutschösterreich,* Wien, 1919.

Nassmacher, Karl-Heinz. *Das österreichische Regierungssystem. Grosse Koalition oder alternierende Regierung.* Köln, 1968.

Pelinka, Anton, Parlamentarismus. In E. Weinzierl und K. Skalnik, eds. *Österreich, Die Zweite Republik,* vol. II, pp. 9ff. Graz, 1972.

Pelinka, Anton, and Manfred Welan. *Demokratie und Verfassung in Österreich.* Wien, 1971.

Shell, Kurt L. *The Transformation of Austrian Socialism.* New York, 1962.

Steiner, Kurt. *Politics in Austria.* Boston, 1972.

Stiefbold, R., et al., eds. *Wahlen und Parteien in Österreich,* 3 vols. Wien, 1966.

Welan, Manfred. *Der Verfassungsgerichtshof-Eine Nebenregierung?* In Heinz Fischer, ed., *Das politische System Österreichs,* 2d ed. Wien, 1977.

Welan, Manfred, and Heinrich Neisser. *Der Bundeskanzler im österreichischen Verfassungsgefüge.* Wien, 1971.

Modern Austria, pp. 261–78

12. PUBLIC ADMINISTRATION:
The Business of Government

Raoul F. Kneucker

Secretary General of the Austrian Science Research Fund

Modern states are administrative states, Austria being an administrative state *par excellence.* Public administration has become a dominant feature of the civic culture, and more than simply a part of the political system. It has become an overpowering and penetrating organization providing for life's happiness and security, and helping against life's risks, excluding in principle no individual or collective sphere from its regulating, ordering, policing, planning, promoting, financing, subsidizing, and restructuring activities. Public administration has become a source both for grandiose political, social, economic, and technological development[1] and for large, cold, and impersonal complexes, rendering for the mass society "industrialized" public services: *"Unentrinnbarkeit der Bürokratie"* (inevitability of bureaucracy)[2] and at the same time *"Ambivalenz des Fortschritts"* (ambivalence of progress).[3]

Public administration is not an entertaining subject; it is more often a topic for lamentation. It is not, however, and should not be, a specialty for students of politics only.

INTRODUCTION TO AUSTRIAN PUBLIC ADMINISTRATION

Österreich wird nicht regiert, sondern verwaltet ...
Austria is not governed but administered ...

—Metternich, *Letters*

There in Cacania, in this much misunderstood state since perished, which was—without recognition—exemplary in many ways, there was tempo but not too much tempo. . . One prepared for the conquest of the spheres; yes, here too, but never too intensively . . . One

9306-6403/81/0415-0261$01.50

did not show economic imperialism or world power ambition; one was Europe's center, where the old axes of the world meet ... One displayed luxury but by no means as overrefined as the French. One went in for sports but not as insanely as the Anglo Saxons ... One spent millions on defense, yet only enough to securely remain the second weakest of the big powers. Too, the capitol city was somewhat smaller than the largest cities of all the other countries, but still considerably larger than merely big cities. And the country was administered in an enlightened and barely noticeable manner—as a gardener who prunes carefully—by the best European bureaucracy, which might be said to have only one shortcoming: it took genius and the genius-like ambitions of private persons, not being charged by birth or decree, as impertinent behavior and presumptiousness. Alas, who does like interference by incompetent people! At any rate, in Cacania a genius was always understood to be a rascal, and never—as happens elsewhere—a rascal immediately understood to be a genius.

—R. Musil, *Der Mann ohne Eigenschaften*

Readers in Austrian modern history and social, economic, political, and cultural development will everywhere be confronted with, or confounded by, Austrian administration and bureaucracy. In particular, readers of modern Austrian literature will encounter numerous passages on the subject; Austrian poets, dramatists, and essayists have captured the spell of public administration and its peculiar atmosphere better than the experts in public administration; for instance, Robert Musil in *Der Mann ohne Eigenschaften,*[4] Arthur Schnitzler in *Professor Bernardi,* or Franz Werfel with the novella *Eine blassblaue Frauenschrift;* Anton Wildgans in *Kirbisch;* Hugo von Hofmannsthal in the play *Der Unbestechliche,* Josef Roth in *Radetzkymarsch,* or Fritz von Herzmanovsky-Orlando in two novels, *Der Gaulschreck im Rosennetz* and *Maskenspiel der Genien;* Heimito von Doderer in *Die Strudelhofstiege* in the essay "Die erleuchteten Fenster," or Alexander Lernet-Holenia in a short story *Weihnacht im Finanzamt.* Franz Kafka has illustrated the predicament of the modern human condition precipitated by public administration and bureaucracy.

Such literary works serve well today as source books on the subject. Indeed, students of Austrian public administration will discover almost empty shelves in the scholarly corners of libraries. Even in German, only a few law books are offered, and some historical accounts are available; however, political scientists and sociologists have only recently begun studying the various aspects of Austrian public administration.[5] (May we assume that expert authors, who could have prepared the scholarly studies, felt conspicuously obligated to the *arcana* and the mystique of bureaucracy, to which they happened to belong themselves? On the other hand, have poets felt free to treat the subject? Have they acted as sensitive eyewitnesses to the phenomena of modern states, and of modern Austria?)

To make the reader who is interested in Austrian history, its social development, politics, and economics aware of the place and role of public administration and bureaucracy, material has been selected to illustrate Austrian public administration, its particular atmosphere and special quality. The material corresponds to two major aspects: Austrian federalism and democracy.

A DIFFERENT TYPE OF FEDERALISM

He established the empire of the tarocks . . . The Constitution was commendable. It was based on the strict laws of this popular Austrian card game, the esoteric meaning of which could contribute much to the solution of the world's riddles.

—F. Herzmanovsky-Orlando, *Maskenspiel der Genien*

Still in force in its basic features, the Austrian federal model of 1920 deviates in several ways from the older "classical" models, such as those of the USA and Switzerland.[6] Some variations directly concern the federal administration and the administration of the states or provinces (*Länder*), and one of them is fundamental in character:

(*a*) Federal constitutions establish a certain division of labor and powers between the federal central and states' spheres of government; they usually distribute legislative powers, and each sphere is then free to organize its executive branch and administrative offices within its jurisdictions. The Austrian Constitution[7] distinguishes expressly between legislative and executive powers and distributes both types of powers; they may be divided independently of each other, the consequence being that the executive administrative realm of the federal or state government does not always follow from the respective legislative realm. For instance, citizenship is a federal matter, but the regulations are administered by state (or municipal) offices; and land reform is a matter of federal legislation as far as principles are concerned, but the states regulate on the basis of such principles and carry out the reform. The state's administration regularly pertains to many more areas than its legislative powers would suggest.

(*b*) Another peculiarity in Austria is that the constitutional division of powers makes the judiciary a federal matter only—there are no state courts —and it refers to the activities of federal and state governments as governments (*Hoheitsverwaltung*) and not as legal entities participating in economic affairs, based on private and commercial laws (*Privatwirtschaftsverwaltung*).[8] This means that important and costly activities, such as theaters, hospitals, railroads, highways, and public housing, are left to the initiative of the state or the federal government as a "private" business concern, although federal acts usually regulate the matter organizationally.

(c) The division of powers favors the federal government, since it must regulate by law and administer considerably more areas than the states may act upon. However, almost all federal administrative matters, which federal laws regulate and with which federal offices would ordinarily be charged, must be administered by the state governments on the district and state level, and may be handled by the federal ministries only in questions of national concern, in planning, in coordination and in administrative review —indirect federal administration (*mittelbare Bundesverwaltung*).[9]

(d) Such constitutional relationships clearly necessitate special financial arrangements between federal and state governments. The division of powers, however, does not include the right to tax (as the most important source of income); a special constitutional law (Finanz-Verfassungsgesetz, 1948), regulating financial questions on the federal, state, and municipal levels, provides that each level must finance its own activities and, on the basis of a number of principles,[10] leaves to federal legislation the solution by which the state governments can support their activities and are compensated for those activities they do carry out because of the peculiar constitutional arrangements, in particular the "indirect federal administration." Money questions do not lend themselves to political sentimentality—the Federal Government clearly dominates the federal structure, and the federal law on financial questions is clearly an antifederal element (but is it more so than the unitary tendencies in other federal states where the Federal Government also rules over states by subsidies?). Leaving aside other forms of financing governmental affairs and distributing financial burdens, a federal law (the Finance Equalization Law or Finanzausgleichgesetz)—which, in spite of its character as federal law, is in fact fiercely negotiated with the representatives of the state governments—distributes tax powers in the sense that it determines which of the various taxes will constitute revenue for which of the governments—federal, state, or municipalities only, or any two or three of them by a certain percentage. Tax powers are, in fact, powers to collect and spend tax revenues, although the states may levy taxes if federal law does not include the source of taxation (*Steuererfindungsrecht der Länder*).[11]

AN ILLUSTRATION, AND MORE FACTS AND EXPLANATIONS

One key to understanding present Austrian public administration is the constitutional concept of "indirect federal administration": the Federal Government, when acting on state and district levels, is divested of most of its executive administrative powers, which have been transferred to the state governments. The imperial and provincial administrations in the provinces of the former Austro-Hungarian Monarchy (1867–1918) were merged into one state administration in 1920–1925.[12] With few exceptions, there are not, and there may not be, federal offices established in the states. Austrian federalism is often, quite derogatorily, termed "administrative federalism"; however, even if the specific historical conditions and developments are disregarded, the constitutional division of powers must be seen as an effective part of the constitutional system of vertical checks and balances, paying tribute to the influential role the administration plays in the daily lives of the citizens. In the Austrian model this role is entrusted to the states, which are closer to the people and which interpret federal laws in the light of state and regional interests. Many overlook the compound administrative organization and, consequently, misjudge the effects of the federal structure. This can be illustrated by the accompanying chart (Figure 1).

Explanation of the Chart (Figure 1)

The chart describes the administrative organization in a vertical sense (federal-state relationships) and in a horizontal sense (organization of the federal and state levels); it also indicates the administrative review system in rule-making and adjudication procedures.

1. Autonomous forms of public administration (not discussed in detail) are exercised by municipalities; by certain interest groups with public-law status, the so-called Chambers (e.g. the chambers of trade, labor, and agriculture, as well as the chambers for attorneys, notaries, and physicians); by other public corporations and funds; by the universities, etc. Certain state activities (e.g. administration of citizenship matters or data collection) or federal activities (e.g. certain income tax matters) may be delegated to the municipalities. Accordingly, there are an autonomous sphere and a delegated sphere of administration. In both of these spheres, administrative review and supervisory action by the delegating authorities are available and, after exhaustion of these remedies, an appeal to the Constitutional or Administrative Court, which usually can be initiated either by the affected parties or the autonomous administration itself by a request for a review of supervisory decisions.

2. Parliament (the National Assembly or lower house and the Federal Council or upper house) and other control institutions for both the federal and state administrations are mentioned here because their staffs belong to the federal civil service, but they are organizationally separate from the federal service in the ministries. The control institutions are parliament for political control actions; the three high courts—Supreme Court (for civil and criminal questions), Administrative Court (judicial review of all administrative decisions), and Constitutional Court (judicial review of administrative rule-making and adjudication involving constitutional questions, as well as elections and impeachment procedures—to name some of the tasks that affect the public administration); the Rechnungshof (Cours des Comptes) for financial control actions and reports to parliament on the legality and optimal use of public funds; the Volksanwaltschaft (the Austrian form of ombudsman) for citizens' complaints against the (federal) administration at large. Review procedures are not indicated on the chart.

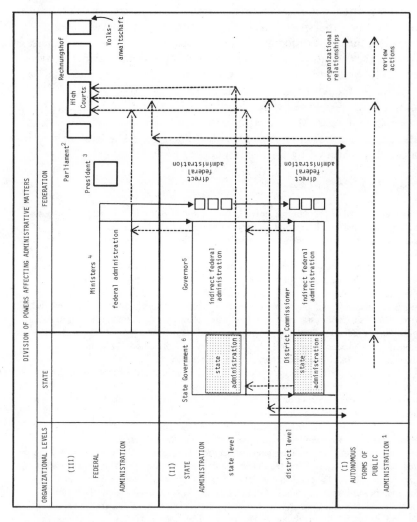

Figure 1 Division of powers in Austrian public administration. See the text for explanations keyed to superscript numbers.

3. The federal level is characterized by a duality of heads: on the one hand, the president of the republic, and on the other hand, the chancellor and the federal ministers. The staff of the president belongs to the federal civil service, but it is organizationally separate from the ministerial service. Political, administrative, and judicial review procedures are not indicated.

4. Federal administration: Chancellory and Ministries for Foreign Affairs; for Federal Buildings, Highways, and Technology; for Finance; for Health and Environmental Protection; for Commerce, Trade, and Industry; of Interior; of Justice; of Defense; of Agriculture and Forestry; of Social Administration; of Education and the Arts; of Transportation; and for Science and Research.

Contrary to the state level, the federal level is structured, in what may be considered the typical European form of administrative organization,[13] solely according to the department, or ministerial, system. The federal ministers, the highest officers, are equal in rank and directly accountable to parliament. They are in complete charge of the ministerial staffs and the internal organization of ministries. Sometimes state secretaries or deputy ministers (*Staatssekretäre*), the second highest federal officers, support the ministers, but they may only act with the consent or on instruction of the minister. At present there are seven such deputy ministers. All other positions are civil service positions. Ministries recruit their staffs directly; there is no central federal recruitment institution comparable to the civil service commissions of other countries.[14] The internal structure of ministries is built on sections (*Abteilungen*), usually with several areas (*Referate,* headed by academically trained staff); groups of sections; and departments. In addition to this linear structure, special staffs (cabinets of ministers, policy-making groups, research groups), or outside offices (*nachgeordnete Dienststellen*) on the federal, state, or district level may exist.[15] The Chancellor is, legally speaking, only a minister, but of course as the political leader he has a different political stature. The cabinet is a political forum and coordinates the activities of all ministries; it is a policy-making body and responsible for the government's draft bills; it may be given specific administrative responsibilities, but would then be another "minister" whose work is prepared and carried out by the chancellery.[16] Administrative review may be obtained in questions of direct federal administration, but as a rule it is not exhausted until the ministry has rendered a decision; then appeals to the high courts are admissible.

5. The larger part of federal administration is transferred to the states or the districts (which are part of the state government) as indirect federal administration. It is carried out at the state level by the governor (*Landeshauptmann*) and the state administration, and at the district level by the district commissioner (*Bezirkshauptmann*) and the district administration. There are at present 97 districts (*Bezirke*) in the nine states (*Länder*). Even federal offices, when established in the states, are placed under the governor's instructions, thus permitting his influence in a direct form. Of course, the governor himself may be bound by instructions of the minister and is accountable to him in this respect.

Administrative review is regularly possible in two steps: district decisions are reviewed by the governor, and the governor's decisions are reviewed by the minister. When the administrative review procedures have been exhausted, appeals to the Administrative or Constitutional Court are admissible in cases involving principles.

6. There are nine state administrations: in Burgenland, Carinthia, Lower and Upper Austria, Salzburg, Styria, Tyrol, Vorarlberg, Vienna. Vienna is at the same time a state and a municipality, and the municipal officers are both municipal and state officers.

The state level is organized by state laws on the basis of provisions of the federal constitution about state government and of a special act on the state offices. (Grundsätze für die Einrichtung und Geschäftsführung des Ämter der Landesregierung ausser Wien, 1925);[17] this includes recruitment of (state) civil servants and personnel administration. Within the framework of a merit system, state offices are staffed from the regional labor market and stress the notion of representative federal recruitment.

As a rule, the state governments (*Landesregierung*) are collegial bodies, formed by a coalition of all political parties in the state parliaments according to their proportional strength and chaired by the governor; their decisions are based on majority rule. The state government as a body is in charge of state administrative matters and is supported by the offices of the state administration. In matters of state administration, administrative review ends at this body, after whose decision an appeal must be addressed to the Constitutional or Administrative Court.

A FEW STATISTICS

A glimpse into the quantitative extent of bureaucratization in Austria is in order here.[18] Personnel expenditure has reached almost 30 percent of the yearly federal budget and is rising. The percentage is even higher in some of the states. Austrian governments are notorious for employing large bureaucracies: today there are about 290,000 federal and 120,000 state employees (excluding municipal civil servants), which is a high proportion in relation to the population and certainly in relation to Austria's active labor force of about 2.9 million people.

However, these figures need interpretation: the total number of public employees increased only slightly from 1930 to 1937 and from 1950 to 1966; recently, it decreased or remained practically stagnant on the federal level and increased steadily on the state level. The figures from which decreases or increases are measured, it should be noted, were the high figures, owing to the situations after two world wars. After World War I, many civil servants returned from the different parts of the former monarchy; after World War II, the war bureaucracy was overexpanded and the personnel demands continued high in a period of reconstruction. The assumption that the secular growth of administrative tasks must be reflected in personnel statistics is generally not supported by facts;[19] only in some instances was it obviously correct (e.g. expansion of the number of teachers for schools, including university staffs, after 1965; creating an army after 1955; police and security problems in the First Republic and extensive personnel changes enforced during the 1934 regime). New needs have been met instead by internal shifts and automation. The Federal Government ceased recruiting for several years, allowing certain exceptions (e.g. for schools, postal service, police force) only in priority cases of personnel policy. The core of public administration, especially the higher civil service, remained stagnant or decreased over the long run; there was expansion of staff in other parts of the public service; for it is by tradition, based on unfortunate economic and political developments, that the Austrian public service includes occupations and sectors that would hardly be included in other countries (e.g. railroads, public utilities on the state level, hospitals, schools of all levels).

ARE THERE DIFFERENT ADMINISTRATIVE CORPS, FEDERAL AND STATE?

Nowhere else had K. seen office and life so intertwined, so interwoven that it could appear at times that office and life had changed places.

—F. Kafka, *Das Schloss*

The federal structure has left its mark on Austria's public service. Of course, there are always general similarities in bureaucracies everywhere, and there is also a good deal of professional cohesion and homogeneity in the Austrian public service. However, there are two tendencies, linked to the federal structure, to be observed in the development of the Austria public services in the Second Republic:

1. *Bureaucratic continuity.* In a discussion of Austrian bureaucracy, a historian with a sense of humor remarked that the Austro-Hungarian Monarchy really died with World War II. There is some truth in this statement. It is remarkable how the style, the ways and means to solve problems or to disregard them, the image and behavior, the format and work ethics were unaffected by the advent of the republic. There was absolute continuity in the day-to-day work. The bureaucracy of an old, large multinational empire adapted itself to a small scale and new governmental outlook. The First Republic, and even the Catholic authoritarian regime after 1934, continued to employ civil servants of former times. Administrative reforms consisted largely in dismissing or retiring personnel. After World War II, that age group left the service. A reconstruction period was both possible and politically necessary. New people came in, and the public administration began changing its character to a truly representative service, with men and women whose historical experience was the small, liberated, and new Austria. A civil service, with the historical background of a privileged group, was gradually transformed into a staff of public employees, which is a professional group like others, talking about salaries and job security —plain, efficient or inefficient, white-collar workers. Privileges were done away with. Looking at the factors of development, we find that they included (*a*) access to the service, open to all strata of society; earlier recruitment grounds no longer existed or had lost their influence (elite schools,

family, academic associations); (b) the Grand Coalition's *Proporz,* shaping personnel policy more or less as a quota system in which people from all political camps had an equal chance to enter the service, thus a step to a fuller application of the merit system; and (c) the labor market situation, since new positions had to be filled in a market characterized by low unemployment rates and by excellent prospects and security in other sectors of the economy. Actually, the public service became for the first time a part of the general labor market and had to compete in it.[20] This development can be noticed earlier in the state administrations than in the Federal Government (social structure studies of the state services are unfortunately still lacking). The recruitment policy of the states was closely related to the regional labor market and to the interests and circumstances of the individual states. The atmosphere was regionalized; mobility decreased. It was customary under the old personnel regulations (*Dienstpragmatik;* 1914)[21] to start service in the provinces and to be called to ministerial service later, if at all; the new unified state administrations ended that tradition. The federal civil servants began to be recruited directly, and largely from Vienna and environs, uncoupling the federal from the state services.

2. *Federalizing the public services.* At the start of the republic, the intention was to establish a unified administrative corps; the mobility between federal and state level was especially to be guaranteed. The federal legislature was charged with affairs of all civil servants, and not only of the federal service. The Constitution provided for such regulations explicitly; the political development, however, was different. Uniform rules were not issued; a constitutional law of 1974 finally acknowledged the, in fact, separate personnel policies and staff regulations. The states, having asked for more federalism for over ten years, are now free to regulate the matter. The federal and state legislatures had begun reforming their respective civil service laws, the federal reforms since 1968 leading the way: provisions against political transfers of public employees, posting of open positions, changes in job classification and performance evaluation, establishing an academy for administration (*Verwaltungsakademie*) for all forms of in-service-training of federal employees, including that of top managers, and abolishing many old, lovely, and in some cases funny, titles. Some of these titles had relevance to functions of former days, but no longer to the functions of a modern bureaucracy. As a matter of fact, such titles had long been scorned and their use ridiculed (especially when they were used to greet a customer of a grocery store or were inscribed on a tombstone), but as soon as they were abolished, as soon as the source of satire and jokes was removed, nostalgia set in, and many now regret the loss of color and historical meanings.

COMMON TRADITIONS AND STYLES

As a butterfly then, Eynhuf should participate in the ball ... 'Alas! I got it,' and he suddenly hopped with joy; 'I go as a swallowtail' ... It seemed to him, a man in an important position, utterly impossible to go to a public dance without tails.

—F. Herzmanovsky-Orlando
Der Gaulschreck im Rosennetz

Common characteristics of the Austrian public services do exist:

(*a*) Some old traditions are still alive, such as a distinctive style of each ministry or each state government in communication, expressed in their statements, in their relationships to the outside world, or to other ministries and state governments; a certain prestige and pride in being a member of certain ministries such as the Chancellory, the Ministry of Foreign Affairs, or the Ministry of Finance, generally held in the highest professional esteem; an extreme consciousness of the hierarchy, a common form of polite behavior, a strong attitude of loyalty to the government, and a strong feeling of being bound by positive law and of only serving the law. To these must be added an incomparably strong sense of ministerial jurisdictions, which are defended as if personal interests of property were at stake. (Interministerial conferences have great importance for the numerous projects that cross jurisdictional lines or involve federal-state cooperation; they tend to start with the question of jurisdiction, and discussions of venue, in which the members of a ministry always behave as dedicated agents of their own house, may easily paralyze any talk. Consequently, a specific Austrian form of cooperation between ministries, *im Einvernehmen*—about as complex as committee work in the legislature—will often lead to the administrative death of a project.)

(*b*) Today, public services comprise a great number of occupations; even more importantly, the spectrum of administrative tasks requires functional expertise in many different disciplines. In Austria, the federal division of powers accentuates a diversity in professional structure. For instance, on the state level certain technological, agricultural, cultural, and medical tasks predominate and require appropriate qualifications; in the higher civil service, on the federal level, legal questions, planning, policy-making, international relations, and commerce dominate the work. The recent reforms paid attention to such changes. Personnel, academically trained in diverse disciplines, now rank equally in career prospects; personnel policy has opened new positions to social scientists. The public services are clearly in a transitory stage. The need for functional expertise will continue to shape the personnel structure and attitudes of public employees.

The character of the Austrian public service has been shaped by the legal training of its top ranks.[22] It is the man trained in law who has played the most important part; it is the legal question at which ultimately everything ends. There are several reasons that explain and support such a development, and the Austrian case is only different in the degree of intensity, but is not otherwise different from general European administrative history. The legally trained bureaucracy increased the viability of constitutional government and helped by its legal expertise to establish legitimate authority and effective control mechanisms.[23] Administrative history is linked with the secular constitutional developments of securing the rule of law (*Rechtsstaat*). The ideal for the higher bureaucrat was, and still is, the type of general administrator who feels responsible for the whole, for the weak individual's procedural rights and for finding compromises, the right proportions (even aesthetic ones), and the politically possible. The higher civil service was not unsuccessful in realizing such ideals. Who, indeed, will be able to replace the legally socialized generalist in the future?

BUREAUCRACY BEFORE DEMOCRACY

He was of the opinion that each production—not only of a civil servant but also of a blue-collar worker or concert singer—constitutes an "office."

—R. Musil, *Der Mann ohne Eigenschaften*

Like the other highest civil servants, the department head did not feel a special respect for the ministers ... Leonidas and others like him ... had learned government as musicians study counterpoint in years of continuous practice; they possessed the sensitivity for the thousand nuances of administration and decision-making. "You have conspicuously changed your point of view, Herr Sektionschef." "Yes, Herr Minister, I did change it in this case." "In politics, dear friend, it is at times quite advisable to cause irritation. But it depends on whom you annoy." "I do not have the honor of being a politician, Herr Minister; I serve the state to the best of my knowledge and conscience."

—F. Werfel, *Eine blassblaue Frauenschrift*

The new democratic states in Europe after World War I, like Austria, continued to employ the large, well-trained, and well-organized, strong and indispensible bureaucracies of earlier constitutional and political systems and of earlier regimes. Would such a socially and politically homogeneous bureaucracy, devoted to the service of the empire and the constitutional monarchy, remain in opposition or alienation, or would it reorient itself? Would it be able to do so, belonging to a specific social elite? Would it stay aloof from party politics, so foreign to its own political outlook? The bureaucracy's inability to understand new political mechanisms, the alienation from them, and the desire to establish or restore "order" contributed to the fall of the Weimar Republic. The changeover in Austria was more successful; political events did not involve the bureaucracy as a party to the process. The succession of regimes—three or more in less than two generations of civil servants—amounted "not only to a change in political leadership, but also to a break with previous ideology." Bureaucracy continued to provide continuity and administrative stability; it was at the disposal of the authorities, loyal and dutiful, "in the spirit of the office." An interesting case of "bureaucratic resiliency"[24] and of administrative ethics! Convenient or not, laudable or not, in the self-image of the civil service the concept of "servant to the state" with a responsibility to the whole and to the "common good," irrespective of political developments "above" administration, prevailed, even when it was confused with the "service of (any) regime." The self-interpretation was linked to constitutional notions of a bureaucracy as the "instrument" of government, in turn based on and applying Max Weber's distinctions.[25]

In today's democracy, the service of the state is at the same time service to any duly elected, democratically legitimate leadership. Indeed, the old work ethic—to be in the service of the state—has undergone (in the self-interpretation of modern Austrian bureaucracy) this very change; i.e. to be the instrument of legitimated leadership is to serve the whole. The change of interpretation was evidently prepared by and connected to the concept of a Grand Coalition after World War II, when the former opposing political camps united in the reconstruction of Austria. Again the bureaucracy proved to be an indispensable and excellent expert help in the process. The civil service remains proud to have been part of this development and an instrument of creating the modern social state.

Two further tendencies after World War II should be considered: the close ties of bureaucrats to the political leadership are, compared to the First Republic, much less a sign of total politicization or the employment of political followers. The elections for the public employees' representation against the state as their employer during a ten-year period of Socialist political leadership, still reveal absolute majorities of the associations affiliated with the People's Party.[26] It is the ability to contribute to political achievements for which the service feels responsible, even if it is often regretted that such achievements in the service of whatever political leadership are never duly attributed to the bureaucracy but always reported as the success of government.[27] If the political analyst of some 15 years ago could notice in the higher civil service a certain contempt for or condescension toward politicians, particularly parliamentarians, the analyst today might well come to different conclusions. Before 1918, it was a quite common career pattern to enter parliament in order to become a top civil servant or minister; it is now usual to become a parliamentarian when as a civil servant one showed organizational and political talent. There is, in fact, even regret that so many parliamentarians are now public employees.[28] In general, the public service has developed into a professional area for career men and women, based on the need for functional expertise in the political process —another indicator for the democratic development of the service.

THE INDISPENSABLE EXPERT

Austrian higher civil service is an action group in the service of the political processes just as other bureaucracies are. Two specific Austrian features are, however, to be kept in mind: (*a*) In policy formation, on the federal and state levels, many functions are *de facto* delegated to the higher civil service. More than 90 percent of all federal bills originate in the ministries; whether or not such bills are politically necessary, the first reading is already a precluded question, and after extensive briefing on the drafts by the ministries and changes according to interest politics, which are integrated by the bureaucracy, the work of the ministry often takes the place of the second reading. The federal legislature begins the legislative process at a later stage, namely with the concrete committee work, and it ends the process with the last decisive political compromise or resolution. Even during this part of the legislative activities, the higher civil servants act as committee experts, committee counsel, and secretaries. The legislative offices are at present not staffed to help the parliamentarians in this capacity.[29] The situation in the state legislature is similar to the federal one. (*b*) The demographic structure reveals that, for the business of government and the political process in general, only two major bureaucracies are available, the federal and state bureaucracies on the one hand, and the quasi-bureaucracies of the big legalized interest groups on the other. The public service has almost a monopoly in providing expertise and organization to the political process. It possesses the field expertise and holds the threads of development; it acts, reformulates, calls outside experts, and integrates all professional views. Its work is checked by the political and common-sense control in parliament; on a professional level, it can hardly be checked by another set of experts, such as is easily available for the political process in many other countries.

THE CONCEPT OF LEGALITY

All open-air concerts (which took place under the balcony of the District Commissioner) began with the Radetzky March. Although it was so familiar to the band members that they could have played it in the middle of the night in their sleep without a conductor, the band master nevertheless considered it essential to read each note from the score.

And as if he had rehearsed the march for the first time with his musicians, each Sunday with military and musical conscientiousness he raised his head and raised his baton and sent his commands to each segment of the circle, in the center of which he stood, as if they needed them.

—J. Roth, *Radetzkymarsch*

In previous sections, elements of the modern Austrian public administrations have been discussed: the vertical/federal system of checks and balances; the political, financial, and legal/judicial controls, the concept of accountability and work ethics; and the changes into a democratic public service, into a professional group of public managers. If the first key to understanding the present Austrian public administration was the concept of a "federalized" public administration, the other key is the constitutional concept of legality.

The relevant constitutional provision reads simply: "All executive/administrative actions must be based on legislative acts and must determine clearly which administrative office may act in a certain case."[30] But what is of interest here is not the provision itself, but rather the conception that created it and that is so fundamental to the spirit and work of Austrian public administration. It is expressed in the tradition of codified administrative procedures, establishing a separate and appropriate procedural law and review system for administrative activities; it was expanded over the years to literally all federal and state offices; its efficacy allowed judicial review to centralize *a posteriori* in only one court, the Administrative Court, for both the federal and state administrations.[31] It is expressed in the doctrine of liability of federal and state offices and officers for administrative activities; assessment of damages, restitutions, and reparations are questions for the law courts.[32] It is expressed in the style, behavior, and mental quality of the public employees: politics, on the level of administration, is a legal question; reforms come principally from above and are an area of politics (even if the higher civil service contributes to it); there is, in fact, to be a division of labor between legislation, the major vehicle of reform, and the administration; the democratic legislation must be administered through a strictly hierarchical, dependent administration in order not to distort the intentions of the parliament.

Interpretations of laws are permissible only within narrow margins for concrete executive actions; response to or the engineering of social change should be based on exogenous political impulses, as is the steering of public administration. Austrian public administration does not differ from others in the sense that legality (or rule of law) is a constitutional feature, which for the political scientist is only a prescription, unable to explain political reality; it differs from others in the sense that the constitutional regulation is applied more strictly and seriously and is thought to be more fundamental than in other administrations, or that it still has a regulative force despite the political realities or expediencies.[33]

TRANSITIONS

It is appropriate, in a time when indispensable bureaucratic organizations have created much ambivalent progress, to conclude by reminding the reader of the transition in the public administration, discussed earlier. The public administration is also in transition from being a legalistic one, for which politics and social reform are legal questions that should more or less lie outside the administration, to a functional one, for which politics is an all-embracing social process in which the bureaucracy must perform a special role and provide specific professional service. It is furthermore in transition from bureaucratic organization to new organizational forms in which it may serve the public more adequately and manage public affairs in new ways.

Notes

All translations of literary quotations have been made by the author.

1. J. LaPalombara, (ed.), *Bureaucracy and Political Development,* chaps. 1–4 (Princeton, 1963).
2. M. Weber, *Wirtschaft und Gesellschaft* (Studienausgabe J. Winckelmann) (Cologne, 1964) pp. 160–66, 1047–62.
3. C. F. von Weiszäcker, *Der Garten des Menschlichen,* 2d ed. (Munich, 1977), pp. 63–140.
4. Robert Musil's great novel, translated by Eithne Wilkin and Ernst Kaiser, has been published in 3 volumes under the title *The Man Without Qualities* (London, 1960). English translations of the works of Schnitzler, Hofmannsthal and Roth, referred to in this paragraph, are also available.
5. An annotated bibliography of recent publications may be found in R. Kneucker, "Öffentliche Verwaltung, 1975/76," in A. Khol and A. Stirnemann, ed., *Österreichisches Jahrbuch für Politik, 1977* (Munich, 1978), pp. 143–45.
6. For details see the chapter by Peter Gerlich in this book. A full account of the federal system is found in E. Melichar, "Entwicklungstendenzen des österreichischen Föderalismus," *Österreichische Zeitschrift für Öffentliches Recht* (Wien, 1967), pp. 220–69; see also F. Ermacora, *Österreichische Verfassungslehre* (Wien, 1970), chap. VI; and F. Koja, *Entwicklungstendenzen des österreichischen Föderalismus. Schriftenreihe der niederösterreichischen Juristengesellschaft* (Wien, 1975).
7. Constitutional texts: H. Klecatsky, *Das österreichische Bundesverfassungsrecht,* 2d ed. (Wien, 1973); F. Ermacora, *Österreichische Bundesverfassungsgesetze,* 8th ed. (Stuttgart, 1979); an official English translation is available. Commentaries: L. Adamovich, Jr., *Handbuch des Österreichischen Verfassungsrechts,* 6th ed. (Wien, 1971); R. Walter, *Österreichisches Bundesverfassungsrecht* (Wien, 1972); R. Walter and H. Meyer, *Grundriss des Verfassungsrechts* (Wien, 1976). Note: To facilitate comparison with other federal systems, the term "state" is used for the subdivisions, referred to as provinces (*Länder*) in other chapters.
8. In addition to the above-mentioned studies, for information on this subject, see F. Ermacora, G. Winkler, H. P. Rill, and B. Ch. Funk, *Allgemeines Verwaltungsrecht* (Wien, 1979), chap. IV; and H. Mayer, Die Kompetenzverschiebungen zwischen Bund und Ländern, in H. Mayer et al, *Neuerungen im Verfassungsrecht* (Wien, 1976), pp. 21–22.

9. Important exceptions are customs and other matters of international trade; federal taxes and other federal financial questions; state monopolies; weapons, ammunition, explosives; trademarks, patents, federal police matters of security, highways and river police; monument protection; military affairs, federal schools, and employment offices (see Article 102, Austrian Constitution). Whenever the Federal Government chooses to establish federal offices for "indirect federal administrative matters" on the state level, the state's consent is required. See R. Novak, "Bundes-Verfassungsgesetznovelle 1974 und Verwaltungsorganisation," *Österreichische Juristen-Zeitung* (Wien, 1975), p. 281.

10. For instance, the types of taxes are constitutionally fixed: e.g. federal, state, and municipal taxes or "taxes shared between federal and state governments." From these the legislative and administrative power is derived.

11. For further details see E. Melichar, "Finanz- und Steuersystem," in Tautscher et al, *Handbuch der österreichischen Wirtschaftspolitik* (Wien, 1961); E. Melichar and H. Wissgott, in C.-A. Andreae, ed., *Handbuch der österreichischen Finanzwirtschaft* (Wien, 1969); Ch. Smekal, Wirtschaft- und Finanzpolitische Probleme des österreichischen Finanzausgleichs, unter besonderer Berücksichtigung der Länder," in E. C. Hellbling, Th. Mayer-Maly and H. Mieshler, eds., *Theorie und Praxis des Bundesstaates* (Salzburg, 1974), pp. 173–219.

12. See L. Adamovich, p. 21; E. Melichar, "Die Entwicklung der österreichischen Verwaltungsorganisation seit 1867," in A. Csizmadia, ed., *Entwicklungsfragen der Verwaltung in Mitteleuropa* (Pecs, 1972), 189–201; and F. Koja, *Das Verfassungsrecht der österreichischen Bundesländer* (Wien, 1967), pp. 221, 269, 317.

13. See F. Morstein Marx, ed., *Elements of Public Administration,* 2d ed. (Englewood Cliffs, N.J., 1963).

14. Recruitment, promotion procedures, and political positions in the Austrian civil service are discussed in R. F. Kneucker, "Austria: An Administrative State," *Österreichische Zeitschrift für Politikwissenschaft* (Wien, 1973), pp. 103–7, 120–22.

15. Details can be found in a reform act, debated since the 1960s, "Bundesministeriengesetz," Federal Gazette No. 389/1973. The official "Österreichischer Amtskalender" (manual of public offices), published each year by the Österreichische Staatsdruckerei in Vienna, contains all federal (and state) offices (with their current activities) and officers (higher civil service included). A detailed study of a ministry is available in S. Titscher (with contributions by R. Kneucker and R. Hiessmannseder), *Struktur eines Ministeriums* (Wien, 1975).

16. For details on the political processes of the federal and state governments, see the chapter by Peter Gerlich.

17. See note 12 above.

18. For a discussion of data and terms, see R. Kneucker, "Austria: An Administrative State," pp. 96–101; and C. H. Ule, ed., *Die Entwicklung des öffentlichen Dienstes* (Cologne, 1962), in which Austria is treated by V. Hackl, p. 358; see also V. Hackl, "The Public Service in Austria," *International Review of Administrative Sciences* vol. 27 (Brussels, 1962), p. 172; and H. Schambeck, "Der Beamte und das Bundes-Verfassungsgesetz," in H. Lentze and P. Putzer, eds., *Festschrift für Ernst Carl Hellbling zum 70. Geburtstag* (Salzburg, 1971), pp. 629–50. For data sources: several publications of the *Statistisches Zentralamt* (Wien); explanatory notes to the yearly federal budgets, Federal Ministry of Finance; A. Teissl, *Personalstatistik der Bundesländer, 1962* (Wien, 1965).

19. While everyone cheered the witty remarks and "tongue-in-cheek" theories of Northcote Parkinson—which make, indeed, brilliant reading—statistics do not bear them out. See F. Morstein Marx, *The Administrative State. An Introduction to Bureaucracy* (Chicago, 1957), p. 7. In the case of Austria the statistics are hardly more alarming than in other countries.

20. See K. Steiner, *Politics in Austria* (Boston, 1972), pp. 378–82; R. F. Kneucker, "Austria: An Administrative State," pp. 101–5; similar views on the intermediate steps to a fuller liberalization and better representativeness of public services are in F. Engelmann, "Austria: The Pooling of Opposition," in R. Dahl, ed., *Political Opposition in Western Democracies* (New Haven, 1966), p. 274. (All references contain additional sources and studies for the interested reader.)

21. See V. Hackl, *Die Dienstpragmatik,* 5th ed (Wien, 1965); with an English translation in L. White, ed., *The Civil Service in the Modern State* (Chicago, 1930), pp. 457, 461.

22. See also K. Steiner, *op. cit.,* p. 382.

23. F. Morstein Marx, "The Higher Civil Service as an Action Group in Western Political Development," in J. LaPalombara, ed., *Bureaucracy and Political Development* (Princeton, 1963), pp. 64–65.

24. Quotes from K. Steiner, *op. cit.*, pp. 378–82. See also R. F. Kneucker, "Austria: An Administrative State," p. 127.
25. See R. F. Kneucker, "Bürokratie und Demokratie," in Gerlich et al., *Dynamische Demokratie* (Wien, 1973), pp. 46–47. See also below. (The categories of "service" are F. Morstein Marx's in *The Administrative State* (Chicago, 1957), pp. 154–70).
26. Statistics are in A. Khol and A. Stirnemann, eds., *Österreichisches Jahrbuch für Politik, 1977* (Munich, 1978) and *Österreichisches Jahrbuch für Politik, 1979* (Munich, 1980).
27. For understanding the moods of the Austrian public service, G. Engelmayer, ed., *Die Diener des Staates: Das bürokratische System Österreichs* (Wien, 1977, published under the auspices of the public employees union), provides excellent material; see especially F. Gasperschitz or the editor's own contribution. (The book contains contributions on other aspects, too; the reader is encouraged to turn to the contributions of H. Fischer and F. Ermacora on politics and bureaucracy.)
28. See statistics in H. Fischer's contribution to the publication in note 27; see also his contributions to the present volume.
29. See R. F. Kneucker, "Austria: An Administrative State," in *Österreichische Zeitschrift für Politikwissenschaft* (Wien, 1973), pp. 124–27; see also the contributions mentioned in note 27.
30. Article 18 of the Austrian Constitution; see the literature in note 7.
31. The codification of originally "judge-made" case law took place in 1925 and had the greatest influence on Central European administration; it was codified again in 1950 and amended several times. Texts are in E. Manlicher and H. Quell, *Das Verwaltungsverfahren,* 2 vols., 8th ed. (Wien, 1978). There is also a very extensive literature on this subject.
32. See the introduction in R. F. Kneucker, "Austria: An Administrative State," p. 120.
33. See also the chapter by Rudolf Strasser in this volume.

Selected Bibliography

LITERATURE IN ENGLISH

Various authors in a special issue, "The Public Service in Austria," of the *International Review of Administrative Sciences,* vol. 27 (Brussels, 1962).
Kneucker, Raoul F. Austria: An Administrative State. The Role of Austrian Bureaucracy. *Österreichische Zeitschrift für Politikwissenschaft,* pp. 95–127. Wien, 1973.
Steiner, Kurt. *Politics in Austria,* specifically Chapter XIII. Boston, 1972.

LITERATURE IN GERMAN

The rigorous selection of references is based on the following considerations: the publications should be oriented toward a *foreign* reader with some working knowledge of German, who is interested in the general political, social, and historical questions but who is not necessarily a scholar in the field. (These considerations have also guided the selection of literature in the notes to this essay.)
Engelmayer, G., ed. *Die Diener des Staates. Das bürokratische System Österreichs.* (Wien, 1977).
Ermacora, F., G., Winkler, F., Koja, H. P. Rill, and B. Ch. Funk, eds. *Allgemeines Verwaltungsrecht.* Wien, 1979. See also the work upon which it was based: W. Antoniolli, *Allgemeines Verwaltungsrecht,* Wien, 1954, which will be revised by F. Koja (2d ed., in print).
Fischer, H., ed. *Das Politische System Österreichs.* Wien, 1974.
Hofmann, A. Bürokratie insbesondere in Österreich. In H. Fichtenau and E. Zöllner, eds., *Beiträge zur neueren Geschichte Österreichs,* pp. 13–31. Wien, 1974.
R. F. Kneucker. Bürokratie und Demokratie. In P. Gerlich et al., *Dynamische Demokratie.* Schriftenreihe des Österreichischen Akademikerbunds, Wien, 1973.
———. Öffentliche Verwaltung, 1975/1976. In A. Khol and A. Stirnemann eds., *Österreichisches Jahrbuch für Politik 1977,* pp. 123–51. München, 1978.
Titscher, S. Gespräche mit Insidern über Verwaltung, Bürokratie und Verwaltungsforschung. In *Österreichische Zeitschrift für Politikwissenschaft,* pp. 141–59. Wien, 1974.
Wandruska, A., and P. Urbanitsch, eds. *Die Habsburger Monarchie, 1848–1918. II, Verwaltung und Rechtswesen.* Wien, 1975.

Modern Austria, pp. 279–98
Copyright © 1981 by SPOSS Inc. All rights reserved

13. THE MEDIA

Hubert Feichtlbauer

Chief Editor, *Die Furche,* Weekly Newspaper for Politics, Society, and Culture

1 THE DEVELOPMENT OF RADIO BROADCASTING DURING THE FOUR-POWER OCCUPATION, 1945–1955

1.1 The First Radio Stations in the Various Provinces

Austrian radio broadcasting was from its beginning a public, monopolistic enterprise, not a part of the private economy. In 1924, a public corporation, the Radio - Verkehrs - Aktiengesellschaft (RAVAG), began radio broadcasting for all of Austria. It was centrally organized, with its center in Vienna. RAVAG was reestablished in 1945, under very confused circumstances. Broadcasting was resumed on 29 April 1945, but programs were limited to the provinces (*Länder*) of Vienna, Lower Austria, and Burgenland, i.e. the three provinces of the Soviet occupation zone, with more than 400,000 listeners at the end of 1945.[1] All attempts to convert this program to an all-Austria radio were futile. In part this failure was the result of disunity and interest conflict among the occupying powers, but in part it resulted also from the dynamic of the broadcasting groups (*Sendergruppen*), which had been established in the meantime in the various occupation zones. With or without occupation, these broadcasting groups did not want to permit the reestablishment of a central radio institution located in Vienna.

After seven years of Nazi rule, the first broadcast of a democratic station in the west of Austria reached Vienna on 2 May 1945, from the French occupation zone, when the Austrian Radio, Sender Vorarlberg in Dornbirn began operation. A day later, Sender Innsbruck, also in the French zone, resumed broadcasting. Both stations then formed the Sendergruppe West, which by the end of 1945 had 65,000 steady listeners. In the British occupa-

Translated by Susan Perkins, Vienna.

9306-6403/81/0415-0279$01.50

tion zone (essentially composed of the provinces of Styria and Carinthia) the studio Klagenfurt and the studio Graz[2] started broadcasting on May 8 and 9, respectively. They became the *Sendergruppe Alpenland.* At the end of 1945 *Sendergruppe Alpenland* had 136,000 listeners.

The studio Rotweissrot broadcast for the first time from Salzburg on 6 June 1945. Studio Linz, which after a brief start had fallen silent again on 1 May, resumed production in August. They were combined into the Sendergruppe Rotweissrot, which had 136,000 listeners by the end of 1945. Initially planned for the American occupation zone (the provinces of Salzburg and Upper Austria), they became the most successful senders, and they were to influence substantially the entire development of Austrian radio. From the beginning they were operated with skill and originality by professional broadcasters of the United States Armed Forces—among them some German-speaking Jewish refugees from the Nazi regime—in cooperation with Austrian broadcasters. Early on, a close relationship to the listeners was established by the often hour-long broadcasts, which facilitated the reunion of families with missing persons—an important concern in the confusion of the immediate postwar period. Later Rotweissrot maintained this relationship by programming that initiated a new style in radio —transmissions from the Salzburg festivals, a new somewhat less rigid news service, racy contemporary music, but also theater productions of cultural value.

1.2   Radio Censorship, Its End, and Preparations for Austrian Television

All Austrian broadcasting stations of the immediate postwar period came under the censorship of the occupation forces in their respective zones. But there were great differences in the skill with which propaganda was dispersed. In Rotweissrot pure propaganda broadcasts were limited to 15 minutes per day, and were explicitly declared as such by their title, "America Calls Austria." Otherwise, valuable programs were sent across the airwaves. As tensions among the Allies increased, the line followed by Rotweissrot became more clearly anti-Soviet and anti-Communist, but there was no need to impose such a line on the Austrian staff. It reflected from the beginning Austrian tendencies.

In contrast, the Russian Hour of the RAVAG became more and more a propaganda tool of the Soviet occupation forces, and the propaganda was rejected by Austrian listeners. Naturally, this rejection increased their attitude of distance toward broadcasts from Vienna. When Communist trade unionists, with obvious encouragement from the Soviet forces, proclaimed a general strike in October 1950, Radio Vienna had to send the proclamations of the Strike Committee, but, in a remarkable act of courage, it supplemented them regularly by the totally conflicting statements of the Austrian government and the Austrian Trade Union Federation (Österreichischer Gewerkschaftsbund, ÖGB). The communist-inspired general strike, which many saw as an attempt to establish in Austria the conditions of a people's democracy, failed owing to the activities of the majority of democratically inclined trade unionists and the government. But these circumstances made it clear that the Austrian postwar radio would not be centrally guided by Vienna in the future.

A grotesque accident, involving a mistranslation by the newspaper of the Soviet occupying forces, led to the end of censorship in the fall of 1953.[3] The Austrian cabinet—which, since 1947, did not include a Communist minister—utilized the error and informed the Soviet forces that no RAVAG manuscript would be submitted for censorship as of 1 October. After some diplomatic maneuvers, this decision was ultimately accepted by the Soviet authorities, and the British and French occupation authorities followed suit. The American authorities were originally reluctant to let go of Rotweissrot, but a *modus vivendi* was ultimately reached with the Austrian government: the radio stations in Salzburg and Linz were transferred to Austria, but Rotweissrot would continue to be operated and financed by the U.S. forces as long as the Russian Hour was broadcast by the RAVAG in Vienna. By the middle of 1955 Austria finally attained full authority over the radio.

In the meantime some developments had favored the reestablishment of a unitary, all-Austrian radio. A judgment of the Constitutional Court in October 1954 declared that broadcasting belonged to the jurisdiction of the Federal Republic and not of its component provinces, in terms of both legislation and implementation. The same year brought a technical innovation that tended in the same direction. The Ultra-Short-Wave Service, which had started in 1953 as an experimental program, was institutionalized. This was a decisive precondition for the initiation of television, and it was clear that even if only for reasons of economy, television could only be operated by a center in Vienna.

The legal fiction of an "Austrian" broadcasting system thus again became a reality, but in a different way from that prevailing before 1938. After the experiences of 1945, the relative autonomy of the studios in the provinces was firmly established. The public corporation, whose shares were held by the Federal Government and the federal provinces, was now called the Austrian Broadcasting Corporation (Österreichischer Rundfunk GmbH.). Television began programming on 1 August 1955 with a discussion of the editors in chief of prominent Austrian newspapers on the topic Will television harm the press?[4]

2   TRIUMPH OF THE INDEPENDENT PRESS; NEWSPAPER MARKET, 1945–1965

2.1   Great Variety and Reader Records after the War

It soon became clear that such fears were completely unfounded. Just as in other countries in the free world, where the advance of television led to increased newspaper circulation, in Austria, too, television had the effect of an appetizer that stimulated the appetite for more information from the papers. Far from disappearing from the scene, newspapers enjoyed an enormous increase in circulation. They only had to adapt themselves to the new medium by providing more background information and commentaries and by taking the illustrations more seriously.

In early 1945, when the Nazi regime finally collapsed in Central Europe and Austria reemerged as an independent republic, there was understandably a record desire for information among the general public. In the various provinces, the occupation forces granted permission for the publication of newspapers to two main groups: trustworthy private individuals and the political parties authorized at that time, i.e. the Austrian People's party (Österreichische Volkspartei, ÖVP), the Socialist party (Sozialistische Partei Österreichs, SPÖ), and the Communist party (Kommunistische Partei Österreichs, KPÖ).

The first paper to appear in postwar Austria was the *Österreichische Zeitung,* but that was the official paper of the Soviet occupation force (the occupation forces published their own German-language papers in Vienna). The *Österreichische Zeitung* (first published on 21 April 1945, i.e. before the end of the war) was followed in August by the *Wiener Kurier* brought out by the US forces, in September by the British *Weltpresse,* and in November by the French weekly paper *Wiener Montag.* Only the *Wiener Kurier* and the *Weltpresse* met with reader success. At the end of the occupation period, the Americans sold their paper to a Viennese industrialist (the paper still exists today as the *Kurier*) and the British sold theirs to the Socialist party (which soon discontinued it).

Out of the 32 daily papers that came out at the end of the first postwar year in 1945, only 6 had been in existence before the war, when the Austrians had had 39 daily papers to choose from. Among the most traditional were the semiofficial *Wiener Zeitung,* which in 1945 was already in its 238th year; the Socialist party's *Arbeiterzeitung,* founded in 1895; and the *Kleines Volksblatt,* which was first published in 1929 and now became the mouthpiece of the Austrian People's party.

In the Western occupation zones, the *Salzburger Nachrichten* and the *Oberösterreichische Nachrichten* became the most widely known; both were papers whose publication by private individuals had been made possible by the US occupation forces. In 1946 the total circulation of the Austrian daily papers reached the record figures of 2.5 million copies, which after the ensuing drop in circulation was only to be achieved again a good 20 years later.

2.2 Fewer Readers and Even Fewer Party Paper Readers

In 1957 the circulation of the daily papers reached its lowest ebb, with 1.2 million, a drop in circulation of 51 percent since 1946. This trend is reflected by the decrease in the thirst for information, which had been at its peak just after the war and had then been difficult to quench owing to the paper shortage—there were days when the newspapers had only four pages. As the supply increased, the demand decreased. This was particularly true of the political party press. In the period of violent party disputes between the two world wars, it was common practice to keep abreast of events through a paper belonging to one's own political party.

At first, postwar Austria followed this tradition. But since the three political parties, legally authorized in 1945, wanted to demonstrate that the formerly bitterly opposed political camps could create a new Austria only through common efforts, they founded a joint paper that they named *Neues Österreich* (New Austria). In this paper political events were commented on by editors from the different parties.[5] Eventually, more and more readers in Austria found that the party papers because of their biases were a less reliable source of information than the independent papers. With the increase in circulation of the independent papers, their revenue also rose, which enabled the contents to be increased and in turn made the party papers seem even more scanty by comparison.

In the meantime, the *Neues Österreich* and the official paper of the Austrian People's party, the *Volksblatt,* have folded. The official paper of the Socialist party, the *Arbeiterzeitung,* is still going today, heavily subsidized by the party and the Socialist faction of the Trade Union Federation.

2.3 The Importance of the Press for the Restoration of Democracy

Through the authoritarian regime between 1934 and 1938 and the totalitarianism of the ensuing Nazi regime, the Austrian people had grown unaccustomed to democracy. It can also be argued that the authoritarian period was at least in part a result of the exaggerated quarrels between the political parties, which in turn were sparked by the precarious economic situation in the period after World War I. In other words, many Austrians had either no memories at all of democracy or not very good ones.

In 1945, however, there could be no doubt that the Austrian people wanted democracy back. The Austrian press played a prominent part in preparing for democracy and in creating an atmosphere that would further democratic development. It also succeeded in arousing understanding of the need for some form of cooperation between the large political parties.

For 21 years (1945–1966) this took the form of the Grand Coalition of the People's party (ÖVP) and the Socialist party (SPÖ). These parties represented almost 90 percent of the electorate and held an even greater percentage of the seats in parliament. The function of an opposition was therefore performed only in a most limited and ineffectual manner by the small parties—i.e. the Communist party (KPÖ)—and, since 1949, by the Union of Independents (Wahlpartei der Unabhängigen, WdU), which in 1955 changed its name to Liberal party (Freiheitliche Partei Österreichs, FPÖ). In this situation the non-party press also assumed the role of a democratic opposition.

In the history of postwar Austria the Grand Coalition had the all-important task of reuniting the people. It enabled the followers of the Social Democratic party, which had been excluded from government power since the foundation of the Republic, to become an integral party of the new state for the first time. When the sole responsibility in the government was taken on, first, by the People's party in 1966, then by the Socialists in 1970, and the period of one-party governments began, the common basis was sufficiently firm to eliminate once and for all the possibility of a return to the situation that had existed in the period between the two world wars, when the country was always close to civil war.

But the Grand Coalition also had certain negative aspects, which in time came to outweigh its positive aspects. The coalition partners haggled about every piece of legislation. Each partner bought the other partner's approval to a law by agreeing to the passage of another law that this other partner desired (*Junktim*). Important positions in the government and in nationalized industries were filled by representatives of both parties according to the system of *Proporz.* All this led to inefficiency and cost increases. Dissatisfaction with these inevitable negative aspects of the Grand Coalition became widespread.

2.4 The National Referendum for an Independent Broadcasting System

This situation was particularly evident in the realm of broadcasting, where both parties were striving to gain influence, the ÖVP dominating radio and the SPÖ dominating television. On the other hand, this also led to a situation in which the news broadcasts were colorless and the commentaries scanty and unexciting. Important investments could not be made, since, with the elections in mind, first one party, then the other, did not want to raise the listening and viewing fees.

The independent papers had criticized this situation for years. But finally in 1964 three of them took action; these were the daily *Kurier* owned by the industrialist Ludwig Polsterer, the Styrian Catholic Press Association's *Kleine Zeitung,* and the newsmagazine *Wochenpresse,* which was closely connected with the Viennese Association of Industrialists (Wiener Industriellenvereinigung). They called upon their readers to sign a referendum against the "party dictatorship in broadcasting" and in favor of an independent, nonpartisan, and high-quality radio and television program.

Right from the start, the Federal Constitution of the Republic had provided for the possibility that, apart from parliament and the government, a certain number of voters could initiate a discussion regarding a proposed law. But up to that time the provision had never been made use of. The papers that now called for an independent broadcasting system (dozens followed the example of the three above-mentioned) could therefore give their plan an additional incentive with the key term "new life for democracy."

Certainly many Austrians were dissatisfied with the situation in broadcasting, but they were even less satisfied with the degeneration of the Grand Coalition as a whole. The issue of a reform of broadcasting assumed the significance of a reform of democracy. The initiative in favor of a liberal broadcasting law was supported by almost the entire independent press, and it produced 832,353 signatures. Considering the complicated bureaucratic machinery necessary, this was certainly more than anyone had expected. Nearly one-fifth of the Austrian voting population could hardly be ignored by the political parties. A new chapter in the history of broadcasting in Austria had begun, and it was the newspapers that had started it.

3   THE NEW FACE OF BROADCASTING: ORF, 1966–1980

3.1   The Broadcasting Law of 1966

The subject of broadcasting played an important part in the election campaign of 1966. The People's party (ÖVP) and the Liberal party (FPÖ) showed strong sympathy with the aims of the national referendum, even though there were several ÖVP politicians who disliked the sometimes excessive criticism of the coalition by the newspapers involved in the referendum. The Socialists on the whole condemned the activities of the "Newspaper party," as they called it, although several of them had to admit that the broadcasting system was in need of reform.[6]

At the parliamentary elections of 1966, the People's party gained the absolute majority for the first time since 1945; after unsuccessful attempts at negotiating a coalition, the Socialists withdrew from the government. The bill for the reform of broadcasting, put forward by the People's party, was truly not commensurate with the referendum in all its points, but was brought more into line with it in the course of parliamentary negotiations. Finally, the People's party, supported on some points by the small Liberal party, decided on the Broadcasting Law of 1966. The Socialists immediately announced that they would change it when they returned to power in the future.

The law maintained the public character of the broadcasting system but obligated it to present "objective information" and "well-balanced" commentaries. Further aims for radio and television laid down in the statutes were "programs to suit every taste," "educational programs for young and old," "programs to promote the arts and sciences," and even "programs to further the interest in sport." The structuring of the programs should take into consideration "the position of Austria as a Federal State" as well as the "importance of the legally recognized churches and religious societies."

These were clearly defined legal instructions that aimed at a high-quality broadcasting system. An efficient administration, kept as free as possible from political influence, should see to it that the program was carried out as planned. To this end, the law also postulated the independence and autonomy of the management similar to that in the British Broadcasting Corporation and endowed the General Director (*Generalintendant*) with sole responsibility and a wide range of authority. In March 1967 Gerd Bacher, a former newspaper journalist from Salzburg, who in the 1950s had been instrumental in founding various boulevard papers in Vienna, was elected the new General Director by the newly formed supervisory board (*Aufsichtsrat*) by 13 votes to 9.

3.2   An International Model

The style of leadership of the impulsive and sometimes aggressive General Director was disputed from beginning to end of his almost eight-year period of activity. In retrospect, however, it cannot be disputed that the Bacher period lent the Austrian Broadcasting Corporation an aura of quality and efficiency that in some respects made it an international model.

The creation of a common emblem or logo and the adoption of an international abbreviation (ORF for Österreichischer Rundfunk, Austrian Broadcasting Corporation) were only formalities but rapidly led to increased self-assurance on the part of the 3000 permanent employees in the ORF. The radio and television programs, hitherto lacking in a clear structural basis, were now adapted to meet the needs of the public. Since then, the differences in the three radio stations have become more sharply defined: "Ö 1" mainly provides serious music, literature, science, art (radio has become the greatest sponsor of every type of art), school, and educational programs, as well as religion in its broadest sense (ecumenical Sunday morning services have been a standard feature for years); "Ö Regional" mostly offers popular entertainment from the various regions in Austria, and it is the station with the greatest number of listeners; and "Ö 3" is a lively pop-sender with an international touch, a great appeal for young people, and an hourly information service. Of the two television channels, "FS 1" was better known for its information programs and attracted the general public, whereas "FS 2" had more of an elite appeal.

The well-known journalist Joseph Wechsberg wrote in *The New Yorker:* "The reformed ORF has extended its information and is now known throughout Europe for the high quality and fairness of its reporting." And it was indeed this "information explosion" that lay at the heart of the reform period. The number and type of information broadcasts were increased and more differentiated, the reporters questioned politicians long and aggressively, in a way hitherto unknown in this country. This brought disenchantment to some politicians in the ruling party, which had brought about this reform, and led many an ÖVP politician to ask himself whether he had perhaps backed the wrong horse. But the new style was certainly good for democracy.

3.3   Economic Basis for Independence

In the first Bacher period, more than 500 transmitters were newly built, and an ORF television center complete with the latest technical innovations was established in Vienna. New studios in Salzburg, Linz, Innsbruck, and Dornbirn and modernization of the old ones in Vienna, Graz, and Klagenfurt, as well as the construction of a broadcasting center in Eisenstadt, used up a lot of funds. The ORF could provide the required capital, since, with the Broadcasting Law of 1966, it had also attained fiscal autonomy and its own authorities could therefore decide on an increase in fees for listening and viewing without waiting for authorization from the government or parliament.[7]

Of course, there are also commercials on radio and television, but they are subject to time limits. This arrangement was negotiated between the papers that were responsible for the reform referendum and the parliamentarians who formulated "their" law. A maximum of 120 minutes a day is allowed for commercials on radio and 20 minutes a day on television; one radio and one TV program have to remain completely free of commercials, and on Sundays and certain public holidays during the year no advertising at all is permitted. The listeners and viewers readily agree to this arrangement, and the papers retained almost their full share of the total advertising activities and proceeds.[8] As far as ORF is concerned, the effect of the arrangement is that only roughly a third of its total revenue comes from advertising, and the remaining two-thirds from viewing and listening fees.

3.4 Austrian Broadcasting for Foreigners

Since 1966 a short-wave service for foreigners has been directly financed by funds from the national budget. It has the task of providing listeners throughout the world (including of course, Austrians on every continent) with an up-to-date picture of modern Austria. To this end, there are daily information programs in German, English, French, and Spanish. In 1979 an attempt at providing foreigners living in Vienna with a non-German-speaking sender met with immediate success: Ö 3 International established the Blue Danube Radio. This sender (which at present can only be received in the Vienna area) offers a mixed program of information and music in English and French morning, noon, and evening, and it uses professional radio journalism of an Anglo-Saxon type to provide foreign residents and visitors with a closer look at everyday life in Austria. It has also become popular with thousands of Austrians eager to improve their knowledge of foreign languages.

In this connection we should remember that the ORF center at Künigl-berg, Vienna, is also the greatest transfer point for news between Eurovision, the international TV network of the Western world, and its Eastern counterpart, Intervision. This, and the fact that ORF radio and television programs are among the most popular even in Eastern and Southeastern Europe beyond the Iron Curtain, illustrates the importance of Austrian broadcasting outside the boundaries of its own territory.

3.5 1974: The Reform of the Reform

In the 1970 election Bruno Kreisky led his party to a narrow victory and formed the first Socialist government in the history of postwar Austria. After the 1971 election, that government had an absolute majority in parliament, and, as was to be expected, the discussions on broadcasting came up again. Two things were particularly criticized by the Socialists in the existing broadcasting system: the strong position of the General Director and the fact that, in their opinion, the contrast between the TV channels FS 1 and FS 2 was not clearly enough defined.

After lengthy negotiations with the People's party and the Liberal party, in which agreement was almost reached, the Socialist majority in parliament finally decided in mid-1974 on an amendment to the Broadcasting Law of 1966. Without change in the basic structures, the power of the

General Director was reduced in favor of two television directors and a radio director, as well as in favor of other organs, and the obligation of producing two programs entirely independent of one another was imposed on the two television directors.

Apart from the board of trustees (*Kuratorium,* formerly the supervisory board, or *Aufsichtsrat*), composed of 30 representatives from the political parties, the federal provinces, the employees, and the listeners and viewers, a new body was formed: the representation of listeners and viewers. Its 35 members are supposed to protect the interests of science, public education, the arts, sports, churches, youth, senior citizens, families, tourism, motorists, consumers, trade unions, and the professional chambers vis-à-vis the ORF. Another body is the Commission for the Observation of the Broadcasting Law, which largely consists of judges who examine complaints pertaining to violations of this law.

In 1974 a new General Director, Otto Oberhammer, was chosen to head this new venture. He led the undertaking with the precise workings of a legal mind but lacked professional dynamism. Much to everyone's surprise, during the corporation elections in the summer of 1978, the former General Director, Gerd Bacher, was reelected to this post by a narrow majority of the board of trustees.[9] Both the government and Bacher understood the significance of this surprising event; it was an open invitation to bury the hatchet and, in the second Bacher era, work together within the framework of the law. It seems, indeed, that both sides are more willing to cooperate than before, and optimists hope that this will result in an even better broadcasting system. That the People's party and the Liberal opposition fear a stronger indirect influence on the part of the government toward the ORF is normal—and even functional—in a parliamentary democracy. It is the listeners and viewers, who at the same time are members of the voting public, who will have to pass final judgment.

4   THE AUSTRIAN PRESS TODAY

4.1   Market Trends: Cost Explosion and Concentration

In the whole of Austria today there are 19 daily newspapers with 31 regional editions,[10] about 130 weekly papers, and almost 3000 magazines, trade journals, and other periodicals of all types. The development in regard to the daily newspapers best reflects the market trends: out of the 32 newspapers appearing after the end of the war, only 19 have remained. Eleven of them are independent papers, which have 14 editions and a total circulation of 1.9 million copies; the 8 party papers with 17 editions have altogether almost half a million readers.

This confirms the development described in sections 2.1 and 2.2 of this chapter; far from pushing the press aside, television has helped increase its total circulation, which, after the drop in 1957, in 1977 again reached the earlier record of 1946. But within this total circulation there was a strong shifting of interests away from the few remaining party papers, which, heavily subsidized by their owners, appear with quite a few local editions, toward the independent papers that today can claim almost 90 percent of the entire newspaper reading population in Austria.

But even within the independent press there was a strong concentration of circulation; more than a third of the daily newspaper readers in Austria take the small boulevard paper, the *Kronenzeitung,* on a regular basis. Fifty-six percent read one of the two largest papers in the country, the *Kronenzeitung* or the *Kurier.* Together with the third most popular paper, the *Kleine Zeitung,* these three make up nearly two-thirds of the total circulation of the daily papers; the other third is composed of the 16 remaining papers, of which the *Presse* is internationally the best known. Austria is therefore among the countries with the relatively highest degree of press concentration. Of course these figures must be seen in light of the fact that more than half the Austrian papers are kept going only because their owners cover the deficits from other sources. This is true for all party papers (even the Communist *Volksstimme* still appears today, although its source of financing is rather strongly concealed), and also for some other papers, which are running at a loss and which groups of businessmen or publishing companies keep going by investing in them the proceeds from other branches of business. The fact is that the Austrian market is over-crowded from the quantitative point of view and has for years been plagued by a cost explosion.

Between 1970 and 1975 printing costs rose by over 50 percent, paper costs went up by nearly 100 percent, but proceeds from distribution and advertising only increased by 57–60 percent. Contrary to the situation in the ORF, roughly two-thirds of an active paper's income derives from advertising and a third from sales. Small newspapers naturally receive fewer advertisements than those with a larger circulation, which renders their economic situation even more precarious. In addition, there are an increasing number of so-called free papers in Austria that are financed only through advertising; in 1979 such papers were distributed to potential customers at the rate of 3 million copies a month.

4.2   Press Subsidies from Public Funds

The pressure of costs and competition as well as public discussions to the effect that a wide variety of papers was befitting a democracy led to press subsidies from public funds. Some view this with reservations, but other democratic countries also subsidize their papers—mostly through tax rebates and reductions in postal charges.

Arguing that tax rebates help those least who pay less tax, owing to the small volume of their business, the Austrian Socialist government has pursued the course of direct sponsorship. Since 1972, periodicals that appear on a fortnightly, monthly, or quarter-yearly basis that, "report exclusively or mainly on questions of politics, culture, or philosophy" and that are distributed in more than one province, receive subsidies from the government's budget. The extent of the subsidy is decided by the government, advised by a 14-member commission. Since 1975 a similar arrangement has also been in effect for daily and weekly papers that "mainly provide political, social, general economic, or cultural information," that have a minimum circulation of 5000 copies, are not just locally distributed, and have at least two permanent editors.

Any unprejudiced observer can see that nothing has changed in the way the papers are written, particularly where the critical attitude toward the government is concerned. But it is still difficult to impress upon a foreign observer that the Austrian press will not at some time be made to toe the line or be threatened with a withdrawal of government subsidies. Such a government has yet to come to power in Austria. However, many a newspaper publisher or editor in Austria would feel more at ease if a less questionable form of promoting a wide choice of newspapers could be found.

4.3   The Press Council as a Means of Voluntary Self-Control

Newspapers are the watchdogs of a democracy. But who barks at them if they themselves steal a sausage? The question extends far beyond the framework of this essay. But just as in other countries, in Austria too the newspapers have tried to subject themselves to a kind of voluntary self-control since they of course reject every kind of state intervention. Therefore the Austrian Press Council, which is composed of equal numbers of members from the professional associations of the newspaper editors and publishers on the one hand and the journalists on the other, was established in 1961.

The Press Council published guidelines for journalistic work (the "Honor Code"), which include a regard for factual truth, the obligation to use correct investigation methods, abstention from every type of discrimination or unproved accusations, and protection of professional secrets. Every person's private sphere should be respected, no one intimidated, no false hopes raised through praise of new medications, no presents accepted, no inhabitants of neighboring totalitarian states placed in difficulty through newspaper photos. Everyone has the right to start proceedings with the Press Council if he feels that these principles have in any way been violated, and the Council itself can initiate action in this respect.

Although sanctions cannot actually be imposed to carry out the Press Council's judgments, the newspapers—in most cases even the convicted ones—regularly publish them. In addition, it is also the task of the Press Council to safeguard the freedom of the press, to ensure unhindered access to sources of information, and to represent the interests of the press vis-à-vis the legislature, the administration, and the general public. The possibility of strengthening its authority and image is discussed at regular intervals, and certainly no one would wish to see it abolished.

4.4   Characteristics of Austrian Newspapers

Are Austrian newspapers different from those in English-speaking democracies? Yes and no. As everywhere, they try to keep apart news and commentaries without forgetting the fact that the choice of subject, method of presentation, choice of titles, etc, involve some value judgments. As elsewhere, they simplify in the presentation of facts, and particularly in the choice of titles. Negative events and developments are emphasized more than the routine case, but space is also devoted to "sensational favorable events" when such are discovered. In Austria, too, the style of investigative reporting has made inroads through news magazines such as *Wochenpresse* and *Profil,* but (following the example of the West German *Spiegel*) in this country articles are written perhaps in a less merciful and more exaggerated style than in Anglo-Saxon countries.

In Austria, as elsewhere, first-page stories about sex and crime attract more readers than *feuilletons* on the purpose of life. There are now only a few papers, such as the *Presse,* the *Kurier,* the *Salzburger Nachrichten,* the *Oberösterreichische Nachrichten,* and the *Tiroler Tageszeitung,* that report fairly regularly on foreign affairs on the first page. Only few papers afford foreign correspondents (usually as a kind of "tenant" to West German correspondents, owing to the expense); the newspapers with the greatest mass appeal prefer to cover a trouble spot only when a crisis breaks out. In the realm of domestic politics, stories about people and straight gags often enjoy priority over more serious factual reports. For most of the papers, culture consists largely of theater, opera, and concerts. Most of the pages on economy are written for insiders with at least some knowledge of the subject, and the uninitiated often remain virtually uninformed. Generous space is usually devoted to sports, but, except for soccer and skiing, some sports receive little attention.

If their own reporters are not directly on the scene, the Austrian media get their information from the Austrian Press Agency (APA), which is a joint association of the Austrian daily papers (with the exception of the *Kronenzeitung*) and the ORF. The APA in turn has exchange contracts with all the important world press agencies. But, in practice, about 96 percent of foreign news reports are received from the four main outside agencies (Deutsche Presse Agentur, Associated Press, Reuters, and Agence France Press), which calls to mind the questionable oligopoly among the agencies.

One difference in Austrian newspapers is a smaller format. Another is the ownership structure: apart from political parties and individuals, as in the case of the *Kronenzeitung, Salzburger Nachrichten, Oberösterreichische Nachrichten, Tiroler Tageszeitung,* and *Vorarlberger Nachrichten,* the Catholic Press Associations also publish papers such as the *Kleine Zeitung* (Graz and Klagenfurt) and the two weekly papers involved in sociopolitical aspects, the *Furche* and *Präsent.* [11]

In some provinces such as Lower and Upper Austria, these Press Associations still occupy a strong position among the politically oriented weekly newspapers. Through indirect sponsorship, some elements of industry and the trade unions also show interest in certain papers. In 1972, for example, when Ludwig Polsterer put the daily *Kurier* on the market, it was bought by several hundred industrialists jointly, since the only persons who could have afforded it were Hans Dichand and Kurt Falk, owners of the rival paper, the *Kronenzeitung.* In the 1960s a court case, whose central figure was the former president of the Trade Union Federation and Minister of the Interior, Franz Olah, revealed something about the amount of trade union money involved at the start of the *Kronenzeitung.* But the fact that political interests can be involved even when there is no political party backing a paper is something not limited to Austria.

Austrian newspapers can be bought at a tobacconist's, at newspaper kiosks, in certain bookshops and supermarkets, and, on Sundays and public holidays, in self-service vending stands on the roadside.[12] Subscribers can have them delivered by mail or, in some cities, by early morning delivery boys. All Austrian newspapers are morning papers, whose first edition is often available the evening before, sold by special vendors (mostly non-Austrians of exotic origin) in the streets and in public places. Distribution is also through so-called reader circles (Lesezirkel), in which chiefly the West German glossy magazines are sold. Certain groups of people get these on a loan basis, and in this way a million readers are supplied with weekly reading material.

4.5   Characteristics of Austrian Newspaper Readers

More than a third of all Austrian newspapers and magazines are sold in Vienna, where every fifth Austrian lives: in rural areas radio, television, and local papers dominate the scene. Since 1965, publishing companies, the ORF, and advertising firms in conjunction with well-known market research institutes have organized regular "media analyses," which reveal which media are read by which section of the public in which areas. These media analyses are also important guidelines for decision-making in the realm of advertising.[13]

For international comparison, in 1976 the Féderation Internationale des Editeurs de Journaux conducted a survey in 16 Western countries to assess the number of daily papers read per 1000 inhabitants. The Austrians proved to be as avid readers as their counterparts in West Germany, Denmark, and the Netherlands. They read less than the Americans, Swedes, Japanese, British, and Russians, but more than the Italians, Israelis, French, Canadians, and Belgians.

4.6   Characteristics of Austrian Journalists

Austrian journalists have one thing in common with the politicians: they do not have to prove their aptitude for the profession through public examination. Although there is no set training course prescribed, today hardly any journalists are employed who cannot prove by means of a *matura* certificate (school-leaving certificate) an eight-year attendance at secondary school, which is roughly the equivalent of a junior college degree. According to a survey conducted in 1974, every fourth journalist had an academic degree, and a further 25 percent had attended a university for several semesters without obtaining a degree.

At two Austrian universities (Vienna and Salzburg) there are Institutes of Journalism and Communication, but this is only one of the possible courses of study in a university to prepare for a journalism career. Law or political science, German or history, the study of theater or musicology, sociology or modern languages are good alternatives, depending on the intended field of specialization.

4.7   The Foreign Press in Austria

For the non-Austrian mass media, Vienna is much more interesting as a center than one would suppose from the importance of Austria in the international community. After World War II most of the foreign correspondents came to Vienna only to get a better view of Eastern and Southeastern Europe behind the Iron Curtain. Today, most of these countries are willing to receive foreign correspondents directly from the West. But even in 1970, 29 out of 100 foreign correspondents stationed in Vienna stated that they were reporting exclusively on Eastern and Southeastern Europe, and a further 23 were reporting on these countries and Austria; only 48 had chosen to report exclusively on Austria.

With the proclamation of Vienna as the third UN city after New York and Geneva and the transfer of important international organizations and congresses to Austria, Vienna has gained additional importance as a center for foreign correspondents. In 1978 the Association of Accredited Foreign Correspondents in Vienna had 163 regular members working for 239 media in 31 countries, two-thirds of them on a full-time basis. The Federal Press Service (Bundespressedienst), with headquarters in the Federal Chancellery, is known for the unobtrusive and efficient way it helps and looks after the foreign correspondents in Austria.[14] In all of Austria's larger cities all the more important papers, at least from the Western world, are available at newspaper vendors. Lack of demand is the only reason for the absence of papers from the East.

4.8   Legal Aspects: The Press Law and the Media Law

The Austrian free press is subject to certain legal regulations. In some respects, this is also the case elsewhere, except that one often does not think of it. Article I of the American Bill of Rights of 1791 stipulates freedom of the press, just as does Article 13 of the Austrian State Basic Law of 1867, which is part of the Federal Constitution. In every country there are also provisions under criminal law, applicable to everyone (including, of course, the mass media), in order to protect individuals or state interests. Since 1922 it has been an Austrian specialty to have a rather detailed press law, which imposes concrete obligations on the newspapers; for example, to publish counterstatements to factual reports (not evaluations of events) if the people concerned so demand, and to indicate the name of a so-called responsible editor, who has to answer in court for unsigned articles (in addition to the name of the owner and publisher).

Since the end of the war there have been frequent discussions about modernizing the Press Law. There have been minor alterations, but only in 1980 did the long awaited complete reform take shape. For the first time the law was to include radio and television in certain regulations: for example, counterstatements and the obligation to publish a report on the acquittal of persons on trial if the trial had been widely reported on earlier. For this reason the bill has since been known as a Media Law instead of a Press Law.

The possibility of confiscating an issue of a newspaper or magazine, which even before the reform was limited to exceptional cases, was to be further reduced and left exclusively to the judges. No radio and television broadcasts shall be allowed in future from the courtroom during criminal proceedings. Regulations that were much debated but finally agreed on by all parties were drawn up to require statements of the exact state of ownership and the political direction of the paper to be published every three months. The freedom of conscience of every journalist was also to be sanctioned by the law: no journalist can be forced to write something against his conscience. Since the beginning of the Seventies editorial statutes have been drawn up on a voluntary basis in several Austrian papers and also in the ORF. They also provide for the right of the journalists to participate in the process of selecting the leading editorial staff.

5   NEW DEVELOPMENTS: DISCUSSIONS OF A BROADCASTING MONOPOLY

The beginning of the 1980s has again led the print and electronic media to a point at which their interests, which are partly common but partly also contradictory in nature, diverge. As a result of new technical achievements, television programs produced in other countries can be transmitted via cable and satellite to a growing number of areas in Austria. The reception is free of charge, and the following questions automatically arise: "Why can't the program production be free too? Austrian lawmakers cannot influence foreign programming. Why should the Austrian domestic programs be produced only by public institutions and not by private companies as well? Doesn't freedom of the media also include freedom of programming?"

Experiments such as those made in Italy with the abolition of the state broadcasting monopoly do not seem to present attractive prospects. For years now there has been frequency chaos in radio and television broadcasting. However, the introduction of a private television system alongside the public BBC in Great Britain has by no means led to the prophesied drop in standards of both programs; rather, it has led to increased competition for better achievement and efficiency. This was achieved by imposing certain obligations on the private television system. In the case of Austria the question arises as to who could act as a private TV producer: presumably only large cities, the federal provinces, and the organizations representing the interests of the employers and employees. Of course, this is potential dynamite for party politics. There is also the fact that a privately organized television system would only be possible if heavily financed by commercials, which in turn could prove detrimental to the financial situation of some newspapers. Therefore, private newspaper owners' TV is also being discussed. The question will probably remain unsolved for some time to come, but it will inevitably arise.

6   OTHER FORMS OF MEDIA

When one speaks of mass media, one usually thinks of the press, radio, and television. But one could say that the media of mass communication in the broadest sense include also mass demonstrations, the theater, posters, and, above all, books, films, records, and cassettes. Space unfortunately prevents more than a brief reference to the latter in this report. Interested readers are invited to refer to some of the publications mentioned in the annex and to the publication of the Institutes of Journalism and Communication at the Universities of Vienna and Salzburg. But a few words about films, books, records, and cassettes may be appropriate in this chapter.

The basic trend in these areas points in recent years to the preference for larger markets, or—to be precise—to the growing dependency of Austria on foreign countries. In 1978 the export of Austrian books, which in 1970 was still greater than the import, was only half the imports. About 85 percent of the imported books come from West Germany and 82 percent of the Austrian exports go there. American-owned companies that operate in Austria publish *Reader's Digest* and *Southern Music.* Austria has an important position in the field of books for young people. In conjunction with UNESCO and UNICEF, the International Board on Books for Young People was founded here in 1952. Its English-language magazine *Bookbird* is sent from Vienna to 46 countries throughout the world.

Austrian film production, which was so well known in the period between the two world wars and just after 1945, has also decreased in quality and quantity (e.g. "1. April 2000" and "Die letzte Brücke" were historically interesting films that met with international success). In 1920, 142 films were made in Austria; in the 1950s, on the average, 23 films a year were made, and in the 1970s only 6 a year. Of the movies shown in Austrian cinemas today, only about 3 percent are of Austrian origin; almost one in every three comes from the USA and one in five from West Germany. The same is true of the films and series shown on Austrian television. About three-quarters of the records and cassettes in Austria are made by foreign firms.

Notes

1. The population of the provinces was, of course, much larger. "Listeners" are owners of receiving sets who paid the requisite small subscription fee.
2. The Red Army reached Styria—and its capital, Graz—first, but later withdrew, and Styria became part of the British zone.
3. On 29 August 1953 the paper reported the lifting of controls by the Allied Council for postal, telephone, and other services, including *Rundfunk* (radio). What was actually meant by this term was "Radio Austria," a company for the transmission of radiograms and thus unrelated to radio broadcasting.
4. At the time 540 registered TV senders already existed. Of these 420 were located in the USA and 80 in Europe.
5. Ernst Fischer, the Communist party's representative, and incidentally a brilliant speaker in parliament, was paid his newspaper salary for years without being permitted to write articles, which, for their political contents, would have alienated readers.
6. One of them was Günther Nenning, long-time president of the Journalists' Union, who was from the beginning among the main protagonists of Rundfunk reform in Austria.
7. Austrians pay the equivalent of two movie tickets to their postal administration to be allowed to listen to radio and watch television.

8. Groups of commercials are scheduled together as part of the programming rather than being interspersed throughout other programs. They are therefore less obtrusive than are commercials in, say, American broadcasts.
9. Obviously, at least one member of the electing body nominated by the Social Democrats must have voted for Bacher.
10. For details consult *Handbuch der Presse* (published by Verband österreichischer Zeitungsherausgeber und Zeitungsverleger, Wien), which for 1979 listed these dailies and circulation figures (weekend circulation in parentheses): *Kronenzeitung,* 584,000 (698,-000, 947,000), independent; *Kurier,* 428,000 (638,000, 692,000), independent; *Kleine Zeitung,* 221,000 (256,000), independent; *Oberösterreichische Nachrichten,* 92,000 (128,-000), independent; *Tiroler Tageszeitung,* 86,000 (96,000), independent; *Neue Zeit,* 79,000 (89,000), socialist; *Salzburger Nachrichten,* 65,000 (100,000), independent; *Kärntner Tageszeitung,* 63,000 (68,000), Socialist; *Arbeiter-Zeitung,* 96,000, Socialist; *Die Presse,* 60,000 (73,000, 79,000), independent; *Vorarlberger Nachrichten,* 53,000, independent; *Neue Vorarlberger Tageszeitung,* 43,000, independent; *Volksstimme,* 43,000 (80,000), Communist; *Südost-Tagespost,* 46,000 (48,000), People's party; *Tagblatt,* 43,000, Socialist; *Neues Volksblatt,* 33,000, People's party; *Volkszeitung,* 33,000, People's party; *Salzburger Volkszeitung,* 9,500 (13,000), People's party; *Wiener Zeitung,* semiofficial.
11. The Catholic Press Organizations were founded shortly before the turn of the century, when Catholic citizens of the country, in order to defend themselves against militant liberalism (central European brand), created political organizations and publishing companies. These publishing companies could sustain papers in the red by making a profit in other lines of commerce such as printing and paper and book dealing. Some are still in existence today, such as the *Kleine Zeitung,* Austria's third largest daily, and *Furche* and *Präsent,* two prestigious political weeklies.
12. Potential newspaper buyers should not be discouraged by the appearance of many of these newsstands as purveyors of sex literature. Quality papers are kept there, too, if less obviously.
13. For detailed information, consult Verein Arbeitsgemeinschaft Media-Analysen, c/o Hager GesmbH & Co., Seilerstätte 13, A 1010 Wien (Vienna).
14. It also regularly publishes information on Austria for Latin American, African and Arab countries, as well as bulletins on specific occasions. The address is Bundespressedienst, A 1014 Wien (Vienna).

Selected Bibliography

Bundespressedienst (Österreich-Dokumentationen). *Massenmedien in Österreich.* Wien, 1978.
Ergert, Viktor. *50 Jahre Rundfunk in Österreich II.* Salzburg, 1975.
Magenschab, Hans. *Demokratie und Rundfunk.* Wien, 1973.
Österreichische Rundfunk GmbH. *ORF-Almanach.* Several annuals.
Signitzer, Benno. *Massenmedien in Österreich.* Wien, 1977.
Steiner, Kurt. *Politics in Austria.* Chapter IX, Political Communication, pp. 257–85. Boston, 1972.
Verband Österreichischer Zeitungsherausgeber und Zeitungsverleger, *Handbuch der Presse.* Wien, 1979.

SELECTED TOPICS

Bundeskanzleramt. *Die Auslandspresse in Österreich.* Wien, 1978.
Gottlein, Arthur. *Der österreichische Film.* Wien, 1976.
———. *Der österreichische Presserat.* Wien, 1979.
Luger, Kurt. *Österreich im internationalen Mediensystem.* Projekt des Instituts für Publizistik und Kommunikationswissenschaft der Universität Salzburg, Projektleiter Benno Signitzer. Salzburg, forthcoming.
Signitzer, Benno, and Pierre Walhöfer. *Structures of the Phonographic Industry in Austria.* Phono Doc. 11. Wien, 1979.

PART IV

SOCIAL EDUCATIONAL, AND LEGAL POLICY

Modern Austria, pp. 301–19

14. SOCIAL POLICY SINCE 1945: DEMOCRACY AND THE WELFARE STATE

Rudolf Strasser

Professor for Private Law, Labor Law, and Welfare Law at the Johannes Kepler University in Linz

1 THE SITUATION IN 1945

In 1945, when Austria was liberated from German occupation, the institutions of social policy presented a contradictory picture. The free trade union movement had been destroyed in 1934, and the Chambers of Labor and the Works-Council organizations in the enterprises had been dissolved in 1938. Regimentation by the authorities of the Reich had replaced the autonomous regulation of the conditions of labor by collective contracts and enterprise agreements by the parties concerned.

In legal protection of workers (regulation of work time, law for the protection of mothers), some progress had been made during the occupation, but these measures had little effect owing to the adaptation of the economy to wartime conditions. The introduction of German legal institutions had finally brought old-age pension insurance and disability insurance to the workers, but in fact this too was of little effect for the time being. The housing situation for workers had dramatically deteriorated because of bomb damage. The task of caring for war victims had grown to a staggering extent.

2 RESTORATIVE SOCIAL POLICY

The period ending in the first half of the 1950s was that of a "restorative" social policy. The primary goal was elimination of certain National Socialist

Translated by Ulrike E. Lieder, Stanford University

9306-6403/81/0415-0301$01.50

institutions in the area of social policy and restoration of institutions of proved value.[1] The accent was on reestablishing a democratic labor constitution or framework for labor relations. The Chambers of Labor were restored in 1945, the labor courts in 1946; Works Councils, which had formed spontaneously in most enterprises in 1945, received legal sanction in 1947; and collective contracts, replacing the former regulation of working conditions by bureaucratic authorities, were permitted and regulated in the same year. The reestablishment of free trade unions required no governmental action once their prohibition during the Nazi period was lifted.[2]

In the area of labor law that deals with the protection and claims of individual employees, the situation was somewhat different for the legislator of the period between 1945 and 1955. Some of the laws that had formed the basis for Austria's earlier world-wide reputation as a country with a highly developed social policy had remained in force during the occupation. A relatively acceptable regulation of the 48-hour work week and a law for the protection of mothers dated from the occupation. Regulation of working conditions, acceptable under the circumstances of the time, was completed by creating a legal claim for leave periods for workers, including building trade workers (1946), by instituting a system of work inspection (1947), and by eliminating the workbook as compulsory identification for employed persons (1955). In addition, some measures of relatively high reform content were instituted even in this restorative period. These measures included a modern law for agricultural workers (1948), comprehensive regulation of the labor relations of contractual (not tenured) state employees (*Vertragsangestellte*) in the same year, and progressive protection for children and adolescents in the work force.

Outside the area of labor relations, the accent was on the Austrification of social insurance institutions that had come from Germany. The introduction of public support for children, at first limited to employed persons (1949), was a remarkable step in a new direction of social policy during this early period.[3]

3   THE PHASE OF DYNAMIC REFORM

3.1   General Characteristics

At the time of the signing of the State Treaty (1955), the restorative phase of the Austrian social policy after the war was essentially completed, as were the most urgent reconstruction and economic stabilization. The social policy of at least the next two decades is characterized by great dynamics and a pronounced element of reform, which manifests itself particularly clearly in the area of social security. Passage of the General Social Insurance Act (Allgemeines Sozialversicherungsgesetz) in 1955 was the turning point and marked the beginning of this phase. This law set an abrupt end to the attempts, made since 1946, to adapt German social insurance institutions to the Austrian situation. It created something entirely new, which is reminiscent of Bismarck's old social insurance only formally and outwardly.

The end of the period of approximately twenty years is characterized by increasingly apparent endeavors to reformulate the labor laws on the books into a labor law code, organized according to uniform aspects. This reformulation would simultaneously abolish the traditional differences between the workers' legal claims and the employees' much more favorable legal claims (e.g. continued salary in case of illness, terms of notice, severance pay).

3.2   The Significance of the Austrian Version of the Legal and Constitutional State

Briefly, the Austria of the First and Second Republic is a legal state (*Gesetzesstaat*). The Constitution mandates that practically every general abstract regulation of social processes be a parliamentary decision in the form of a law. The general authority of the executive branch (ministers and other administrative organs; the minister in charge of social policy is the Minister for Social Administration) to regulate in the form of general administrative action (regulation by decree) is severely restricted. These organs of the State are essentially limited to enforcing the laws passed by parliament, a situation further aggravated by an extremely narrow interpretation of the pertinent passages of the Constitution by the Constitutional Court (an interpretation in favor of parliament). Second, mere tradition, actual practice, or custom has practically no normative importance. This also applies to the verdicts handed down by the highest courts. All of this means basically that everything that is to exist as a reform, as a regulation, in years to come must be "decreed" in the form of a law passed by parliament. This corresponds with a uniform attitude and expectation among the population: matters that have not been promulgated in the form of law but are common practice, be it in the executive branch, in the enterprises or factories, or among the interest associations (Verbände), are considered of little consequence. Although here too there are exceptions to the rule, an abnormally high degree of faith in the law is prevalent in all strata of the population, and thus a permanent wish for social change by the passage of laws.

As for the overly strict limitations of the executive's authority, the situation is changed decisively by the following fact: the priority of parliament, mandated by the Constitution, is factually turned into almost total dominance by the government because of the close ties between cabinet members and members of parliament existing in the organizations of the two large parties. It is ultimately the government that determines whether and how the laws will be passed by parliament.[4]

All of this means that the development of social policy takes place almost exclusively through legislation. Austrian social policy is essentially social legislation, supplemented by regulations of collective contracts. However, its effectiveness is great, owing to an extremely well-functioning administrative machinery.

3.3   The Intellectual Background

3.3.1   PRELIMINARY REMARKS   The comparative strength of the political parties during the two decades (1955 to 1975) of the prime of reformatory social policy makes it imperative that we relate the intellectual background of Austrian social policy to the contents of the political programs of the two large parties. This must be done especially because of the extensive equation of social policy and social legislation in Austria. However, by referring to the party programs we do not mean to indicate that such programs can always be realized in the sense that they can function as guidelines for the social legislator. In spite of all reservations about these declarations of principle, which are primarily intended for members of the organization and for voters, they sometimes contain concrete demands that, sooner or later, appear as topical political demands in daily politics.

However, the role of the Austrian Federation of Trade Unions (Österreichischer Gewerkschaftsbund, ÖGB) is possibly even more important than that of the political groups in developing and realizing the Austrian version of the welfare state (see Section 3.3.3).

3.3.2   THE BASIC PROGRAMS OF THE TWO LARGE PARTIES[5]   Even a superficial comparison of the program contents reveals major differences. The statements on social policy in the program of the Socialist party (Sozialistische Partei Österreichs, SPÖ) are professional, whereas the corresponding passages in the program of the Austrian People's party (Österreichische Volkspartei, ÖVP) sound somewhat amateurish. The SPÖ's program, in other areas just as vague as the ÖVP program on social policy, literally brims with concrete demands in its chapter on social policy. By comparison, the statements of the ÖVP program on social policy appear rather scanty, some being nothing but an enumeration of institutions that already existed at the time the program was approved.

Apart from a few anticapitalist passages, the statements on social policy in the SPÖ program contain neither positive professions nor negative delimitations toward the great secular ideologies, which, in spite of all reservations about such schematizations, usually are the criteria for assessing programmatically formulated systems of values. An objective appraisal of the chapter on social policy must conclude that this catalog of demands is a document typical of the so-called revisionist wing of socialism. It is highly pragmatic and expert in its formulation, and thus it could well serve as a guideline for the government's medium- and long-term practical work.

The difference in the ÖVP statements on social policy is one of degree, yet significant. They, too, are relatively concrete demands for practical social reform, but, compared with the SPÖ platform, they are less numerous and less knowledgeable and are often formulated in more general terms. However, these demands are not statements of economic liberalism or conservatism, just as the SPÖ statements are not statements of Marxism. All in all, this conformity of the programs of the two large parties with respect to the slight degree, if not absence, of ideological ties, in conjunction with their pragmatism, is a good basis for realizing the individual reform plans through parliamentary decisions. This holds true for the era of the Grand Coalition (until 1966) as well as for the subsequent period of single-party majority governments (1966 to the present).

3.3.3 THE ROLE OF THE ÖGB

Character and functions The life of Austrian labor, and thus everything connected with social policy, is characterized by a specific situation with certain peculiarities that distinguish Austria from the Western industrialized nations as well as from the so-called Eastern Bloc.

Disregarding a few, numerically insignificant agricultural workers and several splinter groups of civil servants, there is one unified labor union in Austria, the ÖGB. This is the result not of a legal decree but of its actual development in the aftermath of World War II. The 16 unions for the various industries (*Fachgewerkschaften*) must *de facto* be evaluated as corporate subdivisions; they are, according to the ÖGB statutes, legally set up as its organs. This circumstance, in conjunction with a corresponding fiscal sovereignty of the roof organization, among other things, has resulted in domination by the ÖGB, and not the individual unions. However, in matters of collective contracts and in questions of the membership's immediate concerns, the unions have relatively much latitude. Extensive personnel links between the executive bodies of the ÖGB and of the individual unions make divergent opinions on important issues all but impossible. This is one of the major causes of the monolithic unity of the Austrian labor union movement and thus of its position of great social power in the country. The *de facto* monopoly of this labor union organization could be maintained until this day without requiring any action. Approximately two-thirds of all employed persons in Austria are organized as members of the ÖGB.

Furthermore, there is often a personal union between top functionaries of the ÖGB and of the individual unions, and members of the highest executive organs of the two large political parties. This means that trade union matters can, alternatively, also be realized politically, which, in fact, happens frequently. Moreover, the top functionaries of the ÖGB or the individual unions are generally also members of parliament. This applies in particular to the SPÖ, which has been a governing party from 1945 to the present, with a single interruption from 1966 to 1970. Not only do the leading unionists have great influence in the highest party organs, but they can also voice their views in the SPÖ parliamentary *Klub* (caucus).

This is manifest in two facts whose significance cannot be overestimated. The office of Federal Minister for Social Administration has been held by an ÖGB functionary without interruption since 1945, and the ÖGB president has been the president of the National Council (the primary legislative organ) for a number of years.

During the First Republic, labor unions and Chambers of Labor existed side by side. The former had a largely political party orientation and were divided into many splinter groups, whereas the latter were nonpartisan, and membership in them was prescribed by law. Immediately after the end of World War II, the Chambers of Labor were reestablished. Although their original task no longer exists owing to the absence of competing, political party–oriented labor unions, they have maintained their position and significance to this day by adjusting to the function of a support and advisory organization to the ÖGB. Because of an almost complete personal union between the top officials of the Chambers of Labor, the ÖGB, and the individual unions, there are practically no differences of opinion; and thus this parallel organization only helps to strengthen the position of the ÖGB.

Beyond its function of membership recruitment, the ÖGB has a *de facto* monopoly for the conclusion of collective contracts, which are generally for an entire industry. Again, the only exceptions here are the agricultural workers. The effectiveness of the ÖGB's activities is increased by the fact that the collective contracts negotiated by the labor union also apply to non-union employees ("outsiders") working in a company subject to the collective contract.

For the employers, Austria has a powerful central organization of entrepreneurs, the Federal Chamber of Trade (Bundeskammer der gewerblichen Wirtschaft), which is definitely equal to the ÖGB. Its monopoly position in the commercial and industrial areas is anchored in law; moreover, the principle of *ipso iure* membership applies to it. The person engaged in a trade or an industry acquires membership along with his trade license. Since the parallel employers' organizations, which have voluntary membership, either do not have or do not exercise the ability to conclude collective contracts, the Federal Chamber of Trade also has a *de facto* monopoly on collective contracts, just as the ÖGB does for the employees. The Federal Chamber of Trade exercises its monopoly through its suborganizations, the branch groups at the provincial and federal levels. Owing to the principle of mandatory membership, there are practically no outside employers in Austrian trade and industry.

For years, the ÖGB and the Federal Chamber of Trade, in conjunction with the Assembly of the Austrian Chambers of Labor (Österreichischer Arbeiterkammertag) and the Presidents' Conference of the Chambers of Agriculture (Präsidentenkonferenz der Landwirtschaftskammern), have formed the so-called Joint Commission on Prices and Wages (Paritätische Kommission). The Joint Commission is not mandated by law, yet it is an extremely effective means of coordination and cooperation in economic and social policies. The existence of this top-level organ in economic policy contributes to the subtle increase of the labor union's influence on the enterprises, even though this influence is indirect.[6]

When regulations pertaining to labor law are at stake, the ÖGB, because of this situation, generally has a choice in the way its demands are to be realized. It can have a law passed by parliament, or the Minister for Social Administration, an ÖGB official himself, can issue a decree within the latitude given him by the Constitution, which, however, sets strict limitations. The third option the ÖGB has for the realization of its demands is negotiating a collective contract. There is no great difference between a regulation by federal law and an agreement contained in a collective contract, which is valid in and uniform for the entire federal territory. Their legal force is almost the same, and they are realized in a similar manner. The bills that significantly affect the interests of the nation's employees are generally worked out in a manner similar to collective contracts, i.e. in negotiations between the top organizations of the social partners. These negotiations either precede or take place at the same time as the debates in parliament. The social partners' ideas and compromises in the realm of social policy are, at least in content, frequently realized by the minister in charge or by parliament.

After the above exposition on the specifically Austrian situation, it is not surprising to see that Austria is among those countries in the so-called free Western World that have the fewest strikes. In fact, compared to other Western industrialized countries, Austria can be called an oasis of social peace. This fact cannot be explained by the Austrian employees' especially peaceful attitude toward labor relations. The main reason for the absence of spectacular and lengthy labor disputes is, ultimately, the strong position of the employees' representation of interests. Indeed, it would be paradoxical if the unions were to employ the instrument of a labor dispute in order to realize their demands when they have other means at their disposal, means that may not be as spectacular but are more effective.

Objectives in social policy   Except for its objectives, described in detail in its statutes, the ÖGB does not have a special basic program. Its tasks are adequately defined by "representation of the employees' social and economic interests," which demand permanent activities oriented toward care and support for the members. These activities are defined and directed by various action programs. The guidelines for the social policy of the 1960s and 1970s were fixed at the ÖGB congresses of 1955 and 1959. These are partially rather concrete catalogs of demands, passages of which are similar to the corresponding part of the 1958 SPÖ program. The general objective to be strived for is the "social welfare state," the way to attain it is "progressive social policy." Conspicuous is the constant emphasis on the dependence of any social policy on a productive economy and the emphasis on the priority of full employment. A special characteristic is the program's great number of details in the realm of labor law. The program is so detailed that it takes positions on individual supreme court decisions and demands countermeasures.[7] Furthermore, the restraint in the area of further development of social security is conspicuous, especially with respect to questions of general old-age pension (*Volkspension*) and comprehensive public health service. Altogether, these programs are even more pragmatic and concrete than the corresponding part on social policy in the SPÖ program.

3.4   General Objectives?

A look at the programs of the large parties, responsible for the government, and of the ÖGB, the dominating force in social policy, has shown clearly that uniform general objectives, at least in the area of social policy, are difficult to find in them. However, if the programmatic social policy formulated by the groups primarily involved in the development of political objectives is already antidoctrinaire and emphatically pragmatic, this must be all the more true of the practical political work done in parliament, government, and representations of interests, whose activities are more or less based on these programs. Furthermore, there are practically no specific intellectual trends with socio-reformatory content outside the political parties and representations of interests that have significant social relevance (as for instance, in the churches). Therefore, in summarizing, it can be said that even after the signing of the State Treaty (1955), the phase so significant for development of the welfare state, Austrian social policy working toward its goal of the welfare state was not based on a general doctrine that shaped and characterized it, nor on a social theory by which it was guided, nor on a general ideology that determined it.

3.5   Objective and Personal Range of Social Policy

3.5.1 TARGET GROUPS   As in many other European countries, social legislation in Austria began as labor legislation or, more precisely, as workers' protection legislation. Relatively early, still before World War I, it became a comprehensive employees' protection legislation when white-collar workers were included. This state of affairs remained constant for a relatively long time. Only after World War II, social protection was successively extended to include self-employed persons in the area of social insurance. In 1956, self-employed persons were included in the accident insurance program; in 1957, trade and industry were included in the old-age pension insurance program, and in 1966 in the medical insurance plan. The farmers were included in medical insurance in 1965, and in the old-age pension plan in 1969. Before that time, in 1954, the system of children's allowance and family support measures was extended to cover the entire population.

With these measures, Austrian social policy departed from its limitation to employees, which had lasted almost an entire century. It recognized every citizen, regardless of his function in the total society, at least as a potential object of protection with measures of social policy. Discussions on the introduction of a general old-age pension, housewives' insurance, and comprehensive national health service are the outward manifestations of this basic change of philosophy in regard to the groups of persons that should have, in principle, a claim to protection by social policy.

3.5.2 OBJECTIVE RANGE   Objectively, the social policy typical of continental Europe in the 19th century started out with measures on individual employment relationships. Only subsequently did problems of employer-employee relations on a more general level, and then on the company level, receive attention. The third important area that can be included in the classical contents of social policy before the war is social insurance, which today, primarily under the influence of Anglo-Saxon developments, has been conceptually and actually expanded to a system of comprehensive social security. It is certainly not coincidence that this development took place along with the inclusion of new areas of coverage, as e.g. children, family, and housing, and that it was closely coupled to the inclusion of new groups of persons.

It is at least a legitimate object of discussion whether or not the areas of education (ranging from preschool education to night school, adult education to correspondence courses for working people), and leisure time and recreation (slogan: "social tourism") are also legitimate objects of the activities of social policy.

3.5.3 SUMMARY All in all, Austrian social policy after 1945 has mentally, conceptually, and actually gone beyond the classical target groups and has at least potentially included the entire population as an object of protection. It has also considered new areas of life in which it could become active.

4   DETAILS ON THE MOST OUTSTANDING INDIVIDUAL REFORMS

4.1   Labor Constitution

The Second Republic reintroduced full freedom of association in the sense of the right to form labor unions, to join them, and to be active within their framework. Problems of the so-called negative freedom of association have practically no significance. Union security clauses in any form are not included in Austrian collective contracts; in fact, they would not be permissible under current law. Collective contracts have the effects of law, are generally admissible only for an entire industry, and include outsiders (non-union employees) on the side of employees. There are practically no outsiders on the side of employers in trade and industry, since the Federal Chamber of Trade, in which every employer in trade and industry must be a member, is a party to the collective contract. In practice this means that a collective contract in the area of trade and industry, e.g. for trade workers, includes all employees and employers in the trade sector in Austria. The employees' claims created in this manner can be realized by court order just like legal claims. Sometimes, the top levels of the Federal Chamber of Trade and the ÖGB sign a collective contract in order to implement an important reform (e.g. introduction of the 40-hour work week). In such a case there is no difference between the contract and a federal law, passed by the National Council, with respect to legal range and factual effectiveness.

Strikes are neither expressly permitted nor prohibited by law. Current jurisdiction and doctrine interpret this situation as a system of freedom to strike, with a concurrent neutrality by State authorities toward the groups involved in a labor dispute. Austria is among the countries where labor disputes are extremely rare. Since there has not been a practical need for them, there has so far been no legislation on mandatory arbitration, the regulation of methods and procedures of labor disputes, or the regulation of the labor union system, with the exception of the already mentioned prohibition of union security clauses. These are not necessary anyway, because of the legal status of the collective contract (collective contract for the entire industry, unified labor union, inclusion of non-union employees mandated by law, factual inclusion of outsiders on the employers' side).

In the companies, there is an organization of Works Councils based on legal regulations. These works councils are collegial organs whose numerical composition is determined by the number of company personnel.[8] Enterprises with several operations also have central works councils, which are charged with representing overlapping interests.

The works councils are the organs of codetermination within the company. The Austrian form of codetermination differs in some essential points from the codetermination prevalent in the Federal Republic of Germany. First, it would be better to speak of cooperation or participation. Genuine codetermination, i.e. equal co-decision-making, in entrepreneurial matters is provided only in a few cases. Frequently the issue is one of the employer informing or hearing the works council, or of discussing the matter at hand with the works council. Objectively, a differentiation must be made between cooperation in personnel matters, in social matters, and in issues of the economic management of the company (enterprise). The works council is not represented in the company's executive organs (no director of labor is a member of the board of directors [*Vorstand*] of a corporation, as in the Federal Republic of Germany), but the personnel is represented by members of the works council in the supervisory board (*Aufsichtsrat*) of a corporation or a similar enterprise, the proportion being one-third of the total number of personnel (*Drittelbeteiligung*). This kind of cooperation is linked to the legal form of the enterprise and to the system of strict separation of the enterprise's managing and controlling organs, which is common practice in both Austria and the Federal Republic of Germany. In larger enterprises the works council can raise objections to significant economic measures that could have disadvantageous effects on personnel. However, such objections result in, at most, an independent State commission delivering an expert opinion on the issue, which is not binding for the company.

In summary, the primary significance of the Austrian form of codetermination is found in the areas of personnel and social matters. For instance, in cases of transfers, termination of employment, or dismissals, in cases of disciplinary measures, and in the regulation of work conditions within the company, there can be genuinely equal codetermination by personnel.

4.2 Employer-Employee Relations

The outstanding event in the field of social policy reforms of individual work conditions is undoubtedly the step-by-step introduction of the 40-hour work week at full wages, initiated by a general collective contract in 1969. According to the plan it contained, this demand of the labor unions, which dates back to the 1950s, was realized in 1975. Second, the creation of a general claim to a minimum paid vacation of four weeks per year in 1976 should be mentioned. This was preceded by the introduction in 1964 of a minimum paid vacation of three weeks per year (by general collective contract). In a parallel development, almost all collective contracts for individual industries have also for many years mandated so-called vacation bonuses, an extraordinary additional gratuity from the employer, paid out when the employee begins his vacation.

The third great reform concerns the claim to compensation in case of illness. Here, an important step was made in the direction of giving workers the same rights already enjoyed by employees, something the labor unions had demanded for a long time. The 1974 law, mandating that payment of compensation be continued, guarantees the continued payment of full wages to blue-collar workers in case of illness. Payment continues for four to ten weeks, depending on the duration of employment. A number of other improvements should also be mentioned, e.g. the limitation of employees' liability in cases of slight negligence (1965); expansion of work inspection (1974); special protection of employment for persons doing military service (1956); and improved protection of working mothers-to-be (1957).

4.3   Social Security

In form and structure, the Austrian social security system belongs to the group of social insurances dating back to the 19th century. Since they are based on endeavors within the framework of international organizations, there are indications of an approach to modern social security systems. However, the results of an evolutionary process of almost 100 years cannot be abolished; nor can they be changed radically and abruptly.

Besides the classical branches of social insurance (medical insurance, accident insurance, old-age pension insurance), which are administered by independent social insurance institutions, there are in Austria unemployment insurance and relief payments and pensions to war victims, both of which are administered by the federal authorities. The insurance provisions for civil servants and officials of the Federal State, the provinces, and the municipalities (for death, old age, and disability) are incorporated in the pertinent civil service laws and are traditionally not considered part of social insurance.

Meanwhile, social insurance protection has also been extended to persons who are self-employed (independent businessmen in trade and industry and farmers): accident insurance for independent businessmen in 1955; old-age pension insurance for independent businessmen in 1957; medical insurance for farmers in 1965; medical insurance for independent businessmen in 1966; old-age pension insurance for farmers in 1969. However, this extension program has not yet reached its goal of including the entire population, and there are no plans for a systematic, step-by-step realization of this goal, although a general old-age pension for the entire population and a national health service plan are presently being discussed.

With respect to medical insurance, the present system has almost attained the goal of including the entire population. Persons who formerly carried medical insurance may continue voluntarily in the medical insurance program if they are not old-age pensioners whose insurance coverage is automatically extended. Independent businessmen may voluntarily join the medical insurance program (self-insurance). The immediate families of persons covered by compulsory insurance enjoy the same rights as the persons themselves. The definition of "immediate family" covers a rather large circle of persons, including the female spouse (also the disabled male spouse), the legitimate children, possibly also the illegitimate children, the legitimated children, adopted children, and stepchildren living in the same household, and the grandchildren. Medical insurance covers all these children of persons covered by compulsory insurance until age 18, and possibly, if they are undergoing vocational training or attending the university, until age 26.

Among insurance benefits, monetary benefits dominate, systematized according to amount. There are also, to a certain extent, benefits in kind or services, especially in the case of medical or accident insurance plans. Since 1965 old-age pensions have been adjusted annually to the changed domestic monetary purchasing power (dynamization). Detailed regulations provide that the medical insurance program pay the following benefits according to the event insured against (illness, inability to work because of illness, childbirth, death): medical treatment essentially free of charge, including the services of a physician, medication, and therapy, as well as hospitalization free of charge. In addition, a compensation (*Krankengeld*) is paid in case of inability to work due to illness. In the case of childbirth, the insured is entitled to the services of a physician and/or midwife, in addition to medication and therapy, hospitalization if necessary, and, in any case, maternity allowance and delivery subsidy. In the case of death, benefits include a contribution to funeral expenses. In addition, the medical insurance program sponsors free medical check-ups for adolescents as well as prophylactic medical examinations for healthy persons.

Benefits from workmen's compensation insurance, which covers accidents at work and occupational illnesses, include free medical treatment, further disability pensions, surviving dependents' pensions, and funeral subsidies. It also pays benefits to the family of a disabled person and provides artificial limbs free of charge. The workmen's compensation insurance program is further charged with the organization and implementation of industrial safety measures in order to prevent accidents.

The old-age pension insurance plan pays benefits for old age, decreased ability to work, and death, as well as for health care of persons still working. If certain legal requirements are met, old-age pensions are paid to men at age 65 and to women at age 60. If the person has been insured for a long time, pensions may be paid to men at age 60 and to women at age 55.

Disability pensions are paid regardless of a person's age. The miners' old-age pension insurance program provides for additional benefits, which are meant to offset the particular hardships of this occupation.

The methods of financing are varied: contributions by employees and employers, by employers alone, public funds, subsidies from public funds, and special surcharges. The contributions paid in by employees and employers are adjusted to the changed cost of living at irregular intervals.

With regard to the administration, i.e. payment of benefits, the classical branches of social insurance have been entrusted to special agencies with legal capacity, which have the legal position of corporations under public law. The most important social insurance institutions are the nine provincial health insurance agencies (one for each province), which operate sanitariums, rest and convalescent homes, and outpatient clinics; next come the general accident insurance agency, which maintains hospitals for accident cases and first-aid stations; the workers' old-age pension insurance agency; the employees' old-age pension insurance agency; the Austrian miners' insurance agency; and the Austrian railroad insurance agency. All these agencies have established sanitariums and rest and convalescent homes. All social insurance institutions are united in an umbrella organization, the association of Austrian social insurance institutions (*Hauptverband der österreichischen Sozialversicherungsträger*), whose main task is coordination. Many benefits are paid out by the federal administration, and others are paid directly by the provincial administrations. Here again, the federal benefits are partially administered by the general federal administration and partially by special agencies. This situation is accompanied by an equally complicated system of legal recourse. There are special social insurance courts, general administrative agencies, and special agencies that have jurisdiction over matters pertaining to relief payments and pensions to war victims.

The present Austrian social security system desperately needs systematizing, unifying general reform.[9] However, the most urgent problem at the present time is securing the financing of benefits, which are legally established in the form of individual legal claims. This objective takes priority over all other reform plans.

4.4   Children and Family

The family allowance fund (*Familienlastenausgleich*) pays out various benefits that are dependent on the presence of not fully employed children up to a certain age. It is presently the only branch of the social security system to include the entire population, regardless of citizenship although requiring residence in Austria, and regardless of family income.

Financing is secured by contributions from employers; by special taxes levied on the income of self-employed persons; by contributions for agricultural and forestry enterprises, which are collected in the form of a surcharge on the real estate tax; and by an assessment on the provinces, dependent on the number of adult residents. The funds are administered by the State (Ministry of Finance) in a special category which is not legally independent. The majority of the contributions are structured in such a way that an automatic adjustment to the changes in monetary purchasing power is safeguarded (dynamization). In contrast, benefits from the family allowance fund, unless they are benefits in kind, are determined by fixed amounts of money. These are either increased at irregular intervals, depending on the money available, or expanded to include new and different benefits.

This expansion to include different benefits was begun in 1971. Until then, there were essentially only monetary benefits per month and child. These family allowances, which today are still the core of the family allowance fund, are structured in a slight progression up to the fourth child and then remain the same, independent of the number of children. As a rule, the allowance is given until the child comes of age (presently completion of the 19th year) as long as the child cannot fully support himself. In exceptional cases, the allowance can be extended until the child turns 27, as long as he is undergoing occupational training (e.g. attends a university).

In 1971, these allowances were supplemented by a system of subsidies for trips to and from school or by free trips to and from school. This applies to all trips to and from schools, including universities. The basic requirement for such a claim is a distance of at least 3 kilometers between the student's place of residence and the school. These benefits are systematized monetary benefits in graduated amounts, paid out as subsidies for or in full refunds of travel expenses, or they are benefits in kind in that a free ride on public transportation is provided.

A few years later, in 1974, textbooks were provided free of charge. This system is limited to mandatory schools and secondary schools and does not include universities. The benefits are in kind, in that the actual books are provided or the student is given a coupon for their purchase. There is no interference in the private market sector of textbook manufacturing and trade.

In 1976, a further benefit from the family allowance fund was introduced: birth subsidies. This is a one-time monetary benefit, paid to the mother. The amount is essentially dependent on the mother undergoing a series of medical examinations, prescribed by and entered into a mother-child pass, and on these examinations being continued for the child during the first year of life.

Until the end of the year 1972, the legislator encouraged newly married couples to establish a household by granting special tax benefits, which, however, were more advantageous to persons with higher incomes. In order to remedy this situation, a marriage allowance was introduced in 1972. This entitles each spouse, while a resident of Austria and paying taxes there, to a one-time payment of 7,500 schillings on the occasion of the first marriage.

4.5   Housing

Securing adequate housing for the wage-earning and low-income population has long been regarded in Austria as an important task of the State's and the provinces' social policies, particularly so since the end of World War II.

According to the 1971 count of houses and apartments, there were approximately 2.5 million occupied and 230,000 unoccupied dwellings. Ninety percent of the apartments in multifamily houses are smaller than 90 square meters (about 970 square feet). One-fifth of all dwellings (farmhouses, single-family houses, duplexes, including summer houses and weekend houses) are owned by territorial authorities or nonprofit housing associations; 47 percent are occupied on a lease agreement. The density of occupation amounts to an average of 1.1 persons per room. The central problems of the Austrian housing situation are bad quality of the dwellings and too high density of occupation: 30 percent of all dwellings must be qualified as substandard housing.

Remedies for this state of affairs are measures to maintain and modernize old dwellings, a suitable real estate policy, an appropriate building law and area planning, and measures to encourage the construction of new housing units. These latter measures are particularly relevant in social policy. Shortly after the end of World War II, a special housing reconstruction fund was created by the State, which grants long-term, low-interest housing construction loans (1948). A few years later, in 1954, the State created a general program to promote housing construction, especially of small and medium-sized apartments for low-income groups in the population. As the problems of housing reconstruction receded, this type of promotion came more and more to the fore.

State-subsidized housing construction has been thoroughly reorganized since 1968 by major reform. It is now being supported by 50-year State loans at 1 percent interest. These loans are granted on condition that the builder supply capital of his own in the amount of 10 percent of construction costs. Other measures include annuity subsidies from the State to assist in repaying construction loans secured on the general money market, the granting of State guarantees for construction loans secured on the general capital market, and finally State housing subsidies to individual low-income renters.

5 THE PRESENT SITUATION

5.1 Economic Guarantees for Achievements to Date

The paper on social policy submitted for discussion to the ninth Federal ÖGB Congress in the fall of 1979 contains two subheadings that are characteristic of the present situation in Austrian social policy: "Limits of the Welfare State?" and "New Social Question?" Both questions are formulated accurately and are justified, although the considerations they present of course reflect only the ÖGB's point of view. The question on limits of the welfare state is an indication that the responsible officials of political and other significant groups are acutely aware that the continued swift expansion of the welfare state, in particular in the area of social security, could cease for several reasons. Problems of financing are only one superficial reason. Economic causes, in both the domestic and the world economy, are basic, as are specifically Austrian demographic causes, such as age structure and declining population.

The subheading "New Social Question?" reflects the consideration that among wage earners there is an inadmissable differentiation between the social strata who are secure and those on the periphery who have "remained excluded," for the most part unintentionally by those responsible for social policy measures. This point raises, quite simply, the age-old problem of social outsiders whose presence could not be prevented by the modern, perfectionist welfare state. They are the ones who must receive increased attention in the present phase of the development of social policy.

5.2 Cautious Further Development

In the area of basic labor laws, representation of employees on an equal basis on supervisory boards of corporations and similar enterprises is presently being discussed, although not, according to the prevalent philosophy, in management organs. With respect to individual working conditions, further shortening of working hours has high priority for employees' representations of interests. However, differences are acknowledged between the shortening of a person's working life (owing to longer mandatory schooling and a lowered retirement age), of the work year (minimum vacation is to be increased to five weeks per year), and of the work week (36 hours, or the four-and-a-half-day work week). The goal of shortening the work week must not blindly be given absolute priority. Another important item in the program of Austrian social policy is the so-called issue of equalization, which strives to abolish the differences in labor law between workers and employees, as well as between men and women. This item is closely linked to the creation of a uniform labor law. These endeavors have already made considerable progress.

6   CONCLUSION AND ASSESSMENT

The evolution of Austria into a modern welfare state, based on a progressive social policy that focuses on the human being, his dignity, and his personality, has progressed at different speeds since the end of World War II. The initial phase of the reconstruction of the Republic and of the reestablishment of its social institutions was followed by a dynamic period of great social reforms. Although not everything striven for has been accomplished, and although what has been achieved does not always appear integrated and uniform, such swift expansion is hampered by serious economic obstacles, both at home and abroad.

However, reduction of the achievements to date, or even a total standstill, is not to be considered seriously. On the contrary, as soon as the State has the financial capability, the immense project of social security, which still does not appear to be evenly administered, is to be expanded and implemented. The primary goal in economic policy of full employment is joined by the endeavor in social policy to consider the individual employee, to secure a solid job for the worker, and to give him working conditions, leisure time, and recreation that enable him to freely develop his personality.

All of this means simply that any social policy, including Austria's—and that in turn means the Austrian version of the welfare state—is nothing but the concrete expression of a humanism that alone corresponds to our philosophy of man and the meaning of his life.

Notes

1. Although there was no disagreement on this goal, other priorities (such as stability, economic viability, rapid reconstruction) prevented its immediate achievement, so that such organizations as works councils and collective contracts were without basis in law until 1947.
2. With the lifting of the prohibition, the union could be formed on the basis of the freedom of association (*Vereinsfreiheit*) which existed in Austria since 1867.
3. The Austrification of the German social insurance law had the undesirable result that the regulations became more and more complex, as was soon discovered.
4. See also the section on unseparated powers in Peter Gerlich's chapter in this volume.

5. The following statements are based on the "New Party Program" (1958) for the SPÖ, and on the ÖVP programs entitled "Everything for Austria" (1952) and "What We Want" (1958) as well as on the "Klagenfurt Manifesto" (1965).
6. See the chapter by Maria Szecsi.
7. This may be appropriate for the Anglo-American type of legal system, which follows the principle of *stare decisis,* but not for a legal system of the continental European type.
8. The significance of works council elections for the distributions of positions among the party-oriented groups (*Fraktionen*) within the ÖGB is referred to in Section 4.3 of Anton Pelinka's chapter in this volume.
9. Thus the basic law, the General Social Insurance Law (Allgemeines Sozialversicherungsgesetz), has been the subject of more than 30 piecemeal amendments during the 25 years of its existence. It should be noted that social assistance (*Fürsorge*) supplements the system of social insurance for persons who fall below a certain poverty level, to ensure a minimum standard of living. Social assistance is covered by legislation of the nine provinces, as are certain youth welfare services.

Selected Bibliography

Arbeit und Wirtschaft, monthly. Wien, 1947–.
Brusatti, Alois, et al, eds. *Geschichte der Sozialpolitik.* Wien, 1962.
Burghardt, Anton. *Kompendium der Sozialpolitik.* Berlin, 1979.
Fischer-Kowalski, Marina, and Josef Bucek, eds. *Ungleichheit in Österreich.* Wien, 1979.
Floretta, Hans, Karl Spielbüchler, and Rudolf Strasser. *Arbeitsrecht.* Wien, 1976.
Floretta, Hans, and Rudolf Strasser. *Arbeitsverfassungsgesetz.* Wien, 1974.
Die Industrie, weekly. Wien.
Institut für Sozialpolitik und Sozialreform. *Schriftenreihe.* Wien, 1954–.
Klose, Alfred, ed. *Katholisches Soziallexikon.* Innsbruck, 1964.
Krebs, Edith, and Margarete Schwarz. Austria. In Sheila B. Kamerman and Alfred J. Kahn, eds., *Family Policy: Government and Families in Fourteen Countries.* New York, 1958, pp. 185–216.
Lingens, Ella. Sozialpolitik und Gesundheitswesen. In Erika Weinzierl and Kurt Skalnik, eds., *Das Neue Österreich.* Graz, 1975, pp. 203–24. Also Ella Lingens. Gesundheitswesen, in Weinzierl and Skalnik, eds., *Österreich: Die Zweite Republik.* Graz, 1972, vol. 2, pp. 253–81.
Mayer-Maly, Theo, et al., eds. *Festschrift für Hans Schmitz.* Wien, 1967.
Mock, Alois, and Herbert Schambeck, eds. *Verantwortung in Staat und Gesellschaft.* Wien, 1977.
Österreichischer Gewerkschaftsbund. *Schriftenreihe.* Wien, 1946–.
Strasser, Rudolf. *Soziale Sicherung.* Linz, 1971.
Weissenberg, Gerhard. Sozialpolitik. In Weinzierl and Skalnik, eds., *Österreich: Die Zweite Republik.* Graz, 1972, vol. 2, pp. 231–52.

Modern Austria, pp. 321–34
Copyright © 1981 by SPOSS Inc. All rights reserved

15. EDUCATION AND EDUCATIONAL POLICY

Kurt Steiner

Professor of Political Science (Emeritus), Stanford University

1 JURISDICTION IN THE FIELD OF EDUCATION

The Austrian Constitution of 1920 did not decide the question of the jurisdiction of the Federal Government and the provinces (*Länder*) in the field of education. Rather, it provided that this decision should be made by a "special regulation by federal law." Because of ideological cleavages between the parties, exacerbated by the fact that the Federal Government and all the provinces except Vienna were under conservative control, while Vienna—a province in its own right—was under Social Democratic control, a definitive regulation was not possible within the lifespan of the First Republic.[1]

The Constitution of 1920 was readopted in 1945. But a breakthrough in the field of education did not occur until 1962. After difficult and long negotiations between the partners in the then existing Grand Coalition, a series of laws was passed. Basic to them was the Constitutional Law of 18 July 1962, which assigned educational legislation in principle to the federal level. Such legislation now requires a quorum of half of the members of the National Council (Nationalrat) and a two-thirds majority. In practical terms this means that educational laws can be passed only when the two big parties achieve a compromise. The provincial parliaments (*Landtage*) legislate on preschool education, whereas in school matters they have only the right of subsidiary legislation within general principles laid down by federal law. The administration of compulsory education is, in principle, under the jurisdiction of the provincial governments (*Landesregierung*). The Constitution itself (in Articles 81a and 81b, added in 1962) has provisions regarding education commissions (*Schulräte*) formed in the provinces and their districts (*Bezirke*). These commissions are—significantly—consti-

321

9306-6403/81/0415-0321$01.50

tuted in proportion to the strength of the parties in their respective areas.

Among the various federal ministries, matters pertaining to education at the lower levels—i.e. not including the universities and colleges (*Hochschulen*) of fine arts[2]—belong to the jurisdiction of the Ministry of Education and Art. A number of commissions are attached to that Ministry for purposes of policy-making and planning, and some of these will be mentioned below.

2 THE SCHOOL SYSTEM

For the foreign—and especially the American—reader it is important to keep three important facts in mind. One is the prominent role played by the federal level. As noted, educational legislation is principally a matter of federal legislation, and the educational structure is therefore uniform for the entire country, a uniformity that is reinforced by the existence of a federal ministry of education. Second, most of the elementary and secondary schools are run by "legal school-maintaining authorities" (in the terminology of the law), which may be federal or provincial agencies. (All universities are also state-run.) Private schools, accredited under the Private School Law, are run mainly by the Catholic Church, which also plays a significant role in preschool education and in the training of teachers in compulsory education.

A third important fact is that the Austrian educational system has traditionally been a "two-track system," as is also the case in such countries as Switzerland and Germany. After the four years of compulsory elementary or primary school (*Volksschule, Grundschule*), attended by all children from their sixth to tenth year, a separation occurs.[3] The great majority of children (about 80 percent) go on to compulsory secondary general schools (*Hauptschulen*), and a minority attends upper-level secondary schools (*Allgemeinbildende Höhere Schulen,* AHS), which provide the usual path to higher—and especially university—education. The fateful decision regarding the educational track to be pursued—with all its ramifications for future occupation and income, and thus for social and economic status—made at age 10, used to be irrevocable.

The school reform of 1962 led to a reorganization of much of the school system. Of particular importance is the School Organization Law of 25 July 1962, which contains an all-encompassing enumeration and systematic regulation of most types of schools. This law has been repeatedly amended since 1962, and further amendments are under consideration. However, the "two-track system," although somewhat modified, has remained a basic feature up to the present (see Figure 1). One type of secondary school, the *Hauptschule,* comprises four grades. Most *Hauptschulen* (about 80 percent by 1974) are organized to provide two streams (*Züge*), with academic requirements for the first stream going beyond those of the second stream (e.g. a modern language is compulsory only in the first stream). The assignment to either of these streams is made by a collective decision of the students' *Volksschule* teachers as recorded on their grade 4 certificate.[4] Transfer from one stream to the other (in either direction) on the basis of actual or expected achievement is possible, but actually is rather rare. For students who do not intend to stay in school beyond their compulsory education, a one-year prevocational course has been instituted as a ninth

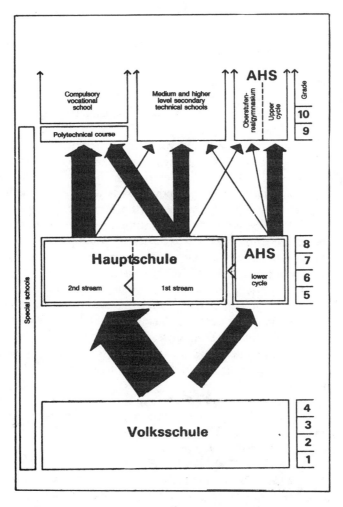

Figure 1   Present school organization (compulsory education).

year of schooling (after four years of *Volksschule* and four years of *Haupt-schule*). This course (Polytechnischer Lehrgang) is oriented toward preparation for work in an occupation. Having completed their compulsory education, the students become apprentices in their chosen occupation. According to the "dual-training principle," the apprenticeship is complemented by compulsory attendance at a vocational school for the branch of business or industry in question.

The other type of secondary school, the *Allgemeinbildende Höhere Schule* (AHS), constitutes the "upper track" and carries a degree of social prestige. In the past it had been necessary to pass an admission test in order to enter the "upper track," but this test was suspended in 1971, and it is not likely to be reinstated. The four lower grades or classes (ages 10–14) constitute the lower cycle (*Unterstufe*), and students may leave school after completing them. Most students, however, continue for another four years (upper cycle, *Oberstufe*), and at the end take a comprehensive written and oral examination (*Reifeprüfung* or *Matura*) that qualifies them to enter (without entrance examination) a university or other institution of higher learning (*Hochschule*).[5]

Actually, the term "Allgemeinbildende Höhere Schule" is the collective designation of a category of various types of schools. The differentiation between the various types previously started in the first year, but in the course of the reforms it has been postponed by two years. The main types are the *Gymnasium* (early-Latin type) and the *Realgymnasium* (standard type), to which a home economics type for girls (*Wirtschaftskundliches Realgymnasium für Mädchen*) has to be added. Within these main types there exist subtypes to accommodate the differing interests and aptitudes of the students as well as the requirements of society for a variety of qualifications. Certain compulsory subjects are common to all subtypes. These include religious instruction, German language and literature, two foreign languages (of which at least one must be a modern language), history and social sciences, geography and economics, mathematics, biology, chemistry, physics, introductory philosophy, music, art, and physical training. The compulsory subjects (totaling 33 hours or more) are identical in the first two years of the lower cycle.

Specifically, students in the Gymnasium study Latin and one modern language in the lower cycle. If the Gymnasium is of the classical subtype (*Humanistisches Gymnasium*), they add Greek as a third foreign language in the upper cycle. But if the Gymnasium is of the modern language subtype (*Neusprachliches Gymnasium*), they add another modern language. A third subtype (*Realistisches Gymnasium*) is characterized by intensified instruction in mathematics and scientific subjects in lieu of a third foreign language in the upper cycle.

There are also two subtypes of the other main type, the Realgymnasium. In both subtypes, students in the upper cycle continue the modern languages taken in the lower cycle. But in the upper cycle of the science subtype (*Naturwissenschaftliches Realgymnasium*) they take up Latin and, in classes 7 and 8, either descriptive geometry or intensified instruction in biology, physics, and chemistry, while in the upper cycle of the mathematics subtype (*Mathematisches Realgymnasium*) they take up a second modern language and, in classes 7 and 8, descriptive geometry. Although such rigorous requirements leave little room for electives and, especially, for frivolous "mickey mouse courses," there is some concern about the overloading of the curriculum and the resultant stress (acerbated by the examination system) on the students.[6]

The decision at age 14 to go or not to go on into the upper cycle, and from there, after the *Reifeprüfung,* to higher education is, of course, also an important one for the future. However, it is no longer unalterable. To facilitate access to the upper cycle even at a later time—e.g. after working for a few years—there is now an independent upper-cycle form, called *Oberstufenrealgymnasium.* It comprises four years (as does the upper cycle of the main types). It is also possible to achieve the education provided by the lower cycle at a later time, by attending an *Aufbaugymnasium* (language-oriented) or *Aufbaurealgymnasium* (science-oriented) in analogy to the two main types mentioned above. These schools have a transitional class, followed by four grades. Furthermore, there is "second-chance education" in schools, offering part-time instruction for employed persons who want to make up for the schooling missed earlier. These schools offer nine semesters.

The schools discussed above all aim at providing general education. There are also schools aiming at vocational training. These are the medium-level secondary technical schools (*Berufsbildende Mittlere Schulen*) and the higher-level secondary technical schools (*Berufsbildende Höhere Schulen*). Training is offered for more than 30 occupations in industry, trade, crafts, tourist industry, social work, agriculture, forestry, and nursing. Normally students enter at age 14, but some enter the higher-level schools after a period of practical work. Attendance usually replaces the period of apprenticeship and beyond, shortening the time required to obtain a certificate for independent exercise of the occupation. The number of grades in the medium-level schools varies. The higher-level schools normally have five grades, and conclude with a comprehensive final examination (*Reifeprüfung*), which gives the student a choice between proceeding to a university or entering an assured middle-level career in an industrial, commercial, or social occupation. The 1979 OECD report on Austrian School Policy[7] states that these schools "are the object of great pride in Austria, and rightly so," and finds that they "provide a carefully thought out, well constructed and richly supported system, intimately articulated with the wishes of the employers and to all appearances meeting in an eminently satisfactory way the needs of the Austrian social and economic system. . . . No other secondary schools in Western Europe offer such advantages to their graduates."

3 TEACHER EDUCATION

The training of teachers depends on the prospective level of employment, i.e. on the qualifications required for teaching at a given type of school.[8] Normal schools (which require only eight years of previous schooling and passing of an aptitude test) train nursery school teachers and handicraft teachers in the compulsory general schools. Since 1968, a new institution, the Pedagogical Academies, trains teachers for primary and secondary schools other than the AHS. There are 14 of these academies, recruiting students after the *Reifeprüfung,* i.e. at ages 18–19 years. (In some cases, e.g. for teachers of fine arts or physcial education, an aptitude test is a condition of admission.) The course lasts four semesters, after which an examination leads to certification as a primary school teacher. A course for teachers at *Hauptschulen* (and special schools for handicapped children) takes six semesters, and is also followed by a certification examination. There is, however, an alternative route for active primary school teachers who wish to achieve the higher status and remuneration of teachers at *Hauptschulen.* They can take courses in their spare time at Pedagogical Institutes and then submit themselves to an examination before a board appointed by the Minister of Education. There are also special pedagogical academies or institutes training teachers in technical schools.

In many European countries, teachers for the traditional academic secondary schools are trained in or in association with universities. Austria is no exception. Future teachers at "upper-track schools" take a nine-semester university course, normally in two academic subjects, and pass a certification examination. The professional training in the subject matters concerned is supplemented by educational training, including basic principles of pedagogy and their application to the subjects in question. A second examination leads to the award of the master's degree (*Magister*). The above-mentioned OECD report finds, as a broad generalization, that the teaching profession in Austria, while dedicated to professionalism, tends to be conservative in outlook and cautious in the face of change. It also notes that the number of pupils is—and in the near future will continue to be— lower than expected in earlier forecasts. Although this, together with a policy of not restricting access to Pedagogical Academies, has brought about a favorable trend in the teacher-pupil ratio, the fact remains that the career outlook for teachers is not encouraging, and this may strengthen the conservative attitudes of older teachers.[9]

4 TOWARD GREATER FLEXIBILITY OF THE SCHOOL SYSTEM

Having presented a brief survey of the school system, we can now return to a discussion of the reforms of 1962 in relation to the traditional two-track system. As the reader may have noticed, it was one of the aims of these reforms to loosen the rigidity of such a system by making the decision regarding the track pursued more flexible than formerly by opening up possibilities of transfer from the lower track (*Hauptschule*) to the upper track (AHS). The School Organization Law of 1962 states that "the acquisition of higher education and the transfer from one school type to another must be made possible for all students suited for it." But transfers were not possible as long as the curricula of the two tracks were quite different. Therefore, curricula of the first stream of the *Hauptschule* and of the lower cycle of the *Realgymnasium* were made identical to a large extent. This, it was thought, would make it possible for first-stream students with above-average marks to transfer, without examination, into the following grade of the lower cycle of a *Realgymnasium*. It would also permit students who, having completed *Hauptschule,* wanted to go on to the upper cycle of a *Realgymnasium* to do so. A transfer possibility was also provided from *Hauptschule* to a *Gymnasium* during the first two years (i.e. during the observation and orientation phase).[10]

The establishment of the above-mentioned *Aufbaugymnasium* and *Aufbaurealgymnasium* was also a measure aimed at increasing the "permeability" of the school system.

5 EDUCATIONAL ISSUES, PAST AND PRESENT

In the past a prominent issue in the area of educational policy had involved State-Church relations. The big parties of the First Republic had traditionally reflected a clerical-anticlerical cleavage. The claim of the Church to a substantial influence on education (such as it had actually exercised in the monarchy before 1867) had been promoted by the Christian Social party, whereas liberal demands for separation of Church and State and, more specifically, between Church and school, had been espoused by the Social Democrats as well as the German nationalists.

The Second Republic brought about a rapproachement between the Church and the successors of the Social Democrats, the Socialist party

(SPÖ). A law on religious instruction was passed in 1949. The great school reform of 1962—which in this aspect if closely connected with the treaty between Austria and the Vatican of the same year—resulted in a legal guarantee of state subsidies to denominational schools, most of which are Catholic schools. Originally, up to 60 percent of the personnel costs of Catholic schools were so subsidized; since 1971 the subsidy has amounted to 100 percent.[11] Today the Church also plays a significant role in preschool education and in the training of elementary school teachers. The law permits the establishment of Pedagogical Academies that are not state schools, and the Church maintains such academies in many of the dioceses, where they function side by side with the existing public academies and train many of the teachers for the parochial schools.

Although this issue has been laid to rest, another issue of great political sensitivity is under discussion at present. It relates to the continuing character of the school system as a "two-track system" and to the early point in the student's life when the decision about the track to be pursued must be made. As we noted in the discussion of the increased permeability of the system, "bridges and crossovers" are now provided in the law. From an overall point of view, the number of students who continue beyond compulsory education has considerably increased. The increase was greatest at the higher-level secondary technical schools, but there was also some increase in the AHS. The percentage of people graduating with a *Reifeprüfung*, which had risen markedly between the censuses of 1961 and 1971, has shown a further increase since then. In 1961, it was 4.9 percent of the population older than 15 years; in 1971 it was 5.9 percent, and in 1977 it was 7.3 percent. Since the *Reifeprüfung* is a precondition for attendance at universities, the percentage of university graduates rose from 1.8 percent in 1961 to 2.1 percent in 1971 and to 2.5 percent in 1977.[12]

To the extent that the decision to pursue education beyond its compulsory minimum is based on financial considerations, the measures for financial relief for the cost of schooling are also significant in this context. A basic rule is stated in the School Organization Law. It provides that "in addition to the exemption from school fees provided for in other statutes relating to public compulsory education, the attendance at any other public schools now covered by this federal law shall also be free of charge." A 1971 amendment to the Family Allowance Fund Law (Familienlastenausgleichsgesetz) provides for free trips to and from schools (including universities), and a 1974 amendment provides for free textbooks. The Student Grants Law of 1971 provides allowances from the 9th grade upward for students in need of financial support who show adequate achievement.[13]

Still, the "bridges and crossovers" provided by the law are, in fact, not effectively utilized. Once students have been allocated to a school with lesser academic demands (and lesser prestige), they accommodate themselves to the assigned role, and transfers to a more demanding school are rare. The increase in attendance at such schools, noted above, is due more to their greater accessibility to hitherto neglected regions and to an increased number of female students who decide to enter them than it is to transfers from the lower track. The early age at which the initial decision has to be made remains a critical issue.

To understand the sociopolitical sensitivity of the issue, one must realize that the various strata of society are disproportionately represented in the higher-track schools. The selection of an educational track at age 10 is closely tied to the social class and family background of the students. While upper- and middle-class families consider it a matter of course that their children select the upper track (or, more precisely, that they themselves select the upper track for them), working-class families are less motivated in this respect. Since educational differences are closely related to future socioeconomic status, it has been argued that the traditional educational system—in Austria and elsewhere in Europe—tends to reproduce the class structure from generation to generation.[14] The selection of the educational track is, therefore, seen as related to the issue of equalization of educational opportunities for all social classes. In reviewing past accomplishments, Hermann Schnell, president of the School Commission of Vienna and an ardent proponent of further reforms, finds that regional inequalities have been reduced by strengthening the network of schools, and inequalities between the sexes have been removed in that the number of female graduates from the AHS equals that of male graduates; social inequalities, however, have not diminished to an equal degree.[15]

The Socialists advocate a postponement of the track selection to age 14 by extending comprehensive schooling—now limited to *Volksschule*—to that age (see Figure 2). For this purpose a new, integrated school type, known as *Neue Mittelschule* would be instituted for all children in the age group 10 to 14.[16] The People's party (ÖVP) opposes this concept, at least partly because of a concern that such integration will lead to lowering the quality of instruction presently available at the AHS. While preferring to maintain a differentiation of schools for those in the age group 10–14, it proposes certain reforms of the *Hauptschule,* including replacing the present streams by *Leistungsgruppen* for certain subjects, where individual students would be placed according to their performance in these subjects.

Because educational laws require a two-thirds majority, the SPÖ cannot realize its plans without the votes of the ÖVP. In the meantime, a parliamentary School Reform Commission was formed in 1969, and a special Center for Pilot Projects and Educational Development was established in the Ministry of Education. Among the pilot projects launched since 1971,

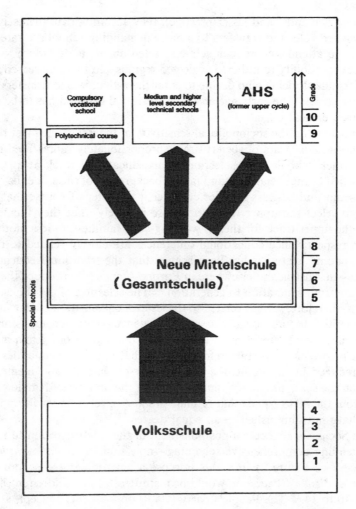

Figure 2   School organization (compulsory education) proposed by SPÖ.

one tests a "school for the age group 10–14 (comprehensive school)" in about 1,200 classes with 48,000 students.[17]

Another controversial issue is the introduction of full-day forms of schools, which would be a departure from the status quo of school attendance only in the mornings. Two types of such schools are being tested, the *Ganztagsschule* (in 165 classes) and the *Tagesheimschule* (in 148 groups). According to the former model, the time for classes, homework, and leisure is distributed over the mornings and afternoons, so that attendance in the afternoon is necessarily compulsory. In the Tagesheimschule the afternoon attendance is voluntary, the school providing supervision and assistance both in school work and in play or other leisure activities, primarily for day-care purposes. The SPÖ is in favor of instituting both models as alternatives. The ÖVP prefers the *Tagesheimschule* as the only full-day model, and opposes the *Ganztagsschule* as leading to an unjustified erosion of the role of the parents. Some spokesmen even accuse the SPÖ of desiring the *Ganztagsschule* as part of a plan for the "nationalization of the child" ("Verstaatlichung des Kindes"). Resolution of this issue is not yet in sight.[18]

6 OVERVIEW

The Austrian school system has a long tradition. In the perspective of the 19th century, it was a progressive system, providing for general education, vocational training, and teacher training. A compulsory minimum of eight years of school attendance had already been introduced by 1869. Attempts at progressive reforms were instituted in Vienna in the 1920s, but this development was interrupted by the emergence of an essentially conservative authoritarian regime in 1934 and by the absorption of Austria into Nazi Germany between 1938 and 1945.

In the Second Republic the process of introducing change has proved to be slow and intricate. This remains the case, inspite of—and to some extent because of—the compromise of 1962. Because the distribution of jurisdictions assigns overwhelming importance to the federal level in educational legislation, reforms depend on the passage of laws by parliament. Educational laws have required a two-thirds majority since 1962, and thus a large measure of consensus between the two large political parties.

The reforms of 1962—one of the most significant achievements of the Grand Coalition—constitute a landmark in the history of Austrian education. Since then, the economic necessity of providing a better qualified work force at various levels, together with sociopolitical demands for equal opportunities, led to great expansion, especially at the level of secondary schools. There is now greater diversity of school types at this level, and secondary technical schools have assumed greater importance. One element in the picture is the increased attendance of female students in upper-track schools; another is the reduction of regional imbalances. School construction was effectively promoted, especially during the last ten years, and the number of teachers at all levels has doubled. This involved the allocation of increasing resources to education, and Austria's educational budget has increased by 200 percent between 1970 and 1980, at an annual rate ranging from 11.5 percent to 21.9 percent.[19]

There is some criticism about the quality of learning conveyed by the schools, including the upper-track secondary schools. The School Organization Law of 1962 sees the task of the schools, among other things, to be "fostering the talents and potential abilities of young persons" and "training them to acquire knowledge on their own initiative." Young people shall be "encouraged to develop an independent judgment and social understanding." But, some critics contend, the system still stresses memorizing encyclopedic knowledge rather than developing the potential for independent thought.[20] Some feel that the aim of equal educational opportunity for all social classes has, so far, been elusive even under a socialist government since 1970. The OECD examiners found that "in relying too much on gradualist development, [the Austrian education system] may not be giving sufficient impetus to measures designed to foster equality of educational opportunity."[21]

This gradualism—which is dictated by constitutional and political requirements—notwithstanding, the Austrian educational system has been anything but static over the last two decades. Much has been achieved since 1962. Perhaps most significant is the basic fact that educational policy and educational reform now have a place in public affairs that is commensurate with their importance for the future of society.

Notes

1. An interim arrangement provided that some matters, especially those pertaining to obligatory education, could be regulated only by identical laws on the federal and provincial levels. This was a virtual guarantee of immobilism. See Kurt Steiner, *Politics in Austria* (Boston, 1972), pp. 100–101.
2. These have been under the jurisdiction of the Ministry for Science and Research since 1970.
3. Primary schools that provide eight years of compulsory basic education have virtually disappeared now.
4. For a critique of this procedure, see the Organization for Economic Cooperation and Development (OECD), *Austria: School Policy* (Paris, 1979), pp. 18–20.
5. This examination by itself is also a prerequisite for certain positions in public service.
6. The upper cycle of the home economic type continues the modern language taken up in the lower cycle and offers in addition another modern language.
7. OECD, *Austria: School Policy* (Paris 1979), p. 28. Realizing that employment opportunities for university graduates are diminishing, more and more young people are opting for vocational and technical educations. It is the policy of the authorities to expand the provision of these schools in preference to the AHS.
8. Teachers at primary schools are classroom teachers, often taking the class from grade 1 to grade 4, whereas those at other schools are typically subject teachers. In the latter case, the training also depends on the subject taught.
9. This chapter is limited to the most important parts of the educational system. It should be noted, however, that there are also special schools for handicapped children, and that Austria has a system of adult education that has a longstanding tradition related originally to the view that adult education could be used as an instrument of social advancement of the working class and the achievement of its class interests. Partly because this motiviation no longer seems pertinent to a working class that has achieved a recognized position of partnership in society, and partly because in society the number of employees

(contrary to that of workers) is steadily increasing, the relative proportion of workers among participants in adult education is dwindling.

10. To make these transfers possible, the study of Latin—which traditionally had started in the first year—was postponed to the third year.
11. See the chapter by Erika Weinzierl in this volume.
12. OECD, *Austria: School Policy,* p. 61.
13. See also the chapter by Rudolf Strasser in this volume. Students at universities and art academies receive stipends (*Studienbeihilfen*) by virtue of a law passed in 1963. On this law and its legislative history, see Steiner, *op. cit.,* pp. 366–70.
14. From the standpoint of society as a whole it has been argued that the traditional system of secondary education with its early selection and channeling fails to develop much of the talent latent in families of lower social class. See the summary of discussion on these questions in Henry Levin, "The Dilemma of Comprehensive Secondary School Reforms in Western Europe," in *Comparative Education Review,* vol. 22, no. 3 (October 1978), pp. 433–51.
15. In "Sozialistische Bildungspolitik für die 80iger Jahre," *Der Sozialistische Akademiker,* vol. 32, no. 11–12, (November–December 1979), p. 4.
16. See, e.g., "Schulprogramm der SPÖ, 1969," *Bildung für die Gesellschaft von Morgen* (Wien, 1969), and Hermann Schnell, "Die Neue Mittelschule als Gesamtschule," in *Der Sozialistische Akademiker,* vol. 33, no. 3–4 (März–April 1980), pp. 5–7. A characteristic of the proposed school type is the placement of students in three groups (*Leistungsgruppen*) according to their performance in various subjects (e.g. language, mathematics) for more individualized instruction.
17. Other projects carry out tests in regard to the full-day forms of schools, discussed below, as well as in regard to preschool classes, prevocational schools, special schools for the handicapped, etc. A pilot project on "early training in foreign language" introduces a foreign language in the curriculum from the third grade of *Volksschule.* In 1978–79, 212,000 students participated in this project. See OECD, *Austria: School Policy,* p. 56.
18. Aside from the reforms of the school structure, accomplished or under consideration, there are also efforts under way to democratize the hitherto somewhat authoritarian decision-making process of the schools themselves in their day-to-day operation through participation of teachers, parents, and students. The School Instruction Law of 1974 contains provisions in this regard.
19. See the Report presented by the Bundesministerium für Unterricht and Kunst at the 37th International UNESCO Conference on Education, *Austria: Organization of Education, 1977–79* (Vienna, 1979), p. 16. The above-mentioned OECD report (p. 15) states that Austria's expenditures in education between 1963 and the early 1970s were already the highest for 13 countries surveyed by OECD.
20. See Steiner, *op. cit.,* pp. 201–6.
21. OECD, *Austria: School Policy,* p. 6.

Selected Bibliography

The survey presented in this chapter is based to a large extent on two sources in English, namely:

Bundesministerium für Unterricht und Kunst. *Austria: Organization of Education, 1977–79.* Vienna, 1979. This booklet contains an extensive bibliography of sources in German.
Organization for Economic Cooperation and Development (OECD). *Austria: School Policy.* Paris, 1979.
A tangential source in English is Kurt Steiner, *Politics in Austria.* Boston, 1972, esp. pp. 62–65, 100–101, 199–206.

In German, useful sources include:

Bundesministerium für Unterricht. *Bildungsplanung in Österreich,* 2 vols. Wien, n. d. (Report to the OECD of 20 December 1963).
Neugebauer, Max. Schulwesen in Österreich. In Erika Weinzierl und Kurt Skalnik, eds., *Österreich: Die Zweite Republik,* vol. 2, pp. 323–45. Graz 1972.
Olechowski, Richard. Schul- und Bildungspolitik. In Erika Weinzierl und Kurt Skalnik, eds., *Das neue Österreich,* pp. 225–40. Graz 1975.
Steindl, Josef. *Bildungsplanung und Wirtschaftswachstum.* Wien, 1967.

Modern Austria, pp. 335–44

16. HIGHER EDUCATION

Kurt Steiner

Professor of Political Science (Emeritus), Stanford University

1 HIGHER EDUCATION: AN OUTLINE

Austria's universities have a long history. The University of Vienna, founded in 1365, is the oldest university in German-speaking Europe. The universities of Graz and Innsbruck were established in 1585 and 1669, respectively. The University of Salzburg, originally founded in 1619, was reactivated in 1962. Most of the other institutions of higher education were established in the 19th century. The most highly qualified engineers for Austrian industry have come from the technical universities in Graz (1811) and Vienna (1815). The Economic University in Vienna dates back to 1873. Also in Vienna are the higher schools for veterinary science (1767) and for agriculture (1872). A university specializing in mining has existed in Leoben since 1840. Two universities are recent creations. The University in Linz, created in 1962, originally emphasized the social sciences, but recently expanded into technical and natural sciences. In 1970 a University for Educational Sciences was established in Klagenfurt. In addition to these institutions, all carrying the title "university," there are six higher schools of art and music (Kunsthochschulen), most of them founded in the 19th century.[1]

The constitution assigns legislation and administration in the area of higher education to the federal level. All schools of higher education are state institutions. Administratively they fall under the jurisdiction of the Federal Ministry of Science and Research, created as a separate ministry in 1970.

Austrian institutions of higher education are in effect graduate schools preparing students for a doctorate in certain fields.[2] There are no exact Austrian equivalents to the undergraduate curricula and students of American universities. Entering students in Austria have normally completed the upper cycle of the "upper track" secondary schools (especially the "all-

335

gemeinbildende h hehere Schulen") and successfully passed the comprehensive school-leaving examination (Reifeprüfung, Matura), as noted in the preceding chapter on education and educational policy.

Traditionally, the universities were divided into faculties (Fakultäten), such as theology, philosophy, law, and medicine.[3] Below the faculties, headed by a Dean (Dekan), were subdivisions, headed by a professor who was the "Professor Ordinarius" for his field. Professors were formally appointed by the Federal President upon proposal by the government, which in turn was based on a list of three candidates submitted by a council of professors at the university in question. This manner of appointment was indicative of the elevated position of the Ordinarius, and the rather authoritarian method of decisionmaking justified the characterization of the system of "Ordinarienuniversität." Far below the professors were the docents (Dozenten), lecturers (Lektoren), instructors (Lehrbeauftragte), and assistants. A highly deferential atmosphere pervaded the universities, including the student body, the composition of which was heavily biased against the lower social classes and against the female sex.

As in the case of the secondary schools, the last two decades were a period of reconsideration of these traditional structures, leading to considerable reformist initiatives. The reform was carried out through the passage of federal laws.

2 REFORMS SINCE 1966

The main laws to be considered in this context were the General Law for University Studies (Allgemeines Hochschulstudiengesetz) of 1966, and the University Organization Law (Universitätsorganisationsgesetz) of 1975, which replaced an earlier law passed in 1955.

The former law unified the organization of institutions of higher learning, codified some existing rules and, to some extent, liberalized the hitherto rigid degree structure.[4] Perhaps more significantly, it provided the framework for further reforms. The responsibility for the degree course structure is allocated to three levels, namely parliament, ministry, and university. In accordance with this allocation, parliament passed special laws for the various types of faculties (i.e. juridical, medical, economic, technical, etc.), and these special laws laid down the main features of study courses for the various disciplines (Studienrichtungen) encompassed by the faculty in question. The special laws in turn provided the basis for ministerial ordinances (Studienordnungen), promulgated by the Ministry of Science and Research. These ordinances prescribed the rules for the conduct of courses and examinations (i.e. subjects to be studied, their relative balance, etc.) in the various disciplines. The more detailed content of courses and the precise pattern of examinations were left for determination by each university.[5] The determination at the university level is now made by the study commissions (Studienkommissionen) established in an effort to democratize the decision making in institutions of higher learning, as discussed below.

The University Organization law of 1975—which made the Study Commissions a general feature of the academic decision-making process—brought about a fundamental change in the general structure of the Universities. Larger faculties were subdivided and new faculties, smaller than the traditional ones, were established in various universities. The faculties are now an intermediate level, because within them a new organizational level in the form of institutes (similar to the departments of US universities) was created. The institutes (Institute) are the basic organizational units for teaching and research.[6]

An important aspect of the law concerned the democratization of academic decision making. Traditionally the main decisionmaking collegiate organs at the university level were the Council of Professors (Professorenkollegium), on which even Dozenten were only minimally represented, and the even more selective Academic Senate, consisting of the top officeholders (such as the Rector and the Deans) and one senator from each of the faculties. The Deans were normally elected by the Council of Professors from among the professors of the faculty. The Rector was indirectly elected by representatives of the faculties (Wahlmänner). The purpose of the University Organization Law was to ensure, according to their qualifications, the participation in decisionmaking of all involved in the scientific process. The basic principle is the parity of all three components of the academic community, namely professors, nonprofessorial teaching staff (the so-called Mittelbau), and students, in the collegiate organs at the level of institutes, faculties, and universities (including the above-mentioned study commissions).

At the institute level, the head (Vorstand)—who is elected from among the professors—is assisted by the institute conference, in which the number of assistants and students is equal to that of the professors in the institute. At the level of the faculties, the rather unwieldy collegiate bodies (Kollegien) can be relieved of many of their decision-making functions by delegating them to standing and nonstanding commissions. On these commissions all groups must be represented, and no single group can have a majority. At the university level, the Academic Senate remains the supreme authority, but provision is made for representation of all groups active in the university.[7]

There was, of course, some opposition to these changes in the structure of universities. A lawsuit asserting the unconstitutionality of the composition of the study commissions was instituted by a group of professors, but the claim was rejected by the Federal Constitutional Court.[8]

There was also considerable concern that the study commissions would be immobilized by "block voting" because each of the three component groups can veto any proposal, provided its members are unanimous. It appears, however, that this has occurred in relatively few cases.[9] While problems undoubtedly exist, the reforms brought about a new spirit of adaptation to the demands of the time and a change in the traditional atmosphere of university life.

The reforms were conducted during an explosion in the demand for higher education (Bildungsexplosion). In 1955–56, the number of registered students (13,888) was at its lowest point. Since then it has risen dramatically. By 1973–74, it reached 58,613; by 1977–78, it stood at 80,553.[10] Adaptation to this situation necessitated an increase in teaching staff (from 2,864 in 1969 to 4,277 in 1973) and in the space made available for higher education (roughly a 33% increase between 1969 and 1973). This, in turn, required additional resources.

In this regard, the OECD Report 1976 found that "the record of the Austrian government in recent years has been impressive."[11] The share of the budget and of the Gross National Product (GNP) devoted to the universities has steadily increased, as shown in Table 1.

3 FROM "ELITIST UNIVERSITY" TO "MASS UNIVERSITY"

The increased attendance at universities has initiated a transition frequently characterized by the slogan "from the elitist university to the mass university." The share of university students per 1000 persons of the resident population rose from 64 in 1970–71 to 87 in 1973–74. This is, however, a smaller proportion of academically trained people in the population than

Table 1 University budget (including research promotion and construction of university facilities)[a]

Year	Budget (in millions of schillings)	Increase compared to previous year (in percent)	Share in the total budget (in percent)	Share in the GNP (in percent)
1970	2,426.729	15.2	2.40	.65
1971	2,770.208	14.2	2.50	.67
1972	3,353.441	21.1	2.73	.70
1973	3,949.936	17.8	2.84	.71
1974	4,727.418[b]	19.7	2.96	.76

[a]Source: OECD Report 1976, p. 77.
[b]According to *Hochschulbericht 1978* (p. 156), the university budget rose to 7,302.121 schillings in 1978.

existed in 1973–74 in the Federal Republic of Germany (102) or in Sweden (121).[12]

The rising demand for higher education and for higher levels of qualification is welcomed by the government. It is a principle of Austrian law that everyone who is qualified has an unrestricted right to study in institutions of higher learning. Access to the universities is unencumbered by entrance examinations for graduates of the "upper track" secondary schools. However, these graduates are still a relatively small proportion of the relevant age group, and this fact goes far in explaining the relatively small proportion of academically trained people in the population.

Under these circumstances the government has steadfastly refused to follow other Western European countries in restricting access by instituting a full or partial "numerus clausus." Such restrictions are usually dictated by bottlenecks in university capacities or by considerations of demand for university graduates in the economy. In the latter regard the Austrian background paper to the OECD Report 1976 states that "in Austria there are at present no signs of unemployment with regard to university graduates" and that "comparisons on an international level show that Austria seems to have a deficit in highly qualified persons compared to other highly industrialized nations."[13] Far from limiting access, the government has assiduously tried to translate the legal principle of free access into reality. University fees have been eliminated, and a system of financial support (including stipends as a matter of right under certain conditions, free transportation, and social insurance for students) has been instituted. Student dormitories and dining halls (Mensen) are subsidized.[14]

The deeply held conviction of the desirability of a continuous expansion of higher education is based on two interrelated considerations. On the one hand, education is considered "an integral part of the quality of life." As the background paper to the OECD Report states, "this calls for a continuous raising of the levels of education of the total population, as this is the prerequisite for the participation of larger sections of the population in the cultural tradition and the innovation as well as in the political and social determination of the future. This is the only way to realize the emancipatory and creative character of education." The long-term prospect is an "educated society." Over-qualification, considered elsewhere a reason for limiting educational expansion, is seen as a constituent of educational policy.[15]

The other consideration—already hinted at in the foregoing by the reference to a "participation of larger sections of the population"—is related to the goal of establishing equality of educational opportunity. The more privileged segments of the population, as measured by the educational background of the students' fathers, are greatly overrepresented in the student body, as shown in Table 2.

Table 2 Educational backgrounds of the fathers of University Students[a]

Educational background	Fathers of university students (in percent)	Male working population age 40–64 (in percent)
Secondary schools without school leaving examination (Matura)	48.9	88
Secondary schools with Matura	19.7	7
University	26.4	5
No data	5.9	—
Total	100.9[b]	100

[a] Source: *OECD Report, 1976*, p. 72.
[b] Column does not total 100 due to rounding.

Thus only 5% of the Austrian male working population of the appropriate age group, but 26.4% of the fathers of university students, had a university education. While almost half (48.9%) of the university student population came from families in which the father had not taken the upper track of secondary schooling, the overall bias in favor of the more privileged strata is still obvious. If the underprivileged strata are to advance in an achievement-oriented society, the formal educational system must offer possibilities for their advancement. In so doing it will also utilize a partially unused talent reservoir of society. The number and percentage of students from working class families have in fact substantially increased over the last years—from 4700 (about 7%) in 1970 to 11.000 (about 14%) in 1977–78. The figures for students from farming families rose similarly—from 1500 to 5000 (5.5%). The social imbalance is thus being reduced, albeit slowly.

There has also long been an imbalance between the sexes. The gap is narrowing because the percentage of the female population that attends universities rises faster than the percentage of the equivalent male population. Thus the latter percentage increased from 8% in 1970–71 to 11.4% in 1977–78, but the percentage of the female population increased during the same period from 2.8% to 7.1%. Similarly, the male students matriculating in 1970–71 constituted 10.8% of the same male age group; in 1977–78 the percentage was 11.6%. For female entrants the percentages were 4.5% and 10.0%, respectively.[16]

Considerable differences continue to exist in the regional origins of the students. On one end of the scale we find students from Vienna (27.5% of the total student population), followed by Upper Austria (16%), Styria (14.2%) and Lower Austria (14.1%). On the other end are Vorarlberg (2.8%), Burgenland (3.1%) and Salzburg (5.3%).[17]

4 PROBLEM AREAS

One problem of Austrian universities is the high rate of noncompletion of their studies and the high drop-out rate of students. In the former regard, the background report estimates that "during the past 15 years, an average of 13% (men) and 11% (women) have completed their studies within five years; 33% (men) and 29% (women) within seven years." To understand this situation, it is necessary to realize that continuation of studies is not dependent on the successful completion of individual courses (i.e. the accumulation of credits for certain units) but on the successful completion of prescribed examinations, which the student may take more or less at his or her discretion. The OECD examiners view the failure to complete the studies by earning a degree within a given time with a concern that is not shared by the Austrian planners of higher education. The latter are reluctant to adopt a formal credit system (which essentially follows the pattern of secondary education) and thus to introduce more rigidity in the way in which students can study. They see no need for measures to curtail the attendance of students who do not aim at a degree but simply want to further their education (possibly after having obtained a degree).[19]

The problem of drop-outs is different. According to the background report, 9% of all Austrian regular degree students dropped out of their studies after the first two semesters; after eight semesters 21% of the students entering in 1967–68 had dropped out (ex-matriculated or not registered in three consecutive semesters). By 1973, 40% of the students who first registered in 1967–68 were no longer registered. Austrian authorities consider this drop-out rate "unacceptably high." The OECD examiners believe that "open access involves wastage," but beyond this suggest that "excessively burdensome academic loads, disappointment with the content of studies, and too heavy a load of extra-mural obligations may be three important reasons."[20]

The Austrian background report sees a juxtaposition of a heterogeneous demand for education to a homogeneous educational system as a cause for the admittedly high degree of dissatisfaction among the students. The following excerpts may indicate the position taken by the Austrian authorities:

> In addition to the general, mainly technocratic, aspects, the possibility of realizing also individual demands as to training and education is an integral part of an educational policy which is not exclusively directed toward the utilization of education. An optimal use of the different individual talents and demands calls for an "individualization" of education.... The counterpart of mass education at the universities will have to be individualized studies, i.e. opportunities to realize individual interests and individual abilities and talents; employment of different learning and study techniques; a varied structure of studies; study possibilities taking into account different social backgrounds,

etc. Yet it will always be necessary to make a compromise between the different requirements of the labor market, the possibilities of the universities, and the qualitatively
differentiated demand for education.[21]

These are, of course, ideas for the future. Their realization depends on the
cooperation of groups of varied interests—cooperation that may or may not
be forthcoming. In the meantime, counselling may mitigate the situation,
and the Austrian authorities are making a determined effort to improve
it.[22]

They are also aware of the need for rationalization of teaching and
instruction. Traditionally, the mass lecture has been the main instrument
for the imparting of information. Now the disadvantages of its impersonal-
ity and its uni-directional character are being realized, and it is being
replaced by seminars with student participation and specific student contribution. The problem here is the size of the seminars—frequently consisting
of as many as 80 students—which limits the student involvement.[23]

Related to this question of teaching style is the question of educational
objectives. It is felt that "the emphasis will have to shift from the availability
of factual knowledge to the capability and readiness to learn and to apply
new findings." With particular reference to the objective of educating students so that graduates can assume special political and social responsibility, the background report states that "precedence must be given to
discussion," including in scientific education "a discussion of the relation
between science and politics and the economic and social utilization of
science and scientific qualification." In the vernacular of students, universities should not produce "Fachidioten," proficient in a narrow discipline but
lacking a wide horizon.

Over the last decades, the field of higher education has been anything but
static. Quite likely more changes have been introduced since 1966 than in
a century before. There were changes in structure and curriculum. The
changes "from elitist university to mass university" and from the "Ordinarienuniversität" to one with participatory decisionmaking did not occur
without controversy. Some critics have been concerned about the effect of
these changes on the quality of university education; others have found the
changes too gradual and not thorough enough.

Still, the balance between tradition and innovation has shifted decisively.
The developments of the past twenty years cannot be reversed. Tradition
is being reconsidered in the light of changing times and demands, and is
adapted to them where rationalization requires it. In the words of the
background report, "reform of university studies is not a one-time event;
it calls for a constant adaptation of the study regulations to changed conditions, above all to the progress of science and new professional requirements."

Notes

1. This chapter deals with university education, which accounts for more than 80% of the students in post-secondary education. In the Kunsthochschulen the percentage of female students (46% in 1977–78) and of foreign students (30%) is high. The three higher schools for music and the performing arts in Vienna, Graz, and Salzburg account for more than 70% of the students. Admission is competitive on the basis of an examination that tests the artistic talent and the level of preparation. See Bundesministerium für Wissenschaft und Forschung, *Hochschulbericht 1978* (Wien, 1978) pp. 90–91. This report, presented to the National Council, is hereafter cited as *Hochschulbericht 1978*. I am indebted to Dr. Sigurd Höllinger, head of the Department for Planning and Statistics of the Ministry, for making it and other documents available to me.
2. Courses supplementing this education can be taken at the Institute of Advanced Studies and at the Diplomatic Academy, both in Vienna.
3. The specialized schools of higher learning (mining, agriculture, veterinary science, and economics) were not divided into faculties. Before its reactivation as a full-fledged university in 1962, the University of Salzburg consisted only of a Catholic-Theological faculty.
4. Thus the "Studium irregulare" makes it possible for an individual student to follow a course that does not conform to any of the prescribed discipline-oriented patterns. Within these patterns, students have now some degree of choice, being permitted to take "elective" subjects—alternative groups of subjects related to the student's main field—and "free" subjects, which may simply reflect the student's personal interest. See Organization for Economic Cooperation and Development (OECD), *Austria: Higher Education and Research* (Paris, 1976), pp. 16 and 25. (Hereafter cited as *OECD Report, 1976*)
5. OECD, *Report, 1976*, p. 31; *Hochschulbericht 1978*, pp. 40–43; Richard Olechowski Schul- und Bildungspolitik, in Erika Weinzierl und Kurt Skalnik, eds., *Das Neue Österreich* (Graz, 1975), p. 237.
6. See *Hochschulbericht 1978*, pp. 54–57, 92, 95. For example, the University of Vienna now has in addition to some traditional faculties (Catholic-Theological and Evangelical-Theological Faculties, Juridical Faculty, Medical Faculty) a Faculty of Social and Economic Sciences, a Faculty for Basic and Integrative Sciences, a Faculty for Humanistic Sciences, and a Faculty for Formal and Natural Sciences, all of them replacing the traditional Philosophical Faculty.
7. Two representatives of the nonscientific personnel are also included in various bodies. One innovation aims at greater continuity in managerial functions. Thus the elected rector now serves first one year as pre-rector, holds his tenure as rector for two years (rather than one year as heretofore), and then serves an additional year as pro-rector. The arrangement for deans is similar.
8. See *Hochschulbericht 1978*, pp. 95–96.
9. A survey in 1976 showed that 8 of the 165 study commissions at various levels existing at the time were blocked in this way. See *Hochschulbericht 1978* p. 44. The *OECD Report 1976* (p. 32) suggests that the nonprofessional teaching staff may not be sufficiently independent in its participation in decision making because its career prospects rest in the hands of the professors. The Minister of Science and Research advanced the explanation that the groups themselves may be subject to political cross-pressures, so that political conservatives from all groups may be on the same side of various issues. Most professors are conservatives, as shown by the 1975 elections for personnel representation, in which 3318 professors voted for the list, close to the conservative People's Party (ÖVP), while only 443 voted for the Socialist list. See Hertha Firnberg, Demokratisierung von Wissenschaft und Forschung, in *Der Sozialistische Akademiker*, Mai–Juni 1978, p. 5.
10. *OECD Report, 1976*, p. 76; *Hochschulbericht 1978*, p. 116 (Table 1.15). The figures are those for Austrian regular degree students. The number of foreign students exceeds 10% of these figures, a higher proportion than in any other European country. Most of them (52.1% in 1973–74) came from the industrialized countries of Western Europe, followed by those from the developing countries (18.4%) and from Southern Europe (15%).
11. *OECD Report 1976*, p. 18.
12. *Ibid.*, p. 75.
13. *Ibid.*, p 89.
14. On the legislative history of the Law regarding Stipends (Studienbeihilfengesetz) of 1963, see Kurt Steiner, *Politics in Austria* (Boston, 1972), pp. 366–370; on recent developments see *Hochschulbericht 1978*, p. 38.

15. *OECD Report, 1976,* pp. 88–89.
16. Hertha Firnberg, Wie sich die Wissenschafts- und Forschungslandschaft Österreichs verändert hat, in *Der Sozialistische Akademiker,* März–April 1979, p. 4.
17. *Hochschulbericht 1978,* p. 125 (Table 1.22); see also *ibid.,* p. 10.
18. *Ibid,* p. 113 (Table 1.12). The percentages are for the academic year 1977–78.
19. *OECD Report, 1976,* pp. 18–26; *Hochschulbericht 1978,* p. 8.
20. *OECD Report 1976,* pp. 19, 74, 93.
21. *Ibid.,* p. 91.
22. *Ibid.,* p. 24, 119.
23. *Ibid.,* p. 21.

Selected Bibliography

Bundesministerium für Wissenschaft und Forschung. 1978. *Hochschulbericht 1978.* Wien
Bundespressedienst. 1976, *Austria: Facts and Figures.* Vienna pp. 147–65
Ermacora, F. 1962. Das Hochschulwesen. In *Mensch und Staat.* ed. B. Pittermann, Vol. I, pp. 446–60. Wien.
Firnberg, H. 1978. Demokratisierung von Wissenschaft und Forschung. In *Der Sozialistische Akedemiker* Mai–Juni:pp. 2–7
——— 1979. Wie sich die Wissenschafts- und Forschungslandschaft Österreichs verändert hat. In *Der Sozialistische Akademiker* März–April: pp. 3–5
Grohmann, K., und S. Höllinger 1970. *Bildungsplanung in Österreich,* vol. II. Wien.
Olechowski, R. 1975. Schul- und Bildungspolitik. In *Das Neue Österreich,* ed. E. Weinzierl, K. Skalnik, pp. 225–40. Graz.
Organisation for Economic Cooperation and Development (OECD) 1976. *Austria: Higher Education and Research.* Paris.
Schilcher, B. 1972. Hochschulen In *Österreich—Die Zweite Republik,* ed. E. Weinzierl, K. Skalnik, Vol. II, p. 345 ff. Graz.

Modern Austria, pp. 345–58

17. LEGAL POLICY SINCE 1970*

Franz Pallin

President of the Supreme Court of Austria

Herbert Ent

Ministerialrat in the Ministry of Justice

I. LEGAL REFORM IN CRIMINAL LAW AND PROCEDURE (Franz Pallin)

1

The most important reform in this area took place on January 1, 1975, when a new penal code was introduced. In order to assess the significance of this legal achievement, its history must be considered. Until that time, a criminal law was in force in Austria that dated back to 1803, which had its roots in the *Constitutio Criminalis Theresiana* of 1768. In spite of various reforms during the 19th century, the decisive break with the spirit of the absolutist and moralistic Theresian tradition never did take place, a break that was to become more and more urgent as intellectual and social developments progressed. On the contrary, in criminal law this spirit weathered all changes and upheavals, as if it dwelt in an untouchable reserve of security. A total reform of the criminal law was begun several times, the first time

Note: Austrian law belongs to the system of continental European law, which has its basis in Roman law. In this system, legal codes, i.e. systematic and comprehensive compilations of norms, play an important role. The Austrian Penal Code dates back to 1803, the Civil Code to 1811. This chapter analyzes the most important recent reforms in the areas of criminal law and criminal procedure in the contribution by Professor Dr. Franz Pallin, and in the area of civil law in the contribution by Dr. Herbert Ent. The spirit of these reforms is illuminated in statements by Dr. Christian Broda, Minister of Justice from 1960 to 1966, and again since 1970, according to which legal reforms adapt the legal order to the social changes that have occurred, thus being the endpoint of social developments, while at the same time being the starting point for new social developments. (See e.g. his statement before the Committee of Social Democratic Jurists in Frankfurt/Main on November 13, 1976.)—Editor

Translated by Ulrike E. Lieder, Stanford University

345

9306-6403/81/0415-0345$01.50

in 1861, but these attempts were thwarted partially by political developments (World War I) and partially by scientific progress in the field of criminology overtaking the drafts, which were then shelved for revision. A final attempt at reforming the criminal law during the First Republic failed owing to the ideological differences between the political forces in the nation, differences that became particularly blatant in the assessment of the penalty for termination of pregnancy.

In 1954, following a resolution of the National Council, a fifth attempt was begun. A commission was formed; its approximately 20 members numbered among their ranks university professors, members of the Supreme Court, members of the procurator's office, top officials of the Justice Ministry, representatives of the bar association and of the political parties represented in parliament. The commission worked for eight years and published a draft in 1962, which was the basis for the 1964 ministerial draft. The commission's draft was a compromise among its members, who, of course, subscribed to different ideologies. Controversies regarding social policy were avoided wherever possible. The commission's objective was to develop a criminal law that was up to date in scientific terms, and that was politically acceptable to the entire population. It was an essential contributing factor to the new law's sociopolitical continuity that it followed the so-called tradition of reform, i.e. the ideas of a hundred years as to how the Penal Code could be improved objectively according to the current state of dogmatics and to the most recent findings of penal policy. But a certain reorientation of the new draft vis-à-vis the old criminal law is evident; it clearly dissociates itself from the mental and political attitude represented by the old criminal law. The old spirit of enlightened absolutism and the police state is replaced by a new spirit of liberalism. Not only is this new attitude tolerant and generous, but it also strives to be rational and to dissociate itself from a basically ideological and emotional criminal law. Through rationality, criminal law serves humanity better than before, because it frees people from unnecessary restrictions. Therefore, the reform is to be regarded as a contribution to more reason and humanity in criminal law, because, as Minister of Justice Broda stated in his preface to the documentation on the Penal Code, "We firmly believe that only that is effective which is reasonable and humane." In our pluralist, or open, society, criminal law must no longer penalize our fellow humans for being different as compared to the ruling strata, but it must give legal protection only, where it is indispensable for the continued existence of society and of individual rights. Criminal law sees itself as a functional law.[1]

However, this functional law was not to be realized without difficulty. In the late 1960s, a veritable storm against the innovations of the draft of the criminal law was unleashed by clerical organizations, partially supported by the official church. Mitigations contained in the criminal law were denounced as reflections of a soft attitude toward crime, the introduction of fines instead of short prison sentences (which had long been accepted in other civilized countries) was decried as the settlement of an offense with money, termination of pregnancy (even on medical or other grounds) was called infanticide, and the impunity of homosexual relations between consenting adults was regarded as an attack on the family. During a political intermediate stage, when Austria had a conservative government (1966–1970), the draft's provisions were tightened on numerous points, following a demand by the Austrian Conference of Bishops, which the Minister of Justice acceded to. In particular, penalties for termination of pregnancy, blasphemy, incest, and other sexual and matrimonial offenses were tightened so much that they partially even exceeded the criminal law in force. The Austrian liberal bourgeoisie remained silent to this "counterreformatory" challenge—an indication of the emphasis of today's society, which protests the slightest tax increase, on material things. The failure of the conservative government's draft to become law (1968) was ultimately due to its determined rejection by the Socialist party.

In the meantime, a small circle of Socialist jurists had worked out a program containing all those demands that, when subsequently realized, gave the new criminal law the character of progressiveness and modernity. Only in the year 1970, when a Socialist government came to power, did a change take place: progress was accepted again, and even the attitude of the conservative party became more lenient. So the criminal law reform was finally realized in two stages. In the first stage, (1971), individual, especially critical, provisions were dealt with. In the second stage (1974), the new criminal law as a whole was passed with the votes of all parties; however, legalizing the termination of pregnancy within the first three months after conception (*Fristenlösung*) was passed with only the votes of the Socialist majority.

2

In its dogmatic stipulations, the new law remains within the borders of prevailing philosophies; the principle of guilt applies, but without a clear position on the question of determinism or indeterminism. Numerous provisions reflect the spirit of a sense of justice and understanding for human beings, as, for instance, the provision making an error in law excusable, or the expanded recognition of an exculpating emergency situation (Notstand). On the other hand, the impunity of self-defense is restricted by the principle of the proportionality between the attack and the permissible defense and by the rule that a possible need for leniency toward the attacker has to be taken into consideration.

The core of the new Penal Code is the chapter on penalties. Article 42 must be considered an innovation unprecedented in the entire area of European law; it stipulates exemption from penalty for an offense if the guilt and the injustice involved are negligible and if there is no other need for punishment. This takes the burden of superfluous work off the courts, and a first offender or an accidental offender is not unnecessarily branded a criminal. In other legal systems, criminal prosecution of comparable cases is left to the discretion of the public prosecutor (principle of expediency). This system creates inequalities, whereas Article 42 provides mandatory grounds for exemption from punishment if the legal requirements are present. The law also grants impunity in cases of physical injury caused by negligence if the injury resulted from no serious fault on the offender's part and if the consequences are not serious or if no one other than a relative of the offender is affected.

Penalties pursuant to the law are imprisonment and fine. In contrast to former times, there is no longer a distinction made between imprisonment (*Kerker*) and confinement (*Arrest*.) Limited prison sentences cannot exceed 20 years; life imprisonment is the sentence for the most serious cases; capital punishment does not exist in Austrian criminal law. In cases where there would be only a brief prison sentence (up to and including six months), the prison sentence is to be converted into a fine unless there are specific reasons (prevention in terms of the individual offender or of society) against it. The fine is set in per diems, one day of imprisonment corresponding to two per diems. The per diems vary between a minimum of 20 schillings and a maximum of 3,000 schillings, depending on the offender's financial situation (actual or potential income), so that he retains only an allowance to support himself and his family. Such a system of fines has an advantage over fixed fines in that it is in accordance with a person's income; it is effective because it lowers the offender's standard of living for twice the period of the prison sentence, but it is not as discriminating and socially stigmatizing and alienating as the latter. The law also provides for the possibility of suspending a sentence of imprisonment or a fine over a probationary period of up to three years. This can be imposed in conjunction with conditions and instructions, e.g. payment of damages, and the offender can also be placed under the supervision of a probation officer.

The law provides for the protection of society from insane or severely psychopathic lawbreakers as well as from dangerous repeat offenders by mandating that such persons be committed to a special institution. There are institutions for lawbreakers in need of drug rehabilitation treatment. Mentally incompetent persons can be committed for life, and dangerous repeat offenders for up to ten years beyond the sentence.

3

With respect to the special section of the Penal Code (dealing with specific offenses and their punishment), the regulations pertaining to termination of pregnancy have been mentioned.[2] These hotly disputed regulations are today approved by a great majority of the population; none of the political parties advocates their abrogation. The regulations concerning homosexuality have also become accepted; only male adults are subject to prosecution if they have homosexual relations with adolescents. In other respects, the provisions of the special section correspond to the pertinent passages of most other European penal codes.

Special mention should be made of the provisions of Article 283 with regard to incitement or agitation. According to Article 283, a person commits a criminal offense if he publicly, in a manner that could disturb public law and order, incites others to hostile actions against a domestic church or religious community, or against a group of persons characterized by their affiliation with such a church or religious community or by their race or their ethnic or national origin. A person is also liable to punishment if he publicly agitates against one of the above-mentioned groups in a manner violating human dignity, insults them, or attempts to expose them to contempt. So far, there has been little need to apply these provisions.

After five years in force, the law has, in general, proved itself. Above all, it gives the judge much more latitude than before; he can impose individually adjusted sentences or other penal measures, or he can altogether forgo the imposition of such sentences and measures. Neither is the judge required to administer justice on the basis of obsolete statutory offenses. We may safely say that the judges have accepted the law inwardly as well. However, some deficiencies in the law can be seen. These flaws became apparent in its application, as for instance in cases of fraudulent misrepresentation (making false statements to the authorities), where the provisions of the law are excessive, or in dealing with repeat offenders, where the formulation of the law does not correspond to its purpose.

Even more important is the fact that scientific findings in the fields of criminal law and criminology are constantly progressing. Alternatives to imprisonment, with its generally recognized detrimental social effects, are being sought for petty and minor delinquencies, and the concept of "diversion" is widely discussed. Proposals are submitted at the Conferences of the Ministers of Justice, at international (Council of Europe) and domestic conferences (7th Conference of Austrian Jurists), and at numerous other meetings of jurists. If Austria is not to again bring up the rear in European developments in criminal law, it should not delay consideration of amendments to the existing Penal Code and of the introduction of new criminal regulations. Certainly, Paul Reiwald's statement that, in the majority of countries, public opinion is a serious obstacle to the development of criminal law and that the public's attitude is "shockingly reactionary and primitive" applies to Austria as well; it is therefore all the more incumbent on science to exert a persuasive influence on public opinion.[3]

4

In another area, however, that of criminal procedure, major reform is in the making. As early as 1971, during the tenure of Minister of Justice Broda, an attempt was made to reduce the inordinately high number of prisoners awaiting trial. Among other things, a certain time limit of detention pending trial was introduced, as was a procedure for review of the remand in custody, a limitation of mandatory detention pending trial of serious cases, a restricted application of the risk of an attempt to escape as a reason for detention of socially integrated persons, and the creation of alternatives to detention. However, the consequences of these measures failed to materialize; the number of prisoners remained high.

For five years a committee on basic questions of reform of criminal procedure has been working with the Minister of Justice. Some professors of criminal law as well as practicing jurists of all categories belong to this committee. Some points of the total reform will emphasize legal tightening of reasons for detention and acceleration of procedures by abolishing the two-track investigation by police and court. The interrogation records are, on principle, to be placed at the disposal of the defense. The right of poor offenders to assistance by a public defender is to be extended to the investigation stage, especially when the offender is detained. Utilization of evidence obtained illegally and in violation of the offender's basic rights is to render the trial void; this evaluation of the evidence is to apply to both primary and secondary evidence ("the fruit of the poisonous tree"). It is also necessary to give the judges more latitude than before on questions of penalty and on assessment of the personality of the accused. Therefore, the so-called interlocutory phase (*Schuldinterlokut*), i.e. dealing with the question of guilt and that of the penalty to be imposed in two separate phases of the trial, should be introduced. The system of appeals against court sentences is to be less formalistic in the future than it has been so far. The possibilities of appeal, especially on the question of guilt, are to be expanded. However, in trials where lay judges (*Schöffen* or *Geschworene*) have been appointed in the first instance, it will not be possible to repeat the trial in the second instance, since it would be impossible to have their evaluation of the evidence replaced by that of other lay or professional judges.[4] Furthermore, the sentences of judges in the court of the first instance must reflect objectively a reasonable certainty of the correctness of their assumptions, in addition to their personal conviction of the offenders' guilt; only this would preserve the principle *in dubio pro reo.* Finally, every person acquitted is to have the right to publish his acquittal at the expense of the court system in order to rehabilitate himself. Furthermore—and this is to be realized in the immediate future—the State is to reimburse the acquitted person for the expenses he incurred for his defense.

A further legal undertaking that parliament will have to deal with soon is an amendment to the law concerning execution of a sentence. This is to establish new procedures concerning the conditional release of convicts who have served two-thirds or, in special cases, one-half of their sentence. According to the present system, this is decided by professional judges in a sort of summary procedure, based only on the files. Conditional release is therefore granted in relatively few cases, but at times in just those cases where severe recidivism occurs, thus causing this important legal institution, which is widespread, to lose credibility with the public. In the future, lay judges (*Schöffen*) are to be included in difficult cases, and the procedure is to become more of a truly legal procedure by mandatory hearings of the convict, the warden, and, if necessary, medical and psychological experts. Other regulations contained in the draft include increased compensation for work done by convicts and facilitation of written complaints to certain legal institutions.

Part of the area covered by criminal law is a 1978 law that improved the legal position of the victim of the crime with respect to his claim for damages. According to this law, the State must advance compensation to the poor victim in cases of homicide, bodily injury, and damage to his health or property, if it can be foreseen that payment of compensation will be obstructed when the convicted person is fined or imprisoned. The claim for compensation—which is not recoverable in most cases—is transferred to the State. This regulation is based on the concept that the victim of the crime is not to be indirectly victimized further by imposition of the sentence on the offender.

5

Finally, we mention the government draft of a media law that should be passed soon. This proposed law is to provide effective protection of the person vis-à-vis the mass media, not only against slanderous attacks but also against intrusions of privacy by the media. On the other hand, the present anti-press regulations on confiscation of newspapers are to be mitigated; in the future, decisions to confiscate because of offensive content of a press organ are to consider the general interest in obtaining information against the private interest of the injured party. The principle of equality is also to be realized in the legal area of the press and other mass media.[5]

In summary, it can be said that, in criminal law (in the broadest sense of the term), Austria has caught up with international standards in the past ten years, during the tenure in office of Minister of Justice Christian Broda. In some areas, such as dealing with petty offenses, it holds a leading position. However, many things still await implementation during the 1980s, for human thought and knowledge do not stand still.

II. LEGAL REFORM IN CIVIL LAW (Herbert Ent)

1 Introductory Note

A significant aspect of the developments in many fields, initiated by Austria's Socialist government in the decade 1970–1980, is the reform in civil law. Like the reforms in criminal law, described above by Professor Pallin, this reform is linked to the name of Minister of Justice Broda, who developed the strategic concepts and guided its course with great tactical skill. The reform is remarkable in scope, but even more so in sociopolitical impact. The legal and judicial reforms fulfilled demands that had accumulated over decades; their social ramifications will make them a lasting component of the Austrian legal and social order.

2 The Reform of Family Law

2.1 The Austrian Civil Code (Allgemeines bürgerliches Gesetzbuch, ABGB) dates back to 1811. One of its original characteristics was that parts of family law were not secularized. Different norms (e.g. in regard to marriage and divorce) applied to Catholics and to those affiliated with other religions and confessions, the norms for Catholics being heavily influenced by canon law. This confessionalization of family law was eliminated after the Anschluss in 1938.[6] However, the heavy hand of the past continued to be apparent in many provisions regarding relations within the family, in which, e.g., the husband was considered the head of the family, and he alone was endowed with paternal power.

Reform of family law has been one of the sociopolitical goals of Austrian social democracy throughout this century.[7] Thus the party program of 1901 demanded the elimination of all laws by which women are discriminated against in public or private law. In 1925, and again in 1927, a member initiative for a "Law Regarding Sexual Equality in Family Law" was brought before parliament, but because of the majority relations in that body at the time, it was never considered. Other landmarks were the 1926 "Linz Program"; the party program of 1958, with guidelines that a commission constituted by Socialist Minister of Justice Tschadek in 1949, developed; and the declarations of the successive Socialist cabinets in 1970, 1971, 1975, and 1979.

2.2 Because implementation of a total reform of family law by way of a statute had no chance of success, the alternative route of amending family law by well-balanced partial reforms was taken. Aside from the amendment to the adoption law in 1960, which was already based on the concept of equality and improved protection for the child, the essential parts of the reform were only realized beginning in 1970. The reforms began with new regulations concerning the legal position of the illegitimate child, continued in 1973 with lowering the legal age, and reached a first climax when Article 91 of the Civil Code, stating that "the husband is the head of the family," was finally stricken from the books. Further steps were the introduction in 1976 of the law regulating alimony advances, new regulations on the status of children, and finally the great reform of marriage law, which came into force on July 1, 1978, and covered the legal effects of marriage on a person, spousal succession, property rights during marriage, and divorce and its consequences.[8]

2.3   The most important principles of the new family law are those that aim at removing the former relations of authority and power (*Gewaltverhält-nisse*) in marriage and family, i.e. the status of the husband as head of family and as wielder of paternal power. These principles are as follows:

(*a*) The principle of equal rights of the sexes. Husband and wife have equal rights and duties in mutual legal relations, including the right of support (Civil Code, Articles 89 and 94); in their relations to the children (Article 137, para. 3); in regard to the law of spousal succession (Articles 757ff); property relations during marriage, where wives had hitherto been discriminated against (Article 1237); and in regard to rights after divorce (Articles 62f of the Marriage Law of July 6, 1938, as amended).

(*b*) The principle of partnership. According to this principle, derived from the equality principle and the democratic principles that permeate public life, husband and wife are to cooperate in marriage as equal and free partners (Articles 91 and 144).

(*c*) The principle of autonomy of the marriage partners and, to some extent, of the children. Every member of the family has the right to the autonomous development of his individual potential, such as the choice and practice of an occupation. However, this autonomy has limits in the concept of the common interests and common welfare of all family members, which provide marriage and family law with positive meaning both for the individual and for society (see e.g. Article 91).

(*d*) The principle of consensus in the actions of the marriage partners. Only responsible cooperation can ensure a healthy marriage and wholesome upbringing of the children.

(*e*) The welfare of the children is the guideline for the parents (Article 137, para. 1) in terms of care and education, administration of property, and legal representation of the children.

In addition, family members affected by social discrimination receive special protection. This applies to children born out of wedlock, to children from marriages ending in divorce, and to the parent who lives with them (see e.g. the regulations regarding consequences of divorce in Article 177). Similarly, the so-called incomplete family is given special attention. Insofar as this is compatible with the welfare of the weaker family members, the ties within the family have been strengthened.[9]

One other principle should be mentioned, that of the autonomy of marriage and the family: society and State have the right of intervention in matters within the family only insofar as this is required for the protection of a weak or disadvantaged family member.

2.4 The 1976 law regulating alimony advances is of great significance, especially for mothers. It safeguards the support of minor children if the person owing alimony according to civil law does not, but is able to, fulfill his obligation. In such a case, the State grants advances to the children in the amount of alimony set in accordance with family law. The State then either collects from the delinquent party or suffers the loss.[10]

2.5 The great reform of the marriage law in 1978 was of special importance. In the area of marital property rights, this reform provided for a claim to appropriate compensation for the partner who cooperated in the earnings of the other partner (Article 98), and it removed discrimination against wives. The rules on causes for divorce were reformulated in regard to the cause of "dissolution of the marital community" (Article 55 of the Marriage Law). The dissolution of a marriage in which irreconcilable differences prevail (*aussichtslos zerrüttete Ehe*) is now possible even against the opposition of the partner, provided that three, maximally six, years have elapsed since separation.[11]

Another trenchant change in regard to divorce was the introduction of a "divorce by agreement" (Article 55a of the Marriage Law). Since July 1, 1978, marital partners who are in agreement in regard to divorce (including alimony claims) may obtain a divorce in a simple procedure before the family affairs department of a district court (*Bezirksgericht*) without going through the formerly customary "pseudo-conventional divorce," which had to be based on the pretense of guilt of one of the partners.[12]

Equally important are the new regulations concerning the consequences of divorce. Basically, the partner who is solely or predominantly responsible for the divorce has to provide to the other partner a degree of support (alimony) that is appropriate to the standard of living enjoyed during the marriage, insofar as the earnings of the latter are insufficient (Article 66, Marriage Law). Generally speaking, the purpose of these and other regulations (e.g. regulations regarding distribution of property and savings) is to arrive at an equitable basis for creating an appropriate starting position for the future, now separate, paths of life.

3 Protection of Consumers

This reform, too, shows the purpose of modern legislation to help particularly those who are in a socially weaker position in an increasingly complex society and economy. Technological and economic developments—especially tendencies toward concentration of enterprises—have lessened personal contact between consumer and provider, who may, for purposes of rationalization, use preformulated contracts. Whatever their advantages even for the consumer, such contracts are often misused for unjustified gains on the part of the provider. The methods used to make the consumer enter the contract are becoming ever more sophisticated and, in many cases, downright aggressive. Consumers often enter contracts without fully understanding the terms. To maintain or restore freedom of contract, the Law for the Protection of Consumers instituted special regulations of private law.[13] Thus it provides the right to withdraw from a contract in "door to door" sales (so far possible only for installment contracts); regulates estimates and the effect of oral promises, etc; it contains provisions against unfair business conditions and allows lawsuits by corporate plaintiffs (such as the Chambers or the Federation of Trade Unions); it regulates separately certain types of contract, such as installment contracts and subscriptions to periodicals. All this is subject to certain procedural rules, protecting consumers in case of lawsuits.

4. Improved Access to the Law and the Courts

A number of measures provide easier access and improved efficiency in the functioning of the courts and thus increase the protection of the individual and the attainment of a greater measure of justice.

4.1   In terms of personnel, modern rules guarantee the independence of judges by being separated from rules pertaining to the activities and salaries of other public officials. *Rechtspfleger,* i.e. officials who are not judges and who have not studied at universities but who have received special training for certain judicial functions, are used, for instance, in regard to the abovementioned matter of alimony advances (see Section 2.4 above). The autonomy of notaries and lawyers has been strengthened.[14] An improved procedure for selection of court experts and interpreters and rules concerning limitation of their tenure have already proved beneficial.[15]

4.2   As in other countries, the Austrian court structure has become antiquated and uneconomical. The present hierarchy of the ordinary courts —all federal courts—has at its lowest level the district courts (*Bezirksgericht*), and rises to the provincial courts (*Kreisgericht* or *Landesgericht*) and higher courts (*Oberlandesgericht*), which are found in Vienna, Linz,

Graz, and Innsbruck, to the highest ordinary court, the Supreme Court (*Oberster Gerichtshof*).[16] One step toward reform was the merger of some courts at the lowest level, courts that were no longer viable. This step was achieved in the face of opposition, based on traditional sentiment and local parochialism.

In terms of functions, the new jurisdiction of the district courts in matters of family law has already been mentioned (e.g. for divorces by agreement, and for cases regarding property distribution following divorce, and questions of alimony). New endeavors aim at providing procedures appropriate for these matters, which would involve judges and *Rechtspfleger* with training in social psychology. In short, the ultimate goal is the establishment of a three-tiered structure of efficient courts with the appropriate personnel and technological equipment.

4.3   In terms of procedural law, the Procedural Assistance Law (*Verfahrenshilfegesetz*) deserves special mention.[17] Its basis is Article 6, para. 1, of the European Convention for the Protection of Human Rights and Basic Liberties of November 4, 1950, guaranteeing to everyone a constitutional right to have his civil or criminal affairs decided by competent and independent courts inexpensively, in a public procedure, and without undue delay. The Procedural Assistance Law improved legal protection for those who lacked the means for court procedures by regulations that apply to civil and criminal matters before the ordinary courts, as well as before the Constitutional Court, the Administrative Court, and before administrative agencies. Procedural Assistance is to be granted when a person cannot participate in procedures without endangering his own appropriate standard of living or his duties of support, provided the procedure is not hopeless or mischievous; where necessary, assistance of an attorney is included. Other regulations pertain to the use of tape recorders in civil cases, as a means of court reporting, and of computers. Thus the registers of landed property (*Grundbuch*) have been converted to this technological innovation. Ultimate goals are greater uniformity of procedural rules (which are still quite diverse for different types of procedures), elimination of antiquated formalism, and narrowing of the distance between the citizen and the courts by procedures that are quicker and less expensive while guaranteeing the greatest possible measure of justice.[18]

5 Prospects

The great reform in civil law is not over. Thus "the improvement of access to the law and courts" remains a focal point. Regulations protecting the rights of psychologically handicapped persons who require institutional confinement are to be reformed by providing rational cooperation between judges, health authorities, and medical personnel of the institution. Reform in assistance to mentally handicapped persons, replacing the "declaration of incompetence" (*"Entmündigung"*) and limiting its effects, is under discussion.[19] So is reform of the youth welfare laws, which would emphasize the "social character" of the relevant institutions, including the courts, dealing with matters of guardianship. The objective would be to help families that, for a variety of reasons, are unable to fulfill their obligations in bringing up the young; the removal of these young family members would be a measure of last resort.

Finally—and on another front—the endeavor to create modern product warranty legislation should be mentioned. The goal is to limit the dangers to the consumer resulting from modern production procedures, and to guarantee compensation for damage caused by faulty products.

Thus, in the broad area of civil law, too, much remains to be done in this decade.

Notes (Part I)

1. Moos, "Die gesellschaftliche Funktion des Strafrechts und die Strafrechtsreform," *Österreichische Richterzeitung,* 1977, pp. 229f.
2. On developments regarding the new provisions on abortion, with particular reference to the attitude of the Catholic Church and Catholic organizations, see also chapter 3 by Erika Weinzierl in this volume.
3. Paul Reiwald, *Society and Its Criminals,* T. E. James, tr. and ed. (New York, 1950).
4. Lay participation in criminal trials is restricted in Austria to cases where the crime is either political or of some gravity. Even in these cases, the lay judges determine only the guilt or innocence of the accused. *Schöffen* are lay persons who sit on a "mixed bench" along with professional judges. *Geschworene* are jurors who decide on the question of guilt by themselves.
5. See also the chapter by Hubert Feichtlbauer in this volume.

Notes (Part II)

6. Since then, to cite an example, marriages, including those of Catholics, are validly entered into only before civil (rather than ecclesiastical) authorities.
7. Christian Broda, "Die österreichische Sozialdemokratie und die Familienrechtsreform: Eine Dokumentation und einige Schlussfolgerungen," in Wolf Frühauf, ed., *Festschrift für Hertha Firnberg* (Wien 1975), pp. 75f.
8. The principal laws, mentioned in this text, may be found in the official Federal Law Gazette (Bundesgesetzblatt, BGBl) in which all laws are promulgated, as follows: BGBl Nos. 372/1970, 412/1975, and 403/1977. The great reform of the laws concerning marriage, effective as of July 1, 1978, is represented in the laws in BGBl Nos. 280/1978 and 303/1978.
9. See, for instance, Articles 148, 166, and 178 of the Civil Code.
10. Up to February 1, 1980, more than 30,000 children had received advances amounting to a total of nearly 560 million schillings, and currently about 20,000 children receive monthly advances. Thanks to the cooperation of the authorities involved, the recovery rate presently lies around one-third of the amount advanced, and it is steadily increasing. Where recovery from the delinquent party is unsuccessful, neither the child nor other persons with a duty of support have an obligation to pay back the advance.
11. The partner who is divorced against his or her will, according to Article 55, but who bears no guilt in regard to the state of the marriage retains his or her claims for support and pensions, as before (Article 69 of the Marriage Law).

12. There were 1,500 divorces according to the amended Article 55 between July 1, 1978, and June 30, 1979, and about 2,200 divorces of this type between July 1, 1978, and December 31, 1979. Divorces by agreement amounted to more than 3,500 for the first period and 6,500 for the second period.
13. Federal Law Gazette No. 140/1979.
14. Notaries (who are legally trained) are especially important in matters of inheritance, which they settle largely without court action. Like the lawyers, they too have their organ of representation (Chamber), which autonomously regulates professional affairs and is officially consulted on draft bills affecting their profession.
15. Law regarding General Court Experts and Interpreters, Federal Law Gazette No. 137/1975.
16. Outside the hierarchy are the Administrative Court and the Constitutional Court. See also Chapter 9.
17. Federal Law Gazette No. 569/1973.
18. In international private law, a law (BGBl No. 304/1978) codified the regulations regarding application of laws in civil cases that involve facts of an international law character.
19. See the press conference of Minister of Justice Broda on April 11, 1979.

Selected Bibliography

I. CRIMINAL LAW AND PROCEDURE
Foregger, Egmont, and Eugen Serini. *Kurzkommentar Strafgesetzbuch.* 2. *Auflage.* Wien, 1978.
Foregger, Egmont, and Friedrich Novakowski, eds. *Wiener Kommentar zum Strafgesetzbuch,* being published as a series. Wien, 1979–.
Leukauf, Otto, and Herbert Steininger. *Kommentar zum Strafgesetzbuch.* 2. *Auflage.* Eisenstadt, 1979.
Serini, Eugen. Entwicklung des Strafrechts. In Erika Weinzierl and Kurt Skalnik, eds., *Österreich: Die zweite Republik,* vol. 2. Graz, 1972, pp. 109–34.

II. CIVIL LAW
Ent, Herbert. Articles in *Österreichische Juristenzeitung.* Wien, 1978 and 1979.
Ent, Herbert, and Gerhard Hopf. *Kommentar zum Unterhaltsvorschussgesetz.* Wien, 1976.
———. *Das neue Eherecht.* Wien, 1979.
Floretta, Hans, ed. *Das neue Ehe- und Kindschaftsrecht.* Salzburg, 1979.
Gschnitzler, Franz, and Christoph Faistenberger. *Familienrecht.* 2. *Auflage.* Wien, 1979.
Koziol, Helmut, and Rudolf Welser. *Grundriss des bürgerlichen Rechts.* 5. *Auflage,* Band II. Wien, 1979.
Ostheim, Rolf, ed. *Schwerpunkte der Familienrechtsreform, 1977/1978—Entscheidungshilfen für die Praxis.* Wien, 1979.

PART V

AUSTRIA AND THE WORLD

Modern Austria, pp. 361–80

18. FOREIGN POLICY

Peter Jankowitsch

Representative of Austria at the Organization for Economic Cooperation and Development (OECD) in Paris

A NEW BEGINNING: 1945 AND THE FOREIGN POLICY OF THE POSTWAR YEARS

Austrian foreign policy in the immediate postwar years had one overriding objective: attainment of independence by ending the occupation by the Soviet Union, the United States, Great Britain, and France, and concluding a State Treaty. This central problem occupied Austrian foreign policy for a full ten years: its realization was soon to be complicated by the falling out of the World War II Alliance and the ensuing cold war, which created a separate "Austrian question."

The eminent role of Austrian independence for the peace of Europe had been highlighted by the fact that the reestablishment of an independent and sovereign Austria became one of the first proclaimed war aims of the allied powers. Acting on a draft introduced by Anthony Eden, Churchill's Foreign Secretary, Great Britain, the United States, and the Soviet Union declared on November 1, 1943, that "they wish to see reestablished a free and independent Austria."[1]

But after the Allied powers, supported by an Austrian resistance movement that coordinated action with their advancing armies, had actually liberated Austria in early 1945, agreement on the future of the country seemed to elude them. Nor did their wartime plans show any cohesive idea on the future shape of the country.[2] The fact that as early as April 1945 a Provisional Government could be formed in Vienna was therefore very largely due to a new spirit of national identity and a new-found belief in the possibility, indeed necessity, of Austria's existence as an independent political body in Central Europe. Contrary to the 1918 situation, the Second Austrian Republic was not forced on an unwilling and doubting people, torn between nostalgia for a lost past and dreams about an unattainable

361

9306-6403/81/0415-0361$01.50

future. The new country was created by the will of its people, united for the first time in many decades into a common feeling of national purpose.

In this period, other aims of Austrian foreign policy remained secondary, with the possible exception of relations to Italy over the South Tyrol and to Yugoslavia over the Carinthian question.

Nor did the material conditions of a country ravaged by war and many years of Nazi occupation allow the conduct of foreign policy on a larger scale. When Austria's first postwar envoys reached their destinations in Washington and Moscow, London and Paris, their primary tasks included efforts to secure the necessities of economic life for the country. Repatriation of prisoners of war was another priority.[3]

Furthermore, Austrian foreign policy remained under the control of the four occupying powers, exercised through an Allied Council and based on Control Agreements. These agreements, after revisions that removed some of the more stifling restrictions, finally gave Austria freedom to establish diplomatic relations with all members of the United Nations and to conclude international agreements—provided no change of the Constitution was implied. There was still no doubt that final authority on many crucial matters had not been returned to Austrian hands.

As negotiations by the four powers to achieve agreement on a State Treaty dragged along, Austrian foreign policy gradually became more imaginative. First, efforts to involve the United Nations and influential third powers such as India to solve the crisis were made. Simultaneously, thinking proceeded on the future international status of Austria. Although there was a clear consensus that Austria should be part of the family of Western industrialized democracies, the idea of neutrality made headway.

In discussion of the most effective policies for assuring a maximum of sovereignty and independence to Austria, the idea of adopting a status of permanent neutrality had appeared as early as 1919.[4] But it was in the new political climate of 1945 that the idea of Austrian neutrality finally gained momentum. Karl Renner, who had presided over the first government of republican and democratic Austria in 1918 and 1945 and who was then elected first head of state of the Second Republic, became one of the earliest and most influential advocates of this concept. He was also the first to draw a clear parallel between a future status of neutrality for Austria and the permanent neutrality of Switzerland. Theodor Körner, who succeeded Karl Renner as president, became equally dedicated to the idea that "Austria, once free and independent, removed from all rivalry and not committed one-sidedly to any one, devoted exclusively to the cause of peace, would be an asset for Europe, for the whole world."[5]

But the idea of Austrian neutrality still lacked appeal to the powers, whose joint action was needed to put an end to occupation. When Austria, during the abortive Berlin Conference of Foreign Ministers in January and February of 1954, made its first firm proposal not to enter into military alliances and not to allow establishment of foreign military bases on its soil, Molotov made countersuggestions that would have extended the occupation of Austria almost indefinitely.

NEUTRALITY: THE NEW REALITY

Although prospects for Austrian independence still seemed bleak at the end of 1954, some of the main elements of a new situation already existed. After the conclusion of the Paris Treaties between the Federal Republic of Germany and the Western powers, Soviet hopes to block West German entry into the Western alliance collapsed and the artificial link between the German and Austrian questions was broken. Furthermore, Soviet leaders, whom the death of Stalin in 1953 had freed from some of the constraints of the past, began to consider possibilities to replace the unproductive policies of the cold war with new avenues to détente.

But a signal was needed to demonstrate the new mood in the Kremlin. It came in an indication of the Soviet Union's willingness to sign the long deadlocked Austrian State Treaty, should ways and means be found to safeguard the independence of the alpine republic against a renewed *Anschluss.*

Sven Allard, a perspicacious Swedish diplomat who had keenly followed Soviet policies in Central Europe, describes how during this delicate period Bruno Kreisky, the main influence on foreign policy among Austrian Social Democrats even before he joined the Federal Government in 1953, impressed Soviet diplomats with his ideas on solving this problem: Austria should simply adopt a form of neutrality modeled on the Swiss example.[6]

When the four most important members of the Austrian Government—Chancellor Raab, Vice-Chancellor Schärf, Foreign Minister Figl, and Secretary of State Kreisky—traveled to Moscow in the spring of 1955 to discuss the State Treaty with Khrushchev and a still hesitating Molotov, their offer to adopt permanent neutrality on the model of Switzerland provided the basis for an agreement to which the Western allies later acceded.

John Foster Dulles, Harold Macmillan, Vyacheslav Molotov, and Antoine Pinay signed the State Treaty in Vienna on May 15, 1955. The result of nearly ten years of arduous negotiations, it reestablished Austria as a "sovereign, independent, and democratic state" within its prewar frontiers. But the Treaty not only restored Austria's political sovereignty with special safeguards against a renewal of *Anschluss;* it also gave Austria full control over its economic resources, including the oilfields and industries that—

claimed by the Soviet Union as German property—had been the subject of much controversy.

On October 26, 1955, one day after all occupying forces had evacuated Austrian territory, the Austrian parliament adopted a constitutional law declaring "on its own free will . . . for the purposes of the permanent maintenance of its external independence and for the purpose of the inviolability of its territory" the permanent neutrality of Austria, which it would be resolved "to maintain and defend . . . with all means at its disposal."[7]

The conclusion of the State Treaty and the subsequent adoption of a status of permanent neutrality were the successful end of the first phase of a new Austrian foreign policy. As Austria launched into a new era of independence, it was entering largely unchartered territory. There was little tradition its foreign policy could rely on. Years of occupation and limited sovereignty had deprived it of the experience other countries had been able to acquire in the changed international environment after 1945. Some early points of reference were offered by modeling Austrian neutrality on that of Switzerland. Another model was provided by the practice of Sweden, a country exercising strong influence on postwar Austria for reasons transcending foreign policy. Austrian foreign policy was thus oriented toward full participation in international affairs. The politics of permanent neutrality were not conceived as a formula for abstention (*Stillesitzen*) but rather as a positive contribution to world affairs.

AUSTRIAN FOREIGN POLICY
IN THE EUROPEAN CONTEXT

Permanent neutrality as practiced in the European context can usually be related to the need to maintain certain regional patterns of equilibrium. Whereas, historically, equilibrium between France and Germany was at the root of Swiss neutrality, the parallel policies of Austria bear a direct relation to the European balance between the Eastern and Western democracies. Within these parameters Austria was forced to develop imaginative new concepts in foreign policy, aware that a strong and independent country had become one of the essential elements for stability and détente in Europe as a whole.

One well-remembered lesson of Austria's interwar history was that independence would remain an elusive goal if not built on solid economic foundations. It seemed imperative, therefore, to create firm and productive links with the new patterns of Western European economic and political cooperation that emerged after the war. A first step in that direction was made as early as 1947, when Austria decided to participate in the European

Recovery Program, the multilateral framework for maximizing the benefits of the Marshall Plan for the economies of Western Europe. Austria thus became one of the founding members of the Organization for European Economic Cooperation (OEEC), which for many years remained the main forum for Western European economic integration.

An adequate formula for Austrian participation in the process of Western European economic integration became one of the main problems of Austrian foreign policy after 1955. The importance of this problem was heightened by the fact that the political divisions of Europe after 1945 had given a new direction to Austria's foreign economic policy, which until 1938 had relied strongly on exchanges with its Eastern European neighbors. Integration of these countries into the Soviet economic orbit reversed patterns of trade that had existed over centuries and forced Austria to seek increased economic ties in Western Europe and other parts of the world.

The main challenge that Austria faced was the creation, in 1958, of the European Economic Community. The fact that a large proportion of Austria's trade was directed toward the six original members of the Community suggested close relationships with the new entity. But like the other neutral countries of Europe, Austria found it impossible to abandon part of its economic sovereignty to a supranational body. Although few of the chartered aims of EEC seemed to be totally incompatible with the demands of permanent neutrality, the proposed transfer of parts of the economic sovereignty of EEC members to a supranational commission was incompatible; full compliance with rules of neutrality requires free exercise of sovereignty.

Austria, like Sweden and Switzerland, therefore had to renounce the idea of acquiring membership in the EEC. Even as this possibility was excluded, Austria took a full part in other efforts to promote the cause of European economic integration. After the failure of efforts to create an all-European trade zone including all members of OEEC, Austria became a founding member of the European Free Trade Association (EFTA), whose establishment Britain had suggested to provide a first bridge to the new Community in Brussels.

During the 1960s much energy was spent on efforts to find a closer relationship with the EEC. These efforts became more urgent when Britain finally decided to abandon EFTA and seek full membership in the EEC. Although there were some hopes that Austria might gain separate access to the EEC, it soon became apparent that its problem could only be solved in the wider context of the relations of Britain and others to the EEC. Such a prospect appeared in 1969, when at The Hague meeting of heads of state and governments of the EEC, not least due to the influence of the new German government of Willy Brandt, a general formula toward opening the Community was found.

The signing by Chancellor Kreisky of a free trade agreement between Austria and the EEC in Brussels in July 1972 concluded the first chapter in Austria's relations with the EEC. It not only provided Austria with access to the growing markets of the EEC but also allowed it to profit more strongly from the dynamics of European economic cooperation. The Brussels agreement was not an end to Austria's efforts to widen and increase economic cooperation with its partners in the West, which also include the industrial democracies in North America and the Pacific region. On the one hand, Austrian foreign policy continued to focus on ways and means to strengthen ties with the countries of the European Communities. EFTA, in continued operation after the concurrent conclusion of free trade agreements between its members and the Communities, has remained an important instrument in this regard. In order to highlight EFTA's role, Austrian Chancellor Kreisky called a meeting of heads of government of EFTA countries, which met in Vienna in May 1977 to promote closer economic cooperation in Europe. Austria took a leading role in EFTA in order to increase its role as a bridge to those European countries that remained outside EFTA and the Communities, such as Spain and Yugoslavia. Austrian foreign policy has also increasingly turned to the Organization for Economic Cooperation and Development (OECD), the geographically widened successor organization to OEEC, so as to strengthen economic cooperation between all members of the family of Western industrialized countries.

Membership in OECD has given Austria an opportunity to cooperate with its Western partners in new areas. One of these is the wide field of development politics and the approach of the Western community to the North-South Dialogue. An area of even greater importance is the cooperation of industrialized democracies in the field of energy.

AUSTRIA IN THE INTERNATIONAL ENERGY AGENCY

The first energy crisis of 1973–1974 underlined the interdependence of the Western economies and demonstrated the extent to which the smooth functioning of the world economy depends upon regular energy supplies. It also made clear that the energy problem could not be solved by national policies alone, and that energy problems were indeed closely linked to policies of a more broadly political nature.

Although the industrialized countries were inadequately prepared to cope with the crisis in a coordinated manner, the basic similarity of their interests was always apparent. Thus initiatives were taken—and supported by Austria—to establish a new foundation for energy cooperation within the Western world. These negotiations resulted in an explicit and detailed agreement on an International Energy Program, which was signed by 16 member countries of the OECD on November 18, 1974. The scope of the agreement is ambitious; it covers every major energy policy issue. The objectives of the program seek to provide assurances against the disruptive effects of oil emergencies; these involve a greater independence from imported oil, the broadening of cooperative relations among the participating countries and between other producing and consuming countries, and the establishment of an international system to make available more information and greater predictability regarding oil market developments.

In deciding to join the International Energy Agency Austria carefully weighed its needs as an oil-importing country against certain demands of a policy of permanent neutrality. Although expressing willingness to fully exploit possibilities of international energy cooperation with its partners in the Agency, Austria made it equally clear that it did not perceive the new organization as a vehicle for confronting oil-exporting developing countries, with many of whom Austria had long maintained close and friendly relations.

Thus Austria continued to call for a more open and understanding attitude toward the needs of oil-producing developing countries, for many of whom oil remains the only means of promoting their economic and social welfare. It insisted on the urgent need of continuing dialogue with those countries, expressing willingness to discuss such problems as are of interest to industrialized countries (such as supply and price of energy) and the larger questions of structural change in the world economy that developing countries postulate.

AUSTRIA AND THE COUNCIL OF EUROPE

Early in 1956 Austria—preceding Switzerland in this move—became a full member of the Council of Europe, having enjoyed observer status in this important institution even before the conclusion of the State Treaty. Austria has found the Council a particularly attractive forum for cooperating with other pluralistic democracies, not only because of its original organizational structure, which allows full participation of governments and parliaments, but also because few other institutions created in postwar Europe have so successfully upheld the basic values on which contemporary Western societies are built. Thus the most advanced mechanisms to defend human rights were developed by the Strasbourg Conventions and Tribunals, forcing member governments in many instances to change their policies and legislation.

It was in the Council of Europe that Austria joined European democracies in urging a return to representative government in Greece after that country had fallen under the rule of a fascist junta. The Council of Europe allowed Austria to contribute to the strengthening of the new democracies that emerged in Spain and Portugal in the second half of the 1970s. The role that the Council of Europe gave to eminent Austrian political leaders is another reflection of the active involvement of Austria in the life of the organization. Thus in 1975 the late Karl Czernetz, one of the most dedicated advocates of West European cooperation, became the first Austrian to preside over the Parliamentary Assembly of the Council. In 1979 Franz Karasek was elected Secretary General of the Council, following Lujo Toncic-Sorinj, who had a few years earlier been the first Austrian to hold this high European post.

AUSTRIA AND ITS NEIGHBORS TO THE EAST

While developing links with Western Europe and the industrialized democracies in the world at large, Austria pioneered an active policy to normalize relations with its neighbors to the east, with many of whom it had shared centuries of history. This policy, the principal architect of which became Foreign Minister Bruno Kreisky after 1959, bore rich fruit and was, after an initial spell of skepticism, quickly imitated by many other Western countries. Although the pace of normalization was quicker in some cases, such as Poland, Romania, and Bulgaria, than in others, it was slowed—not least by the magnitude of problems to be settled—in the case of Czechoslovakia, where complete normalization was only achieved toward the end of the 1970s.

The success of a policy of neighborliness with states operating under different social systems is perhaps best exemplified by current relations between Austria and Hungary. These relations, characterized by a policy of open borders and frequent informal meetings between the leaders of both countries, bear close resemblance to the association that linked Austria and Hungary during a common past of many centuries. At the same time Austria remained careful to keep relations with the USSR on a high and productive level, maintaining a regular pattern of visits and agreements to keep up momentum.

Much of the health of Austria's relations with its Eastern neighbors is built on successful development of trade and economic interaction. Foreign trade, viewed as a whole, is important to the economy. In 1977 exports amounted to 20 percent and imports to 30 percent of Austria's gross national product. The East holds a substantial part of total Austrian trade.

In the 1970s Austria has pioneered new forms of East-West economic cooperation in the field of energy. Austria was one of the first countries to realize that energy resources of the USSR and other Eastern European countries, Poland in particular, represented new possibilities for meeting unfulfilled demand in the Western countries. However, as the Eastern countries moved toward greater dependence on oil and gas, there appeared greater need for investment and technology for exporting their resources.

As the UN Economic Commission for Europe has found,[8] East-West energy cooperation was initiated by the signing of the USSR/Austria gas pipe agreement in June 1968. This agreement provided for the delivery of Soviet natural gas in return for delivery of Austrian pipe. Later, increased deliveries of pipe were supplemented by further deliveries of Soviet gas, electric power, oil, and uranium.

AUSTRIA AND THE EUROPEAN SECURITY CONFERENCE

Devoted to a policy of reducing tensions and strengthening international foundations of peace and security in Europe and the world, Austria became an early supporter of the idea of holding a conference on security and cooperation in Europe. In July 1970, in a memorandum transmitted to members of NATO and the Warsaw Pact, Austria developed its own ideas concerning the conference, which was to be concluded by the adoption of a Final Act in Helsinki on August 1, 1975.[9]

Although the states have developed different types of approaches in implementing the various parts of the Final Act, the Austrian government has repeatedly pointed to the fact that the document provides signatory states with a moral and legal mandate to invoke the Helsinki Act in their relations with other states without fearing accusations of interference in the domestic affairs of others. The most significant advance the Helsinki Act contains is perhaps the fact that it gives an international character to the issue of human rights.

Austria has insisted on the fact that a process of détente such as that emanating from the conference in Helsinki can endure only if similar advances are made in disarmament and arms control. Although the original Austrian suggestions to discuss issues of disarmament in the Helsinki framework were not generally accepted, Austria has never ceased to urge the USA and the USSR to strengthen the arms control system that originated from SALT I and that should now be carried into a second and third strategic armaments agreement. Similarly, Austria has exercised constructive pressure on the talks on troop reduction in Central Europe, which have been held in Vienna for the last few years. It has thus continued active involvement in questions of European security through the Helsinki follow-up process, whose first stage was the meeting in Belgrade late in 1977.

Austria again presented proposals directed specifically to the strengthening of economic cooperation between East and West. Although the Belgrade meeting ended without new agreements, the role of Austria, which was trying actively—without departing from its fundamental basis as a Western democracy—to moderate differences between different perceptions, was highly appreciated.

AUSTRIA AND HUMAN RIGHTS

Confronted with the human rights policies of its Eastern neighbors, which tended all too frequently to discard hopeful beginnings of liberalization, Austria has consistently urged acceptance of the norms of conduct contained in the Helsinki Acts. The promotion of human rights and fundamental freedoms was even more clearly identified as one of the central motivating forces of Austrian foreign policy when Willibald Pahr, an eminent constitutional lawyer, succeeded Erich Bielka as Austrian Foreign Minister in 1976.

Austrian foreign policy has always considered the issue of human rights as one and indivisible. Thus Austria frequently added its voice to those that condemned the abject violation of human rights and fundamental freedoms through the system of apartheid practiced in South Africa and other forms of racism. Nor did Austria remain insensitive to violations of human rights that occurred in Chile after the coup against President Salvador Allende, or in Uganda under the rule of dictator Idi Amin.

When, on the other hand, extremist forces in the United Nations tried to label Zionism a form of racism, Austria reacted with deep moral indignation and did not hesitate to vote against Resolution 3379 of the Thirtieth General Assembly in 1975. Austria has remained no less determined to defend, over the years, another primary principle of its foreign policy, the maintenance of Austria as a haven for refugees from countries as widely separated as those of Eastern Europe, Chile, Uganda, and Vietnam. This traditional policy has also enabled Soviet Jews to find a gateway to new homes in Israel or other parts of the world.

AUSTRIA ON THE WORLD POLITICAL SCENE

Liberated by the conclusion of the State Treaty from the somewhat unidimensional scope of its foreign policy, Austria hastened to join the United Nations: as early as December 14, 1955, the Tenth General Assembly of the United Nations admitted Austria to membership, where it joined other neutrals like Finland and Sweden. Contrary to fears of the authors of the Charter, a system of collective security and the modern concept of neutrality, as practiced by Austria and other European states, have developed a great identity of purpose. From an early moment in the history of the United Nations, neutral nations have been called upon to perform important services within the United Nations.

Not only have secretaries general been drawn from Sweden and Austria, but, increasingly, neutral nations have begun to perform indispensable functions, particularly in the framework of peace-keeping operations in the United Nations, in various negotiating processes, and in many other aspects of its political work. The first instance in which Austria made use of the possibilities of the United Nations was its conflict with Italy over the fate of Austria's minority in the South Tyrol. When it became evident that Italy remained unwilling to enter into genuine bilateral negotiations on implementation of the 1946 Gruber–De Gasperi Agreement, which had promised full autonomy to the German-speaking inhabitants of the South Tyrol, Austria did not hesitate to take the conflict to the United Nations. Despite marked reluctance of Italy's Western allies to expose Rome to this type of pressure and despite a similar lack of enthusiasm on the part of the Soviet Union and its Eastern European clients, Austria, largely owing to Third World support, won its case. On the basis of General Assembly resolutions adopted in 1960 and 1961, a genuine process of negotiation was able to start. Although most of the 1960s were spent in Austro-Italian negotiations and autonomy was granted only after much confrontation and recrimination— at one point in 1967, Italy even blocked Austria's negotiations with the EEC to exert additional pressure—the influence of the United Nations remained decisive in tipping the scales in favor of Austria and its minority in the South Tyrol.

Pursuing a policy of providing services to the United Nations, Austria offered Vienna as headquarters for important UN agencies. As early as 1957 the newly created International Atomic Energy Agency (IAEA) was established in Vienna. A few years later the United Nations Industrial Development Agency followed.

To an increasing degree Vienna became the site of important UN conferences, the last one to date being the 1979 Conference on Science and Technology for Development, which concluded a series of large international meetings on development issues that had been held over a full decade in locations as varied as Stockholm, Bucharest, Nairobi, Vancouver, Mar del Plata, Mexico, Lima, and Manila. But membership in the United Nations also enabled Austria to reenter—albeit in a modest way—the arena of world politics from which old Austria had been evicted and in which the First Austrian Republic never won entry. Austria's willingness to accept some measure of world responsibility soon became visible through the ability of the country to adopt a clear and unequivocal position on most issues brought before the United Nations. Contrary to a widely shared belief that it would be the height of wisdom for neutral countries to follow a path of abstention and thus avoid painful choices in votes in the General Assembly, the record shows that Austria rarely hesitated to take a clear stand.[10]

Emboldened by this experience, Austria as early as 1970 sought membership in the most important political organ of the United Nations, the Security Council. This step led to a certain amount of domestic debate on whether the policies of permanent neutrality would enable Austria to play its role in this body, but practical experience justified the move. While Austria occupied its seat in the Council, two severe crises faced the world community: the 1973 Israeli-Arab war and the 1974 Cyprus crisis. In both instances Austria proved its ability to contribute to the restoration of peace, to the search for peaceful solution of conflicts.

The record of Austria's achievements as a member of the Security Council proved another point that was frequently raised: these policies led to a number of diplomatic exchanges (such as efforts to swing Austria's vote in one direction or another), but they were generally well understood and did not create problems in its relations with other member states of the world organization. Thus, far from having a negative effect, on many occasions they enhanced Austria's standing in the international community and gave Austria a clear and visible profile. It was not least on the basis of these achievements that the organization increasingly called on Austria to perform services for maintenance of peace. Thus Austrian peace-keeping forces were called upon to serve first in Cyprus and later in the Israeli-Syrian disengagement area on the Golan Heights. The appointment of Austria's UN Ambassador and former Foreign Minister Kurt Waldheim as successor to U Thant as Secretary General of the United Nations is another telling example of the high esteem in which the principled and reliable foreign policy of Austria is held in today's world.

Active participation in the work of the United Nations has also led Austria to confront a problem to which its foreign policy had so far paid little attention: the whole range of disarmament questions. Although Austrian contributions to the international debate on disarmament did not acquire any degree of notability for a number of years, the special session of the General Assembly on disarmament held in the spring of 1978 saw a new Austrian awareness of this problem. Proposals submitted by Austria included ideas on strengthening the process of verification of disarmament measures and suggestions toward the total demilitarization of Outer Space.

Another new dimension of Austrian foreign policy was offered by its accepting responsibility for the overall aid effort of the developed world: while still limited in scope, Austria's aid policies reflect a new awareness of

world responsibilities. This awareness is also reflected in the strong contribution that Austria's Chancellor Kreisky has made on many occasions to
the North-South dialogue. Speaking to the 1979 General Assembly of the
United Nations, Chancellor Kreisky called for a "grand design" based on
strong feelings of responsibility and international solidarity.[11] Kreisky expressed the view that "economic and political cooperation is only possible
if the industrialized states are able, through large-scale, joint actions, to
assist in building up the infrastructure of the developing states—and what
we mean here is infrastructure ranging from the building of a subcontinental
system to the development of telecommunication."[12]

In advocating these policies, Austria is assuming a new role in world
politics. Remaining independent of large political, military, and economic
interest groups, Austria has acquired a new moral prestige that it never
possessed in previous incarnations.

AUSTRIA AND THE THIRD WORLD

At an early point, Austrian foreign policy had to react to the change in the
world's political geography brought about by the anticolonial revolution of
the 1950s and 1960s. Even less than in other fields could Austrian foreign
policy rely on historical precedent when forging relations with emerging
Third World nations. The Habsburg monarchy had shown little interest in
extra-European affairs and had always centered its foreign policy on Central
and Southeast Europe and—as far as concerned Turkey—parts of the Middle East.

Thus, in the early 1960s the first Austrian diplomats set up missions in
many of the new countries of Africa and Asia (completing a spotty network
of embassies that had already existed in some of the larger and traditionally
important Third World countries such as India and Brazil). Contrary to an
idea often expressed, Austrian political and economic penetration of these
countries was not always favored by the fact that Austria had rarely possessed colonies overseas or that it was a country committed to a policy of
perpetual neutrality: Austrian efforts to establish closer relations were often
frustrated by the all-pervading influence of former colonial powers, which
continued to exercise strong economic and cultural influence, as well as by
lack of experience in dealing with non-European nations.

Today, half of Austria's 90 world-wide diplomatic, cultural, and consular
missions, not counting specialized missions to multilateral institutions, are
maintained in countries of Africa, Asia, and Latin America. But there is no
doubt that Austria is still behind other industrialized countries in developing its relations with the Third World. Whereas, for example, 15 percent

of Switzerland's trade and 14 percent of Sweden's trade are conducted with developing countries, the share of Third World countries in Austria's foreign trade is only 9 percent.

Wanting to strengthen relations with the main political groups of developing countries, Austria pioneered a new status for itself and like-minded European countries in nonaligned conferences. The Third Conference of Heads of State and Governments of Nonaligned Countries, held in Lusaka in 1970, gave Austria and Finland guest status, allowing Austria to attend all nonaligned conferences held since. The fact that Sweden and Switzerland followed Austria's example is another proof of Austria's ability to develop an original foreign policy of its own, which can in turn be imitated by neutrals and countries with similar interests. Over the last decade, Austria not only has strengthened its political and economic relations with the new nations in Africa, Asia, and Latin America, but has developed understanding and sympathy for the great issues confronting these countries. Thus, Austria in the United Nations and elsewhere early became a strong supporter of the principles of self-determination and independence of colonial peoples and territories.

Through Chancellor Bruno Kreisky Austria took an even stronger stand on the issues of the Middle East. Over the past years its foreign policy—motivated by the immense significance of this conflict for world peace—has made a great number of significant contributions to the promotion of peace in this region. Linked by history and geography to the area and its people, Austria was able to develop a particular understanding of the issues, thus creating a special trust between its leaders and many of the leaders of the Middle East. President Nasser of Egypt was one of the first to acknowledge this potential in his meetings with Bruno Kreisky in the early part of the 1960s. His successor, President Sadat, developed an even closer relationship with Chancellor Kreisky, on many occasions seeking his help and advice. Strongly impressed by the successful social and economic model that Austria presented to the world, he encouraged an increasing volume of Austro-Egyptian exchange so as to learn from Austria's experience.

The strong exposure to Middle Eastern issues through membership in the Security Council gave Austria renewed opportunities to address this question in a constructive way. Thus, in the last major Security Council debate preceding the Yom Kippur war, Austria suggested that the parties, in order to gradually build confidence, adopt a calendar of operations to implement Resolution 242 of the Security Council.

After the 1973 war and the energy crisis had sharpened Western awareness of the need to promote peace in the region, Chancellor Kreisky accepted a mandate from the Socialist International to lead a representative fact-finding mission to the Arab world. These and other experiences generated Austria's conviction that peace in the area was intimately linked to the problem of the Palestinian people. Recognition of the importance of this problem has led Austrian foreign policy to participate actively in efforts to bring the Palestinian question closer to solution. An important element of this policy was to persuade Palestinian leaders to abandon violence and terrorism to achieve their political aims and to embark on a policy of negotiations. By receiving the chairman of the PLO, Yassir Arafat, in Vienna, Chancellor Kreisky demonstrated the value of direct contacts with the Palestinians, thus encouraging other Western governments to do the same and draw the PLO and its leaders into a continuous process of negotiation.

In the latter part of 1979, Chancellor Kreisky took another important initiative by proposing a well-constructed plan for negotiations between Israel and the Palestinians to the UN General Assembly. His plea for negotiations proceeded from recognition that the PLO now represented the Palestinians to a degree that made it the only partner carrying enough international weight to sustain direct negotiations with Israel. Drawing on long experience as an international negotiator, he knew that the discussions would have to proceed in stages and that a phase of exploratory talks would have to precede broader negotiations of the type envisaged in Geneva after the end of the Yom Kippur war. Even in the exploratory stage, certain basic requirements would be needed, such as mutual recognition of the national rights of Israelis and Palestinians, and acknowledgment by both sides that the existence of the other had become a reality. But concessions on other important points of principle, such as acceptance of the idea of a separate Palestinian state might not be necessary to set in motion the kind of dialogue in which the whole range of Israeli-Palestinian questions might be addressed.

The clear and forceful exposition of new avenues to peace in the Middle East has helped to enhance the profile of Austrian foreign policy in the contemporary world. The impact of Austrian participation in these efforts is further heightened by awareness that Austria has remained extremely careful in selecting areas of world policy for its contributions.

Austria can be counted upon to adopt clear attitudes on important issues of the day that contain significant elements of principle. Thus Austria has never remained silent over violations of sovereignty of small countries by bigger powers, such as in the case of the invasion of Afghanistan by the Soviet Union, or the cynical disregard of international law, such as became manifest in the taking of hostages in the American embassy in Teheran. But at the same time Austria has always resisted the temptation to sit in judg-

ment on others or to develop solutions to every crisis. Austria thus continues to heed the warning uttered by Max Petitpierre, for many years
Switzerland's Minister of Foreign Affairs:

> Small states must be able to resist the temptation to assume parts transcending the limits
> of their material resources. This does not mean that they are devoid of responsibility,
> that they have to abandon all forms of international cooperation, and that they have to
> remain passive. On the contrary; while I am convinced that wisdom and prudence would
> urge them to exercise restraint in big political conflicts in which they would try vainly
> to be heard, it would, on the other hand, be their obligation—by their own initiative or
> if so requested—to render services and accept duties conducive to the promotion and
> maintenance of peace.

AUSTRIAN FOREIGN POLICY:
THE NEW DOMESTIC BASE

Much of the success of the foreign policy of the Second Austrian Republic
can be related to a fundamentally changed domestic climate. The broad
national consensus that developed after 1945 was one of the main bases on
which Austria could fight for reestablishment of sovereignty and independence. In the years following the conclusion of the State Treaty, Austrian
foreign policy remained based on the social values to which the overwhelming majority of the Austrian people continued to adhere. The basic principles of Austrian foreign policy thus continued to rest on solid consensus.

It would not be true to state that controversy was totally absent from the
day-to-day conduct of foreign policy in the Second Republic. Such controversies occurred in both forms of government that characterized postwar
Austria: Grand Coalition government and government by one party. This
was especially true when innovative policies were introduced, such as Foreign Minister Kreisky's policy of normalization to the East in the 1960s as
well as the economically painful decision to remain outside the European
Economic Community in 1958. Nor was criticism absent from some Austrian policies in the United Nations, which were hotly debated domestically
although they won Austria increased credit and little criticism abroad.
None of this controversy, however, extended to the fundamental direction
of Austria's foreign policy, regardless of claims on the existence or nonexis-
tence of a "common foreign policy." Some questions may arise, however,
about the place of foreign policy in public debate and the involvement of
wider groups of decision makers in shaping foreign policy. A study conducted by Malcolm G. Koch in the early 1970s presents as a central
hypothesis that "only a small number of the elite have a deep, detailed
knowledge of foreign affairs, and foreign policy decision-making is concentrated in their hands."[13] The creation in 1976 of a Foreign Policy Council

(Aussenpolitischer Rat) is one obvious answer to this dilemma.[14] The questions of stronger involvement of the public at large, as well as of specific interest groups remains, however, in all its acuteness.

AUSTRIAN FOREIGN POLICY IN THE 1980'S AND BEYOND: A RELIABLE PATTERN OF STABILITY AND INDEPENDENCE

The foreign policy conducted by Austria over the past 25 years has given the country a degree of stability and security unparalleled in previous periods of its existence in this century. Although this remarkable result is linked to the absence of major, global international conflicts, especially wars, in the second half of the century, it owes as much to Austria's successful effort to steer, for the first time since 1918, an independent course in foreign policy.

Indeed, the major achievement of this new foreign policy is perhaps the fact that Austria today appears to be one of the few countries in the world that has no conflict with any other nation. Removed by its status of neutrality from the East-West conflict (at least in its military and some political aspects), Austria has succeeded in solving all major bilateral problems with its neighbors. Most of these problems Austria inherited from its multinational past, such as the protection of an Austrian minority in Italy and the status of a Slovene minority in Austria.

Austria's new ability to solve conflicts and avoid being drawn into new ones, of course, does not owe everything to the policies of neutrality. It was to an equal degree made possible by the strength and determination of a country that had gained new self-respect and a new sense of identity.

Another major achievement of Austrian foreign policy is the fact that now, for the first time in its history, Austria has achieved a global economic and cultural presence; this was possible through use of the wide network of international organizations created after World War II as well as through a policy of establishing contact with a growing number of countries on all continents. On the basis of these achievements, Austria has played an international role similar to the one played by Switzerland alone for many decades and, indeed, centuries.

It is the view of Austria that today permanent neutrality can serve the international community well, since neutrality essentially aims at preventing proliferation of war. Also, the functions of neutrality have become much wider today and more universally recognized. The traditional concept of neutrality applied exclusively to the case of war, and was therefore limited in time, space, and scope by its very nature. As opposed to this, permanent neutrality, as adopted by Austria, aims at rendering perpetual service to the international community. It is the proclaimed aim of Austria's policy of neutrality to do everything in its power to prevent the widening of conflict, to achieve a greater measure of international cooperation, and thus, in the words of the Charter, "to maintain international peace and security."

The rise of Vienna as a major new center for international organizations of the UN system (and others such as OPEC and IASA*) and as a site for major international encounters, such as those involving the leaders of the USA and the USSR, is a symbol of this new role. Similarly, the election of Austrians to high international office and the trust placed by nations of strife-ridden regions in the abilities of Austrian statesmen such as Bruno Kreisky to play a moderating role are another indication of the new place of Austria in world affairs.

This has been well understood by contemporary statesmen like Henry Kissinger, who credits Austria's Chancellor with having "parlayed his country's formal neutrality into a position of influence beyond its strength, often by interpreting the motives of competing countries to each other." Kissinger credits Kreisky with "far more geopolitical insight than many leaders from more powerful countries." And he thus regrets the "asymmetries of history" and the resulting "lack of correspondence between abilities of some leaders and the power of their countries."[15]

The success of Austria's foreign policies is therefore strongly linked to its ability to render service and put its potential for moderation and conflict-solving at the disposal of the international community. However, Austrian foreign policy will need much further effort. For one, its efficiency could be enhanced by strengthening the material base on which it operates: whereas Austrian foreign ministers have been used to operating on a tight budget, this constraint sometimes defeats the purposes of good foreign policy. Another imperative is the strengthening of Austria's development aid effort. Although progress was made in the 1970s, Austria has still not reached the impressive aid and cooperation record of some of the smaller industrialized democracies, such as the majority of Scandinavian countries and the Netherlands.

In the 1980s Austria will have to develop new and imaginative policies to cope with qualitative and quantitative changes in the European communities, and it will have to make major contributions to the shaping of a new international economic order, giving the economic effort of developing and developed countries an equal chance. Large as some of the new challenges for Austrian foreign policy may appear, Austria will have to remain within

*IASA stands for International Institute for Applied Systems Analysis. See also the chapter by Gottfried Heindl in this volume.

the basic parameters of its course. Although this course may, on occasion, appear to be unspectacular and even infertile, its long-range gains in stability and respect for Austria's independence will be considerable.

Notes

1. Moscow Declaration, Department of State *Bulletin*, vol. IX (1943), No. 228.
2. Fritz Fellner, "Die aussenpolitische und völkerrechtliche Situation Österreichs, 1938: Österreichs Wiederherstellung als Kriegsziel der Alliierten," in *Österreich: Die Zweite Republik* (Graz, 1972), p. 89.
3. In *Festschrift für Karl Waldbrunner* (Wien, 1971, p. 48), Walter Wodak describes the tenacious efforts of Austria's first postwar envoy to Moscow to secure release of Austrian prisoners of war from Soviet camps.
4. Gerald Stourzh, *Kleine Geschichte des Österreichischen Staatsvertrages* (Graz, 1975), pp. 78ff.
5. Address on the occasion of the thirtieth anniversary of Burgenland's return to Austria. Quoted by Bruno Kreisky in *Die Herausforderung* (Düsseldorf, 1963), p. 84.
6. Sven Allard, *Diplomat in Wien* (Cologne, 1965), p. 171.
7. *The Austrian Federal Constitution* (Vienna, 1967), p. 29.
8. Document, UN-ECOSOC/Energy/R.6/Add, Annex I, p. 1, of August 29, 1979.
9. Rudolf Kirchschläger, "Die Aussenpolitik Österreichs," in *Festschrift für Karl Waldbrunner* (Wien, 1971), p. 169.
10. Felix Ermacora, *20 Jahre Österreichische Neutralität* (Frankfurt/Main, 1975), p. 187.
11. Bruno Kreisky, Address to the 34th Session of the General Assembly; Provisional Procès-Verbal A/34/P.V.49 of October 29, 1979, pp. 92ff.
12. *Ibid.*
13. M. Koch, "Contemporary Austrian Foreign Policy. Elite Attitudes Concerning Consensus and Decision-making" (dissertation, Brandeis University, 1973), p. 222.
14. See also the chapter by Heinz Fischer in this volume.
15. Henry Kissinger, *White House Years* (Boston, 1979), p. 1204.

Selected Bibliography

Allard, Sven. *Diplomat in Wien: Erlebnisse, Begegnungen und Gedanken um den österreichischen Staatsvertrag.* Cologne, 1965. English version: *Russia and the Austrian State Treaty: A Case Study of Soviet Policy in Europe.* University Park, Pa., 1970.
Aussenpolitischer Bericht des Bundesministers für Auswärtige Angelegenheiten. Wien. Successive vols.
Austriaca: Cahiers Universitaires d'information sur l'Autriche. Université de Haute Normandie. Centre d'Etudes et de Recherches autrichiennes, Rouen. Successive vols.
Austrian History Yearbook. Rice University, Houston, Texas. Successive vols.
Bridge, F. R. *From Sadowa to Sarajevo: The Foreign Policy of Austria-Hungary, 1866–1914.* London, 1972.
Ermacora, Felix. *20 Jahre Österreichische Neutralität.* Frankfurt/Main, 1975.
Festschrift für Karl Waldbrunner. Wien, 1971.
Jedlicka, Ludwig. *Vom alten zum neuen Österreich: Fallstudien zur Österreichischen Zeitgeschichte, 1900 bis 1975.* St. Pölten, 1977.
Koch, Malcolm. Contemporary Austrian Foreign Policy. Elite Attitudes Concerning Consensus and Decision-making. Dissertation in political science and international relations, Brandeis University, 1973.
Kreisky, Bruno. *L'Autriche entre l'Est et l'Ouest.* Paris, 1979.
———. *Die Herausforderung: Politik an der Schwelle des Atomzeitalters.* Düsseldorf, 1963.
———. *Neutralität und Koexistenz.* Munich, 1975.
Kreissler, Felix. *De la révolution à l'annexion: L'Autriche de 1918 à 1938.* Paris, 1971.
Luža, Radomir. *Austro-German Relations in the Anschluss Era.* Princeton, 1975.

Matzner, Egon. *Trade Between East and West: The Case of Austria.* Stockholm, 1970.
Mayrzedt, Hans, and Hans Christoph Binswanger, eds. *Die Neutralen in der europäischen Integration.* Wien, 1970.
Schärf, Adolf. *Österreichs Erneuerung, 1945 bis 1955: Das erste Jahrzehnt der Zweiten Republik.* Wien, 1955.
Schausberger, Norbert. *Der Griff nach Österreich: Der Anschluss.* Wien, 1978.
Stadler, Karl R. *Hypothek auf die Zukunft: Entstehung der österreichischen Republik.* Wien, 1965. English version: *The Birth of the Austrian Republic, 1918–1921.* Leiden, 1968.
Stearman, William L. *The Soviet Union and the Occupation of Austria.* Bonn, 1961.
Stourzh, Gerald. *Geschichte des Staatsvertrages.* Graz, 1980.
————. *Kleine Geschichte des österreichischen Staatsvertrages.* Graz, 1975.
Strasser, Wolfgang. *Österreich und die Vereinten Nationen. Eine Bestandaufnahme von zehn Jahren Mitgliedschaft.* Wien, 1967.
Verdross, Alfred. *Die immerwährende Neutralität der Republik Österreich.* Wien, 1966.
Weinzierl, Erika, and Kurt Skalnik, eds. *Österreich: Die Zweite Republik.* Graz, 1972.
Wissenschaftliche Kommission des Theodor Körner Stiftungsfonds und des Leopold Kunschak Preises zur Erforschung der österreichischen Geschichte der Jahre 1927 bis 1938. *Österreich, 1927 bis 1938.* Wien, 1973.
Zöllner, Erich, ed. *Diplomatie und Aussenpolitik Österreichs. Elf Beiträge zu ihrer Geschichte.* Wien, 1977.

Modern Austria, pp. 381–91
Copyright © 1981 by SPOSS Inc. All rights reserved

19. DEFENSE POLICY FROM THE AUSTRIAN POINT OF VIEW

Emil Spannocchi

Commander of the Austrian Army

PREMISES

Today's reader is, of course, interested only in the type of defense policy being pursued in present-day Austria. However, this cannot be understood without some background information on its premises and on its more or less logical development up to today. To this end, a brief retrospective and evaluation of this development are indispensable if we are to correctly assess the significance of the defense policy as an essential part of Austria's neutrality policy.

The initiation of a new defense policy, especially after a ten-year abstinence from such activities, was as surprising to Austria as was the State Treaty in 1955, which brought the withdrawal of the four occupying powers and complete national sovereignty. This event had often been discussed and had always been hoped for. But, owing to a certain justifiable skepticism, the consequences of neutrality, now imminent for Austria, had never been seriously deliberated. Thus unexpected perspectives opened up in the area of defense policy, a decisive part of a neutrality policy.

The first obstacle to be overcome was a rather confused psychological start. The victorious powers with their well-publicized "reeducation" had a relatively easy time convincing a people of seven million, who had mourned 470,000 dead and missing in action, that the root of all evil in the world was the military; that, therefore, nothing was more unnecessary and more dangerous for the nation's future than an army. So, during the entire ten years between the end of the war in 1945 and the beginning of sover-

Translated by Ulrike E. Lieder, Stanford University

9306-6403/81/0415-0381$01.50

eignty in 1955, no one really noticed how inconsistent the superpowers themselves were while reeducating Austria—they maintained, enlarged, and even deployed their own large armies, for instance in the Korean conflict. Let the smaller states begin with disarmament; and the Austrians were willing and ready to do so. Now, suddenly, there was a call for "neutrality patterned after Switzerland," as expressly stipulated in the Moscow Memorandum, armed neutrality that, in turn, required a defense policy. This was a surprising turn of events after the above-mentioned psychological preliminaries.

Second, from a historical perspective, the Austrians were not accustomed to defense policy being part of a neutrality policy. Because of its age-old geographical location on the border between Central and Eastern Europe, Austria had always been forced to deal with the current situation of power politics. It did not have any geographical buffer zones or frequently—at least politically speaking—only limited ones. This situation has left its mark on the land as well as the political leadership, but it has not been entirely without success, for otherwise Austria would not exist after more than a thousand years as a borderland, still in the same spot where Charlemagne founded his march, and—moreover—still in the same European camp. Some of its neighbors have not fared as well.

Holding and maintaining its position were generally only possible through defense, using every military strategy. It would never have been possible by merely following the famous motto attributed to Habsburg policies, *Tu felix Austria nube* (Let others wage war; you, fortunate Austria, marry). The West German news magazine *Der Spiegel* was wrong only with respect to motivation when it mockingly wrote, years ago, that Austria was the most militant country in Europe. For example, the country did not have ten years of peace during the 17th century—not because it did not want peace, but because it had no choice. Even the most tired man will not get any sleep at the main entrance to a major railway station.

This, then, shaped not so much knowledge and planning, but rather the feeling, experienced by generations, that for this country a policy aimed at maintaining the state would not be successful without a defense policy. It was an active defense policy, fully utilizing available military potential for war as history dictated, be it offensive or defensive. But a defense policy for the purpose of neutrality, for the purpose of not waging war—that was a surprising, a sensational, concept for the Austrians.

So the inevitable came about in 1955: an army had to be produced out of thin air. But how? No one, not even the political leadership, had really thought about the fact that an army is the instrument of policy, and, therefore, the objectives of policy are decisive to formation of the armed forces, and that policy would have to determine the formation of its instrument. Since this consideration had been neglected, building up the army was begun in every aspect right where it had stopped as a constituent part of the Hitler state. The same political concepts were used for defense policy, as well as the same structures—even the existing military leadership, since it was available. The hierarchical structures, natural to the military profession, had been destroyed by the end of the war, and the following ten years without an army had done their part to scatter them to the four winds of all professions. So the country had to take those former career officers whom it could find and who were available. Of course, these officers had been molded in the German Wehrmacht, and they picked up where they had left off in 1945 in ideas, military concepts, and behavior. That was at a relatively low level, because they had not advanced much beyond the rank of battalion commander or very young general staff officers. In fact, the text of the State Treaty forbade commissioning officers of Austrian origin who had served as generals and colonels in German uniform during World War II—one entire generation of military leaders.

So the first model of a new Austrian army was not structured according to the demands of future neutrality; rather, it was constructed according to theories derived from the memories of military leaders trained for entirely different tasks. It was a miniature reproduction of a great power's army, but considerably smaller, with antiquated equipment and a shorter training period.

A GAP IN LOGIC—A PAUSE FOR INSPIRATION

At first, no one noticed this from the point of view of theory, at least not in Austria. However, the maneuvers of this new army soon brought fear to the hearts of the military and the political leadership, as well as meeting with disbelief and lack of understanding among the people. It was simply incredible to attempt to prepare for a defensive war with less money, less technology, and a shorter period of service. The uneasiness grew in proportion to the output of inadequately trained young soldiers, the unsatisfactory results of which became the increasingly more credible argument of pacifist opponents of the army. These opponents, proceeding from the attitude that armament even for the purpose of defense is reprehensible, could now sow the seeds of insecurity over the entire political landscape by using the argument of frustrated draftees.

This situation was further aggravated by the unfortunate effect on other countries of Austria's glaring lack of defense against a crisis of even reasonable proportions. Austria itself was at least partly to blame for this defenselessness, which had caused uneasiness among the powers that had signed the State Treaty, owing to its voluntarily entered obligation to remain neutral. They had sought to avoid this very thing: that the military vacuum would provoke an opposing superpower to create a military *fait accompli* on every possible occasion.

It was to the joint interest of the great powers to create stability in this sensitive area along the line of demarcation between East and West; and it had been precisely this consensus of interest that made the State Treaty possible at all. With sovereignty now regained, Austria's most pressing obligation was to maintain this stability. Of course, it requires a functional army to accomplish such a task, with its limited challenge.

It is a fact (a fact, incidentally, of a military bias that Austria must deal with) that the great powers and the readers of their newspapers often have schizophrenic ideas about the defense efforts of small states. In an emotional "all or nothing" attitude, they expect little of the small state's armament, which is not particularly impressive in comparison with their own. On the other hand, they expect the small state to make a positive contribution to the maintenance of peace by all means, even military. This attitude of all or nothing is politically unrealistic, especially in defense politics. Therefore, Austria had to see what was useful and do what was possible.

A brief outline of the strategic position of the country must accompany presentation of the tasks faced by Austria's defense policy, in order to demonstrate what the country, as a neutral state, has to deal with and what is impossible. Henry Kissinger's statement, which said, in essence, that strategy is the utilization of all military and nonmilitary means available to the state in order to attain a political objective, might serve as a useful reminder here. For Austria, this means to avoid doing anything to provoke the world around it to war, and to do everything to keep that same world, or parts thereof, from waging war against Austria or through Austrian territory.

To make this rather general concept more specific, we proceed on the assumption that it is in the interest of the East-West pact systems to respect peace in this country even if they are engaged in all-out or partial conflicts. If this were different, the decision to grant Austria the State Treaty and to stipulate its neutrality would have been absurd. If that assumption is correct, Austria does not need to prepare for defense against a nuclear war, something it cannot do anyway; nor does it have to prepare for defense against an attack by one of the great powers, directed solely against the country. There would be no reason for such an attack unless Austria failed to protect her territory equally against all neighbors who may be political or military adversaries.

Austria must not allow military advantage to accrue to any side. In case of conflict, defense policy mandates that this include the task of immediately warding off or ending wanton or negligent misuse of Austrian territory that is to the advantage of one party in the conflict and to the detriment of the other. It is, therefore, not important to prepare for and fight great battles. That would be the end of neutrality, and thus directly against the strategic interests of at least one side in the present political situation in Central Europe. However, if such battles are to be avoided, or prevented, we must discover where they would take place and how they could be prevented. And here, for the sake of clarity and understanding, we should call a spade a spade.

Austria's main problem area, at least from a strategic point of view, is the Danube valley. This valley has always been a strategic East-West corridor and will most likely continue to be. History has many illustrations of its importance: the Nibelungs are said to have marched through it from west to east, Napoleon tried to do the same, and the Turks and Hungarians tried for centuries to do the reverse. These examples reach into modern times, to the actions of the Russians in 1945. NATO and the Warsaw Pact nations know this and must have an interest in having this corridor blocked by Austrian defense preparations, thus rendering it useless for opponents. A second, although not as important, line runs along the south side of the main crest of the Alps from the Hungarian lowlands to northern Italy. In case of conflict, it could be of interest to the Warsaw Pact nations. Therefore, Austria must block it.

And finally—in spite of obvious friendship with the West and belief in Western ideologies—Austria must keep in mind that its western province of Tyrol represents the shortest line of communication between the NATO sectors of Central and Southern Europe. This line of communication is interrupted by neutral Austria, an area only 50 km wide as the crow flies. In case of an East-West conflict, there could be great temptation to avoid logistic detours by simply negotiating this small barrier, albeit in violation of international law. This is not just a nightmare. In 1958, during the so-called Lebanon crisis, one entire US division was airlifted to the Mediterranean area by exactly this route. It saved quite a bit of aircraft fuel but did great political damage, and the memory remains. But with this knowledge Austria can generate better models than those offered by the old cliché. The insights gained, that the country could not withstand a nuclear war or, without assistance, confrontation with a military pact system, and the fact that it is obligated to and capable of precautionary blocking of known passages and controlling its air space by military means—all these define a task whose dimensions can be encompassed.

The task must also be handled by utilizing an effective military instrument. This is the content of the defense policy of a neutral Austria. It would be a destabilizing factor for the political world around it if the military instrument were not effective and if therefore the defense policy as part of the neutrality policy did not exist. But this would also mean that Austria's national policy itself had been pushed into a gray zone of unpredictability, which would necessarily be a destructive development for the state's continued existence.

The general staff of the new army was the first to perceive the need for reorientation. This did not occur without an argument about which direction to take. But this reorientation had already begun during the 1960's, and proceeded from analysis to planning and from planning to a model of new solutions better suited to a defense policy. Responsibility had to be assumed for subsequent reform of the army—or, ultimately, renunciation of an unfit army, and thus for the possibility of pursuing the defense policy for the sake of protecting neutrality.

A NEW MODEL IN THE 1970s

Now, finally, a sober analysis was begun. It was possible to take stock and to see what had failed, as this report roughly outlines. What was it that this army was to achieve? Or, in military terms, what was its mission?

Now for the first time it became clear that the only task in agreement with the political objective was not to wage war but to prevent war; and that, furthermore, the challenge to the country's defense policy would least likely be a test in a possible third world war, an "all-out war." Such a demand exceeds the potential of any small country on its own. Rather the issue was correct behavior within the framework of a crisis management, appropriate for our neutrality, in the wide range between events with ramifications that affect our territory and actual military conflict outside that territory but within our area of political affinity.

In such a conceivable scenario, a sensible defense policy—and that includes using the military instrument—must achieve the following: full protection of borders against negligent or wanton inclusion in military operations, if necessary through the threat or use of force. This would stabilize at least a section of the European political landscape and would make it predictable. This would be the only contribution to maintenance of peace that Austria, in its sensitive location, would make through a defense policy. But this it must do, for the sake of its neutrality policy and in the interest of the European family of nations.

Dealing with aggression against our country comes at the end of the list of efforts. Such a possibility cannot be excluded, but the probability decreases proportionate to the extent to which the probability of Austria's determination to resist increases. Ultimately, others will come to believe that the country not only will defend itself effectively but can defend itself according to its political values. That means that, as an *ultima ratio,* Austria must also be capable of a credible effort in defensive war.

This insight brings us closer to the objectives of planning and the model of implementation. This was the opening move, which will be followed logically by others, according to the laws of reason. What were the results?

THE MODEL OF A NEUTRAL STATE'S ARMY AS AN INSTRUMENT OF DEFENSE POLICY

First, the demands to be made of the political instrument of the army were defined precisely as follows. (1) Effective management of a crisis affecting the area, including the use or threat of military means: political experiences from the years 1956 (uprising in Hungary) and 1968 (CSSR invasion) provide valuable lessons. (2) Protection of borders and of territory in case political conflicts among neighbors escalate into effective military confrontations: Switzerland's behavior during World Wars I and II is the best demonstration of this. And (3), finally, an effective defense if the country should actually be attacked.

This tripartite challenge was the task the military instrument had to be prepared to deal with in the case of crisis, neutrality (see below), and defense, and it was the basis for the formation of a new Austrian army structured in accordance with the specific requirements of a neutral state. The following will briefly elaborate on this.

First, there must be effective crisis management, since crises can occur again and again after relatively short political preliminaries. In such a case, this country believes it can manage by using a relatively small but always available segment of the army called readiness troops (*Bereitschafts-truppe*). These troops must have primarily conventional equipment, be well trained and highly mobile. We believe that 15,000 men, the fighting sections of two divisions, should be sufficient. Their equipment would be largely armored and mechanized, and the soldiers would be volunteers serving longer than the standard six and a half months of basic training. These readiness troops must be supplemented by a fairly small air force whose task would be to safeguard the country's sovereignty in the third dimension, with a sophisticated air control system (air police). This part of the army would not so much be required to prove itself in battle as to see that Austria is given credence with respect to its capability to end negligent or wanton disregard of its neutrality in a crisis.

In the case of neutrality in an ongoing conflict (when we remain neutral, being surrounded by belligerents) Austria's task would not change so much in essence as it would quantitatively. In this situation, pressure on the 2400-km border (1500 miles) would increase, and an available reserve would be needed to withstand it. This reserve could be deployed fully or partially, depending on the actual threat. Here it is useful to remember that, during World War II, Switzerland's stand-by forces did not in all that time have the same strength as before or afterward. Yet it was always able to adjust to the actual danger.

At this point, a word of clarification on the significance of airspace control is in order. Sovereignty is not two-dimensional; it does not stop ten feet above the ground, but includes air space to the extent that is technically acceptable and feasible. Austria must safeguard its rights to an altitude of 65,000 to 80,000 feet. To preserve its rights, protests alone against violations of air space are not sufficient. It is not a question of foolhardy aerial combat —where we would come out the loser—but of claiming our sovereignty at an altitude of 80,000 feet, if need be, by intercepting. The capability is present for electronic spotting, locating, and directing devices. However, the country needs to catch up in the area of interception in order to be able to stop unsurpation and disregard of sovereignty after twenty protests have been filed.

Only in the third situation, which would threaten the existence of the state, that is, in a case of defense against aggression, is it necessary to deploy the entire military potential available. Here, we use a few truisms to clarify our position on defense policy.

Austria cannot play a role in a nuclear war of the magnitude that is technologically possible today. Even the superpowers cannot deal with it except through mutual deterrence. There is no contribution that Austria can make in this situation. It is, therefore, justified in staying out of the affairs of NATO and the Warsaw Pact. Further, Austria does not delude itself that it could achieve any measurable military successes if one of the two military pact forces, between which Austria lies, were to direct its entire military might toward it alone. However, from the point of view of political reason it seems evident that such a situation would be improbable. Why else would these powers have recognized Austria's neutrality? It must have been in the paramount interest of both superpowers, at odds with each other, to whatever degree of intensity.

In this third situation, that of defense, we can proceed, according to the rules of military policy and operative logic, from the following assumption: aggression would be started with limited forces, because a conflict between the pact systems would be of such dimensions that it would not be strategically decided by the gain or loss of Austrian territory. This territory could only be useful to them as a basis of operations against their real enemy and the attacking forces will have the corresponding strength. This consideration is the starting point of our efforts. If our assumption is correct, it will be important for Austria to have so many forces, adequately trained and equipped, deployed in such a fashion that every potential aggressor, after analyzing the cost effectiveness, will reasonably have to conclude that the advantages to be derived from a military attack on Austria are not in proportion to the expenditures such an attack would require. Which brings us back to our basic principle, that of preventing war. This is something which we must be able to achieve, and we believe we can.

INSTRUMENTS AND DOCTRINE

We believe we have learned the following from these theories. (1) This task could be accomplished by an Austrian army of approximately 10,000 men in the air force (surveillance, support operations, transport, and helicopter systems); in conjunction with 15,000 men in always available readiness troops, who serve as volunteers for longer periods of time; with an additional militia, similar to the Swiss model, of approximately 200,000 men. For the case of defense, as well as for the case of a mere crisis, the entire country has been divided into military zones of different degrees of significance. (2) Along the main paths of conceivable operations, geography is a rather reliable indicator of the type of defense required: it shows where to prepare such zones of genuine defense and where to make a military stand by deploying combat units as is done in a partisan war (but, of course, in compliance with the rules of war, in uniform, and with responsible leadership). This division into genuine defense and territorial defense should be realized in such a way that these areas could be subdued only with the utmost effort after penetration by an aggressor. (See the accompanying map.) (3) We assume further that Austria can maintain a base in the alpine central region, which poses great military problems, and that this base will make the survival of the state possible, if not probable, even after aggression.

Austria has already made good progress in the formation of an army. Mobilization today would put more than 160,000 men at its disposal. The possibilities of their deployment have been tested with positive results in medium- and large-scale maneuvers. This has helped demonstrate to other countries how seriously Austria takes its military and political obligations to preserve its neutrality.

Some things (or, if one wants to be critical, many things) still remain to be done to perfect the military instrument. But the new army has already emerged from the old one, we believe in a positive direction, which has also been recognized by the world around us as a genuine result of this pragmatic defense policy, It seemed to us that we could not achieve more up to now, but we have done what was possible.

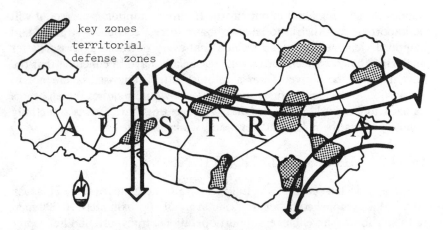

Figure 1 Diagram of the division of the national territory into zones of territorial defense. Key: The *arrows* represent the areas of possible passage, based on the geographical and military situation. The *Key Zones* (shaded areas) are the especially important areas where the defensive battle is carried out, predominantly based on fixed installations. These zones are like plugs, located perpendicular to the direction of possible passage. In the *Territorial Defense Zones* (unshaded areas) Austria's intention is to prevent the invader from freely using the area, primarily by means of partisan combat.

CONCLUDING REMARKS

Austrian neutrality as a predictable factor, and thus a contribution to maintaining peace in the area, can only be effective if Austrians themselves take it seriously. To this end, a small country like Austria must pursue a defense policy. Not only is it unavoidable in a real sense, but it also renders recognizable service to the policy of the great powers in the area. Austria would surely not have received full sovereignty through the State Treaty of 1955 without the pledge to armed neutrality.

Estimating the role of defense policy in relation to overall policy is the responsibility not of the military but of the government. It is understandable, and in many ways legitimate, that there will always be critics at home and abroad who would emphasize different aspects (and, for example, spend more on the instruments of defense policy). Yet this will always hold true: in Austria's democracy, the ultimate decision rests with the political authorities. The military leadership cannot do more and must not do less than consult and implement as optimally as possible the decisions of the political leadership. I have tried to present here the path that these two bodies are following.

Selected Bibliography

Aebi, A. Sicherheitspolitik und Landesverteidigung in der Schweiz und in Österreich. In *Österreichische Militärische Zeitschrift,* Wien, April 1977, pp. 278–87.

Aron, R. *Einführung in die Atomstrategie:Die atlantische Kontroverse.* Köln, 1964.

Bayer, R. Von der Verfassungsverankerung zum Landesverteidigungsplan. In *Österreichische Militärische Zeitschrift,* Wien, April 1976, pp. 316–20.

Beaufre, A. *Totale Kriegskunst im Frieden.* Berlin, 1963.

Brossolet, G. and E. Spannocchi. *Verteidigung ohne Schlacht.* München, 1976.

Chaplin, D. Austria's Defense in Transit. *In Military Review,* Fort Leavenworth, January 1977, pp. 57–64.

Eder, E. Die Rolle des österreichischen Bundesheeres im Rahmen der Strategie. In *Österreichische Militärische Zeitschrift,* Wien, June 1976, pp. 448–50.

Fenkart, E. Austria's Defense. In *Military Review,* Fort Leavenworth, July 1977, p. 111.

Fürlinger, H. and L. Jedlicka, eds. *Unser Heer.* Wien, 1963.

Kahn, H. *On Thermonuclear War.* New York, 1960.

Kahn, H. and B. Bruce-Briggs. *Things to Come: Thinking about the Seventies and Eighties.* New York, 1972.

Kissinger, H. *Kernwaffen und auswärtige Politik.* München, 1959. *Was wird aus der westlichen Allianz.* Wien, 1965.

Korkisch, P. 20 Jahre österreichische Luftstreitkräfte. In *Österreichische Militärische Zeitschrift,* Wien, February 1976, pp. 100–114.

Mao, Tse-Tung. *On Guerilla Warfare.* New York, 1961.

Miksche, F. *Kapitulation ohne Krieg.* Stuttgart, 1965.

Morgenstern, O. *Strategie—Heute.* Frankfurt, 1962.

Ruef, K. *Der Dienst im Bundesheer.* Wien, 1979.

Sokolowskij, W. ed. *Militärstrategie.* Köln, 1969.

Modern Austria, pp. 393–406
Copyright © 1981 by SPOSS Inc. All rights reserved

20. AUSTRIA AND THE WORLD: IMAGE AND IMPACT

Gottfried Heindl

Director for Cultural Affairs, Austrian Federal Theaters

When I took charge of the Austrian Institute in New York in March 1967, for the first time I concerned myself with the questions this contribution is to answer: How well known is Austria in the world? Which achievements of Austrian statesmen, scientists, and artists are known beyond its borders? In short, what is Austria's impact and image?

In order to obtain an answer to these questions, the Austrian Institute sent out a questionnaire to 200 American university professors and students. The most important questions were the following:

1. What comes to your mind first when you think of Austria?
2. What do you consider Austria's most outstanding contribution to Western civilization?
3. Can you name Austrians responsible for such contributions?
4. Can you name an Austrian ruler, statesman, or politician?
5. Can you name an Austrian artist, musician, or writer?
6. Have you read any books by Austrian authors?
7. Can you name an Austrian scholar, scientist, or explorer?
8. Can you name an Austrian product, brand name, or company?

I published an article on the evaluation of the returned questionnaires in the March 23, 1968, issue of the daily *Die Presse,* and would like to excerpt from it a few principal statements that are still of interest today.

The answer to the first question brought the first surprise. One assumes that the name Austria would, above all, evoke association with the concept of music. However, it turned out that the image the persons questioned have of Austria, is, quite literally, an "image"; 178 of the persons polled, i.e. 89 percent, associate the name Austria with countryside and landscape: 93

Translated by Ulrike E. Lieder, Stanford University.

9306-6403/81/0415-0393$01.50

mentioned the beautiful countryside in general, or the mountains and skiing, 58 named Vienna, 14 Salzburg, 10 Innsbruck or the Tyrol.

Of the persons questioned, 150 knew of an Austrian contribution to
Western civilization. The term music was mentioned 114 times, followed,

Figure 1 What comes first to people's minds when they think of Austria: beautiful scenery
(terminal of the Tyrol's Zugspitze cable car).

after a wide gap, by mention of the existence of the Austro-Hunga
monarchy and its achievements (19), psychoanalysis (13), and literary contributions (8).

Corresponding to the answers to question 2, answers to the next question
(Can you name Austrians responsible for such contributions?) gave the
names of composers, for a total of 192 times. The frequency is interesting:
Mozart ranks first with 64 mentions, followed by Johann Strauss with 51
mentions, and Haydn (17), Beethoven (16), Schubert (14), Gustav Mahler
and Richard Strauss (7 each), Brahms (4), Bruckner, Berg and Schönberg
(3 each), Liszt and Webern (2 each).

The fourth question (Can you name an Austrian ruler, statesman, or
politician?) was answered by 119 persons, whose answers can be divided
into four groups: names from the monarchy were mentioned 163 times,
almost four times the number of all other mentions together. Names from
the Second Republic rank second (17), followed by the First Republic (15)
and the Nazi period (10). Again, the frequency of names is interesting: in
the group of personalities from the monarchy, Metternich is first (45),
followed by Maria Theresa (41) and Franz Joseph (33).

Whereas only 119 of the persons interviewed were able to name an
Austrian ruler, statesman, or politician, 141 could name an artist, composer, or writer from Austria. In view of the answers to questions 2 and 3,

Figure 2 Asked for Austrian contributions to Western civilization, most people name music:
the Vienna State Opera (opened in 1869 with Mozart's "Don Giovanni").

Figure 3 When Austrian statesmen are asked for, many people remember Maria Theresa, shown here with her husband, Emperor Franz Stephan. Mother of 16 children, she was the energetic ruler and reformer of the country between 1740 and 1780.

it is not surprising that the composers were again mentioned most often (159 times). Mozart ranks first again (62 mentions), followed by Johann Strauss with 51 mentions; the remaining sequence is approximately the same as the enumeration of the answers to question 3. It is remarkable that composers were mentioned almost twice as often as artists from all other areas combined. The names of writers were listed 61 times, the names of performing artists 14 times, the names of painters 10 times.

Among the writers, Grillparzer ranks first with 26 mentions, followed by Schnitzler (12), Hofmannsthal (6), Musil (4), and Werfel (3). Stifter and

Rosegger were mentioned two times each; Broch, Doderer, Kafka, Rilke, Zweig, and Walther von der Vogelweide once each.

The 14 names of performing artists are exclusively those of contemporary conductors and singers; concentration on one or the other could not be discerned. Among the painters, Kokoschka was mentioned six times, followed by two mentions each of Klimt and Schiele.

Question 6 (Have you read any books by Austrian authors?) was an interesting complement to the question inquiring about Austrian artists: 86 of the persons polled, i.e. 43 percent, answered the question. The frequency of mentions corresponds to that in question 5. Grillparzer again ranks first with 36 mentions, followed by Schnitzler (29), Hoffmannsthal (14), and Stifter (9). Sigmund Freud's works were mentioned seven times, Raimund four times, Kafka, Rilke, Werfel, and Zweig three times each, Musil, Nestroy, and Rosegger twice each, and Altenberg, Doderer, Friedell, Handel-Mazetti, Lernet-Holenia, Alma Mahler-Werfel, Roth, Trakl, and Ziesel once each. There are only two living authors among the writers listed; this fact is all the more remarkable as students of literary history were especially well represented among the persons interviewed.

Only 58 interviewees, 29 percent, were able to answer the question concerning Austrian scientists. Sigmund Freud was mentioned 38 times, followed, after a wide gap, by Gregor Mendel (5), Alfred Adler (3), and Viktor Frankl (2). Ernst Mach, Viktor Kaplan, Ignaz Semmelweis, and Othmar Spann were mentioned once each; the other mentions are the names of Austrian historians. It is remarkable that none of the Austrian Nobel laureates for medicine, physics, and chemistry, many of whom spent the later years of their lives in the United States, were included among the names listed.

Question 8 (Can you name an Austrian product, brand name, or company?) was answered by only 46 subjects, i.e. 23 percent. The answers are quite disappointing with regard to their contents as well. Food items ranging from Sachertorte to Wiener Schnitzel were the largest group, being mentioned 19 times, traditional costumes 11 times, ski equipment ten times, Steyr-Puch three times, and the other answers concern products that are hardly characteristic of Austria.

So much on the evaluation of the questionnaires, on which I then wrote the following summary: "The results of the poll could be summarized in the statement that the interviewed Americans obviously consider Austria a '5M-country: Mountains, Music, Mozart, Metternich, and Maria Theresa.' In fact, the most frequently given answers can easily be condensed in the following image: a piece by Mozart is being played in a hall whose walls are adorned by pictures of Metternich and Maria Theresa, and the beautiful Austrian countryside with its mountains is visible through the open window. A pretty picture, a picture that many a state might envy us, yet a picture not unconditionally satisfying. The incongruity in the knowledge about Austria's past and present is rather depressing . . . The disproportion in information on Austria's artistic substance and the familiarity with its scientific and economic efforts is similarly drastic."

This poll in America brought very typical and generally valid results. During the late 1960s, a polling institute, commissioned by the Austrian trade attaché in Paris, investigated the "Austria image" of one thousand Frenchmen in trade and industry. The evaluation of the poll stated, "The images concentrated . . . unequivocally on history . . . There are almost no concepts of the Austria of the present and of its problems . . . Most persons interviewed did not know what is being manufactured in Austria and had no clear concept of its industrial production."

A report of the Austrian Institute in London, which dates back to the mid-1970s, states, after reference to the decline of foreign language teaching in Great Britain: "In this situation, even intellectuals and experts in the field often do not have the tools to take advantage of Austria's comprehensive scientific literature, of her belles-lettres, her dramas, of primary and secondary historical sources, etc. As the number of persons influencing the formation of public opinion—the 'multipliers'—with a thorough knowledge of Austria is small, it can be assumed that the information on Austria among the general population is correspondingly less than in other Western nations. The exception is, of course, music, and not only Viennese classical music." Later on, the same report states, "It is questionable whether the best way to create an image of present-day Austria in Great Britain is to take the direct route. It seems at times that this route goes by way of Austria's past, which must not be neglected in Great Britain which is so conscious of tradition." The question suggests itself whether Austria is an exception and whether the image that other countries enjoy abroad is more up to date and more influenced by scientific and economic achievements.

In 1968, Manfred Koch published an evaluation of opinion polls taken abroad, entitled "The Image of Germans Abroad" (published by Inter Nationes, Bad Godesberg). For purposes of comparison, the interviewees were also asked what associations were evoked when certain other countries were mentioned. The most frequent responses: England: the royal family, 18 percent; Italy: Rome and food and drink, 21 percent each; France: Paris, 28 percent. Only in the case of Germany were topical political problems mentioned first: 25 percent of the persons polled mentioned the country's division into two parts. Cultural and scientific achievements of all four countries were mentioned by only 4 percent of the persons questioned, economic achievements by only about 2 percent.

Austria is thus not an exception. It is not really surprising that polls about images of peoples and states elicit answers that are influenced by the past and demonstrate very little knowledge of the present. Our knowledge about the world beyond our own borders is based essentially on the information we receive in school and on what we are provided daily by the mass media. However, school has a tendency to convey mainly information on the past, and the media, in this world-wide explosion of communication, report less and less on more and more subjects and thus give only superficial information.

An experiment carried out in the USA demonstrated that this discrepancy can be changed by specific information being conveyed. In early 1969, the Austrian Embassy in Washington, D.C., the Austrian consulates general, the information service, the trade attaché, the tourist office, and the Austrian Institute in New York jointly sponsored an exhibit entitled "Creative Austria—20th Century" in the Philadelphia City Hall. One of the main purposes of the exhibit was to correct the traditional clichés of Austria. Visitors to the exhibit could take part in a drawing; to enter, they had to list, among other things, the names of three well-known Austrians. Analogous to the previous poll taken by the Austrian Institute in New York, 2000 responses were evaluated, and Sigmund Freud, with 1,034 mentions, was the leader by a wide margin.

I published an article on this evaluation as well, again in the daily *Die Presse,* in the May 30, 1969, issue, from which I quote.

"A comparison with the previous poll taken by the Austrian Institute in New York shows that the Philadelphia exhibit caused a temporary and local change in the image of Austria. This change manifests itself in a 'rejuvenation' of the personalities mentioned. Although names from a more or less distant past were in the majority in the earlier poll, this time, under the impression of the exhibit, a pleasingly large number of personalities was mentioned whose work is affecting us even today. The more balanced distribution over the individual subject matters is also pleasing . . .

"In this sense, the Philadelphia exhibit and its concomitant poll can be evaluated as an encouraging local and temporary experiment. The Philadelphia experiment allows the conclusion that it is possible to correct the often jocularly mentioned 3W-Image of Austria (Wine, Waltzes, and Whipped Cream) or the 5M-Image (Mountains, Music, Mozart, Maria Theresa, and Metternich) that emerged from the earlier poll, that these images can be supplemented in the sense of intellectualizing and modernizing them."

This was ten years ago. What is the situation today, 35 years after the Republic was reestablished, 25 years after independence and sovereignty were regained through the signing of the State Treaty? What are Austria's image and impact in the four relevant areas of politics, economy, science, and art?

There have been several developments in the area of politics, so that the mention of the name Austria would do more than merely evoke the association with Metternich and Maria Theresa. The country has taken advantage

Figure 4 Founder of psychoanalysis, the Austrian scientist with the greatest global impact: Sigmund Freud (at his desk in Vienna).

of the neutrality that it voluntarily obligated itself to in 1955; it has become a place of encounter and, within the realm of possibilities, of mediation as well. The International Center, called UN-City by the population, which was opened in 1979, has made Vienna the third official United Nations headquarters, along with New York and Geneva.

Figure 5   Testimony to Austria's present-day involvement in matters of international relations: the Vienna International Center (informally called "UN City"), housing the UN Atomic Energy Organization, the UN Industrial Development Organization (UNIDO), and other international agencies (capacity: 4700 persons).

The International Atomic Energy Organization (IAEO) has been head-quartered in Vienna since 1957, and the United Nations Industrial Development Organization (UNIDO) since 1967. Moreover, the city has been the site of many international conferences and of important encounters. John F. Kennedy and Nikita Khrushchev met here in 1961; the Soviet-American Strategic Arms Limitation Talks (SALT) were held here in 1970 and 1971; the talks on a mutual and balanced troop reduction in Europe have been going on since 1973; and it was in Vienna that Jimmy Carter and Leonid Brezhnev signed the so-called SALT II Agreement in 1979.

The personal involvement of Austrians in international organizations is great. The former Austrian Foreign Minister, Kurt Waldheim, was elected Secretary General of the United Nations in 1972, and he was reelected to that post in 1976. Another former Foreign Minister, Lujo Toncic, was secretary general of the Council of Europe from 1969 to 1974, and this office has been held by the Austrian representative Franz Karasek since 1979. Another Austrian representative, Karl Czernetz, was president of the Council of Europe from 1975 to 1978; and the former chairman of the Socialist party of Austria (Sozialistische Partei Österreichs, SPÖ), Bruno Pittermann, was chairman of the Socialist International for many years. Alois Mock, chairman of the Austrian People's party (Österreichische Volkspartei, ÖVP), is chairman of the European Democratic Union (EDU), the umbrella organization of the Christian-Democratic and conservative parties of Europe, as was his predecessor in office, Josef Taus.

A castle in Laxenburg near Vienna, which formerly belonged to the Habsburgs, is now the seat of an institution that is proof of how little Austria is solely relying on the tradition of Maria Theresa and Metternich in its political presence in the world and on Mozart and music in its cultural presence. The International Institute for Applied Systems Analysis (IIASA) has been headquartered in Laxenburg since early 1973. IIASA was founded in 1972 by scientific institutions from 12 states (Bulgaria, Canada, Czechoslovakia, the Federal Republic of Germany, France, the German Democratic Republic, Great Britain, Italy, Japan, Poland, the Soviet Union, and the USA). Accepting an invitation from the Austrian government, the Institute established its headquarters in Laxenburg. IIASA researches long-term problems of scientific methodology with the assistance of large computers, and it concentrates its efforts on the areas of environmental protection, urban problems, and problems of world-wide food supply. One of its first tasks was the investigation of the world energy supply. The Austrian Academy of Sciences has been a member of IIASA since 1973, when the Institute established its headquarters in Laxenburg.

In the economic sector, Austria's position in the world can best be illustrated by a comparison between the First and the Second Republic. The state that was created in 1918 was hardly viable and was thus especially hard hit by the world economic crisis of 1929. On the other hand, the state that was reestablished in 1945 has been characterized by remarkable economic and social stability and has therefore been in a much better position to deal with the problems arising from the great crude oil shocks of the 1970s than many other countries. A high employment rate, accompanied by a low inflation rate, are typical of Austria. With this secure basis, which is not least due to the so-called social partnership, the cooperation between employers and employees, the Austrian economy is now attempting to hold its own in international markets. It focuses on the sale of know-how, on the development of intelligent and sensible products, and on the production of high-quality merchandise.

For instance, the LD steel-making process, named after the Austrian steel centers of Linz and Donawitz, is being used in license by more than 200 steel mills throughout the world. In 1975, more than 50 percent of the raw steel produced in the entire world was manufactured according to this method, which uses an oxygen top-blowing process in steel production. Austria has also made a name for itself in the field of iron and steel construction, owing to the high quality of its products. It has, for instance, built hydroelectric power plants in Sudan, Greece, Ghana, the Democratic

Figure 6   Modern industrial Austria: United Iron and Steel Works (VOEST) industrial site of Linz (Upper Austria). Its technique of steel production has been adopted by more than 200 steel works all over the world.

People's Republic of Korea, Nicaragua, Chile, Bolivia, and the USA (Glen Canyon); steam power plants in Thailand, the Antilles, and Malawi; steel mills in India, the Soviet Union, the People's Republic of China, and Brazil; refineries in Greece and Switzerland; and chemical plants in Poland and Bulgaria.

A little-known Austrian specialty is theatrical equipment, which was delivered to the opera houses in Sidney, Istanbul, Bucharest, Warsaw, and Zagreb, among others. Austrian lamps supplement this equipment, and they can be found, e.g., in the Metropolitan Opera in New York, in the Kennedy Center in Washington, D.C., in the meeting room of the Supreme Soviet in the Kremlin, in government buildings in Columbia, in Djakarta, Addis Ababa, Kabul, and Kuwait, and in the Hilton hotels in Tunis, Paris, and Athens.

Economic achievement and success can be measured and registered objectively at the time of their accomplishment. Scientific achievement and success are much harder to evaluate. However, the following Austrian scientists have been awarded the prestigious Nobel Prize:

In medicine: Robert Barany for research of the vestibular organ in the brain (1914), Julius Wagner-Jauregg for paralysis therapy (1927), Karl Landsteiner for discovery of the blood groups (1930), Otto Loewi for research on the chemical effects on nerves and muscles (1936), Carl and Gerty Cori for research on enzymes (1947), and Karl von Frisch and Konrad Lorenz for behavioral research (1973).

In physics: Erwin Schrödinger, as one of the founders of quantum mechanics (1933), and Viktor Hess for discovery of cosmic radiation (1936).

In chemistry: Fritz Pregl for developing microchemical analysis (1923), Richard Zsigmondy for research and development of pioneering methods of measurement in colloid chemistry (1925), Richard Kuhn for research on vitamins (1938), Wolfgang Pauli for discovery of the "Pauli Principle" in quantum theory (1945), and Max Perutz for the first determination of the structure of protein molecules (1962).

In economics: Friedrich von Hayek for monetary theory and theory of the economic cycle (1974).

Two Austrians were awarded the Nobel Peace Prize. In 1905, it went to Baroness Berta von Suttner, an author who had published her most significant work *Die Waffen nieder!* (Disarm!) in 1889. This work was translated into almost all European languages. Six years later, in 1911, it went to the Viennese publicist Alfred H. Fried. He was publisher of the magazine *Die Waffen nieder!* and founder of the German Society for Peace (established in 1892).

Of course, Nobel Prizes are imperfect means of measuring the significance and effects of scientific achievements. In his book *The Austrian Mind,* published in 1972, the American historian William M. Johnston presents an "Intellectual and Social History" of Austria for the time from 1848 to 1938. In the final chapter of his book, entitled "Austria's Intellectual Achievement," he presents the following conclusions:

> Which of the innovators chronicled in this book, one may wonder, have most decisively influenced posterity? First place undoubtedly must go to Freud. No other thinker of the twentieth century, Austrian or otherwise, has so impregnated contemporary consciousness, permeating every facet of economic, social, and intellectual life . . .

A second movement claiming innumerable adherents is Buber's philosophy of dialogue: like psychoanalysis it reconciles positivism with impressionism by differentiating levels of the psyche.

Third, reverence for fantasy has sustained Austrian literature. Defying the philistinism of both bureaucracy and the masses, novelists as disparate as Kafka, Musil, and Roth have proclaimed the sovereignty of imagination.

In addition to formulating visions that have come to constitute our self-awareness, Austrians launched major innovations in nearly all fields of thought. In philosophy, logical positivism and linguistic analysis spread from Vienna to every English-speaking university. Brentano opened new perspectives in epistemology, psychology, and ethics, while Husserl's phenomenology has become a discipline unto itself. In legal theory, Kelsen's positivism formulated problems of his field, while in economic theory, Menger and his students collaborated founding marginal analysis.

Going beyond the period of time that he treats in his book, Professor Johnston states, "Since 1945, Arnold Hauser, Michael Polanyi, Friedrich von Hayek, Ludwig von Bertalanffy, Karl Popper, and Ernst Gombrich have crowned their careers with wide-ranging syntheses." I would like to add at least two names to Professor Johnston's enumeration: Alfred Adler as another representative of the time before 1945, and Viktor Frankl for the time after 1945.

The evaluation of artistic achievements and their influences is even more subjective and therefore even more difficult. However, let me venture to make one principal statement: especially in artistic areas, so much is so old and laden with tradition in Austria because it was done there earlier than elsewhere. The Salzburg Festival is an example of this. When it was founded in 1920, the concept of a festival had hardly gained ground elsewhere in the world. It must have seemed to be a superfluous, even disastrous, luxury to establish a festival so shortly after the war, in a country that had hardly overcome the collapse of the great monarchy, that was economically weak and politically divided. This action only seemed to confirm the cliché of an irresponsible people of dancers and violinists.

Today, one generation later, there are festivals throughout the entire world. They are an expression of the leisure-time society, a society that has achieved long weekends and guaranteed minimum vacations. They are an expression of a mobile society that makes festivals possible in the most remote locations; and, not least, they are an expression of a society that is becoming increasingly aware of the significance of the quality of life. As long as belief in purely material, technological progress was unshaken, it may have appeared as if the Austrian way of life was not in keeping with the spirit of the times. However, as the limits of growth, the limits of a purely quantitative increase in goods, were recognized; as concern for qualitative improvement of life, for a healthy environment, and for open space for recreation and reflection in a noise-polluted environment is increasing; there is also increased understanding for a way of life characterized by the poet Anton Wildgans fifty years ago in his "speech about Austria."

He to whom historical consciousness and psychology have become second nature, he would tend not to see progress in every change of affairs; and he who has an old culture, he rests too much in himself and he is too sure of his own taste to think that every innovation might contain the gospel. He lacks that barbaric pleasure in worthless glitter that loudly pretends to be valuable and genuine; he lacks the ostentatious lust of the cultural parvenu for the so-called achievements that generally are only achievements of civilization. He sees through the trash and the fraud by which those who are eternally preoccupied with the present, who have no or only few traditions, are trapped regularly and believingly. It may well be that he is not always quite 'with the times,' but, on the other hand, he will not so easily and unsuspectingly fall into the pitfalls of the times. It may well be that he does not quite keep the pace and does not participate adroitly enough in the St. Vitus's dance of an increasingly desecrating civilization. But he will keep something else, something that might yet be very important, when, in days to come, the peoples of the earth will be counted and measured according to different standards than those of power and competitiveness, namely the standards of the human heart and the human soul!

Selected Bibliography

Austria Today. Quarterly Review of Trends and Events. Wien.
Bundespressedienst. *Austria—Facts and Figures.* Wien, no year of publication.
Johnston, William. *The Austrian Mind.* Berkeley, Calif., 1972.
Spaulding, E. Wilder. *The Quiet Invaders. The Story of the Austrian Impact upon America.* Wien, 1968.
Ungar, Frederick, ed. *Handbook of Austrian Literature.* New York, 1973.
Waldheim, Kurt. *The Austrian Example.* London, 1973.

PART VI

CULTURE AND THE ARTS

Modern Austria, pp. 409–29

21. CONTEMPORARY LITERATURE IN AUSTRIA

Wendelin Schmidt-Dengler

Associate Professor for Modern German Philology and Literature, University of Vienna

1 ANTECEDENTS OF THE PRESENT SITUATION: A RETROSPECTIVE

Austrian authors have caused quite a stir. In a development that by now has continued for 15 years, the public awareness of the writings of contemporary Austrian authors has become much greater than it was immediately after World War II. To put it somewhat crudely: the works of Austrian authors are among the country's highly regarded export items. Not that Austrians have developed a voracious appetite for books, one might add.[1] A development of interest not only to critics and literary historians has brought about a situation in the world of literature that gives us much more justification than was previously the case to speak of the development of an Austrian literature in its own right.

In order to better understand this status quo, it is necessary to make a few preliminary remarks pertaining to the period between 1945 and 1966. The war and the Nazi regime caused heavy losses to the intelligentsia. The experience of this war and the sad economic state of affairs in the postwar period left their mark on the younger generation, for whom there were no ties with the past and no figures in whose footsteps they might follow. However much a number of rémigrés such as Otto Basil (b. 1901) and Hans Weigel (b. 1908) created periodicals and annuals for writers to have a place to publish their works, the lack of public interest and the unfavorable state of the publishing houses led a number of writers to take up residence in the Federal Republic of Germany, where the prospects for work were far better. Thus it was that Ilse Aichinger (b. 1921), Herbert Eisenreich (b. 1925), and Ingeborg Bachmann (1926–1973) went abroad.[2] But the younger generation became more and more conscious of their Austrian identity. There was particular interest in authors such as Franz Kafka (1883–1924), Karl Kraus

409

9306-6403/81/0415-0409$01.50

(1874–1936), Robert Musil (1889–1942), Hermann Broch (1886–1951), and Joseph Roth (1894–1939). It was Ingeborg Bachmann who in 1953 was the first to draw attention to Ludwig Wittgenstein, whose reflections on language came to be binding for many authors. But one particular author who may be considered representative for the 1950s was not at all a member of this "lost generation" of those in their thirties at the time. Instead, he was of a completely different age. It is Heimito von Doderer (1896–1966), whose novels *Die Strudlhofstiege* (1951; the Strudlhofstiege is a flight of steps in the 9th district of Vienna), *Die Dämonen* (1956; in English, The Demons, translated by Richard and Clara Winston, New York, 1961) and *Die Wasserfälle von Slunj* (1963; The Waterfalls of Slunj) portrayed the world of the Danube monarchy and Austrian society between the two world wars. Doderer's works seemed to fit perfectly into the climate, welcoming tradition, of a period striving for a state of equilibrium—the period in which Austria received the State Treaty of 1955.[3] It was around this time that Friedrich Torberg (1908–1979) began to edit and publish the works of Herzmanovsky-Orlando (1877–1954), works full of grotesque satirical visions of an Austrian past, which in their absurdity are for many even today the appropriate expression of Austrian conditions.

2 AVANT-GARDE GROUPS IN VIENNA AND GRAZ

The year 1966 can be regarded in many respects as a year of reorientation. New tendencies began to obtain a foothold. Tendencies that in the Federal Republic of Germany took the form of a student revolt in the political sector and that had their effect indirectly also in the area of cultural policy developed in Austria into a revolt of aesthetics from within. Admittedly it had long been in the offing. In the early 1950s authors in Vienna were already experimenting with language itself. They considered language a changeable material and not something that was immutable because it had been passed down by tradition. The writers in question are Hans Carl Artmann (b. 1921), Friedrich Achleitner (b. 1930), Gerhard Rühm (b. 1930), Konrad Bayer (1932–1964), and Oswald Wiener (b. 1935).[4] The first public appearances of this "group" were scandal-ridden, and from this point up to the immediate present there has been an obvious strain in relations between the general public and a somewhat irritable cultural administration on the one hand and artistic production on the other. The authors comprising the so-called "Wiener Gruppe," along with a few others such as Ernst Jandl (b. 1925) and Andreas Okopenko (b. 1930), found "refuge" in the form of the literary periodical *manuskripte,* which began to appear in Graz in 1960. The *manuskripte* gradually developed into the leading organ of those who saw themselves as avant-garde.[5] It was the Carinthian-born Peter Handke

(b. 1942) who came to be the symbolic figurehead of the upheaval. It was he who at a meeting of the West German "Gruppe 47" (The '47 Club) cast fundamental doubt on its critical and literary principles. Handke's early prose and his play *Kaspar* (1967) captured public attention far beyond the borders of Germany. Interest on the part of West German publishers in Austrian authors began to grow, whereby one might note that the Suhrkamp and Luchterhand publishing houses showed special interest. Aside from Peter Handke, it was Thomas Bernhard (b. 1931) in particular who became a representative of Austrian literature. The image he projected of Austria was at odds with all the clichés, propagated by the promoters of the tourist industry. His first novel *Frost* (1963) portrayed Austria as the epitome of the negative. The critical, sometimes aggressive, attitude taken toward the homeland and tradition gave many authors a significant impulse for their own creative work.

3   LITERATURE AND THE PUBLIC

The reorientation in the mid-1960s, for which mainly those who were between 30 and 40 at the time were responsible, also created poles of literary activities. The existence of writers' organizations in itself indicates little about the literature produced or its quality; however, the development in this field does indeed reveal a great deal about the present situation. The lack of an involved reading public stigmatized Austrian literary production for quite some time. The Austrian Society for Literature, founded in 1961 under the directorship of Wolfgang Kraus, was able to rectify the situation by providing Austrian authors with the opportunity to read before a larger audience. Interested students were also able to hear non-Austrian authors and philosophers such as Hans Magnus Enzensberger, Theodor W. Adorno, Ernst Bloch, Max Brod, Alain Robbe-Grillet, and Nathalie Sarraute, as well as Austrian émigrés, among them Elias Canetti (b. 1905), Erich Fried (b. 1921), Heinz Politzer (1910–1978), and Manès Sperber (b. 1905). This example found followers, and at the present time there are several organizations that arrange readings and symposia. One is the Alte Schmiede (The Old Forge) with its Literarisches Quartier, which has been in existence since 1975. There and elsewhere, less conventional means are employed to bring people into contact with literature. Since then there has been such an overabundance of readings, symposia and the like offered in the metropolis of Vienna that some of them only attract small audiences.

Graz, too, became a focal point of attention with its annual Steirischer Herbst (Styrian Autumn), an event initiated in 1966. It is by and large the gathering of Austrian avant-garde from all areas of culture with the strongest tradition. As part of the Steirischer Herbst a specific topic is dealt with in a symposium by internationally recognized authors and critics in precisely the same spirit that has made the periodical *manuskripte* and the artists association Forum Stadtpark what they are. Attempts have been made in the province of Salzburg through the Rauriser Literaturtage, founded in 1971, to come up with a particularly original form of contact. Authors read their texts and discuss them with professors and students of German literature. Attempts to have the rural population participate in the events have met with varying degrees of success. Both the Steirischer Herbst and the Rauriser Literaturtage are clear indications that the "provinces," as it were, are most eager to compete seriously for the rank of literary capital, which hitherto was unquestioningly held by Vienna. Many people feel that the city of Graz and its inhabitants are synonymous with avantgarde, but such a view represents an unwarranted simplification. The fact is that through the literary magazine *manuskripte* and the activities of the Forum Stadtpark authors from Austria and abroad have been offered the chance to publicize their works. Before that their chances of receiving any response from the reading public were small. The magazine *manuskripte,* now in its 21st year of existence, can be regarded as the leading literary organ. The editors have made it their principle to print only previously unpublished material without an honorarium. Despite this precondition, getting something published in the *manuskripte* is an important boost for a young author. A great deal of credit is due in this regard to the editor, Alfred Kolleritsch (b. 1931), himself a novelist and lyrical poet.

Back at the time when the *manuskripte* first began to appear, there was only one literary magazine to speak of and that was *Wort in der Zeit* (Word in Our Times), which was edited by Gerhard Fritsch (1924–1969) and which folded in 1965. This in turn found a successful continuation in 1966 in the form of *Literatur und Kritik* (Literature and Criticism). The basic concept behind the *manuskripte* led to imitations on the one hand, and to the creation of new periodicals in opposition to *manuskripte* on the other hand. Of these newly founded periodicals, the one entitled *Wespennest* (Wasp's Nest), which commenced publication in 1969, has established itself most firmly on account of its political involvement. Aggressive titles also seem to be the order of the day for other periodicals that are worthy of mention. Take for example *Projektil* (Projectile), which has been appearing out of Salzburg since 1975; *Fettfleck* (Fat Stain), since 1975 in Carinthia; *Löwenmaul* (Lion's Mouth), begun in 1975 in Vienna; *Frischfleisch* (Fresh Meat), which got started in Vienna in 1971; and *Salz* (Salt), which commenced publication in Salzburg in 1975. A further periodical called *Freibord* (Free Board) pays homage to anarchistic tendencies. Then there is *Die Rampe* (The Ramp), which first appeared in 1975 and is produced in Upper Austria, where another series of publications—important for experimental literature in Austria—namely the *edition neue texte* (New Texts

Edition), is also managed. The year 1973 saw the initial publication of *Pannonia,* a periodical edited in the province of Burgenland by György Sebestyén, which aims at promoting cooperation between Austrian and Hungarian writers. A second literary magazine in this easternmost province of Austria began to appear in 1978 and goes by the name of *Wortmühle* (Word Mill). Since 1977, Sebestyén has also been editor of the newly founded Lower Austrian magazine *Der Morgen* (The Morning), which has declared itself to be a "cultural magazine" and which sees itself as a counterweight to all-too-modern tendencies. *Das Fenster* (The Window), which published its first issue in 1968, is a product of Tyrol, and *Die Brücke* (The Bridge) has aimed since 1975 at representing the province of Carinthia. This brief survey shows to what extent those in the "Provinz"—a somewhat condescending term or expression that the Viennese use to describe their "backward" fellow countrymen in the other eight Austrian provinces—are competing with the literary metropolis of Vienna for the lead.[6]

An important annual publication is the *Protokolle* (Protocols), which began to appear in Vienna in 1966. In addition, other gazettes are making an effort to expand their literature sections. One might mention the *Neues Forum* (New Forum), the *Extrablatt* and *profil.* The Vienna daily *Die Presse* started publishing a fortnightly literary supplement entitled "Literaricum" in the fall of 1979.

4 COMPETING WRITERS' ORGANIZATIONS

The variety of periodicals best reflects the wide range of tendencies and positions represented. Austria's literary landscape has become very complex. This circumstance may well dampen the spirits of critics wishing to pigeonhole writers and their works, but at the same time it is a welcome sign for literary production in that both the conception of the texts and the understanding of literature in general are not at the dictate of any kind of uniformity.

The most radical divergences of opinion have manifested themselves from the beginning of the 1970s to the present day in the two main writers' organizations in Austria, namely the P.E.N. Club and the Grazer Autorenversammlung (Graz Authors' Assembly). The latter was founded in February 1973 to represent the interests of those authors who placed more stress on innovation within literary works themselves and also on a more intensive contact between politics and literature.

Attempts to have the Grazer Autorenversammlung obtain recognition from the International P.E.N. as the second autonomous Austrian P.E.N. Club failed once and for all in 1975. Even so, the Grazer Autorenversammlung was able to continue to assert itself because its protagonists had achieved acclaim outside the country. Although it has its base in Vienna, it has retained the name Grazer Autorenversammlung because it was founded in Graz and the movement from which it draws its support had started there.[7]

The willingness of the two groups, which at the risk of oversimplification one might call "traditionalists" and "modernists," to sit down and patch up old differences seems to have more or less declined in the past few years. The ministry responsible for subsidies supports both groups on the basis of a balanced distribution scheme.

5   BUSINESS AND LITERATURE

The abundance of literary publications, the presence of two writers' associations and a whole slate of local centers could lead one to believe that the calling of the author in Austria is one that is financially attractive. Nothing could be further from the truth. Admittedly there has been a manifold increase in the past few years in public funds made available at the federal, provincial, and municipal levels to promote literature through prizes and stipends. But even so, the free-lance writers still lack a living basis. The free-lancer is becoming more and more dependent on mass media such as radio and television. The situation with regard to publishing houses has improved in Austria in the past decade. The Residenz Verlag in Salzburg has done much to promote Austrian authors in particular. In addition, a number of smaller houses have attempted to put out inexpensive books. Nevertheless, most writers have remained dependent on West German publishers and radio stations. Here, the relevant statistics speak for themselves. According to figures from the year 1976, the Federal Republic of Germany tops the list of countries exporting books to Austria, with 84.9 percent of the total volume; 81.8 percent of Austria's total book exports went to West Germany.[8]

The difficulties encountered by an author just starting out to get something accepted by an established publisher have led authors themselves to put forward proposals to improve the situation. These have, however, yet to be discussed. Hans Heinz Hahnl (b. 1923), a writer associated with the P.E.N. Club and culture editor of the Austrian Social Democratic organ *Arbeiter Zeitung,* for instance, conceives of a state publishing house that would receive public subsidies in the same manner as the State Opera or the Burg Theater. The Grazer Autorenversammlung, on the other hand, is in favor of self-help on the model of the Verlag der Autoren (Authors' Own Publishing House), which was founded in Frankfurt in 1969, and in favor of founding an "authors' own book shop."[9]

Although many authors receive important financial assistance in the form of countless prizes, still no basic change in their financial situation results from such awards. The Federal Ministry of Education and Art awards the "Great Austrian State Prize," valued at 150,000 Austrian schillings, once a year for a different branch of the arts. In 1975, the prize went to H. C. Artmann, then president of the Grazer Autorenversammlung. Manès Sperber was the recipient in 1977, whereas in 1979 the award was made to Friedrich Torberg, the protagonist of the Austrian P.E.N. Club, only a few weeks before his death. The honorary prize valued at 75,000 Austrian schillings went for five years in a row, until 1978, to writers belonging to the Grazer Autorenversammlung (Mayröcker, Rühm, Okopenko, Jandl, and W. Bauer). An assistance grant valued at 40,000 schillings is made annually for a different literary genre. In addition, stipends aimed at introducing recipients to the production of television programs, state stipends, and stipends for promising young writing talents are awarded. Up to 18 of the latter, each worth 6,000 schillings per month, are awarded annually. It might be worth noting that there is an Austrian State Prize for European Literature valued at 150,000 schillings, which is presented each year to a foreign writer. The Austrian provinces are doing much the same thing to promote their authors.[10] Both the creation and manner of awarding of the Ingeborg Bachmann Prize, first sponsored by the City of Klagenfurt in 1977, were highly acclaimed and at the same time the object of widespread criticism. The authors read before an audience; the television people are on hand. The winner, who receives the respectable prize money totaling 100,-000 schillings, is announced after the jury has conducted a public discussion on the merits of each contestant. (Marcel Reigh-Ranicki, the prototype of the West German outspoken critic and the target of attacks by Austrian avant-garde writers, proved himself to be a particularly effective opinion leader.) The selection of the jury as well as that of the authors and the form in which criticism is made represented a provocation for many young Austrian writers and compelled them to give a good deal of thought to their own situation.

In 1978, Gerhard Ruiss and Johannes A. Vyoral made public a study entitled "On the Situation of Young Austrian Authors." In it they provided the public with important information on the economic situation of their writing colleagues and gave some of them the opportunity to criticize existing practices in the world of literature. Criticism was directed mainly at the manipulations of various functionaries in influential positions, but also at the now "established" avant-garde of the 1960s. Many a drastic statement to be found in the study is diametrically opposed to the image of Austria as the "island of the blessed," one that the media in this country are so fond of conjuring up. Elfriede Gerstl (b. 1932) has called the writer a "citizen with amputated rights" and has made the following claim: "In happy Austria, the (trade-) names that have been propagated and marketed abroad—with foreign capital—are later advertised as being home-grown products and displayed in the media as the show windows of the nation. This is a mechanism that one can only get away with here in Austria by reason of the confused state of the superstructure. And what chance of escape does the Austrian writer have other than the aforementioned emigration: drugs, booze, insanity, and suicide. They have all been put to frequent use."[11]

Even if the radicalism of the formulation may be shocking and the problem of the artist in society cannot be solved by material means alone, it does become clear that it would be possible to improve the status of the writer. This could be achieved through efforts made by public institutions, especially through schools and universities, as well as through the help of a more considerate public, one more fond of reading, and of a more conscientious brand of criticism than one is accustomed to encounter in Austria at present.

6   AUSTRIAN LITERATURE IN TEACHING AND RESEARCH

Beginning in the mid-1960s new chairs for the study of Austrian literary history were created in Graz, Innsbruck, and Salzburg to complement the one already in existence in Vienna. This fact is symptomatic of the attention being paid to Austrian literature. It was also during this period that the Dokumentationsstelle für neuere österreichische Literatur (Documentation Center for Contemporary Austrian Literature) came into being in Vienna. Its task is to collect the most important material on literature in Austria and to make it available to the general public. Poetry readings at schools and universities are intended to acquaint pupils and students with contemporary literature. Lecture series given by the authors at the universities— something that has long been commonplace in the Anglo-Saxon countries —got off to a hesitating start in Austria in the 1970s.[12]

A number of scholars are also at work trying to determine the inherent properties, as it were, of Austrian literature. Walter Weiss and Sigrid Schmid edited the instructive anthology *Zwischenbilanz* (Taking Stock, 1976), which provides a cross-section of writing in Austria from 1939 to the year of publication. One must point out that viewed half a decade later the accents have changed somewhat.[13] It was in the very same year (1976) that a History of Contemporary Austrian Literature, edited by Hilde Spiel, appeared in a series put out by the Kindler Publishing House. Just as one might expect, critics pounced upon it immediately. Be that as it may, today it is an indispensable reference work owing to the wealth of material offered.[14]

All of these activities, which one can follow up to the present day, serve one purpose: to develop better criteria to determine the peculiarities of literature produced in Austria and its special position within the German-language literatures. Both literary critics and scholars have been dealing with this problem for quite some time. Initially—reference is to a point in time before World War II—attempts were made to describe the Austrian essence, whereby the latter was supposed to be explained in terms of a specific tradition having its roots in the culture of the Baroque period. The term "Austrian national literature" served as a means of protecting the threatened territorial integrity and of proving that Austria could be self-sufficient not only from an economic point of view but also in a literary sense. However necessary this retrospection and dealing with a specific Austrian tradition was, the tendency to promote "austriazensic narcissism" by reference to a glorious past was indeed open to question. In addition, it is difficult to find scientifically unequivocal criteria to distinguish texts from Austria from other texts written in German.

7   HABSBURG: NO END IN SIGHT?

The Italian scholar of German literature, Claudio Magris, set about examining the relations to reality in Austrian literature in his dissertation *Il mito absburgico nella letteratura austriaca moderna* (The Habsburg Myth in Modern Austrian Literature). It appeared in print in 1963. In this study, as in essays that were to follow and that considerably refined what had been said in the initial examination, Magris concluded that Austrian literature as a whole has been marked, right up to the present day, by a certain indulgence in retrospection—in other words, by a transformation of reality under the sign of the "Habsburg myth," even after the disintegration of the multinational empire in 1918.[15] The *Evasionscharakter,* that is the escape from a dialectical approach to reality, seemed to Magris significant. The term "Habsburg myth" therefore does not always mean concrete reference to the dynasty. It evokes a fairy-tale order with both positive and negative effects: praise of being and condemnation of change, cloaked in "disen-chanting irony." According to Magris, this and similar factors have been and still are the determinants of literature in Austria from the mid-19th century to the present. Consequently, Austrian literature was spoken of as having a deeply apolitical character, as for example in a book entitled *The Broken Eagle,* written by the Briton C. E. Williams (1974).[16] The West German critic Ulrich Greiner writes in the same vein in his book *Der Tod des Nachsommers* (The Death of the Indian Summer, 1979), a collection of critiques that first appeared in the *Frankfurter Allgemeine Zeitung,* augmented by an additional essay. In its obvious allusion to the novel *Der*

Nachsommer (The Indian Summer) by Adalbert Stifter (1805–1868), the title says just about everything: Stifter is the "grandfather of Austrian literature, which is dominated by a 'political calm.' "[17]

But aside from these negative definitions of the apolitical character, one ought also to note the positive sides. Whereas Austria's authors took a more retrogressive attitude, they did try to be progressive in the artistic sense; in other words, progress with regard to aesthetic techniques and regress in connection with the political consciousness. But, according to critics, this renunciation of partisan involvement, as expressed by many authors, the emphasis on radical subjectivism, the "privatization" of historical change is, in the guise of the "ideology of a non-ideology," merely a camouflaged conservative world view and, as such, false consciousness. In the case of the Austrian author, the revolt is carried out—or so it is said—in the aesthetic sphere. As has already been emphasized, such a stand became obvious when during the year 1968 in Vienna protests were not voiced in the form of political programs, but instead were celebrated as some kind of "happening." At the political level Austrian students simply borrowed from their West German colleagues the argumentation they used.

8   NEW CONSTELLATIONS

The question arises whether the perspective on Austrian literature that Magris and others have opened up is the only conceivable and valid one. There can be no doubt that Austrian authors have worked very intensively toward the solution to formal problems. One characteristic of many of the most important writers is the consistent reflection upon the medium of language and reference to the philosopher of language, Ludwig Wittgenstein. One need only mention Handke, Bernhard, Bachmann, Konrad Bayer, and Jutta Schutting (b. 1937). The suitability of language as a means of communication came to be a theme of its own. And many were of the opinion they could build their own ivory tower out of it. It was Peter Handke who proclaimed in 1969[18] that there was "officialdom in the very sentences" (*In Sätzen steckt Obrigkeit*), thus making an analogy between the authority of the State and that of language. But what was duly celebrated around the middle of the 1960s as an uprising against authority in general through the criticism of language soon turned out to be more and more a dubious concentration on the medium, whereby a discussion of the content was dispensed with. Michael Scharang (b. 1941) showed in a number of essays just how open to argument this viewpoint was. Later on, though, this linguistic strategy, worked out especially by the so-called Wiener Gruppe and by Ernst Jandl and Peter Handke, turned out to be an effective means of taking to task the social reality in the country.

Photo 1   Peter Handke (Photo: Residenz Verlag, Salzburg)

Seen from the vantage point of the year 1980, Austrian literature is not just a continuation of the "Habsburg myth," that is to say, literature that aims at portraying the unchangeable and that sticks to the priority of form over content. Today the battle lines are no longer drawn between the one-time avant-garde and the conservative elements—a conclusion one might draw from the split into P.E.N. Club and Grazer Autorenversamm-lung. It is not a matter of trying out new linguistic strategies, but instead one of their effective application in the presentation of experiences and of their possible use for didactic purposes. The experiences are for most writers Austrian experiences.

9   MODELS OF AUTHENTICITY

Fundamental differences became evident in the interpretation and portrayal of these experiences. The formalistic experimental literature, which upsets the game of language by an often macabre witticism, seems to have fallen behind realistic literature in terms of popularity. However, it is precisely the procedure employed by Ernst Jandl which is capable of regeneration—a fact he has demonstrated in his *bearbeitung der mütze* (1978; "revision of the cap"). In it he presents us with models of a "damaged language" and in so doing demonstrates the possibilities of social criticism at his disposal. What is striking is the widespread emphasis on autobiographical elements. Biography is serving more than ever as the backbone of a narrative context. Peter Handke's story *Wunschloses Unglück* (1972; Perfectly Unhappy), which tells about his mother's life and eventual suicide, was a harbinger of this trend. Of course, the tendency to use a biographical story line is by no means an Austrian patent, and Handke's book was not a novelty in Austria. Books by the East German author Christa Wolf such as *Nachdenken über Christa T.* (1968; Reflections on Christa T.) and *Kindheitsmuster* (1976; Childhood Pattern) are impressive proof of that fact. What is specific to Austrian authors—and in this regard Handke has laid the groundwork in exemplary fashion in his *Wunschloses Unglück*—is the attempt to test the possibility of expressing something that has been an individual experience through the medium of language, which is common to all. One can scarcely keep track any more of the number of novels that are autobiographical in nature. Several of the most important ones are mentioned in the following. Franz Innerhofer (b. 1944), a native of Salzburg and author of the novel trilogy *Schöne Tage* (1974; Happy Days), *Schattseite* (1975; The Wrong Side), and *Die grossen Wörter* (1977; The Big Words), presented the story of a farm hand who grows up with a mountain farmer, becomes an apprentice, and later takes a job to help finance his studies. Innerhofer presents it as the story of a disillusionment. Gernot Wolfgruber (b. 1944), whose novel *Herrenjahre* (1976; Gentlemen Years) tells the tale of a laborer who builds a house while his wife, who is suffering from cancer, pines away, goes about relating his story in a similar manner, and yet from a psychological point of view more vividly and subtly. Wolfgruber's second major novel *Niemandsland* (1978; No Man's Land) is about an unskilled laborer by the name of Georg Klein. Klein becomes a white-collar worker, then experiences to what extent he has alienated himself from his upbringing without being able to grasp a foothold in the other social class either. Wolfgruber chooses not to follow up on the moral in the sense of social criticism that might have been distilled from these experiences. Instead, he concentrates his efforts on the illustrative detail. Quite the contrary, Michael Scharang supplies us in his two novels *Charly Traktor* (1973) and *Der Sohn eines Landarbeiters* (1976; The Son of a Farm Laborer) with practical recipes for the class struggle. In so doing, he remains the exception among those authors who concentrate their interest on the working world. Wolfgruber, Innerhofer, and Walter Kappacher (b. 1938) treat problems from the viewpoint of the affected individual and offer descriptions rather than concrete suggestions. And that is reason enough to be scolded by politically involved literary critics.

Although they are part of a completely different day and age as well as social and cultural context, older authors have paid tribute to this type of literature, prescribed by the power of memory. One need only mention Elias Canetti with his book *Die gerettete Zunge* (1977; The Rescued Tongue), Manès Sperber with his *All das Vergangene* (1974–1977; All That's Gone By), and Dorothea Zeemann (b. 1909), author of *Einübung in Katastrophen* (1979; Training for Catastrophes).

Thomas Bernhard, who at one time maintained that everything in his books was artificial, has explained his development as an author in three autobiographical works; *Die Ursache* (1975; The Cause), *Der Keller* (1976; The Cellar), and *Der Atem* (1978; The Breath). He has termed them *Erinnerungsfetzen* (scraps of memories).[19] They are the story of a refusal. A young man refuses to follow the trodden path toward an education, and on account of a serious lung ailment he is from a very early age continually confronted with death. The radical tenor of his views and the negative selection he makes from reality—one that is, however, consequent in itself

Photo 2 Thomas Bernhard (Photo: Residenz Verlag, Salzburg)

—has been irritating to many. An equally authentic story—and one that lingers unpleasantly in the mind of the reader—is that of the suicide of two boys in a village. The author is the Carinthian Josef Winkler (b. 1954), and the novel, *Menschenkind* (1979; Child of Man).

H. C. Artmann's *Nachrichten aus Nord und Süd* (1978; News from North and South), a collection of loosely compiled notes, memories of a life that is supposed to be governed only by the laws of poetry, is a further example of this authenticity. Jutta Schutting's *Am Morgen vor der Reise* (1978; On the Morning Before the Journey) is another, with its dreamlike vignettes and word games that end in punch lines.

10   AUTONOMY AND ANARCHY

Anyone wishing to gather an impression of Austria from most of these texts, or to use them as the basis for a sociological study, would most likely come up with a result different from the publicly desired and propagated self-image. It would differ above all from the image of the neutral Alpine republic, attested to by foreigners. The anthology *Glückliches Österreich*

Photo 3   Jutta Schutting (Photo: Residenz Verlag, Salzburg)

(Joyous Austria), published in 1978 by the Residenz Verlag, clearly shows that the contributors take a tongue-in-cheek view of the title.

Although the authors are conscious that the scope of their freedom is relatively large in comparison with other countries, they nevertheless insist on pointing out its limitations. The autonomy of the artist in this society is a mock autonomy. At least that is the basic tenor of the criticism. The artist, it is said, enjoys a type of court jester's license. He receives backing for as long as this happens to serve the greater glory of the patron. The invectives he makes against society are parts of the arrangement for advertising purposes, so the critics say. The entire argument of the authors takes on a concrete form particularly when it comes to vying for positions in the mass media.

The widely criticized answer the artists give is the personal anarchism of the individual. But according to the critics, they usually go along with the game, stage an "uprising" now and again, but then stop short of actually taking the consequences of their solidarity. Because of the advocacy of anarchy, authors such as H. C. Artmann, Peter Rosei (b. 1946), and Helmut Eisendle (b. 1939) turned their backs on the Grazer Autorenversammlung. The dramatic work of Wolfgang Bauer (b. 1941) is likewise committed to this anarchy; radical subjectivism and a Bohemian attitude are the answers given to society, rather than a plan for changing society. Total change in poetry is something that Frederike Mayröcker (b. 1924) considers possible. In her case, as Ernst Jandl once stated, the poem is not a part of the world; instead, the world is part of the poem.[20]

Revolte intern (Revolt Within) is the title the East German critic Kurt Batt has given his book. By that he is referring to the literature of West Germany, but actually he prefers to base his theses on the works of Austrian writers such as Peter Handke, Ingeborg Bachmann, Thomas Bernhard, and Oswald Wiener. In Batt's view, the artist in capitalist society is barred from the real goings on in society;[21] he is dependent on himself and on his artistic production. It would be incorrect to take this charge lightly, but one must also take into consideration the fact that concentration on language itself and the process of creation can contribute considerably to the artistic quality. The revolt against making the element of "order" into such an important theme in Austrian literature is carried out within the confines of the art.[22]

The judgment that Austrian literature is apolitical threatens to become an undesirable cliché. It is thus understandable that a number of young authors are making an emphatic effort in their work to ward off any suspicion of the "Habsburg myth"—that is, of being tied to tradition and a retrospective attitude. To be sure, the Austrian literary scene lacks authors who, like Günter Grass, get involved in election campaigns or who, like

Photo 4   Friedericke Mayröcker and Ernst Jandl (Photo: Murauer, Innsbruck)

Heinrich Böll, unceasingly and with a good deal of verve comment on current political happenings, and who are exponents of firm political beliefs. An author like Günter Wallraff, who sets out to uncover improprieties and abuses, would somehow be atypical for Austria. But then there are a number of indications that a gradual change is definitely taking place in the literature. Wolf Biermann, for example, the singing poet who was stripped off his citizenship in the German Democratic Republic, has found many admirers and imitators among young people in Austria who have adapted his way to fit the Austrian scene. In the summer of 1976, the so-called Arena, a summer cultural program sponsored especially for young people by the city fathers of Vienna, was held on the grounds of the former Vienna Slaughterhouse. The underlying theme of the many events, in which young people took part, was essentially the testing of alternatives—alternative ways of living, forms of art and work. The organizers attempted to reach those young people—among them apprentices, unskilled laborers, workers, outsiders, "rockers"—who otherwise do not attend such artistic presentations. The aim was to animate them into becoming creative on their own.[23] The project soon came to a premature end, for the Municipality of Vienna had already sold the grounds to a large company. A rain of protests followed because this stopped an experiment that promised to bear fruit. Even though much of it may have been mere illusion, the Arena had marked a beginning in the attempt to bridge the gap between the working classes and the "producers" of art. Some incidents that took place were exploited to the hilt by a good part of the press in order to spread prejudice among a wider segment of the public against this experiment, which represented a noteworthy alternative to the image of Austrian culture that is usually summed up in the term *Hochkultur*—more or less the established brand of culture for a relative minority—in particular the State Opera, the Burgtheater, the Spanish Riding School, and the Salzburg Festival.[24]

The German biographer of Kafka, Klaus Wagenbach, and the Austrian Arena protagonist Gustav Ernst (b. 1944) have devoted the 16th issue of the series *Tintenfisch* (Octopus) to literature from Austria. In it, the fervent desire is expressed for an understanding of literature, which is in emphatic contradiction to the platitude about "political calm" in Austrian literature. The target of the editors is mainly the otherwise highly praised model of "social partnership." In the editors' view, the literature can be broken down into two parts: "The one Austrian literature shows everything one can do with language in the social partnership, the other what the social partnership can do with man."[25] Some authors see themselves as opponents of any tendencies to harmonize, to any form of compromise or balance between the classes. In their television series "Alpensaga," Peter Turrini (b. 1944) and Wilhelm Pevny (b. 1944) want for once to go against the grain and depict history from the standpoint of the oppressed. The "Alpensaga" (Saga of the Alps) is an undertaking that through the pronounced rejection of high-flown pretensions hopes to bring about a new historical consciousness in a wider segment of the public. And Barbara Frischmuth's (b. 1941) *Kai oder die Liebe zu den Modellen* (Kai or the Love for the Models) makes a theme out of possibilities of women's liberation.

11 CONTROVERSIES

The exact opposite position to the attitude characterized briefly above is embodied by one author, who, of all the Austrian authors living today, has become best known in countries other than the strictly German-speaking ones. Peter Handke is considered in France to be the German (!) *écrivain* par excellence; his major works have been translated in the Soviet Union, a few of them have been made into films, and a drama version of *Wunschloses Unglück*—the English title was A Sorrow Beyond Dreams—was performed in New York in 1977. Nevertheless, the author, whose works are a source of model sentences for German language primers, has changed considerably of late. Not much has remained of the rebel of former days. The advocacy of subjectivism, the renunciation of any partiality or political action, was one thing he had already illustrated at the very beginning of his writing career. This conviction was put into more programmatic words in his journal with the title *Das Gewicht der Welt* (The Weight of the World), which appeared in 1977 and which is preceded by the provokingly solipsistic motto: *Für den, den's angeht* (To Whom It May Concern). Handke's diary and his latest narrative work, *Langsame Heimkehr* (Slow Homeward Journey, 1979), are typical of this stylized withdrawal of many authors not only from political reality but also from history itself. This process has naturally left its mark on the authors' writings: the effort to dissociate themselves from the historical change is deceptive. About the only thing left of Handke's "timely" criticism is to be found in the formula *Das Fette, an dem ich würge: Österreich.* (The fat mass I choke on is Austria).[26] Thomas Bernhard, who is far less choosy about the means he uses and the way he phrases what he has to say, wrote a poison-pen letter to the Hamburg weekly *Die Zeit,* a letter, it must be noted, that the magazine did not publish until the Austrian general election of 1979 was over. In it, he did not present any criticism with a basis in fact, but he proved himself to be a virtuoso when it came to insults. He called the Austrian Chancellor, Mr. Kreisky, a *Salzkammergut- und Walzertito* (a lake-district and waltz-time Tito). The chancellor was, according to Bernhard, comparable to a clerk out of a Nestroy play and thus not a figure in world history, but only one out of literary history. This judgment is important for the relationship many Austrian authors have to politics: they transform politics and political history into literature or literary history.[27]

The position of Handke and Bernhard, seen as being contrary to that of many young authors, clearly shows to what degree literary life in Austria is characterized by juxtapositions. From what we have said so far, it is possible to determine the poles between which lies the whole range of contemporary Austrian literature: avant-garde and traditionalism, anarchy and ordered thought, formalistically determined literature and realistic content-related texts, radical subjectivism and attempt at objectivity, egocentrism and sociopolitical involvement, parochial regionalism and urbane centralism. Austria's literature provides a comparatively favorable example for studying the state of literature in the Western world. The field is not too large to be surveyed, and it can serve as a model for conflicts, such as that between the generations.

12   APPRECIATION ABROAD

It is satisfying to witness the interest taken in Austrian literature abroad, even in places where one might not have a priori expected it. In 1978, for example, an anthology entitled *Österreich heute* (Austria today) was published in the German Democratic Republic. The authors of the blurb state

with obvious satisfaction: "Now that the big spectacle of the formal uprising is over with and no real change has resulted from it, more and more
writers are taking sides in favor of social and political change. The
profile of Austrian literature has changed fundamentally within the last
few years."[28] At the same time, though, they also include texts that are part
and parcel of this "formal uprising." An Austrian literary history in German is currently in preparation in Poland. In the Soviet Union countless
works of Austrian authors have been translated, printed in large numbers,
and offered to the reading public. The German Democratic Republic supports—for obvious reasons—the thesis of a specifically Austrian literature
and a development peculiar to it. During a symposium in Moscow in 1978,
Soviet scholars in the field of Germanica made a far more pronounced
distinction between Austrian literature and German literature—and more
specifically that of the Federal Republic of Germany—than their Austrian
colleagues would ever dream of doing. English and French translations
would also provide the prerequisites necessary to make authors other than
Peter Handke and Thomas Bernhard (who, in the meantime, have already
become famous and who are considered representatives of Austrian literature), known to a larger reading public. In this regard, the magazine *Austriaca* is pioneering in France, just as the periodical *Modern Austrian
Literature* has done in the USA.

The separation of Austrian literature from the literature of West Germany is no longer of the same nature as that which *mutatis mutandis*
existed between the two world wars, in other words a German/German
problem. Instead it is a German/Austrian problem. In its report about the
awarding in Klagenfurt of the Ingeborg Bachmann Prize for 1979, the West
German weekly *Die Zeit*[29] commented wryly: "3:0 for Austria" because
the three prizes awarded had gone to a native of Saxony living in Carinthia
and two Austrians. The reporter noted that this was by no means atypical
for the situation of contemporary German-language literature. One must,
however, take into consideration that the recognition that Austrian authors
have achieved in German-speaking countries could breed an unhealthy
hubris.

Modern-day Austrian literature does, to be sure, owe a good deal to
tradition, but on the other hand it would be incorrect to try to explain its
current status solely on the basis of the existence of the multinational
empire. The multinational empire is scarcely present in concrete terms in
the writings of today's authors. Let there be no misunderstanding or talk
of chauvinism when we venture to claim that new relations to tradition have
developed in the Second Austrian Republic. The most recent past has
shown that it is no longer necessarily the task of Austrian authors to
administer a "great heritage"[30] or to affirm aggressively an Austrian iden-

tity. On the contrary, their task is to spend all their energies in a critical examination of the basis of this identity.

Notes

1. In his acknowledgment address during the award ceremonies after receiving the Kafka Prize of the province of Lower Austria, Peter Handke wished his fellow Austrians would become a *Volk von Lesern.* The text of the speech appeared in the Vienna daily *Die Presse* on October 12, 1979.
2. See in particular the articles by Hans Weigel, Hans Heinz Hahnl, and Andreas Okopenko in Otto Breicha and Gerhard Fritsch, eds., *Aufforderung zum Misstrauen. Literatur, Bildende Kunst, Musik in Österreich seit 1945* (Salzburg, 1967). For general information, see Walter Weiss, "Die Literatur der Gegenwart in Österreich," in Manfred Durzak, ed., *Die deutsche Literatur der Gegenwart. Aspekte und Tendenzen* (Stuttgart, 1971), pp. 386–99; and Hilde Spiel, ed., *Die zeitgenössische Literatur Österreichs. Autoren. Werke. Tendenzen* (Zürich, 1976).
3. See Walter Weiss, "Die Literatur der Gegenwart in Österreich," p. 389. For an assessment of Doderer today, see Georg Schmid, *Doderer lesen* (Salzburg, 1978) and *Heimito von Doderer, 1896–1966. Symposium anlässlich des achtzigsten Geburtstages, Wien 1976* (Salzburg, 1978).
4. See Gerhard Rühm, ed., *Die Wiener Gruppe* (Reinbek bei Hamburg, 1967).
5. Peter Laemmle and Jörg Drews, eds., *Wie die Grazer auszogen, die Literatur zu erobern, Texte, Portraits, Analysen, Dokumente junger österreichischer Autoren* (Munich, 1975); Elisabeth Wiemayr, *Die Zeitschrift "manuskripte" 1960–1970* (Frankfurt/Main, 1980)/ Wendelin Schmidt-Dengler, *Eine Avantgarde aus Graz* (Klagenfurt, 1979).
6. Gerhard Ruiss and Johannes A. Vyoral present a survey of the periodicals in *Zur Situation junger österreichischer Autoren. Eine Bestandsaufnahme der gegenwärtigen österreichischen Literaturszene* (Wien, 1978), pp. 331–56.
7. See Hilde Spiel, *Die zeitgenössische Literatur Österreichs,* pp. 116–24, as well as Gustav Ernst and Helmut Zenker, "Zur Grazer Autorenversammlung," in *Wespennest,* 6(1974), Heft 14, pp. 25–32.
8. Ruiss and Vyoral, *Zur Situation junger österreichischer Autoren,* p. 114.
9. *Ibid.,* pp. 147f.
10. *Ibid.,* pp. 297–310.
11. *Ibid.,* p. 21. The to some degree successful attempts made by various writers' organizations to have free-lance writers eligible for regular social insurance and pension coverage are important.
12. The results of such a series of lectures have appeared in print. Ernst Jandl, *Die schöne Kunst des Schreibens* (Darmstadt, 1976).
13. Walter Weiss and Sigrid Schmid, eds., *Zwischenbilanz. Eine Anthologie österreichischer Gegenwartsliteratur* (Salzburg, 1976).
14. See note 2. See also the critique by Peter Laemmle, "Die österreichische Literatur kommt nur dem Namen nach vor. Über ein fragwürdiges Beispiel von Literaturgeschichtsschreibung," in *manuskripte* (1979), Graz, H. 63, pp. 51–53.
15. Claudio Magris, *Il mito absburgico nella letteratura austriaca moderna* (Torino, 1963); (German trans., *Der habsburgische Mythos in der österreichischen Literatur;* Salzburg, 1966); C. Magris, *Der unauffindbare Sinn. Zur österreichischen Literatur des 20. Jahrhunderts* (Klagenfurt, 1978); regarding Magris, see also Walter Weiss, "Die österreichische Literatur—eine Gefangene des habsburgischen Mythos?" in *Deutsche Vierteljahrsschrift für Literaturwissenschaft und Geistesgeschichte,* 43 (1969), pp. 333–45.
16. C. E. Williams, *The Broken Eagle: The Politics of Austrian Literature from Empire to Anschluss* (London, 1974).
17. Ulrich Greiner, *Der Tod des Nachsommers: Aufsätze, Porträts, Kritiken zur österreichischen Gegenwartsliteratur* (Munich, 1979).
18. *Der Spiegel* (Hamburg), April 21, 1969, p. 186.
19. See Thomas Bernhard, *Der Atem: Eine Entscheidung* (Salzburg, 1978), p. 87.
20. Ernst Jandl, "Die poetische Syntax in den Gedichten von Friederike Mayröcker," *Manuskripte* 1974, Graz, H. 45, p. 55.

21. Kurt Batt, *Revolte intern: Betrachtungen zur Literatur in der Bundesrepublik Deutschland* (Munich, 1975), p. 132.
22. Walter Weiss, "Thematisierung der 'Ordnung' in der österreichischen Literatur," in Walter Strolz, ed., *Dauer im Wandel* (Vienna, 1975), pp. 19–44.
23. Gustav Ernst's novel *Einsame Menschen* (Lonely People; Frankfurt, 1979) presents the Arena activities in the form of a novel. Of particular note are the efforts of some authors regarding the situation in psychiatric clinics and those interned in them. Werner Kofler (b. 1947) presented the story of a mentally disturbed person on the basis of his own experiences in *Ida H.* (Darmstadt, 1978).
24. See in this connection the "song" "Trara Trara, die Hochkultur!" by Fritz Hermann, which has been reprinted in *Tintenfisch.* 16, *Literatur in Österreich,* edited by Gustav Ernst and Klaus Wagenbach (Berlin, 1979), pp. 60f. The "song" touched off a good number of scandals.
25. *Ibid.,* text on the inside cover. On social partnership, see Chapter 8 of this volume.
26. Peter Handke, *Das Gewicht der Welt. Ein Journal (November 1975–März 1977)* (Salzburg, 1977), p. 21.
27. *Die Zeit* (Hamburg), June 29, 1979, p. 33. The term "Salzkammergut" refers to the vacation land near Salzburg which is the setting of the operetta "White Horse Inn."
28. *Österreich heute. Ein Lesebuch,* edited by Georgina Baum, Roland Links, and Dietrich Simon (Berlin, 1978); text on the inside cover.
29. *Die Zeit* (Hamburg), July 6, 1979, p. 39. The report was written by Rudolf Walter Leonhardt.
30. See Otto Basil, Herbert Eisenreich, and Ivar Ivask, *Das grosse Erbe. Aufsätze zur österreichischen Literatur* (Vienna, 1962).

Selected Bibliography

Best, Alan, and Hans Wolfschütz, eds. *Modern Austrian Writing. Literature and Society after 1945.* London, 1980.
Daviau, Donald, and Herbert Zeman. *Metamorphosen des Erzählens: Zeitgenössische österreichische Prosa.* Special issue of *Modern Austrian Literature,* vol. 13, No. 1. Riverside, Calif., 1980.
Greiner, Ulrich. *Der Tod des Nachsommers. Aufsätze, Porträts, Kritiken zur österreichischen Gegenwartsliteratur.* Munich, 1979.
Magris, Claudio. *Il mito absburgico nella letteratura austriaca moderna.* Torino, 1963. German translation: *Der habsburgische Mythos in der österreichischen Literatur.* Salzburg, 1966.
Ruiss, Gerhard, and Johannes A. Vyoral, eds. *Mürzzuschlager Manifest. Materialien zur Tagung "Die Lage der Schriftsteller in Österreich", 1.-4. November 1979.* Wien, 1980.
————. *Zur Situation junger österreichischer Autoren.* Wien, 1978.
Schmidt-Dengler, Wendelin. Europäische Nationale Literaturen. I, Österreich: Pathos der Immobilität. *Frankfurter Hefte,* 34(1979), No. 10, pp. 54–62.
————. Modern Authors: Battles Public and Private. In *Austria Today,* 2 (1976), No. 3/4, pp. 84–87.
Spiel, Hilde, ed. *Die zeitgenössische Literatur Österreichs.* Munich, 1976.
Suchy, Viktor. *Literatur in Österreich von 1945 bis 1970. Strömungen und Tendenzen.* Dokumentationsstelle für österreichische Literatur, 2. Wien, 1973.
Weiss, Walter. Literatur. In Erika Weinzierl and Kurt Skalnik, eds., *Österreich. Die Zweite Republik,* vol. II. Graz, 1972, pp. 439–79.
————. Österreichische Literatur—eine Gefangene des habsburgischen Mythos? In *Deutsche Vierteljahrsschrift,* 43(1969), pp. 333–45.
————. Thematisierung der "Ordnung" in der österreichischen Literatur. In S. Strolz, ed., *Dauer im Wandel. Aspekte österreichischer Kulturentwicklung.* Wien, 1975.
Williams, C. E. *The Broken Eagle. The Politics of Austrian Literature from Empire to Anschluss.* London, 1974.

Modern Austria, pp. 431–48
Copyright © 1981 by SPOSS inc. All rights reserved

22. MUSIC IN AUSTRIA

Gottfried Scholz

Professor of Music at the Hochschule für Musik und darstellende Kunst,
Vienna

The contemporary Austrian music scene encompasses a vast realm of various and different activities and institutions. Its constituents are the composers and the interpreters, the audiences and the media—which are often involved—as well as formal music training and the publishing world. Ultimately, however, the music scene is influenced by the cultural policies of both the federal and provincial governments. The individual areas constituting the Austrian music scene are briefly outlined here.

CONTEMPORARY COMPOSERS

Other countries often refer to Austria as the country of music. This opinion appears to be justified in view of the great Austrian composers of the past, and of the high esteem enjoyed by premier Austrian ensembles and soloists. But the compositions that are known and performed as "Austrian" the world over are almost exclusively works from past centuries and decades. Are there no composers living in Austria since 1945? Of course many creating musicians can be found, some of whom have become known far beyond the country's borders. However, a history of compositions has not yet been written, since we are still too much a part of the process of evolution to distinguish between the outstanding and the merely good, between the lasting and the passing fancy. There are too many swift changes in technique and style, even within the work of one composer, which make it impossible to establish easily surveyable categories. Who can feel willing, or able, to pick out a comprehensible and manageable number of especially

Translated by Ulrike E. Lieder, Stanford University.

9306-6403/81/0415-0431$01.50

significant persons from the considerable group of creating musicians? Yet it is imperative that it be done if we want to present a concise overview, and it will be done in the following.

Our composers' lives are made difficult by the Austrians' strong adherence to tradition, and by many music lovers' shying away from open-minded interaction with something novel. In the concert hall, in the opera house, and on records, the heritage from the classic and romantic periods dominates. New music is pushed into a marginal role, being performed by specialized ensembles and listened to by few subscribers. Attempts to integrate new music into popular concert programs have only rarely been successful, even though the Federal Government has recently begun awarding premiums to concert promoters for doing so. The stamp of Schönberg's Verein für musikalische Privataufführungen (Association for private musical performances), the ghetto of an exclusive circle, has remained an Austrian, specifically Viennese, fate of modern music. Very few composers are able to avoid this peril.

It would be erroneous to regard the compositions since 1945 as a stylistic unit. When a new Austria gradually emerged from the ruins of World War II, there was also a new beginning in the musical sector. The unfortunate Nazi prohibition of any art not conforming to party standards, which was denounced as "degenerate art," prevented the further evolution of the avant-garde of the 1920s. The Second Vienna School did not stay alive in Vienna; Schönberg (1874–1951), who emigrated to the USA in 1933, was not to set foot on Austrian soil again. Alban Berg (1885–1935) died at an early age, and Webern (1883–1945) fell victim to a soldier's bullet during the American occupation. Their more recent works had hardly been published by the end of the war; their earlier publications had been destroyed by the Nazis. To be sure, advocates and students of the Schönberg Circle pleaded passionately for the conservation and continuance of this heritage. Among them, Hans Erich Apostel (1901–1972) is one of the strictest followers of dodecaphony. Josef Matthias Hauer (1883–1959) also plays a role in the postwar period. Independently of Schönberg, he created a 12-tone technique based on tropes.

Yet it was exactly this violent interruption of a continuous evolution of the Vienna School that made dodecaphony a dogmatic obligation for many progressive composers of the postwar period. The general rejection of everything the Nazi regime had propagated resulted in a strong commitment to those things that had been denounced. A need to catch up intellectually pushed aside the trend toward an independent and critical further development of what had been. As a result, the followers of the 12-tone technique were pitted against the followers of tonal music, and vice versa. At issue were not so much composition techniques as different positions of cultural politics. Two great figures symbolize the gap between the factions: Gottfried von Einem (see Photo 1), whose work is stylistically homogeneous, and Ernst Krenek, who incorporated in his work every possible innovation.

His operatic work has made Gottfried von Einem (b. 1918) known and respected beyond Austria's borders. Opera, a type of music most expensive to produce, cannot exist without being assured of an audience. Einem's moderately modern, neoclassicist style, his dramatic dialogues, and, above all, his lyrical fade-outs and colorful instrumentation have contributed to his success just as much as his preference for libretti from the well-known world literature (for instance, "Danton's Death" based on Büchner, "The Visit" based on Dürrenmatt, "The Trial" based on Kafka). On the occasion of the bicentennial of the USA, he wrote the "Philadelphia Symphony." Although he is being denounced as an eclectic by members of the avant-garde, his independent tonal language has found an audience all over the world, an audience not committed to being avant-garde on principle but feeling more akin to the vanishing late romantic style or to a shock-free modern period.

Ernst Krenek (b. 1900), who has been living in the USA since 1938, is also known world-wide. In contrast to Einem, Krenek shows an extremely pronounced ability in his work to adapt techniques currently in vogue. This

Photo 1 Gottfried von Einem. Photograph courtesy of Fayer, Wien.

becomes apparent in the free atonality in his Symphony No. 2 (1922), the lyrical-romantic cycle on a tonal basis, "Reisebuch aus den österreichischen Alpen" (Journey Through the Austrian Alps, 1929); his opera "Johnny spielt auf" (Johnny Strikes Up), which is permeated by jazz elements (1925–1926); strict dodecaphony in the dramatic work "Charles V" (1931–1933); multiserial techniques in his postwar works, as for instance "Sestina" for soprano and chamber ensemble (1957); aleatory techniques in the TV opera "Ausgerechnet und verspielt" (1961); and electronic sounds in his oratorio "Spiritus intelligentiae, sanctus" (1956). Looking at Krenek's works, one is reminded of an overview of the more recent history of style.

Essential ideas, above all theories of composition technique, were vociferously discussed and criticized in the Federal Republic of Germany. The International Summer Courses for New Music in Darmstadt have been a forum for musical experiments since their inception in 1946. However, significant differences become apparent in a comparison of the Austrian and German modern periods. Hardly any of the younger Austrian composers adhere strictly to any given composition technique. The intellectual aspect cannot eliminate the emotional aspect. Austrian music of any epoch contains a metaphysical element; it can be found not only in Schubert's work, Bruckner's, and Franz Schmidt's, but also in Johann Nepomuk David's work, in Cesar Bresgen's, and György Ligeti's—whom we like to regard as at least part Austrian—and in Cerha's compositions. This element gives Austrian music a transcendental dimension which leads away from a superficial purposefulness. A characteristic just as traditionally Austrian is the absence of national or even nationalist tendencies. Austrian compositorial work has been molded by a receptiveness to foreign influences and a willingness to synthetically incorporate foreign stylistic elements. The different nationalities under the monarchy created the basis for the coalescence of German and Slavic, Italian and Hungarian characteristics. The more pronounced Austrian individualism refuses to prematurely categorize today's creative musicians as belonging to this school or that stylistic group. Although this may be an additional problem for the future music historian, it is a refreshing change of pace for today's interested audience. Today, experimental sound constellations coexist peacefully with traditional tonal compositions. The Austrian meets new ideas with reserved interest. Fashion trends from the USA and the Federal Republic of Germany usually reach Austria after a delay of several years. The passing fancy of a novelty has by then normally given way to sober consideration of what is essential. Perfection in their craft, even pedantry, give the Austrian products something solid and protect the vulnerability of deep emotions.

The great stylistic trends of the period between the wars, late romanticism, expressionism, and neoclassicism, have tended to mingle since 1945.

The above-mentioned concepts have become obsolete. The composers of the younger generation tend to be tolerant of that which is different. The pluralist society has caused tolerance also in the field of music, but this must not be misconstrued as mutual understanding.

There were other models in the early postwar years besides the Viennese School, namely Paul Hindemith (1895–1963), and the French music represented by Debussy (1862–1918), Varèse (1883–1965), Messiaen (b. 1908), and Boulez (b. 1925). In this frontal position described above, Hindemith appeared to offer an escape, since he combined new harmonics with a strong focus on tonality. His mature, neoclassicist style had a profound influence on those composers who experimented with polyphony without traditional tonality, who combined the *cantus firmus* technique with new sound constellations. Johann Nepomuk David (1895–1977) numbers among them. His linear strictness, patterned after medieval music, is apparent in his works for chorus and in the literature for the organ. The amount of his compositions for the church confirms that he is a nondenominational mysticist. Cesar Bresgen's (b. 1913) works are simpler and more popular. Folkloristic elements, religious themes, and a fresh style, influenced by the German "Music for Youth" movement, assure him of a greater audience. His works may well be the ones that reflect most strongly the character of the Alps. David, from Upper Austria, and Bresgen, living in Salzburg, are proof of the fact that good new music is also created outside of Vienna's sphere of influence. Helmut Eder (b. 1916), whose activities have been primarily restricted to his native province, numbers among the most successful representatives of the modern era. He utilizes many novel techniques (clusters, microtonal structures, aleatory music), yet he remains comprehensible to a large, interested audience. Among his best-known works are the Symphony No. 3, "Syntagma" for orchestra, and "Memento" for organ and strings. Robert Schollum (b. 1913), of Vienna, transfers the expressive emotions of his personality to works of all genres except opera. He, too, is receptive to many different techniques, but he adapts them all to his own personal style. His Symphonies Nos. 1 and 4 and his "St. Mark's Passion" are works of note. His works reflect influences from Debussy and from folk songs. If neoclassicism is understood to mean mastering ecstasy, an exactitude of forms, and the solidity of folk art, then the unconventional Marcel Rubin (b. 1905) and the traditional Alfred Uhl (b. 1909) may also be categorized as representatives of this style.

The Austrian avantgarde has many facets. This is apparent in the fact that two stylistically very different composers such as Friedrich Cerha (b. 1926) and Kurt Schwertsik (b. 1935) jointly founded the ensemble *die reihe* (the series) in 1958. To this day, this ensemble offers the most significant performances of new works. Composer Cerha also suffered the fate of the generation culturally damaged by the war. Hungering for something new, he found early inspirations in Satie, Milhaud, and Hauer. The Art Club, starting in 1951, brought together writers, painters, and composers in the basement pub Strohkoffer, and served as a forum for an unconventional exchange of opinions on progressive art. Only later did Cerha become acquainted with Webern's work and used the latter's technique of motives as a guide. The encounter in Darmstadt led to his post-serial phase. In "Relazioni fragili" for cembalo and chamber orchestra, he combines soft, jelly-like sounds with sharply accentuated contrasts. The passage of time is reduced to the moment. "Trois Mouvements" is a step on the way to the New Tonality. The most extreme sound stability in "Trois Mouvements" is found in the third movement, which consists of a single cluster. In "Mirror 5" Cerha combines tape recorder sounds with the big orchestra sound. In his most recent works, "Curriculum" (1972) and "Concerto for Violin and Violoncello" (1976), we again find melodic connections and thematic work. His current project, the opera "Baal," might possibly bring a new stylistic synthesis. Contrary to the wishes of Alban Berg's widow, Cerha finished Berg's opera "Lulu."[1] The critics' reaction was generally positive. Notwithstanding, the Alban Berg Foundation sued Universal Edition, which enabled Cerha to finish the opera. The trial ended—typically Austrian—with an amicable settlement.

Immigrants, too, are part of the development of Austrian music. Györgi Ligeti (b. 1923) came from Hungary in 1956, where he had been composing music patterned after Debussy and Kodaly. It was in the West that he became one of the main representatives of the New Tonality, a development that was influenced to a significant degree by the Darmstadt contacts with Stockhausen, Boulez, and Nono. In his piece for orchestra, "Atmosphères" (1961), he develops iridescent-static sound configurations without a recognizable rhythmic effect. In his "Requiem" and "Lux Aeterna," the listener discerns gliding, micropolyphonic fields of sound, interpreted vocally. Ligeti presents absurd music theater in "Aventures" and "Nouvelles Aventures," in which the singers at times utter nonsemantic complexes of sound. The "San Francisco Polyphony" is one of his most recent works. Roman Haubenstock-Ramati (b. 1919) hails from Cracow and lived in Tel Aviv until 1956. He is one of the representatives of musical graphics, a new notation similar to abstract graphics, which leaves a wide margin of freedom to the musical interpretation. The great variety of his sounds is demonstrated by his opera "America" (1966). Another representative of musical graphics is Anestis Logothetis (b. 1929), who is of Greek-Bulgarian origin. Dieter Kaufman (b. 1949) works mainly with electronic music, concentrating on the emphasis of sound. Kaufmann goes beyond pure music to multimedia productions by including forms of radio theater and gestures. Like many of those mentioned above, he too teaches at the Music Academy in Vienna. Otto M. Zykan (b. 1935) represents the scurrilous, satirical accent of the New Music. His opera "Singers Nähmaschine ist die beste" (Singer's Sewing Machine Is the Best) is novel music theater combining film and pantomime, music and dramatic scenes. His primary concern is taking the profound seriousness out of the New Music.

New Music is faced with a difficult situation in Austria. The highly paid ensembles such as that of the Vienna State Opera or the Vienna Philharmonic meet modern music with great reservation, as do their conservative audiences. Specialist ensembles (die reihe, Kontrapunkte, Schönberg Chor) perform modern works with great enthusiasm, but their audiences are limited. The Vienna festival, too, provides modern music with many an opportunity. However, it is the Austrian Radio (Österreichischer Rundfunk) that gives the modern composers the most exposure. Its symphony orchestra emphatically supports the works of New Music and the marginal areas of music literature, as long as the works in question can be played by the traditional orchestra apparatus. The "Musikprotokoll" (Music Minutes) of the Styrian Autumn in Graz provides a suitable forum for the encounter with international modern music.[2]

The Federal Ministry for Art and Education generously supports the Austrian composers by awarding many financially attractive prizes. The Great Austrian National Prize for Music is awarded in recognition of a lifework, and the National Scholarships are intended to encourage young unknown composers. There are a number of other possibilities of support through the Federal Government or the provinces, which range between the two above-mentioned categories. These measures include premiums for concert promoters if their program includes at least 20 percent contemporary Austrian music each season. Only rarely do living composers gain recognition and praise; their dead colleagues fare better in this respect. The system of premiums protects the composers against starvation, but, in the words of Gerhard Wimberger, "they (the composers) do not really fill a role in society; society keeps them as luxuries, but it does not need them." Yet it is possible that future stylistic trends will be geared more to the comprehension of their potential audiences.

Since 1945, nothing specifically Austrian has been found in the vast area of light music that envelops millions by way of radio and television, records and cassettes. Robert Stolz (1880–1975) may quite possibly have been the last representative of good Austrian light music. Hits, pop, beat, and rock music have always been imports. The trend toward internationalism has generally extinguished all national characteristics, which can now only be found in folk music. In any case, the gap between contemporary serious music and light music has grown to such an extent that composers and

interpreters, organizations and audiences have all become involved. It remains to be seen if future trends will decrease the dangerous tension. A first
step in this direction would be rekindling the public's interest in something
new, and abolition of the arrogant *l'art pour l'art* attitude of some members
of the avant-garde.

PUBLISHING

Two companies stand out among the not too numerous Austrian publishers:
Doblinger and Universal Edition are internationally recognized. The Doblinger Publishing House celebrated its 100th anniversary in 1976. Its main
concern has always been service to Austrian composers, and it is open to
representatives of all genres. By the turn of the century, serious music was
represented among its publications by Bruckner's symphonies, Mahler's
Symphony No. 4, and contemporary chamber music; but its revenue originated predominantly from Ziehrer's operettas and Léhar's "The Merry
Widow." After the two world wars, the publisher has remained equally
devoted to both serious and light music. The house also publishes important
educational materials, modern works for choirs and for performance in the
family circle, as well as rural brass music. Doblinger's policy supports
modern music that can generally be performed by means available through
the traditional practice of music, rather than hits of the avant-garde. Many
composers in this group may not be internationally recognized, but through
their choral and instrumental music, they do introduce new stylistic elements to amateur musicians and to students who play a musical instrument.
The "UE" has existed in Vienna since 1901. Its international prestige is
based on its favoring of what is modern at the time. Quality and progressiveness have always been more important than material success. Between the
wars, UE invested heavily in the publication of works by Schönberg, Berg,
and Webern. Since 1945, the publishing house has been able to plan generously, thanks to the interest accrued from this farsighted investment. The
publishing program includes works of many foreign composers such as
Boulez, Berio, Christobal Halffter, and Wolfgang Rihm. They carry on a
tradition that began with Bartók, Janáček, and Malipiero.
    In the field of trade journals, the *Österreichische Musikzeitschrift* (Aus-
trian Journal of Music) deserves mention, as do a number of publications
for specific areas of interest, such as *Musikerziehung* (Musical Training)
and *Singende Kirche* (Song in Church). The significance of the musical
publishing business is not matched by the Austrian recording industry.
Owing to the financial situation in the aftermath of World War II, the
promising small companies were unable to obtain the support they needed
to compete against the large firms abroad, especially in the Federal Republic

of Germany. So Austria found itself in the paradoxical situation of having top Austrian ensembles record Austrian works of music exclusively on the labels of major foreign recording companies.

MUSIC IN THE MEDIA

Today, music reaches the greatest number of its listeners through the mass media.[3] By its nature, radio has a more direct relationship to music. Ever since the beginnings of broadcasting, radio broadcasts of serious and light music have taken up a major portion of the daily program. At the present time, three different radio programs with different contents are broadcast daily in Austria. The unfortunate separation of serious and light music is, as it were, cast in concrete in both production and programming. In the field of light music—mainly featured by Ö 3, the third radio program—a light, upbeat consumer music is broadcast as a more or less unobtrusive companion throughout the day. This music takes up 81 percent of the daily broadcast time of the Ö 3 stations. A uniform rhythm and easy harmonies make it easy to listen or not, to tune in or out according to the demands of the work day. The titles of the individual programs have no meaning and are as interchangeable as the music they announce. The first radio program, Ö 1, represents "the intellectual and musical Austria; as an educational radio program, it is the country's largest school" (ORF [Österreichische Rundfunk und Fernsehgesellschaft—Austrian Radio and Television Corporation] Almanac, 1974). At times, Ö 1 reaches 30 percent of the potential listeners. Ö 3, on the other hand, has an age-specific audience; it reaches peak numbers among adolescents, up to 88 percent of whom prefer this program. The second radio program is regional, therefore its musical programming can hardly be compared to the other two. The ORF department "Serious Music" programs approximately nine hours a day out of a total broadcast time of 17 hours. Stylistically, the programming ranges from old music to the contemporary avant-garde, which generally receives special support from the European radio stations and their ensembles. But it is especially the amount of serious music offered every day that makes it become background music as well. The autonomous character of the musical work of art frequently takes second place to its service function. It is easier to integrate 17 minutes of Vivaldi into the program than it is to plan a live broadcast from the concert hall. Yet, a certain balance is indeed achieved by virtue of the spectacular broadcasts of festival performances or those from the regular musical season, which number among the highlights of the weekly programs.

Television has rules of its own: music without optical effects is alien to this medium. Moreover, the sound reproduction of television sets is not nearly as technically perfect as that of a normal home stereo system. For this reason, the ORF simulcasts its Sunday morning stereo concerts over television and radio. Austrian television considers itself "the mediator between concert and opera listeners on the one hand and a constantly growing mass audience on the other." In the future, broadcasts from the State Opera are to be increased dramatically—it is the only way to confront the rural population with this type of music. Furthermore, Austria's political position makes it possible to play a certain "bridgehead" role between East and West with regard to television broadcasts. The live telecast of the Vienna Philharmonic's New Year's Concert ranks highest among the domestic productions telecast world-wide; it has an audience of 500,000,000.

Music reporting and reviewing in the newspapers must also be included in a discussion of music in the mass media. None of the major dailies neglect reporting on cultural affairs, the major portion of which has, in recent decades, dealt with the fine arts and the theater rather than with music. Opinions about the music critics are generally influenced by the type of review given the musician. However, it can be said that reviews tend to concentrate on the interpretation of a work much more than on the work itself. Detailed, intelligent reviews of compositions, which were the rule in music reviews around the turn of the century, are rare nowadays.

MUSIC IN TEACHING AND RESEARCH

For Austrian schoolchildren, music is a mandatory subject. At the elementary school level, the 6-to-10-year-olds are to have two hours per week of music lessons—singing, instrument playing, and learning to read sheet music. However, since one teacher teaches everything except religion at this level, the music lessons are often neglected. In the intermediate schools and in the lower division of secondary schools, students 11 to 14 years of age take music one to two hours a week, taught by a music teacher. The curriculum prescribes singing and occasional instrument-playing in ensemble, as well as the basics of the theory of music, simple harmony, theory of musical forms, instrumentation, and a survey of the history of music. In the four-year upper division of secondary schools, the 15-to-18-year-olds are to have two hours of music instruction per week, but students are permitted to substitute art for music during their last two years in school. In the upper-division music courses, the curriculum of the lower division is expanded and deepened, and it is supplemented by the presentation and discussion of exemplary works of music. The training received enables students to choose music as one of the subjects of examination in their matriculation exams. Austrian schools rarely offer individual instrument lessons, but instrument players are often incorporated in a school orchestra where a balance between strings and woodwinds is emphasized. In general, instrument lessons are taught by private teachers or at special music schools, which can be found in the entire country. Approximately 100,000 students—7 percent of all children between the ages of 5 and 15—are enrolled in such schools. The music schools are organized in a three-level system: the basics of playing an instrument are taught at the music schools; advanced classes are taught at the presently seven conservatories, which are generally located in the provincial capitals. The most advanced training is available at the three Music Academies in Vienna, Salzburg, and Graz.* These are organized like universities, but they are independent of the universities. Their curricula include courses of study leading to a degree in all traditional instruments, in singing (opera, Lieder, oratorios), as well as in musical pedagogy. Thirty to fifty percent of the students enrolled at the Music Academies in Vienna and Salzburg are foreigners, an especially large portion of whom are American. The tuition of US $110 per semester is very low for foreigners, and one could say that cultural ties with other countries are being actively maintained at great financial expense. Pure musicology is traditionally taught only at the universities, and it is being offered at the Universities of Vienna, Salzburg, Graz, and Innsbruck. Austria's great musical heritage is also reflected in the holdings of it archives and libraries. Above all, the music collection of the National Library in Vienna should be mentioned, although recently there have been significant finds in city libraries and monastery archives. The scientific processing of the materials in the archives is done by the universities, by the Academy of Sciences and other research institutes, among them in particular the international foundation Mozarteum in Salzburg.

It would exceed the state's financial capacity to sponsor a critical publication of the complete works of all significant Austrian composers. Only the works of Johann Strauss, Anton Bruckner, and Hugo Wolf have been published domestically in critical new editions. Other productions have been entrusted to German publishers, such as the complete editions of the works of Schubert, Mozart, and Schönberg. In such cases, Austrian scientists are only collaborators on the edition; the State of Austria subsidizes the printing. It is obvious that the financial means are insufficient in view of the abundance of Austria's musical heritage. This is evidenced by archives that have not been carefully sifted through, as well as by the short daily operating hours of some collections.

*Translator's Note: The conservatories are private institutions; however, any diplomas earned from them are given state recognition. The Music Academies are public institutions.

Internationally respected and esteemed activities include the symposia and congresses held on the occasion of major anniversaries. Beethoven, Schönberg, Schubert and Berg were recently the focal points of such gatherings of scholars. The chance to exchange opinions in the Viennese atmosphere is attractive.

INTERPRETERS

The star conductors and interpreters are probably the best known among contemporary Austrian musicians. Karl Böhm (b. 1894) and Herbert von Karajan (b. 1908)—both of whom are former directors of the Vienna State Opera—are both internationally celebrated masters of the baton. With concert obligations around the globe, from Washington to Peking, they only rarely find time during the season for a performance at home. But their true domain is the Salzburg Festival. Karajan, from Salzburg, is also the initiator of the Easter Festival in his home town, where great operas and symphonies attract a well-to-do international audience.

The majority of the star singers at the Vienna State Opera are foreigners. Following modern-day trends, they are constantly on the road. Of native Austrians, Leonie Rysanek, Eberhard Wächter, and Walter Berry are internationally acclaimed. Pianists Jörg Demus, Friedrich Gulda, Alfred Brendel, and Paul Badura-Skoda and violinist Wolfgang Schneiderhan give concerts in Austria rather rarely. Recording star Udo Jürgens has become well known as a representative of light music; he appeals mainly to the younger generation.

ENSEMBLES AND MUSICAL INSTITUTIONS

The Vienna State Opera ranks among Austria's best-known cultural institutions. No state visitor leaves Vienna without attending an opera gala. At times, for instance in Washington, D.C. in 1979 and in Tokyo in 1980, the ensemble gives guest performances abroad. It is not as well known that the Vienna State Opera, the Volksoper, and the two leading Viennese theaters are state-run operations. This is the continuance of the former imperial sovereignty. Since the subsidies from the Imperial Purse have stopped, the current sovereign, the people, must subsidize the gigantic deficit. The 1979 national budget provided $105,000,000 for the four state-operated stages. The estimated revenue for the same year amounted to $23,000,000. But even citizens in faraway Tyrol usually approve of these subsidies, since they regard the State Opera primarily as Austria's cultural showcase, and possibly even feel faint traces of the grandeur nostalgically reminiscent of former times, when Austria was a political world power.

The Opera House on the Ring concentrates on the great German and Italian repertoires, having staged 43 different operas during the 1977–1978 season, each performed in the original language. The frequently changing casts generally guarantee first-class performances. The orchestra of the State Opera, with the same personnel as the Vienna Philharmonic, assures the highest perfection; the orchestra plays daily, albeit with different members. A favorite game in Viennese society is intrigue against an incumbent opera director and the search for a possibly better one.[4] Lorin Maazel, who will not take over Egon Seefehlner's function until September 1982, is already the focal point of animated discussions. Although it is customary to have foreign guest conductors, only a few receive an enthusiastic welcome, as did Leonard Bernstein, for instance. The Vienna ballet has traditionally been overshadowed by the opera productions. Comparisons with Paris or Moscow would not be valid.

The Volksoper and the Theater an der Wien offer lighter operas in German, as well as operettas and musicals. The theaters of the provincial capitals—associated in the "Theaterverband österreichischer Bundesländer und Städte" (Theater Association of Austrian Provinces and Cities)—are doing their best to cultivate music theater as well, although they are plagued by a chronic shortage of funds. Opera productions are found mainly in Linz and Graz. There are only two private music theaters: the Raimundtheater in Vienna and the Vienna Chamber Opera.

In the area of concerts, too, Vienna has traditionally played a leading role. The first concert by the Vienna Philharmonic took place in 1842. The orchestra offers approximately ten different concert programs per year, with different conductors, in the Goldener Saal of the Musikverein building. Subscribers to these concerts are part of the Viennese cultural aristocracy; tickets are simply not available at the box office. Especially characteristic of the Philharmonic are the high tuning standard and the particular Viennese sound style, which is different from the usual vibrato by virtue of a smooth intonation of the woodwinds. In accordance with tradition, the repertoire of the Vienna Philharmonic is limited to works of the Classic and Romantic periods.

The other professional orchestra in Vienna, the Vienna Symphony, performs mainly in the Vienna Concert House and is subsidized by the city. Its program also includes more recent works; of 118 works performed during the 1979–1980 season, ten were by living composers. There are also a great many smaller ensembles, which, depending on their individual style, perform in the Barockpalais by candlelight or on rough wooden platforms in blue jeans.[5] The provincial orchestras generally maintain a respectable artistic quality; some, such as the Mozarteum Orchestra Salzburg or the Bruckner Orchestra Linz, are known far beyond Austria's borders.

Photo 2   Brucknerhalle in Linz. Photograph courtesy of Burgl Eder, Linz.

Choral activity has greatly decreased in recent decades. Different leisure activities and TV have made the artistic-social gathering of amateurs less attractive. In particular, men's choirs, formerly very active, have practically vanished. In Vienna, two large mixed amateur choirs are used primarily during performances of oratorios. Some youth choirs represent a slight hope for the future. The Wiener Sängerknaben (Vienna Boys' Choir) is known world-wide. Its members have been singing at mass in the Hofburg Chapel every Sunday for nearly 500 years. By virtue of their extensive trips and many recordings, they have become Austria's cultural ambassadors. The church choirs, too, are active. Their repertoire, especially the great masses by Haydn, Mozart, and Bruckner, has survived the liturgy reform of the Catholic Church. In rural areas, amateur ensembles are quite frequent, in particular brass ensembles playing folk music. At present, there are approximately 2,000 brass bands with more than 60,000 members, one-third of whom are adolescents. Pop and jazz are generally presented in small clubs for young people or in spectacular monster concerts (for which the established Concert Associations only reluctantly rent out their facilities, since at times the furniture tends to suffer from the audience's enthusiasm). Jazz concerts were stimulated after World War II through American aid, and they soon found a lively echo in radio. In the mid-1960s, a Jazz Research Institute was established at the Music Academy in Graz. However, in daily musical life, jazz plays only a modest role.

FESTIVALS

Of Austria's many festivals, the Salzburg Festival is foremost as well as the most traditional one. Since 1920, a select, generally foreign audience has annually been treated to first-class interpretations of well-known works in the setting of Mozart's charming city in the summer. All genres of serious music are represented. Modern music stands modestly in the background; the few events featuring modern works are the only ones for which tickets are still available at the box office on the day of the performance itself.

In recent decades, Austria has been seized by a fit of establishing festivals. Culture and nature, fine entertainment and quality tourism, brought an interested audience into all provinces. The Musikprotokolle in Graz are reserved for the avant-garde;[6] there are Operetta Weeks in Bad Ischl or in Mörbisch, a Festival at Lake Constance in Bregenz. The Vienna Festival and the Carinthian Summer in Ossiach offer broader programs, which include theater and the fine arts. These festivals and summer events generate high cultural prestige, and also serve to guarantee the profitability of the tourist trade. For festival budgets, too, the State is the most significant source of subsidies. There is practically no private patron of the arts left in Austria, and the very existence of theater and concert productions, of ensembles ranging from the Vienna Philharmonic to the Camerata Academica in Salzburg, would be threatened were it not for the financial aid provided by the Federal Government, the provinces, and the communities. The State even grants a "relief for losses due to inclement weather" to some open-air theaters. The vacationer is the main beneficiary of the summer festivals. The plan of making the rural population consumers of art by offering a multitude of performances during the summer has met with little success. If this were to be pursued seriously, the festivals would have to take place far away from the main stream of tourism during the quieter season. This way, the experience of a festival has become mainly a dislocated enjoyment of art for domestic and foreign connoisseurs.

CLUBS AND ASSOCIATIONS

The number of musical societies and associations is immeasurable. Some are interest groups, such as the Austrian Composers' Association or the Association of Austrian Teachers of Music; some are devoted to a particular composer, such as the International Gustav Mahler Society. Of a more general nature are the Austrian Music Council, which acts as the joint forum for the various musical institutions and as liaison with the International Music Council; the Society of Authors, Composers, and Music Publishers, which represents the authors' rights for approximately 3,500 musicians; the International Music Center, which promotes music in the media; and MEDIACULT, a research center studying the media.

MUSIC IN CULTURAL POLICY

By a look back to the postwar period, it becomes clear that, for more than a decade, cultural reconstruction, regaining former cultural significance, was of paramount importance. In 1955, to the cheers of the entire population, the cultural symbols of the State Opera and Burg Theater, which had been bombed during the last year of the war, were reopened. The top institutions with their star artists are still considered national symbols. Austria has remained a world power in the arts, even though it ceased being a political world power in 1918.

In recent years, this enthusiasm has given way to a more sober look at the actual cultural behavior of the Austrian population. Empirical research shows that in all the arts, passive consumption far outweighs an active desire to create. Only 13 percent of the population play an instrument. Enjoyment of the rich and varied program of music being offered is largely dependent on a person's education—persons with higher education prefer opera and concerts, those with an intermediate school background like operetta and musicals, and those with mandatory minimal schooling prefer folk and pop music. City dwellers enjoy easier access to cultural events than does the rural population.

Therefore, particular emphasis must be placed on confronting the general population with good music. In order to reach this goal, unconventional methods are sometimes employed. In September 1979, Bruckner's 8th Symphony was broadcast over the entire city of Linz, his home town, like a cloud of sound. Emanating from hundreds of loudspeakers in hot-air balloons, as well as from radios which the population had been asked to place in open windows, the sounds enveloped more than 100,000 listeners. It is still an open question whether this has made Bruckner any more popular, and whether the enthusiasm was generated by the elitist work or by the technical spectacle.

All political parties strive to reduce the difference in cultural levels. This explains the high subsidies provided for in the federal budget as well as in the individual province and city budgets.[7] The principle holds true that any type of education—in school as well as adult education—must never be a business but must always be a human concern of a democratic society.

Photo 3   Arnold Schönberg's grave in Vienna. Photograph courtesy of W. Schollum.

Therefore, the lack of cultural consciousness and insufficient cultural offerings must be changed. To be sure, such an immense project cannot be implemented with money alone, but requires goal-oriented ideas, suitable cultural managers, appropriate stimulation, and planned coordination of all initiatives. A significant step in this direction would be more frequent telecasts of operas and theater productions, in spite of legal and financial obstacles. Another positive factor is that the large State Theaters give guest performances in small towns in the provinces. It is in accordance with the spirit of federalism that cultural activities are not left to the central government but are supplemented by the initiatives of the provinces and cities. The term "Austria, country of music" must not contain simply historical facts; it should also describe the musical consciousness of contemporary Austrians.

Notes

1. The premiere took place in February 1979 in Paris.
2. For more on the Styrian Autumn (*steirischer herbst*), an annual festival, see the chapter by Haeusserman and Wiesmann and the section on Festivals in this essay.
3. On broadcasting in Austria, see the chapter by Feichtlbauer.
4. Former directors of the Vienna State Opera, such as Gustav Mahler, Richard Strauss, and Herbert von Karajan, had similar experiences.
5. The well-known special ensembles also include the Alban Berg Quartet and the Concentus Musicus under the baton of Nicholas Harnoncourt.
6. See note 2 above.
7. Financial subsidies for cultural activities from public funds are specifically Austrian. A few industrialists are private patrons of the arts. However, since tax legislation does not tend to encourage such activities, private subsidies are limited.

Selected Bibliography

Blaukopf, Kurt, ed. *Soziographie des Musiklebens.* Schriftenreihe. *Musik und Gesellschaft,* vol. 17. Karlsruhe, 1979.
Goertz, Harald. *Österreichische Komponisten der Gegenwart.* Wien, 1979.
———. *Österreichisches Musikhandbuch.* Wien, 1971.
Grundlagenforschung im kulturellen Bereich. IFES Report. Wien, 1975.
Klein, Rudolf. Musik. In Erika Weinzierl and Kurt Skalnik, eds., *Das Neue Österreich.* Graz, 1975.
Kulturberichte der einzelnen Bundesländer (Cultural Reports of the Provinces).
Kulturpolitischer Massnahmenkatalog (Catalog of Cultural Policy Measures). Bundesministerium für Unterricht und Kunst. Wien, no year of publication.
Österreichische Komponisten des 20. Jahrhunderts. Wien, 1964–. Up to the present time, 23 volumes have been published, dealing with the following composers: J. Marx, E. Wellesz, J. N. David, H. E. Apostel, H. Gál, J. M. Hauer, J. Lechthaler, A. Uhl, O. Siegl, E. W. Korngold, G. v. Einem, E. Krenek, J. Bittner, G. Mahler, A. Berg, K. Schiske, F. Schreker, A. Webern, E. Marckhl, C. Bresgen, M. Rubin, A. Zemlinsky, F. Schmidt.
Wagner, Manfred. Musik im Rundfunk. In *Österreichische Musikzeitschrift,* vol. 3, No. 3.
Wiesmann, Sigrid. From Clavichord to Electronic Music. In *Austria Today.* Wien, 1975.
———. Music: Conditions and Changes from Schönberg to Liberda. In *Austria Today.* Wien, 1978.

Modern Austria, pp. 449–70
Copyright © 1981 by SPOSS Inc All rights reserved

23. PERFORMING ARTS AND ·FESTIVALS

Ernst Haeusserman

Director of the Theater in der Josefstadt, Vienna

Sigrid Wiesmann

Lecturer at the Hochschule für Musik und darstellende Kunst, Vienna

1

Thirty-five years of Austrian theatrical history are a comparatively small section of an intensive, eventful, and continually evolving tradition spanning many hundred years, a tradition that has been equally generous in giving and in receiving.

If one were to look for a characteristic of Austrian theatrical history that all epochs have in common, one would find the trait of bipolar openness, as I like to call it. Austrian theater has always been open toward the outside, open to the entire German-speaking area but also open to other linguistic areas, to other cultures. Yet it always had enough strength for self-assertion, strength to find itself again, to make its own what it had adopted from the outside, and to possibly hand it on. (A case in point would be Mozart's "Italian operas" or Nestroy's adaptations of French and English models.)

However, Austrian theater has also always been open toward the inside, with—one is tempted to say—stubborn persistence. The much discussed crisis of confidence between the stage and the audience, which has become increasingly more noticeable throughout Europe in recent decades, remained a phenomenon without far-reaching effects in Austria. It was an argument gratefully taken up by theater managers looking for subsidies and by politicians attempting to assuage their voters. However, traces that could

Translated by Ulrike E. Lieder, Stanford University

449

9306-6403/81/0415-0449$01.50

have been proved statistically were faint and unspecific. The reason for this development may be the fact that from the point of view of its audience Austrian theater has always been people's theater, although surely never merely that, and that Austrian theater was regarded only secondarily as an educational instrument, and, even less, as a political tool. The relation of the Austrians and in particular the Viennese, to the theater is so intimate that one would assume they would go to the theater more often than, say, the Swiss or the Italians. However, our admittedly unreliable statistics on theater attendance, computed for the entire population, do not present a very different picture than what we are accustomed to elsewhere, be it east or west. Nevertheless, even the Viennese who never sets foot inside a theater during his entire lifetime feels a certain pride of ownership, follows with curious interest the not infrequent management crises, which tend to create a great fuss in the country, and shows interest in the fate of "his actors." For instance, it is typical that, in spite of periodically repeated appeals to economize, the theater budgets have increased rather regularly under each government and have now reached a level that is probably unique in the world. Again and again, the opposition proposes cuts in the State theater budgets. However, it can be predicted with reasonable certainty that, if the opposition should come to power, not only would it not execute those budget cuts, but it would increase the budget year after year, following the trend of many years.

This ultimately positive basic attitude toward the theater is expressed visibly in an almost fetishist love for the theater building. When the old Hofburg-Theater was torn down and the company moved into the pompous building on the Ring, which stemmed from the period of rapid industrial expansion, a veritable cultist trade with souvenirs from the old house developed. Half a century later, a decision had to be made whether to raze the ruins of the State theater buildings, which had been destroyed by bombs and fires, thus gaining a free hand for the construction of modern, technically up-to-date buildings. But it was decided to reconstruct the old buildings. This attachment to a building, this attempt to cling to familiar things, this not unsentimental persistence is also manifest in a number of more or less successful attempts at reconstruction: in Graz, the old dilapidated theater, built in the Classicist style, was faithfully reconstructed optically but with different materials, and something similar was done to Vienna's oldest theater, the Theater an der Wien. This phase of reconstruction, necessitated by war and dire times, has a precursor as amiable as it is curious in the history of architecture. When Max Reinhardt (whose plans to take over management of the Burgtheater had not materialized) found a theater in the Viennese district of Josefstadt, he did not have the dilapidated building restored; rather, he had Carl Witzmann turn it into a rococo theater in the

Venetian spirit. For the sake of an intimate atmosphere, many inconveniences and discomforts had to be put up with. These inconveniences would not have existed in a new building that would have been hardly more expensive. Reinhardt made his decision in a spirit that not only was typical of his endeavors to create the intimacy of a little theater but also was genuinely Austrian.

A brief statistical item serves as illustration: Of the medium-sized and large theaters that are today still in full use or fully usable, six were built during the 18th century or during the first years of the 19th century and are fully preserved or, at least, their building materials have been preserved; two were built during the first third of the 19th century, one during the second third. No fewer than ten theaters date back to the last third of the 19th century, and another five to the first decade of the 20th. Four theaters from the 1920s have been preserved. During the 1940s, one theater was built, three (plus three open-air theaters) during the 1950s, two during the 1960s, and only one theater was built during the first half of the 1970s (this item does not include three very small theaters, places for experiments in drama, built for the provincial theaters in Salzburg, Linz, and Graz). The second half of the 1970s brought a veritable theater building boom. At the Academy of Music and the Performing Arts Mozarteum in Salzburg, a well-built medium-sized theater hall was constructed, which is also being used for performances of the Salzburg Festival. In Vienna, the Schauspielhaus opened in a remodeled movie theater in 1978, and a new basement theater was opened, which can seat an audience of about 100. In Bregenz, the new lake stage, part of a complex of festival theaters, was opened in 1979.

This survey has quite consciously left out festival open-air theaters, the two Passion Play theaters in Erl and Kirchschlag, and, above all, the numerous basement, chamber, and experimental theaters that exist everywhere, oftentimes have a long tradition, and usually seat an audience of 49 to 150. At present, there are ten such theaters in Vienna alone. No fewer than 23 of the still existing theaters are thus older than the Republic, and only eight were built after the war. Even taking into consideration that the interiors of the large houses in Linz and Innsbruck had to be totally renovated, these facts are still quite impressive. The vast majority of the Austrian theater buildings manifest a bygone concept of the theater, have ostentatiously pompous rooms for an audience that no longer goes to the theater to see and be seen. This "obsolescence" of the theaters is remarkable because it did not come about naturally, but is the result of an artificial extension of their lives. As already intimated, most of the old houses were more or less severely damaged by the effects of the war and many could only be used again after years of reconstruction. Others had to be extensively remodeled in order to meet safety standards and the demands of modern stagecraft and of a contemporary administration.

Another indication of the Austrian's rather peculiar attitude toward the theater also deserves attention: the few new buildings are hidden behind old façades. Disregarding the little theaters in Linz and Innsbruck, which have partially dissociated themselves from the old style, there has not been an architecturally unique theater built in Austria since the expansion of industrialism. The theaters built during the 1920s are hidden behind apartment or office buildings or historical façades.

This means that, in the very recent past, Austrian society obviously only accepted in their cities theater buildings authorized by tradition. People were not willing to express architecturally the new tasks of the theater; rather, they attempted to preserve the "old" image of the theater as much as possible.

When an attempt is made at characterizing an epoch in theatrical history, the architectural element is usually considered incidental. Yet, the acoustic character of a house, the depth and architectural peculiarities of the proscenium, the arrangements of the seats in the orchestra, and the viewing angle very much determine the style of staging and acting.

This argument should not be overemphasized. However, it is significant that the vast majority of theaters still in use today were constructed when Vienna was the capital of a great empire, when the imperial city had to be a unifying model influencing a number of very independent cultures, when aristocrats and patricians gathered for political, economic, and social reasons, and when the theater had a social function.

2

This tradition, which has remained alive, may also be the reason why there was never the often quoted Point Zero for the Austrian theater (the term *Stunde Null* is an evasion for those who thought that by the use of such expressions they could absolve themselves from their share of guilt for the recent past and to begin again at zero). The ban on all theaters, cabarets, nightclubs, and schools of drama, imposed by Goebbels on August 24, 1944, this decreed asceticism of an absolutized egoism, was not treated with the same zealous seriousness in Austria, above all in Vienna, with which it had been dictated in Berlin. A number of grotesque excuses were found in order not to lose contact with the audience.

Still, it is amazing how quickly the theaters opened their doors again. Performances began barely two weeks after the fighting in and around Vienna had ceased, even before the declaration of a truce. Reinhardt's theater, the Theater in der Josefstadt, opened on May 1, 1945, with a sentimental drama reminiscent of the Vienna of the Biedermeier period,* with Martin Costa's *Hofrat Geiger.* The Burgtheater ensemble had already played before an audience one day earlier, in the Ronacher establishment, which was to become its "exile for ten years," since the Burgtheater had burned down during the last days of the war in Vienna (April 11 and 12, 1945). The State Opera ensemble gave a guest performance on May 1, 1945, in the other State-operated opera house in Vienna, the Volksoper, since the State Opera House had burned down on March 12, 1945. The first *Figaro* seems like a preface to an important chapter in Austrian operatic history. A new style was found for Mozart's work in Vienna and Salzburg, a style that helped the Vienna Opera considerably in regaining its world acclaim.

Other theaters too opened their doors surprisingly soon, such as opera and drama in Graz (May 31, 1945), and theaters in other provincial capitals (Innsbruck, Salzburg, Klagenfurt, Linz), all of which had a three-purpose theater (exceptions being Bregenz and Eisenstadt). Even more amazing than the fast reopening of the theaters, which generally took place at the express order of the occupying forces, was the holding of the Salzburg Festival, which took place with only a slight delay between August 12 and September 1, 1945, and which featured no fewer than five concerts by the Mozarteum Orchestra, one concert of solo performances, one choral concert, five serenades, six so-called Austria evenings, each of which featured a well-known soloist, and one concert with church music. It is significant that both drama and opera found their place in this first program. Hofmannsthal's atmospheric drama in verse, *Der Tor und der Tod* (The Fool and Death) was performed, with Albin Skoda, one of the Burgtheater's masters of diction, in the role of Claudio, and Mozart's *Abduction from the Seraglio* followed one day later. Mozart and Hofmannsthal have remained basics of the program, as they had been during the interwar period. These first, still somewhat improvised, events already point to the structure of future events: a return to tradition, emphasis on the musical sector, the search for a balanced relationship between internationalism and specifically local elements. The tradition of the period between the wars was consciously continued, yet the accents are different: for many years, the spoken drama, Max Reinhardt's true domain, loses weight in the total concept.

But let us return to the first Burgtheater performance after the war, which was brought about under circumstances typical of the early days. Management had been taken over by Raoul Aslan, the grand seigneur of the house, famous for his diction, an exceptionally intelligent actor of great integrity, the ideal embodiment of the old Burgtheater, as it were. In his brief opening speech, he implored everyone to maintain tradition and the old fame, saying

*The Biedermeier period extended from 1815 to 1848.

that the Burgtheater must remain a theater of acting personalities working together as an ensemble. To him, the return to the house on the Ring was not only a necessity but a matter of course.

The opening, intended to be programmatic, was an Austrian classic, Franz Grillparzer's *Sappho,* the tragedy that once had its celebrated première in the Burgtheater. However, the reasons for this choice not only were patriotic but were dictated by necessity, since it was easy to cast. An outstanding protagonist was available in Maria Eis, the queen of tragedy and the champion of comedy, who resolutely swept away all illusions. Decorations had to be and could be done without; one relied on the power of the poet's words. As in the other theaters, performances began at 5:30 in the afternoon, since there was neither public transportation nor street illumination, and martial law went into effect in the city at 10:00 P.M. Curiously, the performance was begun twice: Soviet Marshal Tolbuchin was late, and to honor him, the performance was interrupted and the first 150 verses were repeated.

In the Akademietheater, the little theater of the Burgtheater, performances resumed with two exemplary productions from 1941, with Nestroy's *Mädel aus der Vorstadt* (Girl from the Suburbs) and Kotzebue's *Die beiden Klingsberg* (The Two Klingsberg). The third revival, also from 1941, was Tirso de Molina's comedy of errors, *Don Gil von den grünen Hosen* (Don Gil of the Green Pants), performed in the late baroque Redoutensaal of the Hofburg, which had been rediscovered for theater by Max Reinhardt. That same year, there were no fewer than five openings each in the Burgtheater itself and the smaller Akademietheater and also one in the Redoutensaal. With the exception of two new plays that were performed in the Akademietheater, dramas that had proved themselves in the house were presented. The repertoire was build on works by Molière, Goldoni, and Nestroy, Lope de Vega and Calderon, Ibsen and O'Neill, Schnitzler and Schiller. This program of dramas from the world theater, a very demanding one for the audience, was realized in careful productions that concentrated on the poets' words.

The State Opera, now without a home, was to move initially to the Volksoper on the Währinger Gürtel; its building and general equipment had remained largely intact. The new director of the State Opera, composer and conductor Franz Salmhofer, continued to search for a central location in which to hold performances, thus ensuring the independence of the second opera house. In the following years, a certain division of labor developed between the two institutions. The Volksoper concentrated on well-produced and well-cast operettas and smaller comic operas. But *Porgy and Bess* was successfully produced in the house on Währinger Gürtel, as were Carl Orff's *Der Mond* (The Moon) and *Die Bernauerin.* There are today two other institutions dedicated to operetta and musicals, the Raimundtheater, located near the Westbahnhof, and the Theater an der Wien, where now Broadway hits are introduced to Viennese audiences in carefully executed productions, usually graced by a world-famous star.

Salmhofer found his central location for State Opera performances barely five minutes by foot from the ruins of the opera house: the Theater an der Wien. It is an old house, ennobled by tradition: here *Fidelio* premiered in its original version; the Pastoral Symphony and many other works by Beethoven were heard for the first time; Grillparzer's *Ahnfrau* (The Ancestress) was first staged; and Nestroy's best farces had their première. The most important operettas of the golden and silver ages* were first rehearsed on this stage. However, the house was so dilapidated that it could not be used; renovations were carried out with the entire ensemble pitching in, and they continued for the entire summer. Finally, on October 6, 1945, the curtain rose on a *Fidelio* that was memorable for its artful ensemble work (Leonore—Anny Konetzny; Pizarro—Paul Schöffler; Marzelline—Irmgard Seefried; Jaquino—Anton Dermota; conductor—Joseph Krips). Another eight openings followed the same year, two of which were devoted to the ballet, which merited more attention in the Vienna of the postwar period than in other epochs of Viennese operatic history.

3

By the second year after the war, a new development began that for a while gathered momentum: many new theaters were being founded. By the fall of 1949, there were no fewer than 32 ensembles in Vienna, all of which had their own, albeit often very primitive, stage, and 23 traveling theater troupes, 15 studio and chamber theaters, and 19 summer and impromptu ensembles. In addition, there were 5 theaters in adult education institutes, which were often used by several groups, and 28 amateur theater groups. This enumeration does not include several ensembles that played exclusively children's theater.

The economic basis of most of these ensembles was narrow, and their chances of survival minimal. Members frequently participated in several projects at once, and many practiced a trade in order to be able to stand on the stage at night. In spite of this situation, which was a constant challenge to idealism, in spite of the pressure of competition, and in spite of the pent-up demand resulting from years of isolation, the programs

---

*Translator's Note: Vienna's "golden age" of operetta began about the middle of the 19th century, its primary representatives being Franz von Suppé, Johann Strauss the younger, and Carl Millöcker. The "silver age" started around 1900 and is characterized by the increased influence of foreign elements (gypsy music). The leading figure of the silver age is Franz Lehár.

remained surprisingly conservative. Returns to expressionism and to new objectivity (*neue Sachlichkeit*) were regarded as self-evident amends to those authors who had been banned and denounced by the Third Reich, and their dramas were predominantly staged in the small theaters. This conservative tendency was even more pronounced in the large theaters; people seemed to trust only that which had already proved itself. They were more receptive to experiments in the production, since the monumental lack of material constantly necessitated improvization. In spite of this, theater of stage direction (*Regietheater*) in the sense we know it today did not gain ground. The individual actors' personalities remained decisive, although they subjected themselves to an ensemble spirit often strengthened by similar shared philosophies. This ensemble spirit was especially strong in the so-called basement theaters (*Kellertheater*), the best of which became stepping stones to the large theater companies for young actors. This was the case with the Young Actors' Studio in Vienna (which then changed its name to Scene 48, and finally to Theater of the 49; it is now the Ateliertheater), where attempts were made to deal critically with the recent past and the present from an Austrian point of view; and plays like *Barabas* by Hans Weigel, *Weltuntergang* (End of the World) and *Glückliche Reise* (Bon Voyage) by Jura Soyfer, and *Das sind wir* (That's Us) by Helmuth Schwarz were presented. This theater, operated primarily by students, finally merged with the studio of the university, to which an experimental opera theater was added later. Directors like Erich Neuberg, Michael Kehlmann, and Herbert Wochinz, and actors like Helmut Qualtinger gained their first experience here while doing experimental productions. Ödön von Horváth was first remembered here; Franz Theodore Csokor's *Medea Postbellica* successfully premiered here, and here also works by Elmer Rice and Carl Sternheim were performed for the first time in Vienna.

The University Studio, founded by Heinz Gerstinger, fulfilled a similar function in Graz. Like its Viennese counterpart, it presented a multitude of cabaret programs, dared to dig out interesting plays such as Rilke's *Das tägliche Leben* (Daily Life) and Kaltnecker's *Bergweg* (Mountain Path), and tried Sartre's *No Exit*. Another university studio in Leoben functioned in a similar manner for ten years.

4

Vienna's largest dramatic theater, the Burgtheater, still without a general manager, began with a 50-year-old comedy in order to keep the house for the ensemble, and continued with another comedy. The next production— in the meantime, the manager, who had been in office before the Anschluss, had taken over the reins again—was *Des Meeres und der Liebe Wellen* (The

Waves of the Sea and of Love) by Grillparzer; it opened on June 21, 1945, and was intended as a statement, as were the last four scenes from *Die letzten Tage der Menschheit* (The Last Days of Humanity) by Karl Kraus, that apocalyptic epilogue of his monumental work. After the continued existence of the house had been ensured, Rolf Jahn turned its management over to the actor and director Günther Haenel, who restructured its profile. He emphasized modern thesis plays (Priestley, Anouilh, Hay, Lunatscharski), but also determinedly continued the tradition of the house, presenting many Austrian dramas and especially Old Viennese popular theater (Nestroy, Raimund). His plan was completely successful, the more so as he was able to attract an ensemble of extraordinary quality. He hired Attila Hörbiger, Ernst Deutsch, Hans Thimig, and Adrienne Gessner from Reinhardt's ensemble; Karl Paryla and Wolfgang Heinz came from Zurich, which had boasted the best theater in the German-speaking area during Nazi times; Annie Rosar and Karl Skraup stayed with the company; and the stars of the future, such as Oskar Werner, Inge Konradi, and Josef Meinrad, were given their first major assignments.

In 1948, Haenel, whose persistent struggle for social realism was not approved of by everyone, moved with most of the "Zurich people" to the Theater in der Scala in Vienna's 4th District, where he gathered a first-class ensemble which was politically aware and active. The house was subsidized by the Russian occupying forces and presented outstanding productions of works by Brecht and Gorki. Here, the aggressively enlightening undertones of Old Viennese popular theater were rediscovered, as was Grillparzer as a realist, and the program was devoted to Russian drama and topical drama of social criticism.

5

The phase following the immediate postwar period was characterized not only by the hectic state of new beginnings, described above, but also by the establishment of new cultural centers. A not insignificant number of artists working in Vienna had fled to western and southern Austria. They played a decisive role in the activities of the first beginnings, but they also continued to maintain their ties to the theaters that had given them shelter in time of need. The quick reestablishment of the Salzburg Festival after the chaos of war's end was possible only because a number of well-known artists had fled to Salzburg. On the other hand, a surprising remigration of those who had fled from the Nazis began early. Hans Weigel explains his precipitous return from safe Switzerland to starving Austria as a "blatant case of love" because he did it against his better judgment. Like him, others have no plausible explanation for leaving a secure existence, which they had painfully established, to help with reconstruction of a country from which they had been expelled.

The importance to theatrical history of these returnees in love with Austria cannot be overestimated. By their work, they had furthered the development of art. Now they could help to break through the crust formed during the Nazi regime, which was nothing more than a protective wall against the demands of totalitarian rule, of an absolutized ideology.

Bridging the gap was easiest in opera, not least because of the conservativeness of the genre. The pillars of the institution came from the period between the wars, the bases of which date back to the last years of the monarchy. In the person of Josef Krips, who had rushed from London to Vienna immediately after the end of the war, a man from the best Viennese musical tradition took over the baton. He took advantage of the intimate atmosphere of the Theater an der Wien to create a new, unpretentious style of performing Mozart's works, a style that was visualized on stage by Oscar Fritz Schuh, chief producer of the house. The success of the Mozart repertoire in particular is partly due to the fact that Salmhofer and Krips succeeded once again in forming a genuine ensemble. The reestablishment of the Strauss and Wagner repertoire was taken care of without much ado by Richard Strauss's nephew, Rudolf Moralt, who had remained in Vienna. Fritz Busch, Hans Knappertsbusch, Wilhelm Furtwängler, and Clemens Krauss returned as guest conductors. Karl Böhm started regular visits to Vienna in 1948, and Otto Klemperer, Georg Solti, and Erich Kleiber were frequent guests. Great artists, like Maria Jeritza, returned from their new homes to Vienna to give guest performances, and many donated their fees to the reconstruction funds. General Manager Salmhofer was successful not only in keeping many stars in Vienna but also in securing the services of a multitude of new talents, so the State Opera again enjoyed world-wide acclaim before the 1950s. The institution was asked to present guest performances throughout Europe, especially of its authentic interpretations of Mozart and Strauss. Tradition was consciously emphasized; accordingly, genuine novelties were rare, although they were still more frequent than they are now. The first step was taken in 1947, when the Salzburg Festival production of *Dantons Todd* (Danton's Death) by Gottfried von Einem was performed; it was followed by *Joan d'Arc au bûcher* (Joan of Arc at the stake) by Honegger. The following year, Menotti's *Konsul* (Consul) was presented, one year after that Stravinski's *The Rake's Progress,* and in 1953 von Einem's *Der Prozess* (The Trial), again in a production by the Salzburg Festival, as was Rolf Liebermann's *Penelope* one year later. All told, modern works including works for the ballet were allotted 89 evenings during the ten years of the State Opera's exile, as many as were allocated to *La Bohème.* The focal point of that era was clearly Mozart's work, which was performed on no fewer than 560 evenings, surpassed only by Verdi's works, which were presented on more than 600 evenings; and 250 evenings were devoted to Richard Strauss's works.

In the Burgtheater in the Ronacher house, under Aslan's management, the stage directors were almost exclusively those whose ties to the house dated back to the time between the wars. However, in 1947 a gradual change set in, a change that was ultimately to change the profile of the house decisively. Ernst Lothar, who had returned to his home as an American cultural officer, was the first of the new stage directors. He was asked to produce O'Neill's *Mourning Becomes Electra.* He was followed by Walter Felsenstein from Berlin, who directed Schiller's *Räuber* (The Robbers), which he staged brilliantly, with the great attention to detail so characteristic of him. In the summer of 1947 a third director, who came from Vienna but who had lived in Zurich during the decisive formative years of this artistic development, began working for the institution to which he has remained loyal until this day—Leopold Lindtberg. He put on Shakespeare productions, crowned by a cycle of the king dramas, the *Wallenstein* trilogy, and Anouilh's *Beckett,* in cooperation with Teo Otto, also from Zurich. Lindtberg, a master of dramaturgic analysis, had proved himself with his first production, *Hamlet,* by the transparent structures of the plot, a sense of mime, a clear concept, and a unified performance by the ensemble.

In 1948 Raoul Aslan resigned as general manager. After a brief interregnum, the office was taken over by Josef Gielen, who had done a few successful Burgtheater productions before being forced to emigrate. He had been a stage director at the Teatro Colon in Buenos Aires for ten years. One of the chief merits of his almost six years as general manager was the significant expansion of the ensemble. In spite of considerable political resistance, in the Burgtheater itself as well, he succeeded in having Werner Krauss return; he hired Reinhardt's Salzburg Faust and Gretchen, Attila Hörbiger and Paula Wessely; he brought Käthe Gold to the Burgtheater as well as the great tragic actress Liselotte Schreiner. Gielen was a knowledgeable conveyor of the poet's word, who carefully, yet boldly, translated dramatic literature into the language of the stage. He preferred grand concepts to finely differentiated psychological interpretations; yet he knew how to maintain human moderation even in monumental productions. This was especially apparent in his production of the *Seidener Schuh* (Silken Shoe) and in his productions of Shakespearean works and classical dramas.

Another merit of equal significance was his hiring of Bertold Viertel, the former collaborator of Karl Kraus, who had won international acclaim before the war as an expressive lyricist and novelist as well as a movie and theater director. He was in charge of the Akademietheater, and almost solely responsible for it. His productions were forums of psychological interpretations, of ruminations on the meaning and the meaning behind the meaning. Through his translations and productions he introduced Tennessee Williams to Vienna, he directed Chekhov's *Seagull* and Strindberg's *Kronbraut* as tension-laden plays of silence, and he produced notable and valid interpretations of works by Anouilh, Cocteau, and Eliot.

Novelist and critic Ernst Lothar decisively influenced the fate of the State Theater as well as that of the Salzburg Festival as a director of classical drama, but even more so as the possibly most sensitive interpreter of the Austrian psyche (Grillparzer, Beer-Hofmann, Schnitzler).

His counterpart and counterpole was Adolf Rott, the impulsive director of grand scenes, to whose temperament and convincing power is ultimately owed the accelerated completion of the renovations of the house which had been postponed again and again. He was responsible for a number of productions distinguished by their bursting realism, movement, and effects. Under his direction Fritz Hochwälder's *Heiliges Experiment* (Holy Experiment) achieved the convincing success in 1947 that opened up the world's stages for it and made the poet Austria's most successful postwar dramatist. Two years later, it was again Rott who staged Hochwälder's most successful drama, *Öffentlicher Ankläger* (Public Prosecutor) in the Burgtheater, a "tragic self-judgment" of an Eichmann of the French Revolution. And finally, he directed the performance of *Donadieu,* with Ernst Deutsch in the title role, in 1953.

Rott's work at the Burgtheater concentrated on the modern era, and, above all, on classics, which are expensive to produce. However, he also worked at the State Opera, and primarily at the Volksoper, where he developed a new operetta style: histrionic, dynamic, unsentimental. He transferred these ideas on a larger scale to the lake stage in Bregenz, where he won glowing victories in battles for effective theater, using veritable armies of extras, thus pleasing the audience in the 6,400-seat auditorium. In 1954, Rott was appointed manager of the Burgtheater (originally along with the poet Friedrich Schreyvogl).

6

It is not untypical of Austria and its theater that they proceed together through decisive stages of their history. In 1955, the year of the State Treaty, a singular event in world politics, both Burgtheater and State Opera houses were completed after almost ten years of construction. Their reopenings were thus more than a mere signal of the successful completion of reconstruction in the alpine Republic. In and by the theater, the reestablishment of the State was celebrated; the spirit of understanding, which had made the political event possible, was feted.

The opening festivities, which lasted weeks, also made clear a willingness to achieve but a lack of courage for decisively new perspectives. The opening ceremonies of the Burgtheater and the State Opera thus became statements of their position vis-à-vis tradition. Proved directors and unique ensembles presented climaxes of cultural history. Beginning with *König Ottokars Glück und Ende* (King Ottokar's Success and End), Franz Grillparzer's tragedy of the Habsburg State, on October 15, 1955, a whole series of exemplary productions was presented. It was followed by *Don Carlos,* produced by Gielen, with Werner Krauss and Oskar Werner; *Torquato Tasso* by Goethe; Raimund's *Der Verschwender* (The Squanderer); and *Das Konzert* (The Concert) by Hermann Bahr. The three openings of modern works were not daring experiments, but were satisfied with mere representations of contemporary literature: Henri de Montherlant's tragedy of faith, *Port Royal;* Carl Zuckmayer's drama of political decision *Das kalte Licht* (The Cold Light), a play about nuclear espionage for the Soviet Union, which had had its world première a few weeks earlier in Hamburg; and finally the world première of J. B. Priestley's *Take the Fool Away,* an existential farce which became a circus adventure in Rott's production.

On November 5, 1955, the State Opera opened its doors under the management of its new director, Karl Böhm. According to tradition, the first performance was *Fidelio,* with the master of the house conducting; the stage sets were by Austria's most successful architect, Clemens Holzmeister, and Heinz Tietjen was responsible for the not totally successful production. It was a final example of perfected, artful Viennese ensemble work. It was followed by *Don Giovanni,* again with Böhm at the baton, *Die Frau ohne Schatten, Aida, Die Meistersinger von Nürnberg,* and *Der Rosenkavalier:* after that *Wozzeck,* a reproduction faithful to the smallest detail of a 1951 Salzburg Festival production; and finally by a ballet evening.

When the echoes of the festivities of the year 1955 had died down, speculations about the management of the Burgtheater and the State Opera began anew. Böhm resigned in the spring of 1956 and gave way to Herbert von Karajan as the new artistic director, but he maintained his ties to the house as a conductor. Instead of using the principle of ensemble work, advocated by Böhm, Karajan tried to achieve superior performances by utilizing a modified *stagione** principle. He hoped to realize this in cooperation with the Milano Scala and intended to broadcast it world-wide through the technical media. In fact, several exorbitant series of performances came about. Karajan was assisted by Egon Hilbert, the most prominent cultural official of that time, who managed the house for another four years after the maestro's abrupt departure in 1964. Following his death,

Stagione, or season, principle.

another top official, Heinrich Reif-Gintl, took over management; he was followed by Rudolf Gamsjäger and Egon Seefehlner, who is still in office. Lorin Maazel will take over in the fall of 1982.

The manager of the Theater in der Josefstadt, Ernst Hauessermann, succeeded Rott as manager of the Burgtheater in 1959. He remained in that position until the end of the 1968 season and then returned to the Theater in der Josefstadt. Under his management, a number of planned great cycles was created, most of which remained impressive torsi. The most significant of these is probably the cycle of king dramas, which was performed *in toto* between May 18 and 22, 1964, on the occasion of the 400th anniversary of Shakespeare's death. This monumental enterprise was realized by Leopold Lindtberg and Teo Otto. Lindtberg, who is considered the most important director of the Haeusserman era, also staged with Teo Otto the *Wallenstein* trilogy in an adaptation for two evenings. The cycle of antique dramas, which was realized by Gustav Rudolf Sellner in cooperation with the sculptor Fritz Wotruba and the translator Rudolf Bayr (*Oedipus Rex, Antigone, Electra* by Sophocles), remained a torso. This was also true of a cycle of Raimund plays, which was started by Rudolf Steinboeck and Hans Thimig, with stage sets by Oskar Kokoschka.

Haeusserman's tenure concluded with an impressive undertaking: a world tour by the Burgtheater. In 79 days, 79 performances and 52 readings by poets from their works were given in 64 cities on three continents. Many of the stars hired by Haeusserman did not remain at the Burgtheater. Yet we owe the thorough rejuvenation of the ensemble to him.

Paul Hoffmann, the incumbent grand seigneur of the house, became Haeusserman's successor. Like Aslan, he accepted the burden for only a short time. He was succeeded by director Heinz Klingenberg, who attempted to present alternative styles by engaging prominent directors. To name a few, Strehler, Ronconi, and Giucardini, Wood and Hall, Barrault and Swinarski directed productions. These attempts at using varied methods were not always immediate successes, but it is apparent today that the ensemble has profited from them. Klingenberg provided a great service especially to Thomas Bernhardt's work, whose *Jagdgesellschaft* (Hunting Party, 1974) and *Präsident* (President, 1975) had their world premières here. Achim Benning has been manager since 1976. He has successfully emphasized the hiring of German-speaking directors, bold new production concepts, and a program that does justice to modern works.

Besides these central events of cultural policy, the achievements of the other Viennese theaters should not be overlooked; the two most important ones, whose development has been undisturbed and consistent, will be briefly described here.

The Josefstadt remained the actors' theater *par excellence,* and the profile of the Volkstheater was increasingly shaped by its program. Management of the Josefstadt had been taken over in 1945 by the sensitive director Rudolf Steinboeck, who turned over the reins in 1953 to the management team of Franz Stoss and Ernst Haeusserman. Like most Viennese theaters, the house is a repertory theater, in contrast to the Chamber Theater (Kammerspiele), which became affiliated with the Theater in der Josefstadt in 1949, and which presents boulevard plays in succession. Between 1946 and 1950, there was an experimental stage in a small house in the center of the city; and the Bürgertheater, with 1,134 seats, no longer in existence, was also affiliated with the complex of theaters for a brief time. In 1957, a basement theater, the Kleine Theater im Konzerthaus (Little Theater in the Concert Hall) was added as an experimental theater. The Theater in der Josefstadt remained the ideal stage for Schnitzler's and Hoffmannsthal's pictures of the soul, painted in subdued colors, for Horváth's imperiled characters, for Pirandello's complex figures, as well as for old and new conversation pieces, for the Old Viennese popular theater, and for Anouilh's and Shaw's works.

After Leon Epp took over management in 1952, the Volkstheater turned vehemently to the topical drama. Epp, founder and director of the little theater Die Insel (The Island), which could claim a secure position in Viennese theatrical life with its courageous program and well-balanced ensemble, had one un-Austrian characteristic: uncompromising inflexibility. This was apparent in his clear, sometimes coldly aggressive productions as well as in his programming. He was devoted to humaneness; he was a vehement warner of Fascist tendencies until his unexpected death in 1968; he fought against any threat to human dignity and freedom by totalitarianism and collectivism. He left his mark on various levels of cultural politics through the establishment of institutions still in existence today. One innovation was the establishment of a special subscription series where he dared carry out bold experiments without alienating the broad masses of his audience. Another one was a series of performances in Vienna's outlying districts, begun in 1954 in cooperation with the Chamber of Labor, where the theater went out to its audience.

Epp's importance is illuminated by the fact that more than a third of the works performed in his theater were either world or Austrian premières. His program was divided into four blocks of different weight: coming to terms with the present was of paramount importance to him, so he presented plays such as Sartre's *Dirty Hands,* Koestler's *Sonnenfinsternis* (Solar Eclipse), Genet's *Balkon* (Balcony) and *Wände Überall* (Walls Everywhere), Frisch's *Andorra,* and Hochhuth's *Der Stellvertreter* (The

Deputy). The second bloc attempted to reflect the present through great allegorical dramas, and works by Dylan Thomas, Sartre, O'Neill, Brecht, and others were presented; whereas the third bloc consisted of classical works of the world theater (Shakespeare, Schiller, Grillparzer, Büchner, Ibsen, Strindberg, Hauptmann, Wedekind). The fourth bloc was comprised of popular plays in the broadest sense of the word. Epp's successor, stage designer and director Gustav Manker, faithfully continued this concept, albeit with a few restrictions. Paul Blaha took over management of the Volkstheater in the fall of 1979.

Of the theaters in the provinces, the most prominent might well be those in Graz. The opera there achieved a considerable standard of excellence, and the dramatic theater proved itself more courageous in many respects than the theaters in the capital. Taking the brief period from 1968 to 1972 as a typical example, it can be seen that the promotion of young Austrian drama was a focal point of the program. The Graz theater has always had the courage to tap the great pool of talent that forms again and again, surrounding the cultural magazine *Manuskripte* (Manuscripts). Moreover, the dramatic theater is an outstanding institution devoted to the preservation of old Viennese popular theater, while the opera concentrates on Richard Wagner's work and on the early Italian operas of the 19th century.

The Linz theater, a three-branch operation like all provincial theaters, has for years experimented successfully with children's and young people's theater, not only in its "Theater Basement" but also by allowing schoolchildren a peek behind the scenes. "A day in the theater" has become a fixed institution which demonstrates work and working conditions in the theater.

Only recently has the Austrian theater begun to dissociate itself from the old houses. It was and is searching for a new concept of the theater and for a new audience. The first postwar experiments date back to the 1950s, when Artmann, Rühm, Bayer, Wiener, and Achleitner (the subsequently much acclaimed Viennese Group, which hardly attracted any attention at that time) carried out their first anti-theater experiments. They countered traditional theater with language plays and montages, experiments that were more along the lines of an audio play or that developed into the first happenings. During the 1960s, there were attempts—partly unsuccessful—to establish coffeehouse theaters after the Paris model. At the beginning of the 1970s, Conny Hannes Mayer finally made an essential contribution with his Theater im Künstlerhaus (Theater in the Artists' House), which can be formed and shaped in multiple variables. The Dramatic Center, which promotes the most varied activities, ranging from target group theater to a creative center is an institution that attempts to provide a basis for the multitude of creative attempts at development. It has been in existence for almost ten years now.

Many of the revolutionary and evolutionary activities have centered in the Arena (1976), which was created spontaneously. It is a cultural center that settled in the abandoned buildings of the municipal slaughterhouse after the Vienna Festival had produced some avant-garde events there. Theater and music groups sprang up, pictures were painted, discussions were held, and newspapers and a film distributors' company evolved. After 109 days, the buildings were vacated again. The artists have since returned to their customary stages and studios.

7

Referring to the festivals that were mushrooming 30 and 40 years ago, Clemens Krauss once spoke of a "furunculosis." The conductor did not choose a very pretty metaphor, but he seemes to be right, at least as far as the high degree of contagion is concerned. On the other hand, the concept of the festival has a healthy element: a magnificent idea which offers all kinds of advantages to art, the artists, and international understanding, to intellectual stimuli of all sorts, and, not least, to tourism. For us, today, the idea that art—music and theater—is to be enjoyed in well-organized cycles during the winter only is obsolete. Many of the modern festivals are trying new paths; they provide the somewhat sterile musical and theatrical life with new impulses. They invite those who were formerly spectators or listeners in the past century to participate more actively; they stimulate listeners to think along, to discuss, because they have advanced to new forms in some places, to forms that attempt to reduce the barriers between performers and audiences. The concept of the festival as it is understood today is a truly dynamic one. To be sure, material considerations may have played a role. A new world is demanding new forms and shapes and is not afraid of experiments. In exchange, we must expect many things that appear artificially construed and mistaken. The creatively active person must not shy away from taking risks; the discoverer of new land must not shy away from shocking discoveries. Festivals are springing up everywhere in Austria, in every province, in large cities, and in small towns.

There cannot be another town the size of Mozart's home town of Salzburg that offers as many festival events. Salzburg has established a series of festivals that span the major part of the year. They are based on Mozart and encompass a multifaceted devotion to art and, above all, to music, which has made the old baroque residence of the prince-archbishops a world symbol of music. Mozart's character is most purely preserved in the Mozart Weeks, which have been held annually since 1956 in the last days of January. They are more intimate and less spectacular than the summer festival.

The Salzburg Festival, which is held from the end of July until the end of August, was founded in 1920 by Max Reinhardt. Hofmannsthal's *Jeder-mann-Das Spiel vom Sterben des reichen Mannes* (Everyman—The Play about the Rich Man's Death) has since been performed every year on Cathedral Square. August 22, 1920, can be considered the true birthday of the Salzburg Festival. Hofmannsthal established a program for the Salzburg Festival which contains a legendary sentence, "He who says Austria, says yes: a thousand years of struggle for Europe, a thousand years of missions through Europe, a thousand years of faith in Europe." There are guidelines for the program: Mozart as the musical focus, as befits the *genius loci*. The Salzburg Festival has become the most comprehensive show on earth: theater and opera, concerts and serenades, open air theater and impromptu plays in the streets, soloists, chamber music, Lied recitals, lectures. The program unites music for drama and drama for dance, concerts in all shapes and forms.

The Salzburg Festival was reestablished as early as the summer of 1945; it opened with the *Abduction from the Seraglio*. Since 1947, there has been an innovation which met with interest at first, but quickly became old: the inclusion of one contemporary opera each season. The beginning was promising; Gottfried von Einem's *Dantons Tod* was very successful.

In the summer of 1960, after four years of construction, Clemens Holzmeister's impressive great Festival Hall was dedicated. It is an amphitheater in warm wood tones, with festive foyers. The managing board of the Salzburg Festival consists of five persons; the president is Joseph Kaut, Herbert von Karajan is in charge of the musical sector, and Ernst Haeussermann is responsible for the dramatic sector. All great conductors come here to conduct the Vienna Philharmonic, the Berlin Philharmonic, and the Salzburg Mozarteum Orchestra. Prominent foreign orchestras, be it the New York Philharmonic or the Chicago Symphony or the Dresden Staatskapelle, are also invited.

On Palm Sunday, March 19, 1967, a new European and yet another Salzburg Festival opened its doors. It is the "festival of a single man," that of Herbert von Karajan. Salzburg was chosen for a number of reasons. Sentimentality may have played a role, since Salzburg is the town where Karajan was born; practicality, since a magnificent concert hall and opera hall in a great Festival Hall was not in use at Easter time; and publicity, since the musical world was well acquainted with this town as the location of festivals. Here, in his Easter Festival, Karajan sought to realize one of his old dreams: an interpretation of the *Ring of the Nibelung* that was modern yet true to the original. In the selection of the artists, their suitability for recording was also considered, since each performance was recorded first. However, three decisive factors remained constant in the course of all events, be it Wagner, Beethoven, Puccini, or Verdi: the orchestra was the Berlin Philharmonic, the chorus was the Wiener Singverein der Gesellschaft der Musikfreunde (Viennese Choral Association of the Society of Friends of Music), and the stage sets were created by stage designer Günther Schneider-Siemssen, who often created overwhelming sets in cooperation with Karajan. Their stage ranges from the most minute to the metaphysical; it is a realistic painting and cosmic space at the same time. However, this Festival may not be considered a model. It was and remains a unique case, for this close community, which has evolved here from among thousands of people who were strangers and which bears the mark of true community life and cooperation more clearly than can be found anywhere else—this is the achievement of one man.

Since 1946, the Vienna Festival has been held in Vienna at the end of May and during the month of June. In 1947, the Vienna Philharmonic, Clemens Krauss conducting, opened the Vienna Weeks of Music and Theater with a festive concert. In 1950, the Viennese Musikverein, which can look back on a rich tradition, held an international Bach festival. Herbert von Karajan produced the "Mass in B Minor," using no fewer than 80 rehearsals. But it can be said that 1950 marked the beginning of a real festival because from then on it was an uninterrupted chain of festive events of all kinds. In order to give a connecting element to the extremely varied events, each festival was to have a theme. It could be a commemorative of Haydn or Mahler, or the title could be something like "Beginning of Our Century," "Art in Freedom," "Neighbors on the Danube," "The 20th Century," "Biedermeier and Vormärz," "Ballet Festival," or "Schubert and His Times," but it would always describe only some aspects of the festival, for a thousand events cannot have a common denominator.

The intention to democratize the Festival dates back to 1951. It was based on the idea that there are enough elitist festivals, which are, moreover, behind the times in the second half of the 20th century. Decentralization was sought: topnotch events in the center of the city, which, owing to its architectural and cultural significance, attracts tourists, but on the other hand, radiation of the ideas into the districts, the suburbs that, like suburbs everywhere, lead their own lives and have little personal or cultural ties to the center of the city. A genuine people's festival was to be thus created, the festival of an entire city, as it were. The Festival management invited all districts of Vienna to participate with their own events, and it created Festival theater troupes that traveled to countless corners of the sprawling city.

Salzburg and Graz demonstrate the extremes of the concept "festival," which are inadequately characterized by the words enjoyment and experiment. In any case, the Styrian Autumn, founded in 1968, with its "musikprotokol" (Music Minutes), organized by the Österreichischer Rundfunk (Austrian Broadcasting Company), is an exhibition of achievements by Modern Music and the avant-garde. It was not merely the motive of a socially responsible commitment to the present and the future, but also an attempt to bring about international understanding at the regional level that was the decisive factor in the 1968 decision to institutionalize an avant-garde festival in Graz. Many of these "Autumns" have a theme, or are dedicated to a retrospective, which sometimes brings about a rediscovery; 1974, to Alexander v. Zemlinsky, would be a case in point, as would that to Hanns Eisler or Franz Schreker. However, the Styrian Autumn offers not only the "Musikprotokol" but also world premières in the dramatic area, of Austrian playwrights such as Gerhard Roth, and, earlier, Peter Handke and Wolfgang Bauer. The dramatic sector is now more committed to experiments than before. There is at least one world première every year during the Styrian Autumn. The fine arts constitute another major part of this festival.

Owing to limitations of space, not all festivals held in Austria can be enumerated. The following rank among the most important ones. The Bregenz Festival was founded in 1946, shortly after the war. A large, spacious stage was constructed on Lake Constance. The audience sat on the banks of the lake, in an open-air, stepped amphitheater, and only the orchestra pit had a roof. The atmosphere of the "Performance on the Lake" is the focal point of this festival, which features not only operettas but also opera and ballet. The new lake stage was opened in 1979, and the new Festival Hall is scheduled for dedication in 1980.

Since 1976, the month of June has been reserved for the commemoration of Franz Schubert's work at Castle Hohenems. Hermann Prey, the popular and famous singer, discovered this place, where he could realize a long-time favorite dream, a festival. The Schubertiade has meanwhile become a permanent fixture among Austria's festivals.

The Bruckner Festival in Linz takes place during the second half of September. Linz has named its beautiful concert hall after its famous son, Anton Bruckner, and the concert hall is the center of the festival that is dedicated to Bruckner's work and features a high standard of excellence in concerts by symphony orchestras, choirs, soloists, and chamber orchestras.

Thanks to the initiative of a former member of the Vienna Philharmonic, Helmut Wobisch, the Carinthian Summer was founded in 1969 in Carinthia. This festival quickly became one of the most significant in Europe, owing to its unusually interesting program, but also owing to its suitable facilities. The festival is held primarily in Ossiach and in the nearby town of Villach. Musical events of surprisingly great interest, rarely heard works, and unusual guest artists are being presented in the beautiful Ossiach Cathedral and in Villach's modern congress hall. The program offers an impressive and well-balanced array of opera, chamber opera, oratorio, sacred music, church opera, concerts, and seminars.

The Carinthian chapter of the International Society for New Music has been holding courses and seminars in New Music in the alpine spa of St. Leonhard since 1977. Another summer event is a festive week of old music in Innsbruck. This festival originated from the Castle Ambras Concerts, founded in 1963, and concentrates on music from the Middle Ages, the Renaissance, and the Baroque. It is held in the traditional and atmospheric setting of Castle Ambras. Friesach, one of the oldest towns in Carinthia, has an old amateur theater tradition. Since 1975, this tradition has been enlivened every summer by performances of the young students of the Max Reinhardt Seminar of the Academy of Music and the Performing Arts in Vienna, who offer mainly comedies in the spacious courtyard of the Dominican Monastery.

The late Herbert Alsen created two festivals, called the "Burgenland Festival," which rank among the most original and successful festivals in Europe: the Lake Festival in Mörbisch on the Neusiedler See, and the Castle Festival in Forchtenstein. The Lake Festival was founded in 1957; a large stage (75 m by 35 m), supported by pilings, was constructed on the lake, similar to the stage in Bregenz; the lakeshore was banked up in order to gain space for bleachers. The seating capacity was 1,200 at first, then 1,800, and finally had to be increased to 30,000 because of rising demand. This festival —located in the province, bordering Hungary—has always been dedicated to operetta, since the classical Viennese operetta of both the golden and silver ages is the result of a combination of Austrian and Hungarian elements. The festival in romantic Castle Forchtenstein, under the direction of Ernst Haeusserman, cultivates in particular the works of the classic dramatist Franz Grillparzer.

Bad Ischl, the former summer residence of the Austrian Emperor and Franz Lehár's chosen home, has since 1962 been the site of an annual operetta festival. Performances are held each summer on a makeshift stage in the spa's casino. The lovely court theater was converted to a movie theater.

This is only a small part of the festivals offered in Austria. In the area around Vienna alone, there are the following smaller festivals: Summer Festival Melk, Open Air Festival Krems, Open Air Festival Stockerau, Castle Festival Neulengbach, Chamber Music Days Castle Eckartsau, Carnuntum Festival, Nestroy Festival Schwechat. In other provinces smaller festivals are held following local initiative. These do not compare with the great festivals, nor do they want to, but they represent proof of local creativity.

Selected Bibliography

Breicha, Otto. *Protokolle,* Wien, 1970/I.
Greisenegger, Wolfgang. Die österreichischen Bühnen seit 1945. Unpublished lecture, held November 8, 1978, at the University of Stockholm as part of the Austrian Week (Literature and Theater in Austria).
Haeusserman, Ernst. *Das Wiener Burgtheater.* Wien, 1976.
Haider-Pregler, Hilde. *Theater- und Schauspielkunst in Österreich.* Wien, 1970.
Jahrbuch der Gesellschaft für Wiener Theaterforschung. Wien, 1947 and following years.
Kathrein, Karin. All Vienna's a Stage. In *Austria Today,* vol 5(1979), No 1, pp. 46ff.
————. Theater since 1955. In *Austria Today,* vol. 6(1980), No 1, pp. 55ff.
Österreichisches Theaterjahrbuch. Wien, 1963 and following years.
Prossnitz, Gisela. Salzburg Festival: 60 Years Young. In *Austria Today,* vol. 5 (1979), No. 3, pp. 20ff.

Modern Austria, pp. 471–83

24. CONTEMPORARY ART*

Georg Eisler

Artist, Vienna

INTRODUCTION

It is by no means an easy undertaking to summarize the development of visual art in a particular country over a limited span of years. The history of modern art is not an isolated phenomenon confinable within the boundaries of one city or one state: the interplay of the most diverse factors and influences makes it difficult to define boundaries and there is a danger of overstressing local characteristics, which can lead to a provincial point of view.

To define modern art in Austria to a discerning public outside that country is made more difficult by the fact that musical tradition and reputation have tended to obscure other aspects of cultural creativity. The relatively late and recent emergence of Austrian literature and art into increasing international interest is partly explained by the fact that for a long time Vienna has been instantly associated with music in its most varied if conservative forms—of late predominantly with opulent performances.

The geographical situation of Austria—on the crossroads between East and West, North and South—has been reflected in painting and sculpture as in architecture from the Middle Ages onward. In many subtle ways composite influences produced art styles that can be seen as specifically Austrian: late Gothic painting, for instance, which holds an intermediate position between Northern severity and Italian early Renaissance elements. Examples of this type of cross-fertilization are numerous and, in all their diversity, form a characteristic element in Austrian art.

This close contact with the European mainstream of art has been the consequence of another symptomatic aspect: the surprising number of indi-

*This chapter is based on a paper presented at the Conference on Tradition and Innovation in Contemporary Austria, Stanford University, May 1980. Grateful acknowledgment is made to Dr. Heribert Hutter of the Akademie der bildenden Künste in Vienna for providing the illustrations.

9306-6403/81/0415-0471$01.50

vidual achievements anticipating later important developments. To name two examples: Raphael Donner's already classicist figures, created during the reign of high baroque, and, in the second half of the 19th century, Anton Romako's disturbingly proto-expressionist portraits. On the other hand, Austrian artists were prone to cling to already prevalent forms and achieved in many instances a late flowering in elsewhere obsolescent styles. Within the framework of this polarity the modern movement in Austrian art is situated.

In the first years of the 20th century the Vienna Secession, and its off-shoot, the Wiener Werkstaette, represented the only concerted effort of artists, architects, and designers to create a contemporary style. Considerable achievements in architecture and design also represent this intermediary position: Vienna was the last stronghold of the international Art Nouveau style and at the same time the scene of numerous pioneering feats in modern design. Here the elsewhere almost exhausted Art Nouveau found its late and perhaps most perfect expression, at the same time serving as a steppingstone to modern design. This period has left its mark on contemporary Vienna like no other since the baroque.

The final decade of the Austro-Hungarian Monarchy, while providing the setting for what Karl Kraus called the "laboratory for the end of the world," also engendered a great flowering of art and science, of literature and medicine, in a veritable "bravura of fin de siècle"; to quote Nicolas Powell: "this flowering cannot be explained except in terms of the feverish peak of a dying epoch, and the compensation for loss of political power that goes with such an end, and which constitutes a beginning. . . ."

For subsequent generations of Austrian artists such a legacy was not only a source of pride and inspiration—it was also an awe-inspiring challenge. It was above all the triumphal arch for the passage of the arts into the more precarious 20th century. The year 1918 saw not only the end of the Empire, but also the death of some of the leading exponents of its art, Otto Wagner, Egon Schiele, Kolo Moser, Gustav Klimt.

The 1920s and 1930s were in many ways lean years. Kokoschka and Thoeny spent most of their time outside Austria; Loos and Plischke received few opportunities to build; patronage and commissions reflected the crisis-ridden epoch, with the notable exception of the Municipality of Vienna, which launched a grandiose scheme for social housing, employing numerous Viennese architects on large projects (which today are becoming internationally recognized as aesthetic and social pioneering efforts). By the early 1930s this too had come to an end, and the short span of years leading up to the occupation and liquidation of the First Republic were poor in artistic creativity and reception, apart from relatively isolated important personalities such as Alfred Kubin, Herbert Boeckl, and Paris Gütersloh.

The disastrous years of the Third Reich and the war drove creative

Picture 1   Herbert Boeckl, "Der Dominikaner." Osterreichische Gallerie, Wien.

activity underground and into emigration. In its place the provincial and
bombastic trash of Nazi art had its brief and ruinous heyday. All Austrian
art—not only modern art—ceased to exist as a national concept; what
appeared desirable to the new rulers was grafted onto the established canons
of German and Nazi art. Modern Austrian art, as all modern art, was
labeled "degenerate" and disappeared from museum and gallery walls.

Nevertheless, there were small pockets of survival; one of them, Herbert

Boeckl's class at the Academy, became the nucleus of postwar Austrian modernism. The stolid academism of the middle and older generation of the art establishment, having made its lucrative peace with the then prevailing powers, found itself doubly discredited.

2 A NEW BEGINNING

Austria's reestablishment in 1945 brought a radically new beginning for the visual arts as well. The renewal of contacts with art centers of the world came, to quote Werner Hofmann "too late for some and as a surprise to others: fear of being left behind occasionally led to changing horses in midstream." The break with the past became in some cases total, and sometimes grotesque in a constant tug-of-war between tradition and assimilation of new influences.

The focal points were concentrated at the Academy of Fine Arts in Vienna: Fritz Wotruba, returning from Swiss exile immediately after the war, established his master class for sculpture; Paris Gütersloh, also new to the Academy, made his class the hotbed of that specifically Viennese variation of surrealism later to be termed "Fantastic Realism"; and Boeckl's life class became the center for reestablishing the strong tradition of draftsmanship leading back to Klimt and Schiele.

Before describing in greater, if by no means exhaustive, detail the developments in recent Austrian art, I should draw attention to the situation immediately following the end of the war. In spite of great deprivation and the military occupation, cultural life, released from the shackles of the Third Reich and of total war, experienced a great upsurge. What had been banished and maligned was eagerly brought back; the allied powers vied with each other to demonstrate their cultural achievements. Younger artists and students, many with years of war service and captivity behind them, gave the cultural scene new impetus. With the exception of a handful of venerated father figures, they had no older generation of established artists to contend with. Traditions in this first phase of creative activity were considered at the least questionable and conformist. In those days of want and little or no money for the actual buying of art, conformism was relatively easy to reject.

The powerful personality of Fritz Wotruba dominated postwar Austrian sculpture, through the example of his own work as well as the central role of his teaching. His virile personal style developed from a monumental neoclassicism to a completely personal articulation of blocklike forms. The human figure was always at the center of his formal experiments—the rugged angular steles of his later style can be interpreted as the sculptor's personal vision of the dignity of man. Wotruba found many adherents among the young sculptors; the forcefulness of his character made "the gifted aware of his talent and gives him confidence in his own personality, but it paralyzes the mediocre . . ." (Werner Hofmann). Wotruba created his own tradition: as a pupil of the only prewar sculptor of importance, Anton Hanak, he was not burdened by any strong tradition, sculpture having played a minor role until then. A measure of his achievement can be seen in the statement of the French critic Michel Seuphor, who referred to Vienna as one of the centers of contemporary sculpture.

The first generation of Wotruba's pupils produced a number of strong personalities. Rudolf Hoflehner's iron sculptures are also variations on the proportions of the human body. A new and original use of cast iron enables Hoflehner to combine monumental intractability with sensitivity. Joannis Avramidis developed his own formal canon to form the human body out of clearly defined segments. His sculptures have a strong sense of the architectural. More recently Avramidis has concentrated his figures in groups, achieving a sense of harmony and archaic simplicity. The great promise of Andreas Urteil was cut short by his early death. His sculptures set the strong constructive elements, derived from Wotruba, into an almost baroque sense of dynamic motion. Alfred Hrdlicka was the first to break out of the concepts of the Wotruba school. After working as a painter, Hrdlicka developed a strong naturalistic style, working directly in stone. His figures are the antithesis of his contemporaries' severe formal restraint. They are anguished mementos of the violence and brutality of common experience. His mastery of detail and composition is matched with a creative violence of temperament. Mention should be made of Hrdlicka's prolific graphic work. Karl Prantl's "meditative sculptures" represent another extreme position: complete emancipation from anthropoid images, carefully worked simple forms in stone with indentations and hollows, sculptures with a considerable tactile appeal. More recently Walter Pichler and Bruno Gironcoli have created a new form of sculptural cult-object, employing new materials, which they imbue with a personal imagery of metaphysical stylization. These new sculptors, or should we say image makers, were the first of a group of young artists whose formal innovations reveal a pessimistic view of the world—others work in a diametrically opposed way, trying to redefine realistic, mimetic concern with the human figure. This polarity is characteristic of the vitality of contemporary Austrian sculpture.

3 THE BACKGROUND FOR ARTISTIC ACTIVITY

Before continuing with this cursory and, of necessity, incomplete review of modern Austrian art, I will try to sketch in the background of all this varied

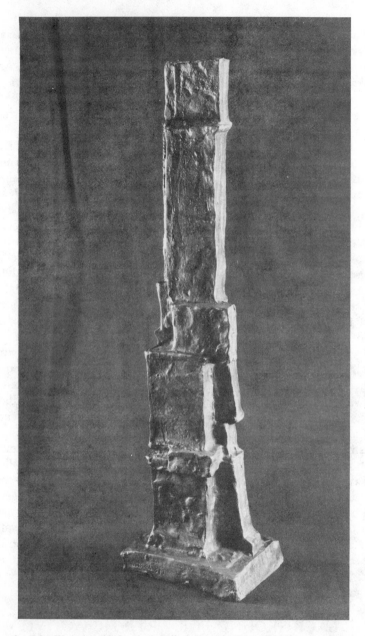

Picture 2   Fritz Wotruba, "Gehende." Gallerie der Akademie der bildenden Künste, Wien.

and rich activity, without which the picture would appear two-dimensional and euphoric. With a population of over seven million, Austria is also the home of 3000 painters, sculptors, and graphic artists. This is a far greater number than in the period between the two world wars. The cultural explosion after 1945 should not detract from the reality, that only a very small proportion of these 3000, something like 2.5 percent, can be said to make a good living from their artistic work. Teaching accounts for a much larger percentage, but the majority derive their income from other sources: other jobs, wives working, family support; and some are living in meager circumstances. The state, local government, and other public institutions yearly allocate more or less modest sums for stipends, the acquisition of works of art, pensions, etc. The distribution of these funds can be said to be fair and democratic, inasmuch as no suppliant artist is turned away empty-handed. Government sponsorship—along lines that have been not incorrectly named the "watering-can principle"—is the subject of heated discussion. Some find that, in spite of some holes in the "watering can" being larger than others, the principle assures on the whole a fair distribution of what little there is. Others want to modify, some to abolish it altogether. The Austrian solution occupies a middle-of-the-road position between state-controlled art support, with all that this can imply, and the sink-or-swim attitude adopted by other states toward its artists. These problems were first systematically researched in a recent study commissioned by the Austrian Ministry of Education and Art.

Art dealing plays a minor role in Austria—speculation and imperative trends are not of primary concern.

Although public interest in art has increased considerably during the last ten or 15 years, contemporary visual art as yet has not reached a wider public and figures low on the list of cultural priorities.

Art does not play a role in Austria's political life. The years of the Cold War, whose frontiers ran through Vienna, have resulted in a widespread, although not total, political abstinence on the part of artists. Political and social questions are still instinctively shunned in art, whereas in contemporary Austrian literature they are increasingly voiced among the younger generation.

4 UNITY AND DIVERSITY

Modern Austrian art can be viewed as a continuous confrontation with and reaction against tradition: the strong tradition of expressionism, Art Nouveau's tradition of sensuous decoration, the tradition of Austrian baroque. These essential characteristics cannot be ignored; they can be either

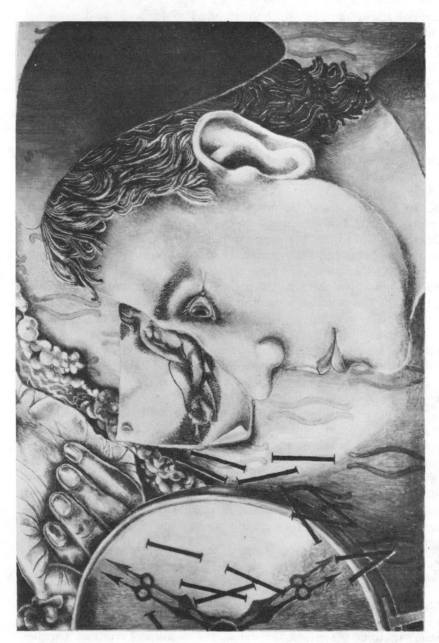

Picture 3   Paris Gütersloh, "Bildnis des Malers Obdetürkis."

Picture 4 Rudolf Hausner, "Forum der einwärts gewendeten Optik." Museum der Stadt Wien.

adopted, changed, or destroyed, and their rudiments remain something specifically Austrian. This is exemplified particularly well in contemporary Austrian painting.

The first group of younger painters to emerge in a stylistically unified grouping were the adepts of a new Viennese version of surrealism. They were pupils of Paris Gütersloh at the Vienna Academy, whose poetic, minute, and somehow ominous genre scenes reflect his work as novelist and grand old man of Austrian literature. Rudolf Hausner's essays in psychoanalytical self-examination, with its acute self-centered iconography; Wolfgang Hutter's gardens of wax fruits and flowers, peopled by beings hovering on the borderline between the oversweet and the horrific; Ernst Fuchs' ecstatic paraphrases of retrospective mannerism, rendered with old-masterly painstaking detail; Arik Brauer's vegetative and brilliantly hued allegories; Anton Lehmden's dream landscapes of geological structures and dense vegetation covering the ravages of war; the Vienna "Fantastic Realists," as the art critic Johann Muschik, their champion from the start, named them, have become nationally and internationally famous.

Of the same generation, Friedensreich Hundertwasser has achieved perhaps even more acclaim: his spiraloid figurations echo the decorative elements of Klimt, his imagery is one of vegetation and meandering lines, with intense and intricate coloring, bordering on but never crossing into abstraction.

A group of young artists based themselves on the Galerie St. Stephan in the early 1950s. This gallery, under the guidance of Monsignore Otto Mauer's charismatic and immensely knowledgeable personality, became the center and laboratory for abstract expressionist art in Austria. Various factors combined to give this movement relevance: the growing influence of American color field and action painting, the international importance of which Mauer was one of the first to appreciate, the desire to break away from representational art, and the metaphysical implications of a modern inconography with its meditative and emotional content. Josef Mikl organically transformed the geometric structure of surface planes into free-flowing strokes of color; Wolfgang Hollegha works in transparent swathes of pigment, using natural forms as a point of departure; Arnulf Rainer, starting as an adherent of the Fantastic Realists, evolved a violently personal system of "overpainting," a form of painterly concealment in shrouds of broad color planes. Later he broke away from the St. Stephan group and developed a facial sign language of personal mythology, overpainting photographs with bizarre and slashing lines.

The third grouping of artists to emerge from the postwar generation began from the unpromising position of outsiders: as late adherents of a realistic style, widely held to be outmoded. Their breakthrough thus came

Picture 5   Josef Mikl, "Studie nach van Dyck." Photo Marianne Haller.

relatively late, in the early 1960s. Works of this group include Fritz Martinz' monumental figure compositions, Rudolf Schoenwald's exuberant
graphics of acute sarcasm and offbeat humor, the work of the present writer,
and Alfred Hrdlicka's violent and critical cycles of etchings and drawings.

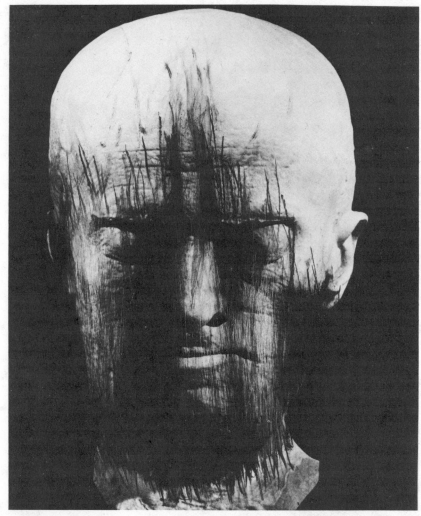

Picture 6   Arnulf Rainer, "Totenmaske." Gallerie Ulysses, Wien.

These artists are concerned with a critical commentary of contemporary life, social consciousness, and formal explorations into the old-new field of realistic figuration. Adolf Frohner's expressive and caustic sublimations of what is otherwise considered ugly are also politically relevant. Mention should also be made here of the distinguished draftsman Kurt Moldovan and the subtle satirist Paul Flora.

I have tried to trace the predominant trends, but it would be only confusing to name numerous other painters, sculptors, and graphic artists whose work is of at least equal significance. That strange interdisciplinary phenomenon of the 1960s, Vienna Actionism, which proved to be a unique and forceful contribution to the then emerging method of stylistic transgressions and happenings, can also be mentioned only in passing. The Viennese variant (Mühl, Nitsch, Schwarzkogler, Brus, and others) was an individual and creatively vicious reaction to the spirit of unrest and breakout then manifesting itself all over the world.

I hope I have given some idea of the multiplicity of styles and tendencies that characterize modern art in Austria within the polarity of tradition and innovation—both elements vital to the development of a broader visual culture.

Selected Bibliography

Breicha, Otto. 1963. *Finale und Auftakt.* Salzburg.
Hofmann, Werner, 1965. *Moderne Malerei in Österreich.* Wien.
Feuerstein, Günther, Heribert Hutter et al. 1965. *Moderne Kunst in Österreich. Wien.*
Breicha, Otto, and Gerhard Fritsch, eds. *Aufforderung zum Misstrauen.* 1967. Salzburg.
Waissenberger, Robert. 1971. *Die Wiener Secession.* Wien.
Powell, Nicolas. 1974. *The Sacred Spring. Arts in Vienna, 1898–1918.* London.
Vergo, Peter. 1974. *Art in Vienna.* London.
Schmied, Wieland. 1979. *Nach Klimt.* Salzburg.
Eisler, Georg, Harold, Sterk, et al. 1979. *Die unbekannte Sammlung,* Materialien zur Staatlichen Kunstförderung in Österreich. Bundesministerium für Unterricht und Kunst. Wien.

Modern Austria, pp. 485–507

EPILOGUE: INTELLECTUAL TRENDS IN AUSTRIA SINCE 1945

Norbert Leser

Professor of Social Philosophy, University of Vienna

Any attempt at a survey of the intellectual trends that played a role or were even decisive during the first quarter of a century of the Second Republic must begin with a retrospective of the First Republic. Only a comparison will elucidate the progress made in Austria's political and intellectual life, as well as the setbacks suffered. After the turning points and collapses of fascism and war, a new order was established in Austria, an order different in many respects from that of the First Republic, but one that undeniably also contained strong elements of continuation of the interrupted past. Indeed, the postwar order of the Second Republic is characterized by a high degree of continuity in the midst of change. It would be more appropriate to speak of a modification and continuation of the past under different circumstances and with consideration of historical experiences, rather than of a total break with the past or of overcoming it.

However, referring back to the First Republic and comparing it to the achievements of the Second Republic, it must be kept in mind that this Austria, which is now being used for purposes of comparison, did not come out of the blue in 1918, and that fateful year does not represent the zero hour of Austrian history. For the collapse of the Habsburg Empire and the break with its traditions, caused by the "Austrian revolution" and proclamation of the Republic, by no means ended the struggle with the Habsburg inheritance; on the contrary, they started it. "The Habsburg Myth" was echoed in Austrian literature, as was proved by the Italian Germanist

Translated by Ulrike E. Lieder, Stanford University

9306-6403/81/0415-0485$01.50

Claudio Magris,[1] who hails from the old Austrian territory of Trieste; furthermore, sociopolitical reality itself, which was reflected in the literature, was under the spell of a great past from which it either definitely wanted to free itself or which it yearned to restore—or at least preserve in the form of nostalgia and transfigured reminiscence. Even during the Second Republic the Habsburg question triggered a government crisis and strained the framework of the otherwise solid Grand Coalition.[2] How much more unrest must the struggle with the Habsburg inheritance have caused during the First Republic; how much more divisive and provocative it must have been!

Attempts by the two great political camps to successfully overcome the past failed. The third political camp, the German-Nationalist one, with its one-sided concentration on the concept of incorporation into the German Reich, was the least able to deal with the past. The political and intellectual forces of the First Republic, which were still living off the substance of the traditions of the multination state, were not capable of truly coming to terms with the values of their reference system, which had collapsed but which was still very influential; nor were they able to creatively adopt these values. Instead, they were mired on both sides in that ambivalence and halfheartedness that permeate Austrian history and negatively influence the Austrian character, as was noted by Grillparzer as well as by the analyses of many others.

Both the political right and left wing reinterpreted the circumstance of the old Austria according to their needs. In fact, in the course of this process of reevaluation of the monarchist past, both sides stylized their own role. The living lie of the Austrian bourgeoisie and petty bourgeoisie, primarily represented by the Christian Socialist party during the First Republic, consisted of the plaintive illusion of having become victims of world history and of sinister political forces and of having lost their well-deserved social standing through hostile intrigues. They failed to consider that the collapse of the old Austria was not least the fault of those who had failed to take the necessary measures to support and strengthen the faltering state. They also failed to realize that the hated social democracy and the "proletarians" it represented were, at best, the beneficiaries of the collapse of the Habsburg Empire, and not its cause.

However, Social Democratic propaganda did its part to strengthen the bourgeoisie and petty bourgeoisie in this complacent view of their own past. In its demagoguery, social democracy assumed the role of destroyer of the monarchy and creator of the Republic; in order to give moral support to its own followers and to strengthen its self-image, it assumed a role it had never played in the past. On the contrary, in the old Austria, social democracy had long been the unacknowledged supporter of the State and had made the most realistic proposals to save old Austria. Its proposals had met with little echo among those in power; nevertheless, it had remained loyal to the old State almost after the State's demise. In the course of the enormous and abrupt increase in the State's power after 1918, the Habsburg past was more and more denounced. In fact, it was just this polemic against the greatness of the old Austria that discredited social democracy with the middle classes, which had preserved a sentimental attachment to the old Austria and which deprived social democracy of the well-deserved recognition of its historical merits. These merits included, after 1918, the fact that social democracy prevented the development of a Communist Soviet republic, but again, its own radical propaganda killed a not insignificant portion of these merits.[3]

Naturally, under these circumstances, a uniform political culture could not develop, nor could that minimal consensus so imperative to the existence of a community evolve. Yet, however divided the political forces of the First Republic may have been, this division was not an obstacle to the development of creative intellectual forces, which produced an extremely high degree of variety and achievement in a historically rare manner within a short period of time and a restricted space. In this First Republic there was a unique flowering of schools, tendencies, and personalities, most of whom had already begun to influence the old Austria and now affected the First Republic, whose political darkness and economic poverty they eclipsed by their brilliance.[4]

To cite a few examples, there was the Viennese School of National Economics, as well as Hans Kelsen's "Philosophy of Pure Law"; there was the "Vienna Circle" of positivist philosophy, as well as psychoanalysis and psychology of the individual; there was Austro-Marxism, as well as a lively Catholicism, which acted in power politics with a unilateral base among conservative forces.[5] However, all these achievements were overshadowed by the political reality in which they existed. And since the signs of the times bode no good for them, these blossoms and achievements were threatened by the dangers of the times. They were caught in the maelstrom of political catastrophe, and in these confused times they suffered the fate of being scattered and forgotten. It turned out that even the greatest intellectual achievements could not halt the fateful course of events but, instead, fell victim to it.

The real reason for the destruction of Austrian democracy and the unresisted annihilation of Austrian independence was the adverse constellation of the year 1918, which did not permit a uniform interpretation of the events. Another reason was the lack of faith in the viability of the new State in whose independent existence no one believed. The prevailing German nationalism, the result of many traditions, did its share to subvert the beginnings of Austrian willingness to accept independence, and to drive Austria into the arms of its stronger German brother, even given the circumstance that Hitler was in power.

When the State, which had been overrun in 1938, had to be reconstructed in 1945, the historical and psychological circumstances were quite different and much more favorable, even though Austria had to accept the presence of foreign occupying forces and limitation on its independence and sovereignty after 1945. But in contrast to 1918, when the new State fell upon the people as an unexpected burden and when it was considered the remnant of a great empire that was still effective as an element of comparison (even if hindsight condemned it), the independent Austria of 1945 was welcomed by the vast majority of Austrians and was considered an improvement. The collapse of the Third Reich was not regarded as the end of the world but as the inevitable consequence of an unsuccessful policy.

The consensus that had been lacking in 1918 developed quickly and naturally after 1945. Turning away from Germany was an action that was politically opportune; it was also the result of insight that the Austrian people had acquired step by step through the bitter experiences of war and oppression, insight that was confirmed by those with political responsibility and that was secured in world history by the victorious powers. The intellectual political tendencies that, according to Adam Wandruszka's analysis, had developed out of the disintegration of the old liberalism and that found their locus in the three political camps in the First Republic had demonstrated an amazing viability in spite of all the changes and upheavals of world history.[6] How did these tendencies develop after 1945?

Austrian social democracy was the political force that had been least compromised by historical developments. On the contrary, it could, in fact, boast that it had resisted fascism on February 12, 1934, and that it had thus given clearly visible support to democracy, which had vanished in Europe. This support was too late to prevent the impending doom, but it was still an act of resistance unparalleled in Europe. In spite of a change in the party's name ("Socialist" instead of "Social Democratic" party), the leadership of the party (Sozialistische Partei Österreichs, SPÖ) after 1945 professed loyalty to this tradition, which had been so gloriously defended and which had been destroyed only by violence. Indeed, the party leadership capitalized on the moral values that the fighters of February had accumulated by their deed and by their heritage, for the purposes of reconstructing the party. This reconstruction proceeded more swiftly and smoothly than had been thought possible during the times of emigration and resistance.

Social democracy was thus the only camp in Austrian domestic politics that was able to formally continue the tradition of the party that had gone down with honor and to claim continuity of political attitudes and actions.

However, this formal and moral continuity obscured a discontinuity of content that can be described as a swing of the pendulum to the other extreme. During the First Republic the rejection of the State, based on Marxist reasons, prevailed, and the postwar coalition of 1919–1920 was regarded as a temporary anomaly. After 1945, Karl Renner's concept gained ground, namely that labor and its party had a right to the State and that the State could become the "lever of socialism." The opposition on principle was replaced by the concept and practice of the permanent coalition, an alternative to which was considered inconceivable for 20 years and which was ended through the voters' decision in the 1966 elections.

The SPÖ leaders, who were in power after 1945 and continued to be for a long time, paid their respects to the past of Austro-Marxism on holidays in order to legitimize their own actions. However, in everyday political life, they pursued policies that did not have much in common with Austro-Marxism—indeed, that deviated from its program and practice in almost all essential points. This erosion and overcoming of the content of classic Austro-Marxist positions, combined with a nonbinding reverence for the greatness and the great ones of the past, was facilitated by the fact that those who had been mainly responsible for the political course of Austro-Marxism between the wars, like Otto Bauer and Robert Danneberg, were no longer alive and that others did not return home.

Events at home were influenced by Adolf Schärf and Oskar Helmer, Theodor Körner, and, not least, Karl Renner himself. Renner saw not only rehabilitation of his ideas, which had been underrated during the First Republic, but also his own advancement to the highest government positions of Chancellor and Federal President. These were men who had been in opposition during the First Republic to Otto Bauer's collision course, which had simultaneously been a course of constant retreat.[7] The work of integration, which social democracy accomplished without and within, might have been impossible had Otto Bauer returned to Austria, which would have made inevitable a discussion about the mistakes and failures of the old leadership. This discussion did not take place in 1945, so that the peace within the party would not be disturbed and the healed wounds would not be reopened.

This careful and selective treatment of its past brought the SPÖ the disadvantage of a continuing intraparty traditionalism, in spite of the discontinuity of the policies it actually pursued. For a long time, this traditionalism prevented the party from being the effective integrating force it has become since the 1970s. On the other hand, the advantages of this touching up of its past are obvious: since delicate questions were excluded from internal discussion, the party's past and the requirements of the present could coexist peacefully.

The party's emancipation from its past took place *de facto* and without formal renunciation of the reclaimed past. In the later party programs of 1958 and 1978, it assumed a form that strove to keep up appearances and continuity, and thus made the difference in the content appear less blatant. In registering the process of emancipation from the past, it should also be noted that the premises of Austro-Marxism were quietly dropped, and the determinist, even fatalistic, belief in the inevitable advent of socialism was replaced by a sober assessment of the party's own chances of success.

This dual aspect of social democratic postwar policies, which had to mediate between emancipation and continuity in order to effectively integrate the party from within, must constantly be kept in mind. It is essential for the understanding of the fact that Karl Renner could succeed and dominate with his practice and his theorem of development "from the liberal to the social state." But, at the same time, Karl Czernetz, who monopolized and thus partially paralyzed the educational system and thus also the party's intellectual life for three decades, advocated an ideology of integration that was still very much under the spell of Bauer's Austro-Marxism, and that was intended to keep the older generation of party officials loyal and to reconcile them to the party's extensively pragmatic policies.[8] Czernetz knew how to spread an effusion of words and phrases over the current party policy and party line and to immunize them against criticism from the left. This continuation of the verbal radicalism of Austro-Marxism did not prevent Czernetz from advocating a definitely pro-Western and anti-Communist course in questions of foreign policy, which he analyzed astutely.

On the other hand, the left-wing Socialist theoretician and speaker Josef Hindels took up Bauer's Austro-Marxism with respect to the slogan "Hands off of the Soviet Union," which had been the official party maxim during the First Republic. Hindels, whose past influence on the young people in the party must not be underestimated, maintained that the Socialist experiment in the Soviet Union and in the other "Socialist countries" should be accorded moral and political solidarity.[9] It is an open question whether Hindels is actually Otto Bauer's ideological successor with this attitude, which has grown to an outright Soviet partisanship in recent years (but which makes Hindels a relatively isolated case in the SPÖ). Otto Bauer based his benevolent assessment of the Soviet Union—which, incidentally, he never accepted as a model for socialism in other countries—on the assumption that the dictatorship would give way to a Socialist democracy once it had been rendered superfluous by external circumstances, especially by the victory over fascism. Hindels not only was a follower of Otto Bauer's in regard to his orientation to foreign policy, but was one of the few opponents of the Grand Coalition. Even after he had been forced to resign himself to its existence, he fought the spirit of the coalition, the spirit of opportunism and pragmatism. In this criticism, Hindels is linked with the criticism of others who, based on different intellectual premises, have also opposed the erosion of the idealistic substance in the party.

Moreover, the example of the national economist and political theorist Eduard März, whose philosophy also has Bauer's Austro-Marxism as its starting point, demonstrates that maintaining Bauer's historical position is by no means a necessary immanent consequence, but rather only reproduces the letter, not the spirit, of Bauer's thinking.[10] As Soviet policy began more and more to reveal its true face, März became one of the most outspoken critics of the Eastern degeneration of communism and, without giving up his Marxist basis, gradually developed into a humanist Socialist capable of constructively criticizing all sides.

Benedikt Kautsky, a Socialist theoretician, authored the rough draft of the 1958 party program, which was submitted for discussion to an extraordinary party convention in 1957 in Salzburg, and he also played a decisive role in the final wording of the program. Being the son of the great Karl Kautsky, he seemed predestined by birth to carry out, even symbolize, the continuation of the great heritage of the past, but also—protected by this authority—to make possible and bestow blessings on the breakthrough to revisionist positions.[11] The editor in chief of the *Arbeiterzeitung*, Oskar Pollak, had the important function of bringing into agreement the past of the Socialist party with the demands of the present, and, above all, to represent a strictly anti-Communist line vis-à-vis the Soviet occupying forces in eastern Austria. This anti-Communist line was also advanced in the administration by Minister of the Interior Oskar Helmer.

The incisive change after 1945 was not only the result of the transition from the sterile attitude of opposition of the First Republic to a coalition policy at any price. The "social partnership"—the organized and institutionalized cooperation of capital and labor that in this highly developed form is unique to Austria—is a reversal of the class struggle policy, supported by party-oriented labor unions, characteristic of the First Republic. This policy during the First Republic was still based on the perspective that the separation of capital and labor would finally be overcome.

The leading unionist and later banker Fritz Klenner may be characterized as the historian and programmatic commentator of this established social partnership. There is no lack of critical overtones and testimony in his work, and he registered relatively early the "discomfort in democracy" that has not lessened today but that has grown.[12] Felix Butschek takes an even more revisionist stand than Klenner. He considers postwar capitalism, which has been reshaped by social democracy, to be an appropriate basis for the future as well, and he subscribes to an explicitly optimistic view of economic and political developments. It was not least the phenomenon of the "new left," which became virulent also in Austria during the 1960s, that ideologically separated the former revisionist co-combatants Felix Butschek and Günther Nenning, both of whom came from the party's right wing in Styria. In a fluctuating transition, Nenning developed into an ideologist and a focus of the "new left," which found shelter in his center and the opportunity to articulate its opinions in his magazine *Neues Forum* (New Forum).[13]

The differences between the Socialist technocrats, who tend toward confirmation and continuation of the status quo, and the thinkers, who advocate reconsideration of the issues of nuclear energy and economic growth in the economic sector, have also erupted again. A case in point would be the director general of the National Bank, Heinz Kienzl, who is striving to work out the newly emerged facts intelligently and in the spirit of social partnership, and to continue in the path that has been so successful so far. On the other side, Egon Matzner, an economist and political analyst, questions the development to date and attempts to integrate the important premises of the present in a leftist but undogmatic view of the times. In his function as coordinator of the Socialist party program of 1978, Matzner found that some of his ideas and those of his friends from the new left were not included in the final version of the program and that political practice does its part to water down the remaining concepts aimed at restructuring society. It is for this reason among others that Egon Matzner is a critic of nonegalitarian developments in the party, because they prevent the party from pursuing further its Socialist objectives.[14]

In his work and in his philosophical basis, the political scientist and philosopher Norbert Leser, too, feels obligated to this endeavor of keeping the socialist idea pure, although he is more influenced by religious-ethical elements than by leftist and Marxist ideals. As a historian of Austro-Marxism, he sees a danger that the party, which failed in the First Republic owing to the contradiction between a radical phase and a retreating practice, might end up in a historical impasse.[15] This impasse might be brought about if the party uncritically adapts its no longer revolutionary but still anticapitalist and egalitarian program to the existing society and its standards, which are oriented toward profit and consumption, thus making its program lose credibility and effectiveness.

In his integrating function as patron, Bruno Kreisky has made possible the pluralism based on a variety of different premises. Future developments will show which trends will actually be realized and what possibilities they will accord to the further development of these premises.[16] Of all the Socialist politicians of the present, Heinz Fischer seems to be most able to find the fine line between theoretical foundation and practical politics and to demonstrate a creative synthesis of theory and practice. However, there is an inherent danger in the combination of theory and practice, of science and politics, chosen by Fischer, namely the danger of manufacturing the ideology of one's own practice and of shying away from analysis, but even more so from dealing with determination with the critical points of our social structure, a decisive part of which is the party itself.[17]

A reminder that effectiveness and critical function are difficult to reconcile and that collisions of different, possibly equally important, issues are inevitable in this area is the case of Christian Broda. He was successful as a reformer of the law, but he gave up his attempts to bring about party reform; and he no longer is a critic of the excesses of the "new class," like his former client Milovan Djilas. Rather, Broda joins the "new class" in order to implement his long-term plans.[18]

However, Austrian social democracy has so far been able to make acceptable even compromises between ideology and expediency and to keep these compromises from growing to uncontrollable dimensions. In contrast, Austrian partisans of Soviet communism who were endowed with a heart as well as a brain saw their loyalty put to a severe test, in which the idea had to be victorious over remaining within a party machinery that had become separated from the idea. The political theoretician Franz Marek and the economist Theodor Prager, who left the Communist party of Austria (Kommunistische Partei Österreichs, KPÖ) without finding a new political home, shared this fate with the brilliant Communist Ernst Fischer. Eurocommunism, which never gained a foothold in Austria, is a demonstration rather than a solution of the problems of leftist existence in today's world.[19]

Austrian social democracy was able to accept its own past, albeit without dealing with the question of guilt, which was left untouched, and to utilize it for the political present. The traditionally bourgeois conservative camp, on the other hand, which found a firm organizational basis in the Austrian People's party (Österreichische Volkspartei, ÖVP), founded in 1945 and recognized by the occupying powers, had to constitute itself into a new party and to establish a new self-image. It was not opportune for the conservative forces to continue the tradition of the Christian Socialist party, which had compromised itself in the experiment of the corporate State and which had, moreover, voluntarily dissolved itself. Continuation of that tradition would have meant presenting to the voters a party burdened with an authoritarian past. Besides, such continuity would not have corresponded to the self-image that leading representatives of the non-Socialist sector of the population had developed in the resistance movement against and in the concentration camps of the Third Reich.

Therefore, in spite of the extensive sociological and personal identity with the substrate of the old Christian Socialists and of the corporate State, a new party was founded that was different from the old Christian Socialist party in some essential points. One difference was the fact that the ÖVP, without denying its close ties to the Church and to Christian philosophy, no longer included the word "Christian" in the party name. In this action the party was in agreement with the Church, which no longer wished to identify with one particular party. Furthermore, from the very beginning, the ÖVP has always been much more of a popular and mass party than the Christian Socialist party, which had considered itself primarily a bourgeois class party and had not nearly as many members as the ÖVP.[20]

The People's party also freed itself of the reservations against parliamentary democracy and the party state, which had originated in the resentment of the Republic, which many felt had been forced upon them. Such reservations had been felt by many Christian Socialists, and had facilitated the slide into authoritarian government. The new party professed its loyalty to democracy and to the Republic. A conscious Austria ideology, coupled with a profession of loyalty to the Austrian nation, also played an important role during the founding phase of the People's party and during its early years. This ideology was advocated by theoreticians such as the editor in chief of the then still influential Österreichische Monatshefte (Austrian Monthlies), Alfred Missong, and by politicians such as Minister of Education and secretary general of the ÖVP, Felix Hurdes.[21]

During its first years, the People's party, being new, had to establish a profile and to credibly dissociate itself from a problematic past. This necessity brought a period of intellectual ferment and programmatic activity to the ÖVP, so that, in contrast to the traditional intellectual and programmatic reserve of the conservative parties, it even surpassed the Socialists, who are usually more articulate in their programs. It is also very much an open question whether the party in this early phase (when the party paper, Das Kleine Volksblatt [The People's Small Paper], congratulated the British Labour Party on its 1945 election victory) can even be characterized as a conservative party, or if it should not be seen as a parallel to the left-wing Catholic French Mouvement Républicaine Populaire (MRP). However, it is not mere coincidence that the men of the first hours, who shaped the new face of the ÖVP, gradually disappeared from the political stage or were, like Felix Hurdes, slowly pushed into the background.

By the first postwar years there were already harbingers of the transition to the Raab-Kamitz line of economic liberalism and to a pragmatism unburdened by ideologies, that took place during the 1950s.[22] When the process of creating a new party profile, which had brought a new image for the People's party in 1945 and which had helped it in gaining the absolute majority, was completed, some of the persons who had rendered valuable services in 1945 were retired. In addition, the clear delimitation from the political right and the openness to the left that had been prevalent in 1945 were ended when the less incriminated National Socialists were allowed to again participate in the 1949 elections, which made the ÖVP hopeful of drawing from this new reservoir of voters. The traditional Catholic social theory functioned only as an ideological bridgehead, but it still had some prominent political representatives such as Alfred Maleta, who was the ÖVP secretary general during the Raab administration.[23] In contrast to neoliberalism, Catholic social theory had always been more inclined to side with the employees and had always had less difficulty with parliamentary democracy than the representations of interests that were based on mere economic considerations. However, during the 1950s, neoliberalism in its older version was prevalent. It considered questions of ideology a burden and special Catholic wishes a problem rather than a concern. Its representative was Minister of Finance Reinhard Kamitz, who shaped Austria's political landscape and even partially restructured it. Yet even the economist Kamitz, who clearly was on the side of the entrepreneurs, was not able to push through his preferences (which were directed at the private sector of the economy and not at the public sector, which was now gaining strength, following the 1946 and 1947 nationalization acts) to the point where he would have been able to upset the public sector and the social partnership, so firmly established in Austria. However, the direction of his economic and financial policies ran counter to the trends that the Socialists advocated and promoted.

After putting its house in order in its relationship to democracy and social partnership, the People's party turned to questions of cultural policy, the link between political and intellectual life in the state. In spite of the new self-image, according to which the party was no longer a self-declared Christian party, the socialization of the ÖVP functionaries and leadership in Catholic schools, organizations, and associations continued to have its effect. This characterized the party as being still close to the Church and distinguished it from the traditionally secular Socialists, who, to an increasing degree, came to terms with the Church but still considered it an alien rather than a friendly power.

The Christian Socialist party had not only fought against the economic objectives of social democracy, but had also resolutely opposed cultural liberalism, which had wanted to deprive the Church of its terrain of social effectiveness, or at least reduce it. The traditional union of Throne and Altar had been replaced by the alliance of the Church and the Christian Socialist party during the First Republic. This alliance culminated in the person of the priest/politician (and at times Chancellor) Ignaz Seipel. During the First Republic, both party and Church fought against the secular cultural liberalism that would have deprived both of valuable support and security for their activities.

During the Second Republic, this phase of clerical orientation and of cooperation between political Catholicism and clerical hierarchy was replaced by a network of Catholic organizations that, without any affiliation, maintain loose ties to the ÖVP. This organized Catholicism acted as spokesman for the Austrian Catholics; it backed the Catholic Church in spite of the latter's party-political neutrality, often on request but often without it. It attempted to pin "Catholic Austria" down to a line of maintaining traditional positions in society (e.g. in criminal law) and almost always defended the status quo.

Among leading ÖVP politicians, Heinrich Drimmel, Minister of Education from 1954 to 1964 and a determining factor in the ÖVP's cultural policy owing to this function, was the primary representative of the forces that based their antisocialism not so much on economic interests as on concerns of cultural policy.[24] Heinrich Drimmel is the intellectual successor of Catholic thinkers and journalists of the time between the wars who, like the editor in chief of the *Schönere Zukunft* (Better Future), Josef Eberle, were primarily antiliberal in the European sense and regarded socialism as the continuation and aggravation of the evils and errors of cultural liberalism. On the other hand, Eberle and his like-minded friends had felt a benevolent empathy for those right-wing circles that wanted to leave the territory of party democracy and establish authoritarian rule. The link between this form of Catholic and authoritarian German-nationalist tradition (which later succumbed to national socialism or at least underestimated its danger) was the ideology of the Reich, which also had a Catholic-romantic side and a German-nationalist aggressive side. The right-wing Catholic and National Socialist groups and trends were further linked by anti-Semitism. Based on religious, economic, and racist nationalist roots, anti-Semitism played a fatally important role in the political and cultural life of the First Republic and paved the way for Hitler's bloody crimes.[25]

Drimmel's political and cultural line was dictated and characterized by an uncompromising rejection of "sinistrism," which he dated back not just to the French Revolution but as far as the new humanism of the Renaissance and the Reformation. Drimmel's philosophy was also manifest in his personnel policy as Minister of Education and left clearly visible marks in Austria's academic life. "Sinistrism" (derived from *sinistra,* left) was to be categorized also as something sinister or disastrous by this choice of terms. It was considered by Drimmel to be the great enemy, which had to be pushed back. Authoritarian "deviations to the right," such as fascism and national socialism, were recognized as essentially healthy movements, which were condemned only because they deviated from the Church and because of the resulting violations of the principles of humanitarianism. This principal intellectual attitude of Drimmel's could actually coexist with a coalition policy that was inclined toward compromising, just as it could exist in the People's party itself, where Kamitz and Drimmel, in a kind of tacit division of labor, fulfilled different tasks and integrated different social strata into the party.

The preponderance of Drimmel's line was an essential contributing factor in isolating the People's party from the intellectual and social forces that demanded liberalization in State and society and in later facilitating the Socialist link-up to these groups. It was not least the development in the World Church itself, which had been advancing since the Second Vatican Council and which has a representative in the person of Cardinal Franz König of Vienna, who is effective far beyond Austria's borders, that finally bypassed Drimmel and pushed him on the defensive.[26] With the advent of the "New Left" movement—which reached Austria belatedly and in weak manifestations, but affected every country and every party—Drimmel's attitude became a completely anachronistic counterposition to the important trends of the times. Yet Heinrich Drimmel, the person and the politician, deserves a special place in Austrian intellectual and cultural history: the determined attempts to go against the trends of the time, which do not always bring pure blessings but often dubious changes and successes, merits respect. Although Drimmel's concept was not trend-setting for his party and for Austria but was, in retrospect, a battle of retreat, at least it was a concept. How many politicians of the Second Republic can claim with a clear conscience that they have consistently followed a line—albeit a wrong one—and that they have not just paid homage to the political expediency of everyday life?

In a simplification of the ideal type, Heinrich Drimmel (who, incidentally, after retiring from political life has become an immensely prolific writer of high literary and philosophical standards) could be characterized as the representative of a militant right-wing Catholicism that still thinks in prewar categories of friends and enemies. The representatives of left-wing Catholicism, who wanted to free the Church and the Catholic camp from its traditional narrowness, cannot be found in the upper ranks of the ÖVP and of Catholic organizations but primarily on the periphery of this frame of reference. This is a further explanation of the fact that the SPÖ won the battle for the "liberal" marginal strata, which determined the outcome of the elections during the 1970s. The most interesting representative of such an open, left-wing, and liberal Catholicism is Friedrich Heer, who is probably the greatest talent not only of Catholic Austria but of the entire intellectual life after the war. In his booklet *Gespräch der Feinde* (Conversation among Enemies), published in 1949 and only one example of a production of amazing quantity and quality, he anticipated the subsequent opening up of the Church to the world and to the ecumene, but he also laid the groundwork for the breaching of traditional political borders.[27] In spite of his brilliant work and in spite of his world-wide fame, Friedrich Heer has not succeeded in establishing himself at an Austrian university, a fact that is poor testimony to this country's academic and political climate during the first two postwar decades.

The Vienna psychologist and humanist Wilfried Daim and Viennese professor of sociology August Maria Knoll joined Heer during the early 1960s in demanding reform of the Church, a demand that did not always win them friends in "Catholic Austria." August Maria Knoll in particular, who criticized the ecclesiastical natural law and looked with a critical eye at the ideology of Catholic social theory, had some bad experiences—yet the developments that have taken place in the Church since then have caught up with Knoll's criticism and have rendered it obsolete. This development is, with increasing frequency, connected to an attack on the basis of the faith, something that was foreign to Knoll as a devout son of the Church.[28]

During the time of the corporate State before 1938, Ernst Karl Winter had worked for reconciliation between government and labor, and he had been proved right in his rejection of the unimaginative bourgeois anti-Marxism as well as in his warning not to capitulate to Germany. In spite of this, or possibly because of it, he was not reintegrated into Austrian society in a manner befitting his stature when he returned from American exile in the mid-1950s. He died in 1959, after completing a pioneer work on Saint Severin (d. 482), who, in Winter's interpretation, was one of the spiritual and intellectual ancestors of the specifically Austrian development and of the Austrian State. Another left-wing Catholic who played a role in the intellectual and political reality of the time between the wars and of the corporate State but who missed the boat to the future during the Second Republic, is Graz professor of national economics Joseph Dobretsberger. He tried his own way politically as well when he founded his own, left-wing bourgeois party, which, like all other parties founded outside the traditional "camps," was not very successful. Dobretsberger demonstrated in his own person the problematics of the "Catholic social policy at the crossroads," which he had treated scientifically.[29]

Developments in the world-wide Church have changed Austrian Catholicism and have also pushed in a different direction the leading personalities of clerical life, who had originally held intransigent positions. This change could be observed, for instance, in the career and personality of Monsignore Otto Mauer. As the ecclesiastical assistant to Katholische Aktion[a] and as

---

[a]Translator's Note: The Katholische Aktion is the official Catholic lay organization, with a structure that reaches from the federal and diocesan levels to the parish level. It has a number of subdivisions (e.g. Catholic Workers' Movement, Catholic Action for Men).

the spokesman of the Church on controversial matters and in public discussions, he had originally represented a hard and traditionally Catholic line, but during the 1960s he became more and more an advocate of reorientation and of reform within the Church. With his friend Otto Schulmeister, also a prominent representative of the Austrian Catholicism that had been purified by experience, Mauer published and edited from 1946 to 1973 the Catholic cultural magazine *Wort und Wahrheit* (Word and Truth), which was not continued after his death. Mauer might well be the most interesting, most multifaceted figure of the Austrian clergy, which, like the Catholic laity during the Second Republic, does not have as much talent and as many representatives of the younger generation as it used to have.[30]

After 1945, Friedrich Funder, former editor in chief of the Christian Socialist party paper *Reichspost,* founded the Catholic cultural and political weekly *Die Furche* (The Furrow). Experiences in the concentration camp had changed Funder from a militant anti-Marxist of the interwar period to a forgiving man, willing to compromise, and to an open-minded Catholic. In combination with the Church's changed attitude, *Die Furche* provided parts of Austrian Catholicism with the broadness and open-mindedness it had lacked in its rigid positions of the past, thus enabling enlightened conservatives to work fruitfully, unencumbered by pitfalls of the past, and to overcome within Catholicism itself the dichotomy of right-wing and left-wing Catholicism.[31] Among the personalities who followed such a line themselves in *Die Furche,* or who were inspired by the atmosphere that *Die Furche* had created to the type of work appropriate for the times, are Funder's colleague and successor Kurt Skalnik and the historian Erika Weinzierl, and, in addition, the sociologist Anton Burghardt and the economist Alfred Klose. Erika Weinzierl is meritorious especially in her consistent antifascism and in her endeavors to shed light on the anti-Semitic tendencies that darkened and burdened Austrian Catholicism and Austrian history in general.[32] In his textbooks on economics, social policy, and sociology, as well as by writing on social ethics and on questions of private property, Burghardt sought renovation of old Catholic traditions in the light of new and changed experiences. Klose, as a social scientist as well as an influential man with leverage in social partnership by virtue of his position in the Federal Chamber of Trade, continued the Catholic social theory and adapted it to the reality of Austrian postwar society.

This represents a continuation of social theory and ethics in the sense of Christian "social realism" that is aware of the limitations of human nature but that also takes into consideration historical changes that have occurred; this theory was developed by the Nestor of Catholic social theory in Austria, Professor Johannes Messner.[33] However, even this purified social theory is dominated by tendencies of the entire Christian tradition in favor of private property, although tendencies skeptical of private property are also represented. This fact is probably explained not only by considerations of justification of private property but also by the interests and economic dependencies that motivate ecclesiastical and conservative attitudes.

These internal developments of Catholicism, in conjunction with concentrated efforts by the Socialists (who had, in the person of Bruno Kreisky, since 1967 a party chairman who was very attractive to undecided voters), represented a dangerous challenge to the People's party. This challenge was still contained and covered up by the ÖVP's victory in the 1966 elections. Josef Klaus and Hermann Withalm, the two representatives and architects of the 1966 election victory,[34] were unable to take advantage of the time thus granted them to strengthen the position of the ÖVP, which owed its victory primarily to the weakness of the SPÖ following an internal crisis. On the other hand, the SPÖ, under the leadership of Bruno Kreisky, succeeded in 1971 in extending its initially relative majority and in crowning it by a series of unparalleled election victories. These successes are due not only to Kreisky's outstanding personality but also to the fact that the Socialist policies were more in keeping with major contemporary trends than were the ÖVP's policies. Furthermore, the structure of the Socialist party appeared better suited to integrate conflicting interests than that of the People's party. The SPÖ outdid the ÖVP as the party in power and as a popular party because there are fewer obstacles and hurdles to the implementation of progressive social trends in its internal structure.

However, this relative lead does not mean that the People's party will never regain the lost terrain or that progress must always be on the side of the Socialists. This fact applies all the more as the ÖVP presently has, in the persons of Alois Mock and Erhard Busek, men who have learned from the party's mistakes, are resilient in their thinking, and have already proved able to transcend effectively their own past.[35]

The issue at stake in the referendum of November 5, 1978, was whether or not the nuclear power plant at Zwentendorf should be put into operation, but beyond this it was to decide the entire energy and environmental policy. This referendum demonstrated that historical fronts and pro-and-con attitudes can also reverse themselves; for whichever reasons, the Socialist party with its appeal to vote Yes on nuclear power isolated itself from the younger generation's dynamics, and the People's party at least did not counteract these dynamic forces.[b] The ongoing historical development makes possible not only a reversal of the classical positions but also another trend, namely the shake-up of the entire traditional party system, which might no longer be able to cope with the problems that lie ahead.

[b]Translator's Note: Those opposed to putting the plant into operation won a narrow victory.

Simply because everything has gone well so far, we should not lull our-selves into a false sense of security regarding the future, but rather, we should assume, with purposive pessimism, that our instruments to date might not be sufficient to meet the challenges of the future. During times of abrupt change, surprising turns of events with unforeseen consequences take place, even when there are no tangible alternatives to the status quo. Not only bridges[c] but political structures may lose the function they were intended to fulfill and may no longer be of service in their accustomed manner.

However, without anticipating future developments, and remaining within the traditional Austrian party structures for the purposes of this essay, a few remarks on the third camp in Austrian domestic policy are in order. The third camp constitutes those groups who, before 1938, without reference to Hitlerism, advocated a pan-German Reich that incorporated Austria, but who, after 1938, merged largely into national socialism. Of all political groups in Austria, this camp was the most burdened and compro-mised in 1945. Whereas it would have been risky for the People's party to continue the tradition of the authoritarian Christian Socialist party, it would have been an outright impossibility to base a political party on the traditions that had led to national socialism and to the Third Reich. The impossibility of recuperating credibly from the moral beating the German-Nationalist camp had suffered, and to dissociate from it, was one of the main reasons why the allies allowed only one non-Socialist party, the Peo-ple's party, in 1945. Only in 1949 was the Verband der Unabhängigen (Association of Independents, VdU) founded, thus restoring the third camp in Austrian domestic politics. This took place with the active support of the Socialists, who wanted to break the ÖVP's absolute majority; although they succeeded in doing this, they also were weakened by the emergence of the new party. This newly founded party was intended as an organization to attract former National Socialists, those who had been expelled from their former homelands, and other groups that were not attracted by the system of the two large parties. The VdU actually did fulfill this function, but the tone was set by liberally minded men like Herbert Kraus and Viktor Rei-mann, who wanted to overcome national socialism in the ranks of the third camp. However, Kraus and Reimann were soon pushed aside by representa-tives of just that past they had been trying to overcome. This new direction was expressed especially clearly in the 1954 "Aussee Program."

After the Verband der Unabhängigen collapsed, the Liberal party of Austria (Freiheitliche Partei Österreichs, FPÖ) was founded in 1955. This

[c]Translator's Note: The reference is to the unexpected collapse of the main bridge across the Danube in Vienna.

new party's ties to a brown (Nazi) past were not least evident in the person of its first chairman, Anton Reinthaller. Reinthaller had been Reich leader of the farmers and a minister in the Seyss-Inquart administration, which had been forced upon Austria in 1938 by Hitler. Only under the leadership of Friedrich Peter, who succeeded Reinthaller in 1958, was the attempt made to liberate the party from a past that had no future. In spite of, or possibly just because of, his controversial political origins, Peter was in a position to make the FPÖ a liberal party rather than a German-Nationalist party. If a person is to be judged not by what he has done in the past and where he comes from, but rather by what he has made of himself and where he has gone, then it must be admitted that Friedrich Peter not only purified and detoxicated the Liberal party, but even made it a pioneer of reform on some issues. Today, the FPÖ is the Austrian party that works most energetically for the maintenance and increase of parliamentary rights. This is understandable since parliament is the FPÖ's most effective forum and is much more important to it than to the other large parties, which have plenty of other bases.

Today, the liberals are the standard bearers of parliamentarianism, whereas in the period between the wars, the Nazis denounced and ridiculed parliament as a "bull dump" (*Quatschbude*). This shows that there is a world of difference between today's liberals and the political forces that deprived the German-nationalist camp of its liberal backbone between the wars and finally pulled it into national socialism. But it should not obscure the fact that there are significant and quite unpleasant remnants of an unfortunate past. Nevertheless, the trend toward dissociation from these remnants is clearly discernible, and the recognition of this fact cannot be diminished by disturbing terminological concessions to this past, which were made and are still being made.[36] In historical perspective we should not be petty in regard to this matter, nor should we overlook the possibility that a rigorous and clean-cut separation and terminology would probably have resulted in stronger right-wing radical competition for the FPÖ, a competition not limited to existence as a mere sect, as is the case with neonazism and right-wing radicalism today.

However, in spite of these positive signs, the question of survival remains. This question should be directed to the party system as a whole, but it should be addressed specifically to the FPÖ, which is torn by struggles for direction and leadership. It would be desirable if the FPÖ developed into a liberal party as a corrective to the large parties' power, since the latter's ability and willingness to reform seem to be quite restricted. It is to be hoped that the appearance on the scene of the long-time leader of the FPÖ parliamentary group, Wilfried Gredler, who was nominated as the FPÖ candidate in the 1980 elections to the office of Federal President and who has always represented the liberal element in the FPÖ, has helped to enliven the discussion about the execution of the State's highest office, and to leave a mark on the party that lasts beyond the elections.[d] This would also put an end to the apparent problem of dual loyalty to the Austrian State and to the German cultural community; this problem still burdens the FPÖ and keeps it from integrating fully into the unquestioning Austrian national consciousness of the younger generation in particular.

It is an indication of the overly great influence exerted by the political parties on the social and cultural life in Austria that discussion of intellectual trends remains, of necessity, predominantly within the sphere of influence of the three traditional political camps, and that intellectual trends, although not exhaustively represented by the existing camps, are primarily found within them. Since its collapse after the turn of the century, Austrian liberalism as a formative social force outside the political camps has been active only through individual personalities who were strong and consistent enough in their liberal substance to resist illiberal trends. The great Austrian jurists Hans Kelsen and Adolf Julius Merkl come to mind as examples. As university teachers and men in public life, Kelsen and Merkl always spoke out when liberal values were threatened.[37] Moreover, liberalism in its various manifestations has permeated the three camps: the conservative camp primarily as economic liberalism, the Socialist one as cultural liberalism. However, in spite of liberal influences, the mass character of the large parties tends toward concentration of power and totalitarianism, both of which become apparent whenever and wherever this power is exercised over a long period of time without disturbance. This fact in particular should make it all the more tempting for the third camp in Austrian domestic politics to take up the fallow liberalism in the sense of creating more tolerance and controls of power—for practiced tolerance and effective control of power are the most valuable and important bequests of liberalism.

By comparison to the First Republic, the intellectual life within the political camps has become diluted and impoverished. This could still be accepted with the argument that the intellectual richness and engagement of the interwar period were a symptom simultaneously of political fanaticism and of an overestimation of questions of political orientation, which today, in a reversal, threaten to drown in the leveling reality of pragmatism. More serious is the fact that there are no new creations and original achievements comparable to the great trends and schools of the past, and that continuation of the old schools, which can be perceived in Austria, is often characterized by sterility and epigonism. Yet, in spite of this, one should

[d]Translator's Note: In the presidential election of May 1980, Gredler obtained 17 percent of the vote against 80 percent for the incumbent president, Rudolf Kirchschläger.

not be entirely blind to the times and overlook the fact that, during the Second Republic, Austrians have developed ideas and concepts that have echoed throughout the world. Two examples of this are the logotherapy and philosophy of the meaning of life, developed by Viktor Frankl, and Konrad Lorenz's theory and practice of behavioral research.[38]

In order not to be unfair in arriving at unjustifiably negative conclusions in assessing present intellectual trends, it must be admitted that the Austria of the Second Republic, unlike that of the First, no longer lives off the cultural background of the Danubian monarchy, that it has the normal proportions of a small nation, and that it can still boast considerable achievements in spite of being such a small nation. To name just one area, which influences intellectual life more than other individual scientific disciplines, leading representatives of Austrian philosophy have creatively developed further the prevailing contemporary trends: in his monumental work *Die beiden Labyrinthe der Philosophie* (The Two Labyrinths of Philosophy), the Viennese philosopher Erich Heintel presents an overview and reconciliation of transcendental philosophy and classical existential philosophy. Leo Gabriel, who teaches at the University of Vienna, has attempted to fuse traditional Christian and existentialist trends. And Ernst Topitsch has applied modern sociology and ideological critique to cosmological images and ideologies and has thus contributed to the genesis and critique of the human self-image.[39]

Still, the Second Republic does not approach the cultural prime of the time between the wars. This is due not only to a definitive separation from a spacious and generous past, but also to the personal bloodletting suffered by Austrian intellectual life through the expulsion of its important representatives by war and fascism. For instance, the above-mentioned jurist Hans Kelsen was forced to leave his home country by increasingly authoritarian developments during the late 1920s; he only visited a few times after World War II. But his theory of pure law (*Reine Rechtslehre*) has permeated legal thought throughout the world to such an extent that Kelsen has repeatedly been called the "jurist of the century." The appreciation this trend-setting Austrian enjoys today in his home country was expressed by the Federal Government when an International Hans Kelsen Institute was founded on the occasion of his 90th birthday.

Many of the most eminent emigrants did not return home. The schools of thought they founded and advocated are often cultivated abroad more than in their country of origin. The history of Austrian thought, which was to remain, or to become, a domain of the Austrians, is no exception. In this sense, this essay is to be seen as a sketchy attempt to overcome this deficit in the evaluation of the Austrian past and present.

Notes

1. Claudio Magris, *Der habsburgische Mythos in der österreichischen Literatur* (Salzburg, 1966).
2. Margarete Mommsen-Reindl, *Die österreichische Proporzdemokratie und der Fall Habsburg* (Wien, 1976).
3. Norbert Leser, *Zwischen Reformismus und Bolschewismus. Der Austromarxismus als Theorie und Praxis* (Wien 1968); Alfred Diamant, *Austrian Catholics and the First Republic* (Princeton, 1960).
4. William Johnston, *The Austrian Mind. An Intellectual and Social History, 1848–1938* (Berkeley, Calif., 1972).
5. Emil Kauder, *A History of Marginal Utility Theory* (Princeton, 1964); Victor Kraft, *Der Wiener Kreis. Der Ursprung des Neopositivismus. Ein Kapitel der jüngsten Philosophiegeschichte* (Wien, 1950); Wolfgang Huber, *Beiträge zur Geschichte der Psychoanalyse* (Veröffentlichungen des Ludwig-Boltzmann-Institutes für Geschichte der Gesellschaftswissenschaften in Österreich, IV). (Wien, 1978); Erwin Ringel and Gerhard Brandl, eds., *Ein Österreicher namens Alfred Adler. Seine Individualpyschologie—Rückschau und Ausblick* (Wien, 1977).
6. Adam Wandruszka, "Die politische Struktur Österreichs," in Heinrich Benedikt, ed., *Geschichte der Republik Österreich* (Wien, 1954).
7. Fritz Kaufmann, *Sozialdemokratie in Österreich. Idee und Geschichte einer Partei von 1889 bis zur Gegenewart* (Wien, 1978); Adolf Schärf, *Österreichs Erneuerung, 1945 bis 1955. Das erste Jahrzehnt der Zweiten Republik* (Wien, 1955); Oskar Helmer, *50 Jahre erlebte Geschichte* (Wien, 1957); Erich Kollman, *Theodore Körner. Militär und Politik* (Wien, 1973); Karl Renner, *Die neue Welt und der Sozialismus, Einsichten und Ausblicke des lebendigen Marxismus* (Salzburg, 1946), and "Vom liberalen zum sozialen Staat," speech presented at the first Congress of the Austrian Federation of Trade Unions, May 23, 1948 (Wien, 1948), and *Wandlungen der modernen Gesellschaft. Zwei Abhandlungen über die Probleme der Nachkriegszeit* (Wien, 1953).
8. Karl Czernetz, *Die sittliche Kraft des österreichische Sozialismus, 75 Jahre österreichische Sozialdemokratie* (Wien, 1963), and *Vor der Entscheidung. Welt in Wandlung. Sozialismus im Werden* (Wien, no year of publication).
9. Josef Hindels, *Der Sozialismus kommt nicht von selbst* (Wien, 1959), and *Was ist heute links? Sozialistische Strategie im Spätkapitalismus* (Wien, 1970).
10. Eduard März, *Die Marxsche Wirtschaftslehre im Widerstreit der Meinungen. Ist sie heute noch gültig?* (Wien, 1959), and *Einführung in die Marxsche Theorie der wirtschaftlichen Entwicklung. Frühkapitalismus und Kapitalismus der freien Konkurrenz* (Wien, 1976).
11. Benedikt Kautsky, *Geistige Strömungen im österreichischen Sozialismus* (Wien, no year of publication).
12. Fritz Klenner, *Das Unbehagen in der Demokratie. Ein Beitrag zu Gegenwartsproblemen der Arbeiterbewegung* (Wien, 1956), and *Denkanstösse zum Überleben. Diskussionsbeitrag zu einem neuen SPÖ-Programm* (Wien, 1976), and *Die Österreichischen Gewerkschaften, Vergangenheits- und Gegenwartsprobleme,* 3 vols. (vols. 1, 2, Wien, 1951; vol. 3, 1979).
13. Felix Butschek, *Der gelenkte Mensch von Marx bis heute* (Wien, 1962); Günther Nenning, *Anschluss an die Zukunft. Österreichs unbewältigte Gegenwart und Vergangenheit* (Wien, 1963), and *Realisten oder Verräter? Die Zukunft der Sozialdemokratie* (Munich, 1976).
14. Heinz Kienzl, *Gesellschaft am Wendepunkt? Wirtschafts- und Gesellschaftspolitik bei sinkenden Wachstumsraten* (Wien, 1975); Egon Matzner, *Notizen zur Gesellschaftsreform. Aufruf zu einem zeitgemässen Humanismus* (Wien, 1976), and *Wohlfahrtsstaat und Wirtschaftskrise: Österreichs Sozialisten suchen einen Ausweg* (Hamburg, 1978).
15. Norbert Leser, "Sozialismus und Staat," in *Rote Markierungen, '80* (Wien, 1980).
16. Bruno Kreisky, *Aspekte des demokratischen Sozialismus. Aufsätze—Reden und Interviews* (Munich, 1974).
17. Heinz Fischer, ed., *Das politische System Österreichs* (Wien, 1974), and *Positionen und Perspektiven* (Wien, 1977).
18. Christian Broda, *Demokratie—Recht—Gesellschaft. Ausgewählte Aufsätze, Vorträge, Reden* (Wien, 1962).
19. Ernst Fischer, *Von der Notwendigkeit der Kunst* (Hamburg, 1967), and *Das Ende einer Illusion. Erinnerungen, 1945–1955* (Wien, 1973); Franz Marek, *Was Lenin wirklich sagte*

(Wien, 1969), and *Was Stalin wirklich sagte* (Wien, 1970); Theodor Prager, *Zwischen London und Moskau. Bekenntnisse eines Revisionisten* (Wien, 1975).

20. Ludwig Reichhold, *Geschichte der ÖVP* (Graz, 1975).

21. Alfred Missong, *Die Österreichische Nation* (Wien, 1946), and *Die Weltverpflichtung des Christen* (Wien, 1948).

22. Reinhard Kamitz, *Grundlagen der sozialen Marktwirtschaft* (Berlin, 1961); Julius Raab, *Selbstporträt eines Politikers* (Wien, 1964).

23. Alfred Maleta, *Entscheidung für morgen. Christliche Demokratie im Herzen Europas* (Wien, 1968).

24. Heinrich Drimmel, *10 Reden wider den Geist* (Wien, 1965), and *Der konservative Mensch und die Revolution* (Wien, 1970), and *Die Häuser meines Lebens* (Wien, 1975), and *Gott sei uns gnädig. Die Welt von Joseph Stalin bis Jimmy Carter* (Wien, 1979).

25. Heinrich Busshoff, *Das Dollfuss-Regime in Österreich in geistesgeschichtlicher Perspektive unter besonderer Berücksichtigung der "Schöneren Zukunft" und der "Reichspost"* (Berlin, 1968).

26. Cardinal Franz König, *Worte zur Zeit. Reden und Aufsätze* (Wien, 1968), and *Kirche und Welt. Ansprachen, Referate, Aufsätze* (Wien, 1978).

27. Friedrich Heer, *Gespräch der Feinde* (Wien, 1949), and *Aufgang Europas* (Wien, 1949), and *Europäische Geistesgeschichte* (Stuttgart, 1953), and *Land im Strom der Zeit. Österreich gestern, heute, morgen* (Wien, 1955), and *Der Glaube des Adolf Hitler. Anatomie einer politischen Religiosität* (Munich, 1968), and *Scheitern in Wien* (Wien, 1974).

28. Daim/Heer/Knoll, *Kirche und Zukunft* (Wien, 1963); August Maria Knoll, *Katholische Kirche und scholastisches Naturrecht zur Frage der Freiheit* (Wien, 1963), and *Zins und Gnade. Studien zur Soziologie der christlichen Existenz* (Neuwied, 1967).

29. Ernst Karl Winter, *Christentum und Zivilisation* (Wien, 1956); Joseph Dobretsberger, *Katholische Sozialpolitik am Scheideweg* (Wien, 1947).

30. Otto Mauer, *Krise und Chance der Kirche heute* (Freiburg, 1971); Otto Schulmeister, ed., *Spectrum Austriae* (Wien, 1957), and *Die Zukunft Österreichs* (Wien, 1967), and *Der zweite Anschluss. Österreichs Verwandlung seit 1945* (Wien, 1979).

31. Friedrich Funder, *Von Gestern ins Heute. Aus dem Kaiserreich in die Republik* (Wien, 1952), and *Als Österreich den Sturm bestand. Aus der Ersten in die Zweite Republik* (Wien, 1957).

32. Kurt Skalnik, *Dr. Karl Lueger. Der Mann zwischen den Zeiten* (Wien, 1954); Erika Weinzierl, *Österreich—Zeitgeschichte in Bildern 1918–1968* (Innsbruck, 1968); Weinzierl/Skalnik, eds., *Österreich—die Zweite Republik,* 2 vols. (Graz, 1972).

33. Alfred Klose, *Die katholische Sozialehre. Ihr Anspruch. Ihre Aktualität* (Graz, 1979); Johannes Messner, *Das Naturrecht. Handbuch der Gesellschaftsethik, Staatsethik und Wirtschaftsethik,* 3d ed. (Innsbruck, 1958).

34. Josef Klaus, *Macht und Ohnmacht in Österreich. Konfrontationen und Versuche* (Wien, 1971); Hermann Withalm, *Brennpunkte* (Graz, 1975).

35. Alois Mock, ed., *Die Zukunft der Volkspartei* (Wien, 1971); Erhard Busek, *Wien—ein bürgerliches Credo* (Wien, 1978).

36. Friedhelm Frischenschlager, "Funktion- und Inhaltswandlungen von Parteiprogrammen am Beispiel der FPÖ-Programme," in *Österreichische Zeitschrift für Politikwissenschaft,* No. 2/78, pp. 209f.

37. Rudolf Aladar Métall, *Hans Kelsen. Leben und Werk* (Wien, 1969); Max Imboden et al, eds., *Festschrift für Adolf Merkl zum 80. Geburtstag* (Munich, 1970).

38. Viktor Frankl, *Man's Search for Meaning. An Introduction to Logotherapy* (New York, 1973); Konrad Lorenz, *Das sogenannte Böse. Zur Naturgeschichte der Aggression* (Wien, 1973).

39. Erich Heintel, *Die beiden Labyrinthe der Philosophie. Systemtheoretische Betrachtungen zur Fundamentalphilosophie abendländischen Denkens,* vol. 1 (Wien, 1968); Leo Gabriel, *Existenzphilosophie. Von Kierkegaard bis Sartre* (Wien, 1951); Ernst Topitsch, *Vom Ursprung und Ende der Metaphysik. Eine Studie zur Weltanschauungskritik* (Wien, 1958).

Selected Bibliography

This essay refers to the pertinent literature *passim,* and the notes can therefore serve at the same time as a basic bibliography for works in the German language.

OTHER RELEVANT WORKS BY NORBERT LESER INCLUDE
THE FOLLOWING:

Die Odysee des Marxismus: Auf dem Wege zum Sozialismus. Wien, 1971.
Reine Rechtslehre und Sozialismus. In Salo Engel and R. A. Métall, eds., *Law, State and International Legal Order: Essays in Honor of Hans Kelsen.* Knoxville, 1964.
Sozialismus zwischen Relativismus und Dogmatismus: Aufsätze im Spannungsfeld von Marx und Kelsen. Freiburg i.B., 1974.
Zwischen Reformismus und Bolschewismus: Der Austromarxismus als Theorie und Praxis. Wien, 1968.

WORKS IN ENGLISH THAT ARE AT LEAST TANGENTIALLY
RELEVANT AS FOLLOWS:

Bluhm, William T. *Building an Austrian Nation: The Political Integration of a Western State.* New Haven, 1973.
Buttinger, Joseph. *In the Twilight of Socialism: A History of the Revolutionary Socialists in Austria.* New York, 1953.
Diamant, Alfred. *Austrian Catholics and the First Republic: Democracy, Capitalism, and the Social Order.* Princeton, 1960. German translation by Norbert Leser, Wien, 1965.
Fischer, Ernst. *An Opposing Man,* trans. by Peter and Betty Ross. London, 1974. German original: *Erinnerungen und Reflexionen.* Reinbek bei Hamburg, 1969.
Gulick, Charles A. *Austria from Hapsburg to Hitler,* 2 vols. Berkeley, Calif., 1948.
Leser, Norbert. Austro-Marxism: A Reappraisal. In *Journal of Contemporary History,* vol. 1, No. 2.
Moody, Joseph A., *Church and Society: Catholic Social and Political Thought and Movements, 1789–1900.* New York, 1953.
Pinner, Frank A. On the Structure of Organization and Beliefs: *Lagerdenken* in Austria. Paper presented at the 1967 meeting of the American Political Science Association.
Shell, Kurt L. *The Transformation of Austrian Socialism.* New York, 1962.
Whiteside, Andrew. Austria. In Hans Rogger and Eugene Weber, eds., *The European Right.* Berkeley, Calif., 1966.

Index

A

Abortion
  church and, 101–2, 108–11, 114–15
  controversy over, 346–49
  and population policy, 83
Accident insurance, 309, 312, 314
Achleitner, Friedrich, 410, 464
Adler, Alfred, 397, 405
Administration
  See Public administration
Administrative Court, 213, 265–68, 275, 356
Adoption law, 352
Adorno, Theodor W., 411
AEG Corp., 160
Aehrenthal, Count, 8
African nations
  relations with, 373–74
Aggstein Castle, 65
Aging
  See Elderly; Population
Agricultural Marketing Order, 193, 195
Agricultural workers
  laws protecting, 302, 309, 312–13
  voting trends of, 229–29
Agriculture, 28–31
  arable land for, 29, 34, 36, 39, 41
  area map of, 45
  and economic structure, 145–46, 152
  employment structure in, 131–32, 144, 152
  in history, 11, 142
  income differentials in, 48–50
  labor in, 48
  in mountain regions, 51–53
  population statistics in, 26
  productivity in, 48, 152–53
  regional divisions of
    population movements in, 86
  structural changes in, 47–52
  training in, 52
  U.S. aid to, 127
Agriculture, Chamber of, 186–87, 217
  party representation in, 235–36, 254
  President's Conference of, 233
Aikfeld-Murboden regional program, 46
Aichinger, Ilse, 409
Aircraft production, 161

Air force, 387–89
Air police, 387
Air space, 385
  defense of, 387–88
  See also Defense policy
Aktion Leben, 109–11
Allard, Sven, 363
All Austria Assembly of Chambers of Labor, 187, 307
Allende, Salvador, 370
Allgemeinbildende Höhere Schule (AHS), 322–24, 326–27, 329–30
Allied occupation period, 15–16, 488
  broadcasting during, 279–80
  censorship of, 280–81
  control agreements during, 362
  and foreign policy, 361–64
  economic development in, 174–75
Allies
  air raids of, 14
"Almen", 52
  See also Pastureland
Alpine Mountain Steel Company, 155, 161
Alps
  and Austria's image, 393, 397, 399
  Central, 31–34
  ecosystem of
    and tourism, 61
  farming in, 51–3
  Northern limestone regions, 32–33
  Southern, 35–6
Alsen, Herbert, 469
Altenberg, Peter, 397
Alte Schmiede, 411
Aluminum industry, 43, 45, 47, 128, 156, 166
Ambras Castle concerts, 469
Amin, Idi, 370
Amstetten, 30, 46
Andau, 30
Androsch, Hannes, 196
"Angerdorf", 39–41
Anouilh, J., 460–61, 463
Anschluss, 12–13, 100, 352, 363
Anti-semitism, 18, 496
Apostel, Hans Erich, 432
Arafat, Yassir, 375
Arbed Corp., 160
Arbeiterzeitung, 282–83, 414, 491
Arena cultural program, 424–25, 465

Arlberg area, 56, 61
Arlberg Tunnel, 63
Armaments industry, 47
Armenian Apostolic Church, 117
Army, 381–82, 387, 398
  See also Defense policy
Art
  and Austria's image abroad, 395, 397, 405
  baroque, 477
  contemporary, 471–74
    background for, 475–77
    new beginnings for, 475–77
    unity and diversity in, 477–83
  educational institutions for, 324, 335
  jurisdiction of, 322
  gothic, 471
  nouveau style, 472
  See also Education and Art, Ministry of
Artmann, Hans Carl, 410, 415, 423
Aslan, Raoul, 453–54, 459
Assembly of Austrian Chambers of Labor, 187, 307
  See also Labor, Chamber of
Association of Accredited Foreign Correspondents, 295
Association of Austrian Teachers of Music, 445
Association of Freethinkers, 112
Association of Independents
  See Verband der Unabhängigen (VdU)
Aufbaugymnasium, 325, 327
Aufbaurealgymnasium, 325, 327
Augsburg Confession, 99, 115
  subsidy to, 106
Augsburger Bekenntnis
  See Augburg Confession
Ausgleich of 1867, 6–7
Ausländerbeschäftigungsgesetz, 91, 95
Austria
  area of, 23
    by province, 26
  climate and vegetation of, 30–31, 39
  historic self image of, 1–3
  image and impact abroad, 393–406
  land use in, 28–30
  location in Europe, 23–25

physiographical divisions of, 27
Austriaca, 427
Austrian Academy of Sciences, 402, 441
Austrian Composer's Association, 445
Austrian Central Bureau of Statistics, 82, 84–85, 194
Austrian Council of Bishops, 109–10, 347
Austrian Embassy, Washington D.C., 399
Austrian Federation of Workers and Employees, 197
Austrian Institute, London survey of Austria's image in U.K., 398
Austrian Institute, New York Creative Austria-20th Century exhibit, 399 survey of Austria's image in U.S., 393–98
Austrian Institute for Regional Planning, 50, 84–85
Austrian Katholikentag, 102–3
Austrian National Bank, 174–75, 182, 193
Austrian People's Party See Österreichischer Volkspartei (ÖVP)
Austrian Press Agency (APA), 292–93
Austrian Radio See Österreichischer Rundfunk (ORF)
Austrian schilling, 174 See also Monetary policy
Austrian Society for Literature, 411
Austrian State Prize for European Literature, 415
Austrian Trade Union Federation See Österreichischer Gewerkschaftsbund (ÖGB)
Austro-Hungarian Empire See Habsburg Empire
Austro-Marxism, 237, 487, 489 Linz program of 1926, 102–3
Avramidis, Joannis, 475

B

Babenberg dynasty, 3
Bacher, Gerd, 286, 289
Bachmann, Ingeborg, 409–10, 418, 423
Bachmann Prize, 415, 427
Badgastein, 58

Bad Ischl, 58 Operetta Week, 445, 469
Bad Kleinkirchheim, 56
Badura-Skoda, Paul, 442
Bahr, Hermann, 461
Balance of payments economic policy on, 135, 150–51 in history, 142, 145, 149–50
Banks and economic development, 148–49 nationalization of, 128, 157, 166
Baptist Church, 117
Barany, Robert, 404
Bartok, Béla, 438
Basil, Otto, 409
Batt, Kurt, 423
Bauer, Otto, 10, 489–90
Bauer, Wolfgang, 415, 423, 468
Bauernbund, 188
Bayer, Konrad, 410, 418, 464
Bayr, Rudolf, 462
Beer-Hofman, Richard, 460
Beethoven, Ludwig van, 395, 442, 461
Benelux countries industrial investment by, 159
Benning, Achim, 462
Bereitschaftstruppe, 387, 389 See also Defense policy
Berentsen, W. H., 71
Berg, Alban, 395, 432, 436, 438, 442, 461
"Bergmähder", 52
Berio, Luciano, 438
Berlin Conference of Ministers, 363
Berlin Philharmonic, 466–67
Bernhard, Thomas, 411, 418, 421–23, 426–27, 462
Bernstein, Leonard, 443
Berry, Walter, 442
Bertalanffy, Ludwig von, 405
Bezirke, 266–67, 321 See also Local government; Municipalities
Bezirksgericht, 355
Bezirkshauptmann, 266–67
Biedermeier period, 453
Bielka, Erich, 370
Biermann, Wolf, 424
Blaha, Paul, 464
Bloch, Ernst, 411
BMW Corp., 162
Bobek, H., 25, 68–70
Bodensee, 56
Boeckl, Herbert, 472–74
Bohemia in Austrian history, 3–5, 10, 24

Bohemian Granite Massif, 25–28
Böhm, Johann, 189
Böhm, Karl, 442, 458, 461
Böll, Heinrich, 424
Bookbird, 297
Boulez, Pierre, 435–36, 438
Brahms, Johannes, 395
Brandt, Willy, 365
Brauer, Arik, 480
Braunau, 47
Brazil relations with, 373
Brecht, B., 457
Bregenz, 25, 56, 69 Lake Constance Festival, 445, 451, 453, 460, 468
Brendel, Alfred, 442
Brenner Highway, 62–63
Brentano, Franz, 405
Bresgen, Cesar, 434
Bretton Woods system, 136, 149–50, 174, 181
Brick making industry, 166
Broch, Hermann, 397, 410
Brod, Max, 411
Broda, Christian, 345–47, 350–52, 493
Brown-Boveri Corp., 160
Brücke, Die, 413
Bruckner, Anton, 395, 434, 438, 441, 444, 446
Bruckner Festival, Linz, 443, 446, 468
Bruckner Orchestra, Linz, 443
Buber, Martin, 405
Büchner, G., 464
Buddhist Temple, 117
Budgetary policy, 178–79, 181–82 See also Monetary policy
Building materials industry, 157, 166
Bulgaria relations with, 368
Bundesrat. See Federal Council
Bund werktätiger Juden, 115–16
Bureaucracy See Civil service; Public administration
Burgenland, 3, 66 Apostolic Administration of, 105 church in, 107 development and land use in, 29, 41, 44, 49–50, 56 population shifts in, 76, 87, 92–93 student population of, 340 urban development in, 64–66 vital statistics on, 26

See also Eastern Austria;
Provinces
Burgenland Festival, 469
Burghardt, Anton, 499
Busch, Fritz, 458
Busek, Erhard, 500
Butschek, Felix, 141–54,
491–92

C

Camarata Academica, Salzburg,
445
Canetti, Elias, 421
Capitalism
growth of, 5–8
Carinthia
geography and land use in,
25, 29, 31, 34–37, 69
history of, 3, 10
tourism in, 54–56, 58
transport in, 62–63
vital statistics on, 26
Yugoslavian relations of,
362
See also Provinces; Southern
Austria
Carinthian Summer Festival,
445, 468–69
Carnutum Festival, 469
Cartel Commission, 193
Cartel Court, 193–94
Cartel Law, 193–94
Catholic Church, 12, 99
and abortion issue, 101–2,
108–11, 114–15, 346–49
and criminal law, 108–11
and education, 101, 103–4,
107–8, 111–12, 322,
327–28
and marriage law, 352
and political parties
membership patterns in,
224, 228–29
policy of, 237, 486–87,
493–501
relations with state, 99–100,
105–6
legal issues concerning,
349
Catholic Men of Austria, 112
Catholic movement
in social partnership, 187
Cattle breeding, 39, 45, 52
Cellulose manufacture, 45, 47
Celtic culture, 3
Cement production, 163, 166
Central Alps, 31–34
Central Office of Statistics, 82,
84–85, 194
Cereal cultivation, 36, 39, 45,
49, 132
Cerha, Friedrich, 434–36

Chambers
in government structure,
265–66
legal status of, 355
in social partnership, 186–88
See also Agriculture,
Chamber of; Labor,
Chamber of; Trade and
Industry, Chamber of
Chancellory
See Federal Chancellor
Charles, Emperor
abdication of, 9–10
Charles V, Emperor, 4
Charles VI, Emperor, 4
Chekhov, A., 460
Chemical industry, 43, 45, 47,
128, 147, 156–57, 161–63,
166
See also Petrochemical
industry
Chemistry
and Austria's image abroad,
404
primary and secondary
training in, 324–25
Children
laws protecting, 302, 309,
313, 352–54, 357
Chile
relations with, 370
Choral activity, 444
Christian Socialist Party,
224–25, 237, 327
in Austria's history, 10–12,
15, 17, 100
in elections of 1919–1930,
241–43
traditions and policy of, 486,
493–96, 501
See also Österreichischer
Volkspartei (ÖVP)
Civil Servants
statistics concerning, 268
voting trends of, 228, 254
Civil Service
background in history, 269,
272–74
open advertisement of
positions in, 252
training for, 219, 270–72,
274
See also Public
administration
Clemenceau, G., 1
Clothing and apparel industry,
47, 50, 162
Coal
current production of, 163,
203
deposits of, 42, 46
imports of, 138, 203
industry, 127–28

nationalization of, 157,
166, 206
Cocteau, J., 460
Codetermination, 196, 199, 311
Cold War, 14–16
See also Iron Curtain
COMECON countries, 24–25
energy imports from, 203
Commerce, Chamber of
See Trade and Industry,
Chamber of
Common Market
See European Economic
Community (EEC)
Commission on the Reform of
the Criminal Law, 108–9
Communications industry,
127–28
See also Media;
Österreichischer
Rundfunk (ÖRF)
Communist Party of Austria
See Kommunistische Partei
Österriechs (KPÖ)
Consociationalism, 217–19
Constitutio Criminalis
Theresiana, 345
Constitution, 209–10, 252
election law in, 241–43, 249
See also Legislation
Constitutional Court, 213, 251,
265–68, 303, 356
Consumers
laws protecting, 355–57
Copper production, 163
Corporatism, 217–18
See also Chambers; Social
Partnership
Cory, Carl, 404
Cory, Gerty, 404
Costa, Martin, 453
Council of Europe, 365–68, 402
Council of Ministers, 189, 256
Courts, 213–14
administration of, 263
in government structure,
265–66
structure of, 355–56
See also Administrative
Court; Constitutional
Court; Supreme Court
CPC Corp., 160
Crafts education, 325–26
teacher training in, 326
Creative Austria-20th Century
exhibit, Philadelphia, 399
Creditanstalt, 11, 162, 166
Criminal law
church and, 108–11
penalty reforms, 348–49, 351
procedural reforms, 350–51
See also Legislation, Penal
code

Croatians, 2
Croat minority, 92–93
Csokor, Franz Theodor, 456
Cyprus crisis, 372
Czech minority, 93
Czechoslovakia
  imports from, 203
  relations with, 2, 8–9, 24,
    368
Czernetz, Karl, 368, 402, 490

D

Dachstein, 32–33
Daim, Wilfried, 498
Dairy farming, 39, 132
Danneberg, Robert, 489
Dantine, Wilhelm, 115
Danube River, 65
  development of, 69
  in history, 3
  hydropower on, 204
  and transport, 61, 64
Danube valley, 25, 28
  strategic importance of, 385
Darmstadt
  International Summer
    Courses for New Music,
    434, 436
David, Johann Nepomuk,
    434–35
death benefits, 313
Debussy, Claude, 435–36
Defense policy
  background of, 381–83
  instruments and doctrines of,
    389–90
  neutral state model of,
    386–89
  premises of, 383–86
  territorial zones of, 389–90
Dellepiane, Giovanni, 105
Demographic factors
  birth rates, 77, 82
    migrants and, 91
  divorce rate, 82
  fertility rate, 77, 82–85, 94
  marriage statistics and
    trends, 77, 80–82
  mortality rates, 77–78
    infant and child, 80
    in 1919–1951, 75–77
    in 1951–61, 77
    in 1961–78, 77–78
  See also Migration
    movements; Population
Demus, Jörg, 442
Dermota, Anton, 455
Deutsch, Ernst, 457, 460
Disabled persons insurance,
    313–14
District government
  See Provinces

Divorce
  laws on, 110, 352–54, 356
  rates of, 82
Djilas, Milovan, 493
Doblinger publishing house,
    438
Dobretsberger, Joseph, 498
Doderer, Heimito von, 262,
    397, 410
Dokumentationsstelle für
  neuere österreichische
  Literatur, 416
Dollfuss, Engelbert, 12, 17
Dollfuss Concordat, of 1933,
    105
Donner, Raphael, 472
Dornbirn, 47, 69
  broadcasting from, 279, 287
Drau valley, 37
Drimmel, Heinrich, 105, 107,
    496–97
Dual Monarchy, 7
Dulles, John Foster, 363

E

Eastern Austria, 78–80, 86–87
  See also Burgenland, Lower
    Austria; Regional
    structure; Vienna
Eberle, Josef, 496
Eckartsau Castle
  Chamber Music Days, 469
Economic and Social Advisory
  Board, 170, 180, 189,
    192–93, 195–96
Economic Association, 229
Economic Commission, 188–89
  See also Joint Commission
    for Prices and Wages
Economic development
  achievement period in—
    1950–1978
    growth rates in, 129–30,
      139, 147
    inflation and stabilization
      in, 128–29
    investment and
      employment rates in,
      132–34
    structural changes in,
      130–32
  beginnings of, 123
    and German rule, 124–26
    nonviability doctrine in,
      123–24
    and economic policy, 135
    crisis management since
      1974, 136–38
    full employment priority
      in, 136
    problems and perspectives
      of, 138–39

and European integration,
    134–35, 145, 147,
    149–50, 157–58
  reconstruction phase, 126
    Marshall Plan in, 126–27
    nationalization acts in,
      127–28
    recovery period from 1945,
      123–24
  See also Industry
Economic partnership
  See Social partnership
Economic policy
  See Monetary policy
Economics
  Austria's image in, 402–5
  intellectual trends in, 487,
    491
  primary and secondary
    training in, 324
Economic structure
  characteristics of, 144–49
  historical determination of,
    141–44
  problems of, 149–53
Eden, Anthony, 361
Eder, Helmut, 435
Edition neue texte, 412–13
Education
  church and, 101, 103–4,
    107–8, 111–12, 322,
    327–28
  higher, 335–36
    budgetary statistics on, 338
    dropouts from, 341–42
    increased demand in,
      337–40
    problem areas of, 341–42
    teaching style in, 342
    university administrative
      structure and
      curriculum, 336–38
    university student's family
      study, 339–40
  jurisdiction of, 321–22
  national support for, 331–32
  population trends in, 84–85
  postwar expansion of, 148,
    151
  research and reform in,
    327–30
  social benefits in, 315–16
  social policy in, 310
  subsidies for, 95
  system of, 322–26
    attendance scheduling in,
      330–31
    in earlier history, 6
    increasing flexibility of,
      327–30
    of teachers, 326–27
    two track system, 322–27
      controversy over, 329–30

university entrance and,
324–25, 335–36, 339
Education and Art, Ministry
of, 322, 415, 437, 477
Center for Pilot Projects and
Educational
Development, 329
Department for Religious
Affairs, 117–18
Egypt
relations with, 374
Einem, Gottfried von, 432–33,
458, 466
Eis, Maria, 454
Eisendle, Helmut, 423
Eisenreich, Herbert, 409
Eisenstadt, 26, 66
radio in, 287
theater in, 453
Eisenstadt Diocese, 106
Eisler, Georg, 471–83
Elderly
population statistics on,
80–82, 84–85
See also Population, age
structure in
Electrical engineering, 147,
161–62, 166
Electrical equipment industry,
128
Electric power
import of, 369
industry, 45, 50, 127
supply balance of, 203–5
See also Energy production;
Hydroelectric power
Electronics industry, 161
Eliot, T. S., 460
Employee protection insurance,
309–12, 314
Employer-employee relations,
309–12
Employment
and economic development,
148
and economic policy, 135–36
prognosis for, 50–51
rates of, 132–34
statistics on, 276
structure of
by province, 26
of university graduates, 339
See also Labor
Energy policy
and foreign affairs, 366–69
Energy production, 138
organizational structure of,
205–6
sources and supplies of,
203–5
See also Coal; Electric
power; Hydroelectric
power; Natural gas; Oil

Enns valley, 56
Ent, Herbert, 345, 352–58
Environmental concerns
in Alpine environment, 61
in Danube valley, 64
and social partnership, 197
Enzensberger, Hans Magnus,
411
Epp, Leon, 463
Erl passion play, 451
Ernst, Gustav, 425
Erzberg, 34
Ethnic minorities, 92–94, 349
Europe Bridge, 62–63
European Democratic Union
(EDU), 236, 402
European Economic
Community (EEC), 24–25,
134–35, 365–66, 371, 376
Agricultural Market, 135
and economic development,
145–46, 158–59, 177
European Free Trade
Association (EFTA), 24,
365–66
and economic development,
134–35, 145–46, 158–59,
177
European Payments Union
(EPU), 127, 176–77
European Recovery Program
(ERP), 126–28, 174, 193,
364–65
Investment Program, 128,
167
European Security Conference,
369–70
European Union of Christian
Democrats, 236
Extrablatt, 413
Exxon Corp., 160

F

Fachgewerkschaften
See Labor Unions
Family law, 309, 315–16, 347,
352–54, 356–57
Fantastic Realist School, 480
Farmers' Association, 229
Federal Chancellor, 211–12,
266–67, 271
and social partnership, 189
Federal Civil Service Academy,
219
Federal Council, 211, 241, 256,
265–66
Federal President, 212, 243,
248, 253, 266–27
Federation of Industrialists,
188, 285
Feichtlbauer, Hubert, 279–98
Feldkirch, 69

Feldkirch Diocese, 107
Fellner, Fritz, 1–20
Felsenstein, Walter, 459
Fenster, Das, 413
Ferdinand I, Emperor, 4
Fesl, M., 69–70
Festival performances, 465–69
Fettfleck, 412
Fiat Corp., 162
Figl, Leopold, 257, 363
Finance, Ministry of, 315
Finance Guarantee Company,
168
First Republic, 10, 42–43
and Austria's image, 395
brief history of, 10, 12–15,
18
and economic development,
123–24, 142–43, 150
and industrial development,
155–56
intellectual trends of, 237,
485–92, 495, 502–3
party politics in, 242–43
union structure and
government in, 306
Fischer, Ernst, 493
Fischer, Heinz, 241–59, 492–93
Flora, Paul, 482
Food
and Austria's image, 397
Food and tobacco industries,
162, 164
Food Codex Commission, 194
Forchtenstein Castle Festival,
469
Ford Corp., 160
Foreign investment, 159–60
and industry, 159–60, 165
Foreign laborers, 133, 137
problems of, 86–92, 95
regional concentrations of,
85–86
Foreign policy, 490
domestic basis of, 376–77
European context of, 364–66
Council of Europe in,
367–68
Eastern Europe in, 368–70
European Security
Conference in, 369–70
future trends in, 377–79
and human rights, 370
and International Energy
Agency, 366–67
neutrality in, 362–64, 367,
377
parliament in, 253
postwar beginnings of,
361–63
and world political scene,
370–73

and Third World nations,
    373–76
Foreign Policy Council, 376–77
Foreign trade
  exports
    production structure of,
      163
    regional structure of, 146,
      158
    and development, 134–35,
      158, 175
    and foreign policy, 368–69
    and Gross Domestic
      Product, 144–45
  imports
    regional structure of, 146,
      158
  policy on, 137–38
    in history, 141–42, 149,
      176–77
  with Third World nations,
    374
Forestry, 163
  and economic structure,
    146
  employment structure in,
    131–32, 144
  and land use patterns, 28–31,
    34, 36, 39, 45, 49
  population statistics on, 26
  training in, 325
  See also Paper industry
Fortune magazine, 165
Forum Stadtpark, 412
Foundries, 147, 157, 162–63
  See also Metal products
    industry
Fractionen, 188, 230, 235
  See also Chambers
France
  Austria's image in, 398
  occupation by
    broadcasting under,
      279–81
    and press, 282
  trade with, 158
Frank, Wilhelm, 203
Frankfurter Allgemeine
    Zeitung, 417
Frankl, Viktor, 397, 405, 504
Franz Ferdinand, Heir
    Apparent, 8
Franz Joseph, Emperor, 7, 395
Franz Stephen, Emperor, 396
Freibord, 412
Freiheitliche Partei Österreichs
    (FPÖ) 102, 108–9, 224,
    244–45
  and election law reform,
    250–51
  financing of, 230–231
  ideology and platforms of,
    223, 237–38, 501–3

in Grand Coalition, 244–45,
    247
  and media, 284–85, 288–89
  membership rules of, 226
  in ÖVP government, 216,
    247–48
  in SPÖ government, 216, 249
  voter profile of, 227–29
Freud, Sigmund
  and Austria's image abroad,
    395, 397, 399–400, 405
Friedell, Egon, 397
Frisch, Karl von, 404
Frisch, M., 463
Frischfleisch, 412
Frischmuth, Barbara, 425
Fritsch, Gerhard, 412
Frohner, Adolf, 482
Fuchs, Ernest, 480
Funder, Friedrich, 499
Fund for the Promotion of
    Research, 193, 196
Furche, Die, 293, 499
Furtwängler, Wilhelm, 458

G

Gabriel, Leo, 504
Gamsjäger, Rudolf, 462
Ganztagsschule model, 330–31
Gastarbeiter
  See Foreign laborers
Gastein valley, 56
Gatt treaty, 134, 177
General Motors Corp., 44,
    160–62, 168
General Zionists, 116
Genet, J., 403
Geneva Protocols of 1922, 11
Geographic divisions
  Alps, 25, 27–28, 30–36
  basins and valleys, 27–28, 30,
    37
  granite uplands, 27, 30,
    36–38, 46
  high mountain areas, 27
  North-eastern hills and
    lowlands, 27–28, 30,
    39–41
  Northern Alpine Foreland,
    27, 30, 38–39, 49
  South-eastern hills and
    lowlands, 27–28, 30,
    41–42
  See also Regional structure
Gerlich, Peter, 209–21
German-Austrians
  and Habsburg collapse, 1–3
  See also German nationalism
German Confederation, 7
German nationalism, 11, 16,
    224–25, 237, 242, 327,
    486–88, 496–502

See also Freiheitliche Partei
    Österreichs (FPÖ)
German Reich, 9–13, 43
  See also National Socialist
    period
Germany, Federal Republic of
    25
  codetermination in, 311
  investment by, 159–60
  and media in Austria,
    297
  tourism from, 54, 58
  and trade and development,
    39, 43, 47, 62–63
  trade with, 146, 158, 203
Gerstinger, Heinz, 456
Gerstl, Elfriede, 415–16
Gesellschaft für
    Fertigungstechnik und
    Maschinenbau, 163
Gessner, Adrienne, 457
"Gewannfluren", 41
Gielen, Josef, 459, 461
Gironcoli, Bruno, 475
Glass industry, 45–46, 162
Glockner, massif, 56
Gmünd, 46
Goebbels, J., 452
Goethe, J. W. von, 459,
    461
Gold, Käthe, 459
Gombrich, Ernst, 405
Gorbach, Alphons, 257
Gorki, M., 457
Government and politics and
    Austria's image abroad,
    395, 399
Government structure
  constitution and politics in,
    209–11
  outlook for, 219–20
  principles and trends of
    consociationalism and
      corporatism, 217–18
    democracy from above,
      211–13
    liberal to welfare state,
      218–19
    strained local government,
      216–17
    symbolic federalism,
      214–16
    unseparated powers,
      213–14
  See also Chambers; Courts;
    Federal Chancellor;
    Federal President;
    Ministries; Parliament;
    Party system; Public
    administration
Governors, provincial, 212
Graduate education
  See Education, higher

Grand Coalition, 1945–1966, 232–34, 244–45, 247–48, 273, 486, 490
Coalition Committee, 246
crisis of, 246–47
educational accomplishments of, 331–32
government structure in, 211–14, 217, 219
in media, 284
prime of, 246–46
Proporz system of, 214, 270
Grass, Günter, 423
Graz, 26, 36
development and industry in, 42–43, 46, 62–64, 69
festival performances in, 467–68
literary avant-garde in, 411–14
music theater in, 443
Muskiprotokolle, 445
performing arts in, 464
population development of, 85
radio in, 280, 287
technical universities, 335
theater in, 451, 453, 456
University of, 335
music training in, 441
Grazer Autorenversammlung, 413–15, 419
Graz Music Academy, 441
Jazz Research Institute, 444
Great Austrian National Prize for Music, 437
Great Austrian State Prize, 415
Gredler, Wilfried, 105
Greece
relations with, 367
Greek Orthodox Church, 117
Greif, E., 49, 52
Greiner, Ulrich, 417
Grillparzer, Franz, 396, 454–55, 457, 460–61, 464, 469, 486
Gross Domestic Product, 144–45
agriculture in, 152–53
international income comparisons of, 147–48
Grossglockner peak, 32, 35
Gross National Product (GNP)
and econimic development, 124, 129, 142–44, 161, 178–79, 181–82
educational expenditures in, 338
industry and manufacture in, 42, 44
international comparisons of, 131

investment component of, 133
taxes as percentage of, 219
Gruber–De Gaspari Agreement, 371
"Grundenlastung" of 1848, 51
Grundschule, 322
"Gruppe 47", 411
Gulda, Friedrich, 442
Gurktaler Alpen, 86
Gutenbrunn, 30
Gütersloh, Paris, 472, 474, 478, 480
Gymnasium, 324

H

Habsburg Empire
administration of, 265, 269
and Austria's image abroad, 395–96
and Austria's self image, 1–3
brief history of, 3–9
culture under, 7
dissolution of, 9, 24
expansion policy of, 382
myth of, 485–87
in contemporary literature, 417–19, 423
relations with Catholic church, 100
Habsburg-Lorraine, 4
Haenel, Günther, 457
Haeusserman, Ernst, 449–70, 462–63, 469
Hahnl, Hans Heinz, 414
Halffter, Christobal, 438
Hallstatt period, 3
Hanak, Anton, 475
Handel-Mazetti, Erica, 397
Handicapped
education for, 326
laws protecting, 356–57
Handke, Peter, 410–11, 418–20, 423, 425–27, 468
Haslauer, Wilfried, 111
Haubenstock-Ramati, Roman, 436
Hauer, Joseph Matthias, 432, 436
Hauptmann, G., 464
Hauptschule, 322–24, 327, 329–30
Hauser, Arnold, 405
Hausner, Rudolf, 479–80
Hausruck range, 42
Haydn, Joseph, 395, 444
Hayek, Friedrich von, 404–5
Health services, 148, 151, 314
See also Social security
Heer, Friedrich, 497–98
Helmer, Oskar, 489, 491
Helsinki Act, 369–70

Heiligenblut, 35
Heim, Bruno, 105
Heimwehr, 242–43
Heindl, Gottfried, 393–406
Heintel, Erich, 504
Heinz, Wolfgang, 457
Helvetisches Bekenntnis, 99, 106, 115
Hermann Goering Werke, 125–26
Herzmanovsky-Orlando, Fritz von, 262–63, 271, 410
Hess, Viktor, 404
Hilbert, Egon, 461
Hindels, Josef 490–91
Hindemith, Paul, 435
Hitler, A., 12, 18
See also German Reich; National Socialist period
Hitler Youth, 100
Hochhuth, R., 463–64
Hochkönig, 32
Hochschule, 322
Hochwälder, Fritz, 460
Hoechst Corp., 160
Hoffman, Paul, 462
Hoflehner, Rudolf, 475
Hofman, Werner, 474–75
Hofmannsthal, Hugo von, 262, 396–97, 453, 463, 466
Hohe Tauern range, 32–33, 35
Hollegha, Wolfgang, 480
Holy See
relations with, 99, 104–7
and education policy, 328
Holzmeister, Clemens, 461, 466
Homosexuality
laws concerning, 108, 110, 347, 349
Hörbiger, Attila, 457, 459
Horváth, Ödön von, 456, 463
Hospitals, 263, 269
See also Health services
Housing, 130
of migrant workers, 89–91
public, 263
second home ownership, 56
social policy on, 316–17
subsidies for, 95
Hrdlicka, Alfred, 475, 481
Humanistisches Gymnasium, 324
Human rights
in foreign policy, 370
Hundertwasser, Friedensreich, 480
Hungarian speaking minorities, 92
Hungary, 2, 7, 10
relations with, 368
Hurdes, Felix, 494
Husserl, Edmund, 405
Huttner, Wolfgang, 480

Hydroelectric power, 33, 46, 138, 203–5
installations abroad, 403–4

I

IBM Corp., 160
Ibsen, H., 454, 464
Illwerke, 204
Income
and agricultural development, 49–50
in agriculture and industry, 48
per capita, 144
and production structure, 147–48
from tourist trade, 58
India
relations with, 373
Industry
and Austria's image abroad, 402–4
codetermination in, 196, 199, 311
current policy debate on, 169–70
education for, 325–26
and European integration, 157–59
and foreign investment, 159–60
in history, 11, 17, 141–44
and international recession of 1974–5, 169
nationalization of, 127–28, 137, 156–58
post 1918 development of, 155–56
post 1945 development of, 156–57
post 1969 development of, 161
provincial statistics on, 26
reconstruction and nationalization of, 156–57
and State Treaty of 1955, 157–59
structural change in, 150–51, 161–65
growth of and, 160–61
in World War II period, 125–26
zones of, 35–36, 39, 41–47
in broader areas, 50
core areas of, 69–71
See also Economic development; Economic structure; individual industries by name
Inflation
current rates, 181

during reconstruction period, 174–76, 180
and economic policy, 135–36
postwar, 128–29
Innerhofer, Franz, 420
Innitzer, Theodore, 112
Innsbruck, 26, 36
and Austria's image, 394
development of, 56, 64, 69
music festival, 469
population development of, 85
radio in, 279, 287
theater in, 451–52
University of, 335
musicology at, 441
Innsbruck Diocese, 107
Inn valley, 36, 46–47, 69
Institute for Empirical Social Research, 91–92
Institute of Economic Research, 189, 194
Intellectual history
and Austria's image, 404–5
of current political divisions, 485–89
Interior, Minister of, 189–91
International Energy Agency, 366–67
International Gustav Mahler Society, 445–46
International Hans Kelsen Institute, 504
International Institute for Applied Systems Analysis (IASA), 378, 402
International Music Center, 446
International Music Council, 445–46
International Unification Church, 118
Investment
rate of, 132–34
tax concessions for, 167, 176
See also Foreign investment
Iran
relations with, 375
"Iron Curtain", 24–25, 38, 44, 69
Iron manufacturing industry, 34–35, 43, 45–46, 125, 128, 147, 155, 161–63, 166, 169
Islamic Center, 117
Islamic faith, 116–17
Israel
relations with, 375
Israeli-Arab war, 372, 374–75
Israelitische Kultusgemeinde, 115–16
Italy
in history, 2, 10–11, 25

relations with, 362, 371, 377
in trade and development, 62, 146, 158
ITT Corp., 160

J

Jahn, Rolf, 457
Janáček, Leoš, 438
Jandl, Ernest, 410, 415, 418–20, 423–24
Jankowitsch, Peter, 361–80
Japan
trade with, 146
Jehovah's Witnesses, 118
Jewish population
and anti-semitism, 18, 496
Viennese
emigration and resettlement of, 78
Jewish religion
relations with state, 115–16
subsidy to, 106, 116
John XXIII, Pope, 105
Johnston, William M., 404–5
Joint Commission for Prices and Wages, 188–91, 194, 217–18, 307
Economic and Social Advisory Board, 192–93
membership of, 234–35
Joseph II, Emperor, 6, 106
Josephinism, 6
Journalism, 294–96
See also Media
Judenberg basin, 46
Judiciary
See Courts
Jürgens, Udo, 442
Justice, Minister of
and reformed civil code, 352
and reformed penal code, 346–47, 350

K

Kafka, Franz, 262, 269, 397, 405, 409, 425
Kahn, R. A., 4
Kaltnecker, Hans, 456
Kamitz, Reinhard, 494–95, 497
Kapfenberg, 46, 69
Kaplan, Viktor, 397
Kappacher, Walter, 420
Kaprun, 33, 56
hydropower installation at, 204
Karasek, Franz, 368, 402
Karawanken range, 35
Katholische Aktion, 113, 498–99
Kaufman, Dieter, 436–37
Kaut, Joseph, 466

Kautsky, Benedikt, 491
Kautsky, Karl, 491
Kehlmann, Michael, 456
Kellertheater, 456, 464
Kelsen, Hans, 195, 405, 487,
    503-4
Kelsen Institute, 504
Kennedy, John F., 402
Keynesianism, 136, 138
Khal Israel, 116
Khruschev, N., 363, 402
Kienzl, Heinz, 492
Kindler publishing house, 416
Kirchschläger, R., 111, 503
Kirchschlag passion play,
    451
Kissinger, Henry, 378, 384
Kitzbühel, 34, 56
Klagenfurt, 26, 36, 64, 415
    population development of,
    85
    radio in, 280, 287
    theater in, 453
    University for the
        Educational Sciences,
        335
Klagenfurt basin, 28, 36
Klaus, Josef, 17, 108, 257, 500
Kleiber, Erich, 458
Kleines Volksblatt, 282-83, 494
Kleine Zeitung, 285, 290, 293
Kleinwalsertal, 56
Klemperer, Otto, 458
Klenner, Fritz, 491
Klimt, Gustav, 8, 397, 472,
    474, 480
Klingenberg, Heinz, 462
Klose, Alfred, 499
Klostermann, Ferdinand, 112
Klubzwang, 255
Knappertsbusch, Hans, 458
Kneucker, Raoul F., 261-78
Knoll, August Maria, 498
Koch, Malcolm G., 376
Koch, Manfred, 398
Kodaly, Zoltan, 436
Koestler, A., 463
Köflach, 42
Kokoschka, O., 397, 462, 472
Kolleritsch, Alfred, 412
Kommunistische Partei
    Österreichs (KPÖ), 17,
    102
    associations in, 236-37
    in Grand Coalition, 244
    intellectual trends of, 493
    international ties of, 237
    interparty relations of, 235
    and media, 282-86
    opposition roles of, 225,
        232-34
Konecny, Albert, 112
Konetzny, Anny, 455

König, Franz, 101, 109,
    111-13, 497
Konradi, Inge, 457
Kontrapunkte ensemble, 437
Koren, Stephan, 111, 173-83
Körner, Theodor, 362, 489
Köstner, Josef, 112
Kotzebue, August von, 454
Krammer, J., 48
Kraus, Herbert, 501
Kraus, Karl, 409-10, 457, 472
Kraus, Wolfgang, 411
Krauss, Clemens, 458, 465, 467
Krauss, Werner, 459, 461
Kreisgericht, 355
Kreisky, Bruno, 17-18, 195,
    257, 288, 426, 492, 500
    and church relations, 105,
        107-8, 110-11
    and foreign relations, 363,
        366, 368, 373-76, 378
Krems, 64
    Open Air Festival, 469
Krenek, Ernst, 433-34
Krips, Joseph, 455, 458
Kronenzeitung, 290, 292-93
Kubin, Alfred, 472
Kufstein, 69
Kuhn, Richard, 404
Kulturkampf, 100, 109-10
Kunsthochschulen, 335
Kurier, 282, 285, 290, 292-93

L

Labor, Chamber of, 186-88,
    196, 217
    All Austria Assembly of,
        187, 307
    Economic Research
        Department, 192
    party membership in, 235-36
    and social policy, 301-2
Labor force
    commuting by, 50-51
    foreign workers in, 62
    participation in
        age structure and, 82,
            84-85
    productivity of, 145-46,
        148
    structure of, 131-32
Labor law, 309-12, 317
    in constitution, 310-11
    early reforms of, 302-3
Labor market, 132-34
    and nearby countries, 47
    policy on, 136, 168-69
    See Also Employment;
        Unemployment;
        Vocational education
Labor unions

contract coverage of, 306-7,
    310-11
    in ÖGB structure, 305-8
    political ties of, 224
    strike activities by, 257,
        307-8
    voting trends of, 228, 254
Lacina, Ferdinand, 155-71
Lake Constance, 56
    Music Festival, 445, 451,
        453, 460, 468
Lake Neusiedl, 55
Länder
    See Provinces
Länderbank, 166
Landesgericht, 355
Landeshauptmann, 233, 266-67
Landesregierung, 266-68
    See also Provinces
Landsteiner, Karl, 404
Langen/Arlberg, 30
Languages
    education in, 323-25
    See also Linguistic minorities
Latin American countries
    relations with, 370, 373-74
Law
    civil, 352
        consumer law reform, 355,
            357
        family law reform, 352-54
        improved access to courts,
            355-56
        prospects and trends in,
            356-57
    criminal, 345
        penal code reforms since
            1970, 345-51
        See also Legislation, Penal
            code
    rule of, 213, 272, 274-76
    and social policy, 303-4
LD steelmaking process, 126,
    163, 403
Lead industry, 45, 163
League of Nations, 11, 13
Leather industry, 45, 50, 147,
    162
Legislation
    Broadcasting Law of 1966,
        286-87
    Civil code
        reforms of, 352-57
        See also Law, civil
    Education Acts of 1962, 107
    Family Allowance Fund
        Law, 328
    Finance Equalization Law,
        264
    General Law for University
        Studies, 336
    General Social Insurance
        Act, 302-3

Labor Market Act, 137
Law Concerning a Person's Civil Status, 103
Law Concerning Ethnic Minorities, 93
Law Concerning the Employment of Foreign Workers, 91, 95
Law for the Protection of Consumers, 355
Law providing for the Equalization of Family Burdens, 95
Law Regarding Sexual Equality in Family Law, 352
Law to Promote Family Counseling, 95
Laws concerning the Protestant Church, 106
Media Law, 295–96
Official Languages Law, 93
Party Law of 1975, 230–32, 252–53
Penal code, 345
  abortion issue in, 346–49
  adoption of, 347
  criminal procedure reforms, 350–51
  media law in, 351
  salient provisions of, 347–49
Procedural Assistance Law, 356
School Organization Law of 1962, 322, 327–28, 331–32
State Basic Law of 1867, 295
Student Grants Law, 328
University Organization Law of 1975, 336–37
See also Nationalization Acts
Legislation process, 251–52, 255–56, 274
  and state administration, 263–64
See also Parliament
Léhar, Franz, 438, 455, 469
Lehmden, Anton, 480
Lehne, Friedrich, 109
Leistungsgruppen plan, 329
Leitner, Helga, 75–97
Lenzing, 43
Lernet-Holenia, Alexander, 262, 397
Leser, Norbert, 485–507
Liberalism, 218–19
  intellectual tradition of, 242, 488, 496–97, 502–3

Liberal Party of Austria
  See Freiheitliche Partei Österreichs (FPÖ)
Liberal World Union, 236–37
Lichtenberger, E., 51, 56, 60, 68
Liebermann, Rolf, 458
Lienzer Dolomiten range, 35
Ligeti, György, 434, 436
Lindtberg, Leopold, 459, 462
Linguistic minorities, 92–94
Linz, 26
  Bruckner Festival, 443, 446, 468
  development of, 38–39, 43, 47, 64, 66, 69
  music theater, 443
  performing arts, 464
  population growth, 85
  radio, 281, 287
  theater in, 451–53
  University of, 335
Linz Program of 1926, 102–3
List Simon Wiesenthal, 116
"Literaricum", 413
Literarisches Quartier, 411
Literature
  and Austria's image abroad, 395–97, 405
  contemporary
    antecedents of, 409–10
    appreciation abroad of, 426–28
    autonomy and anarchy in, 422–25
    avant-garde in Vienna and Graz, 410–11
    business and, 414–16
    competing writers' organizations, 413–14
    controversies in, 425–26
    and the Habsburg myth, 417–18
    models of authenticity in, 419–22
    new constellations in, 418–19
    and the public, 411–13
    teaching and research in, 416–17
  primary and secondary education in, 324
Literatur und Kritik, 412
Lizst, F., 395
Local government, 216–17
Loeben mining school, 335
Loeben-Donawitz, 46, 69
Loewi, Otto, 404
Logothetis, Anestis, 436
Lombardy, Kingdom of, 5, 7
Loos, Adolf, 472
Lope de Vega, 454
Lorenz, Konrad, 404, 504

Lothar, Ernest, 460
Löwenmaul, 412
Lower Austria, 10, 42
  development and land use in, 29, 44, 50
  student population in, 340
  tourism in, 55–56
  transport in, 63–64
  vital statistics on, 26
See also Eastern Austria; Provinces; Regional structure
Low Tauern, 86
Lunatcharski, Anatoli Vasilyevich, 457
Lungau area, 56

M

Maazel, Lorin, 443
Mach, Ernst, 397
Machinery industry, 128, 162
Machsike Hadass, 116
Macmillan, Harold, 363
Magister degree, 326
Magnesite mining, 128, 147
Magris, Claudio, 417–18, 485–86
Magyars, 23
Mahler, Gustav, 8, 395, 438
Mahler-Werfel, Alma, 397
Maize crop, 36, 39, 41
Maleta, Alfred, 495
Malipiero, Gian Francesco, 438
MAN Corp., 160
Manker, Gustav, 464
Manufacturing
  centers of production in, 45
  employment structure in, 131–32, 144
  growth of, 147
Manuskripte, 410, 412, 464
Marchfield basin, 39, 41
  development of, 39, 41, 49
Marek, Franz, 493
Maria Theresa, Empress, 4, 6, 395–97, 399
Mariazell Manifesto of 1952, 103
Marriage
  church and, 103–4, 108
  laws concerning, 347, 352–4, 356–7
Marriage benefits, 316
Marshall plan, 15, 126–27, 157, 175
Martinz, Fritz, 481
Marxism, 18, 199, 489, 491
See also Austro-Marxism; Kommunistische Partei Österreichs (KPÖ); Social Democrat Party
März, Eduard, 123–140, 491

Mathematics
    education in, 325
Matzner, Egon, 492
Mauer, Otto, 112, 480, 498–99
Maximilian I, Emperor, 4
May, Gerhard, 107
Mayer, Conny Hannes, 464
Mayröcker, Frederike, 415,
    423–24
Mechanical engineering, 163
Media
    advertising in, 287–88, 290
    film production, 297
    and government awareness,
        248
    laws concerning, 295–96, 351
    music in, 439–40
    other forms, 296–97
    press
        characteristics of, 292–93
        current market trends of,
            289–90
        foreign, 294–95
        freedom issues in, 291
        and independent
            broadcasting
            referendum, 284–5
        journalist characteristics,
            294
        legal aspects of, 295–96
        post WWII, 282–83
        press council and
            self-regulation of,
            191–92
        public of, 293–94
        readership and party
            papers, 283
        and restoration of
            democracy, 283–84
        subsidies to, 290–91
    publishing
        of books 414
        of music, 438–39
    radio
        censorship period of,
            280–81
        financing of, 287–88
        first stations in various
            provinces, 279–80
        for foreigners, 288
        international model for,
            286–87
        referendum on, 284–85
        See also Österreichische
            Rundfunk (ÖRF)
    television
        administration of, 284–87
        financing of, 287–88
        laws concerning, 285–86
        preparations for, 280–81
        referendum on, 284–85
        reforms concerning,
            288–89

MEDIACULT, 446
Medical insurance, 309, 312–13
Medicine
    and Austria's image abroad,
        404
Meinrad, Joseph, 457
Melk
    Summer Festival, 469
Mendel, Gregor, 397
Menger, Karl, 405
Merkl, Adolf Julius, 503
Messiaen, Olivier, 435
Messner, Johannes, 499
Metal products industry,
    43–47, 162
    See also Foundries
Methodists, 117–118
Metternich, Prince, 261, 395,
    397, 399
Michels, Robert, 188
Middle East countries
    relations with, 373–76
Migration movements
    historic, 76–78
    international, 85–92
    regional, 36, 71, 78–80
Mikl, Josef, 480–81
Milhaud, Darius, 436
Militia, 389
    See also Defense policy
Millöcker, Carl, 455
Millstat, 56
Millstättersee, 37
Mining education, 335
Mining gear production, 163
Mining industry, 32, 34–55
    centers of, 45
    development of, 147, 157,
        162–63
    employment structure in,
        131–32, 144
    nationalization of, 166
    provincial statistics on, 26
Ministers, Council of, 189, 256
Ministries
    in federal structure, 266–67
    functions of, 274
    traditions and styles of, 271
    training for, 273–74
    See also Education and Art,
        Ministry
        of; Finance, Ministry of;
        Interior, Ministry of;
        Justice,
        Ministry of; Science and
        Research,
        Ministry of; Trade and
        Industry,
        Ministry of
Minority groups, 92–94
    legal issues concerning, 349
Misrachi, 116
Missong, Alfred, 494

Mobil Corp., 160, 205
Mock, Alois, 402, 500
Modern Austrian Literature,
    427
Moldavian, Kurt, 482
Molotov, V. I., 363
Mondsee, 56
Monetary policy, 136–37, 158
    and budget, 178–79, 181–82
    current, 170, 181–82
    and economic structure, 150
    in growth periods, 176–81
    and post WWII
        reconstruction, 156,
        173–75
    inflation during, 175–76
    See also Economic
        development
Montherlant, Henri de, 461
Moon, S. M., 118
Moralt, Rudolf, 458
Moravia, 5, 10, 24
Mörbisch
    Lake Festival, 469
    Operetta Week, 445
Morgen, Der, 413
Mormons, 117–18
Moscow Declaration of 1943,
    13
Moser, Kolo, 472
Motor vehicle industry, 44–45,
    47, 147, 161–62, 166
Mozart, W. A., 395–97, 399,
    441, 444, 449, 453,
    458–59, 461, 465–66
Mozarteum, Salzburg, 441, 443,
    451, 453, 466
Mozart Weeks, Salzburg, 465
Mühl, Otto, 483
Munich, 47
Municipalities
    in federal system, 265–67
    government of, 216–27
Mur-Mürz valley, 35–36, 63
Mürzzuschlag, 46
Muschik, Johann, 480
Music
    and Austria's image abroad,
        394–97, 399, 402, 405–6
    clubs and associations for,
        445–46
    contemporary composers,
        431–38
    cultural policy on, 446–47
    ensembles and institutions of,
        442–45
    interpreters of, 442
    in the media, 439–40
    national scholarships in, 437
    opera, 395, 432–33, 440,
        442–43, 453–54, 548–61,
        466–67

operetta, 395–96, 438, 441,
    445, 455, 469
publishing of, 438–39
teaching and research in,
    440–42
training institutions for, 324,
    335
jurisdiction of, 322
Musikerziehung, 438
Musil, Robert, 261–62, 272,
    396–97, 405, 410
Muslim faith, 116–17
Muslim Social Service, 117

N

Nasser, G. A., 374
National Council, 16
    Committee on Foreign
        Policy, 253
    in government structure,
        211–12
    and provincial affairs, 215
    and ÖGB, 306
    outlook for, 257–58
    in ÖVP government, 247–48
    President's Conference of,
        234
    procedural reform in, 251–52
    in SPÖ government, 249
    seat allocation in, 249–51
    structure and methods of,
        254–57
    See also Parliament
National debt, 136
National elections
    of 1970–71, 18
    voter turnout in, 257
    yearly comparisons
        of coalitions, 233
        in First Republic, 242
        party concentration in,
            226, 245
        seat allocations in, 251
        trends of
            parliamentarianism in,
            253
        vocational comparisons in
            results of, 255
Nationalism
    growth of, 10–11, 16
    in Habsburg Empire, 6–9
    See also German-Austrians;
        German nationalism
Nationalization Acts, 127–28
    administration of, 161–62
    and energy production,
        205–6
    and industrial development,
        156–58, 160
    role of nationalized
        industries, 165–66,
        169–70
National Library, Vienna, 441

Nationalrat
    see National Council
National Socialist party, 242,
    496, 501
National Socialist period,
    12–14, 18
    and the arts, 456–58, 473–74
    church in, 100
    "final solution" of, 115
    and industrial development,
        124–25, 143, 156
    and present army, 383
    social reforms following,
        301–2
NATO, 24–25, 369, 385, 388
Natural gas
    deposits, 41, 158
    imports, 138
    production, 203–6
*Naturwissenschaftliches
    Realgymnasium,* 325
Nenning, Günther, 492
Nestlé Corp., 160
Nestroy, Johann Nepomuk,
    397, 449, 454–55, 457
Nestroy Festival, Schwechat,
    469
Netherlands, tourism from, 54
Netherland, Spanish, 5
Neuberg, Erich, 456
Neue Forum, 413, 492
Neue Mittelschule plan, 329–30
Neues Österreich, 283
Neugebauer, Max, 104–5
Neulengbach Castle Festival,
    469
Neusiedler See Festival, 469
Neusprachliches Gymnasium,
    324
Neutral status
    background of, 381–83
    defense posture for, 383–86
        instruments and doctrines
            for, 389–90
    and economic development,
        134–35
    model for army's defense of,
        386–89
New left movement, 492, 497
Newspapers
    See Media, press
New Yorker, The, 287
Nitsch, Hermann, 483
Nobel Prizes
    Austrian Winners of, 397,
        404–5
Non Aligned Status
    See Neutral Status
Nono Luigi, 436
Northern Limestone Alps,
    32–33
Nuclear conflict, 388
Nuclear power referendum on,
    500

and energy policy, 138,
    204–5
Nursing
    Training in, 325

O

Oat crop, 36
    See also Cereal cultivation
Oberhammer, Otto, 289
Oberlandesgericht, 355
*Oberösterreichische
    Nachrichten,* 282–83,
    292–93
Oberstergerichtshof, 356
Oberstufenrealgymnasium, 323,
    325
October Manifesto of 1918, 9
OIAG national holding
    company, 162, 165–66
OIL
    deposits, 41, 45, 128
    imports, 138, 367
Oil crisis, 136, 138, 144
    and monetary policy, 181–82
Oil industry, 128, 158, 162,
    203–6
    See also Petrochemical
        industry
Okopenko, Andreas, 410, 415
Olah, Franz, 104
Old Catholic Church, 117
O'Neill, Eugene, 454, 459, 464
OPEC, 378
    trade with, 146
Opera, 395, 432–33, 440,
    442–43, 453–54, 458–61,
    466–67
Operetta, 395–96, 438, 441,
    445, 455, 469
Orchards, 28–39, 41
Orff, Carl, 454
Organization for Economic
    Cooperation
    and Development
        (OECD), 134, 366–67
    agricultural labor
        comparisons, 151–52
Austria: School Policy, 325–26,
    332
    and development, 177
    and GNP increase, 178
    national growth rates,
        129–30
Organization for European
    Economic Cooperation
    (OEEC), 365
Örtz valley, 56, 61
Ossiach
    Cathedral, 468–69
    festival performances, 468–69
Ostarrichi, 3
Österreichische
    Elektrizitätswirtschaft, 205

Österreichische
    Investitionskredit AG,
    167
Österreichische
    Kommunalkredit-AG, 167
Österreichische Kontrolbank,
    168
Österreichische
    Mineralölverwaltungs
    (ÖMV), 205–6
Österreichische Monatshefte,
    494
Österreichische Musikzeitschrift,
    438
Österreichischer
    Arbeiterkammertag, 187,
    307
Österreichischer
    Gewerkschaftsbund
    (ÖGB), 129, 187–91,
    193–94, 196–97, 199, 217,
    237, 281
    Fraktionen, 230, 235
    of Socialist Trade Unionists,
    231–32, 255
    legal status of, 355
    party membership in, 236
    and social policy, 304–10,
    317
Österreichische Rohöl AG,
    205–6
Österreichische Rundfunk
    (ÖRF), 194, 279
    administration of, 286,
    288–89
    foreign broadcasting by, 288
    founding of, 281, 285–86
    FS 1 and 2, 287–88
    funding of, 287–88
    general director of, 286,
    288–89
    international model for,
    286–87
    monopoly issues of, 296
    music programming on, 437,
    439–40, 468
    "O 1", 287, 439
    "O 3", 287–88, 439
    reforms concerning, 288–89
    regional broadcasting by,
    287
Österreichische Volkspartei
    (ÖVP), 15–17
    and Catholic church, 101–6,
    108–9, 111, 114–15
    democracy within, 231
    education policies of, 329,
    331
    external relations of
    associations and, 227,
    232–33, 235–37
    government opposition
    roles of, 216, 232–33,
    244–47

international ties of,
    236–37
    interparty relations of,
    233–35
    financing of, 230–31
    in Grand Coalition, 216,
    244–47
    intellectual trends within,
    223–25, 237–38, 493–97,
    500–1
    and Jewish community, 116
    and media, 282–86, 288–89
    "Salzburg program" of, 237
    in social partnership, 188,
    194–95, 197
    and Social policy, 304–5
    voter-member ratio, 225–27
    voter profile of, 227–29
Österreichische Zeitung, 282
Otto, Teo, 459, 462
Ottokar Přemysl, King, 3

P

Pahr, Willibald, 370
Palestine question, 375
Pallin, Franz, 345–51, 357–58
Pan-Germanism, 13, 16
    See also German nationalism
Pannonia, 413
Paper industry, 45–47, 147,
    157, 162–64, 166
    See also Forestry
Paris Peace Treaties, 10, 363
Parliament, 265–66
    and election law reforms,
    249–51
    Federal Council, 211, 241,
    256, 265–66
    in Grand Coalition, 244–45
    crisis and later years of,
    246–47
    prime of, 245–46
    historic development of,
    241–44
    outlook for, 257–58
    ÖVP era in, 247–49
    procedural reforms in,
    251–52
    SPÖ era in, 249
    See also National Council
Party system
    developmental trends of,
    224–25
    distribution in government
    levels, 213, 216–18
    external relations of parties
    in, 232–33
    historic continuity in, 223–24
    interconnections with
    associations in, 235–36
    internal party structure
    democracy within, 231–32

platform and ideologies of,
    237–38
    social components of,
    227–29
    voter-member ratios of,
    225–27
    international ties of parties,
    236–37
    interparty relations, 233–34
    reforms of 1974–75, 252–53
    voting obligations within
    parties, 255
Paryla, Karl, 457
Pastureland, 28–29, 39, 45, 52
Pauli, Wolfgang, 404
Pelinka, Anton, 223–39
P.E.N. Club, 413–15, 419
Pension program, 308–9,
    312–14
Performing artists, 442
Perutz, Max, 404
Peter, Friedrich, 502
Petitpierre, Max, 376
Petrochemical industry, 45–46,
    166, 206
    See also Oil
Pevny, Wilhelm, 425
Pflieger, Michael, 112
Philips Corp., 160
Philosophy
    in Austria's image, 404–5
    intellectual traditions of, 487
Pichler, Walter, 475
Pick, Anton, 116
Pinay, Antoine, 363
Pirandello, Luigi, 463
Pitterman, Bruno, 402
Pius XII, Pope, 105
Plasser and Theurer Corp., 163
Plischke, Ernst, 472
Ploier, Eduard, 110
Poland, 219
    imports from, 203
    relations with, 368–69
Polanyi, Michael, 405
Political mass organizations,
    212, 217–18, 235–36
    See also Party system
Politzer, Heinz, 411
Pollack, Oskar, 491
Polsterer, Ludwig, 285
Polytechnischer Lehrgang
    See Technical schools
Popper, Karl, 405
Population
    age structure of, 50, 78,
    80–82, 151
    of migrants, 91
    prospects for, 84–85
    cultural mix of, 23–25
    density of, 23
    by geographic division, 28
    by province, 26

development of
  by region, 78–80
drift of, 36, 71
employment statistics for,
  276
future trends of, 84–85
growth patterns of, 75–80
migrant
  in agriculture, 145–46
national policy on, 94–95
sex structure of, 80–82
Pörtschach, 56
Portugal
  relations with, 368
Postal Savings Bank, 193
Potato crop, 36, 45
Powell, Nicolas, 472
Power plants
  See Electrical power;
    Hydroelectric power
Prager, Theodor, 493
Pragmatic Sanctions of 1713, 4
Prantl, Karl, 475
Präsent, 293
Pregl, Fritz, 404
President's Conference of the
  Chambers of Agriculture,
  307
  See also Federal President
Press
  See Media, press
Presse, Die, 292, 393, 399, 413
Prey, Hermann, 468
Price and wage controls,
  128–29, 132
  See also Joint Commission
    for Prices and Wages
Price Commission, 189–90, 195
  See also Joint Commission
    for Prices and Wages
Priestley, J. B., 457, 461
Proclamation of the Republic,
  1918, 9–10
Profil, 292, 413
Projektil, 412
Proporz system, 214, 270
  See also Grand Coalition
Protestant Church, 99
  relations with state, 106
  social policies of, 114–15
Protestant Patent of 1861,
  106–7
Protokolle, 413
Provinces, 25
  administration of, 256–57,
    263–64
  and chamber organizations,
    186
  and election reforms of 1970,
    250
  government of, 211–12,
    214–16

1979 election results in,
  226–27
party affiliation in, 232
radio broadcasting by,
  279–80
relations with federal
  government of, 265–68
social welfare activities of,
  312, 314
student population
  comparisons, 340
vital statistics on, 26
Provisional Government, 361
Psychoanalysis, 487
  and Austria's image abroad,
    395, 399–400
Public administration
  in Austria's history, 5–6,
    10–11, 261–63
  bureaucracy in, 272–74
  between the wars, 10–11
  continuity of, 269–70
  establishment of, 5–6
  statistics on, 268–69
  expertise in, 274
  indirect federalism in, 263–64
  division of powers in,
    264–68
  of public services, 270
legality concepts in, 274–76
Public expenditures
  of federal, provincial and
    local governments, 215
Public housing, 263
  See also Housing
Public utilities, 128
Publishing houses, 414
Puccini, I., 458
"Puszta" steppes, 39

Q

Quakers, 118
Qualtinger, Helmut, 456

R

Raab, Julius, 104, 189, 257,
  363, 494–95
Radio
  See Media
Radio-Verkehrs-Aktiengesell-
  schaft (RAVAG), 279–81
  See also Media
Radstätter Tauern range, 56,
  61
Rahimsai, Abd el, 117
Rahner, Karl, 112
Railway carriage manufacture,
  166
Railways, 63–64, 66
  subsidy of, 151

Raimund, Ferdinand, 457,
  461–62
Raimundtheater, Vienna, 443,
  455
Rainer, Arnulf, 480, 482
Ramako, Anton, 472
Rampe, Die, 412
Ranshofen, 43, 47
Rauriser Literaturtag, 412
Reader's Digest, 297
Realgymnasium, 324–25, 327
Realistisches Gymnasium,
  324–25
Rechnungshof, 251, 265–66
Rechtspfleger, 355–56
Rechtsstaat
  See Law, rule of
Referendum process, 212–13
  on independent broadcasting,
    284–85
  on nuclear power, 138,
    204–5, 500
Reformed Confession, 99, 115
  subsidy to, 106
Regietheater, 456
Regional development, 50, 71
  and migration movements,
    86–89
  population movements in,
    78–80, 84–86
  tourism in, 53–61
Regional structure
  alpine agriculture, 51–53
  eastern areas, 50–51
  and population
    development, 78–80,
    86–87
  east-west divisions, 29,
    42–44, 54
  industrial divisions, 44–47
  roadways and transport,
    61–64
  rural and agricultural
    divisions, 47–50
  tourism in, 53–61
  urban growth in, 64–71
Reifeprüfung, 325–26, 328
Reif-Gintl, Heinrich, 462
Reigh-Ranicki, Marcel, 415
Reimann, Viktor, 501
Reinhardt, Max, 452–54, 466
Reinthaller, Anton, 502
Reiwald, Paul, 349
Religious instruction, 324, 328
  See also Catholic Church;
    Jewish religion;
    Protestant Church
Renault Corp., 162
Renner, Karl, 9, 11, 15, 362,
  489
Research and Development,
  139
  promotion of, 161, 165

Residenz Verlag, 414, 423
Retz, 40
Rhine-Main-Danube Canal, 47, 64
Rhine valley, 43, 47
Rice, Elmer, 456
Ried-im-Innkreis, 47
Riehe, Die, ensemble, 435, 437
Right to Life Movement, 109–11
Rihm, Wolfgang, 438
Rilke, R. M., 397, 456
Roadways, 29
    Brenner Highway, 62 –63
    Grossglockner Hochalpenstrasse, 33, 35
    interregional network of, 70
    Phyrn Pass expressway, 46, 62–63
    South Expressway, 63
    West Expressway, 62–63
Robbe-Grillet, Alain, 411
Rodund, 204
Rohracher, Andreas, 112
Roman Empire, 3, 66
Romania
    relations with, 368
Romanians, 2, 9, 23
Roman Law, 345
Rosar, Annie, 457
Rosegger, Peter, 397
Rosei, Peter, 423
Roth, Gerhard, 468
Roth, Joseph, 274–75, 397, 405, 410
Rott, Adolf, 460–61
Rotweissrot studio, 280–81
    See also Media, radio
Rubin, Marcel, 435
Rudolf, Karl, 112
Rühm, Gerhard, 410, 415, 464
Ruiss, Gerhard, 415
Rural development, 47
    of eastern border areas, 50–51
    industrialization of, 48
    and population shifts, 87
Rusch, Paulus, 103–4, 112
Rye crop, 36
    See also Cereal cultivation
Rysanek, Leonie, 442

S

Saalbach, 56
Sadat, A., 374
Saint Germaine State Treaty, 10
Saint Severin, 498
Salmhofer, Franz, 454–55, 458
Salt agreements, 369, 378, 402
Salvation army, 117–18
Salz, 412

Salzburg, City of, 26, 30, 39
    and Austria's image, 394
    development of, 59, 64, 66
    Easter Festival, 442, 466
    Festival, 405, 442, 445, 453, 457–58, 460–61, 466–67
    Festival Hall, 466
    Mozart Weeks, 465
    radio in, 280–81, 287
    theater in, 451–453
    University of, 335
        Institute of Journalism and Communication, 294, 297
    music training in, 441
Salzburg Catholic Academy, 109
Salzburger Nachrichten, 282–83, 292–93
Salzburg Mozarteum, 441, 443, 451, 453, 466
Salzburg Music Academy, 441
Salzburg Province, 3, 10, 66
    land use and development in, 28–29, 36, 43, 47, 51–52, 69, 85
    student population of, 340
    tourism in, 54, 56
    transport in, 62–63
    urban development in, 64
    vital statistics on, 26
    See also Provinces; Regional structure; Western Austria
"Salzkammergut", 55–56, 58
Sarraute, Nathalie, 411
Sartre, Jean Paul, 456, 463–64
Satie, Erik, 436
Sauberer, M., 85
Scharang, Michael, 418, 420
Schärf, Adolf, 104, 363, 489
Sheer, G., 48
Schiele, Egon, 397, 472, 474
Schiller, F., 454, 464
Schladming, 56
Schmid, Sigrid, 416
Schmidt, Franz, 434
Schmidt-Dengler, Wendelin, 409–29
Schneiderhan, Wolfgang, 442
Schneider-Siemssen, Günther, 467
Schnell, Hermann, 329
Schnitzler, Arthur, 8, 262, 396–97, 454, 460, 463
Schoenwald, Rudolf, 481
Schöffler, Paul, 455
Schollum, Robert, 435
Scholz, Gottfried, 431–48
Schönberg, Arnold, 395, 432, 438, 441–42, 447
Schönberg Chor, 437
Schönere Zukunft, 496

School Reform Commission, 329
    See also Education
Schreiner, Liselotte, 459
Schreyvogl, Friedrich, 460
Schrödinger, Erwin, 404
Schubert, Franz, 395, 434, 441–42, 468
Schuh, Oscar Fritz, 458
Schulmeister, Otto, 499
Schulräte, 321
Schuschnigg, Kurt von, 12
Schutting, Jutta, 418, 422
Schwarz, Helmuth, 456
Schwechat
    Nestroy festival, 469
    refinery, 41, 46, 158, 206
Schwertsik, Kurt, 435
Science
    and Austria's image abroad, 397, 402, 404
    primary and secondary training in, 324–25, 335
Science and Research, Ministry of, 335
Scientology, Church of, 117–18
Sebastyén, György, 413
Second Republic, 13–19
    See also First Republic; Government structure; Grand Coalition; Public administration
Seefehlner, Egon, 443, 462
Seefeld, 56
Seefried, Irmgard, 455
Seipel, Ignaz, 10, 100, 495
Self-employed
    social policy for, 309, 312
Sellner, Gustav Rudolf, 462
Semmelweis, Ignaz, 397
Semmering areas, 55
Semmering Pass, 41
Semmering rail link, 64
Sendergruppe Alpenland, 280
Sendergruppe West, 279–80
    See also Media, radio
Services
    employment structure in, 26, 131–32, 144–45, 148–49, 151–52
Seuphor, Michel, 475
Sexual conduct
    laws concerning, 347
Seyss-Inquart administration, 502
    See also National Socialist period
Shakespeare, W., 459, 462, 464
Shaw, G. B., 463
Shell Oil Corp., 205
Siemens Corp., 160, 165–66
Singende Kirche, 438
Skalnik, Kurt, 499

Skiing, 57, 60, 61
  and Austria's image, 394, 397
Ski production, 47, 163
Skoda, Albin, 453
Skraup, Karl, 457
Slavic peoples, 23
Slavs
  in Austrian history, 8–9
Slovak minority, 93
Slovene minority, 92–93, 377
Social Administration, Minister of, 303, 306
Social Affairs, Minister of
  and social partnership, 189
Social Democrat Party, 237, 486–87
  and Chamber organization, 186–87
  and educational policy, 327
  in First Republic, 241–43
  and foreign policy, 363
  German-Austrian, 9
  historic role of, 9–11, 15, 100
  Republican Defense Corps, 243
  See also Sozialistische Partei Österreichs (SPÖ)
Social insurance, 218, 312–14
Socialist International, 236, 402
Social partnership, 136, 220, 491
  beginnings of, 129, 150, 157
  chambers and voluntary associations in, 186–88
  criticism of, 198–200
  Economic and Social Advisory Board in, 170, 180, 192–93
  in government agencies, 193–94, 217–18
  and industrial development, 168
  Joint Commission for Prices and Wages in, 188–91, 217–18
  and party politics, 232
  recent experiences with, 194–98
Social policy
  assessment of, 318
  dynamic reform stage of
    general characteristics of, 302–3
    general objectives of, 308–9
    intellectual background of, 304–8
    legal and constitutional issues of, 303–4
    targets and objectives of, 309–10

individual reforms in
  of child and family law, 315–16
  of employer-employee relations, 311–12
  in housing, 316–17
  labor constitution, 310–11
  of social security, 312–14
  in 1945, 301
present situation
  economic guarantees for, 317
  further development of, 317–18
  restoration period, 301–2
Social sciences
  and administration, 271
  training in, 324, 335
Social security, 309, 312–14
  financing and administration of, 314, 318
  See also Social policy
Social work
  training in, 325
Society of Authors, Composers and Music Publishers, 446
Solti, George, 458
Sonnblick, 30
Sophocles, 462
South Africa
  relations with, 370
Southern Alps, 35–36
Southern Austria
  population development in, 78–80, 86–87
  See also Carinthia; Regional development; Regional structure; Styria
Southern Music, 297
South Tyrol, 10, 25
  relations with Italy, 362, 371
Soviet Mineral Oil Administration, 156
Soviet Union
  imports from, 203
  of energy, 138, 369
  occupation by, 363–64
  and broadcasting, 279–81
  and economic recovery, 125–28, 156–57
  and population development, 78
  relations with, 368–69, 375
SALT agreements, 369, 378, 402
Soyfer, Jura, 456
Sozialistische Partei Österreichs (SPÖ), 15–18
  budget and monetary policy of, 180–81
  and Catholic church, 101–5, 107–13
  and civil law reforms, 352

"Committee of Socialist Catholics", 103
"Committee on Christianity and Socialism," 103,115
  and criminal law reform, 347
  democracy within, 231
  and education policy, 327–31
  and election law reform, 249–51
  external relations of
    associations and, 235–37
    government and opposition roles, 216, 232–33, 244–47
    international ties, 236–37
    interparty relations, 233–35
  financing of, 230–31
  in Grand Coalition, 244–47
  intellectual traditions of, 223, 237–38, 488–93, 495, 497, 500
  and Jewish community, 115–16
  "Linz program" of, 237
  as majority party, 249
  and media, 282–84, 288–89
  parliamentary reforms, 251
  and social partnership, 188, 195–98
  and social policy, 304–6, 308
  voter-member ratios, 225–27
  voter profile of, 227–29
  Women's Movement in, 109
Spain
  relations with, 366, 368
Spann, Othmar, 397
Spannocchi, Emil, 381–91
Sperber, Manes, 411, 415, 421
Spiegel, Der, 382
Spiel, Hilde, 416
States
  See Provinces
State Treaty of 1955, 16
  church reparations in, 103
  and industry, 157–59
  and military, 381, 383–84, 390
  negotiation of
    and foreign policy, 361–64
    and Vienna's development, 68
Steel industry, 43, 45–46, 125–26, 128, 147, 155, 157, 161–66, 169, 403
Steinboeck, Rudolf, 362–63
Steiner, Kurt, 203–6, 321–44
Steirischer Herbst, 411–12, 437, 467–68
Sternheim, Carl, 456
Steyr, 43, 47
Steyr-Daimler Puch Corp., 162
Stifter, A., 396–97, 418

St. Leonard Spa
music festival, 469
Stockerau
Open Air Festival, 469
Stockhausen, Karl Heinz, 436
Stolz, Robert, 437
Stone and clay industry, 162
Stoss, Franz, 463
St. Pölten, 43, 46
Strasbourg Conventions and
Tribunals, 367
Strasser, Rudolf, 301–19
Strauss, Johann, 395–96, 441,
455
Strauss, Richard, 395, 458, 461
Stravinski, Igor, 458
Strike of October 1950
broadcasting during, 280–81
Strindberg, A., 460, 464
Styria, 3, 10, 42
land use and geography of,
25, 29–30, 34–36, 41,
44, 56, 69
student population of, 340
tourism in, 55–56
transport in, 62–64
vital statistics on, 26
See also Provinces; Southern
Austria
Styrian Autumn, 411–12, 437,
467–68
Styrian Catholic Press
Association, 285
Subsidies
in art, 477
to churches, 106–8, 116
for concert promoters, 432,
437, 445
in housing, 317
to industry, 151, 167–69
in literature, 414
for mountain farmers, 53
for music instruction, 442
to political parties, 230–31
to press, 290–91
for students, 328, 339
for theaters, 449–50
Sugar beet cultivation, 39, 45,
49
Supreme Court, 213, 356
Suttner, Berta von, 404
Swiss cottage architecture, 36,
38
Switzerland
and development, 43, 47
investment by, 159–60
trade with, 146, 158
Szecsi, Maria, 123–40, 185–201

T

Tagesheimschule model, 330–31
Tamsweg, 30

Tauern Expressway, 62
Taus, Josef, 402
Taxes
administration of, 264–65
and family benefits, 95
and industry, 159, 167–69
Technical schools, 323, 325,
328, 330
Television
See Media
Temmel, Leopold, 115
Ternitz, 43
Textile industry, 43, 45–47,
157, 162–64
Theater, 263, 449
building of, 450–52
in Provinces, 450–53, 457,
464–69
in Vienna, 451–65, 467
Theater Association of
Austrian Provinces and
Cities, 443
Theatrical equipment
installations abroad, 404
Thimig, Hans, 457, 462
Third World nations
competition with, 164
and foreign policy, 371,
373–74
trade with, 146
Thoeny, Wilhelm, 472
Thomas, Dylan, 464
Tietjen, Heinz, 461
Timber production
See Forestry
Tintenfisch, 425
Tire production, 166
Tiroler Tageszeitung, 292–93
Tobacco products, 162, 166
Tolbuchin, Feodor Ivanovich,
454
Toncic-Sorinj, Lujo, 368, 402
Topitsch, Ernst, 504
Torberg, Friedrich, 410, 415
Tourism, 53–61
and economic development,
145, 148–49
education in, 325–26
and geography, 28, 33
and housing patterns, 58–60
lake districts in, 55–58
mountain farms in, 52–53
spas and health resorts in,
57–58
winter sports and, 57, 60–61
Trade
education for, 325
See also Foreign trade
Trade, Chamber of, 129,
186–88, 196–97, 217
and ÖGB, 306–7, 310
and party structure, 233,
235–36

Trade and Industry, Minister
of and social partnership,
189
Trakl, Georg, 397
Transcendental Meditation, 118
Transport, 263, 269
interregional networks of,
61–64
Rhine-Main-Danube Canal,
47, 64
U.S. aid to, 127
See also Railways; Roadways
Tschadek, Otto, 104, 352
Turkey
migrant labor from, 62,
87–89, 95
Turrini, Peter, 425
Tyrol, 3, 10
and Austria's image abroad,
394
land use and development of,
25, 28–29, 31, 35–36,
43, 47, 51–52
tourism in, 54, 56
transport in, 62
urban development in, 64
vital statistics on, 26
See also Provinces; Western
Austria

U

Uganda
relations with, 370
Uhl, Alfred, 435
Unemployment
and foreign migrants, 90
historic trends in, 142–43
rates of, 132–34, 136
See also Employment; Labor
Unilever Corp., 160
Unions
See Labor unions; Trade,
Chamber of
United Kingdom
Austria's image in, 398
investment by, 159
occupation by
and broadcasting, 279–81
and press, 282
trade with, 146, 158
United Nations
Conference on Science and
Technology for
Development, 371
Economic Commission for
Europe (ECE), 369
Industrial Development
Organization, 401–2
International Atomic Energy
Agency (IAEA), 371,
401–2

presence in Vienna, 69, 400–402
relations with, 362, 370–73, 376
in General Assembly, 372–73
in Security Council, 372, 374
Relief and Rehabilitation Administration, (UNRRA), 15, 126
United States
aid from, 177
Austria's image in, 393–98
and Austria's media, 297
and Austria's recovery, 14–15, 126–27, 144
investment from, 159–60
occupation by
and broadcasting, 280–81
and press, 282–83
SALT agreements, 369, 378, 402
tourism from, 58
trade with, 146
violation of airspace by, 385
See also Euroepan Payments Union (EPU); Marshall Plan
Universal Edition, 436, 438
Universities
See Education, higher
Upper Austria, 3, 10
development and land use in, 29, 38–39, 43, 46–47
student population of, 340
tourism in, 55–56, 58
transport in, 62–64
vital statistics on, 26
See also Provinces; Western Austria
Uprawlenije Sowjetskowo Imushtshestwa Awstrii (USIA), 156
Uranium imports, 369
Urban development, 63
population movements and, 85–91
and regional structure, 64–71
and suburbanization, 85–87
Urteil, Andreas, 475

V

Vacation benefits, 312, 317–18
Varese, Edgard, 435
Vegetable farming, 49
Velden, 56
Venezia, 7
Verband der Unabhängigen (VdU), 16, 233, 244–45, 501
Verdi, G., 459

Verein für musikalische Privataufführungen, 432
Vereinigter Judischer Wahlblock, 116
Verlag der Autoren, 414
Vermunt, 204
Versailles Peace Treaty, 10
Vienna, City of, 39, 41
administrative areas, 66–68
Akademietheater, 459–60
Arena cultural program, 424–25, 465
Ateliertheater, 456
and Austria's image abroad, 394
Blue Danube Radio, 288
broadcasting from, 280–81, 287–88
Burgtheater, 66, 453–54, 456–57, 459–62
Chamber opera, 443
church membership in, 114
Concert House, 443
development of, 61
Dramatic Center, 464
Economic University of, 335
"Fantastic Realist" School, 480
Heldenplatz, 66
Hofburg Palace, 66
Chapel, 444
Redoutensaal, 454
Die Insel Theater, 463
higher education in, 335, 340
Karl-Marx-Hof, 68
Klein Theater in Konzerthaus, 463
literary avant-garde in, 410, 412
Music Academy, 432, 437, 441
Goldener Saal, 443
Philharmonic Symphony, 443, 466–67
New Years Concert broadcast, 440
population of, 80–82, 87
Jewish, 78, 116
immigrant, 89, 92–93
Raimundtheater, 443, 455
Ringstrasse, 66
Scene 48, 456
Schauspielhaus, 451
St. Peter's Church, 60
St. Stephen's Cathedral, 60, 66
Symphony Orchestra, 443
Theater an der Wien, 443, 455, 458
Theater im Künstlerhaus, 464
Theater in der Josefstadt, 450–51, 462–63

Theater in der Scala, 457
Theater of the 49, 456
theaters in, 451–65, 467
United Nations activity in, 69, 371, 378, 400–402
University of, 66
Department of Protestant Theology, 106
Institute of Journalism and Comminication, 294, 297
music training at, 441
University Studio, 456
urban growth in, 64, 66–71
views of, 60, 67
Volksoper, 442–43, 453–54, 460
Volkstheater, 463–64
Vorstädte, 66
Young Actors Studio, 456
Vienna Actionism, 483
Vienna Basin, 25, 39, 41, 44–46
Vienna Boys's Choir, 444
Vienna Festival, 69, 437, 465
Arena programs, 424–25, 465
Vienna Innovation Corp., 168
Vienna Province, 3–4, 7, 10–11, 42
land use and geography of, 26, 28–29, 44
student population of, 340
tourism in, 54
transport in, 62, 64
vital statistics on, 26, 80–82
See also Regional structure
Vienna Secession, 472
Vienna State Opera, 395, 442, 453, 458–61
broadcasts, 440
Vienna Weeks of Music and Theater, 467
Vienna Woods, 41
Viennese Association of Industrialists, 188, 285
Viennese Musikverein, 467
Viertel, Bertold, 459
Vietnam
relations with, 370
Villach, 36
festival programs, 468–69
Viticulture, 28–29, 39–40, 45, 49
Vocational training, 313, 323–26, 330
Vöcklabruck, 47
VOEST-ALPINE AG, 43, 126, 161, 163, 165, 403
Vogelweide, Walter von der, 397
Volksanwaltschaft, 213, 253–54, 265–66
Volkspension, 309–9, 312–14
Volksschule, 322–23, 329–30

Volksstimme, 290
Voluntary association
  in social partnership, 186–88
Von Karajan, Herbert, 442,
  461, 466–67
Von Suppe, Franz, 455
Vorarlberg, 3, 10
  development and land use in,
    28–29, 36, 43, 47, 51, 69
  population development in,
    76–77, 78–80, 89
  radio in, 279, 287
  student population of, 340
  tourism in, 54, 56
  vital statistics on, 26
  See also Provinces; Western
    Austria
Vorarlberger Nachrichten, 293
Vyoral, Johannes A., 415

W

Wachau valley, 65
Wächter, Eberhard, 442
Waffen nieder!, Die, 404
Wage Commission, 189–91
  See also Joint Commission
    for Prices and Wages
Wagenbach, Klaus, 425
Wagner, Juregg Julius, 404
Wagner, Otto, 472
Wagner, Richard, 461, 466–67
Wahlpartei der Unabhängigen
  (WdU)
  See Freiheitliche Partei
    Österreichs (FPÖ)
Waidhofen, 43
Waldheim, Kurt, 373, 402
Wallraff, Günter, 424
Wandruszka, Adam, 488
Warsaw Pact, 369, 385, 388
War victims' benefits, 301, 314
Weber, Anton, 395, 432, 438
Wechsberg, Joseph, 287
Weigel, Hans, 409, 456–57
Weinviertel, 39–41
  See also Viticulture
Weinzierl, Erika, 99–120, 499
Weismann, Sigrid, 449–70
Weiss, Walter, 416
Weiz, 46
Wedekind, Frank, 464
Welfare state, 218–19, 308
  See also Social policy; Social
    security; Subsidies
Wels, 47
Weltpresse, 282

Werfel, Alma Mahler, 397
Werfel, Franz, 262, 272,
  396–97
Werner, Oskar, 457, 461
Wespennest, 412
Wessely, Paula, 459
Western Austria
  population development in,
    86–87
  fertility and age structure
    of, 78–80
  See also Regional structure;
    Salzburg, Tyrol, Upper
    Austria; Vorarlberg
Wiener, Oswald, 410, 423, 464
"Wiener Gruppe", 410–11, 418,
  464
Wiener Kurier, 282, 285, 290,
  292–93
Wiener Montag, 282
Wiener Singverein der
  Gesellschaft für
  Musikfreunde, 467
Wiener Werkstätte, 472
Wiener Zeitung, 282
Wildgans, Anton, 262, 406
Williams, C. E., 417
Williams, Tennessee, 460
Wimberger, Gerhard, 437
Winkler, Josef, 422
Winter, Ernst Karl, 498
Winter Olympics, 1964, 1976,
  56
*Wirtschaftskundliches
  Realgymnasium für
  Mädchen,* 324
Withalm, Hermann, 108, 500
Wittgenstein, Ludwig, 410, 418
Witzmann, Carl, 450–51
Wochenpresse, 285, 292
Wohlschlägl, Helmut, 23–73
Wolf, Christa, 420
Wolf, Hugo, 441
Wolfgangsee, 56
Wolfgruber, Gernot, 420
Women
  in Austrian population,
    80–82
  education of, 329
    higher, 340
    primary and secondary,
      324
  laws protecting, 313, 316,
    318, 352–53
  in National Council, 255
  pregnancy and maternity
    benefits for, 95

Woodworking industry, 147,
  162–63
Woodlands, 29–30
  See also Forestry
Works-Council organizations,
  301–2, 311
Work week, 193, 310–12
World Union of Christian
  Democrats, 236
World War I
  and population growth,
    75–76
World War II
  and economic development,
    124–25
  population effects of, 76–78
  See also National Socialist
    period
Wörthersee, 56
Wortmühle, 413
Wort und Wahrheit, 499
Wotruba, Fritz, 462, 474–76
Wurzer, R., 69–70

Y

Ybbs, 43
Yugoslavia,
  in Austrian history, 2, 10, 25
  migrant labor from, 62,
    87–89, 95
  relations with, 362, 366

Z

Zauner, Wilhelm, 113–14
Zeeman, Dorothea, 421
Zeit, Die, 426
Zell-on-See, 56
Zemlinsky, Alexander, von, 468
Zemmwerke, 204
Zentralsparkasse, 168
Ziehrer, Carl Michael, 438
Ziesel, Kurt, 397
Ziller valley, 56
Zinc industry, 45, 163
Zionism, 116, 370
  See also Jewish population
Zsigmondy, Richard, 404
Zuckmayer, Carl, 461
Zurich, 47
Zweig, S.. 397
Zwentendorf nuclear plant,
  138, 204, 500
Zwischenbilanz, 416
Zykan, Otto M., 437

DATE DUE

SEP 1 '84			
DEC 5 85			
FEB 21 '86			
JUL 9 '86			
SEP 1 7 Reserve			
NOV 23 '87			
NOV 1 '88			
GAYLORD			PRINTED IN U.S.A.